THE REALIZATION OF ONENESS WITH THE BOOK OF JOHN

VOLUME 2

by Herb Fitch

Edited & Compiled

by Bill Skiles

from the

46 Taped Seminars of 1972

To order additional copies of this book, contact:
Bookwhip
1-855-339-3589
https://www.bookwhip.com

DEDICATIONS

Mystical Principles would like to thank Wilhelmina Litam for her dedication and hard work transcribing these forty-six Realization of Oneness talks by Herb Fitch. It was truly an act of Love and appreciated by us all.

In addition, we wish to thank Alan B. for his work in proofing and editing these talks and keeping us all on track.

Also Paul Liga for the beautiful pdf booklet for reading and forwarding to the publishing company.

And finally, Martin Damboldt for his gorgeous photograph which encompasses the cover for this book.

Bill Skiles
Robbinsville, NC
07/18/2019
Link: http://www.mysticalprinciples.com
(click the above link to go there)

TABLE OF CONTENTS

FOREWORD

By Bill Skiles

"..*That which is born of the Spirit is Spirit. Marvel not that I said unto thee, Ye must be born again..*"
— *John 3: 6-8*

"*This mortal must put on immortality...when this mortal shall have put on immortality, then shall be brought to pass the saying that is written, Death is swallowed up in victory [in Spirit].*"
— *I Corinthians 15: 53-54*

"*Be willing for the harmonious as well as the inharmonious conditions of mortal existence to disappear...[for] above this mortal hypnotism, there is a universe of Spirit governed by Love.*"
— *Joel*

"*Within you is the sacred Fire of Christ. You have passed the dawn, you're into the sunrise which actually becomes a visible event within you rising out of material sunset, out of materialism, out of the belief in all that is unlike God. In our Consciousness only God exists. This is the rising Christ. This is the mystical Easter. This is the Resurrection of Christ in you.*"
— *Herb*

As many as receive Him, to them gives He power to become the sons of God..which are born, not of blood, nor of the will of the flesh, nor of the will of man, but of the Spirit of God.
— *John 1:12*

In this series of talks reviewing the book, Realization of Oneness by Joel, combined with The Book of John in the Bible, Herb Fitch gently lifts us beside the Invisible River of Spirit within our Being, there to be Spiritually Baptized by the Holy Ghost which is the power that transforms us into the Son of God.

When you are entirely ready to turn away from mortality; it's good as well as it's evil, then you are ready to be transformed by the Spiritual Renewing of your Eternal Self. As mortality is surrendered you stand very still, and listen...

Bill Skiles
Robbinsville, NC
09/07/19
Website : http://www.mysticalprinciples.com

Class 24

If Ye Love Me

Herb: You are in a state of meditation and within you the Voice says, *"If you love me, keep my commandments."* Suppose you heard this within, *"If you love me, keep my commandments."*

It's very unlikely that you would ever forget it. It is also very unlikely that you would disobey. You would know this is the voice of the Father within, I am being instructed from on high that the way to the kingdom of God on earth is to be receptive to the inner Voice, be obedient, to be obedient, not out of a sense of duty, not out of a sense of fear, but out of a sense of the rightness of it. Of the love of Truth, of the joy of being taught by the Infinite. And you would say to yourself, "What are the commandments that I am to follow?" And because the Voice which speaks within you always goes before you, it would present to you those commandments which you are to follow. It would further elaborate that all of the Bible speaks one message; to join you in conscious union with your own Immortal Spirit.

That Word which is the Word in the beginning, with the Father, is your Immortal Spirit. And that's all the Bible has been trying to do for us; that's all those who have come to earth Christed, aware, enlightened, have tried to do - to awaken us to the fact that our own Immortal Spirit is the key. No person, no idol, no outer teaching. All these may be ways to awaken you in some way to the Presence of your own Immortal Spirit. And when you are awakened to it, you are ready to obey the commandments of your own Spirit. You as a human being, can never obey the commandments of Christ. And the only way you will obey them is to be united with your Spirit that's becoming the Son of man instead of son of the woman. And then as the Son of man, one with the eternal Spirit, the very Spirit of your own Being from the Infinite flows through guiding, leading, dissolving that remnant of human consciousness which still believes in a material world of material objects and material conditions which are not the Father's creation.

And so we are opening ourselves to our own Spirit learning how it is to be in Oneness with that which is everlasting. And as we begin to accept the challenge of obedience only to Spirit, we walk in a different universe than the world around us. We may be seen in it, we may act in it, we may even be an effect in it but something else is functioning in us and through us and as us, that is unseen. It is that Immortal Spirit that we are.

If you love Me - your Immortal Spirit - obey my commandments. Your Immortal Spirit which wrote the Bible, which functioned on earth as Christ Jesus, which functions on earth as your identity, must have commandments for you or It would not instruct you to obey them. And you find that these commandments are not in yesterday, they are not only commandments issued on the earth in a previous era. The commandments of the Immortal Spirit are continuous and they are within you now. To obey my commands then is the call to withiness. It is the call of Spirit to Spirit, saying, "Turn ye and with joy, with anticipation, with the sure knowledge that I am not separated from you by space or time. That there is no distance between us, that I am a present Spirit, a now Spirit, a here Spirit. It says, "Rest back on the sea of your own Spirit."

With confidence, with trust, with the awareness that this is the way. And you will receive my commandments. You will receive those secret impulses that come up only to those who are listening, aware. Not in a dream consciousness, but conscious that present where they are is the Spirit of God, now, always, without ceasing. And then you are lifting yourself out of the dream consciousness, reminding yourself that you are not a human consciousness but where you are is your spiritual Consciousness present now, waiting to be obeyed, to be listened to, to be worshipped. And it's just like turning the channel of your TV set to another. "No, I am not a creature consciousness. I am not a dream consciousness. I will listen to my Immortal Consciousness."

You're in your overdrive, your back where you belong; listening, ready, willing to be fed from within by My continuous commandments within you.

And this is the call to withiness which opens an infinite method of communication for Infinite Spirit which indwells us all to guide us in its own Divine plan. In this Oneness with the Infinite we are in conscious union with God, we are one with Source, we are one with All cause and we are one with All that is. As you touch God now where you are, in Consciousness, knowing that God is All, that God is Infinite you are touching All that God is everywhere.

And in that Oneness with God where you are now, you instantly are one with God everywhere and you are in a position to obey the commandments of the Father. If God is not where you are, in your consciousness, you can never obey the Divine commandments. You are separated and you are unaware of God presence. "But if you love Me, if you love the Father, if you love the Spirit, if you love the Truth, if you love Life put yourself in the position of being conscious that God is where you are."

And in that union, in that realization, All that God is everywhere is where you are. And wherever God is you are. You are transplanted out of a dot, a point; a limited, finite area; a lacking, limited consciousness. And you are in the Divine flow. The Divine Consciousness individualizing where you are functions as your very Selfhood; flowing, overflowing and Truth fulfills Itself.

You do not fulfill Divine commandments as a mortal being in a human mind. It cannot be done. You cannot sit there and say, "God now you tell me and I will do it." The mortal consciousness must be dissolved in the knowledge that here is God, here is Divinity, here is Divine Consciousness, and it is one with Itself everywhere. No mortal consciousness is present.

And then we need no words. All responsibility is gone from your mortal consciousness; you are not depending on it. You are letting the Divine fulfill Itself. You are letting the Father within actually perform, perfect and do, all that must be done. You are removing human will, human desire, human ambition, human fear, human doubt; you are removing humanhood in all its completeness and all its incompleteness. You are accepting your own Immortal Spirit as identity. Immortal Spirit is the only one who fulfills the commands of Immortal Spirit. You can only fulfill the words of Christ by being Christ.

And therefore in order to fulfill the words of Christ you are forced to that position where having failed to fulfill those words, you finally come to the only place where you can fulfill them; the Christ that must fulfill these words, I am.

You are joined with your Immortal Spirit, forever. For this is the meaning of Grace and Life eternal.

We see Christ as the identity of all. We know the Immortal Spirit stands where the form seems to be and therefore in the obeying of the commandment, *"Acknowledge me in all thy ways,"* and the obeying of the commandment, *"Love thy neighbor as thyself,"* we never deny the Immortal Spirit as the Presence where the form appears to be.

There stands the Immortal Spirit invisible where the form appears to be. Here where I stand, is the Immortal Spirit where the form appears to be. The Allness of Spirit is the command of *"Acknowledge me in all thy ways,"* and therefore to fulfill that command you must acknowledge the Allness of Spirit everywhere. When you are not acknowledging the Allness of Spirit everywhere you are crucifying God. You are crucifying Spirit in your consciousness. You can only acknowledge the Presence of Spirit or you crucify its Presence. That means there is no second presence.

We are training ourselves to live in the conscious awareness of the Presence of Spirit. And to further comply with the statement, *"If you love me, obey my commandments,"* we know that every time we accept a condition that is not present in Spirit we are denying the Presence of Spirit. When you accept an imperfection - because there is no imperfection in Spirit - you are saying that "Spirit is not present."

Every form of imperfection, every fear, every quiver of doubt, every concern, every limitation, every lack is a denial that Spirit is present. And so we can never accept in consciousness the lacks, the limitations, the imperfections; we cannot even accept fulfillment in time. Spirit is already fulfilled. We must accept, I am already fulfilled, because that is the acceptance of Spiritual identity. The appearance may not show it but the appearance is not what we judge by. My Immortal Spirit is fulfilled and Self fulfilling and in the acceptance of it, I accept that I am now Self fulfilled.

I cannot have lingering beliefs in lack or limitation while I am accepting Spiritual identity.

And you continue in this vein knowing whatever you seem to need – every need that you have – is a denial of Spiritual identity. You have no need. The you that has a need is the dream consciousness and therefore whenever you have a need, it is a sign that you are not in Spiritual identity. What can Spirit need if Spirit is all?

You can go a step further and an important step, whenever you feel a need, it is time to realize that this which needs is not my Self. Whatever needs is not Me. Whatever lacks is not Me. Whatever is limited is not Me. Whatever is imperfect is not Me. Whatever is faulty or defective is not Me. And as you know, that these imperfections, lacks and limitations are not you and are not part of your Being, you are again obeying the commandment of loving the Spirit of God beyond all else. Loving God supremely. Not crucifying God while you declare you lack and you are limited. Because the you who lacks is never You.

Every error, every evil, every problem, every suffering, every pain does not occur ever in You.

And when you step out of that false you which experiences these things you are obeying again that commandment, *"If you love me, obey my commandments."* You are upholding the one true, eternal Spirit as the only.

And when you do, and especially those who have had the experience of doing so, know there is a moment of Truth testing, when the very Christ in you walks out testing the very Truth It has spoken through you, confirming to you that what It has said is the Truth. That when you accept no power because only Spirit is power, you discover the Truth that there is no power but your own Immortal Spirit. You discover too, that you are Self complete. Your Spirit being All, your Spirit embodying all that Spirit is, all that you need is present in your spiritual Self. The moment you declare a need, you are declaring your incompleteness and you are declaring your unspiritual identity.

And so we begin to be very careful of what we accept in consciousness. The acceptance of that which is not my Self is the way I deny what I am. These are some of the ways that we learn to love the Father. You can see that it is a complete denial of personal sense or it is a denial of Spiritual identity. We're not trying to ride both horses.

Now in your silence, you may have discovered that you are not able to really attain the right quality of silence. And that is because the mission of Christ is to enable us to break through the world mind. And while you're being silent, the world mind is not being silent and there is this inner conflict between the world mind and your attempt at silence. And although you may have a high state of mental discipline and a strong human will and a great idea of being dedicated, you cannot humanly break the world mind. Only the advent of Christ in you, the Light, breaks the darkness. And therefore the silence which is only a stillness of your mind to some degree, may not penetrate deeply enough to release in you the Light of Christ. That Light which alone breaks the world mind. And you may find your silence not productive.

12

But you can release the Light of Christ through silence when you are consciously practicing the presence of Christ everywhere. If you have not practiced I, Christ everywhere, you do not have the leverage in that silence.

Now last week, last Sunday, we had a little exercise which those who were present learned to practice this week. And it was quite unusual. I here, am the Life of that one there. I am the identity of that one there: and that one isn't there because I, the Spirit of God is there and that is my name.

And so we practiced this week. We took one individual, we took a loved one, and we rested in the knowledge that I am the identity of that person there which happens to either be my husband or my wife or my child or my mother – but they are not there. The Immortal Spirit is there and that Immortal Spirit I am. And we live with that. Some of us tried it for three hours.

Now when you have attained a measure of awareness of that, you can quickly see that this is the Truth that exists where you are, for every individual on the earth. There is no individual on the earth who is not the Immortal Spirit of You. And until you are aware of that, until you have practiced the contemplation of that, until you have lived with that, your silence doesn't deepen enough to permit the advent of the Christ. You see, a human being, being silent is just a physical exercise. But when you are aware that your Immortal Spirit being everywhere is all there is and that it's never divided from Itself; that it is the Spirit of everyone that walks the earth, then you come full circle to the fact that wherever there is a form it is I, invisible. Every form you see is You. There's not a form on this earth that is not your invisible Self.

God is the substance of every form. God is your Immortal Spirit. Your Immortal Spirit is the substance of every form. And when you are not practicing the knowledge that wherever form appears your

Immortal Spirit is there, you are not loving God supremely and you are not obeying God's commandments.

And so this becomes a very urgent practice. Yes, I see that person there but it is not a person - it is my Immortal Spirit. And now I cannot treat that person as a person. It is my Immortal Spirit. I cannot judge that person. I cannot condemn, I cannot in any way slur that individual. Why? Because that individual isn't there. My invisible Self is there – the Immortal Spirit of God. Because God is All there is. The Allness of Spirit is what I am upholding. I am upholding my own Spiritual identity there, as well as here. And when you do this you begin to get your leverage.

It doesn't matter who that individual is, a loved one or an enemy, friend or foe, Greek or Jew, white or black, Democrat or Republican, priest or rabbi, fool or genius; there, invisible is your Immortal Spirit and you make no differentiation. And when you learn this and live with this, the Spirit of God that you recognize there, recognizes you.

Then your silence is an Infinite silence. It is a silence of Spirit. Not just trying to black out a human mind. It's the silence of Light. You're in your Holy Mountain. You can be told your Everlasting Name. You can go from Glory to Glory because you are in the One: you are in conscious union with the One. The everywhere One, is your name.

The whole Bible is in this verse, *"If you love me, obey my commandments."* And the whole Bible is in us.

So this week we have another exercise. As you have been able to practice for three hours that you are the identity of this loved one you worked on this week, now see that every form everywhere is your invisible identity. And don't be fooled by that form even if it seems to, in some way, be unfriendly toward you. You'll find it has many tricks to fool you, to make you think that You are not there invisibly where it appears. And if you can overcome the deception, simply by faith in the Word, you will be lifted higher and you'll be lifted above the deception. And you will discover that your identity where that form appears begins to exert an invisible influence. A subtle, emanating activity.

It begins to bring the Divine influence to bear; not through your effort, not through your will, but simply through your recognition. We never make an effort to influence the Spirit in any way. We do not even ask the Spirit to make us a demonstration or give us a desired manifestation. We rest in the knowledge of unbroken Spirit everywhere as my identity. Everywhere you go, your Spirit is. And only your Spirit is there – your Spirit is the one inhabitant of the universe. Find a second and you will be separated from your own Spirit.

Now this is the one Spiritual identity that we learn to accept for ourselves and we know it to be that the identity of everyone who walks the earth. Every flea. Every fly. Every animal. Every bird. It is the identity behind all that appears in this world.

Who was your Father on this earth? Your own Self. Who was your mother on this earth? Your own Self. Who are your children on this earth? Your own Self. There is only one Self. You were all your own ancestors. You are all there is and you must know it. Only the one infinite Spirit is. And that is your Self.

As you practice this knowingly, meeting your Self everywhere, you will find a Power and it will flow and it will change your life into the Divine image and likeness expressing. Every imperfection that you find is a lie. It is a denial of your identity; of your spiritual infinite Being. Do not accept it, as the Truth of your Self. Rather than get rid of the imperfection, know that the self having such an imperfection is not You and you're well on your way to finding it dissolve. For that self is never you who is imperfect. Do not accept such a self.

If you love the Spirit of God, accept no other identity; for the Son of God is the Spirit of God.

Silence, (pause) …

You may find you can easily rest in your Divine Consciousness. There are moments when it's so clear, so easy and you know you're there. And you can quickly snap out that human consciousness that tries to creep in. And then the flow is open. Omniscience is working full time.

The Power is there. The Power of maintaining its own perfection is ever present just as long as you're not on the floor but up on the ceiling, up on the high mountain top of your own Consciousness. In the upper firmament of Consciousness. Just resting confidently that the Father is doing the Father's job in his own Spirit; your Spirit.

This is an inner baptism; a continuous one and the more faithful we are to it, the higher the revelation that flows through us. The more we are lifted. The more is dissolved of the remnants of the human. Light replaces the unenlightened darkness of the old consciousness. The miracle of his Presence transforms us. We find that we have no fear or if momentarily we succumb to fear, it quickly can know the Truth that fear is not part of my Being; that being which fears is not me. That is not me at all and I step out of the false self. A need creeps up, quickly recognized, but Spirit is my name and Spirit has no need. Spirit is the fullness of God now. Therefore that need is trying to make me accept a false sense of self. There is no 'me' to need.

I am the child of God, the Spirit, the Immortal, the now of God. I'm not in that which expresses a need. I am Self fulfilling perpetually. I'm back where I belong in Self, one with Spirit. I am in the Source, in the Cause. And that cause being Spirit, it must manifest perfection. There is no other me here. The human creature image ceases to have the magnetism to draw us into it as an accepted self.

We begin to feel ourselves more as a living consciousness instead of a form, instead of a finite body. We feel our own conscious Oneness with the Infinite and we have a new intuitive sense of life into which things can flow from within, into the without, manifesting, taking form. And the forms that this innerness takes, conform to the new enlightened realization within. They are Christed forms. They carry with them their own fulfillment, their own Grace. They go before everything we do. They are magically sustained from the Invisible. The Christ which says, *"If you believe on me.... if you love me, obey my commandments,"* is taking us out of mortal, dying consciousness. It is revealing the Immortal Consciousness of God where we stand. It is fulfilling its mission every moment. It is dissolving the dream of lack, limitation, mortality, disability; it is revealing that where his presence is realized, his qualities are manifest.

Where you are is God. To be aware that God is where you are is the key to the Kingdom. To be aware that God will always be where you are and that wherever you go, God will always be.

"I, give you the keys to the Kingdom. I, your Immortal Spirit, tell you, that I am always where you are. And if you love me, you will know this; you will be aware that I, your Immortal Spirit, is always present everywhere until the false film of materialism no longer can trick you."

Joel tells us that. we can. through our ignorance or through our enlightenment. release the forces that curse us or bless us. Our ignorance of the presence of my own Immortal Spirit, releases the forces that curse me. My awareness of the presence of my own Immortal Spirit releases the forces that bless me.

How beautiful to know that if you are conscious that your Spirit is present, you release the forces that bless you.

And so with your exercise to know that your Spirit is where every form appears, you learn that wherever you go there's no one there but your Spirit. And this is the God awareness which releases the forces that bless you. Until all that functions in your life is Divinity expressing. Immortal Spirit living your life.

Is it within reach of us? It's more than that. It's inevitable. You cannot stop it. The moment you are touched by the knowledge of It. It is yours forever. And you will not rest until you have attained it because once you know it is attainable, it is because Christ has touched you; Christ has opened your eyes. And Christ says, "It is attainable, it is already attained and the attaining is merely coming into the realization of that which already is."

Silence, (pause) …

"[And] I," says the Christ within, "I will pray the Father, and he shall give you another Comforter, that he may abide with you for ever…. If you love me obey my commandments. [And] If you obey my commandments …. I will pray the Father, and he shall give you another Comforter that he may abide with you for ever…. Another Comforter who will abide with you for ever."

The disciples had more or less accepted Jesus as their Comforter. Their first Comforter was external to their Being. They saw Jesus but did not really see who was there. They heard Jesus but did not hear who was there. They knew him but did not know him. They had what they thought was their Comforter. Just as many of us have accepted external teachers, external authorities. Yes, they are perhaps our first comforters but the Spirit says, "No, I will pray unto the Father."

And this praying unto the Father is just another word for You when You are in a state of awareness of identity. Christ in you, is one with the Father and that conscious Oneness with the Father is all that prayer really is. When you are in conscious Oneness with God you're in prayer. I, the Christ, the Spirit, One with the Father; I am in a perpetual state of prayer. That is a state of Consciousness called conscious union. I, pray unto to the Father. As you dissolve your dependence on the external - the external dollar, the external form of power, the external material aid, the external help from outside of your Being, you are looking to a higher Power, a Power called the withiness of your own Being. Self power. And you are finding another Comforter. This Comforter who will be with you forever. This Comforter is identity. This Comforter is Immortal Spirit. This Comforter is Son of God. This Comforter is Christ. And so the Master within, appearing as the Master without, teaches us that we must now come to the point of walking in conscious awareness of the inner Spiritual Self.

The new Comforter is your own Being realized. The highest aspect of the Holy Ghost. The Comforter. Identity. Infinite Spiritual identity accepted. Everywhere is my Self. Not even Jesus can take you to heaven. No individual on the earth. Heaven is the Comforter within and when you have been willing to test the outer words by living in the within, not accepting the limitations of the without as part of Being, you are turning your life over to the inner Self, the new Comforter, the awareness that I can never be less than the Immortal Spirit. Nothing can make me less. Every claim that says, "I am not the Immortal Spirit," is a lie.

This acceptance becomes a living Light. Turning from the without, even from Jesus. "No," he says, "You cannot come into heaven through Jesus. I pray unto The Father and he will send you a new Comforter." You cannot come in through Jesus. You must come in through Christ within your Self. That is your new Comforter - your own Selfhood realized. And that Selfhood will be with you forever because it is your eternal Self. Your eternal Self is the only Comforter acceptable unto the Father. To be lived in, to be trusted, to be accepted as the only You that ever will be.

And then you know you are the eternal Life of God. You are no other. You are no second. You are that eternal Life ever expressing. And all that denies it now is a lie. All that ever denied it was untrue. The Christ is opening the way to Christ.

Silence, (pause) ...

The one Infinite Source is functioning our Being now, perfectly. The mind that does not know this perfection has no existence. It is a counterfeit, a pretender with no validity whatsoever. The mind that does not know perfection is a mind that does not exist. It is the false mind of the world expressing as the false mind of the individual. There is no such mind. There is no mind that can know imperfection. That mind which knows imperfection is not the Divine mind and therefore has no existence and you can look at it and say, "Who convinceth me of imperfection?" Only Spirit, only the mind of Spirit is present. And that is your mind. And you can rest in It confidently because where God is, the mind of God is. Where God is, the power of God is being the power of God. The mind of God can only be present where you are. No other mind is present.

The power of God can only be present where you are. No other power can ever be present. And only the qualities of God can be present so the Master always says, "Fear not, fear not." The qualities of God are present, the power of God, the love of God, the very presence of God. Immortal Spirit is your name and it is God Itself. Your Immortal Spirit is God. God is your Immortal Spirit.

And so I in the Father and the Father in me. At all odds we defend this identity against every appearance the world can throw at us. Because that's all these appearances are for. To force us to accept our true identity or to reject it. Every appearance is saying to you, "You are not the identity that God tells you you are." And God is saying, "I tell you who you are and I expect you to look at these appearances and accept my word. *If you love me, obey My commandments.* My commandment is that you are my Immortal Spirit. You cannot be another."

Every appearance in the world has been lying to us. Making us, through the world mind in us, deny the commandments of the Father. But you will notice that you have changed. You've grown aware. You have become Spiritually knowledgeable. You are seeing through the deceit of the world mind. And only Christ in you can do that. And that is the sign to you that Christ in you has been lifted up. The fact that you can see through the deception of the world mind is evidence of the Presence of a consciousness of Christ. And the more this Consciousness is lifted the more the revelation intensifies, further dissolving the power that the world mind assumes in our human sense of life.

"I pray unto the Father, he will send you a new Comforter." This new Comforter is the raising of Christ within you. Until the exultant Self within proclaims I am come. I am the Self. I am all there is of You. Christ Infinite. Spirit Immortal. And the inner lifeline of Omnipotence is established. There's no break, there's no missing link. Omnipotence is established as the nature of Being where You are.

The world of matter loses its dominion. Grace replaces the law of matter. Karma is no more. There's nothing to expiate any more. Karma becomes simply that residue of human consciousness which no longer exists. There is no karma in the Immortal Spirit of God. We don't have to live another thirty lifetimes to pay our karmic debts.

Now let us once again establish that between you and God there is no distance - in space or in time. Never feel that between you and God there is space or time because there never can be in the Omnipresence of Spirit. The Spirit of God which is where you are, now, is never separated from You. It is your Being. The word G-O-D, God, the word Spirit are one and the same. Where are you are is God. Where are you are is Spirit. God is that Spirit. That Spirit is your Being. And the word S-E-L-F is your Spirit, your Self and that is the only God there is. Outside of your Self there is no God. Your Spiritual Self and God are one and the same.

That is why the Grace of your own Self realized is your sufficiency, in all things.

Now we are not separate from each other because we are the Self. And it matters not what forms you see, they are your Self. And that

Self where the forms appear is the same Self where you appear. But you are the Self and not the form - just as they are the Self and not the form. And therefore you are One everywhere. You are unseparated Being. There is no individual on this earth from whom you can ever be separated. And if you think you are, you are losing Spiritual Selfhood. You are a becoming barren.

Now do not misunderstand. If a form is doing what people call something good or if a form is doing what people call bad; you must know that neither the good nor the bad are happening. No form does good and no form does bad. Because only your Spiritual Self is present. The Father's Kingdom is never of this world. We're not trying to make the good of the Kingdom spill over into this world. Don't fall into that trap. We're trying to live in the Spiritual kingdom. We're trying to have that vision of the Christ which can see what is happening in the Spiritual kingdom. We're not trying to look for visible manifestation in the world. We want to see what is happening in Reality. We want to experience what is happening in Reality. We're not trying to transform this world into a better world. We are trying to live in the Kingdom of God where the world seems to be. And for a while it may seem as if you're trying to make this a better world. But you're not trying to heal that which is not there. You're not trying to improve an illusion. You're resting in the Spirit of God that it may manifest it's Spiritual kingdom which is not of this world. That you may awaken in that Kingdom, literally. Not in this world. That you make transition to that Kingdom which is not of this world. You see what we're doing? You see what we must learn to do? And every time we try to bring something of the Spirit into this world we're accepting that there is a world here when you must learn to accept that only the Immortal Spirit is here. You can even, while trying to do good, step out of Spiritual identity and lose that which you are seeking to attain.

You will know when you are walking in the Spiritual Kingdom. And you will know that it is not this world. And every moment that you find yourself led closer and closer to that which is the Kingdom be sure of this: when you are conscious. but for a moment. that you are walking in the invisible Kingdom of God; you have ensured your transition. The moment you have touched the invisible kingdom of God in your consciousness your transition is assured. For you the world will slowly dissolve and the Kingdom will take its place.

"If you love me, obey my commandments. And I will pray unto the Father and he will send you a new Comforter who will be with you forever." Those meaningful words, active in your consciousness, accepted, with reverence and devotion, with fidelity should be your spur and your reward. They are the gift of God to everyone who has an inner ear. And the very heart of us will bring into remembrance the Truth of those words as we proceed along that path so designated by the inner Spirit.

For he who has spoken to us is the voice of God within us. The only Voice we learn we can trust. All else is of the dream world. And only the voice of the Father within you, leading you through your own Christhood to Himself, can lead you into his Kingdom where you stand.

Now then, are you receiving the Comforter? Are you accepting the Comforter? Are you aware that only the Comforter will do? The Comforter can be only the one authority without opposite. Only the Comforter is the Way, the Life, the Truth, the Resurrection, the everlasting Self. And whatever you do to accept, receive and live in the Comforter, as the Comforter; is the Way.

Without the Comforter we are blind. Without the Comforter we are dead, walking images. With the Comforter we are Sons of God living in the Father, Divinely inspired, Divinely maintained, eternally. This is the promise of the Christ. When we accept that promise we have no other path but to find the Comforter who will be with us forever.

— End of Side One —

We'll be able now to conclude the eighth chapter of Joel's book. This is the "Sea of Spirit" and it follows right along with the high demand of scripture. *"We have,"* says Joel, *"no right to have desires."* You see if we're going to let the Immortal Spirit which we are, run its own Life, then we have no right to have human desires. So the minute you go off that direction with human desire you're not accepting Immortal Spirit as your Self. Joel catches us the minute we move out of Immortal Spirit by having a human desire. *"We have no right to have a will of our own.... We have no right to know lack, limitation or unhappiness. We lose the privilege of having fears or doubts or of losing hope, [because] if we indulge in those temptations we are taken back to our mortal selfhood, the one [that is] supposed to be 'dying,' or already 'dead.'"*

And so that clarifies the fact that we must make a conscious effort not to indulge our human wishes. And although it's difficult to discern the difference between a Divine desire, a Divine Impulse, a Divine Will and your own, it's a lot less difficult than if you're not conscious of the fact that you're to have no human will.

Now you can carry this to the point of absurdity. If you're very literal minded, you will say, "Well, do I have to say to the Father, I'm thirsty, do I need your permission to get a drink of water?" - and so forth. And that would be to the point of absurdity because if you are conscious of yourself as Immortal Spirit you will be given the way to obey the commandment of having no human will. And you'll find that there is a path laid out invisibly through which you walk, in which you might appear to be in some way fulfilling human desires but you'll know that this is but an outward appearance to other eyes that whatever you're doing is not humanly motivated. And whenever you find the human motivation creeping in, it isn't so much that you stop that human motivation but that you return to the Father's house which is, Immortal Spirit is my name.

When you're in identity you will not cast a shadow of human motivation. When you're not in identity, you will. Every time you find human motivation creeping in, that's to remind you that you are subtly being a prodigal from your own Self. You're not living in your Immortal Spirit. No will, no human desire, no human needs; living in your Immortal Spirit.

And now let's say that you have no capacity to do this throughout the day. You've got to then develop that capacity and the only way you can develop it is to practice it. And so you must make it a point that a day that goes by in which you are not conscious of your Self as Immortal Spirit, is a day in which you are again crucifying the Father, in you.

You're letting personal sense still permeate. You're saying to world mind, "You've got a home in me friend, just come right through and do what you will." Now we're patching that vulnerability until we can discard it. Consciously, daily, we practice – I am the Immortal Spirit. Consciously daily we practice because I am the Immortal Spirit, I have no human selfhood, no human desire, no human wish. Yes, I'm going to get hungry, I'm going to want a second portion, I'm going to do human things. I know it. But I will suffer this to be so now while I am still conscious of the fact that world conditioning is so strong that I must still go through some human footsteps – maybe for quite a while.

But even while I go through these human footsteps, while I eat, while I sleep, while I behave as a human being in appearance, I am consciously sowing to the Spiritual nature of my Being. This is our constant awareness day by day.

And you can measure your progress by those things which come to you in your inner revelation. You will know you are being lifted to glory after glory by the sublime nature of the revelations that come. They will be the sign that even though you appear in human flesh, you are making Spiritual progress in the knowledge of Spiritual identity. You will never have to feel a sense of guilt that you made a mistake; because you don't make mistakes. You are Spiritual identity.

World mind makes the mistakes and they appear as you making the mistake. But you are always Spiritual identity regardless of what mistakes appear to be there. You do not change. You only change to other people's concept of you. You never change. You are always Immortal Spirit.

And that must be your conscious identification regardless of what the outer picture says. You will find you are cracking through that veil of the world mind until it no longer has the power to create the false sense of its power in you.

"In the degree that we have human desires, human will, human ambition, human fears and human doubts ....we are denying and crucifying our Christhood." That's Joel's statement.

If God is individual Selfhood - which is the Truth we have learned to accept - then how can there be a human selfhood at all? The Truth is that God is individual Selfhood and human selfhood is the counterfeit concept we have entertained. And all that goes with that counterfeit concept is part of the false world belief that we have suffered through. Even the suffering is counterfeit. You are always Immortal Spirit.

"Unless we are able to rest back and float on the Sea of Infinity, we have no conscious awareness of our hidden manna."

What is that hidden manna? Well, he just said we can't know what it is unless we float back on the Sea of Spirit. In other words it must be revealed within what your hidden manna is. Even though the Master has told us what our hidden manna is. It is still but a word to us when we say, "Spirit." It must be the experience of Spirit and then you are in identity. Then you are in your hidden manna. Your experience of Spirit is hidden manna. This is the realization that, *"Greater is he that is in us than he that is in the world."* Your Spirit is greater than your flesh. And the more you come to that realization the more you realize that your Spirit is all there is of You. And your flesh is the world concept.

We're being taken out of the perishable, out of the transient, out of the temporary. We're being lifted into that which is the imperishable, the indestructible, sense of Self. And from this comes the conviction, the understanding, that because God constitutes our Being, God is the very substance of Life.

And then Joel says and, *"And that in the presence of our very own consciousness there is rest, quiet, contentment, peace."*

Now we are being lifted to the realization that there is another Consciousness present than the one which we call our human consciousness. In our human consciousness there is not quiet, rest and peace. There is disquiet. There is turmoil, there are questions, there are fears, there are doubts; there's a feeling of impermanence. That's the wrong consciousness; it's not our true consciousness. In the presence of our Consciousness there is quiet, rest and peace. Our Consciousness is God. And only when you're in your Consciousness instead of your false human sense of consciousness, are you in the quiet, the peace, the true silence. When you are not in peace, quiet, silence, rest, absence of fear, you're not in your Consciousness; you're in your sense mind. And although your sense mind is often called your consciousness, it isn't at all; it's the counterfeit of your Consciousness. It's but the shadow, with shadows of thought. And every time you are in some form of disquiet, remember you're not in your Consciousness; you're in an imitation consciousness which is not your Consciousness. Your Consciousness is Divine Consciousness because you are Divine Spirit. And right where you are, (sound of click of fingers) you can switch channels like that.

Right where you are that disquiet is the wrong channel, the wrong consciousness, the false, the untrue and in the upper firmament right where you are is your Divine Consciousness if you will but rest. And wait. And listen. And trust.

Here I am – I am the Divine flow. Right where you are I've always been present. I, God, am present. And my Consciousness is Divine and I share no consciousness with a second consciousness. The one Divine Consciousness I am, God, is here now as your Consciousness and my Consciousness.

There is no other consciousness present.

In that Consciousness we learn to find our Being. We find the Living water. There's where you find the real Comforter. That's where you find the Spirit of Truth. Not the truth of the mind, but the Truth of the Spirit. The real Comforter comes as the Spirit of Truth, heralding the presence of all that is Real.

Silence, (pause) …

And we find that the serpent who deceived us has no power when we are in the Divine Consciousness. All of its claims and all of the beliefs that it engendered in us are recognized as false. We lose belief in those concepts which said we were other than the pure, perfect Spirit. We lose belief that there is a power beside the pure, perfect power of Spirit. We lose all belief in anything other than Reality. And when there's that click in you that tells you you've lost the belief in unreality you will find it loses its power to manifest where you appear. It can only manifest where you appear while it still has you in a state of believing in its unreality; in its false power. In its capacity to do something not ordained by the Spirit of God. This belief we are slowly rooting out so that we have a pure Consciousness and pure motives.

"The more we live in the conscious awareness of God as constituting our Being" - just the sound of those words to me is music – *"the more we live in the constant awareness that the consciousness of God is our Being."* - this is stated by Joel as a fact – *"The consciousness of God is our being."* And the more we live in that awareness *"The more the 'natural man' is being loosed until finally it fades away entirely."*

28

Here's the Master telling us that the natural man fades away entirely as we abide in the conscious awareness that Divine Consciousness is my Being.

It doesn't leave room for doubt. The natural man is dissolved away entirely. Silence, (pause) ...

So even if we have not been there, one who has tells us; the natural man dissolves. Silence, (pause) ...

That means there's a change of consciousness that takes place; an anointing. An inner Self replaces the outer appearing self. And then a transformation takes place. You live and move and have your Being, your activity emanates from the Divine center, which is the All, and this outer form though still present in appearance, is an instrument of the Infinite Spirit.

And so there's a Christ appearing as Jesus. Why? Because the natural man has dissolved. All that is present there is Divine Consciousness functioning, appearing as a form. And that form as we learn, is not subject to the evils of this world. For it, death has no power.

As the natural man is dissolved in Consciousness death has no power. Disease has no power. Pain has no power. The powers of this world are revealed to be without power. Why? Because Divine Consciousness has replaced human consciousness. The human consciousness that was never there but only seemed to be, can no longer report those defects or problems that were never there but only seemed to be, within that human consciousness.

The new Consciousness reveals the qualities of the new Consciousness made manifest. And the consciousness of God presence is Life Eternal and therefore death has no place. And the conditions that lead to death have no place. And if this were not so we would have no purpose in studying this message because the purpose of the message is to reveal Life Eternal. You cannot reveal Life Eternal if death is a reality. You can only reveal Life Eternal because it is the Reality. And incorporates all of the living qualities which are ever present in our true Divine Consciousness.

So we're trying to stay, if we can, in that upper firmament.

"We maintain and [we] sustain the evils, the errors, the discords of our life by thinking about them, but as soon as we no longer think about them, they cease to be because they never existed [at all] outside our thinking. As we stop dwelling on our triumphs and on our failures, they no longer exist. Instead, Christ lives our life."

Now here Joel identifies that all error is in thought. It never gets outside of thought. Everything we experience is our thought. That is our total human experience, our own human thought. Which in itself is not free thought because it is world thought. We are imprisoned in our own human thought. And it reports those things which are not true because our human thought is not Divine Consciousness expressing. And so the world thinks of the evils that are in the world only because the world is disconnected from its own Divine Consciousness which would reveal to it that there are no evils. There is only Divine manifestation seen through the veil of human thought. As we stay in the upper firmament accepting Spiritual Selfhood, accepting Divine Consciousness, we are stepping out of human thought and stepping out of the conditions which exist in human thought.

"Christ-Self," says Joel, *"is our true identity... Christ Self is our true identity. The 'natural man' is that part of us which was imposed upon us at birth and to which we are now 'dying.' To the degree in which we lift up the I in us, are we 'dying daily' to the personal sense of 'I' [And] in the degree that we take no thought, but rest in the Sea of Spirit, are we letting the Christ live our life, and then each moment of the day we do these things [that are] given us to do [by the Christ within.]"*

That's the method always. Obedience to the Christ within, taking no human thought, no human desire, no human belief, learning that world mind is only the thought that we have thought to be our own thought. We are really bypassing the world mind by taking no human thought.

Now let's sum it up with these phrases of Joel's. *"God is fulfilling Himself and His destiny as our individual experience. This is not your life or my life to do with as we would like: this is God's life which God is living as us. [And] once we begin to perceive this, we will understand Immortality."*

Now then, everything that we think is our life, is not. Because God is living God's life as us. And God's life is perfect and that which we consider our life which is obviously imperfect, is not our life. Because it isn't God's life. Superimposed on what is God's life where you are, is your sense of life and as you turn from your sense of life to the acceptance that God is living your perfect Life now, you find yourself separated from that false sense of life gradually. It sort of falls away. You begin to know your own perfection, the perfection of your neighbor; the hard crusts of human belief slowly dissolve.

Christ in us is bringing forth that imprisoned splendor. Blessing, where the world mind curses.

Now Joel identifies the hidden manna which we have done before many times knowing our true identity is the hidden manna. Knowing yourself as Immortal Spirit it is your hidden manna. Immortal Spirit everywhere. Knowing God has no limitation, that God lives our Life, that God cannot die, God cannot sin. God cannot be sick, God cannot be in pain. This is God life and all that is not perfect God life is not your Life. Withdraw belief that it is your life. For God-consciousness is appearing as us.

Now when Joel says, *"God-consciousness is appearing as us,"* that does not mean what it seems to mean. If you took that as the words sound, you would say, "God- consciousness-appears-as-us." Take that word 'appears' and see what it means. God- consciousness is what is here. What appears is not God-consciousness. God-consciousness is living as us, but what appears is the us that isn't. The us that isn't is what appears where God-consciousness is. God-consciousness is here and there is a false appearance called us. God-consciousness is all that is here. And what it is, is it's perfect Divine, Spiritual manifestation. What appears as us, is not that God-consciousness. That's why the word 'appears' is there. What **seems** to be us, is not that God-consciousness. What we **are,** is that God-consciousness. We are something other than what we appear as. We are Divine Spirit manifesting Itself and no human eye can see that. No human mind can know that and so that which is here as us, Divinely manifesting, is never seen by the human mind. That's why it sees us as we seem to be instead of as we are.

But as we know that we are God-consciousness, God manifestation, even though this appears to be us, eventually, until we then lose concern for our life in the realization that God knows how to maintain and sustain his Life which is ours. We begin to live that invisible Self.

Each of us is that invisible, immortal Self now. The feeling of this should begin to develop and deepen until you can know that you are not embodied in transient form. You never were in a perishable form.

Your exercises this week then are to expand last week's exercise for three hours of knowing that I am the Life of that one there. I am the very Presence where that one appears - to extend it to this universe - wherever form appears you invisibly are. This is a Truth someday must be constant consciousness.

Try it for a couple of hours and I think, what comes to me on it is, that there is a sort of a process called 'thought adjustment.' If you look out of a window at a person, you're going to see a person. But if you don't make the thought adjustment, consciously, you're going to continue seeing person. If you make the thought adjustment you will consciously look at person and say, "There is my invisible Self." That is the thought adjustment. And you should begin making total thought adjustment about everything you see until the realization in you is positive that wherever I see form, I am. You must consciously make this thought adjustment; it doesn't just happen. There'll be more to say about thought adjustment. It's a conscious practice.

You should constantly look at every form - even inanimate objects and know that inanimate object is not there. It cannot be because my Spirit is all that is there. There is no place where my Spirit is not and I must make a thought adjustment every time so that I am aware of my present Spirit everywhere. If I do not make the thought adjustments, I'll find I'm not in a position to fulfill the commandments of the Christ. And I'll find subtly that there develops the consciousness of space between God and myself. Time between God and myself and I start to think in terms of fulfilling myself in time and in space instead of knowing that I am already perfectly fulfilled. And letting that fulfillment then manifest as I know the Truth of Self.

You might not even like me next week after this exercise because I find it very difficult. You might say, "Oh I have a headache," or "This is too much," and it really is too much. But somewhere along the line you'll find a little oasis, you'll find new capacity to do this and there is a place where you're so grateful that you stayed with it. You find that you have greater powers of endurance than you realize. And in a moment, you'll find the power of endurance was fictitious, it never existed. That's what you thought the human being was doing because you weren't being your Spiritual Self. So vicious, so complete and so deep is the world conditioning that we have to sometimes suffer through these things to come to the other side of Reality. And it gets tighter and tighter and tighter. And while it gets tighter something gets looser somewhere else.

There is an Invisible universe right here. And that Invisible universe few of us have touched enough to know what is there. And it is Infinite and our experience in that invisible Infinite is the prize that awaits being willing to identify with it and to accept no substitute. Then the Spirit of Truth will come upon us, It will teach us all things and lead us into a remembrance of the Reality that in our Soul we already know.

The chapter next week is number 9; "Spiritual Identity." We might even be able to get a little further in 14 of John, but if we do or not, we'll stay with it. Let's see where we are in John – we're up to the 17th verse of John 14. That's where we'll begin next week and with chapter 9 of "Realization ."

Thought adjustment is the conscious willingness to look at an object, a form, a condition, a person, a thing and adjust your thought instantly to know - there is my invisible Spirit. And in that moment you are accepting the omnipresence of the Spirit of God. To that we learn to be true.

And so now we are in our ninth year of this teaching. Today was the first day of that ninth year.

Thank you very much.

CLASS 25

TRUTH IS ALWAYS PRESENT

Herb: If that meditation is an indication of today's class, then we have a fine class ahead of us.

I want to welcome all of our new friends again. There seems to be a special something in consciousness which many of us are feeling now as if we were entering a new threshold. Perhaps it's a measure of that inner Peace, a measure of assurance that we are really making spiritual progress and that impossibilities are becoming very meaningful now as present possibilities.

In this chapter, the fourteenth of John, we hear again of the Comforter. We remember in the Beatitudes we were told, *"Blessed are they that mourn for they shall be comforted."* And always the Master is telling us that he's going to leave and now he tells us that not only will he leave but when he leaves, the Father will send the Comforter in my place. And then he begins to tell us more about the Comforter.

In the seventeenth verse, he gets very specific. He says, referring to the Comforter, *"Even the Spirit of truth; whom the world cannot receive, because it seeth him not, neither knoweth him: but ye know him; for he dwelleth with you, and shall be in you."*

You remember the line before, *"And I will pray the Father, and he shall give you another Comforter, that he may abide with you for ever; Even the Spirit of truth; whom the world cannot receive, because it seeth him not, neither knoweth him: but ye know him; for he dwelleth with you, and shall be in you."*

And so, he has identified the Comforter as the Spirit of Truth. He will add more to that definition as time goes on but at the moment he has called the Comforter the Spirit of Truth.

Now the world has a letter of truth. The world has truth as the human mind knows truth. And we're being told here that the way the human mind knows truth is insufficient. The human concept of truth is not the Spirit of Truth. The Comforter is the Spirit of Truth.

And now we're being lifted to the awareness that we must receive a higher level of truth than we can know in the human mind. And if there is a degree of unrest, discord, concern, doubt, a sense of insecurity, a sense of no purpose, whatever we have entertained in the way of not knowing God aright, has been the lack of the Spirit of Truth.

Not having the Spirit of Truth, we wander off in that human sense of things which tries to make its own limited human judgments and regardless of how high we mount in human truth, until it becomes not human, but the Spirit of Truth, we actually do not know Reality.

We are always in a limited, finite universe. We are always in the opposites of health today and bad health tomorrow or limitations today and some degree of fullness tomorrow but never in the wholeness of our own Being. And that lack is always the lack of the Spirit of Truth. This then is the Comforter.

However, we find behind these words something more. We find for example that we have no capacity to receive the Spirit of Truth in our human mind. And as a result, having lived most of our adult lives in a human mind, we have been without the Spirit of Truth. You might say we're been poor of the Spirit, poor in the Spirit of Truth. We've had no faculty to receive it. The Spirit of Truth cannot enter a human mind.

The Spirit of Truth can only enter the Christ mind. And then we have to say to ourselves, "Well, do I have the Christ mind? Is that why I have not received that Comforter? That Spirit of Truth which knows all, which goes unto the Father, which is the will and fulfills the will of the Father which is Grace itself? Is this why I haven't received it, because I'm not in the Christ mind?"

And then comes a very shocking truth.

If I'm not in the Christ mind, what mind am I in? You can scan the world today and ask yourself, "Who is in the Christ mind?" You can look in religion, you can look in science, you can look in industry, you can look in government, you can look everywhere and say, "Who is in the Christ mind? Who is receiving the Spirit of Truth?" And then sadly you must say, "Very few that I known are in the Christ mind." A Joel was in the Christ mind, a Jesus was in the Christ mind, a John was in the Christ mind; but how many can I name who are in the Christ mind? Then what mind are they in? What mind have we been in ourselves?

The admission is sad but it must be made. If we're not in the Christ mind, we must be in the anti-Christ mind. We who say we love the Father but live in the anti-Christ mind and you can judge yourself from that point. If I'm not receiving the living Spirit of Truth, I'm in the anti-Christ mind.

What is the new Comforter? The Christ mind. The mind that takes you out of the anti-Christ mind which receiveth not the things of God. Why have I had fluctuations in my health, fluctuations in my relationships, why have I had doubts and concerns and even deep fears? Because that's the nature of the anti-Christ mind. It is not the nature of the Christ mind. We're being told, "Have ye that mind that was in Christ Jesus."

When you are in the Christ mind, you have walked through the threshold; the threshold of all that is untrue, the threshold of all that denies the presence of God where you stand. We have walked through the threshold of false powers. We learn that matter is not at all what it seemed to be. We learn that evil is not at all what it seemed to be. We learn about a deathless universe. We learn about an Immaculate creation which the anti-Christ mind has no way of discerning.

And then we say, "Is that Christ mind too difficult to come by if that's the mind I need to receive the Spirit of Truth?" We find that it was the mind of those disciples of John. In all his letters, he addresses his words to those who among us have received the inner unction, the anointing, those who have been born of the Spirit, those who are in the Spirit of Truth. Are we any less than students of John?

And Paul, he too was teaching the inner anointing. Are we any less than students of Paul?

We begin to discover that until you are consciously alert to the difference between the Christ mind and the human mind, you sort of float off in human thought trying to live with your own brilliance and never receive that living Spirit of Truth which lifts the veil, which reveals that here, now is the Kingdom.

Reality is here. Reality is perfect. Reality is infinite. This infinite, perfect Kingdom of Reality is here now and discernible only to the Christ mind. The human mind which receiveth not the things of God is unaware of the presence of the Kingdom of God on earth and is therefore incapable of transforming this earth into the activity of heaven.

But not the Christ mind, the Christ mind goes unto the Father, the Christ mind is the instrument of God on earth. The Christ mind of you is the only way in which you receive the living Spirit of Truth direct from the Father.

And then scripture becomes alive in your consciousness for you know it's telling you that God speaks only to the Christ mind. God reveals only to the Christ mind. God functions only through the Christ mind. Peace, Beauty, Truth, Harmony, Life, Love can only function in and through the Christ mind and until we are in the Christ mind, we are divorced from the presence of Reality even though we think we're walking in Reality.

So, it becomes necessary to establish that conscious awareness of the Christ mind in us, as the focal point from which we operate. As creature minds working out of a human brain and a five-sense mechanism, we are not the Christ mind and we are only aware of the realm in which the physical senses can function. And so, we're aware only of the realm of the body, of material forms, material objects and we're aware of the activity of the human mind. We cannot come into that realm which transcends, that realm which is above the present, that realm which is the basic cause of all that appears in the visible world. We cannot live in cause, we can only live in effect until Christ mind is that mind through which we function.

Now, Truth has to be our basic yardstick. We have to know how to identify Truth. We have to know how to identify untruth. We have to be able to say that is not Truth and that is Truth and until you can do this, you are not opening the door which leads to the experience of the Christ mind.

Now, Truth begins with the Word of God. It doesn't begin with human opinions. If we try to establish our concept of Truth, we find that we're on a foundation that wilts. But if we live in the concept not of our mind, but in the statement of Truth given to us by the Christ, then we have a foundation - a dependable foundation. When the rains come, it does not wash this foundation away.

And the Truth of God given through Christ is that God is the one Life.

And so, you start with that Truth - God is the one Creator, God is the one Being, God is the one invisible Substance, God is the one invisible Cause, God is the one Law, God is the one Power - and you have a basis for the beginning of Truth in consciousness.

Now then, there are three things that I can think of at the moment that will help us to identify that which is true and that which is not true. You look at something no matter what it is and you must say, "Did God create it?" Now, if God did not create it, it is not true. You look at something and say, "Is that the substance of God?" If it is not, it is not true. You look at something and say, "Is that temporary or is it permanent? Is it eternal?" If it is temporary, it is not true.

Truth is the substance of God. Truth is the creation of God. Truth is eternal because all that God creates is eternal. Truth is infinite. Is it finite? Then it is not of God.

Now, this is where we have to come face to face with Truth. We have to begin at a place where Truth is so firmly embedded in our consciousness that we can look at all that is not Truth and know it is not Truth and until we can do that, we can't take the necessary next step.

Out here, we look at form and we say, "Did God create it?" And in this level of our work, you cannot quibble. Did God create form? And if you're in doubt, ask yourself if that form is eternal. Ask yourself if that form is the substance of God. Ask yourself if that form is finite and you'll find the answer's clear. It's just a matter of learning that you must accept Truth. That which is finite is not of God. God is infinite. That which is temporary is not of God. God is permanent, eternal. That which is material is not of God. God is Spirit. God did not create form. Therefore, it's not true. Whatever is not true is not here. That's the level of the work where you open the way to the Christ mind.

Whatever is not true cannot be present. It doesn't matter what it looks like or what your feelings about it are. Only Truth is present. God is Truth. God is All. Only Truth is present.

Untruth never changes Truth. Untruth never removes Truth. Truth remains. Truth is permanent. Truth is always present and it's not sharing its place with untruth. Untruth is the false concept entertained in the natural mind. But Truth is there and does not change because the natural mind has no faculty to witness that

Truth. Right where form appears to be, something else is. Yes, Spirit Itself. Spiritual form, Spiritual body, Spiritual individuality,

Spiritual substance and only the Christ mind which discerns that, knows that. The human mind looking at Spiritual substance sees material form but they're not both there.

Now that is what I mean by living in Truth. Did God make it? If God made it, makes it, how can it die? How can it suffer? How can it be sick? How can it be imperfect? Don't play games with yourself. Don't turn away from Truth no matter how it hurts. You'll find this is how you come to the Christ mind.

As you pare away untruth, ultimately only Truth is left and when you're in Truth, why you're in the Christ mind. The Christ mind can only witness Truth and until you are only witnessing Truth, you're in the anti-Christ mind.

Now, we're coming then to a realm which is different that the human mind's knowledge. We learn to identify everything. We look at it. And all we want to know about it is, is it true? Is this situation true? Is this object Truth? Is this condition Truth? Everything must be identified as Truth or untruth. And when you discover that it's not Truth, you're ready for the step, the important step. Whatever is not Truth, is not here. It cannot be. Only Truth can be present.

Once you identify Truth and untruth, you know what is here and what is not here. The Comforter, the Spirit of Truth is that awareness now, that what is here is what God placed here and nothing else. You are not accepting a second creator or a second creation. You are being lifted to the awareness of Divinity. Behind the mortal form, the non-divine form is the invisible Divine and unless you're willing to look at and through the non-divine which is not of God, you will not know the Divine which is of God. You will not enter that realm which is Reality.

And so, many of us have learned to train ourselves to look hard at the fact and to accept that when the Master says, *"My kingdom is not of this world,"* the Master means precisely that. That there is no Truth in this world. No matter what you look at, it is not true. No matter what you see, it is not true. No matter what you touch, it is not true. It is not true because you are looking at it through a human mind and you are only seeing to the capacity of that human mind and what you are seeing is not there. It is in your human mind. You are looking at your thought.

Now, we've been through this study of looking at our thought, learning that everything we see and touch and feel is within our thought. We are looking at a thought form. But you remember here in this verse, the Master tells us that the world cannot receive the Spirit of Truth. And therefore, if we are in the world, if we are accepting the forms of the world, we are those who are in the world and cannot receive the Spirit of Truth.

The Spirit of Truth is not in the world. It is in the Kingdom. It is in the Kingdom which never perishes. It is eternal. It is permanent and it is not moved or changed or altered in any way by what happens in the world. When there is a condition in the world which appears to be one of sickness or suffering, it is not changing the permanent Truth that is there present. Untruth never changes Truth. Truth is ever present, ever perfect, ever infinite, ever real, ever made of the living Spirit and it does not change because the human thought patterns see something untrue.

So, we become aware of the patterns of thought which though they present pictures that are untrue are not changing the presence of the Spirit of Truth which is ever there, awaiting recognition by your Christ mind. It's as if you were to pick up the telephone book and look for a number and then dial it and someone on the other end says, "I'm sorry this isn't the party you wanted," and then you go back to the phonebook and you discover that you dialed the wrong number. You couldn't read the print; it was too fine for you. The correct number was there but you couldn't read it and so you squint some more and you dial again and each time, it's because you can't read the little five or the eight or something - you dial wrong numbers. The right number is always present while you're dialing the wrong numbers because your vision is insufficient. And then, you take a glass or a pair of eyeglasses and you look at it again and you get the right number and you dial and now you are put through directly. So it is, in fine print you might say, is the invisible Kingdom, ever present but if we don't have that vision which can see it, everything that we see is wrong. If we can't see what is there, then whatever we do see isn't there. The wrong number isn't in the phone book. The right number is there but if you can't see the right number, you get the wrong one.

The Kingdom is here but if you can't see it, you cannot see what is Real. Everything you see must be unreal. If you cannot touch the Kingdom, everything you touch must be unreal. If your human mind has no capacity to make contact with the present Kingdom of God, then everything your human mind makes contact with is unreal. And this is the revelation again of that mind which is called the universal world mind. The world mind which is the father of the human mind. The missing link in all of our problems.

Always, what you're looking at and which you think to be present is not what is there but what the world mind is picturing to you. God didn't make the suffering but the world mind presents a picture of suffering. You cannot see the God present, the Power present, the Truth present, the perfect, Immaculate Conception present but you do see the suffering that God didn't put there. You can't see the fine print so you see your concept of it. The suffering is your concept about what you cannot see. The lack is your concept about what you cannot see. The earthquake, the flood and the fire are our concepts about what we cannot see. Bad weather is our concept about what we cannot see. Every disease on this earth is our concept about what we cannot see. If we could see the fine print, if we could put on the Christ mind and look at what is there, you would not see the disease.

You would not see the cripple. You would not see the withered arm, you would not see the blind man. You would not see a dying person. They aren't there. To be there, they would have to be God created. They would have to be the substance of God. They are not.

And so, we see this world is our inability to see the fine print of the Kingdom and everything we see in this world represents the world mind, out-picturing itself as the things we think we're seeing.

The trick then is to know that we are imprisoned in the world mind and that the purpose of our being lifted up to receive the Spirit of Truth is that until we do, we remain imprisoned in the world mind. We remain a part of the world mind's false concept about the Kingdom it cannot see. Each one of us, instead of being heir to the fullness of God, as a creature we are heir only to the false concepts of the world mind.

Now, to look then at what is untrue and to recognize it as the world mind appearing to us as this form, this person, this condition, this thing, this lifespan is to correctly identify untruth. It isn't there. What put it there? If God didn't put it there, what put it there? A counterfeit world mind had to put it there for you to see it.

Now, while we're identifying Truth, we have to see that the Father, being Life, could not create death. That the Father being Peace, could not create discord. The Father being Harmony, the Father being Love, could not create hate. The Father being Eternality could not create age, could not create time. The Father being Infinite could not create finite space.

Infinity never becomes less than itself. It never becomes finite. Eternality never becomes time. Peace never becomes war or discord. Life never becomes death. These things never change but world mind makes us think they change. World mind presents the picture of time. World mind presents the picture of constant change. World mind presents the very opposite of Truth and we are imprisoned in those opposites without the Christ mind. You cannot come out of the opposites presented by world mind while you remain in human mind because world mind is your human mind. Only when you step out of human mind are you out of world mind.

And that's the importance now of this Comforter, the Christ mind. The Christ mind will look at all of the lies presented by the world mind. The world mind will present finitude. It will present forms coming into the world and forms going out of the world and the Christ mind will say, "Those forms are not created by my Father. They're not immaculate. They're not eternal. They're not life. They are concepts in the mind."

The Christ will look at the human concepts of disease and say, "That's not by my Father. My Father created perfection and perfection includes the capacity to maintain perfection." Maintaining its own perfection is the power of Christ and therefore what is this which is diseased? It's a world mind hallucination and each individual mind, each human mind, in the world mind must see this hallucination and react to it.

But we, as we are receiving the Spirit of Truth, we learn that the Christ mind in us can look at the untruth without being hypnotized by it. The Christ mind can look at all disease and say, "My Father didn't create it and therefore only what my Father created can be present.

This, not created by my Father is a world mind idea. I only suffer from it as I rest in that human mind which cannot see the fine print. I have a wrong number but I don't know it. As I find the fine print because the Christ mind can and does, I have the right number and the right number shows me that right where the world sees disease, there is perfect, Spiritual flesh."

Wherever the world mind presents a picture unlike God, the Christ mind finds the total opposite is completely true and no second.

In your Christ mind, you know the cripple, the blind man, the deaf man, all those who suffer from famine and poverty are world mind shadows seemingly real only to the mind that perceives that; the mind that is still the natural mind which is not capable of receiving the Spirit of Truth, the Comforter.

Identifying Truth then, is the way you open the portals to the Christ mind. Wherever you look, take a moment, no matter what it is, do not be afraid to face it with Truth. Is it God created? Is it God substance? Is it permanent?

Whatever does not answer that, is not Truth and is not present. And then having identified untruth properly, the question is how are you going to face untruth? How are you going to meet it? What are you going to do about it?

And this is where only the Christ mind can take you through the next threshold.

The Allness of God is the Law, the Reality, the Truth of Being. That which is untrue is not changing God. That which is untrue exists only in the mind that perceives it. It has no real existence. The Truth is still there where the unreal seems to be. And therefore, what you are going to do about it, in the Christ mind, is absolutely nothing. That's what you do about it - absolutely nothing.

You have confidence in the power of God to maintain the Kingdom of God. You have confidence in the Christ of your Being to remain Immaculate through all of the seeming outer imperfections. You have confidence that the word of God, the power of God, the presence of God, the law of God, the government of God is functioning right there. And all that is necessary for you is not to change what is out there but to change minds. To change from the mind which perceives to the Christ mind which knows only what God placed there is there. And as you change minds, you don't have to change any of the forms.

The changing of minds is the change of consciousness. The changing of minds is the place where the Comforter comes unto you. This new mind is the Comforter because it dissolves the world mind. When the Christ mind is in you, when you are standing fast in it, aware that only Truth can be present, only Reality can be present, that that which is imperfect is unreal and therefore only exists in the mind that perceives it, no where else, then you can face the fire and the flood, the tidal wave and the inclement weather and the unfortunate situations. You can face every catastrophe, knowing that in your Christ mind these do not exist. Your Christ mind breaks the veil of hypnosis. Your Christ mind lives in the Kingdom of God on earth as it is in heaven. And it is your function in that Christ mind to transform every false outer appearance by resting in the conscious awareness that the Comforter within me can be trusted. The Comforter can be trusted to reveal God's present Kingdom where the human mind was revealing the false concept called world.

Now this is the importance then of John 17 to us. We're being lifted into a new mind. A mind which knows the Father, which is the instrument for the Father, which doesn't stand there denying the world but is actively bringing forth that which is of the Father. Never accepting untruth as being present or possibly present.

And so, corporeality, material form, material objects, material conditions, all these which are perishable and not of the Father, in the Christ mind, are not accepted as being present.

We come to that Power, that Christ power which is perfect Power as being the only present activity. No matter what activity appears visibly in your Christ mind, you know that only Christ power is present and that when you know this, you are knowing the Truth which will reveal the presence of that Christ power.

Your function is not to go beyond knowing the Truth. The Truth will make you free but you will not know the Truth in a human mind. You will know it in your Christ mind and it will make you free. It will reveal the Self that was born of a Virgin immaculately, the Self that did not depend on human conception, the Self that did not begin with your birth certificate, the Self that does not end with your death certificate, the Self that is independent of the world that is not the creation of God. That is the high place to which the Christ is leading us now.

I can assure you that once you can identify Truth and untruth, boldly, and stand on that which is untrue is not here, you'll find that there are times when you'll lack the confidence to do that and you'll find there are times when your words seem as if they're just words without any realization behind them and you will also find that there are times when there's no power in your words. But you still must make that step until your words are not just words, until they are backed with discernment, until they are substantial, until they are borne out of conviction, until you feel a Spiritual awareness and then you discover you're not uttering words but the Word is functioning itself through you. And there's a backbone to it, a Spiritual backbone and then you will discover you have opened the way to the Christ mind. These are the footsteps you take.

We become receptive only to Truth, responsive only to Truth. That which is untrue cannot awaken a response from you. You do not react to that which is untrue. It isn't there. So, become Truth conscious because Truth in consciousness dissolves the world mind and dissolves the presentations of the world mind which are anti-Christ. If you're not in this new Christ mind, you're in the world mind which is the anti-Christ mind. This is the separation from the Kingdom.

I think the Master will accentuate these points now so that we can clearly grasp that unless I am responsive only to Truth, and consciously, every moment, looking at everything I see and touch, knowing the Truth or untruth about it, consciously, continuously, I will be forced in some way to accept and respond to the world mind. I will respond to sickness and suffering. I will think that things are bad today but they'll be better tomorrow. I will think that time is running short. I'll be capable of all kinds of human equivocations because if I am not conscious of Truth, untruth will make me conscious of it.

World mind is unceasing and continuous and it controls our thoughts subconsciously, invisibly, involuntarily so that our thoughts as human beings are never our own. We think they are. All our human thoughts are not our own. Our thoughts are never our own until we become conscious of Truth and then the thoughts that come through us are not the involuntary thoughts of the world mind. They are the thoughts of the Father, the invisible angels, the purifiers, the Light. And they lead us to our new glory.

"I," says the outer Jesus, "Will go away now." The outer Jesus represents the visible activity of the Christ but the visible activity of the Christ is not enough. We must be turned now to the invisible activity. The invisible activity of Jesus is the invisible Christ. We must be turned to the invisible Christ of our own Being. We must be turned to be taught directly by the Father. All must be taught by the Father within through the Christ mind. The Christ mind listening to the Father, instead of the human mind listening to the world mind. A complete new system, a complete new way of life for the Christ mind listens to God, the human mind listens to the world mind. The Christ mind lives in the Kingdom of God. The human mind lives in the world. The Christ mind lives in eternity. The human mind lives in time. The Christ mind lives in Reality. The human mind lives in its own thought concept.

We're being lifted out of the human mind, dependence on the human mind, dependence on human authorities with human minds, to our own Christ mind which receives the bread of Life, the Power, the Wisdom, the Truth, the Love, the Infinity of God. Our Christ mind is the heir to all that God has and the Christ itself is turning us to that Christ mind.

Now it's saying, "Have ye that mind which I am demonstrating on this earth as being independent of all form, independent of death, independent of body, independent of human circumstance, independent of matter, independent of time and space. There is such a mind. It is your mind. Have ye that mind."

And to get to know it, to live in it, look at all things and separate them, the sheep from the goats, the Truth from the untruth, the wheat from the chaff. Respond only to Truth. To that which is untruth, pay no mind. Respond not. It has no power because it is not there. Untruth has no power. All power is in Truth and when you have trained yourself to respond only to Truth, you discover the non-power of untruth, the non-power of disease, the non- power of pain, the non-power of suffering, the non-power of lack, the non-power of limitations and that non-power means that because Abundance is present, that which presents lack cannot present a real lack.

There is no real lack. There is no power on earth to create a real lack. There is no power on earth to move away Abundance . It is present and that is the Truth. That is the meaning of non-power. Abundance is present. That is Truth. God is present and God is Abundance therefore lack of Abundance is impossible. You simply have no capacity to see the Abundance in the human mind or to experience the Abundance or to be an instrument through which the Abundance appears in the human mind. But in the Christ mind, the Abundance is made visible as loaves and fishes coming from the sky, gold in the fishes' mouth, a raven feeding Elijah. That which is the need fulfilled is the evidence that Abundance is always present, that the Grace of the Father is always our sufficiency without exception in all things. But if we think that there is a power to remove that Abundance, we're not in Truth. That is the Law. In all things my Grace is thy sufficiency. There is no power to remove the sufficiency.

Then why don't we experience it? We're in the wrong mind. We're in the mind which cannot receive the sufficiency. It has no capacity to see the fine print. No capacity through which Spirit can flow because it's a mind made of a physical brain, of physical senses. Spirit does not flow through physicality.

The Christ mind is not made of a physical brain and physical senses. It is the mind of Spirit and the Spirit of God flows through the Christ mind and the sufficiency appears as the need fulfilled.

Non-power means that whatever denies the presence of that sufficiency is a lie and has no capacity to remove that sufficiency. You can be in dire poverty and that sufficiency is there. You can be in dire famine and the sufficiency is there. There is no power to remove it but you cannot experience it until you know the Truth that it is there and then rest in the knowledge that because it is here, that which says, "It is not here," **it** is not here. You have differentiated between the wheat and the tare. You have isolated the Truth. Sufficiency is here. Food is here. That which I need is here. The rent is here. The harmony is here. The beauty is here. The peace is here. The Truth is here. The perfection in all of my Being is here. I'm not fooled into being this temporary mortal self.

You're lifted back up into your only and eternal Self. And your eternal Self is here even though the world mind, echoed through the human mind makes you appear as if you're not eternal Being. You cannot remove your eternal Self and the knowledge that your eternal Self is here reveals that there is no power to remove it.

We must know there is no power to remove the presence of God. It's just a matter of being in that mind which is willing to be trained until you release the creature mind.

In our meditation before we have a short recess, let us take the subject which is true; that God is my sufficiency in all things and see that this Truth never changes. There are two minds that look at it, the mind which is not mine and cannot see this Truth and comprehend it and that developed state of mind called Christ mind which is automatically in this One Divine Father. It is the very mind of the Father and it is ever fulfilling Itself, effortlessly through Grace.

One mind knows only the power of Grace, the power of the Father and the other mind thinks there are other powers and by these so-called other powers, it is hypnotized into the belief that there is a power that can keep Grace away, push it aside, that something besides Grace is present. That mind, you must learn is not mine at all. It is the pretender. It is not the mind of God, the creation of God and when you have that mind still, you find you are lifted into Christ mind.

When the false mind is still, I am in my Father without a second. The Father is my Father, your Father. There is only one Father, not two. There are no human fathers in Reality. There is only the eternal Father, Spirit of God. That is my Father. That is the knowledge in the Christ mind. God is my Father and God is the Father of the one who calls himself my father. God is the Father of the one who calls himself my son. We have one Father. That is what the Christ mind knows and we are all heirs because we have one Father. We are heirs to all that is in the Kingdom of God here, now because the Father said so.

As Christ Jesus taught, my Father and your Father so the Christ mind in us accepts my Father and your Father are one Father. We are all the activity of God on earth. Nothing is withheld. The fullness of God Being is always where we are. Whatever denies this is not only untrue but is not even present but seems to be. All that could be present is that which is of God.

You put up your sword and you stand on this without defense, without reaction, without response to the invading thought no matter what it says. It has no power. All power is in the awareness that God is present now without a sword, without a plan, without a defense, without a scheme. You already have all that God has, here and now. All that I have is thine, here and now. It is a Truth that never changes. There is no power on earth to change it. It is true now. And in your

Christ mind you rest in this Truth and then you have found the inner Comforter who expresses God on earth as it is in heaven.

Whatever you need, I, the Christ mind already Am. Rest in me. Whatever you need, I Am. This is the Comforter within you, assuring you. Whatever you need, the Christ in you already is. Rest in who you are.

— End of Side One —

Then you find you're in the Christ mind because the words of the Father accepted open you to the Christ mind and that is how the realization of Truth comes. Truth is then realized and you can feel the inner Spiritual substance of the Truth.

Yes, God is my sufficiency. In all things. And it's like the sunrise bursting, the inner realization that this is the Truth, a permanent Truth, an indestructible Truth until all doubt and fear become obsolete.

Always, God is the substance of my form, the sufficiency of my Being. Always, I am Divine governed, Divinely sustained, Divinely fed, Divinely directed.

There's no shadow. There is only the pure Christ mind.

This meditation, that God is the substance, the sufficiency in all things, when realized, is another great key to that great emancipation that comes when you are in your Christ mind knowingly, consciously, independent of all world thought, all shadows of thought, all negatives, all that is unlike God. When the cripple, blind man, the deaf man to you are unreal, untrue and therefore not present but where they appear to be, the Christ mind of you knows the invisible Light of God.

Where lack appears, you know the invisible Abundance of God. Where discord appears, you know the invisible Harmony of God and this is how you break the back of the world mind.

I in the midst of you, I who am mighty, I take you into the Kingdom where you stand.

Silence, (pause) …

Before I forget it, in the chapter, "Revelation of Spiritual Identity," which we brushed through to some extent today, Joel made a suggestion that we also look at the chapter in "The World is New" called "Conscious Union." That's chapter three in the book "The World is New," and in as much as we're going to stay with this chapter of Joel's, at least another session, this will be a good time for you to look at "Conscious Union" in "The World is New," chapter three in conjunction with "The Revelation of Spiritual Identity."

Now as you read through this chapter nine, there was a place where there seemed to be a sudden turning in Joel. He had been discussing things of the world, it's like a sort of a warm up. Suddenly he sort of became, you might say, impatient with the things of the world and there was an abrupt change into which he began to state things like the following:

"If you die while still in material sense, you can only awaken in that same material sense, a materiality which can be greatly intensified. The belief in limitation with which you leave this plane becomes greater limitation, but the degree of freedom with which you leave here becomes greater freedom. The person who goes on from here in material sense, fearing, hating the experience, squeezing himself into it, finds himself more tightly bound than before the transition; whereas the person leaving this plane in spiritual light is wide open for the experience, open to receive more light, more light, more light, and thereby finds himself less fettered on emerging from this plane into his own new experience."

Now, when I read this, the thought that struck me most was something similar that had been given to me within; that wherever you are now, you are merely your own thought appearing and you will always be your own thought appearing no matter where you are, on which side of the veil you are. You are either the thought that you entertain here as mortal or the thought that you entertain here as Immortal and where you go on the other side of what is called the veil is into the thought universe that you are entertaining. You always live in your own thought universe.

Every belief you have, is the universe in which you live. You are a thought form living in your own thought environment. The environment you have around you is your thought. That environment only changes as your thought changes. And if your environment is paradise, that will have to be your thought. It will not be while you're thinking in terms of a material environment.

In this rising Christ mind, you become aware that Christ mind is not conscious, as you have been, of physical environment. Christ mind is not conscious, as you have been, of physical images. The Christ mind does not live in a physical body. The Christ mind does not live in a physical environment. And if to some degree you are aware now that you do not live in a physical body or in a physical environment, you have been touched by the Christ mind.

The importance of Joel's statement is, that *"As a man thinketh... so is he."*

Everything you're doing, thinking, seeing, feeling, touching, experiencing is the quality of your own thought. And as that thought becomes more Divine, less world mind, more Christed, less creature, your universe is changing and being transformed into a Spiritual universe. And the lacks and limitations, the opposites, the vulnerabilities, the discords do not exist in that Spiritual universe. So, we're learning to watch our thought, to identify Truth, to identify non-truth.

And now that we've come that far, we can say this; as you identify that which is untrue, remember this, the mind which has experienced that untruth is not a mind. The mind that experiences untruth is not a mind because the untruth is never present. Only Truth is present. The mind which experiences that which is not present but seems to be, is not a mind. It is as non-present as that which it experiences. When you experience non-truth, you're experiencing it in a non-mind and the value then of seeing non-truth and identifying it, is now to take the step of saying, "Because this is non-truth, I will rest the mind that perceives this non-truth." That's all you do. Rest the mind that perceives that which is untrue. As you rest that mind, you are stepping out of the mind which is not the Christ mind.

And, as you continue this practice you find that as you perceive non-truth, your mind goes into a standstill. It looks at non-truth and rather than trying to change it, the mind sort of freezes. It sees non-truth without accepting it and now you're coming to the place where you're not even accepting the mind that perceives the non-truth. This is a delicate but important exercise.

When I perceive a non-truth, I'm perceiving it with a non-mind. Instead of changing the non-truth, I must stand in the stillness of the non-mind. You learn to practice the stillness of the non-mind. You begin to feel the activity of the real, the Christ mind.

Everything that is untrue, exists only in a mind that is untrue. When Joel says. "Get the axe at the roots," and when the Master says in the Bible, *Agree with thine adversary,*" they're both saying get to the mind that perceives untruth. Don't worry about the untruth. Just identify it. That'll tell you you're in a wrong mind.

And then when you've identified the wrong mind which is perceiving untruth, rest that mind. Be still. Take a sabbath. Fast from that mind and you find you have got to the root of the untruth. You have silenced the mind which is the instrument through which world mind is making you perceive an untruth. And your thoughts will be different. Your thoughts will change because they will not be the thoughts of that mind. Therefore, they will be thoughts of the Christ mind.

And then what Joel is telling us here that whatever universe we are in is our thought universe, you'll find your universe is the universe of the Father. When Divine thought is flowing through you, you're in Divine creation where the law is always perfection. Slowly perfection replaces the opposites of perfection and imperfection, of good and bad. Your universe changes because you learn to be still in the mind that has perceived untruth.

The false mind is nullified. The carnal mind ceases to have power. All its implied power ceases to function in your Being. When your carnal mind is still, the world carnal mind has no power to function in you.

Joel says, *"The Soul or the life of an individual never dies."* Interesting is that he says the soul or life as if they were synonymous. *"The Soul or the life of an individual never dies, nor does it lose its attained development."* So that as you are able now to be still in the mind that perceives untruth, first recognizing untruth and then being still in the mind that perceives that untruth, you're attaining a new level of consciousness. You're dying to the old. Being reborn to the new and whatever you're reborn to will be a level that you never lose. You never lose your attained development.

Jesus the Christ who had this experience in full illumination still exists and lives not in any place but in and as consciousness. And since consciousness is infinite, he lives and exists in your consciousness and in mind.

Now, there's a flat statement that in your consciousness and in mind, Jesus Christ now exists. If you haven't had the benefit of that it's because you have been in your human sense of mind which sees that which is untrue and that's not your real consciousness.

Your human sense of mind is not receiving the intelligence or love or wisdom of Jesus Christ but when you are still to untruth, you'll find that you are in the Christ mind which does receive instruction. Possibly from Jesus Christ, possibly from others.

Joel goes on, *"And it is within our power to receive light and instruction from that consciousness....Gautama the Buddha still teaches, still performs his mighty works....in consciousness...in your consciousness, in my consciousness. We,"* he says," *are being illumined and instructed by that state of consciousness and all who have attained illumination and left this plane fully illumined are right here where we are....facing us through our consciousness, and if we have not yet known that all spiritual light is embodied within our consciousness, we should become aware of it now."*

When Joel says 'we,' it's often the editorial 'we.' He is telling us that he is being fed by the consciousness of Buddha, the consciousness of Jesus Christ and the consciousness of other illumined individuals who have ceased to appear physically on the earth but who are present and function and teach through consciousness.

But Joel has already gone past the point of living in untruth, of being tempted into the belief that untruth is possible. He has stilled the mind which was in untruth and therefore he is in pure Consciousness and in pure Consciousness, you are taught by those who have walked on before us into pure illumination.

And so, an added advantage of stilling the mind to untruth is that you open the Christ mind which now instead of being limited to what the human mind thinks it knows, receives Infinite wisdom from Infinite source and is constantly in the Light of those who have attained the highest degree of awareness in the universe. You are taught direct from illuminated souls, instead of through the channel of the human mind.

This is where revelation comes from and this is another meaning of the Comforter. Another meaning of the Comforter will be the Voice. When within, the Voice speaks, that is the Comforter within. When you receive instruction, sometimes the individual will identify himself. Jesus Christ will identify himself at certain times if you receive instruction from him. And people you may never have heard of will instruct you and identify themselves. Not always, but Joel didn't make this statement because they didn't identify themselves. He made this statement because they have.

And so, the livingness of Spirit is not a matter of guesswork to those who are living in Spirit. And if we're not receiving our instruction this way from within, we are very limited and we are forced into false judgments about things that we cannot discern.

All of us should have, as part of our goal, that clarity of consciousness which is not in material form, not in material objects, not in material conditions, so independent of the material consciousness that we can receive instruction from on high. And if we can maintain this inner listening by always identifying Truth and always identifying untruth and knowing untruth is not there, we will find that we accelerate our capacity to be taught from on high. We deepen our consciousness. The lines of communication become more infinite, more diversified and more immediate so that now, now becomes very important. Always now your line of communication is open because you are living in Truth and Truth is always self- fulfilling.

Now is the Presence. Now are you the Divine Son. Now is the Spirit of God fulfilling itself where you stand. Now is the Spirit of God the invisible identity of everyone you know. Now is Truth omnipresent. It never is budged away. Now is Peace everywhere. That is the Christ mind in you accepting God everywhere now, in all his fullness. In the complete fullness of God everywhere your Christ mind rests with confidence.

Trusting Truth, it always be present everywhere, never moved away, never changed, never altered, never yielding its position for nothing else exists. And you'll find the illumined ones are teaching you to the level of your capacity to receive, to the willingness, to the level of your willingness to obey, until you're ready not to hear words anymore but to go forth and do the living acts of commitment. To let the Christ which speaks within prove Itself in the without, using you as the instrument.

"There's really only one freedom in all this world," says Joel. *"Freedom from the belief in good and evil."* That's an astounding statement. *"When we are free of that,"* he says, *"We are truly free of physical, mental, moral and financial limitations."*

Now, if we were take this, just as he says it, that when you're free of the belief in good and evil, you're free, it would have to mean then that there is no good to believe in and there is no evil to believe in. These are human thoughts. When you don't believe in good and you don't believe in evil, what do you believe in? You believe in Truth. You believe that only Truth exists. There are no degrees of Truth. There's not good truth and then bad truth. Truth is good the way God is good. Of course, Truth is good but it's always good. It's not a variable. There's no such thing as a variable good.

What good is health if it's only good health? That's a variable. It's good health when you're twenty years old and it's bad health when you're seventy-five years old. That's not good. How could good health become bad health. It cannot. That's because we made the mistake of calling it good health. It became bad health because it never was good health. But if you're in Truth at the age of twenty or at the age of seventy-five you're the very same Self. You're the Life that is the Spirit of God. And if your consciousness rests in the knowledge that I am that Life, you're in Truth. That Life is not good today and bad tomorrow. That Life is always that Life and that Life has no age in it. There's no twenty and seventy-five in that Life and that is Truth. Unchanging. When we accept the Truth then we must reject the untruth. I am not changing Life. I am Divine Life. I don't have the belief in a good which can become a bad. You see, if you're working on a level of a good that can become a bad, you're still in the human mind and you're not differentiating between Truth and untruth.

Any good that can become a bad is not Divine. Truth is Divine. There is nothing that can be true if it is not Divine. The only Truth must be Divine Truth. And there's no good that becomes a bad in Divine Truth and therefore you drop the belief.

I'm not interested in good health, anymore than I'm interested in bad health. I'm not interested in that which is un-divine. And so, right where the good health seems to be or the bad health seems to be, the Christ mind is where you rest. That mind which was seeing good health or bad health is where you're still, until the Christ mind says, "Here is the invisible Life of God, always perfect as the Father."

Then you're looking past the good and the bad. You have dropped the belief in good and bad. Joel says, "This is the only freedom. The only freedom is when you overcome the belief in good and evil."

You come to that which is eternal. You live in the eternal Truth and your Consciousness being in the eternal Truth, that is what you manifest. Anyone who knows Joel knows that at the age of seventy-four, he wasn't what we would call a seventy-four-year old. Anyone who has the Spirit is never thinking in those terms or showing it in human terms. Anyone who is in the Spirit is not in the good or the bad but is in the eternal and the eternal is manifesting as the present harmony, the now harmony.

Don't be fooled by good and bad. Anything that is not Divine is a temptation to keep you in the mind that is not the Christ mind. The anti-Christ mind lives in the belief in good and bad. It doesn't know it's an anti-Christ mind and so it's always trying to make the bad into the good. It's never going to the root. It's never agreeing with its adversary. It's never seeing that the same world mind which presents the bad is the mind that presents the good. It's always presenting the transient and making us label it good and bad.

The Christ mind looks at the transient and says, "You were not created by God therefore you are not Truth." What God creates is eternal and you go directly to Source, to Reality, to the Invisible, Spiritual Selfhood that is there. That is where you rest in Consciousness. That is where you accept your Self at all times.

And you find, you're not stigmatized with the ups and downs of good and bad. It may not be as spectacular for you as others but you'll find there's an even keel of sureness. An even keel of health; not up and down, not tragedy one day and sublimity the next but an even keel. Spirit maintaining even that which appears in the visible.

So, it is with every other facet of life, as we have seen it in the human sphere. When you are accepting the Spiritual identity behind the visible without the judgment of this being good or bad, resting in your Christ mind that only that which is of the Father can be your Life, the Life of all you know, you find your life is manifesting those qualities of the Father which you have accepted as being present now. That becomes your thought and then your visible manifestation.

Good must be overcome. Evil must be overcome. Only that which is Divine is Real. Never variable. Not changing with years. Not perishing. Not deteriorating. Not good today and something else tomorrow but always pure, perfect invisible Spirit seen through the human mind which cannot discern the Spirit that is there.

We're sowing to the Spirit which opens the Christ mind. *"There's no life,"* says Joel, *"but the Life of God."*

If you think you've got another life, you're in the anti-Christ mind. If you know anyone who has another life, you're still in the anti-Christ mind. There's no life but the Life of God. Whether it's a twelve-year old girl who seems to be dying, that the Christ has to say now, "Awake little girl." Or whether it's your twelve-year old or whether its you, your life is always the Life of God. And if that Truth is not firmly embedded in your consciousness, you're in the untruth.

You have no other life. You see how by facing the Truth, accepting it, protecting the sure knowledge of it against all invading thought, you keep all of the weeds of falsity out of your consciousness. Your life is the Life of God and any word, thought or deed, in you which denies that is untruth. You are eternal Being. Unless you accept yourself as eternal Being, you are rejecting yourself to be the Life of God.

Now, can the Life of God be good today and bad tomorrow? Is the Life of God ever sick or lacking? The human concept is what is sick or lacking. The Life of God is as perfect tomorrow as today - has ever been perfect. You don't have a past which is black or a past that you have to bury or a past that you have to want to hide from people and you haven't committed any great sins because your life has always been the Life of God.

You see, we wash ourselves clean of all misbelief, of all untruth. We can't linger in a past that was inglorious if we are the Life of God. We see that was all part of growing up into Spiritual awareness out of the false mind of the world into the knowledge of identity.

Again, Joel states, *"That is why you will learn that there is no such thing as young life or old life. There is only life, and it is an immortal and eternal life [from] which we cannot escape by dying."*

You cannot even escape from Life because that's your name. It's forever. This must become Consciousness.

"It is true that our physical body is left for burial or cremation, but actually it is not our body that is left," says Joel. *"It's [our concept that is left,] our concept of what body is.*

And then the reminder which we all seem to turn away from. *"We are not now in the body at all; we never were and we never can be.*

We exist separate and apart from the body, but we use the body as an instrument." And when the day comes for us to lay down the body, it's because we're ready for another experience. We will not then be bodiless. Through our consciousness we will have built for ourselves another body. We will never be without a body even if a person should learn how to travel through the air without an airplane. He will find that he is still embodied.

Now, I feel the statement is Joel's statement that he has done just that. Of course, you know Christ did travel through the air without an airplane. And so, I feel we're being told here that we are learning to develop that body which is not of weight, of density, of texture, of size and shape but is a body which moves through what may be called the invisible without aid of any physical transportation.

I feel this statement was injected with a purpose to tell you that that is the nature of the true body of the Soul. After all, how are you going to travel without a physical body? There's going to come a day when you don't have one. How are you going to move? You're going to have a body that can move even though it's not a physical body. And that body is not going to require physical assistance but we're learning now that if we're not in this body - but we are always embodied - we must be in another body right now. We must be in a body which is capable of just that right now, a body that moves without necessity of physical aid from another source. There is such a body. It is the Christ body. It is the body that walks on water. It is the body that steps on a ship and then the ship is on the shore without a minute's delay. It is the body that transcends time and space and the force of gravity.

And in the Christ mind, you experience that Christ body. It is the body that knows no death. It is the body that you move in your transition from physicality to the Spiritual universe. It is the body that was not born in the mother's womb. It is the body that Jesus claimed by saying, *"Woman what have I to do with thee?"* It is the body that we are being led to. It's the fine print again. You have such a body but your human mind cannot discern it. Only your Christ mind is aware of that body and can function that body. That body cannot function except in the Christ mind.

All good and evil is a barrier to the knowledge of the invisible body of the Soul. Anything that keeps us lingering in the finite sense of life, the changing sense of life, the perishable sense of life, the mortal, human, non-divine sense of life prevents our preparation for the sublime transition while still appearing here in the flesh.

We're not talking about going to heaven tomorrow or going to heaven after we die. We're talking about living in this Christ body here and now. The Comforter will prepare us for that. The Comforter will bring us into remembrance of all things of the Christ body, the glory we had with the Father before the world was. We are going to be opened up to be aware of the fullness of our own Being.

Now, if you know Joel, you know that he can talk for forty minutes on one subject but he'll always find a way to slide in what he's really getting toward and then there's an accumulation of these little recurring implications until those who are ready are able to receive that inner teaching which is behind all of the words he speaks.

And so, it is with the Christ in the Bible, just as with the Christ in Joel, it is always lifting you to a fuller realization of the Truth of your own Selfhood. It is showing that the Immaculate Conception revealed by Jesus Christ on earth is the Truth of you. That there is a Self which emanates from God and is God and that God is the Selfhood expressing where you now appear to be. And as the false mind is dissolved and the Christ mind replaces it, you become aware of that great Truth that you are the living Son of God. And as such, imperishable.

In the Life of God, I in the Father and the Father in me, suddenly, your true Self is discerned and the Light of the Father, from that moment on, continues to be the Emanation, the guiding Light, the Food, the Law, the Substance and the Power that governs all you do.

Joel said that his mission on earth, given to him from within, was not to bring illumination to one person or ten but that his mission was to release the world from the carnal mind. That the Christ may be seen to be the identity of each individual who walks the earth. He felt that he had reached the point where this was assured within a short time. He said so. And if we can trust his words to be the words of the Christ then it is true that within a short time each individual will either realize he is the Christ and lives in the Christ body or he will not know this and there will be a turning over, a new age. There will be an age in which those who have come into the realization of Christ will walk in their Christ Self, will make a transition out of this world into a universe which is called the first heaven. Actually, it's the fifth heaven, there being the fifth, sixth and seventh.

But our transition into this fifth heaven only comes about through the realization that I must now be still in the mind that is not, the mind that perceives untruth and awake in the mind that is Christ mind which perceives the invisible heavens of the Father here on earth.

I think we, to some extent, are feeling a degree of that more positively, more confidently and I think you may find in today's lesson, you have travelled a long distance. You will find that as you can identify Truth and untruth, a stability within you grows. Signs that follow deepen your confidence and then the word "Peace" becomes significant. You find you have that Peace because you are confident that some way or another, something in you knows the way and you know that something is working. *"My peace I give unto you,"* becomes meaningful, a new Peace. It's a Peace born of confidence, of Christ experience. A Peace that you begin to suspect makes you independent of the changing world of form. You are emerging in your true Self.

This is the peace that is meant when the Christ says, *"My peace I give unto you: not as the world giveth, give I unto you."* This is the peace that we are coming into. It's the new foundation of Truth that we live in. Christ mind, accepted and lived in, brings that Peace and the world ceases to have power.

For my Peace flows to him who is in the Christ mind and my Peace is your Grace, your sufficiency. No matter what appears in the world, my Grace flows through your Christ mind to be the manifestation of every need and as that is flowing and you experience it, you know *"The peace... that passeth all understanding."*

"Infinite Way," says Joel, *"is preparing consciousness for the day when no one will have to think in terms of a carnal mind because there will not even be the temptation of the carnal mind there."*

Now, that carnal mind, remember is the universal world mind. "There will be no universal world mind there." That is a statement from Joel.

What does he mean when he says "there"? Does he mean in this world? No. When there is no universal world mind here it won't be this world. He's talking about the Kingdom of Heaven on earth. When the world mind isn't here, there is no world here. He's talking about our transitional experience in which we pass out of the world mind and we awaken in the Spiritual universe where there is no world mind. *"Infinite Way.... is preparing consciousness for the day when no one will have to think in terms of a carnal mind because there will not even be the temptation of a carnal mind here."*

In that state of mysticism, the individual will no longer have to impersonalize. You won't have to talk about there's no form there or there's form there because there won't be a form there. There won't be matter. There is no matter in the Christ universe. Is this five hundred years away? You're not going to make transition five hundred years from now. This is in our transition out of untruth into Truth because in a God realized Consciousness, there is no evil to behold. In that state of mind, evil has no Reality. It has no power, law, person, no cause. That mind which was also in Christ Jesus can look at your

67

particular Pilate and say, "Thou hast no power." That mind can look at the cripple and say, "What did hinder thee?" Can look at the blind man and say, "Open your eyes." In that state of Consciousness there are no opposing powers because *"I and my Father are one."* God is recognized as the Self of everyone.

I wouldn't want these to be just nice sounding words. They've got to be experienced.

In the Bible, the Christ says, *"I will not leave thee comfortless."* That means when you have overcome all reliance on a human consciousness, someone will be there to be your consciousness and it is I, who will not leave you comfortless. I, the Christ mind, will be there when you have moved out of your reliance on human mind, when you have stilled the human mind which sees untruth, you're moving out of there and you're opening to the Christ mind which knows only Truth which can never leave you comfortless because It is the very mind of God.

Now, we're going to deepen again by continuing in this fourteenth chapter, by intensifying in chapter nine, "Spiritual Identity Revealed" and by looking at Joel's chapter in "The World is New" called "Conscious Union" - putting it all together and this is what we're going to do. We're going to study the nature of the Christ mind. How will you know if you're in Christ mind? Everything that tells you you're in Christ mind should be known to us so that we can say. "Because this is what I believe I must be in Christ mind." And we must know the nature of the carnal mind. We just cut it right down the middle; this is Christ mind, this is carnal mind - so that we can recognize where we are and who we are. And every time we find ourselves in carnal mind, be still. We're coming to that place where we can identify the carnal mind, where we can look out at anything and say, "That is the world mind appearing as. And that is carnal mind. That is not Christ mind." And every time you identify what is carnal mind you can put another niche in your belt. You have come closer to Truth.

The more we keep identifying untruth the more we be alert to it. You see what we're coming to now is we're not saying that form isn't there, that disease isn't there. We're looking at it and we're seeing that carnal mind has placed something there and carnal mind which has placed something there isn't there itself. You're beginning to see the nothingness of the carnal mind and its method of operation. Though invisible, it places a form before you. Though invisible it places a disease before you. Though invisible it places a limitation or a lack before you. You say, "That's a disease, that's a lack, that's a limitation," and that's not true. That's carnal mind placing these things before you. That's the disguise of the carnal mind and that carnal mind is your mind. Get out of it. Take all of the diseases and see they're not different diseases. They're just one carnal mind making different presentations. Identify all that is untrue as carnal mind and then get out of carnal mind by being still in the human mind and you're in Christ mind, the miracle worker which replaces carnal mind presentation with the Christ mind presentation which is the image and likeness of God.

We're looking past all of the so-called problems at the cause of them which is carnal mind. The invisible carnal mind projecting these things into appearance using your mind as the guinea pig. The proper identification gets the axe to the root of the problem to the cause of the false appearance and by identifying the false Father of these false causes, these false effects; you have agreed with your adversary. You have come to that place where you can say, "I know what that is, that's carnal mind appearing as this problem or that problem, or that disease or that illness." And the answer is never to change the illness or the disease but to get into the Christ mind. When you're in the Christ mind, you have overcome the carnal mind and its complete presentation of the falsities of the world.

Now, we hope this is another stride today. If you feel a growing, deepening confidence, it is another stride. Give yourself a couple of days of working with it and you'll find that is exactly what's going to happen. We'll be silent now.

I'm interested in Truth. Nothing else. What is Truth? Truth is of God. Whatever is not true has no existence, for it is not of God, therefore it is not here. All I need do is look at it and know that it isn't here. It is being presented to me by a carnal mind which also is not here. I can be still. There is no power in that which is not here. I'm in the one Power, the power of God. What God did not place here does not have power.

As we move in this direction faithfully, you will find you are anointed from within. The Spirit descends and it blesses you.

And so thank you again to my many wonderful friends.

Class 26

Beyond World Consciousness

Herb: Good afternoon everybody.

In your preliminary meditation, if you find you are unable to make God contact, there are things that you must do about it. Now, usually, we do not make God contact unless we have fulfilled certain requirements. The lack of God contact is a separation or division from Divine power and we are not an instrument for that Divine power if we meditate as a mortal human being. There's no contact between the Father and a mortal, human being. You might as well face it, you cannot, as a mortal being, be in contact with God. You cannot be a mortal being and expect Divine power to express in you, through you and as you.

And so, when you sit down to meditate, even with the best of intentions, if you're carrying with you the concept that little you, the person who goes to work in the morning or the person who stays at home and takes care of the house is going to now meditate, you're wasting time. Oh, you might get a quiet, you might get a feeling of no pressure but you're not going to make the God contact. You've got to sit down with the consciousness that I am the Child of God. There's no contact otherwise and you cannot be a human being and the Child of God. We've all been trying to be both human and Divine as if humanhood is a passing phase we go through in order to attain a sense of Divinity. That isn't true. We're not going through humanhood. The Child of God is not human. The Father has no human children and never has had any.

Now, let us suppose that you were on the last twenty five percent of this lifespan. Many of us are. Now according to the authorities, there are various ways we can pass out of this lifespan. They have all of these methods by which we can lose this life. It can come through a disease. It can come through a war. It can come through alcohol. It can come through drugs. It can come through accident. It can come in at least four or five hundred different ways.

And so, if you were to make up a chart which says, "These are the killers of man," you would list all of the physical methods, all of the emotional methods, all of the mental methods and you would say these are the most likely causes. And in that chart, after you had completed it, you would have left out the only killer of man that there is. You'll never see a chart which is made up by science or religion listing the causes of death which will be accurate. The only cause of death is that God did not create a human being. That is the only cause of death there is and when you face it, you must go that extra step. Who am I? If God is no respecter of persons, if God says, *"Henceforth know ye no man after the flesh,"* am I not being told that there are no human children? That I the Child of God must be something else?

The Child of God does not die. There are no causes for the death of the Child of God because the Child of God is immortal now.

When you meditate, if you're not that immortal Child, who's meditating? Someone uncreated by God. And how can creation pour into un-creation? You see your separation is before you even start to meditate.

And so, we need this new Comforter. The Comforter who will bring all things unto remembrance. And then, we should hear the Voice. As we are in Divine Sonship, living it, rejecting all that disclaims our Sonship, rejecting even the mind that says, "We are not the Divine Son," rejecting every appearance that says, "We are not the Divine Son," then we are living faithfully as the Divine image and likeness. We are rejecting anti-Christ. We are rejecting the universal belief that God created something that can die. We live in that Consciousness. We earn the right to hear the Voice, to be in oneness with the Father.

Then it says, what we hear here in the 14th chapter of John. *"Peace I leave with you, my peace I give unto you: not as the world giveth, give I unto you. Let not your heart be troubled, neither let it be afraid."*

Now, this Peace then which the Father gives, is not as the world gives. This Peace has a meaning beyond all else. We are told here and we must never take this statement out of context. When you do, you don't have the fullness of it. When you see it where it is in this chapter with what is around it, what leads up to it, the advent of the Comforter, the Spirit of Truth "bringing all things unto remembrance." Then you have the full scope of that Peace "bringing all things unto remembrance," bringing you back to the conscious knowledge that your Life did not begin at a time and a place. Before Abraham was, your Life is. We're not speaking of this form now. We're speaking of your Life and the Comforter brings to remembrance that your Life, being the life of God is without beginning, without the possibility of sickness, without the possibility of creature limitations and the realization of that Life which is Life eternal is my Peace.

My Peace is *"not as the world giveth."* The world gives you a lifespan. My Peace gives you Life without end. My Peace is the realization that the life of God is your Life. My Peace is the end of the search. There's nothing more to look for. It is all yours. My Peace is the realization that there's no distance between God and my Being. There's no time between God and my Being. There's no absence of God. There's no moment when God is present and another moment when God is absent. My Peace is permanent, beyond the grave, beyond the lifespan. My Peace is the now realization.

"Thou seest me, thou seest the life of the Father."

It isn't something you memorize. The Peace that you receive from the Comforter is the realization of your permanent Self. That permanent Self is not going to become you tomorrow. That permanent Self is all that you can ever be and ever have been and that permanent Self, being imperishable, is not a mortal self.

Every word that you utter, every thought that you accept, every appearance to which you respond which is directed at the impermanent you, is your denial of your own identity.

That's why we all go round this merry-go-round of matter. We're not living in the conscious awareness that I am not a human being. We're all accepting that we are human beings and in that, we're saying, "Being a human being, I am not the Christ of God."

You see, then, when you choose which you are, you are choosing everything that you will experience. You're even choosing the universe you live in. When you choose humanhood, you're choosing the world. When you choose Christhood, you're in Truth and you're choosing the universe of Christ. You're choosing the Kingdom of God. For you, the Kingdom of God is not tomorrow. It is now where Christ is. For you the qualities of God are not tomorrow. They are now where Christ is. And the deepening awareness that where Christ is, I am. Where God is, I am. Where the Kingdom of God is, I am, becomes an experience. Peace is an experience. It is an infinite awareness that I am the living Spirit of God, that I move and have my Being in the Kingdom of God and this is it. I'm not going there tomorrow. I'm not going there after death. I'm not going there because I'm going to live an exemplary, human life. This is it. That's who you must be when you meditate.

Then meditation is merely the acceptance of your identity, where you are, where God is, the nature of God, the qualities of God, the all-presence of God. You're accepting Infinity. Infinity is the measure of God. Infinity is the measure of Son. Here where I am, is the miracle of Infinity. Nothing is missing.

Now look at it another way. The entire Christ message is that God is All.

Where can error be if God is All? Where can matter be if God is All? Where can mortality be if God is All? God is not error. God is not mortal. God is not material. Where are these things if God is All. When you accept error, matter, mortality, you are denying the Allness of God and you're walking in the hypnotized mind which does not know or experience the Allness of God. In that mind you cannot have my Peace. You earn my Peace by living in the knowledge that God being All, matter which is not God is not where God is. Error which is not God is not where God is. Corporeality which is not God is not where God is. Other powers, powers of evil, which are not God cannot exist where God is.

You reconcile yourself to your perfect universe where you are. God being all there is no place in your consciousness for error, for matter, for division, for separation, for evil, for sickness, for death. Where can these occur if God is All?

And as you maintain fidelity to the Allness of God, you can finally come to the conviction that God being everywhere, there's no place for error to be. There's no place for anything ungodly to be. And you've come upon that great understanding that where these things appear to be, there must be a mind perceiving them and the mind perceiving them has no real existence either because God being All, there being no darkness in God, the Father being too pure to behold iniquity, the mind which beholds that which is not God is a mind that has no real existence.

You're facing the fact that's there's a you with a mind that has no real existence. It perceives what God did not place there. You're looking out of a mind that is mortal and there is no mind that is mortal. It never has existed. It sees what God didn't place there. It's never in Peace for that reason. Its sense of peace is always impermanent, never deep, never forever.

75

So, we look at this mortal mind and we recognize that the mind I have looking out at the world is non-mind. It is the mind of the anti-Christ and I've got to face this. The day must come to face this. The human mind is anti-Christ. It does not see Christ. It does not know Christ. It does not know God.

While we are dwelling in human thought, we are totally controlled. There is an activity going on; an activity which exceeds all human understanding. It is an activity of which we are not conscious. The power of that activity is so great in our consciousness that it actually becomes us. It becomes our consciousness. The world consciousness becomes your consciousness. The world consciousness makes your heart beat. The world consciousness moves blood through your veins. God isn't doing it. If God were doing it, God would never stop doing it.

The complete human body is developed and evolved out of the world consciousness. It is maintained up to a degree by the world consciousness and then that same world consciousness that creates the human body destroys it. This is the fate of every body born of the world consciousness. It is destroyed by its own creator.

We've been blaming God for all this because we have been unaware of the world consciousness. We hadn't reached the level where we could receive the Comforter. But this is the age of the Comforter. We've come of age.

The world consciousness is that which eclipses the Divine Consciousness just as a heavenly body moves across the sun and the sun is blacked out or earth passes between the moon and the sun and the moon is blacked out. So, world consciousness blacks out for us the Divine Self and it recreates this self that we walk around in calling it our self, this mortal being. This mortal being is the creation of the world consciousness. This mind that runs this mortal being, is the accomplice of the world consciousness. It is the instrument of the world consciousness. It doesn't take its orders from God. It doesn't know God. It's under the delusion that it knows God but it has no capacity to right the wrongs of the world consciousness. It is a prisoner. It doesn't recognize its own adversary.

And while you and I walk the streets, we are world consciousness appearing as mortal beings who have been persuaded that in some way we are the Divine image and likeness, even though every one of these Divine images and likenesses is to be destroyed by the world consciousness that created it.

It is only when we come out of that brainwashing to prepare the way for the Spirit of Truth, the Holy Ghost, the new Comforter, that the light of God within us dissolves that which has eclipsed the Divine Consciousness and the Light shining through reveals I am not this mortal self at all. I do not live in this mortal body. I do not have a mortal mind. I am and always have been the living Child of God. A completely different Self than the one that has lived at this point in time and space.

You begin to open to being that Divine Son which has no human birth, no human death. You begin to see merit in the statement of Paul's *"to be absent from the body, [and to be] present with the Lord."*

But now, we're going a step further than being absent from the body. You can't be absent from the body when you're in a human mind. You must be absent from the mind to be absent from the body. You must be absent from the carnal mind. Then you're absent from the carnal body. And you must be absent from the carnal body to be in the Christ body.

Always, we're grateful to Paul. In Ephesians, 4:4, we have this statement, *"There is one body, [and] one Spirit, even as ye are called in one hope of your calling; One Lord, one faith, one baptism, One God [and] Father of all, who is above all, and through all, and in you all. But unto every one of us is given grace according to the measure of the gift of Christ."*

Unless we're in the Christ mind, we never become aware of that one, Infinite body. We live in separated, recreated bodies of the world consciousness. We do not know my Peace.

But, my Peace comes to those who have been living in the awareness that Spirit, being All, this is where my fidelity lies. Spirit is All. The belief in the power of evil and the power of good or two powers, is removed by the knowledge that Spirit is All. There is no good power of matter. There is no evil power of matter. There is no good matter and no evil matter. You look through without judgment and if the path you have selected is to walk in the Kingdom of God, you do not walk today consciously in a material universe. That is not where you are.

Last week, we learned to look at Truth. This week is the other side of the coin. We're looking at Truth, not from the standpoint of the human mind. At Truth from the standpoint of God. We're looking at Divine Truth and there are no human footsteps in Divine Truth. You cannot find any.

In a Spiritual universe, there is only your Father's Spirit. And if you think you're not in a Spiritual universe, then you're in division. You're on the merry-go-round. Your peace will be temporary. Your peace will not be the *"Peace… that passeth all understanding."* Your peace will simply be that kind of peace which is better humanhood, a better human life. You all know by now that we're not here for that.

A better human life is the trap. Why? Because when you seek a better human life, what are you saying? You're saying you are not the Christ, you are not the Divine Son. You're saying God is not your Father.

Well why come to a Spiritual message? The purpose of the Spiritual message is to lift our vision to Truth that is Divine, not concept, to lift our vision to Life that is eternal, not temporary, to realize the teaching of Christ, not to talk about it. To learn how to live it, to experience it.

And so, every time you make the mistake of saying you want to make something better in your human life, you're falling into a trap. It's a very normal desire but it isn't for those who have received the inner knowledge that Spirit is my name. They don't waste a moment trying to improve their human situation. Why? Because there isn't any. It's an illusion. Not that they're indifferent to their human situation, but because they know this is the trap of the mind. The mind sets before us a desirable human situation. And as you move toward it, to attain it, you're not being the Spiritual Child of God. And even when you attain it, you've got your claws into something that isn't going to remain permanent. It's going to be destroyed someday.

We're not looking for the kingdom that can be destroyed. We don't want temporary possessions. We are seeking to walk in that which is now present called the Kingdom of God and we can't walk in it as mortal beings. We can only walk in it as the Spirit for this is a Spiritual universe and what is not Spirit, only seems to be.

You notice that the Master here is on his way to crucifixion. But he stops long enough to have a long discourse. In fact, its taken us four weeks to come through the 14th chapter. A long discourse to prepare those who are moving into Spiritual awareness for his resurrection and the understanding of its meaning. He's teaching each of us that we, are going through a period of transformation. The transformation is not the transformation of our Reality but is the transformation of our false consciousness to our true Consciousness.

In human consciousness, we are in the false which knows not the Father nor the Kingdom of the Father. In our Christ consciousness, we have stepped out of the false, out of the transient. We walk in a perfect universe which is heaven on earth, in my Peace - without disturbance, without the need to plan, without effort, under Grace, being fed by the Infinite, by the Eternal so that all things happen under the Divine plan and Divine will in the Divine sequence expressing outwardly as what the world would call harmony and yet, we do not seek that harmony. We do not entreat for that harmony. We do not plan for that harmony. It simply is the nature of Divinity. Divinity expresses as harmony. But to seek that harmony, to seek human betterment is the way you push that harmony away because the moment you seek it, you are unaware that it is the natural quality of you now and you're only seeking it because you're not knowing who you are now.

When you are Christ, you don't seek human betterment. When you are Christ, you're not seeking human improvements. And as long as you're seeking them, you are boldly declaring, "I am not the Christ." And the whole Christ message is that you are. Not that you will become, not that you will earn the right to be the Christ, not that God will suddenly appoint you: but that you are.

"My peace I give unto you."

I give it unto you who know you are the Christ. And when you know you are the Christ, you are in the Kingdom of heaven on earth. And for you, the whole world of matter is an appearance only in the human mind which is the anti-Christ mind which knoweth not the Father. And because for you Spirit is All, God is All, whatever appears that is not Spirit, the total world that appears to you, is not here. The world cannot be here if you dwell in your Christ awareness. You will still have a body moving through that world that is not here. That will not be your body. That will be the outer appearance of your consciousness to man.

We walk in the Christ body. We step out of the concept called human body. We step out of the concept called human mind. We find ourselves not in these things until that Self that we find is a real Self, a Self we know exists. That Self is my Peace. That Self is independent of the world. That Self is always present. That Self can say, "I am Infinity here and now." That is your Self. The Infinity of God expressing here and now - not in form, not in human mind, not in the world.

For you there is no form, no mind, no world. There is your Being. My Peace breaks the illusion of the world. My Peace removes the karma of a hundred lifespans. My Peace takes time and space and reveals that they do not exist. Only the Eternal and the Infinite I here.

Now, this is different Truth than mind truth. This is the Truth in which Grace functions. This is the Truth in which Christ pushes back the mountain, in which Christ parts the Red Sea, in which Christ raises the dead. Why? Because there were no dead. Because there was no Red Sea. Because there was no mountain. These were the appearances of the world consciousness.

The Christ mind is not barricaded by all physical appearances of the world mind. The Christ mind does not know there's a wall to walk through. The Christ mind does not know there's an ocean to walk upon. The Christ mind does not know there is someone sick or someone dying. The Christ mind does not know that there are continents separated by oceans. The Christ mind knows the one Infinite body and knows it now and never leaves it. And that Christ mind, knowing the one Infinite body appears to human sense as what the human considers a harmonious physical body, a body that appears to be under Grace.

The Christ mind does not waste a moment in the world and then comes your great secret. And this is something that you must know. Something you must come to know well. Your Substance becomes every form you need. The Grace of Christ being your sufficiency in all things, your Substance which is Christ, your Substance which is the Holy Ghost becomes every form you need. There is no need that you have which is not made and formed of your own Christ substance when you're living in your Christ awareness. Your form changes, your environment changes, your Substance becomes an invisible, Spiritual activity which appears as a new home. Your Substance becomes an invisible, Spiritual activity which appears as a heart that functions well. Your Substance becomes an invisible Spiritual activity that appears as a new working organ so that that very heart which didn't beat well yesterday beats well today. Your Substance becomes new tissue. Always, the invisible activity of your Substance appears through human consciousness as a new, revitalized you. Nothing is impossible to the living, Spiritual substance of Being. It is the Kingdom and when we find our own Substance as Christ, our Substance is the very Grace unto all that we are.

My Peace is my Substance realized as your Substance. When you know that you are Christ substance and that Christ is the infinite, individuality of God, that all that the Father hath is functioning as the Christ of your own Substance, then you know that Grace is ever present, you know the meaning of imminence, of Emmanuel, of omnipresence as a fact, not as a word.

Now, you will find that your conscious awareness of this grows. The awareness that I need take no thought for this lifespan. I need take no thought for my business. I need take no thought for my marriage. I need take no thought for my children. I am the substance of God. That Substance is perfect. If I don't eclipse it with human thought and blot it out of my experience, it will form itself invisibly as Spiritual manifestation and that Spiritual manifestation which is the Holy Ghost will appear visibly to human sense as that which I need called the added thing. This is the miracle of my Substance.

Everything comes out of your Substance or it comes out of the world consciousness and then it's in division and cannot function under Grace. My Peace then takes me into Self-realization.

Now, I know that all of us have a mixture of Divine and human. That is our division. The human is something super imposed upon us by world belief, the Divine is the Truth, the Reality. And we find that, everything in our lives that we consider to be part of our Being, part of our experience, in the mystical light of Truth is revealed to be only our own consciousness turned into the visible world. It's like that reversible raincoat. Your consciousness turned outside becomes your experience, your life. Your own business is in your consciousness. Your form is in your consciousness. Your marriage is in your consciousness. Your family is in your consciousness. There isn't a thing in your world, including the world itself, that exists outside of your consciousness.

Your consciousness is every moment of your world and if that consciousness is not Divine, then you're not living in the Creation. But you're living in that which is the re- creation of the world consciousness. And as you live in re-creation, you're in the good and evil, the two powers, corporeality, life and death, sickness, disease, disaster, destruction, the good and the bad; the opposites.

Now, take your business. You think it's out there. Now, think of it for a moment as not being out there. Think of all the physical things that you own in that business and try to see that God did not create them. The building can burn down. The vehicles can have accidents. The assets can melt away. God created nothing in your business. The world consciousness through you created it and the world consciousness through you can also un- create it and someday will.

Now, try to see that business exists only in your consciousness because God not having put it there, it isn't where you think it is. It can't exist where God didn't put it and if God put it there, it would be forever and forever perfect. That means it exists in your thought. It exists in your thought and you think it's at a certain address. You think it's a building. You think it has certain physical qualities. But all of that, mystically, is in your thought.

Now, the quality of your thought is the quality of that business. If there are certain qualities in your thought, those qualities appear as the sturdiness, the progressiveness, the dependability of that business. But unless those qualities are Divine, that business is not under Grace. That business can lack one day. That business can be successful for a moment, for a year, for ten and then it can be subject to the winds of the world conditions.

Now, suppose you could bring that business under Grace so that no matter what happened in the world, it would be sustained by the invisible activity of Spirit. Your Substance, your Divine substance becomes the invisible activity of Spirit which outwardly then becomes your business. That would mean that your consciousness would have to be separated from the world consciousness. You have to learn how to do that.

When you separate your consciousness from the world consciousness, you bring your business under Divine consciousness, under Grace. And because the mind of the Father, the power of the Father, the presence of the Father becomes the law unto you, it becomes a law unto your consciousness and just as your human consciousness had out-pictured the kind of business you had, now your Divine consciousness out-pictures what appears to be a same, physical business but it isn't. It is now the Divine consciousness made manifest and it is under Grace. It is maintained by invisible, Spiritual activity. Your Substance unfolds as the business. Between your Substance and the business, there is no separation. It is one, continuous activity of the Father appearing only because the world mind is going to look at your invisible consciousness and see your visible business.

My Peace maintains everything that emanates from the Divine consciousness. There isn't anything that is in the Divine consciousness that is under the powers of this world. A fire cannot burn down a business that is directed by Divine consciousness. A flood cannot come through such a piece of property. There is no possible destruction to that which Divine consciousness out-pictures and Divine consciousness is the only Reality of your consciousness in Christ.

Now, this is the age in which what had seemed to be miracles of yesterday, are going to be made visible as common place events. You will discover that things that seemed impossible only were impossible in the human sense of things, in the human mind, which had not received the Comforter, which knew nothing of my Peace. And my Peace is introduced to us now at this moment to make us all aware that there is a Divine grace functioning in the human consciousness when it steps aside and permits Divine consciousness to be the only Consciousness there.

To be Christed, to be ordained, to be anointed is the acceptance that there is no mortal being here. Don't make your business the business of a mortal being. Don't make your marriage the marriage of two mortal beings. Don't make your children mortal beings. Don't make anything about your life mortal because it's untrue, it's transient, it's not of God, it does not have the Divine blessing.

But when you are willing to accept yourself as the Spirit, the Child of God, you have the total Divine blessing. Everything you do is under ordination and must prosper in the Divine plan. Everything.

Bring everything you know into that awareness that, "I am the Spirit of God." You know, it is often thought that Jesus did all that healing. And you know better. It was the absence of Jesus which did the healing. Jesus represents the place on this earth where there was no me. There was only Christ. But the Way shower was teaching us that when you want Grace, there must be a place where you stand where there's no you; there's only Christ. That's the healing. When there's no you but Christ, just as there was no Jesus but Christ, then the Father within can do the works because the Father within is Christ. Then the Father within shows you why I, Christ in you can heal the sick. I, Christ in you can raise the dead. I, Christ in you can open the eyes of the blind. Didn't I show you I can do it?

Am I different now? Am I not the Christ of your Being? I, Christ in you. Why don't you let me run your business? Why don't you let me run your marriage? Why don't you let me run every relationship you have? And behold, the perfection of Christ in you becomes the perfection expressed in the visible.

Don't try to be human and Divine. You can't be both. You can't be a divided self. And your secret then is you are Divine. And I say secret because it takes a long time to come to the willingness to accept Divinity. Let's not push that on anyone else. We will either accept it for ourselves and for all we know, but we will never try to push it upon them. It takes years to build the awareness of how to accept Divinity with humility, with obedience, with a consecration that is all within.

"The [new] Comforter," says the Master here, *"which is the Holy Ghost,"* and that's an extension of the previous statement, "The Spirit of Truth was the Comforter." Now, you know the Spirit of Truth is the Holy Ghost, *"whom the Father will send in my name."*

Now, how does the Father *"send in my name?"* We're being told that the Father, which is unconditioned, infinite Spirit has an instrument through which the Father works and that instrument is your Christ Self. Your Christ Self must be the Holy Ghost. Your Christ Self must include the Holy Ghost. Your Christ Self is the perfect instrument through which the Father functions. The Father *"sends in my name."* The Father sends that instrument which is the Christ mind through which you receive the Father.

"He shall teach you all things."

Clearly, the Christ mind enables you to be taught all things. Without it, you're in the world consciousness, separated, divided. Only in the Christ mind can you be taught all things and *"Bring all things to your remembrance, whatsoever I have said unto you."* So that you meet Christ out here in a book or if you walk the streets of Jerusalem. But now you meet Christ within your Self and Christ within you reminds you of those days, of the words said out here, of the deeds shown out here. Christ within you reminds you, brings them to remembrance means: repeats them, does them again. Christ in you pushes back the mountain. Christ in you solves the insoluble problem. Christ in you reveals that what you thought was a division of good and evil is only invisible Perfection waiting to be manifest through your Christ mind.

"Brings to remembrance all things."

And so, Christ in you reveals my Kingdom. Christ in you reveals why the world was under the illusion that there were four or five hundred ways to die when all there is, is the Life, the substance of God where you are.

All things that are not of the Father are revealed to be non-existent. Christ in you then becomes your Illumination.

How many times when you have received a phone call, did you, before you picked up that phone, remind yourself that where call was coming from, only God could be? Try it sometime. You'll have a different telephone conversation. How many times before you went out to see somebody did you remind yourself that where you were going to see that person, that friend, that client, that prospect, that associate, only God could be? Remind yourself of it and notice the difference in your reception, the difference in your relationship. How many times before you went from one room to another did you remind yourself that only God can be where the other room seems to be? Try it. It's the Truth. God being everywhere, it doesn't matter what seems to be happening. The moment you know only God is there, you bring yourself back into my Kingdom and the laws of my Kingdom then must express.

Consciously, you must be aware of the presence of God. And, where are you? Is God there? Are you aware of God being there? Is there any distance between you there and God there? Are you two or can you like the Master say, *"I and the Father are one."*

If God is there and God is the Spirit, and you are there and you are the Spirit, that knowledge, that oneness, that acceptance brings the law of Grace functioning. And when you meditate again, who is meditating? I, the Spirit, am being still. I, the Spirit am releasing the sense of humanhood. That's what your meditation really is - releasing the sense of humanhood. I, the Spirit, have nothing to seek. I'm all there is.

And you know, when you dial that phone and you dial long distance and you hear all those little clickity, click, click, clicks all over, all of the circuits are being opened up to send your call through. The minute you catch the Truth of Being, there's an Infinity of clickity- clicks throughout the Father's universe. You're one with it. You're in that automation whereby having accepted the presence of God where you are, where everyone is, my Peace can come to you. You're accepting the miracle of Infinity where you are. No less. Infinite God where you are, always. You can even feel the change in your consciousness when you do. There's an inner response.

Now, this moves us up beyond all of our rational thinking, all of our rational planning into that realm which is beyond mind and beyond form. We're not fed by the world. We're fed by the Word of the Father. The infinite, inner Word of the Father becomes our Substance and it carries with it infinite, Divine power of Perfection. It doesn't depend on human beings. It functions where the human being is absent and then present with the Lord, because of it.

Exit mortality, enter Divine. That's the universe of Light we should now be experiencing frequently as a preparation for my Peace.

The chapter in Joel is called, "Revelation of Spiritual Identity." Spiritual identity has no second identity. Spiritual identity walks through the grave, through the tomb. Spiritual identity has no life to lose. It has no physicality to lose. It has no human experience to lose. It is all totally Divine.

That is where our consciousness should be resting, in the Divinity of Being.

Maybe we ought to pause here. We're going to finish the fourteenth chapter of John. We're going to finish the chapter, "Revelation of Spiritual Identity." We want to prepare for next week so that we can proceed with the fifteenth chapter of John, "I am the Vine" and the next chapter of Joel which is, "It Shall Not Come Nigh Thee." So, I hope that this will be our schedule for the next session after the intermission to complete these chapters.

— End of Side One —

An important thing we want to remember is that always invisibly the world consciousness is functioning. It isn't consulting us. It isn't asking for our permission. It is functioning no matter what you do. And while it functions, it brings fifty percent of the evil and fifty percent of the good. And you have no way, if you're not in Truth, to prevent that from flowing through you as your experience.

Now, it's important to get a good feeling of what this world consciousness is. It will enable you to know that without the Christ mind, you're at the mercy of a force that controls you.

The world consciousness is functioning now, all around us and to the degree that we are not in the Christ mind, we are in that consciousness of the world. And so, everything in our life that is negative, is the degree to which we are not in the consciousness of God but are in the world consciousness instead.

Now, when you look out and do not see God, you'll actually fall into opinions about what you do see. When other people look out and do not see God, they form opinions about what they see. This thought, these opinions, these sensations become active in the world mind. They feed back and become the world mind.

You might say that from the moment of birth, every sensation you have felt accumulated, is what you are this moment. You are the accumulation of every sensation since the moment of birth as a human being. Most of that, being unaware of God, becomes nothing more than mental opinion. Dream consciousness and yours, mine, his and hers, all of this mental opinion become world consciousness. And then world consciousness feeds it back to us. And this continues to flow and flow and flow. It lives out its world which is not the Kingdom of God. It recreates images which are not the Kingdom of God inhabitants. It recreates forms. It recreates conditions. All of this is in the dream world consciousness. And that's where we have our businesses. That's where we have our human relationships. And when you leave them there, they're at the mercy of the world consciousness, they're at the mercy of the whirlwind. They're at the mercy of all of the conditions of the world consciousness. That's why these inexplainable events occur when we're wiped out. When we lose important possessions. When relationships are broken up.

The world consciousness has no regard for what we consider important to us. It's running its world government completely independent of God. And unless we have a change of consciousness, we leave ourselves in a world that God didn't create, in a world of imagination.

And so, the change-over, the pass-over, the new Consciousness is the preparation for the way in which the Comforter comes unto you and lifts you out of the world consciousness. And lifting you out of the world consciousness, it lifts everything that you are. It lifts all of your relationships, all of your possessions, all of your life experience out of the world law of good and evil into the law of my Perfection in all things. Your new Consciousness is no longer world consciousness but God consciousness, Christ consciousness. That's the meaning of this line:

"Ye have heard how I said unto you, I go away, and come again unto you. [And] if ye loved me, ye would rejoice, because I said, I go unto the Father: for my Father is greater than I."

You're being told that the Christ consciousness makes you one with the Father. You don't go unto the Father, you don't find Source without Christ consciousness. You're in world consciousness but when you find Christ in you you're in Christ consciousness which goes unto the Father. And you're one with the Father. You're in the Christ consciousness which becomes the law unto you.

"[And] now I have told you before it comes to pass, that, when it is come to pass, ye might believe."

The visible makes known to us, so that we will turn to the Invisible. When the visible is no longer with us, we must find in the Invisible, our way. Your Christ consciousness is your Invisible way. You've been trying all the visible ways. Some work and some don't. The Invisible way through Christ always works. It lifts you out of the fifty percent universe, out of the fifty percent good and the fifty percent evil. It lifts you out of the action of the world consciousness because it goes unto the Father. It lifts you out of sickness. It lifts you out of fear. It lifts you out of worry. It lifts you out of the conditions of being human.

"I've told you before it comes to pass, that when it is come to pass you might believe."

The Christ is going to reveal that there is no corporeal body, that you're living in a dream body when you think you're living in a physical body. I've told you in advance so that when it comes to past you will believe. I'm going to show you that they can't keep me in a tomb. Why? Because I have no body to put in a tomb. This body you're looking at is the Christ body. This is the Christ body standing before you teaching you. "Your name may be Peter, your name may be John, and you may think I am a man," he's saying, "but this is the Christ body. It is not the same kind of a body that you think it is."

Why is it a Christ body?

"Because I have taken it out of the world consciousness. I was in the world consciousness as a man called Jesus. I took it out of the world consciousness. I became Christed. I became aware of my Christ body. The Divinity of my Being expresses as the Christ body and the Christ mind. And this is the Christ body and the Christ mind that is yours because my Father and your Father are one. And now I tell you this in advance so that when my Christ body cannot be entombed and kept there, you will know why. It is under the law of Divinity. It cannot know death. It can never know death. And I tell you this so that you will know it is the truth of your Christ body. But I, the Christ appearing to men as Jesus, I can walk through the tomb because I am in the conscious awareness of that Christ body."

There's no point in teaching you about the conscious awareness of it after death. That won't do you any good. It's the conscious awareness of it before the entombment. The conscious awareness of Christ before, which makes impossible the experience of death, which makes impossible those conditions which lead to death.

"I, Christ am revealing these things that the world may be Christed, aware of its Christ identity."

"Hereafter I will not talk much with you: for the prince of this world cometh, and hath nothing in me."

He is describing for us a change in consciousness that we must be ready to accept. The prince of this world must come and find nothing in us.

Christ has revealed through a form called Jesus the miracle of Perfection on earth where the world consciousness paints a picture of good and evil.

But now the work has been demonstrated and the Christ in the form called Jesus is leaving because there is nothing more to do. The work is done. There is nothing more that the form called Jesus can do in the visible for the disciples.

This is the place in consciousness where you begin to realize there's nothing more you can do in the visible. You must now come to that Invisible. The visible is departing for you to turn to the Invisible. The prince of this world is the world consciousness. The prince of this world is the carnal mind of the world, the universal carnal mind. But it will come and find nothing in you. It will come and you will not be subject unto it. The dominion of the world mind is broken by your awareness of Christ in you.

The prince of this world cometh and finds nothing in you. The prince of this world, the carnal mind cannot for you, present pictures of evil that you will accept, pictures of lack that you will accept, pictures of bad health that you will accept. That's the prince of this world. But in your Christ awareness, it finds nothing in you. This is the Christ consciousness that must be developed day by day until the world mind finds nothing in you, until every evil on the face of the earth is instantaneously known to be, impossible. Whether it's in your body or someone else's body because Spirit, God, is everywhere and there is no place where God and evil can exist at the same time.

There is no place where God and error can exist. There is no place where God and a flood and a fire can exist at the same time. There is no place where God can be and cancer at the same time. It is impossible.

The world mind will say, "Here is the cancer." The Christ mind will say, "No, here is God." The world mind will say, "Here is the lack, here is the famine, here is the poverty." The world mind is lying. The Christ mind will say, "No, here is God."

The appearance of these things is because of the separation of our thought from God. Our thought being separated from God where the avenue through which world mind expresses these lacks, these limitations. But when you're in your Christ consciousness, conscious that Christ is where you are, that God is where you are, expressing as Christ, world mind, the prince of this world, finds nothing in you. It can't express through Christ. That's not its instrument. Its instrument is the human mind. When you're in the Christ mind, it cannot express in you. It cannot express bad health. It cannot express poverty. It cannot express famine. It cannot express fear. It cannot express the opposites.

The prince of this world cometh where there is Christ consciousness and finds nothing in you. You don't need any human protection. You don't need any human improvement. You have to be in the consciousness which world consciousness cannot penetrate to enter or defile. And obviously, such a Consciousness exists.

"Hereafter, I will not talk much…. for the prince of this world cometh, and hath nothing in me."

Now, even the appearance of corporeality is to be removed; the last outpost of the world mind. Even corporeality is to be removed. All of the work then is turned into the invisible Christ.

"But that the world may know that I love the Father; and as the Father gave me commandment, even so I do. Arise, let us go hence."

"Arise," is a commandment. It is the commandment to rise out of corporeal sense into the constant, conscious awareness that here, now is no human mind. Here now is the Christ mind. Here, now I will recognize all that is of the world and know that it has no place in my Consciousness for I am that expression called the Christ mind. The Christ mind expresses God. The Christ mind expresses God's Self

where you are. The Christ mind expresses Divine wisdom, Divine love. The Christ mind does not express the good and the bad of the world consciousness. Whatever you perceive that is of the world consciousness, you stand still, until you make that reconciliation, that adjustment.

Now, let's go back to your business for a moment. The world consciousness has painted your business in a certain way. Now, let's walk out of one consciousness into the other and bring that business into the Divine consciousness. Let's see how we can do that.

In a human consciousness, we have certain concern about our business. That concern is not the Christ consciousness. That concern is because we're still a remnant of the world consciousness expressing. The world consciousness expresses that concern. The world consciousness expresses certain problems. There are no problems in the Christ. The world consciousness paints pictures of good and of bad. The world consciousness presents a physical business.

Now, let's take it out of physicality. Let's see that there is no physical anything. Spirit, being All, that which appears physical as a business, as customers, as patrons, as services, all of that is world consciousness expressing its concept and it will continue to govern its own concepts but I'm taking it out of the physical universe. Spirit is All and therefore, right where all of the physical quality of the businesses is, all its sales charts, all its customers, all its services, there is only invisible Spirit: God. Ever perfect, ever harmonious, ever self-fulfilling in every detail. Nothing missing. Every need fulfilled and now, I'm taking myself out of the physical universe.

I am Spirit and therefore, I have no human mind here. The only mind that is here is the Christ mind. The Christ mind knows nothing about a physical business, nothing at all, about a good business, a bad business, a successful one or a failing one. The Christ only knows about God's business. The Christ mind is the only mind I will accept as my mind.

95

I have no concept about a business, none whatsoever. Just resting in the Christ mind. Now, if I can stay in the Christ mind, I will know that the Christ mind is under the governorship of the Infinite Father.

When I have no sense of physicality, I will have a feeling of the real existence of a universe made of Spirit. Nothing is happening physically in my universe. There are no physical customers, there are no physical sales, there are no physical services. There's no physical building. It's a complete Spiritual universe and it's functioning now right here, everywhere perfectly. Nothing can ever go wrong because I am the invisible Christ of God and the only way I can express is to express what God is expressing which is Perfection.

Whatever I do will manifest in the visible as Righteousness, as Goodness, as a visible expression of invisible Love, as Fulfillment. It must because it is born of the Father in the Christ mind. It's independent of the world consciousness.

Now, I dwell here until I have that inner response that I am truly in the Christ mind. And as long as I can maintain the thread of consciousness in Christ, I can accept with confidence that the outer manifestation of all that concerns me will be a Christ expression.

I started with a business but it is really the wholeness of my Being. Nothing can happen except the Divine activity in the Christ mind. Now, then, do you go out of the Christ mind or do you stay there? That will determine the manifestation in the visible.

Your capacity to stand in this lifeline, which is the Christ mind, will determine the outer manifestation. If there are going to be fluctuations, it's because you are fluctuating in and out of the Christ mind. The more you remain in it, the more faithful you are to consciously remaining in it, the more you will notice your world is taking shape from that activity. Your Spiritual fidelity in the Christ mind becomes your new Consciousness unfolding as the expression of the Divine.

Consciousness of the Divine unfolds or consciousness of the world unfolds. You're really choosing your whole life, your whole world, your whole universe when you decide to consciously stand in the Christ mind or to revert to a human consciousness. This is the crux. This is where it all happens. This is where the Substance flows.

Now, it's the same in healing. Healing is nothing more than standing in the Christ mind knowing, that where the illness appears, it's only because there is someone there that I have accepted out of my Christ mind. In my Christ mind, I don't know any ill people. I only know them in a human mind. Now, they seem to be out there. Let's get them back in consciousness. There's nothing except in your consciousness.

And so, let's take that sick person, no matter how far away and see that they are in your consciousness. Now, if they're in your consciousness, you're not going to help them out there. You're not in a Spiritual consciousness if they're in your consciousness. You're in a human consciousness. You have been deceived. You are the world consciousness individualized and you have in your consciousness a sick person. You're not in Christ mind then, are you?

Now, how are you going to heal that person if you're still aware of a sick person? World consciousness is governing them and you're not doing anything to stop it.

Now, for you to be in the Christ mind, you'll have to drop your consciousness of a sick person. There isn't any in the Christ mind and then it looks like you're losing control. You don't have your hands on the problem. That's how you do it. You get out of the consciousness of a sick person. Christ consciousness has no sick people. And if you're in the awareness that there is no sick person, you're moving into Christ consciousness. As long as you've got a sick person, you're not in Christ consciousness.

And so, you're crucifying the world mind which says, "There's a sick person." You're saying, "No, no. Spirit is All." Right there where the sick person is, is God. That's your Christ consciousness and now you will rest there. But don't go back to having a sick person. Christ consciousness says, "Only God is present, here and there." Don't look for improvement or else you've still got a sick person. Rest in the knowledge that here is Christ. That's my name and there is the Spirit of God. There's no person there. There's the Spirit of God. Rest in it. Don't go back to the old consciousness.

Now this fidelity is how you develop your Christ consciousness. Every evil on the earth is attacking not you. It's attacking Christ in you. It's attacking your belief that you're not Christ. It's trying to make you believe Christ isn't where you stand. And so, everything that comes at you that is not of God is the way the world mind or the anti-Christ attacks the Christ, in you.

"Arise and let us go hence."

Let us come out of the lower consciousness called the world consciousness, the mortal, the carnal. Rise to the Christ awareness that nothing is present but the Spirit of God. Live with that, awake and asleep until it's solidified, until it's dependable, until you know this is my Consciousness. Nothing exists but God. If that phone rings, wherever it's coming from, God is there and only God. This is God's universe, this is God's substance everywhere. Not what I'm seeing, that's world consciousness. And you're identifying carnal mind.

Now I think we have time to look at some quotations from Joel.

"Limitations are brought about not because your mind and body are evil or sick, but only because your mind and body have been conditioned by the belief of two powers."

Now if you're in God consciousness, God is the power. So, there's no other power to change that which is God and therefore, what

98

appears to be the power of having changed something is impossible because there's no other power. You're looking at the illusion of a power, the illusion of a condition caused by the illusion of power. There's no power to change Spirit. Spirit is everywhere.

If God is everywhere, error isn't there. If Spirit is everywhere, and this is the hard part, if Spirit if everywhere, matter isn't there. How can you heal what isn't there? Do you see you're trying to heal what isn't there? And if you're tempted to heal what isn't there, you're not in the Christ mind. Spirit is there. There's nothing to heal. Rest quietly in the consciousness that Spirit is there until you have the feeling of it. This feeling intensifies. The more you practice, the more you have the assurance.

Now, carnal mind is the belief that there are two powers. Christ mind is the knowledge that God alone is the power and there is no other possible power. There's only the power of God which is perfect. And so, I don't need a power to overcome something that is no power. That which it seems to be a power unto, is only because I'm in the false mind. All right? Out of the false mind. In the Christ mind.

Stand ye still. There are no powers to overcome. There is my Power, being my Power right where the false power seems to be operating. Right where the sickness seems to be, my Power is being. Rest in it until you have the assurance of it from within.

Don't heal. That's the human mind. Don't be tempted to heal. The Christ mind reveals that only my Spirit is present. There's no power to cause anything to be wrong. You're looking at the illusion of wrongness. You're looking at the illusion of lack, the illusion of limitation, the illusion of unemployment, the illusion of poverty. Get into Christ mind accepting the power of God is functioning. It is here. It is there. It is everywhere. Until Christ mind reveals the Truth. And then you'll find that which appears is healing is your Christ consciousness made visible.

A belief in the carnal mind which is belief in good and evil, good powers and bad powers, when actually there is no power to cause your problem. There is no power to cause your problem. It's all universal, carnal mind presenting the illusion of problem and you'll never know it in the human mind because it's the same mind. It's always the **illusion** of sickness, the **illusion** of lack. It's all re-created through world mind to appear 'as.' And only Christ mind is the answer.

Christ mind doesn't fight, doesn't protect, doesn't battle. Christ mind rests in the knowledge that God is present doing a Perfect job of running his Perfect universe now. To the degree that you can maintain that inner assurance in the face of what appears to be the problem, you're in the Christ mind and you're breaking the carnal mind. The prince of the world is finding no place in you.

Now, this you may not like but he says it. "*If, at this moment, you could be made whole, nothing would stop you from [going out tomorrow and] becoming sick or poor again, unless you, yourself, had come to the realization that the healing which had taken place was not one of lack or limitation, [was not one] of fear, sin or false appetites, [was not a healing of] of polio, cancer, blindness, or deafness: the healing was in being freed from the belief in two powers - good and evil.*"

Now, deep in our subconscious, we believe in two powers. You believe your business could be bad tomorrow. You believe your health can be bad tomorrow but your Christ mind doesn't believe that. That's the remnant of the human mind. You've got to work with that belief. It's the denial of who you are, you see. If you believe you can be sick tomorrow, you don't believe you're the Christ, do you? You're talking about a mortal being. You're fooled into the world consciousness which says, "You are a mortal being." And so, the you that's going to be sick tomorrow in your belief, or could be, is your denial of Christhood now. You've got to repair that belief.

"No, I am the Christ and I'm not going to be sick tomorrow or any day. I'm not even going to be a day older tomorrow." That you have to constantly work with until you know it's the Truth. That's how you recognize your attainment of the realization of Christ identity.

Always, the world mind is forcing false beliefs through you and you inadvertently accept them by your latent fears or doubts and yet, Christ isn't going to be any different tomorrow than Christ is today. If you're not anchored on that realization, you're in duality.

See how all the work becomes an inner working in the conscious re-awareness, the constant reminder of your true identity until you can be awakened in the middle of the night and you're still the Christ before you open your eyes?

You are the living Spirit of God, the Child of God, the Son of God. You have one Father, the Divine Father and every time you walk out of this realization and are caught napping, it's the world consciousness still sending its tide of thought through you, fooling you into mortality.

"Our whole consciousness is built on the realization of God constituting all being, therefore there is neither good nor evil. There is only God."

God constitutes all Being. Now, let's take our sick friends and see that God constitutes all Being. We are mal-practicing them by thinking they are sick. We're not helping them. We're not helping ourselves. We're letting the world mind express through our unenlightened consciousness. God constitutes all Being. Now, if I wrote that on the blackboard, that wouldn't heal anybody, would it? So, I can't write it on the blackboard of my mind and expect it to heal anybody either. There has to be a change in consciousness, not writing it on the blackboard. You have to dwell with it. The fact that we say it now doesn't make it a power. It's the daily dwelling in the conscious awareness that God constitutes all Being.

And as you dwell with it daily, you're praying without ceasing. You're abiding. You're resting. You're being faithful. You're standing in the secret place of the Most High. You're building that foundation which suddenly becomes so firm that when the news hits you, so and so is sick, it hits that consciousness, then you don't have to recover. It hits it then and it is dissipated by your conscious awareness that "No, no, no - God constitutes all Being," and you're not trapped. Then, you're not mal-practicing anybody. Then the tides turn.

"Evil power cannot have any existence outside the mind that believes in it."

That's pinning it right down on the false consciousness. The only evil power there is, is in the false consciousness, the mind that believes in it. That's not the Christ mind. So, it's not the mind you want to be in.

"You are never dealing with floods, tidal waves or typhoons: you're dealing with a universal malpractice which is made up of the belief in two powers."

Now, let's get rid of that second power. There's only God power. God power isn't making anybody sick. Therefore, what's making somebody sick if there's no power to do it? We're looking at a universal sense of things, a universal malpractice, a universal belief which we are calling sick person and the only reason we call it that is because we believe that such a thing is possible. We believe there's a power to make a person sick. We believe it and our belief is false. There's only God power. There's only Spirit.

We must come to that side where we know God power is all that is here. God power is the Power behind my life, my business, my relationships. Everything in this world is but the outer appearance of what I know to be invisible God power and therefore, that God power being the only Presence, there's no other power to make anything evil or bad. Only thinking makes it so.

Right where every evil appears, invisible God power is - in your consciousness. You're purifying your thought. You're preparing a habitation for God in your consciousness. You're opening the way for the Comforter.

Anti-Christ is the only cause of discord in the world, that means the universal world mind. Anti-Christ is the only cause of discord in the world. So, now you identify everything you see as universal world mind or anti-Christ or belief in two powers. They're all saying the same thing. Do not battle it. All of this is mirage. Rest in the Word. Do not go out to fight the enemy. This is malpractice. This is a belief in two powers. This is anti-Christ. This is universal hypnotism. Drop it. Do not sit up and do not fear it. Do not protect yourself from it. There is no reality to it. *"There is no it."* This is Joel talking. *"There is no it."*

How can there be a sick person if all there is, is Spirit? There is Spirit which we are misconstruing as a sick person because our human mind is geared to the world mind. Out of the human mind, our Christ mind reveals the perfect Reality that is there.

"And so, once it is recognized that the so-called powers of this world are not powers," Joel says, *"it will not be long before heaven is established on earth…. No material or mental powers can operate in the consciousness of an individual who lives in the realization that God's grace is his sufficiency."*

We had that meditation last week and now, I think there's probably a good way to end today.

God's Grace is our sufficiency but it's of no value to us if we're in the human mind. Spiritual Grace does not function that way. Spiritual Grace did not heal a cripple through that cripple's human mind. Spiritual Grace through the Christ revealed that there was no power to keep that individual as a cripple. Spiritual Grace through your Christ mind reveals there is no power to limit you or make you lack. There's no power to kill you. There's no power to make you sick or suffer. Spiritual Grace reveals through your Christ mind that you are perfect as your Father.

Christ mind. That's our chapter five. Fifteen is going to begin, *"I am the [true] vine."* The Christ mind is the Vine. You want fruit? You want grapes? They come off the Vine. The fruitage only comes from the Christ mind which is the Vine and my Father is the husbandman. The infinity of God through the Christ mind produces our fruitage, the blessings of Grace as we walk in the Light. and then, *"It cannot come nigh thee."*

We're going to take the advice of the Master. *"Arise and let us go [from] hence."* And that means take up your Divine selfhood. Rise to your Divinity. Let us not look back at mortality.

There is nothing happening except the perfect activity of God everywhere. That is the Christ consciousness.

Silence, (long pause) ….

Please bear with me just one minute. Silence, (pause) ….

He that believeth on the Son of God," meaning on Christ as his identity, *"hath the witness in himself: he that believeth not God hath made him a liar; because he believeth not the record that God gave of his Son. And this is the record, that God hath given to us eternal life, and this life is in his Son. He that hath the Son hath life; and he that hath not the Son of God hath not life."*

That's the first Epistle of John, the fifth chapter, verses 10 - 12. As you come into the Christ mind, you come into the awareness of Life eternal. Without it, we're running in lifespans.

Class 27

The Invisible Path To Grace

Herb: It's good again to see some new friends in the house and to all of you, a very cordial welcome.

You know, of course, that there have been many attacks upon the Bible, many statements and many of them proven to be true, that the Bible in its present form is mutilated. It is been altered by many hands, often by political regimes. It has been translated from one language to another and then still to another and finally to the English. Began in the Aramaic, and then the Greeks translated it to the best of their ability and then the Vulgate Roman into Latin and most of the translations that we have today are from that Vulgate Latin which was twice removed from the original.

In spite of all this, the Word of God is never tarnished. Over two thousand years have elapsed and still it reaches us in such a way that its authority, when understood, is never questioned. And though it may be mutilated on the surface, it's like a shell of a nut - when you open the shell, there's the nut. When you open the words, there's the Truth shining at you.

And that's the kind of a chapter we have today.

"I am the vine." The fifteenth chapter of John. It occurs at a very strategic moment between the Last Supper and the crucifixion and so it obviously is a preparation of the disciples and we may consider ourselves to be those disciples - a preparation for an understanding of what is to follow. So that, in understanding the crucifixion and all that follows it, we may have a clear picture of what is expected of us in order to walk in the Master's footsteps.

"I am the vine" tells you instantly that in this room there is a Vine. There is an invisible Christ and that makes each of our human selves branches on this invisible Vine. There's nothing you can do to make yourself better than your neighbor or worse. Each is connected to the invisible Vine. It makes no difference whatsoever what country you came from, what race you came from, what religion you came from. The fact is that there is an invisible Vine called Christ and we are one in that Vine. And now, this chapter beautifully gives us a perfect summary of the complete Christ message.

When you look at it, not casually, you discover that all of the major points of the Christ message are included. It is the way to the first resurrection and every word, every paragraph is another subtle point adding up to a path, a path to a new kind of Freedom, a path to a new Selfhood through the Vine.

And so, the identity of the Vine must be clearly established in our minds in order to understand where the power of Spirit is going to come.

The Vine, speaking to us, is the invisible Christ. If you have no feeling for that, then the words that are to be spoken by the Christ will indicate that you're not ready to be moved by them in the path they designate. If you have been chosen and you will understand more about that by the way you react to those words. If you have been chosen, then these words to you mean more than any human words on this earth.

The Christ says, "I am the Vine" and this is not an external Christ. This is not a Christ external to you. This is the kingdom of God within you speaking. This is the Christ of your Being, telling you, giving you the great key. Everything you seek and beyond what you have ever imagined is available only if you understand the identity of the Vine. The grape that is not on the Vine will not live long. The branch that is not on the tree cannot survive. If you are the branch on the tree, if you are the grape on the Vine, you must be one with that Vine, one with that tree and you must, in this work, be conscious of it.

Everyone who walks this earth is one with the Vine but being unconscious of it, they live in a sense of separation from the Christ. It is only in our conscious awareness of the Presence of the invisible Vine that we are sustained and nourished by it.

Let's read a few verses, maybe about ten or fifteen of them to get the feel of it, so that we can then backtrack and let it feed us its Divine manna.

"I am the true vine," it says. *"And my Father is the husbandman. Every branch in me that beareth not fruit he taketh away: and every branch that beareth fruit, he purgeth it, that it may bring forth more fruit. Now ye are clean through the word which I have spoken unto thee. Abide in me, and I in you. As the branch cannot bear fruit of itself, except it abide in the vine; no more can ye, except ye abide in me. I am the vine, ye are the branches: He that abideth in me, and I in him, the same bringeth forth much fruit: for without me ye can do nothing. If a man abide not in me, he is cast forth as a branch, and is withered; and men gather them, and cast them into the fire, and they are burned. If ye abide in me, and my words abide in you, ye shall ask what ye will, and it shall be done unto you. Herein is my Father glorified, that ye bear much fruit; so shall ye be my disciples."*

That's only the first eight verses. We'll probably go beyond that.

Now, let's see that there is a careful plan, a structure to this, to lead us infallibly to the fulfillment of the Father's plan for us. The Word of Christ is more accurate than a guided missile. It has a target. It hits the target. And here, the target is to awaken us to what may be called the buried God within us, the Divinity to which we are asleep. The Spiritual power that is on the earth awaiting whoever is ready to lay down his personal concept, his way and accept the Divine plan.

The first verse tells us the nature of God and Christ. The relationship between Christ and God. I, Christ, am the Vine. My Father is the Husbandman. The Husbandman is the Source, the eternal Caretaker, the Owner, the Creator, Infinity itself. The Husbandman is Divine Self, Infinity, without limitation. The Husbandman is the perfect God and the expression through which that perfect God flows is the Vine, the Christ, the only begotten of the Father.

Now, because this is the word of Christ, this is the Truth that you learn to accept without human interference. If you're going to sit back and say, "Now how do I know I could believe that," that's your privilege. As I say, if you have not been touched by the Spirit to know this is the Word, it is of no consequence to you. But if this for you is the Gospel, then you know now and forever that the one Creator functions through the Vine, the Christ and no grape will touch the Father except through that Vine. No branch will touch the Father except through that Tree.

God does not function in the grape except through the Vine. God does not function in the branch except through the Tree. God does not function in us except through Christ. And this is the point of the first verse. This is setting the Law, the infinite Law, the Law that must be fulfilled. You can only break it at the peril of your lifespan. You cannot violate Divine law and this is giving you the Law. You come to God only through Christ.

And the second verse tells you what happens if you do and what happens if you don't. The second verse is the explanation of the karmic law, how it operates. First, the Divine law and then that Law which assures that the Divine law is going to operate or else you must suffer through the violation.

And so, the second verse tells us *"Every branch in me that beareth not fruit he taketh away: and every branch that beareth fruit, he purgeth [it], that it may bring forth more fruit."*

And now, let's look at the subtleties there. You'll notice that both branches are purged, the ones that don't bear and the ones that do. But the ones that do bear fruit are purged so that they can bring forth more fruit. And that should tell you then that the branch that is taken away because it bears no fruit, is the statement that this branch must reincarnate. It has broken the Divine law. It is not bearing fruit. You cannot frustrate the Divine plan. You are sent back onto this earth in form again to bear fruit. You reincarnate.

But the other that is bearing fruit is purged and the word "purged" fools us. It means cleansed. This branch which is bearing fruit fulfills its destiny at this level and is raised higher into the next level where it bears more fruit. And so, this is transition. If you're not bearing fruit, human death and reincarnation. If you're bearing fruit, that which is called human death but is actually lifted to the next level or transition.

Now, that should be clear. These are the ground rules being laid down for us by I, the Christ, the Vine. You come to God through the Vine. That's how you bear fruit. If you don't come through the Vine, you don't bear fruit, you are purged, you are removed. And if you come through the Vine and bear fruit, you are rewarded. You are lifted higher into another sphere of consciousness, into the fourth dimension, into the Spiritual universe.

Then he says, *"Now ye are clean through the word that I have spoken unto you."*

And this clean is the same as purged. He's speaking to those who are his disciples there, here or anywhere saying, "Because you have received the word of Christ in you, because you have been willing to follow my commandments to this point, because you have turned within to the inner kingdom, because you have purified, because you have removed human concept, because you have been faithful to my Word, ye are clean. Ye are bearing fruit and you are now being prepared to be lifted to the next level to bear more fruit. You are clean through the words that I have spoken unto you."

And so, Christ is saying to disciples of Christ, "You have abided in me to this point. You are unconditioned, clean, without human concept to the best of your ability at this level. And now, I am prepared to take you higher, to show you how to fulfill the Divine plan which is established before the world was."

We're still in the metaphysics of the message of Christ and of the Infinite Way.

Now, at this point, let us try to see the picture. You would appear to be a form that ultimately dies. Christ says to you, "Don't believe it. I am the Vine. I am the invisible Self of you and I'm not going to die." Now if you're going to die, it's because you're not going to be one with the Vine. You're going to maintain a sense of separateness from the Vine and then you will die. It says so. You will be removed. But it also says that if you bear fruit which can only be done if you are connected to the Vine, you'll be lifted higher, to bear more fruit. Now that's not dying, is it? That's an extension of life, not an end to it. That's not extinction, that's progression.

And so, if we accept the Word again, Christ in you is saying, "If you stay connected to me, abide in me, you'll find that I, the Vine, will nourish you with whatever flows through me from the Father and that which nourishes you will bear more fruit in you."

And so, we begin to feel now this isn't a hopeless lifespan with an ending and then knocking on some pearly gates somewhere with the hope that somebody says, "You may come in." We are being told that Christ here, now, is the invisible Vine - the invisible Self, if you will, of your own Being. The Christ Self doesn't stop at a certain point and then you begin. This is all your Being. Christ Self invisible, flowing out appearing to human sense as individual branches or forms.

But now this human consciousness, this Adam consciousness, this devil mind consciousness which is unaware of its Divinity is being alerted, opened up to reveal that within what I thought was a human body, there is a Consciousness of the Christ and that when I become conscious of that Christ, I and the Vine are one, just as the Vine and the Father are one. And then the Father flowing through the Vine, flows through me and I and the Father are one and I am in Life, not in a dying form. I am in Divine government, not in a human sense which is separated from the Father.

No longer is there a God up there and a me down here but I and the Father are, through the Vine, one. I am nourished by Divinity, by Divine Grace. All that the Father has can flow through Christ as the expression of my Being.

Suddenly, the doors are open. The mortal sense of life with all its limitations is shown to be a limited point of view of a limited sense of mind. Christ says, "It isn't true."

"[If you] Abide in me, and I in you. As the branch cannot bear fruit of itself, except it abide in the vine; no more can ye, except ye abide in me."

Now, look carefully. *"Abide in me, and I in you."* How can Christ abide in us if Christ is not in us now? Is Christ going to come from somewhere?

Now, Christ in you is present and here is where you pause, to establish the awareness that Christ has been present where I am since before the beginning of time. I have been too busy to notice. I have been too forgetful. I have been too occupied with glorifying myself to be about the Father's business. And so, I in my haste, I have not known my own invisible Self. And now, my invisible Self says, "Abide in me. I've been abiding in you since before the world was. It's time for you to awake and know that I am here."

"Abide in me. Be conscious that I am present." And as the mind wishes to rove, run out into the world, there must be a conscious awareness on your part that this is the mind of the world in you which strives to turn away from the invisible Christ of your own Being. That run-away mind that refuses to be still, accept, know, believe, rest; abide.

And so, we plant the seed of belief that Christ is in me now. I have an invisible Self and I let that seed germinate, take root in my consciousness until this being the Word of the Father through Christ, I say, "Amen Father. It is the Word in me. I accept it."

The invisible Self of me is Christ ever abiding where I am. This is holy ground. This must take root in your consciousness. This is a demand of the Christ that you abide in me. I in you. This is the demand that in order to abide, you must do something you have not been perfectly willing to do. You cannot abide in Christ and also abide in a human sense of self. You are not two selves. You are not the invisible Christ Self and a visible human, mortal self. This is the trap, the belief that I am both. When you abide in Christ as Christ abides in you, you are accepting one Divine identity. Henceforth, you cannot know yourself after the flesh.

Christ is not your flesh. Christ is not your blood. Christ is not your human lifespan. Christ is Christ. Christ is Spirit. Christ is Immortal. To abide in Christ is to accept I am Spirit. I am not flesh and blood. I am Immortal.

This is where we founder on the reefs unless we take the time to let this seed of Truth germinate until we have not given it lip service but have discovered it to be so deeply embedded in our conviction that we're now willing to go forth and live from that knowledge.

I am the invisible Spirit of God. I am the Child of God. God is my Father. Every concept I've had about who I am changes when you accept the invisible Christ. Even the concept of human birth must change because human flesh can never give birth to the Christ. Matter never gives birth to Spirit. To accept the Christ, you give up the concept of human birth, of human flesh, of mortal self. I, Christ am the immortal Self, invisibly present here.

Remember, you cannot be connected to the Vine of Christ as a physical, mortal being. You are only connected to the Spirit as Spirit. This is how we now are learning to fulfill Divine law. We may not yet know what to do with our physical self, where to put it, how to react in it but be sure that the Divine plan will show you and so, we cut the ties of mortal belief. We obey. Yes, I am abiding in Christ. Not a Christ who will come a second time, not a Christ who left the earth and is coming back on a white horse. I'm abiding in Christ here, now, as the Spirit of my Being. That's the only Christ that I can accept. The Christ who said, *"I can never leave thee,"* and meant it. The Christ who is limitless, without boundaries. The Christ through whom the infinite Grace of the Father is ever flowing. The Christ who is the only key there is to the Kingdom of God. In that Christ, in that identity, I abide.

Now, you're not reading the Bible and saying, "That's it." You're not studying and saying, "That's it." You're not making loud noises about something and saying, "That's it." You're learning you must **be** that invisible Christ. That is the purpose of the fourth verse. Until you accept the Christ identity you are not abiding in the Vine.

"As the branch cannot bear fruit of itself, except it abide in the vine; no more can ye, except ye abide in me."

Now, how do you abide in Christ? You can't memorize it. You have to be it. And because you can do nothing of yourself, if you are not being Christ, the invisible Son of God, then whatever you try to do of yourself is nothing. Every success you call your success is a nothing success because it lacks the substance of your own Being. You're being opened to the infinite nature of your invisible Self.

There should be a growing awareness that Christ where you are, is ever present as the invisible Self that your eyes cannot see, that your hands cannot touch but is the Life of you, just as what you have called your body is the visible form of you. Now, beside the visible form, you have the invisible Life. You are told now to rest not in the form or the consciousness of the form but to rest in the invisible Life which is Christ as your Life.

And so, the form or the outer branch is resting in the awareness of the invisible Christ which is the Vine, as identity, and through that identity which is the Vine, the Father flows. Infinity pours its Divine plan under its Divine law fulfilling Itself in and as You. This is the way and any other way is described as a way which cannot succeed because of yourself as a human branch, ye can do nothing.

In the fifth verse, *"I am the vine"* is repeated. The human branch is not connected to God. Only the Vine is. *"Ye are the branches."* Now, that branch that we speak of here is the human sense of life, the human consciousness. At the moment, it's treated as a branch and you being a separate branch and another, being a separate branch and a third and a fourth and a fifth - all these separate branches, unaware that there is one invisible Vine, are ever afraid and must preserve themselves. They're all depending on their individual action for safety, for supply, for health. As human branches, unaware of the invisible Vine to which we are one, we all fear. We don't know where the next dollar will come from. We don't know if tomorrow will bring us a thunderbolt out of the sky or a lightning rod. We know we're in vulnerable bodies. We know there's a time limit on these bodies. We know accidents strike from nowhere without provocation. That's because we live as human branches.

You see, the form consciousness is living as a human branch. If you're in a form consciousness, an Adam consciousness, you are the world mind expressing as an individual, separated person. Living that way, we are subject to karmic law. Living that way, we cannot bear fruit. The fruit that we bear that way is false fruit. It's the fruit of good and evil.

If we make a success of our human self, that's not the fruit of the Father. That isn't spiritual fruit. We, in our own lives, must be Divine fruit. That's the only way you bear fruit and the human branch doesn't bear Divine fruit.

So, the devil mind, the serpent mind, the world mind, the Adam mind, the human mind, the human branch must learn that it is cut off. It will be purged. It will be removed. It cannot bear Divine fruit and as long as we continue to be human branches we cannot bear Divine fruit. We are committing suicide. We are living in dying forms. We're being told it in a very specific way.

"Unless you bear fruit"

Now, what kind of fruit does God have? Divine fruit. What kind of fruit must you bear? Divine fruit and no human being can do it.

The call to transform, *"Be ye transformed,"* out of a human branch by the renewing of the mind into the awareness of the invisible Vine of Christ within you and behold, you will bear Divine fruit and you will be lifted higher.

Christ acceptance, now, must be understood and that is why the Christ itself now will explain to us how we accept Christ, how we are given the faculty which enables us to accept Christ and how we can be trapped into thinking we're accepting while we're not. Be sure that every necessary teaching, every facet will be uncovered to us once we are willing to accept that there is an invisible Christ which is my invisible Self and unless I live in it consciously, I am never going to be in union with God. I'll be talking about union with God but it will never be consummated.

"He that abideth in me, and I in him, the same bringeth forth much fruit: for without me ye can do nothing."

Now just take your last twenty, thirty, forty or fifty years. In those years, were you abiding in Christ?

Is there any more that need be said to you if you have not found the heavenly Kingdom of God on earth? There's no other way to find it. There's no other way to walk in safety. There's no other way to feel the flow of Grace. There's no other way to lose the fear of the so-called power of sickness or death. There's no other way to walk in the Kingdom of God except through your conscious awareness that Christ, I am. That living Child of God, I am. And we who have not done that have discovered that we were unprotected. We were subject to the whims and the wills of external powers.

But as a measure of Christ is sown in you, a change begins to be very apparent. The hand of the Father begins to enter your experience. The Presence begins to guide you. The Power begins to dissolve all false powers around you. Invisible doors are opened. The magic of the presence of God through Christ in you becomes to you the only important reality of Life. The core out of which you live and the fruit is that Truth; expresses where you are. Harmony expresses where you are. Peace expresses where you are. Fulfillment expresses where you are. You are being made whole by the activity of the Christ.

I think many of us have passed the point where death has any significance at all. Absolutely none. The point where Paul says, *"Death where is thy sting?"* I think many of us have passed that point. Strangely, even though we can accept that in many cases, lesser things than death give us more trouble than death itself. Possibly because in a sense, these lesser things may instill in us some kind of a subtle fear about a level of consciousness we thought we had passed. But don't think that because it isn't true.

Many students have often said to me, "You use the word 'initiation' very often. I wish you'd tell us why." These so-called lesser things are your initiation. They're very necessary. You remember how we once heard Joel say, "Problems are opportunities." And the manner in which that was given to us was, that in seeing a problem, you are really being presented with an opportunity to know the Truth behind that problem.

Now, when a child in school has a problem, it's not really a problem. It's something to be solved. It's not a problem in the sense that it's irritating. It's a problem in the sense that when the child solves the problem, the child demonstrates the capacity to learn. And these problems should be accepted in the same way. They're really like Algebra problems or Geometry problems or English problems. They are given to us so that we may solve them and in solving them, we come to a higher level of consciousness. If you accept the problem in a different spirit, as a disturbance, something you wish weren't there, you're missing the point. These are necessary problems because you'll find the only way to solve problems is to be one with the Vine. And so again and again and again the problem will come to force you to be one with the Vine and when you're one with the Vine, you wonder where did the problems go? They're not necessary anymore when you're one with the Vine. They only come because you have strayed from your conscious awareness that Christ in me is the Vine which is husbanded by God.

So, don't feel that your problems are signs that your consciousness is not high enough or that you're guilty of some offense. You're not. There is no one, even Jesus Christ, who doesn't have problems because every problem is a lifting up. It's only personal sense in us that reacts to the problem and says, "Gee, I thought I was higher than this. Why did this have to happen to me?" That's personal sense. And the fact that that personal sense is there is the reason the problem is there. When that personal sense isn't there, the problem won't have to hit us.

Now then, let's not react to the problems in the wrong way but let's accept them in the spirit of, "Well here's something that I have to come above. This is part of my test, my trial. Do I believe it's real?"

Now, if you believe it's real, you're going to have ten more problems after it. If you can face the problem and get out of the hypnosis of believing it's real, you'll discover that you have solved the problem. Now, there it is. It's very real to the personal sense but that personal sense to which the problem is real is not in the Vine. It hasn't taken root in its Christ Self and so, the Christ Self which doesn't have the problem is abiding in you but the human sense of self is not abiding in the Christ. And so, the human sense of self is hit by the problem.

And after you get rid of the band aids and all the rest of the material ways of fighting it, you'll come to the place where, you know that where Christ is, there is no problem. And all you've been saying when you said I had this problem was, "Christ is not here." You have denied the presence of the Christ as your own Being. You lived in the false human sense of self instead of in your immortal Christ Self and the problem has brought this to your attention. Be grateful and make your adjustment. Abide in the Vine which has been abiding in you and you will bear fruit.

And so, we find we are being lifted to a place where we may even see that this whole world is our initiation. The temptations of the good and the temptations of the bad. They're equal lures but in different directions. In order to experience the power of Spirit, the power of Life, we have to learn to bypass the lures of the good and the lures of the evil. We have to learn to bypass the personal sense of self. We have to learn just as the Master demonstrated on the cross, "I certainly do not want to be crucified but nevertheless, not my will but **Thy** will be done."

If the will of the Father is that you abide in the Christ, do you have a second will that says, "I will not or I shall not or I don't know how?" Every ounce of energy you have must be turned in that direction because this is the Father saying through Christ to you, "Abide in the Christ."

And there will be more tests and more trials. Be sure of it because you must learn to abide in the Christ through every test and every trial. That is the meaning of initiation, to look out upon every trial, every test, every so-called error with a sure-footed knowledge that it is impossible. It's a test of my integrity in Christ or my separation from Christ. If I accept the test with wisdom, it will make me come closer and closer and closer to the acceptance that I, being Christ, am not the human self which is so undergoing the problem. I will not accept that self which is undergoing that problem as my Self. I will not deny my identity as the Spirit of God. And when I can come to a measure of accepting that, then I will be given greater problems because I must be tested again and again and again right up to the cross - until even the cross.

The final test says, "Are you this mortal self or are you the Christ? Are you the invisible Self or are you this visible form?" And the answer we are being prepared to give is "I am the invisible Christ." There is no form here to be crucified. There is no form here to drown in a flood. There is no form here to burn in a fire. There is no form here to carry a germ. There isn't any. My identity is the invisible Child of God, the Christ. This is abiding in the Vine and only then, do we bear fruit richly. We are being sealed into Oneness, an invisible Unity in which the one Self of the universe called the Father and I, through Christ, are one.

Now, isn't that clear that this is the path that the Christ has given us up to this point? To build our confidence in the invisible Christ as present and then to build our awareness that this invisible Christ that is present is your own Being, your own invisible Self, the living invisible Child of God; Spirit. We're being lifted out of mortality, out of the limitation of a human mind into immortal Spirit which is not a change in your Being but a change in your knowledge of who you really are. For when you know that you are immortal Being, how can there be a problem? And as long as there is a problem, are you're not saying, "I am not immortal Being."

And so, this becomes the conflict, the mind and the Spirit, the flesh and the Spirit, the senses and the Spirit, the limited human sense mind and the Word of the Father. To those of us who have come to grips with this conflict, there is definitely an awareness that the problems of the world are diminishing in my consciousness. Regardless of their nature or their depth, they are initiations we face with the knowledge that Christ here is never to be denied and where Christ is, the power of Christ is functioning. You cannot block it out. You cannot stop its flow. You cannot ever prevent Christ from being Christ. You cannot prevent God from being God. You cannot stop the power of God from being its own perfect Self. And where it is, it is maintaining that perfect Self. Every problem is an illusion in the human mind.

Why do we still have a human mind to contain illusions? Abide in the Christ and you will find the mind that contains the illusions slowly dissolves. Christ breaks the veil. Christ breaks the karma. Christ breaks the material mortal sense. Through Christ flows the Divine Kingdom on earth.

This is the fruit we will bear; Wholeness, Fulfillment, Life eternal realized, Immortality realized, Heaven on earth realized. These are the fruits of the Spirit. They are not human fruit. They are God expressing through Christ in you.

There should be now a change-over from the human mind because how can you abide in Christ unless you're abiding in the mind of Christ, the Mind too pure to behold iniquity, the Mind in which there is Light and no darkness, the Mind which loves and never condemns, the Mind which sees the Kingdom, knows the Kingdom, the Mind which separates the wheat from the tares.

To abide in Christ is to abide not in a human mind but in the Christ mind. And so, one notch higher, back deeper into Self transcending the human mind, I abide in the Christ mind. That is where you say, "Speak Father, thy Son heareth." In the Christ mind, above the human sense mind, you rest. You are abiding. You can be nourished Divinely.

John, again was different than the synoptic three Gospels. In the Last Supper, in the other three there was more space given to "Eat of my flesh and, drink of my blood." He held up the bread and said, "This is my flesh. Eat of my flesh." He held up the wine and said, "This is my blood. Drink of my blood." This has become the sacred Eucharist.

But what does it mean to anyone? John wouldn't let it go at that and so John didn't take us into that level of it, although twice he mentioned, "Drink of my blood and eat of my flesh." Instead, John did something the other three Gospel writers didn't do. Instead of giving us the outward ceremonial, his entire chapter fifteen is the explanation, the within, the esoteric explanation of "Drink of my blood. Eat of my flesh."

When you accept Christ within, when you rest in the Christ mind, above your human sense mind, you are drinking of Divine blood, eating of Divine flesh. You are being nourished at a different level of yourself. You are no longer living in human flesh, in human blood. You are not living in a dying body but you are being nourished with the ingredients of your eternal Body through the Christ mind.

This is the blood of Immortality. This is the flesh of Immortality. This is Spiritual blood, Spiritual flesh and it flows through your Christ mind establishing your new Spiritual body. This is the Body you are building in your consciousness when you rest in the Christ mind, one with the Vine.

The fruit you will bear is the Body that never dies. That is how eternal Life comes about. The deathless body of the Spirit is made of the flesh and blood of Christ. It is an inner process. Slowly you become aware of that Spiritual body. You're not really building it. You're building your conscious awareness that it exists already. The invisible body of Christ is what we learn to walk in consciously as that Body guided by the Christ mind. This is what is meant by the Philosopher's stone. This is what Paul spoke about, the invisible body of Christ in which we are all one. This is what is meant by Life without end. This is the fruit that does not come to a human branch and this is the Word of the Father assuring us that it is so, *"If ye abide in me."*

"If a man abide not in me, he is cast forth as a branch, he is withered; and men gather them, and cast them into the fire, and they are burned."

The human body is what he's describing. The human flesh is what he's describing. Human blood is what he's describing. A human lifespan is what he's describing. But he's also told us about another way which is not a human body or human blood. He's told us about a Spiritual way which builds a Spiritual body which is the Divine fruit. And this is the Divine plan that we be that Divine fruit.

— End of Side One —

And the great knowledge that we are that Divine fruit is the acceptance of your identity. The knowledge that I am that now, is the knowledge that when I came into form, that was the first death. That was the moment when I parted from the knowledge of my identity.

I am the living Spirit of God. I am a Divine body and you can't see it with your eye. You can't look in the mirror and find it. But that is your identity. That is your Divine Self which lives eternally while there is a sense of self walking around in time and space, disconnected from the Vine, unaware of itself, living in its dream sense of life, separated, not fed, not nourished by Divine flesh and blood, which withers, which dies.

The words are clear. It is a branch cut off. Humanity, collectively and individually is a branch cut off and all you need to do is look out and you see it is a branch cut off. Why? Because it is not living as the invisible Christ. It is not one with the Father. It is not being fed Divinely. It is undernourished and therefore, it becomes barren.

"If ye abide in me, and my words abide in you, ye shall ask what ye will, and it shall be done unto you."

Now, we have this covenant, you might say then, that if I abide in Christ, if you abide in Christ, you may ask what you will and it shall be done unto you. It's almost like, "Ask, seek and knock" in the Sermon on the Mount.

Now, this asking, you must see, is a different asking than we have thought about as human beings. When you're in Christ, we must remember that Christ says, *"And I will pray [unto] the Father."* You see, you're in automation when you're in Christ. There's no need to ask. The moment you're in Christ, Christ is already the total fulfillment of God on earth. The asking is already done in Christ.

And so, anything you might ask, meaning your complete fullest expectations, all your unspoken hopes are already in a state of fulfillment in Christ. Anything you can ask will be done unto you. Nothing is withheld. This is the statement, "That fulfillment, wholeness is inevitable in Christ."

We are being shown a fool-proof way to heaven on earth. Nothing is withheld in Christ. If we look around us and we see great personages, who somehow could not find this protection, the answer is that of mine own self, as a human being, I can do nothing. But in Christ, the Father doeth the works.

Every tragedy in our human scene is the absence of the understanding that I am not a human being. I am not a man or woman among men and women. I am not a mortal creature. I am not a form born in a mother's womb. This is sense hypnosis. This is the first birth but the resurrected Self is that Self which knows Christ in me, not born of woman. Christ in me born of the Father, not having two fathers. Christ in me, omnipotent with dominion over all that appears to be land, sea and air. Omnipresent, knowing all because Christ rests in the Father and the Father rests in Christ.

The Christ mind is how you rest in Christ and that is how you rest in the Father. Above the human mind is the way you abide in Christ. Wholeness, Fulfillment, Life eternal, Heaven on earth, these are the fruits that flow through that awareness beyond the level of the human mind. Or else, there'd be no point to chapter fifteen of John or to the rest of the New Testament.

Those who feel it, know it - even if they cannot at the moment seem to do it - are chosen. Those who say, "Well, I'll get that the next time around." That's fine. They are not chosen. You can tell by whether it's for you or not. If it's for you, you are chosen. This is your sequence. There's no guilt or lack of guilt in it. It's simply a matter of Divine sequence. We're not all ready. But those of us who are ready know we are ready and no one can tell you. The bell rings in you and you know this is my sequence. This is my time. My time has come. My hour has come to live in that state of Consciousness which is called conscious union with God. Not a separated branch at the mercy of the world. Not in a dying form but in a living temple, the temple of the living God, a Reality.

"Herein is my Father glorified, that ye bear much fruit; so shall ye be my disciples."

Now, you may not have thought of it just that way but your human success is not glorifying God. Your human success is not bearing much fruit. Your human success means nothing, a great big zero. The only success you can ever be is to glorify the Father and you glorify the Father by bearing his Spiritual fruit which is your own Divinity.

"Herein are ye my disciples." In your Divine identity, you bear Divine fruit. You are disciples of Christ.

Let's pause a moment with this quiet time. Silence, (long pause) ...

Be sure now that as we continue in this second half, there will be methods for us to do this abiding. The Christ leaves nothing unfinished. So, we'll be back in a few moments, say five or six, to continue our oneness with the Father through the Vine.

(Class break)

We want to know how to live in the Christ mind and not in the human mind because the Christ mind is our oneness with the Father. The Christ mind is fed by the Father. Through the Christ mind, we become conscious of our deathless body. Through the Christ mind, we come under the government of God and there is no power on the earth that can function destructively against us when we are in the Christ mind.

And so, we say, "Father what is your method? We're willing." And the Christ answers. The Christ gives us the answer in the ninth verse.

"As the Father hath loved me, so have I loved you: continue ye in my love.... continue ye in my love"

Now we love our children, we love our relatives, we love those who agree with us. We love those who are doing the things we like them to do but there are many we do not love. They have a way of doing things we don't approve of. Some of them we call enemies. That's the human mind saying that, but Christ was loving every moment that Christ walked on earth in a form that we call Jesus. Christ loved the cripple. Christ loved the blind man. Christ loved the leper. These were not healings. These were acts of love. Love revealing the identity that stood there where human eyes said, "Cripple, blind man, leper." That identity was the invisible Spirit of God. Love is the recognition of the invisible Spirit of God where your human eyes see a form. That is not human love. That is Christ love. And that is the key to every healing, the love of Christ which sees what God put there, not what human eyes think is there.

Christ love says, "Yes, I see the cripple but did God make a cripple? Who created that cripple? God is the only Creator. Did God create a leper? Did God make blind people?"

And therefore, Christ love says, "I love the Father supremely and I express that love by knowing only what the Father placed here." Christ love says, "There walks the invisible Child of God appearing to human eyes blind, leper, crippled, lacking, hungry, sick, suffering, dying." And Christ says, "That isn't love accepting that. That's not loving God." Christ says, "As I have loved you, as I have washed your feet, as I have recognized the Spirit of God in you, love ye one another."

And when you're in that Love, you find you're in the Christ mind. And when you're looking around and picking flaws in your neighbor, when you're looking at them who persecute you, and defending yourself against their so-called evil, when you're seeing the beam in your neighbor's eye, when you're calling one a fool or a scoundrel or a thief or a cheat, you're not seeing what God placed there. You're not in a state of Love. You're not loving God supremely, God alone. You're accepting the hypnosis of the human mind. You're in a human mind seeing what God did not place there and you are living the dream life. You're in the form consciousness, the Adam consciousness.

In Love, you do not judge by the form. In Love you judge by the Word of God which says, "All that exists is My Spirit." In Love, you look through the form of matter. You look through materiality, through mortality, through conditions and you see with the eyes of Christ what the human eye cannot see. You see it first with faith. Seeing nothing but knowing this is the Word of God that I accept.

And so, you rob the world of all its murderers, all its thieves, all its criminals. Why? Because you're in the Christ mind.

Do you want to bear fruit richly? These are the conditions that you be in the Christ mind and the way to that Christ mind is to express Love. Love of Reality, love of the invisible Spirit where the mind sees an image called form.

To the thief on the cross, your Christ mind takes him into paradise. In your Consciousness, you see him as the invisible Spirit of God. You see the Spirit of God where the world says, "She is an adulteress." You are living in Love, not in judgment. Judgment is of the form. Love is of the Spirit and when you're living in that capacity to judge not, to *"Know no man after the flesh,"* you're looking through the single eye of the Christ, the eye of the Soul. You're seeing what no eye can see and you're seeing, on the strength of your faith, that only God is there.

God is where the adulteress appears to be. God is where the thief on the cross appears to be. You're accepting that All is God and God is not a thief. God is not an adulteress. God is not a warrior. God is Love. Christ is Love. The Christ mind is loving. And to bear Divine fruit, you must be that loving Christ mind. All human judgment is set aside.

"Who convinceth me of sin?" No matter what you look at, your Christ love says, "There invisibly is God." This is the way outlined by the Christ.

"As the Father has loved me and I have loved you." And that is how Christ has loved us. Just think if Christ hadn't loved these human branches, it would be like the Christ saying to those who condemned the adulteress, "Let him who is without sin throw the first stone." If we hadn't been loved, could we be sitting here? As Christ has loved us, we must love one another.

And then, you see the great glory behind those words. Did Christ love the cripple? No. Did Christ love the blind man? No. Christ loved the Spirit of God that was there. Christ knew there was no cripple there. There was no blind man there. There are no judgments in the Christ mind because there is no material, mortal there. And further still, who stood there where the cripple seemed to be? The invisible Christ. Can we reach the place now where we set aside judgments and know that wherever you look, the invisible Christ is there? Do you see that your Love is loving your Self everywhere?

Christ loves Christ because only Christ is. Christ acknowledges only Christ because only Christ is. There is no thief on that cross. That is the world illusion. There is no adulteress. That is the world illusion and you cannot in the Christ mind see one - for there is none there. That Love is a different kind of Love than we know as a human being. That's usually the kind of love we're only willing to afford those close to us. My child, I can overlook all my child's faults but the Christ mind says, "You have no personal child."

Your child is your Self and every child is your Self and everywhere you look, you're looking at your Self for Christ is one. The Christ that looks through you, at the Christ of another is looking at your Self and until you are willing to accept that all is your Self, you're not in the Christ mind.

Everywhere is You. Everywhere is You. There's no other being on this earth than Christ your Self. That is the invisible Vine.

"I am the Vine." We read it here. Somebody reads it in Asia. Somebody reads it in Africa. Somebody reads it in every nook and cranny of the world. Who are they speaking to? To everyone.

I am the Vine. I am the Christ of you and you and you and you. What is it saying? I am the Christ everywhere and I am the Self everywhere. And that consciousness of you which looks out must know that everywhere is the Christ of you spanning six continents, spanning the planets and the stars. I, Christ is the only inhabitant of the universe and when you're in the Christ mind, you will develop the habit to recognize your Self everywhere and then you're loving God supremely.

"Continue in my love" is the beginning of the understanding that when you're not seeing Christ everywhere, you're not continuing in the Love of Christ. That would be like saying, "Well God is over there, on that side of the street but not on this side of the street." or "I love God more in Asia more than I do in Africa." You can't do it. All you can do when you do that, is cut yourself off the Vine.

The Vine is Infinite. There's no place where the Christ Vine is not and every human branch, every animal branch, every branch of what we call nature is one with the Vine, the invisible Vine everywhere.

The acceptance of the omnipresent Christ is continuing in my Love.

Now, when you know this is a Divine law, you don't waste time trying to decide if you're going to follow it or not. You either follow it or you're the branch that is removed. At least you know what the stakes are. This is why the fifteenth chapter is so vital. It lays it on the line where anyone with a degree of preparation for the Truth can see it and say, "Well, that's it. Either I live by it. That's the code of Christ or I don't." But you cannot say you weren't told, it wasn't brought to your attention because it has been brought to our attention for thousands of years and it has been camouflaged by false teachings so that we do not know we have to see that there is no Catholic, there is no Protestant, there is no Muslim, there is no Hindu, there is no Buddhist, there is no Jew. These are the false garments of the flesh where stands the invisible Christ.

You can make no differentiation. You cannot single out a group and exalt them. The Love of the invisible Christ must be as impartial as the shining of the sun, as the falling of the rain. That's how it is. That is the law of Divinity. You either abide in it or you cut yourself off from it and then you're back in karmic law.

So, you'll find first the exhortation, *"Continue[ye] in my love."* And it will be repeated and then repeated again for the third time.

The emphasis saying that, "Unless you capture the understanding that unless you're in the Christ love, you are rejecting Christ, piercing Christ. You are denying yourself and that is again suicide."

"As the Father hath loved me, so have I loved you: continue ye in my love. If ye keep my commandments, ye shall abide in my love; even as I have kept my Father's commandment, and abide in his love."

And so, we see why Christ Jesus is called the *"Only begotten"* in the Christian Bible. The capacity to go through the initiation of seeing the problem here, the problem there, the catastrophe there and saying "No." My human senses say, "I can feel it and see it and touch it. I can feel the warmth of the fire. I can smell the smoke." But is God absent there? Did this fire push God away? Did this germ push God away? Did this malfunction of the bone push God away? Your Christ mind says, "God is there. I am honoring the presence of my Father."

What power pushed God away to make a fire, to make a flood, to make a hurricane? No power can do it. God is there and God is maintaining God's perfect universe there. What is this fire, this flood, this hurricane? It's the human sense mind which does not know the Father is there, accepting the power to create an evil. That mind is declaring the absence of God. The Christ mind is declaring the presence of God and in the presence of God, the fire and the flood and the hurricane are revealed as images in the human mind, without substance, without power to burn, without power to drown. One in the Christ mind is the majority standing there with that knowledge. We are to be that One.

Spiritual power is in the Christ mind which looks at the cripple, the blind man and the adulteress and refuses to accept that God was pushed aside so that these people could become that way. The Christ mind can stand firmly in the Presence without opposite and where that Presence is, Perfection always is. Where God is, Perfection is. God is everywhere. Perfection is everywhere. The Christ mind accepts that and therefore, honors God supremely.

The human mind does not accept it, cuts itself off from the Vine and invites its own destruction. Which mind are we in determines whether we live in Heaven on earth or in the transient sense of mortality.

The power of God is always where you are, always being perfect, awaiting only your Christ mind awareness to love God supremely. When you look out and see evil, error, any form of malfunction, you are looking through your human mind. You are not in the state of Love. You are in a state of human mis-concept. Make your adjustment. Don't mind how difficult.

The Word of the Father in you is, *"Continue ye in my love. If ye keep my commandments, ye shall abide in my love; even as I have kept my Father's commandments, and abide in his love. These things have I spoken unto you, that my joy might remain in you, and that your joy might be full."*

The state of Love, the state of Joy is the natural state of Christ. It may shock you to find out that you really don't love yourself because you don't know who you are. And if you don't love your Self, how can you love another? What kind of love can you offer? A limited, temporary love? For when you know who you are, when you learn to love your Self, you have Christ love to offer. You're in that other dimension where the Love you have to give is the Love you're going to receive for as Christ's Love pours out of you, that's what flows back into your awareness. If you're not receiving Christ Love, it's because you're not giving it. To give is the way you receive. The Love that pours through you as Christ Love is the Love that knocks upon your door.

Let it flow. Abide in me. You can only abide in me because I am present where you are. The full infinite Love of Christ where you are, is waiting to flow and it must flow for that is the way you are opened to your Self. God's infinite Love in Christ where you are must flow through your conscious awareness. You must open out a way for this Love to flow into everyone through recognition of their invisible Christ Self. And then that Vine will be working overtime for you because that is the way to Grace. Grace is Love flowing consciously, returning as the added things.

Rise up now to this capacity to let Divine Love flow through, that means impartially, not with favoritism. Not the first and the third and the eighth and let the second and the sixth and the fifth go by. You love the ugly ones as well as the pretty ones. You love the unhealthy ones as well as the healthy ones. You love the beggars as well as the princes and the kings. Why? Because you're going through the forms. You're letting impartial, Divine Love flow and you're not interfering with human pleasure, human will, human concepts.

I know it's hard but it's beautiful and it's the way the Father is instructing us. This is the practice we develop, to love everyone. To talk not to their minds, but to their hearts. To see them as the Father sees them is to love them. Every creature, every plant, every fish, every fowl, - you must see the invisible Self that is there. And as we learn to do this, Love is flowing and blessing us.

Again, the Christ speaks, *"If you keep my commandments, ye shall abide in my love."*

So, it's more than lip service, isn't it? You can't say it. To keep the commandments is the call to action, to deeds; deeds of Love. We can't get by with a few words. Our entire way of life must follow through to express the Love so that we are in a sense of universal, spiritual brotherhood and there's no way out. That is Divine law. You can have human law but that's breaking off from Divine law and violating it and the price is extinction. The reward of not breaking it is preparation for transition, resurrection, lifting up into higher mansions of Reality.

And so, we, who have caught the Word, we are loving and we are loving, perhaps, maybe even out of a selfish motive but at least it's in accord with the Spiritual injunction to *"Love our neighbor as ourselves."* Now, we must obey the commandments in order to abide in the love of the Father, in the love of the Christ.

"This is my commandment," repeated again, *"That ye love one another, as I have loved you."* And remember how Christ has loved us. What has Christ asked of us? What did Christ ask of the disciples? Did he say, "In return for what I'm doing for you I want you to do this for me?" Did he ask for reward? What was he seeking for himself after having given up the kingdoms of the world in time? Do you see the selflessness of Divine Love? It isn't asking for anything. Divine Love is a giving, a flowing, a bestowal. It's not a request for something in return.

You see the purifying nature of that Love? How it unselfs you from the personal sense of self? That's why it fulfills the law. It gets you out of person into Christ. It takes you out of the one there who's planning something for a reward. It takes you out of the sense mind.

When you are loving Divinely, you're above the personal sense of self which dies. You're in your own true Self. You have your glimpse of paradise when you're in Divine Love. You'll feel it and know it and you'll feel it and know it many times until you know you've got to live that way, until you don't feel comfortable unless you're living that way.

And finally, the great commandment that follows: *"Greater love hath no man than this, that a man lay down his life for his friends."*

Now that's far deeper than saying to your friend, "I'll take the punishment, not you." Or "I'll volunteer and you don't have to be drafted." No, this is deeper than laying down your life physically for your friends. This means that a new Self must be born where you are, a totally new Self and that new Self is Christ itself. This is the call to rebirth, to transformation. If you want to love God supremely, you must lay down your mortality because if you don't, you're saying, "There is God and man. There is immortality and mortality. There is Spirit and matter. There is Divinity and humanity." Oh no. God is All.

Greater Love hath no man than to lay down his mortality and to look out only through his Christ Self so that now you begin not only to live in the Christ mind but in the Christ body. The body that never knows pain. You lay down your personal sense of self because now strengthened by the Christ mind you have the capacity. You put on the garment of Immortality while appearing in the flesh.

The only way you can honor God is to remove that which is un-Divine and so there's no greater Love than to remove the false sense of humanhood, mortality, transient matter, to come in to that great awareness that I am the immortal Self. To live in this conscious awareness is the supreme love of the Father.

That is why, here the Christ says, "Remember what I'm asking you to do has been done before." Christ Jesus laid down his sense of mortality for his friends. Christ Jesus laid down his human selfhood and took upon himself the robe of Immortality and it took him right through the grave untouched. That was Divine fruit.

Now, that's where these first thirteen verses of *"I am the vine"* take us. I think that's where we'll stay for a while to assimilate them, to deepen them as next verses in this chapter will do for us. And I'd like you, in your studies this week, to do this: Take the first thirteen verses and look at them carefully and then write one to thirteen numbers and for the first verse, put down its basic meaning to you. For example, here would be, the nature of Christ. Christ relationship to God. *"I am the [true] vine, the Father is the husbandman."* The next verse, what is its basic idea until you've got thirteen meanings of the verses. Not a long exhortation, just briefly, what is the purpose and meaning of that verse to you?

Trace it so that you can see this is the Divine law, number one, this is number two, the karmic law of how we break Divine law or accept it; three, is how we stand in Divine law, how we bear fruit; four how we commit suicide; five, so on. Continue until you can just take these thirteen points of yours and you'll see you have a metaphysical chart leading you to the complete Christ message. Every verse has a meaning and be sure when they repeat, that you see the distinction between the repetition of seven in nine. It's not repeated precisely the same way. There's always a subtle change, a subtle expansion of idea. Catch it and you'll see clearly that God is talking directly to you and saying, "You are my immortal Child." And don't let the world fool you.

Don't wake up in the morning thinking that this day you've got to protect yourself against this or that. You don't. This day you are my immortal Child. Now, that's the only protection you need but you must remain in the conscious awareness of it. This is the abiding.

It doesn't matter what anyone says to you, how many people frown at you. You are. The Father says so and you must implant this in your consciousness so that you are faithful to it. And then, when they frown at you, love them. When they persecute you and use you despitefully, love them. Why? They're not there. The Christ is there. They just don't know it and you do.

Wash the feet of the world. Love where every form appears. Speak to the Truth that is there, not to the appearance and you will be loving God supremely. You will be recognizing your Self in all. And as you recognize yourself in all, you will be finding your Self. You will discover that you are the immortal Child of God as a living experience. You will be beyond study.

Do that with the first thirteen verses. Now, if you're really ambitious, complete the chapter. Do it with next twelve verses because that's what we'll do next week. You might compare your twelve verses with the ones you hear. And you'll find that's how you cement it into your consciousness. Until out of these twenty-five verses, you have the plan of the Bible, the whole mission of Christ explained and you'll see that all that is left after that is for you to carry it out, fulfill it, to permit yourself to be that Divine instrument which the Father says you are.

I in the midst of you, I your identity realized, I am the Vine. Your immortal Self realized here and now, is the Vine through which the Father flows. Then you are that seed which bears fruit, some thirty, some sixty, some one hundred percent; not a seed fallen by the wayside.

We'll probably also get into Joel's chapter which we weren't able to do today, "It Shall Not Fall Nigh Thee." That's the tenth chapter.

(Herb talks about dinner to say "Bon Voyage" to some who are travelling overseas with the teaching.)

And I'll see most of you next week I hope. Thank you.

CLASS 28

NO LONGER SERVANTS
BUT FRIENDS

Herb: Now, let's take an Arab, something plants within him the idea that he has to go out and kill a Jew and we say, "What plants this idea?" God said, *"Thou shalt not kill."* Therefore, it wouldn't be God planting an idea to kill.

And then, we go to the other side and we see the same idea is planted in the mind of the Israeli. It says, "Now, you go out and kill that Arab." But God said, *"Thou shalt not kill."* So, therefore, God didn't plant that idea in the mind of the Israeli.

In fact, the whole Old Testament is completely devoted to, *"An eye for an eye and a tooth for a tooth."* And so, we see the Arab and the Israeli living in the Old Testament of *"An eye for an eye and a tooth for a tooth."* Ignored, is *"I say unto you, you have heard it said of old an eye for an eye and a tooth for a tooth.... but I say unto you turn the other cheek."*

Now, then, the Christ message is not only in the Christian Bible. It's in the Koran and the Arabs can read it. It's in the Old Testament and the Hebrews can read it. It's in the Torah. It's in the Talmud. It is in the scriptures of the world. It makes no difference where a human being is on the face of the earth, there is a scripture presented by the Christ within, coming forth in the form of a Bible, a Bhagavad-Gita, a Koran. Always, the celestial Word is present. And, it does not say, "Thou shalt kill." It says, *"Thou shalt not."*

Now then, when the Arab kills the Jew, when the Jew kills the Arab, your next question might be, "Inasmuch as God didn't plant this authority or this desire within a man, what did?" And finally, to face the fact that God did not protect the Hebrew against the Arab and God did not protect the Arab against the Hebrew. The Israelis may send planes into villages and kill people who have no knowledge whatsoever or even a desire to kill. They can be children, they can be mothers and the Arabs can be just as indiscriminate. Why isn't God protecting the underprivileged or the ones who are without the desire to kill who have not earned the right to be killed?

And finally, we face that far away which we're not willing to face in our own backyard. God does not protect what is not God's creation. The human form is not protected. It's very clear that eleven human forms in the Olympic village were not protected by God. It's very clear that those who received death through retaliation in the Arab countries were not protected by God. Why? They were not created by God.

Now, once you face this, you must look around you and say, "Did God not create those eleven and create all the rest? Did God create everyone else on earth but those eleven?

And finally, you see the message clear that God did not create human form anywhere. And in this class, this is what we learn to accept.

There is no human form created by God. And it is important at this level of our work to come to grips with this and to either accept it and abide by it and act accordingly or to realize that you are pursuing a teaching of your own which is not the Christ teaching.

"Know ye henceforth no man after the flesh," for the simple reason that *"My Kingdom is not of this world."*

Now, if we can proceed from that point of view that the human form is not a Divine creation and that no human being is empowered by the Divine to bring forth human forms, we can begin to get an idea of what the human form is, so that we cannot be mesmerized into treating the human form as a Divine Reality.

Now, in our fifteenth chapter of John, we find that *"I am the vine,"* the invisible Self of every man, is a fact not accepted on the earth. The Arab who kills the Jew and the Jew who kills the Arab or when our own nation kills in the Vietcong, we are also being led by an impulse which is not Divine. It matters not what our motives may be, even if they were protections, specific protection of our own lives.

"Thou shalt not kill" is a deeper revelation of a fact that there's no one there to be killed. The Self that is there is invisible and all we're doing is not recognizing the omnipresent You. We're turning away from your own Self which is there and killing that which we think is there. And so, in the process, Christ is unrecognized. I, the Vine, remain unrecognized because there is a world mind.

Now, most of us have at least been alert enough not to blame the Arab and not to blame the Jew. We have learned by now that world mind is that which out-pictures itself as person and if you've at least come that far where you know form is an out-picturization of world mind, then you're really in the mysticism of the Christ message.

Every form you're looking at is world mind made visible and it is necessary to pierce the veil of that form, to place no guilt upon that form, to place no guilt upon the person who kills, to place no guilt upon the person who retaliates because this is the world mind in us placing guilt upon what it itself has performed. We are alert to the many disguises of the world mind when we are living in the Consciousness that Christ is present.

Now, where the Arab attacks the Jew and vice versa, where the white attacks the black and vice versa, where one nation attacks another and vice versa, you are watching the performance of world mind and it is the tempter. It is saying to you, "Watch, here's this man with a gun. He pulls the trigger. Watch that man over there fall down." And world mind is saying to you, "Where is God in this picture? Why is God watching one kill another?"

And when you put the guilt on this one or that one, you're falling into the trap of believing that this is happening in the Kingdom of God or you're falling into the temptation to believe that the Kingdom of God is not there but what you are witnessing is there. You're accepting form. You're accepting physical senses which perceive form and what you're not accepting is the invisible Kingdom of God present, completed, perfect, imperishable, indestructible and without opposite.

You're watching the world imagination in form present the drama of lies, the temptation to believe that matter is here and Spirit is not and in your highest state of Consciousness, you can look at this and place no guilt on that one, no guilt on this one but rather see the non-life that appears to human senses in form. There's no life performing these acts. There is animated images called form and this is an essential of the Christ consciousness.

Now, we have to proceed to build a permanent consciousness that all that I perceive as form in this human world is not Divine creation and therefore is non-life, non-existence appearing to mortal sense. Unless I can accept this and practice this knowingly, world mind in me is going to continue its delusion and wear its many disguises. It is going to create and it is going to destroy what it creates and I'm going to bear witness to this falsehood unless I am enlightened, lifted above the world mind.

And so, this inner teaching in chapter fifteen is to lift us out of the world mind, out of the forms of cosmic imagination, out of the forms that are created by, not God, but the world mind wearing a disguise called the Lord God. The world mind disguised as the Lord God appears right back there in Genesis to Adam and Eve dividing them into the belief in good and evil, appearing to them as form, tempting them with deceit and finally, condemning their complete progeny to perdition.

How stupid of us to have not recognized that this is not God. This is a disguise of the world mind which has convinced our world that it is God. And every day we find our world worshipping this Lord God which is the invisible world mind, praying to it, asking it for help and receiving no help. You can be sure the entire nation of Israel has prayed but it hasn't helped. The Arabs in their fashion must pray but it hasn't helped. The Vietcong is praying. We are praying. The world is praying and we can't even keep afloat an athletic competition on an international scale in spite of all our prayers. Why? Because the ultimate fact must be faced that there are no human methods to solve the problems of the human race. You cannot do it humanly and you will be tricked again and again to try to do it. There are no human methods that will work. Only the invisible Vine. The world mind is exposed in chapter fifteen as never before.

"Now," says the Christ in us, *"Ye are my friends, if ye do whatsoever I command you. Henceforth I call you not servants; for the servant knoweth not what he [his lord] doeth: but I have called you friends; for all things that I have heard of my Father I have made known unto you. Ye have not chosen me, but I have chosen you, and ordained you, that ye should go and bring forth fruit, and that your fruit should remain: that whatsoever ye shall ask of the Father in my name, he may give it you. These things I command you, that ye love one another. If the world hate you, ye know that it hated me before it hated you. If ye were of the world, the world would love his own: but because ye are not of the world, but I have chosen you out of the world, therefore the world hateth you. Remember the word that I said unto you, The servant is not greater than his lord. If they have persecuted me, they will also persecute you; if they have kept my saying, they will keep yours also. But all these things will they do unto you for my name's sake, because they know not him that sent me. If I had not come and spoken unto them, they had not had sin: but now they have no cloak for their sin. He that hateth me hateth my Father also. If I had not done among them the works which none other man did, they had not had any sin: but now have they both seen and hated both me and my Father. But this cometh to pass, that the word might*

be fulfilled that is written in their law, They hated me without a cause. But when the Comforter is come, whom I will send unto you from the Father, even the Spirit of truth, which proceedeth from the Father, he shall testify of me: And ye also shall bear witness, because ye have been with me from the beginning."

In these words, the Christ in us awakens us to be alert to the disguises of the world mind. This is the revelation of that mind of the world which functions as the individual, human mind of every person who walks the earth. So that when the world mind speaks through one saying, "Kill," it is really speaking to everyone on the earth and in greater or lesser degrees, we are in our subconscious hearing, "Kill." If we have progressed beyond the point of responding, all the better. But the latent impulse is always there when it says to one Arab, "Kill" it is saying it throughout the world. That is why it comes to the surface as war or as permissiveness to let nations go to war, as a capacity to stand aside and watch your own nation go to war. The word "Kill" is spoken universally when it is heard by even one. And so, with hate and so with fear, and so with lack, and so with limitation. We're all glued into one world mind through our individual human mind and unless you're conscious of it, you are a servant of that mind.

But now, those who follow the inner Christ, here called the disciples, are told, "You are no longer servants. I have taken you out of the world mind. You were wired to the world mind and all its evil, all its anti-Christ, all its ignorance of God and you were servants of the world mind."

And this then applies to us. To the degree that we are not aware of Christ within, we are servants of the world mind even though we may not know it. It is not a voluntary condition. It's a subconscious condition. Each person born into form is not in the Kingdom of God and is therefore in a state of servitude to the world mind. And make no mistake about it, that person born into form, that form is a creation of the world mind. And the world mind is going to run that form unless there is a consciousness born in that form that takes it out of the world mind. We may be a little late in getting started in our own forms but nonetheless, if we have followed the Christ within to the best of our ability, Spirit within is saying to us at this moment, *"Ye are my friends if you do whatever I command you. Henceforth, I call you not servants; for the servant knoweth not what his lord doeth."*

Now, take an ordinary servant and see the comparison. The servant has a job to do, a duty. He has no choice. This is his job. And his lord and master says, "Do this" and the servant does this. We have not known that but this is what the world mind has been doing with us. We have been servants of it, separated from our own Selfhood, servants to the world mind; mesmerized. That is the state of hypnosis into which every child is born in the world consciousness that we have had up to this point.

But having accepted the inner Christ, now the Spirit says to us, *"The servant knoweth not what he doeth: but I have called you friends; for all things that I have heard of my Father, I have made known unto you."*

Having been alerted, having been opened, we now obey the Christ, not as a servant would; a servant does it because he must, a servant does it for duty, a servant does it for reward. We elect to obey the Christ. The understanding of Christ within gives us a choice. You can, or you cannot, follow the Christ. And if you elect to follow the Christ, you are called the elect because you have elected to follow the Christ. And that is not out of servitude but out of wisdom. Not out of duty but out of knowledge and not for reward but because something inside is opened to understand that this is the way to Fulfillment.

And so, now, Christ in us makes us friends rather than servants. In our Spiritual freedom we elect to choose Christ. We elect to step out of the world mind which enslaves mankind, the mind that makes man do what man does not know he is being made to do. Now, we are no longer dominated - we are taking our dominion. And so, we are now to say we are either servants of the world mind or friends of Christ.

And then, a strange thing. *"But ye have not chosen me, [but] I have chosen you, and I have ordained you, that you should go and bring forth fruit, and that your fruit should remain: and whatsoever you shall ask of the Father in my name, he may give [it] to you."*

Now, many have often wondered about, what does it mean that *"You have not chosen me. I have chosen you."* And even though there have been many explanations, there are certain factors that we still haven't clarified.

Now, remember, if we abide in Christ, we bear fruit richly and we are lifted higher. If we do not abide in Christ and do not bear fruit, we are purged. Now, this choosing refers to that. The fact that you have been chosen means that you have borne fruit. You are not cast away. You are not a branch cast away because you are a chosen branch. Chosen because in some way, you have managed to sever the bonds of world karma, of world dominion, of world mind and to proceed into your own inner drummer, to march to the invisible impulse of the Christ within, to make that effort. And so, those who have done this are chosen. They're not cast away, is the meaning of chosen.

And then because I have chosen you, all that goes with this choosing is included. Once you are chosen, once you are accepted as a disciple of Christ, that means the government is no longer on your shoulders. That which chooses you sustains you. All this is implied in *"I have chosen you."* Do you not realize that by being chosen, you are given all of the weapons necessary to attain total fulfillment? Once you know you have been chosen and not discarded, then you must know that the Infinite with its omnipresent Mind and omnipresent Power and omnipresent Love is guiding and leading and directing you to the Fulfillment of that choosing so that you can rest back in the ever present invisible arms of the Father saying, "I recognize the presence of God and if I were an Israeli, if I were in the Olympic village and if there were an attack, I, in Christ, would be maintained by That which has chosen me." How? By the invisible spirit of God. By living in the inner place of the Most High in the knowledge that I in the invisible Vine are one with the Father. I would find that the Spirit of God cannot be penetrated by those who have the desire to kill.

And this is the point then, that when you have been chosen because of your fidelity to Christ within, you are not under the law of man. You are not under the dominion of a world mind impulse coming through the law of man as a desire to kill. It cannot find you. It cannot contact you. There's no way for material man to make contact with Spiritual consciousness. And the miracle of the form that is guided and sustained by Spiritual consciousness is demonstrated again and again by those who are faithful to the inner Christ. *"It shall not come nigh thee."*

But that isn't our purpose for being faithful. That's one of the happy by-products. Our purpose is to be the individualization of the Infinite Self, to bear fruit richly in Spirit, to live in that which is imperishable. And there's the word here about "remaining. That is implying the chosen One is not in a temporary capsule or form. The chosen One is going to find themselves in the eternal body of the Spirit.

"I have chosen you, and ordained you, that you should go and bring forth fruit, and that your fruit should remain."

The knowledge that you are chosen, that you are Spiritually conscious, brings with it the certainty, the awareness, the conviction that you are in an imperishable form of Spirit which is not the visible form. That you have found Life which is not transient, Life that remains and this carries with it an immunity - even in the form - through the action of the Holy Ghost; not only to the man who would shoot but to the germ that would infect, to the pestilence, to

145

the poverty, to the famine, to the limitations of the human mind, to the obstacles that normally press everyone on this earth because they are functioning as individuals separated from their own Self.

Now again, when the Israeli attacks, when the Arab attacks, when the Vietcong attacks, when the United States attacks, we are going to learn in this work - to a place where we can actually know it - that we are attacking our Self. We are declaring war against our own Self. The world mind in us has so disguised itself that we go out and we shoot at our Self, thinking we're shooting at an enemy. Now, we've got to come to that place where we can see all that is out there is your Self. There's no Arab out there. There's no Israeli out there. There's no Vietcong out there. There's no white and there's no black. There's no Christian and there's no Jew. There is only our Self.

And this is going to become more and more a literal fact in consciousness so that everywhere we look we will recognize Self invisible; the invisible Christ Vine. There's nothing to shoot at. There's nothing to raise our back up at. There's nothing to be offended by except the illusion of separate selves. There aren't any. That is the reason we are being prepared, ever so slowly but firmly, into the knowledge of the one, infinite Self.

It is going to be imperative for each of us to develop the Consciousness that I am the one, infinite Self. And the reason that it is imperative is because there's no other way to transcend the human experience. The 'hu' of a man called human must give way to the Christ man. And the Christ man is the one, infinite Self. A measure of awareness of being the one, infinite Christ man is the inner Saviour. This is how transformation takes place. This is how the Holy Ghost is invited into our experience. This is how we are placed in that cocoon that is not touched by the evils of the world. This is the miracle of how you walk without the need for protection while walking in a world of hate and animosities. You are hid in the one, invisible Self even though appearing in the outer form. And the government of God is your sole protector.

We can even come to the place where we know we are in a Body which is indestructible, a Body that is eternal and you will come to this as you practice the knowledge that the invisible Christ everywhere is not an Arab, is not a Jew, is not a killer, is not a human form, is not a person. You come to the awareness of the impersonal Christ who is where the persons appear to be. The constant practice of it gives you the feel of it. And then the works, the words, the deeds of the Christ begin to show you that they are the works and the words and the deeds that can function in your own individual experience.

Not friends anymore in the human sense, not servants in the human sense but friends in the Spiritual sense. Friends of Christ means we are aware that the one infinite Christ which is invisible everywhere is my name, is the name of the Arab who doesn't know it is his name, the name of the Jew, the name of the Christian, the name of the Hindu and you wipe out all these labels. You can look at iniquity knowing it is not happening in the invisible Christ. If you still are seeing individual, divided selves and accepting that, you are turning against the infinite, undivided, invisible Christ. This is how we're crucifying our own Self daily.

But being friends now, friends of Christ and not servants to the world mind, we find a capacity to transcend these appearances that are creating animosity in our world. We look at them without judgment for our only judgement is here in me Christ stands, there in him Christ stands, that which is performing is a world-wide illusion. It was an illusion before it killed and it will be illusion after it kills. It will continue to be an illusion because it is not my Father's kingdom.

Now, then we are friends of Christ to that extent that we are willing and able to look through these world appearances without reaction, without animosity, without fear knowing that we could be right there perfectly safe and that if Spirit needed us there, we would be there and wherever Spirit needs us, we will be. Always, this knowledge that Spirit sustains those whom it has chosen for *"I have chosen you, and ordained you, that you go and bring forth fruit… fruit that remains."* You will not work and have your fruitage taken away. The fruitage that remains is your indestructible Self.

We're coming out of form into Life, into Christ Life; not human form but Christ Life. We identify as Christ Life. We identify everyone we see as invisible Christ Life. We are not letting the world mind persuade us, fool us, present its imagined world where we know the invisible Kingdom of Christ to be. We are the one who is the majority with the invisible Christ.

"That whatsoever you shall ask of the Father in my name, he may give it to you."

That's interesting. In the fourteenth chapter, the Christ says, *"If you shall ask anything in my name, I will do it."* Here, *"That whatever you shall ask of the Father in my name, he may give it to you."*

Now this is a step up. First, we're told that what you ask in the name of Christ, Christ will perform. Now, we're told what you ask in the name of Christ, God will perform. Do you see how Christ is just another word for God. God individualizes as you and we call it Christ but it's still God. I, Christ and the Father are one. Christ and God being one, You being Christ, Christ where You are and God being one, You and the Father are one.

But, that's true of the Arab. The invisible Christ there is one with God. And so, do you know him after the flesh or do you know him as the invisible Christ? And now, go that extra step. If he is the invisible Christ and You are the invisible Christ, who is he? It's You. The invisible You, is there. There's no Arab killing anybody. There's no Israeli being killed. That is the invisible Christ too. The whole world picture must be seen this way or else you've got two universes; God's universe and another one, God's creation and another one.

God doesn't create death. It isn't there. We've got to look through this world. Now, we've got to look through it now, not tomorrow because the time cometh when no man can be about the Father's business unless he has been in the Christ.

We are told that flesh and blood cannot inherit the Kingdom of God. And so, if we remain as flesh and blood in our own mind, we're kissing the Kingdom of God goodbye. We're going to reap of the flesh corruption. The belief in flesh and blood, the belief in matter is a world mind disguise in us, posing through our human mind as our belief. It must be broken. We cannot accept flesh and blood. We're told instead to drink of the Christ flesh, the Christ blood and that means to live in the constant awareness of that invisible Kingdom of Spirit here and now as our native land.

We're Americans, or we're Hollanders or we're Germans or we're something else in this world but in our consciousness, we are inhabitants of the Kingdom called Spirit. We must consciously be that. You must place your consciousness at that level which stands facing world mind so that world mind presenting all pictures of destruction to you make no impression, evoke no reaction because Christ heals by self-recognition. Christ doesn't heal by miracle work. Christ heals by recognizing Christ everywhere. You carry your own healing with you. You heal by recognizing your Self where the world sees someone else. Where the world sees hate and war, you recognize your invisible Self. That is your healing of the lie of the world mind.

In this, you are one with the Vine, one with the Infinite and the Grace of the Tree of Life flows through you. You have seen the temptation, witnessed the temptation and you've be able to stand and face the temptation with the knowledge that all that is ever present is the Spirit of God. The Allness of God, the one, invisible, permeating, Allself of God as the only Life becomes the deep God-centering of our Consciousness.

Friends of Christ, not servants of the world mind bowing to its every impulse, to its every false picture. Naturally, it's difficult so the Spirit pre-warns us. *"These things I command [you] that ye love one another.*" This is a third repetition, *"Love one another.*" It doesn't say, "Except that Arab or that Israeli or except this particular individual and not that one." It says, *"Love one another.*" This is unqualified because one another is the revelation of Spiritual identity. One, unseparated, seamless robe. The seamless robe of Spirit, in your Christ awareness, is what you recognize.

So, you love the invisible Spirit where the world sees a killing Arab or a dead Israeli. You love it simply by recognizing All that is there is your invisible Spirit. This is the acceptance of one, infinite Self and that's why it is repeated three times that *"Ye love one another.*" This is the revelation of one, invisible Self.

We're always caught unawares when we see injustice. You may think that Father Berrigan was not guilty. And there was a government conspiracy against him. You may feel that in some way, others may have done what he finally did and not have received the same punishment. You may feel many kinds of injustice but the only real injustice is the belief that injustice can exist. You must overcome the belief that it exists. It cannot exist. If it exists, you have denied your Self. There is no injustice being done there where Christ is. This takes you out of being a servant to the conditioned world mind. It makes you look foolish to your contemporaries and this is the cause of many of the persecutions.

"If the world hate you, ye know that it hated me before it hated you."

There you are. The world will say, "Well how can you say that that was the right thing for them to do or that they were justified in killing or that they were justified in retaliating? How can you say that?" So, don't say it but know the Truth. Wherever Christ is, the world mind will hate that Christ. Wherever Truth is, the lie will hate that Truth. The world that hates us, we let to live in Christ, has always hated Christ. It hates Christ for many reasons, just as darkness would hate Light. But this is telling us that the hate of the world should not leave you with a sense of guilt for this reason:

that there is no one out there to hate you. There is no one out there to be unfriendly to you. There is no one out there to deprive you of anything. There is no one out there to kill you. There is nobody on the face of the earth who can kill you. There is no germ on the face of the earth that can infect you. Why? Because you are the invisible Spirit of God and as long as you think you can be killed or infected, you're in your false identity. You're not in your true identity.

All hate coming against us, all animosity, all lack, all limitation is nothing more than world mind picture and all it needs to evaporate is our conscious awareness of its nature. Unless we can recognize it, it continues to move through us and expressing in us and the world that hates you isn't external to you at all. It is your own human mind hating the Christ. Your own human mind is the servant of the world mind. Whatever is in the world mind, your human mind is in one way or another being subject to and this is the eternal inner conflict between the Spirit and the flesh.

The flesh hates the Spirit because the Spirit will deprive the flesh of its pleasures. The flesh is the world mind in us personalized as our person and it turns against the Spirit. The hate is within our own self. It is never out there. There is no external. The external is nothing but the world mind in ourselves.

And so, the Christ wants us to know that if you think you're being hated, remember, it has always appeared that way on earth that Christ was being hated. Christ was never being hated except by the false world mind, a mind that has no presence and no capacity and no power. When you're in Christ, you know there is no such thing as hate because all is Christ and therefore for you, hate has no meaning. You turn this Truth around to know that what is being revealed here is that where Christ is felt, understood, accepted, Love will shine through.

Now what we're doing is building a Consciousness of the invisible Christ Self as a bulwark against the domination of the world mind which has made every man on earth a servant. There's no way out of it except through Christ Consciousness, the invisible Vine.

Now, there are going to be continued killings on this earth and they're all a sign or should be a sign to us that where a killing appears, it is a temptation to believe in its reality. It is telling us that God is not there. We cannot accept a killing as a reality. Therefore, we cannot retaliate against the killing. We resist not evil. Why? Because the Christ in us says, "Only the invisible Christ is there, no one is killing and no one is being killed." And this makes no sense to the human consciousness. Nonetheless, it is the Christ method and you will discover if you have a need to, that it is better protection than an arsenal of artillery.

The anti-Christ is the world mind but don't mistake it as out there. The world mind is your human mind and the anti-Christ is within our human selfhood and it hates the Christ. The battle of consciousness against the anti-Christ is right where you are. Not out there. You have to overcome the anti-Christ mind in you, not in the world and that anti-Christ mind in you wants to see an Arab killing and positively identify it that way. That mind you must overcome. Then you've overcome the world mind in you. It won't make any difference - once you've overcome the belief in an Arab killing, you've overcome the whole, complete illusion of form. Then you can look at the body being attacked by a germ the same way.

"If we were of the world, the world would love his own: but because ye are not of the world, but I have chosen you out of the world, therefore the world hateth you."

Once Christ in you has become more dominant and you are awake to Christ, this other side of you, this human self, seems to be in a higher reactive stage. There's a heightening of the inner conflict. They're never expressing a conflict out there. It is an inner conflict between the rising Christ and the descending sense of humanhood. The personal self puts up the fight but the real battlefield is in the world consciousness and in the Christ consciousness which meet in you as the human sense of mind and the Christ mind. In you is the battlefield and when you solve it in you, Christ in you has overcome the world.

Now, let's not make the mistake then of identifying evil in this world. Let's not fall into the human trap. That would be letting Christ in us die while we live in the human consciousness, letting the tempter within fool us into living in the kingdom of the world instead of the Kingdom of the Father. *"I have chosen you,"* and therefore, if you live in Christ, "I who go unto the Father, will perfect and perform all that concerneth thee." Our faith in Christ includes with it the capacity to know that the Christ which is present brings with it the power to overcome the world illusion.

Let's try a meditation now.

One of the great illusions of the world mind is time. We all have a sense of time but Christ doesn't and so, let's make this meditation a beginning effort to step out of time. Let's see that right now in Honolulu, it's about three hours earlier. So, if it were two o'clock here, it will be eleven o'clock there. And in Denmark it would be another time and in every other country another time. So, we that we have different times and yet, those different times are all right now. So that now, it is this time here but now it is that time there and another time somewhere else. We can have ten or fifteen or twenty different times on the earth but they're all at this moment of now.

Now, let's get out of the changing times. And let's just substitute the word "now" because it is now in every country of the globe. It may be three hours less in Honolulu but it is now. Now, just as it is now everywhere but three hours less in Honolulu, let's go ahead to two a.m. this morning or tomorrow morning. It will tomorrow here at two a.m. but it will still be today in Honolulu and yet, while it's today here, and yesterday there or tomorrow here and today there, it is always now, the same now.

Now, let's stretch that three hours to three centuries and let's see that it's conceivable that it being now in God, it is always now in God regardless of what time it is on the earth. Whether its twentieth century or seventeenth century, in God it's now. And so, when you're in Spirit, you're not in the time of day or in the time of day in the country you happen to be in. You're in the Now of God. And so, whatever happens in Now of God is happening.

Now, the things that happen here today in this world, in this so-called twentieth century are distorted out-picturings of the world mind about what is in the Now of God. The things that happened in the first century were distorted out-picturings of the world mind about what is in the Now of God. And that Now which was counterfeited in the first century by the world mind and counterfeited in the twentieth by the world mind, that Now is now. You can't change it. There's only Now in God.

And so, your past is not a past at all. Your future is not a future. There's no time differential in the Now. Everything that is existent in God is Now and because you exist in God as the Christ of God, everything is Now. You are walking just as much in what came forth as the first century as you are walking in the twentieth. You are walking just as much in the thirtieth century as you are walking in the twentieth.

You see, we walk in the Now of Infinity in Spirit and the way that comes forth in your experience is very amazing when you are living in that Now. In the time picture, you came forth into form, you grew up and you will go out of form. But that only happens in time. Nineteen-twenty you came, Nineteen-something you go. This is the time picture. But in the Now, that isn't happening. In the Now, you didn't come into form and go out of form. In the Now, you are always existent.

What we want to do in this meditation is to get the awareness that in my spiritual Self, I am in the Now which remains, which is always existent. I'm not in the changing time form which comes and goes. I'm not a servant of the world mind because that's all changing time form is. I'm a friend of Christ. As a friend of Christ, I really am that living Christ which lives in the Infinite Now, not in changing time. In that Now, I am always existent. I have a complete total Life which extends far back beyond recorded time. *"Before Abraham was, I am."*

— End of Side One —

I have a complete Life which extends far beyond this world. Even unto the end of this world, I am. I am that Life which is eternal because it is always Now. It doesn't become a past life, a present life and a future life. It is always a continuing Now Life. That is my Self and that is the Self that is everywhere and that is my Self. That Now Self is not the self of an Arab who kills or an Israeli who retaliates. It is not the self of boys who go to war and is not the self of boys who don't come back from war. But it is the invisible Now Self throughout Infinity and Eternality. That Now Self, I am. I always have been, always will be.

You step out of the changing form, out of the time structure. You live for a moment in the infinite Nowness of your Being and as you do, you are a friend of Christ. You are a Child of God but not one child, you are the Child.

And just as He said, first *"Whatever you ask in my name, I will do."* and then later, *"Whatever you ask in my name, my Father will do."* It was being revealed that the Child of God is God. All there is, is the one God Life. It is Now. It will never stop being Now. It does not function in time. It is eternal, timeless and just to clear out all the concepts of the world mind by resting in this Now Life, does unusual things, in different ways to many people. Always harmonious. Always good.

We transcend the limitations, the false boundaries of the human mind. We rest in the Infinite mind which is Now and we rest in its Nowness. We know that It has chosen us, for It is us. And we learn to depend on it. It goes before us because it is there already. It remains behind us because it is always there, too. We are accepting an omnipresent Now Self, with no boundaries in time anywhere.

When Jesus walked the earth, your Life now exists at that moment. Whatever will happen in a million tomorrows, your Life now exists in that moment. We are now Life and we are one Life and there's nothing in the world that's going to change that - although visibly it will appear to be changed by many circumstances. We are to live in the invisible assurance of the one, now Life. There's no hate in it. There's no animosity in it. There's no lack or limitation in it. There's no birthing and deathing. There's no sickness and suffering. The illusions of the senses are forestalled when you live in the Now consciously.

And this week, you should be able to develop this idea. This what I've given you about the Now is only a surface, a starter. You should develop your own conscious awareness of your Now Life which extends far back beyond all recorded history. Never was in the past. That's a human concept and it can never be in the future. That's a human concept. When you try to thread Infinity through the little needle of the human mind, that is what creates the illusion of past, of future, of present. There isn't any. It is all Now. It is Now throughout the universe this instant no matter what time of day it appears. Right now, throughout the whole universe, it is Now and also in universes we know not of. It doesn't matter what time it is on Mars, it is Now. In Mercury it is Now. In Jupiter, it is Now. In invisible worlds unknown to man, it is Now and all of this Nowness has always been Now. We've only seen it come as time but it hasn't. It has seemed to be time to the human mind because the world mind cannot embrace the Nowness of God - but Christ can. The Christ mind does and you're separating yourself from time as you rest in this. It's one way to bear fruit.

When you do it during the week, you'll find that you're pioneering. You're marching into new frontiers and you won't know where to go because the human mind cannot go into Now. It only knows time. It creates its creatures in time and it destroys them in time. But those who stand in Now find that they're not killed in time at all because they don't live within it. They see it. They seem to move within its rules and regulations but they are conscious of their Nowness. And you may have to go above your human mind to get any results out of this. You may have to finally say to your human mind, "Well this is as far as you can go. You can't think your way into Now so I'm going to have to leave you here because that's where I am going." And you rest until the Christ mind lifts you into its awareness of Now. You'll find there's no world in Now. There's only My Kingdom. The Kingdom of Now is and always has been present, out of time. It is inviolate, indestructible. It is totally governed by Love. And there's no power on this earth that can enter it to defile it. That is where we are going to live as friends of Christ.

In your exercise, repeated I hope more than once, you will slowly penetrate this other Realm of Now and you will discover what cannot be discovered in the human mind; that only in the Now are we the Son of God. Now are we the Sons of God. Not in time. In time, we're under the world-mind domination, still servants. But Now, without time, without past, without yesterdays, without tomorrows, we find this moment is Infinite and covers all that exists. It isn't changing. It is imperishable and whoever walks in time has no existence to you.

We're going to see later why we have to do this, right in this chapter of *"I am the vine."* Now you'll find that you cannot feel the Nowness at first, in many cases and you may feel that it's difficult for you to do it on your own but please do it because even if you don't succeed, you'll find you have succeeded. Your human mind may not know you've succeeded but when you plant the seed, it begins to germinate and in ways you know not of, Nowness draws from its infinite Self and brings it forth into manifestation as the activity of Spirit in your Life. This is one time where we go out beyond our human capacities for sure, into the unknown.

We'll rest now before we continue for five or six minutes. (Class break)

In the book of James, the epistle of James, the second chapter, twenty-third verse, *"And the scripture was fulfilled which saith, Abraham believed God, and it was imputed unto him for righteousness: and he was called the Friend of God. Ye see then how that by works a man is justified, and not by faith only."*

A friend of Christ isn't one who says, "I am the Christ," but who, by works, reveals that this belief has become a way of Life. Abraham's fidelity to Christ said, "That in God, there is no destruction." And the symbol of him sacrificing his son was the acceptance that there is no destruction in God. It was a revelation that form was the illusion and that Life, which was indestructible is the Reality. By acts of faith, we demonstrate that we are friends of Christ.

These things have to be thought upon before all of the human ideas we attach to them are dissolved. You might think, "Well, do I have to put my child on the block for God's sake?" and you know that's nonsense. We're being shown that there is a perfect invisible Self and that only world mind asks us to make such sacrifices. The world mind says, "Sacrifice this one or that one." But God doesn't. God is demanding no sacrifice of anyone. There is no separate God, separate from your Self to demand such a sacrifice.

"Greater love hath no man and that he lay down his life for his friends" was where we ended last week and it was the revelation that we are to lay down our sense of mortality to pick up our identity as the immortal, invisible Self and this is the continuation of that idea; that by deeds, we demonstrate who we know our selves to be, by the capacity to look through error. That is a deed. By the capacity to look through the illusion of killing. That is a deed. By the capacity

to remain untouched by the world of form, even though you may be persecuted by others as being incompassionate or inhuman. You must know the Truth that Christ in you knows only the perfection of God's present kingdom even to the point of knowing that time and space and motion are all ideas only within the world mind.

We're only working with the Now idea because when you get the Now idea, the idea of space and motion being equally counterfeit will come upon you. Form, time, space, motion will be revealed to you as activities of the world mind making us servants to them. But break one and you break them all. Touch Christ and you dissolve all illusion. And this is what the Christ words are now penetrating into our consciousness to do.

"Remember the word that I said unto you, The servant is not greater than his lord. If they have persecuted me, they will also persecute you; if they have kept my saying, they will keep yours also."

Now, the persecutions are not outer. There is in us the world mind and it is the persecutor. It is the opposite of the disciple in us. The disciple in us is hated by the persecutor, the world mind in us. The persecution then is within you by your own human thought. Your own human thought is the anti-Christ which is against the disciple in you which is the Christ. You must learn to distinguish which you are and which you seem to be.

If we make the mistake of thinking someone out there is going to persecute me, we're wrong. They cannot persecute you out there because there's no one out there except the Christ. World mind is painting forms out there and world mind in you is making you see the forms it has painted out there. The persecution is world mind in you giving you false vision, false thought which is not of the Father and this persecution within you must be faced with the knowledge that only Peace, only Truth, only Beauty, only Harmony, only Now in the Kingdom of God is present, no matter what the time picture seems to be.

That is how the tempter, the persecutor, the world mind individualized in us as human mind is overcome. Only Now is the Kingdom of God everywhere. There is no time picture that is true. We're being separated from the time picture into the Nowness of the Kingdom, separated from making ourselves higher than God and the persecutions continue within us to heighten the conflict, to force us to be lifted so that we make ourselves subordinate to God, so that we learn not to put our personal knowledge above Goodness, not to put matter above Spirit, not to put human above Divine.

The persecutions continue within us until all that is not human, all that is not Divine, until all that is untrue, is slowly eliminated from our senses, until we no longer believe in the world mind within us, until Christ is awakened and we are awake to Christ, until we are Divine Being and not flesh which cannot inherit the Kingdom of God. This is the knowledge that we should be in at this moment, that I am not the flesh that cannot inherit the kingdom of God. I cannot be that flesh because I am the Spirit of God, the Christ of God, the Nowness of God expressing and everything connected with that flesh is the persecution, the tempter within, trying to perpetuate the illusion but really a blessing in disguise that forces us eventually to be lifted above the persecutor into the Nowness of Being. We must be lifted into the Nowness of Being because we're in a world of time that cannot survive and if you're caught flat-footed in the world of time that cannot survive, you're in that flesh which cannot inherit the Kingdom of God.

If you can escape this minute of time you can escape the world in time and stand in the Reality of Being untouched. The symbol of a body buried and yet not buried, not touched, but free is a symbol of the friends of Christ who stand in the world of time untouched when it perishes.

However strong the words may be, that is what the Christ is preparing us to do. You cannot live in that which was not created by God because it doesn't exist and what doesn't exist cannot continue to seem to exist forever. As it had its birth, it must have its death and only in the Now of Spirit outside of changing time are you independent of the changing time picture because when you're in the Now, you're in another Consciousness. You're in the indestructible Consciousness and you out-picture your own Consciousness instead of the world consciousness of a changing form in time that perishes.

And so, we're hanging on to I, Christ, no matter what the world may present. I, Christ here and I, Christ there. That is no Arab, that is the invisible I, Christ and it isn't killing. That is no Israeli. That is the invisible I, Christ and it isn't dying and that I, Christ and that I, Christ and this I, Christ are one and the same. One indivisible I, Christ. This is your constant Consciousness and if it isn't, then world mind will continue to persecute you and that's the meaning of what Christ is telling us here.

"All these things will they do unto you for my name's sake, because they know not Him that sent me."

In the inability or capacity to live in the conscious awareness that I, Christ here, there, everywhere am the one Self, we are not knowing God aright. And because Divine law must fulfill Itself, there will be a continuance of error within us until we reach that point where we can look at the error and know it has no validity, no substance and no law.

All persecutions are the inevitable result of our ignorance of I, Christ here, there and everywhere and as we violate identity, the opposite strikes against us always with the purpose of calling that violation to our awareness. We call it persecution. It is a time signal saying, "You have violated identity." And you can see how the world has violated identity. You can't turn anywhere without something going wrong in this world. But we will accept that we are being chosen. We learn not to violate identity even though the pictures are harsh at times.

"If I had not come and spoken unto them, they had not [had] sin: but now they have no cloak for their sin."

As human beings under the law of good and bad - material law - we went to human authorities. And the human authorities said, "Here are the ways in which you should live." And so, we have man-made laws. Man-made religious laws. These are the things you must do. And then when we found that when we did them or not, we were just as much subject to destruction. Why? Because they were the man-made laws and those who thought they were authorities were really giving us their concept of what was right. It wasn't God's will. It wasn't God's law. This one said, "This is our religion. Let's do it this way." And the other one said, "This is our religion. Let's do it that way." And so, each was forsworn unto his own doctrine. And none of the doctrines were the Word of God. For as the Word of God is, "I am present as perfection now and beside me there is no other." The word of man is, "There is good and there is evil." And so, man extolled the good and decried the evil and if he happened to be a Pharisee, if he happened to be the ruling sect of a religion, he said "This is the way you do it and if you don't you get stoned." Or if he happened to be another religion, he said, "If you don't do what we want, we'll kill you; we'll go to war against you."

But those who declared that their way was right were not able to remove the evils of the world. They have shown by their incapacity that they had no capacity to raise the dead, to heal the sick, to feed the hungry. They can't overcome famine. They can't overcome poverty. They can't overcome death. All they have is a word called religion and they could get away with it until there was Christ walking the earth showing that these evils can be exterminated.

Who said "There is sin over here? Watch. Who said there is error over there? Watch. Who said there is hunger over here? Watch. Who said there's blindness? Who said there's death? This girl isn't dead. Rise up little child." Now, when there is a power shown on earth that can counter-act all of the knowledge of man, all of the belief in death, all of the belief in sickness and reveals that this sickness isn't there and this death isn't there, when there is Christ there realized. This is giving us the understanding that there is a transcendental Spiritual power on the earth everywhere.

It produced loaves and fishes on one side of the lake for the Hebrews and on the other side of the lake for the Gentiles. It never said to a man before it healed him, "What's your religion? What's your code? What's your morals? What did your father do?" It never even diagnosed him and, in most cases, all healing was done without prayer to God showing the futility and stupidity of a person here praying to a God there. It showed the power of Spirit within a man heals Itself by maintaining Itself because *"I have chosen you."*

And therefore, once the Truth is revealed, there is no cloak for the authority to hide his sin. The authorities can continue to turn away from the Truth and that is their sin. Once the Truth is exposed, that God is present everywhere and those who turn away from that knowledge are in sin. The sin is rejecting the Presence of God everywhere.

And so, we who have not accepted the Presence of God everywhere are still in that conditioned mind that follows the old authorities of good and evil. Having heard that God is everywhere, having known that there was a demonstration on the earth that God is everywhere, that enlightened ones have followed who in many cases have also demonstrated the Power of the invisible Christ. We who do not follow have no cloak for our sin. We are still in that inertia of the world mind.

Before, when we were ignorant of such demonstrations, we had a cloak for our sin. We could say we didn't know but we do know. We do know that religion, that science, that all human authorities are rejecting Christ within each individual and if we continue in that rejection, we are in the same sin. Christ within is the Reality and the outer manifestation of the world mind is the illusion. This is the message. The cloak has been removed. We can look at the Truth and say. "There it is." Now, follow and do likewise and heaven will open up like a scroll.

There are no human authorities. They were wiped out when Christ walked the earth in the form of Jesus Christ and previously in other forms and demonstrated the Power of God is present. And therefore, where that Power is present, evil does not exist because that Power is not a dead power but a living Power. All evil is a lie, a non-existence appearing in the human mind. Every headline tomorrow that shouts of evil must be met with that Consciousness that the world mind no longer has power to fool you.

"He that hateth me, hateth my Father also."

We cannot hide behind the cloak that we love God or we love Truth and still accept evil because Truth has no opposite. God has no opposite. Perfection has no opposite. You're looking at the illusion of a mortal mind.

"If I had not done among them the works which none other man did, [then]they had not [had] sin: but now have they both seen and hated both me and my Father."

To continue then to believe in evil as an existent thing is to reject Christ in you and to reject the infinite Spirit of God. You cannot accept the presence of evil without rejecting Christ in you for the acceptance of Christ in you is the sure knowledge that there is no evil present. You cannot have evil and Christ. You're making your selection and having been enlightened, your sin has no cloak to hide in. The world mind is still dominating that individual who cannot see that Christ is here and therefore the opposite of Christ is not here.

When you stand on Christ, you stand on the knowledge that all evil I see is not here. Confident that this Christ which has permitted you to find Christ, having chosen you, is sustaining you in the Truth that you are willing to declare until such time as the Comforter comes unto you.

"But this cometh to pass," this state of consciousness which we're turning from, *"that the word might be fulfilled that is written in their law. They hated me without a cause."*

If you go back into the Psalms, you'll find in two of the Psalms the same statement, *"They hated me without a cause."* Now this was in the Psalms before Christ Jesus walked the earth and he is revealing that there is no cause to hate Christ. What does that mean? It means that the hating of Christ is as imaginary as all form. It is all within a world mind which itself is an illusion. There's no one hates Christ. The hating of Christ, the anti-Christ is illusion. Anti-Christ means illusion. Anti-Christ means world imagination. There isn't any anti-Christ. There's nothing to be present beside Christ. *"They hateth me without cause."* This was said back in the Psalms; the 35th Psalm and the 69th Psalm. But look at the years between it being said again. *"They hateth me without cause."* And this is to fulfill the prophecy in the Psalms that, *"They hated me without cause."*

Now, why do you think from time to time, we always see that statement? This is to fulfill the prophecy in scripture and that it refers to whatever prophecy it's fulfilling. It's to show you, gradually, to let it sink in, that every prophecy in scripture is fulfilled. Don't ever think it isn't.

Now go back to your Mathew 24, the prophecy in that chapter. There's always this continuous hinting, this is that the prophecy should be fulfilled because you're going to be hit with one grand wallop one day when it tells you, "The end of the world is a prophecy and it must be fulfilled in you." Always, this is the reason we're being so carefully prepared, to step out of time, to step out of form, to step out of that which is not Christ. Don't think these words are here with a lesser purpose. There is no lesser purpose.

"When the Comforter is come, whom I will send unto you from the Father, even the Spirit of truth, which proceedeth from the Father, he shall certify [testify] of me."

So, there is that grand, glorious, supreme realization when all of your effort to know and accept, to believe and to act as the living Spirit of Christ here and there and everywhere that form appears, becomes a ringing realization of Oneness. "I AM THAT I AM," everywhere. The Comforter in you is the Holy Ghost realization that everywhere is My Spirit. There are no Arabs. There are no Hebrews. There are no Armenians. There are no Americans. There are no Englishmen. There is I, the invisible Christ, everywhere and that is your New Kingdom. That is your indestructible Self and that remains as the world passes in time, as you stand in the Now with Christ.

And will you do it? Yes, because *"I have chosen you…. that your fruit should remain."*

"And ye also shall bear witness, because you have been with me from the beginning."

Now, that goes back to a long time before your birth certificate. Ye have been with me from the beginning. This which says, *"Before Abraham was, I am,"* says *"Ye have been with me from the beginning…. Before Abraham was, I am."* Before Abraham was, you are. Why? Because this I am which speaks to you is You. The Self of you is the Bible leading you to Itself. Every Word of the Christ is your own Self enlightening you, breaking through the clouds of human consciousness to release all that is not You, to stand in the Now of time, independent of the world, unused by the world mind, no longer a servant of false authority, liberated out of humanhood, by the Vine which is everywhere present Now.

And this is only the 15th chapter. We have the 16th, the 17th, before that body which is indestructible is subjected to the belief that the world can destroy it. That body is a symbol of many things; one of them is the symbol of your indestructible body. All of this must be given to disciples of Christ, friends of Christ before that particular demonstration can take place so that we are in that state of

Consciousness which understands. We are learning not about a man. We are learning the nature of our Self, of which that man is a symbol.

And I think now, we can do Joel's chapter next week, "It [Shall] Not Come Nigh Thee."

Silence, (pause) ...

When we have put on the garment of Immortality, death will have lost its victory. Fortunately, there have been so many before us who have known the Truth now that the words are no longer hollow. We can look at those who have walked this path and we can say, "I can follow with them. They have blazed the trail but I must blaze that same trail within my Self."

Silence, (pause) ...

I think we've had our message for today and next week we're going to have that dinner at the Mark you know, so all those who have already told me they're coming, that's fine and those of you who still are mulling it over, take all the time you want. Tell me today or next week or even Sunday at 4 o'clock next week, it's fine. And then we're going to have quite a number of people there it appears. And I think we're all going to have a pleasant time. It'll be 5:30 next Sunday at the Mark. Usual class here at 2 o'clock.

Thanks again.

Class 29

The Secret Place of the Most High

Herb: Good afternoon everybody.

The importance of today's class is manifold. One of the major points of today's class is that we are preparing for the higher message that is to be given the disciples before the crucifixion of Jesus Christ. That would be the 16th and the 17th chapters and we are taking this pause to consolidate our gains and to take our checkpoints and find out, if up to this point we have been following the Master.

And so, today, we will review many points that have been coming up within our consciousness and review some of the attitudes we have been forced to take, some of the false methods we have used to protect ourselves against the evils of the world so that finally, out of this, we can evolve into a state of consciousness which is ready and can say to the Master, "Now, I'm ready for chapter 16. I'm ready for this sermon from high Consciousness, preparing me to walk through the Master's experience."

Now, Joel's chapter is the 10th and that's what we're going to discuss today because it will prepare us for the 16th chapter of the Gospel of John, "It shall not Come Nigh Thee."

And you might think that this is a promise that if you go to church on Sunday or if you read your Bible or if you're a diligent student who believes in God, that you're protected from the so-called evils of the world. However, that is not the promise of the statement at all. It does not say if you believe in God, that you will be protected from the problems of the world and that they shall not come nigh thee. That is our misconstrued concept of what is says. It does say, that *"It shall not come nigh thee…. if you live…. in the secret place of the Most High."* And that is not just believing in God. It is living in God.

And to illustrate the meaning of that, there's a story told by Joel. It's about a businessman, who being very successful in his own business was also a seeker of the Spiritual Life and there came a moment when he was ready for a big weekend vacation. It was July 4th and he and his family were going to take this long weekend and take a motor trip. And being very diligent, very sincere, he got up at 5 am on Friday morning and he did what he called his protective work. From 5 to 6, he dwelled deeply in the understanding of Truth, protecting himself and his family. The Bible had said, *"It shall not come nigh thee."*

And so, he was trying his best and then about 6 or 7, the family got in the car and they started on their weekend vacation. On Tuesday morning, he awoke in a hospital and he discovered that he had been in a car wreck. The car had been demolished. Everybody in the family was in a different room of the hospital. And for the months that followed in convalescence, he kept asking himself the question, "Why did this happen when I even did my protective work?" But he couldn't find an answer and so he sought out a practitioner and inasmuch as Joel was telling the story, presumably, the practitioner was Joel. And he said to the practitioner, "I did all I was supposed to do. I even did my protective work before the trip. What went wrong?" And the practitioner said to him, "Oh, what kind of protective work did you do? What were you protecting yourself against?" "Well," he said, "the drunks on the highway, the alcoholic drivers, the bad drivers, the accidents that could happen."

Now we, when we do our protective work, must understand where this gentleman fell into the trap so that we do not make the same mistake. Protective work is not protecting yourself against the evils of the world. And when this practitioner told the businessman that protective work means to know that there is nothing against which you must protect yourself, that was the beginning of a new insight for this individual. He learned a lesson and he learned a lesson which made him later a very competent spiritual healer.

Now, perhaps we can, through his experience and his mistake, learn the same lesson. What are we protecting ourself against? The moment you have something against which you're protecting yourself, you've denied the omnipresence of God. *"It shall not come nigh thee,"* if you live in the secret place of the Most High. And the secret place of the Most High is <u>the Consciousness of the presence of God</u>.

Now, we'll go through seven points and each of these seven points is very simple and after you have them and know them, you'll find they become one point because they all mold together and then as you practice them first as seven points and then integrate them into your consciousness and finally make them one point so that you are single-pointed, you'll find you won't be doing the false kind of protective work that many people think they are going to use as a protection against evil.

Let's start with our first point. God is omnipresent.

This is the crux of your work. God is omnipresent. That means that it doesn't matter whether you see God or hear God or touch God or whether you have evidence that God is present. It doesn't matter if you feel the presence of God any more than it matters if you feel the presence of the sun in the sky. It's going to be there whether you feel it or not. God is going to be present whether you feel it or not. And so, number one is to definitely establish that without this point that, God is omnipresent, you are not going to go anywhere in Spiritual living. That is the cornerstone. You're going to have to live by it and even be willing to die by it, that you may live. God is omnipresent. If in any way you fail to be conscious that God is omnipresent, you will be separated from the very God you're seeking.

And so, first, God is omnipresent. That means here and there, around the corner, up in the sky, under the ocean. Whether you're in a submarine or an airplane makes no difference. God is present where you are and God is present where you came from and God is present where you're going, all the way. Nothing will change it. God is present everywhere and now. This is the cornerstone of the Christ message. Who convinceth me that God is not present?

Now, once you have established this so that this is your living Bible, God is present here and God is present there. I care not what I see. I care not what picture comes to my attention. That has nothing to do with the fact that God is present.

Two. Where God is present, the power of God is present.

And so once you've established the presence of God as a fact, a fact that can never change, a fact that can never yield to any other so-called fact because it is the only fact there is; God is present. Then you know that the power of God is present where God is present and you've got your second point. God is present. The power of God is present.

Now, the nature of God Power is perfection. That means perfection is present where the power of God is present. Always, wherever you are, God is present and the power of God is present, functioning, being Itself, maintaining its perfection in all things. Nothing changes that. It matters not what you see or touch, what you hear, what you feel. That is the fact, the Divine fact. God is present. God's perfect Power is present, too. Over there and over there and over there, up there and down there - in the four corners of the earth, now, the perfect power of God is present.

Now, further, wherever the perfect power of God is present, the very nature of perfection means that no imperfect power can be there. The functioning of that Power is that it maintains its perfect Power at all times. It is the governor of its own government. There is nothing present ever to upset or dethrone that perfect Power.

So, that's the law. We have the law of God, I am present. My Power is present. Everywhere in the universe. And then, comes the world mind picture and now evil appears. But stay with your law. Do not waiver. Perfect power of God is present and therefore, there cannot be an evil power present.

That's number three. There is no evil power present because the perfect power of God is present.

I'm still not looking at appearances. I'm still not making judgments. I'm taking pure Divine law and staying with it. God is present. God's Power is present. Evil power cannot be present. Power is another word for cause; an evil cause cannot be present. There is no power to cause an evil because God's Power is present.

And therefore, the fourth point is because there is no power of evil present to cause an evil, evil is not present.

Once you have established the omnipresence of God, you can work your way to the fourth point that evil cannot be present. It is impossible and that word evil has no cause because there is no evil power present to cause evil. Only the power of God is present. This is your Divine law.

Now, what does evil include? It includes the alcoholic on the driveway, the alcoholic on the road. It includes the accident on the freeway. It includes unemployment. It includes limitation. It includes lack. It includes everything that is unlike God and it is impossible because there is no evil power present because God Power is present and so, every evil that you may see is not present. The moment you think it is present or believe it is present or accept that it is present, you have committed spiritual adultery. You have walked away from the Divine Truth that God is present, that God's Power is present, that there is no power of evil present to cause evil and therefore the evil you see is not present. It simply is not there.

Your fourth point is evil is not there.

Evil is impossible and it makes no difference whether that evil is war, or genocide or manslaughter or rape or arson or flood or fire. It could only be there if God were absent and God is present. Therefore, the chain of command establishes that the evil must be something other than what it seems to be and that's your fifth point. The evil which is not there is temptation. It is a temptation to make you believe it is there. It is a world mind picture coming through as a shadow of thought within your individual mind, appearing as a shadow of thought within your individual mind as the accident, as the flood, as the hurricane, as the problem, as the lack, as the limitation, as the unemployment, as the argument, as the dispute, as the error. Always it is world mind presenting a sense image - sometimes a group sense image, a national sense image, a cosmic sense image - but always, it is a sense image whether it is five million people seeing it or one. It cannot be there because the power of God is there and so, it is a temptation to make you believe it is there.

And the fifth step then is evil being temptation, it cannot be there.

Evil is the denial of the presence of God. That is the temptation coming to you and at that point, your fifth point is to recognize evil as temptation. Recognize evil as temptation; the temptation to believe that God is not present, God's Power is not present, there is another power to cause evil, that the evil is there, all of this is the temptation coming to you as the appearance of evil. Recognize evil as temptation. That is your fifth point.

And then your sixth point is obvious. Reject it. Reject that temptation. Not the evil.

You can't reject the evil. It isn't there. Reject the temptation to accept it and that is where we want to pause and see what that means. Reject the temptation to accept it.

Now then, there is a point, a moment, sometimes just an instant, a flick of an eyelash when you unwittingly accept evil. That moment is when you must learn to stand still. There it is. It appears and if you are asleep, you accept it. It's like opening a door. You open a door of your mind and you let the evil in. Now, you've got to get it out somehow. Why go that far. We are to be awake, not asleep. Evil is temptation and the only reason it gets that far is because we had not dwelt in the secret place of the Most High; that God is present. And if we dwell in it, there is a way so that you can stand alert, awake, not asleep and at the appearance of evil, the temptation to accept it comes directly to you but you do not open the door of your consciousness.

You are able to observe what appears to be the evil, recognizing the temptation that is now presenting itself to you as a hurricane, as a flood, as anything wrong in your life, anything wrong in the lives of the world around you and you look at it and say, "No. This I will not accept into my consciousness as a reality." Why? God is present. God's Power is present. There is no power of evil present. Therefore, evil has no cause and cannot be present. That is the temptation of the world mind and I have caught it. I will not let it enter into my consciousness."

The rejection of the temptation is your sixth point. It is your refusal to be moved by the appearance.

And the seventh is to rest in the knowledge that God is present. God is Power. God is all and beside God nothing is present.

Rest in the knowledge that God actually is. God is present. You come right back to your first point and you rest in the assurance of it. And when you have practiced these points sufficiently, you won't have to go through seven points. You'll simply know God is present because that's all that omnipresence means. When you unravel it, you get the seven points and when you have the seven points, you can come back to the one: God is present. There's no other presence where God is present and everywhere God is present.

Now, then, this is what the Bible means when it said, *"It shall not come nigh thee."*

When you dwell in the conscious awareness that God is present, then you're not tempted to believe God is not present. You're not tempted to accept an error which can never occur in the presence of God. On the other hand, when you accept the error, in that moment you have accepted that God is not present and that acceptance, although not conscious, not voluntary, that acceptance is your way of saying, "God and I are separated." You see, if God isn't present, then you and God are separated and that separation is the result of your belief, though unconscious, that you and God are not one. The inner belief that I and God are not one becomes the belief in the separation from God and then what happens? Your separation from God becomes visible as the problem. That's what the problem is. The problem is the external evidence that you have permitted yourself to be separated from the presence of God.

Every discord in your life, every limitation, every lack, every major and minor state of illness or emotional upset, whatever the problem might be, it is your outer manifestation from this invisible pyramid of first, the unconscious belief that I and the Father are separated, widening into the acceptance of a situation which could not occur in the presence of God, finally being manifest as your problem. Your sense of separation externalizes as the problem.

Now, then, let's practice this very carefully. Instead of going into three meditations a day, as a human being, or going into protective work as a human being, let us recognize that we must dwell in the conscious awareness of the presence of God. Our secret place is making God our constant companion, living in God, abiding in the conscious awareness that here God is. There's no other way for the power of God to express in you and through you.

Now, another example is an individual who tried again and again and again to secure some kind of support for a business he had in mind. And no matter what he did, there was no support coming and he was like the man doing protective work. He knew that he was honest and sincere and diligent. Why couldn't he get the support? He was not conscious of the fact that God is present and the way he was unconscious of the fact is the way we are unconscious of the fact. He thought he was present. You see, if you think you're present, where's God? To be conscious of the presence of God means where you stand, where your neighbor stands, where your children stand, where your parents stand, where everyone you know stands, is the presence of God. God is omnipresent means that there's no other presence. This is the fact of the Allness of God.

You see why it's the cornerstone? And when you're not conscious of it, then the world mind functions subliminally and operates through you and as Joel puts it, "We become a blotting paper for all of the thoughts of the world."

Now, let's go back to number 6 or 5, whichever it was, when the temptation of evil presents itself, learning how to not accept it. We're looking at, oh, let's take a case that happens many times. You hear footsteps while you're in your house alone, right outside your door, in the back of your yard. Who would be there? Nobody's supposed to be there. You thought you locked the doorway to the patio and you're alone. The temptation now is to, "What am I going to do about this? In fact, I hear someone stealthily walking up the patio." The mind runs wild with its imaginative ideas about what can happen. You're caught unaware and now you're thinking, "Should I get to the phone and call the police station? Dare I open the door and peek out. Won't that give them an entrée to the house? What shall I do?"

Point number one. Only God is present. God is omnipresent. God isn't permitting burglars to enter your home. God isn't jeopardizing your Life. God is present. The power of God is present. There is no power of evil present. Therefore, no evil can be present. What is happening is, point 5, the temptation to believe that God is not present, the power is not present, the evil is present and there's a power causing it. You recognize this temptation and now, you do not accept this temptation.

If you do, you step out of creation into recreation. If you do, you step out of Divine thought into human thought. That's the switch-over. The minute we think the evil is present, we're not in creation - we're in recreation. Recreated thought. When we know the evil is not present, we're in Divine thought. And then, when within we have the assurance that I know the Truth and I can look at that which appears to be footsteps on the patio, knowing only the presence of God is, I come to my sixth step, therefore, there is no threat outside my door. It simply isn't there even though I heard it. It cannot be there. And your seventh step is resting that God is.

What happens to the person who is creating the footsteps? You can ask the Holy Ghost. I have no interest in what happened except that you'll find it's either somebody to deliver the groceries or it's just a child who happened to stray in or you heard something that wasn't there or something of that nature but the threat will dissolve. Why? Because the law is infallible. And every time you practice these seven points, even if you just get right down to the nitty gritty of it, God is present now, here, there, everywhere, I don't need any more points than that and rest in the knowledge that this being so, all is well, the picture dissolves. Oh, there are so many little things and big things that happen. You could go on forever making a catalogue of the wonderful things that happen as you rest in Omnipresence.

And then you have so many by-paths to take from there. God is present and therefore, the intelligence of God is present. Right here, where we are, is the intelligence of God. That Infinite intelligence is always present. Is it permitting anyone to break its Divine law? You see, the breaking of the Divine law is the illusion. Divine law can't be broken. It simply isn't here to break Divine law.

Now, as we dwell in these things and you discover that you can depend on the presence of God always to dissolve the illusion or temptation of appearances that come to you even to the point of miracles or what would appear to be miracles to others, then your confidence becomes unbounded and you're ready to live in the foundation stone that because of the omnipresence of God, I can now move to a higher level of activity than I had been dwelling in. Before, I used to do protective work. That's a sort of a negative way of living, isn't it? Protecting ourselves against this and that, even by knowing the omnipresence of God. Suppose we now turn that around and do progressive work. Supposing we now can accept that because God is present, whatever God wills in me today is going to be done and even if it's something I've never been done before, it's going to be done. Supposing we begin to live in the positive side of Spirit instead of the negative side of protection.

The presence of God is the only protection we need. Now, let's see that we were trying to protect our human selfhood. When all your protective work is complete and you know in the presence of God no protection is needed, just a conscious awareness of God's presence, there is no longer anyone there to protect. The real trap of the businessman who came to Joel because his protective work hadn't worked, was that he was protecting his human self instead of going to God to realize his spiritual Self. Translated, if you were unemployed or limited in some way and you wanted to go to God within to the realization of the Omnipresence in order to remove that condition, you would have fallen into the identical trap. That would come in your number five place. There is no such condition except in a human self. That's the temptation to believe that you have such a condition and the purpose of today's class is to make clear to you that there are no conditions in the presence of God and there is no other presence.

Every condition that we accept is the false acceptance that we are a second self and that where we are, the presence of God is not the only self. We have no protective work to do at this level because we are that Self which is the Self of God and if we're not that Self, we are denying that God is the only Presence. God is omnipresent.

Where are you? If you're trying to protect your visible self, you are not accepting God is omnipresent. And if you are willing and determined to accept it, you must finally come to the conclusion that you are an invisible Being. You can never be a visible being. The visible you that's trying to protect something is not You. You are invisible Self.

And so, we graduate above protective work in the knowledge that the presence of God which is omnipresent is the invisible Vine, the Christ, the Self and I being that Self, I am all that the Father is and I have no lack or limitations. There is no evil in my Selfhood which is the infinite Self.

You're still at the place of five or six where you're able to look at temptation knowing that it's trying to tempt you into being a visible self. The word "invisible" now becomes very important. If you had all of the material things of this world, there would come a day when you would have to lose them, give them up. The Christ message isn't to try to show us how to have all the material things of this world, it is to try to show us that our destiny is to be independent of the material things of this world; to live in God Being.

"I live; yet, not I." And if you look at that statement by Paul, you might be surprised to find that there's something in that statement you had overlooked. We all remember to say, *"I live; yet not I, Christ liveth my life."* We forget a few words that he said just a moment before. He said, *"I am crucified with Christ: [and] therefore, I live; yet not I. Christ liveth my life."*

"I am crucified with Christ." I, too give up the physical, visible sense of me. The fellow who is worried about the accidents, the alcoholics on the road, the national budget or who is going to get in as president or vice-president. Who is that fellow worried about these things? That's the one who doesn't know God is omnipresent as the Only.

"I am crucified with Christ." As Jesus refuses to be a visible person, I refuse to be a visible person. For Spirit is God and Spirit is omnipresent and Spirit is invisible and I am Spirit.

Now, you must have your seven points as your foundation in order to be able to come higher to the invisible nature of your Being so that all evil presenting itself to you is now presenting itself to the invisible Self, the invisible Self who can say, "Only Spirit is here. Only the Spirit of God is here and it is I. Only the Spirit of God is there and it is I."

Now, the world has tried to overcome the evils of the world. For instance, you might take any prominent person in religious work and if you ask him one question, you will discover quickly where he stands in Truth. You might say for example to a clergyman, "Please tell me why God permits one million people each year to die of cancer. Please tell me why God permitted six million Hebrews to be burned in German ovens. Please tell me why God permitted nations to go to war against each other. Tell me why." And I can assure you the answer you got would be a very stock answer. Something like, "Well, let's see. In the first place, we must be humble. We must trust God. We must trust His infinite wisdom to know what is right for us." That might be one stock answer. Another might be, "Well, punishment. The world has to be punished for its sins." Another might be that we've given our souls to the devil. And you could go down the list of the vague answers that would be given provided the individual you asked even deigned to give you answer. They might look at you with a paternal glance and think, "How naïve a question. Why did God permit this, that and the other atrocity?"

But I want to tell you this; that any answer of that nature is really a statement that the individual giving you that answer does not believe in the presence of God. There's only one answer that's true. The answer that is true is that God does not permit nations to go to war. God does not permit one million persons to die of cancer every year. God does not permit genocide. God does not permit manslaughter. God does not permit the evils of the world and therefore - and this is the answer that you will never get from all of the religions of the world - therefore, these things cannot be happening.

Now, if you think they're happening, you also think that God is impotent or that God is indifferent or that God is cruel. If they are happening, you are saying God is not God. If they are happening, if one single child in this entire world dies of cancer, we have said that we are atheists and it doesn't matter how many clergymen in the world think that these things are happening, they are practicing atheism.

Atheism is the belief that God is not present. You can believe in a God in the sky but you've got to believe in a God on earth, too. If you don't have a God on earth, you don't have a God; you've got chaos.

Now, most of us have been practicing the presence of God sufficiently to know that God *is* present, not as an abstract idea but as a living force maintaining a perfect universe wherever there is a witness, an individual, a consciousness that can abide in the secret place of the Most High. Any clergymen can prove it when they can abide in the presence of God as a fact, not a word. Then all that is unlike the presence of God cannot be here. Its very existence would be a denial of the Presence or else it would be a statement that it being here, God is permitting evil to be here.

So, these seven points are going to be the fulcrum from which we function in preparation for the higher message, the liberating message. In a way, you might say that as you learn to practice only the Presence and see that all temptation is the material action of the world - all of it, the good material action and the bad material action - is the temptation to deny the presence of God.

And when you are able to give yourself to this work, not on a part time basis because you think that you've got eight hours of work to do at an office, but to make it your constant companion no matter what you do and where you do it, never being asleep to the presence of God, then you'll find that you are really the forerunner of a new age, what is called the remnant; the enlightened remnant, the seed of a new age. Those who will stand in the conscious knowledge that here, right in my office, right in my home, right on the freeway, right in the ghetto, right on the battlefield, the presence of God is all that is present, the power of God is all that is present, there is no power of evil. There is no evil to be here. That which is presented to me as evil or error or accident or lack is a hallucination of the world mind coming through my mind as a shadow, a temptation which I now reject. God is present. God is All and there I rest with confidence.

Sometimes it will come to you as an instantaneous awareness without having to go through point by point. It'll be just a quick shift of the gears and it may even reach you at a point where you don't have to shift because that is to become your permanent Consciousness. God is, period.

That's how you start your day. You spend as much time in it as possible and you continue in that awareness no matter where you go. God is present.

You're not protecting against anything. You're recognizing that my only protective work is the knowledge that God being present, there's nothing here to protect against. The universal intelligence of the Father is on the road. Where's a bad driver? That's the temptation to believe that the universal Intelligence is not here. Why is there a bad driver? Because there's no one aware that the universal Intelligence is here. Aware of it, you discover the bad drivers aren't bad drivers at all. They were separated appearances but the moment you were aware of universal Intelligence present, somehow, something happened to the bad drivers. They became aware. The alcoholic drivers weren't drunk anymore. Why? Because the power of God is the only Power that's present. In the absence of it in your consciousness, you have the chaos of the world. In the Presence of it, you have the government of God functioning through your Consciousness and then you discover that the whole world is in your Consciousness. There are no cars on the road. There are no people. They're all in your consciousness. And because your consciousness is the consciousness of God, they're all brought into the government of God in your Consciousness. You find why one is a majority, when that one is in the conscious awareness of the presence of God.

And so today, if you still insist that you have something wrong in your life, you're merely saying that you're not conscious of the presence of God. The remedy is, be ye conscious of the presence of God, for if you will abide in that secret place you will find that you are under the shadow of the Almighty. The power of God functioning, maintaining becomes the very law of your Being.

Every healing of the Christ is the conscious, continuous awareness of God being present, nothing else is here. I don't have to remove the evil, correct the evil, improve the evil. I must know that God is here. The evil cannot be here, too. It didn't even stray in. It just never was here.

"Thou will keep him in perfect peace, whose mind is stayed on thee." Not strayed but stayed. We stray out of the conscious knowledge of God's presence or we stay in the conscious knowledge and that makes the difference between employment and unemployment, lack or abundance, Truth or the falsehood, happiness or sorrow, success or failure.

You can turn the blackest moments into sunshine but not by trying to do it out there. You've got to do it in your consciousness and have faith that when you touch the consciousness of God within your Self, its Power will manifest out there and change the blackness to sunshine. If you try to do it out there, you've fallen into the temptation to believe that it has to be done out there. There is no out there. There's only God. Don't reach out to the world that isn't there.

Go back to that Matthew statement. *"Lay up your treasures in heaven."* Why? For there, there is no moth or rust to corrupt. There, there are no thieves to steal. You can have all the material possessions in this world but they will run through your fingers like grains of sand. Time runs out. You've got to lay up your treasures in your knowledge of the presence of God as the very invisible Presence of your own Being. That's your treasures in heaven. The knowledge of the presence of God as the invisible Presence of your own Being is the revelation of your Spiritual identity as living Spirit, invisible Being possessing all that is of God because Oneness is the Truth of Being.

You don't have to get an invisible Self employed. You don't have to remove lack from an invisible Self. You don't have to heal the bone of an invisible Self and when you are that invisible Self, it will prevent the bone fracture. It will prevent the unemployment. It will prevent the error. And if by chance you stray instead of stay in that consciousness, the moment you return, it will remove the result of your momentary separation. You are never unemployed. You are separated from the knowledge that the presence of God is standing where the world sees you. You are never lacking. You are never limited. You are never in error. You are simply unaware that where you stand is the invisible presence of God. Holy ground. And when you know it and when you live with it, not just in three meditations, not before work and after work but always, then you are crucifying your visible self.

"I am crucified with Christ: I live; yet not I. Christ liveth my life."

All temptations of the world are meaningless when you know your Self. And then, *"It shall not come nigh thy dwelling,"* neither the accident nor the unemployment, nor the pain, nor the sorrow because these things are in the false sense of self that we entertain.

Now, practice those seven points please until you can reel them off so fast without much thought that it becomes effortless. Catch yourself when you stumble. Repair the damage until you have this

Consciousness with which to face the world. Nothing in this world can convince me that God is not here functioning as God.

And with that level, you'll find when Jesus Christ speaks to us, within or without, in the Bible or within our own Consciousness, we have ears that can hear. We have removed all of the barriers of conditioned world mind, the concepts, the clutter and the pure words of the Christ then fall in a habitation that is ready for them.

Crucify yourself with Christ. Crucify the world with Christ. Crucify all false situations with Christ. Crucify matter and time and space with Christ. Get out of atheism, out of Spiritual adultery, accepting God twenty-four hours a day every second as the Presence. Then we're not atheists. And the power of God will shine through you totally.

As we quietly meditate, first run through in your mind your seven points so that it becomes easy, quick. They move in quick succession, one after the other and this time I'm not going to remind you. You do it yourself. Let's just dwell in that consciousness of those seven points.

Silence, (long pause) …

When you get to the seventh, you just sit back and you rest in God. The Peace usually comes when you do that. It is a sign that you have really cleansed your house. Now we are not tempted but faithful; not believers only in the Word of God as a noun but as a living Reality here on earth as in heaven. We become faithful witnesses of the living presence of God. Disciples, friends of Christ ready to prove by living in Christ that God is here on earth, that we walk in God and God in us. The remnant, the seed of a new age.

— End of Side One —

In the tenth chapter we have a number of statements by Joel, all of which relate to, *"It shall not come nigh thee...*[if you].... *abide in the secret place of the Most High,"* which is the knowledge that God is present where I am, where everyone appears to be, God is.

Now, let's look at some of these statements.

"A person who leaves his home in the morning has no positive assurance that he will return safely at night.... Man has become a statistic.... And how, then, can mishaps and catastrophes be avoided? Is there a way?" And he says, *"Yes, there is. There certainly is a way.... Break through your mental inertia in the morning."*

And he emphasizes *"in the morning."* In other words, it's not two hours after you get going. In those two hours, the world mind has got you trapped. Break through your mental inertia in the morning to consciously realize there is one Power operating in this universe. That of course is the power of God. It is operating. God is present. God is the Power operating and what you're seeing therefore, which is unlike the power of God is your temptation. It isn't what's there. It's your temptation. *"There is no power in any mesmeric suggestion of accident."*

Now, catch the words, *"the suggestion of accident....the mesmeric suggestion of accident."* He's telling you accident is not accident. Accident is suggestion. And the suggestion is a mesmeric suggestion and there is no power in it, meaning there's no power to cause that accident. I know all about the statistics but there is no power to cause those statistics. It is mesmeric suggestion, temptation being presented through the world mind in you, to turn you from the belief that there is only the power of God present. That's what he said.

And therefore, you look at the accident which is happening in your mind. It's not six cars lined up on the freeway. It's the freeway and six cars all lined up in your mind. That's where the mesmeric suggestion is. And there is no power to cause that fact and therefore it isn't a fact. The only Power is God. That's the consciousness you're to develop.

"No power in any belief of infection or contagion." Same thing with infection or contagion, it's a temptation coming to you to make you believe there is another power beside the perfect power of God. And there isn't any other power. *"There's no power in the carnal mind,"* and the carnal mind is the world mind functioning in you. It has no power. It cannot create an accident. It can only create the appearance of an accident in your mind. And the only reason it does that is because you're not in the Christ mind.

The carnal mind is the opposite of the Christ mind and the Christ mind has no opposite and so, we look at the accident, the infection, all that is out in the world and know it to be a picture in the world mind in me. I'm looking at the false mirror of my own mind. And I'm not going to accept another power beside the perfect power of God. *"There is no power in the carnal mind or in any of its forms, or in any of its beliefs, whether individually or collectively."*

So, that's laying it on the line. There is no power to cause evil. Evil is an appearance within the mind of each individual person placed there by our separation from the knowledge of the presence of God.

This is the first step in the elimination of that separation.

"Your experience" says Joel *"is going to be your own state of consciousness objectified."* That which you have in your consciousness will be that which you experience as if it were out there. It will be objectified. It will come into material form out there apparently because it is in your consciousness in here. Your state of consciousness objectified is your experience and if you want your experience to be harmonious, then your state of consciousness must be the conscious awareness of the presence of God. That will objectify as Harmony. That will objectify as the qualities of God made visible.

If you insist however, on walking around all day without consciously living in the realization of God, the presence of God, the omnipotence of God, the omniscience of God here and now, the all and the only Power, you will not bring Harmony into your experience.

So, this is part of what we have today made our seven points. This very second, God is Being. We must know this consciously. Not knowing it consciously is the error. For when you're not consciously aware that this very second God is Being, that is when you become the *"blotting paper"* for world thought that just flows right through you. God is being all that God can be. There's no way for God to change. God will be the same, God is the same yesterday, today and tomorrow. God is from everlasting to everlasting. Do not try to get God to do anything for you. God has already done it. God is. Period. You see, the isness of God is the fact. God is.

And always, the world mind is saying, "God isn't. Look at this, this and this." And that's where you have to tighten up and say, "No, no, no. I'm not looking at this, this and this. God is this, this and this invisibly. That's all that God is everywhere. I don't care what I see. God is."

And so, this is the tightening of that consciousness which won't be budged by the tempter in the appearance.

And the minute you find that little word "but" beginning to creep up, and you go "What about this?" That "but" is the tempter again. There is no about this. God is. Period. The "but" is that little wriggly human mind that won't accept that God is. Period. There's no anything else. God is.

"Protective work is the realization that there's no power from which to protect yourself. It is a living in the realization that because there's only one Power, there are no powers to do anything or to be anything and every suggestion of some other power is a mesmeric influence."

Now, he underlines a certain phrase here "*Without this realization, even though you do not consciously think of accidents, of discords, of diseases, sins, or temptations, you are permitting yourself to unconsciously accept, to subconsciously or unconsciously accept the world's mesmeric and hypnotic suggestions.*" The moment you're not realizing that there's only the power of God present, in that moment you open the door to the world mind flood of lies even though you're not conscious of them. They capture your subconscious. They become the food that feeds your mind and the rift between you and the presence of God just widens and widens and widens until this great big dragon appears called lack or limitation.

Now, we go into some of the mysticism of it. Is weather external to you? Now, we all think the sun is out there, it's external to me. The sky is out there, it's external to me. It's not raining inside me, it's raining out there. But here's a question; is weather external to you? It's external to the false sense of you. If you're living in the sense of a human selfhood, weather is external to you. Is weather external to Christ? Is weather external to God? What's outside of God? Weather not being external to the Spirit of God, how can it be external to you? It's only because you entertain the notion that you're not the Spirit of God. And so, the answer must be, "No, weather is not external to me." Or how can employment be outside of your Self then? How can lack or limitation be outside of your Self? How could anything be outside of you if everything is within the Spirit of God and you are the Spirit of God?

And so, this is to turn us to the fact that nothing is outside of you. It's just the right You that you have to know about. The right You, the Spirit of God includes all that is. Then what is the unemployment? Employment is within the right You. To seek employment out there before finding the right You, is trying to do it the hard way. It won't even be the right employment when you get it because it has to be that which is within your spiritual Self. It has to be that which grows out of the tree of Life. The fruitage must come from the Spirit of your Being. So, the startling thing is that weather is not external to you.

Weather is only external to the image called form which we have learned we are not. We are that Spirit of God to which nothing is external. Nothing in the whole world is external to the Spirit of God which is Infinite. And in this identification, you can trust the Power of that Spirit to manifest Itself, to fulfill Itself. You see how you're in God government when you're in your Self? The legal entanglements out there are for the human self. The spiritual Self dissolves the seeming legal entanglements because there is no power present but the Power of your Spirit even where there seem to be antagonists elsewhere.

So, Joel is opening up to the startling Truth that nothing in the world is outside of your true spiritual Being. Don't reach out for the treasures of the world that moth and rust will corrupt and that thieves will break in and steal, meaning time and space aren't there. Matter isn't there. A human lifespan isn't there. Your Spiritual treasure is the knowledge that I am the Life itself. That Life which is the life of God complete in Self, seeking nothing in the world but accepting these added things if they flow from my Spiritual enlightenment.

"No, weather" says Joel, *"is an activity of the mind…. Weather is an activity of the mind…. The only reason we behold imperfect weather is because there is a belief in two powers which makes for good weather and bad weather."* His reason for stating this is followed by this statement, *"Some of us have…. proved that destructive and injurious forms of weather can be dissolved through the understanding that weather exists as an activity of the mind."* Not the mind of God, mind you. The world mind and the mind of man. *"Anything that exists as an activity of the carnal mind can be nullified in proportion to the degree of your awareness of these principles."*

And so, I've tried to give you those concise seven principles. These principles can nullify any activity of the weather or any activity unlike God. Tidal waves, storms are quickly dissipated when someone knows and understands that they are not conditions of matter. See, they're conditions of the mind which we think are conditions of matter. But they are not conditions of matter. Vast areas in storm and tidal waves, they're not conditions of matter. They're conditions of the collective mind. Activities of the mesmeric mind and often they stop instantaneously because they cannot last long in the face of this realization that they are images in thought and images in thought have no power.

This sounds like a colossal thing, you know. I actually think it's harder to take care of a head cold than a tidal wave. It's really the same problem. One just has a vaster area in seeming space than the other. But mind you, these statements by Joel are not made from opinions. They're made from day in and day out work along these lines which every word was long proven by him.

"Weather is an activity of the mind. It is not an activity of matter. Matter is the appearance to the mind which does not know that the weather is within that mind that perceives it as matter. This is a misperception."

Now, when you face it as an activity of mind, that doesn't mean you're going to make it shine when it's shady. There's a word in it that's very important, "destructive" weather. If the weather is "destructive," you have the capacity in your knowledge of these seven steps to change the weather. You're not changing Reality. You never change Reality. You're simply admitting into consciousness the power of God in which there is no power of destruction and destructive weather no longer is destructive.

Really, it's no more difficult than taking care of a head cold. The scope of it seems bigger. It's no more different than taking care of any form of error or evil that enters your consciousness because it's all made of the fabric of mental imagination. Only God is present. It never happens. Only God is present. That which seems to happen, happens in the human sense of self in those who have not yet learned how to crucify with Christ.

These are the great secrets of the Infinite Way.

"God knows nothing" says Joel, *"about rain."* You can get into many an argument on that statement. *"God knows nothing about rain."* Remember in this chapter, I think it was in this chapter, yes, he told about that city for eighteen months that was deluged with rain. It never stopped raining. It was ruining everything. Nobody could function and again, they called somebody and that somebody, through the knowledge of Truth, being able to rest in the principle that God is and the power of God is never destructive, lo and behold with the sky still grey and sullen, no rain. Only three days after the rain stopped did the conditions that appeared to be causing the rain disappear but the rain stopped for three days before the conditions disappeared. Why? Because the collective mind of that city had rain and the mind of one individual with God had only God and the false mind came to the true mind and said, "Help us." and it stood in the silence of the presence of the Father doing nothing but being conscious of the Presence and the Presence could not manifest as destructive rain. It manifested as the absence of rain.

So, it was with every healing in the Bible and every healing that you are called upon to do. You never do it. The presence of God in your consciousness reveals the absence of error.

There's a reminder if I recall that it doesn't mean because you close your eyes and say, "God is here and God is there," that the errors disappear. He reminds us of the necessity for doing your work and then if the situation doesn't yield, you've got to do it again and again and again. You've got to be as patient as the lie is - until it yields. But the yielding will come provided you will stand in the Truth of that Presence.

This is another way of saying, *"Forgive seventy times seven."* Stay there. You see, in unseeing the lie, you're forgiving. You're erasing the lie. You're wiping out the lie. This is forgiveness. You're forgiving a karmic debt. You're looking through the lie. You're forgiving seventy times seven if necessary until the lie is no longer visible, no longer objectified.

All these things are the tempter. The temptation is the suggestion of a power and a person and a presence apart from God. Reject it in the realization that it is nothing but the fleshly mind, the carnal mind. Then dismiss it. And that's the end of it. It takes only a minute to consciously recognize within your Self that God, Truth, being Infinite - nothing else can enter.

The hardest part is to dismiss it. We want to mull it over, you know. We want to revive those images. Sometimes, even though we try, there's something holds us to them. We keep saying, "That error isn't there. That error isn't there. That error isn't there." Until we've actually almost made it appear there by the repetition of the fact that it isn't there. Get out of the negative side of it. God is there. God is there, the Presence is there, the Power is there until all idea of error is out of your consciousness because that's the only thing that makes the error appear. It's in your consciousness. When it's weeded out by the positive action of knowledge that God is there, then we have dismissed it. And when it pops back in again, you have to go back to the knowledge that only the Presence is there.

One point that should be clarified is that the error out there and the Presence out there is always pushing you away from your consciousness here. You've got to see that God is present where you are. First, here where I am, is the Presence. Here where I am, is no error. My consciousness here is the presence of God. I am conscious of the Presence and that's God consciousness and in my God consciousness here, there is no error. And then over there, it will disappear because your God consciousness here is God consciousness there. You've got to have it where you stand, closer than breathing. Your consciousness of God where you stand does the miracle work even though the storm is over there three thousand miles away. You must have the consciousness of God here and It will manifest as the absence of the storm there.

"The principles you are learning will eventually bring freedom to every individual on the face of the globe." So, start observing what happens when you acknowledge His Presence in all your ways. The miracle worker is the presence of God acknowledged by you to which you crucify your human selfhood until the presence of God you're acknowledging is your invisible Self and there is no second. Then, *"It will not come nigh thee,"* the accident or the flood and we're being pushed to this consciousness not to avert the disasters of the world alone but those disasters are pushing us to the invisibility of our Being that we may establish the Kingdom of Heaven on earth as an objectified Reality.

I want you to hear a Proverb which might sound a little different now. It's the third Proverb. We'll just start it at the thirteenth verse. It sounds so simple and yet what it's been trying to say to us all these years is very close to what Joel has been saying and what we have talked about during this session.

"Happy is the man that findeth wisdom, and the man that getteth understanding. For the merchandise of it is better than the merchandise of silver, and the gain thereof than fine gold. She is more precious than rubies: and all the things thou canst desire are not to be compared unto her. Length of days is in her right hand; and in her left hand riches and honour. Her ways are ways of pleasantness, and all her paths are peace. She is a tree of life to them that lay hold upon her: and happy is every one that retaineth her. The Lord by wisdom hath founded the earth; by understanding hath he established the heavens. By his knowledge the depths are broken up, and the clouds drop down the dew. My son, let not them depart from thine eyes: keep sound wisdom and discretion: So shall they be life unto thy soul, and grace to thy neck. Then shalt thou walk in thy way safely, and thy foot shall not stumble."

All of it is telling us to be conscious of the presence of God. We had thought that that was all a moral thing. Be good. Be virtuous. It isn't that at all. You can be upright. You can be good. You can be church going but if you're not in the secret place of the Most High, it will come nigh thee. We do not stumble when we are in the presence of God and that Presence must be your invisible Presence because there is no selfhood apart from God. The self of you that is not the invisible presence of God must be crucified daily until you are willing to accept "Thou seest me, thou seest the Father." You cannot walk in the presence of God unless that Presence is your invisible Self because that invisible Self is the presence of God called Christ. That's the only way you are in the secret place of the Most High.

The top secret is that you can only be free when you are Christ.

Another assignment I'd like to suggest to you for this coming week is please read the 91st Psalm. You'll find it's the same as this third Proverb. Just another way of saying unless you are in the conscious awareness of the presence of God as your very Being, you're not in the secret place of the Most High. You're in a second self, a separated sense of self, a vulnerable self, a dying self that never existed and never can exist and in that false self are all the problems that you have found. They do not exist when you practice your seven points until "God is" is your living Bible day in and day out.

From this point, I think we have an opportunity to open doors in the 16th chapter of John and to let ourselves be moved into the deep peace of the Presence, out of the temptation of the mind into fidelity to Identity.

Silence, (pause) …

Whenever you run into a problem that you don't seem to be able to solve well even when doing what we talked about today, remember, you're thinking about a visible you instead of an invisible Self. When you come to the place where you know the invisible nature of all Being, those insoluble problems melt away. Invisible Self is the real Self. The permanent, the eternal, the deathless Self, now without problems and there is no second.

If you are going now to be with us later, suppose you spend another ten minutes and we'd like to make a little presentation to the Fosters. The idea emanated with Claire Balance and Lucy Beverage and Lucy, I believe has probably written a little poem, although I haven't read it or heard it and so, Lucy's going to make the presentation to the Fosters.

Class 30

If I Go Not Away

Herb: We're beginning today a very different level of this work. It's going to be very difficult.

It's going to require within you a very different kind of activity than you may have been used to. Up to now, you have been assimilating knowledge and to some degree, opening yourself to the Spirit but basically, the work for a long time remains learning more and more and more of the meanings that were given to us by the activity of Christ on earth in the form of Jesus.

There comes a time when the meanings are somewhat clear and after that, you're merely repeating more and more and mostly because the next step, the ascendancy, is the step that we don't know how to go about. It's so easy to memorize something and it's easy to practice principles. Even if you fail in the practice, at least you can practice them.

But now, we reach a point where it isn't enough to practice the principles themselves. We have to develop the faculty to receive another level of the teaching. Now, we have to practice to develop that faculty for without it we cannot receive a higher teaching.

And so, Jesus goes away. Even Jesus says, "There's nothing more I can do for you. I've got to leave. I cannot give you any more information. In fact, my presence here is a barrier. If I were to stay with you, the only thing that would happen is that you would keep leaning on me, the form and really there's nothing more that I can give you as a person. I can heal another cripple. I can take another person who's in the tomb and raise them out. I can open the eyes of another blind man. But what's the point of it? I can't do it for the whole world."

And so, now I've got to bring you into that place where you are Self-reliant; where everything you have seen Jesus do, you learn is within the realm of your doing and for you to do that, you must now make a very distinct effort in a different direction. That's why this is difficult. It breaks away from our normal pattern of behavior.

Now, let's just look at the beginning of this 16th chapter. Try if you will to get the feel, not of Jesus speaking to the disciples, although that appears to be what's happening. It is really the Spirit of God in you speaking to the disciples in you. Now, the disciples in you are represented by Peter, by John, by James. Each one is a conglomerate of different qualities so that you might say Christ is speaking to that in you which is emotion, emotional love, that in you which is intelligence, that in you which is integrity, that in you which is a desire for Truth. Those basic Divine qualities which are in you, not fully matured, are the disciples in you and Christ speaks to these Divine qualities or disciples in you.

Now, you sort of do this as if you were an actor or an actress on a stage. Instead of seeing an outer Jesus talking to disciples in antiquity, bring it into the now and see that the I of you is speaking to the remnants of human consciousness in you and there's also a you standing back watching this so that you're developing now another level of meditation. You're listening to I in you speak to the human sense qualities in you and really speaking past and through them to another level of yourself. And all of this you're standing back to be a witness of.

And as you do, you are learning that the human sense of you is the composite of all the disciples of Jesus. And this human sense of you is to be lifted up, each disciple within you to its own innate perfection and the Soul of you is speaking to these disciples so that there's no longer an outer activity. It is you having a talk with your

Self within yourself. I, the Soul of me, am speaking to the disciples within me, to teach them, to lead them, to give them information they can not get any other way, to break the fetters that bind them, to release them as a captive to the world mind, to remove the yolk of false thought that has made them seem limited. But I'm not doing this as a me. I'm doing this as an I. I am speaking to the disciples within me and you must now establish that

I-Consciousness which in this book appears to be Jesus speaking to disciples. This is what you do within your Self consciously.

I now speak to my disciples. And if you will hold that, you will see you have established two firmaments, the lower and the upper. The lower is the disciple or disciples in you and the upper is the I of you speaking from the upper firmament to the lower where the disciples are. And as you do this, you become more aware of I in you and ultimately, that will be the Consciousness you retain. That is the new level you will establish. I, in me, must guide these inner disciples of the sense mind, to take them out of the sense mind. I'm not seeking a human authority to do this. I, in me goes to the Father. I in me is the one with the Father. I in me is the Teacher. I in me is my true Consciousness. I in me can never leave me. I in me is here now to teach every facet of my humanhood the true identity of Being, the fullness of my own Self.

And now, let's hear His words because they are the words of I in you, to the disciples within you and if you will hold that upper firmament as you listen to the words, you will see you are establishing a new level of Consciousness, the Christ mind.

"These things have I spoken unto you," - the I, of you has spoken to the disciples within you - *"that ye should not be offended. They shall put you out of the synagogues: yea, the time cometh, that whosoever killeth you will think that he doeth God service. And these things will they do unto you, because they have not known the Father, nor me."*

Those qualities in you that will be battered and shattered and pressured by the world are being reassured that when they know You, they will know You and the Father and they will find a new kind of protection, a new immunity. The more you become "I conscious" now, the more you'll find that every quality within you will borrow from that I Consciousness and find its own peace, its own way to grow, its own way to fulfill Itself. The capacity of Love within you will expand to the capacity of I. The capacity of Intelligence within you will expand to the capacity of I. Every limited, finite human capacity in you as it becomes conscious of I within you, will expand to the fullness of I. Human intelligence will become Divine wisdom. Human limitation will become Divine un-limitation. I in the midst of you am the assurance that this is so. It is I speaking apparently as Jesus, but I in the midst of you speaking to all of the qualities that you are.

"But these things have I told you, that when the time shall come, ye may remember that I told you [of them]. And these things I said not unto you at the beginning, because I was with you. But now I must go away to him that sent me; and none of you asketh me, Whither goest thou? But because I have said these things unto you, sorrow hath filled your heart. Nevertheless I tell you the truth; It is expedient for you that I go away: for if I go not away, the Comforter will not come unto you; but if I depart, I will send him unto you. And when he is come, he will reprove the world of sin, and of righteousness, and of judgment: Of sin, because they believe not on me; Of righteousness, because I go to my Father, and ye see me no more; Of judgment, because the prince of this world is judged. I have yet many things to say unto you, but ye cannot bear them now."

Now, if you've managed to hold on to the upper I, you have found another level of yourself which ultimately is the pathway to heaven. And today, we are going to live in that upper level a little more than we have in the past.

We have here a man named Jesus telling his disciples that he is leaving them for their own good. And now, we want to see that he is leading them into this upper level of themselves. His real secret is that I, Jesus am going away but I, Christ, am remaining with you. The form is leaving but not the Spirit and of course, all of this symbolic of you in your change of consciousness from form to Spirit. The belief in form goes away and is replaced by the conscious awareness of Spirit. If Jesus does not go away, faith of the disciples remains in the flesh, in the form, in the person. As long as you are in a material consciousness depending on the material world for sustenance, as long as material consciousness does not go away, you cannot find your Spiritual consciousness. And so, in the outer, the Master moves away from the disciples that they, losing dependence on the outer, are forced to discover the inner and we are to follow that example, to drop dependence on the outer that we may discover the inner.

And now, we're going to look at his words very closely. *"These things have I spoken unto you, that ye should not be offended."*

The key to the word "offended" is given in Isaiah. He says that Christ is a stumbling block to evil, an offence to all that is unlike God. And Christ is saying to the disciples, that "I am an offence to evil. Evil shudders when I approach. Evil attacks when I approach. Always, when I approach, evil is offended but I have taught you the Truth of your being so that when I approach to you, there is no evil in you to be offended. I have taught you these things so that you will not be offended because only evil is offended and there is no evil in my disciples."

And so, we learn again that we are offended only when there is a sense of evil in us. When we have reached that level which is not offended by evil, it is because the Light within has been touched. He has brought them to a place where they can know the non-reality of evil and therefore, they are not offended by evil.

"I have taught you the Truth of your identity, the Truth of the presence of God where you stand so that when the appearance of evil comes to you, it cannot offend you because you know the Truth."

Now, last week we had a seven-point program. God is always present and there is no other presence. Where God is present, the power of God is present. Where the power of God is present, there is no power of evil present. Finally, fourth, because the power of God is always present, there is no present power to cause evil and therefore, evil cannot exist. It can only appear but it cannot exist and evil is everything that we would consider wrong; every disease, every problem, every error, everything that is unlike God. And so, evil not existing but only appearing, the fifth was it is temptation, the sixth was to observe the temptation without accepting it in the knowledge that only God power is and finally, to rest in that assurance until you feel that absence of the power of evil, that absence of that pressure of evil, that Peace ultimately which lifts you above the illusion of evil.

Now, watch how subtly these seven points change as you accept I, in you. I is the level from which you meditate now. You rest in the I of your Being. That's not a human person waiting for God to do something anymore. That's I, the Spirit of God itself. That is my name and I rest in I.

I, the Spirit of God am present. That's your first principle; only instead of God being present, I, the Spirit of God is my name and I am present and where I, the Spirit of God is, the power of God is, the power of I is present. The I of you is present and it is the Spirit of God. The I of you is the power of God and it is present. And therefore, there is no evil power present because I, the Spirit of God am present and therefore there is no evil present because I, the Spirit of God is present.

Now, when you come to your fifth point, evil appears only for one reason. It only appears because you're not living in I, the Spirit of God am present. And it's also your remedy for that appearance. That appearance of evil is the subconscious denial within you that you are I, the Spirit of God and that I of You is present. All evil that appears in your life is a denial of the I consciousness that you should be in.

In your sixth point, you are to reject the evil. Now, the sixth point changes. Instead of rejecting the evil, you accept I am the Spirit of God. That is the rejection of the evil. The acceptance of the evil is the rejection of I am the Spirit of God and conversely. But I am the Spirit of God. There's no evil where the Spirit of God is. In my own I am Spirit, I rest.

Now, you make these seven points again using I the Spirit of God wherever you had God until you begin to feel there is a level called I, the Spirit of God which is my true Soul consciousness and when I rest there, I am leaving the world mind. I am breaking the karma of the world mind. I am breaking the belief that I am limited to a human mind. I am stepping out of the personal sense of mind, into the I mind, the higher level, and resting there.

And the reason this is difficult is because we're used to thinking with the personal mind making decisions with the personal mind and the personal mind is separated from God. I, the Christ mind, this mind that you are touching, I am your only mind and I go to my Father. I am one with God. I synchronize you with the Infinite. When you rest up in the upper firmament of I Consciousness, you are synchronized with the Infinite. You transcend evil just by being there. It has no place to go in your Consciousness. We are learning to have that mind which was in Christ Jesus which transforms our earthly life.

Jesus is going away but I, Christ remain. Jesus goes away that you may discover that I, Christ is the identity of Jesus and that as I, Christ dwell in Jesus,, I, Christ dwell in you, that everything Jesus did on the earth, I, Christ did where he appeared and I, Christ who did these things am your Self ready to do these same things where you are - if you will dwell in me. As you develop the capacity to make the great shift from the mind of the personal self to I, the Christ mind in you, every miracle that walked upon this earth where a human body seemed to be in some form of limitation, I removed and I am ready to do that work again and again and again through any individual on the earth who will abide in I, here, now. Have that mind which was in Christ Jesus and that mind knows that no evil is present where I am.

There are no intermediaries. There's no one to pray to. There's no clergyman who can go to God for you. When you do that, you are denying that I am the Spirit of your own Being. This is your Kingdom and you must live in it to be under the government of God.

"These things have I told you that you would not be offended, that evil would not stimulate you into reaction or belief, that you would rest in I, the Spirit of God, present now, knowing that where I, the Spirit of God is realized, accepted as ever present, as functioning, as all Power."

Evil is only a false appearance without substance. This was the heritage from which we all turned away when we came into form into the personal sense of mind. But nobody can ever take it away from us. The power of the Christ mind in us is ever ready to reveal that it is the miracle worker, the Father within.

This is what we all share. No one gives it to us. We learn that we were in this Christ mind before the world was. We have ever walked this earth in it unaware of it but now Jesus, to his own disciples says, "This mind that I have shown on this earth is your mind, too and you won't believe it until I walk away and you have to find this mind and so, I am walking away. I am removing your crutches."

You cannot lean on Jesus anymore but you won't understand this until, for a short time, you have been forced to live without the outer Jesus, without the material consciousness. When you leave this personal sense of mind, you're like the disciples, stranded without Jesus, wondering what's going to happen next but in that moment, in that gap, the Christ in you is rising. The awareness will suddenly come forth and you will discover what you can discover no other way. You need no might. You need no power to remove the evils in your life. You need no force. You need no material effort of any kind.

If you were to try to remove those evils, you would be leaning on Jesus, leaning on the material form, the material power, the material weapon or the mental method.

You need no might or power of mind or body to remove evil from your life but rather, to let the need for a material power go away. And this is where the difficulty comes, the confidence to turn instead to the higher level of your own consciousness, I; and know that I, as of old, dissolve every seeming error with no need for physical power or mental power on your part. I reveal the nothingness of all evil in your life. I reveal the nothingness of error. I reveal the non-power of all that you had thought was limitation or lack. In other words, I am a new faculty. The old faculty, the personal sense of mind, saw the evils because it could not perceive the Reality.

"I, your Christ mind, I perceive that which the human mind could not perceive. I perceive the disciples in you at their full, complete, unlimited potential, realized. I perceive the fullness of your Power. I perceive the fullness of your Harmony. I perceive the fullness of your Love. I perceive the fullness of your Abundance and I perceive it because I, the Christ mind of you, walk now here in the Kingdom and I bring forth from the Kingdom that which I perceive. I externalize into the outer that which I perceive in the invisible Kingdom here now. I make the Word flesh. I send the Holy Ghost to do these things. I am the power of Grace within you and instead of removing evils, I reveal they never were there."

This is the level from law to Grace, from Jesus to Christ, from physical power to Spiritual power. That's why it's so necessary for Jesus to withdraw from the disciples that they find their own Spiritual power instead of resting on his. That's why you must withdraw from the personal mind to find your own Spiritual power instead of resting on that mind which receiveth not the things of God.

And so, your work is cut out for you. There's no Jesus can do it for you or anyone else. If you want to walk on the waters of Truth there must be a switch, a shift, a change and it's a conscious change from the thinking human mind to the awareness that I'm in the wrong level of myself. The thinking human mind will just go so far. It can read all the Bibles in the world and just go so far. But I've got to break the barriers and I cannot do it with this thinking mind. And so, consciously I rest that here where I appear to be, is the invisible Spirit of God. Its name is I and I have disciples within me and I am going to train these disciples. I'm going to bring every quality I have up to the level of Divinity by refusing to accept any other level and always then there is this meditation in which I rest in the I-ness of my Being. There's never a person meditating. I'm resting in the I-ness of my Being. Somehow, I'm less aware of form, less aware of the world, less aware of a desire or a need, simply resting in I.

I am the light of God. I am the invisible presence of God. I must rest in that I, until the very invisible atmosphere seems to be moving through you.

You're not cramming a human brain with facts. You're absent from the brain. You're absent from the human sense of self. You're surrendering to I. You're almost out of this mind universe and there's a great gap there between the mind universe and the Soul universe, a vast interval. You're leaving one and haven't yet found the other and that's the journey within that you must take.

You know when you're thinking out of a human mind and that's not the Christ way. The Christ way is to think out of the Christ mind for the Christ mind is the expression of Divine will. Jesus couldn't do this for the disciples. He could meditate with them. He could correct them. He could lift them Spiritually but he could never take them into Christ Consciousness while they thought of him as a human form, as a person, even a God-endowed person, even a Messiah. You can never do this while you think of yourself as a human form, as a person, any more than they could thinking of Jesus as a person.

There must be an acceptance that I, the Spirit of God, is my name and identity and then you give yourself, all of you, to that I. You surrender to your Self and you rest in that meditation and you let little I die in the I that you are - many times. That is how we interpret Jesus' departing from the disciples. The surrender of your form, your person, your humanhood, all concepts about it to the knowledge of the I that You are. You're developing your I Consciousness.

There is no feeling of great personal strength or of any major achievement. It's mostly a giving up and it is slowly replaced by receiving, multiplied and running over that very self that you gave up in a new way. What you give up, you receive to overflowing.

We're giving ourselves to the government of God so that Grace may replace the struggles of the human mind and in so doing, we do it not on faith that is blind but on the knowledge that I, the Spirit of God that indwells me, is present now and I'm accepting its Presence as the power of God where I stand, as the mind of God where I stand. I'm accepting God presence as the I that I am and all that God is, here I am. This is your transformation in Consciousness and from your own experience, you will discover that if you do this frequently, you will develop an awareness of it and it will in some way communicate so that you have a conscious knowledge that there is present where you are, a living Spiritual Being called I and you will know that this is your Infinite twin. It is the twin of you, the twin of this appearance called form and you will learn to let this twin guide you in the form until you one day, will be less conscious of the form, until the very twin you have accepted, you learn to be your very Self.

We all have an infinite twin called Christ. Our unawareness of it is what causes the problems of our human lives. Your twin Christ is my twin Christ. We all have the same twin. But each one has that twin and until we find I, Christ, the twin, I the human being, is a separated mortal subject to the law of mortality.

Jesus must go away. Yes, even Jesus must go away. Your mortal self must go away that your immortal Self may be lived in consciously. And you do not do this except through consciously living in the Christ mind which knows no evil, which knows only the presence of Power ever functioning. This is your break with yesterday, the break with all that is mortal.

"They shall put you out of the synagogues: yea, the time cometh, that whosoever killeth you will think that he doeth God a service."

Now, the synagogue means the holy place. And they who shall put you out of the holy place is not some external power. Yes, that's included but also there is this inner conflict. The self of you, the disciples in you and the I of you are always being besieged by the world mind in you. It is the world mind in you that is trying to put the disciples in you who are trying to learn the I-ness of Being out of the synagogue. The world mind in you which says, "How can you be sure?" The world mind in you which tries to ostracize the disciples for trying to learn the Truth and wants to cast them out. This is speaking again about the inner conflict between the Spirit and the flesh, the doubts, the uncertainties, the failures, when we think we have missed the way. The disciples in you are being forewarned, "This will happen. Expect it. Expect hostility. Expect difficulties. Expect opposition."

But always remember that opposition, hostilities, persecution is the myth of the world mind. All opposition is an image in the mind. There is no real opposition. There is no real tribulation. All that happens to the human happens in the mind and externalizes where the form appears. The worst that can happen to you is always happening in the mind and when you're in the I mind, instead of the personal mind, you find it doesn't happen. That's the point of the transition in Consciousness. In the I mind, that which happened in the human mind does not happen because the I mind is your secret place. That is the miracle of the change in Consciousness.

All that seems so difficult to our human mind vanishes when we attain the level of the Christ mind and that is why it's worth the effort consciously to continue to step out of the human mind whenever it occurs to you and to develop the habit of pattern that enables you to practice this so frequently that living in the Christ mind instead of the human mind becomes more possible for you.

The Christ mind is always I, the I that is speaking to the disciples in you and that's how you can re-establish it. The moment you start thinking of the I that is speaking to the disciples in you, you hold yourself at that level. I am that I speaking to the disciples in me. I'm not the disciples. I am the I, teaching the disciples. That's your Christ mind and that's where you try to stay. You find the evils of the world have no personal mind in you through which they can enter your Consciousness. When they squeeze through this I mind dissolves them. However difficult it is, it falls into a groove later which enables you to stay there. Now this is what the disciples in the Bible are going through with Jesus.

"These things will they do unto you, because they have not known the Father, nor me."

Not knowing Christ, which is the activity of God in an individual, we are persecuted by the world. But when we know Christ, then the world's persecutions do not come nigh us and the world persecutes us because it does not know Christ within itself and therefore, does not receive the influx of Divine love. The world, having no Divine love flowing through its Christ Consciousness because it is in human consciousness, it can only externalize that which is in its consciousness. It being Spiritually barren, that's what it shows forth. And so, there's no Divine fruitage in the world. But if you are not Spiritually barren, that is what will come through you. Your Divine Consciousness will bring forth its Divine fruitage and it is independent of the world's Spiritual barrenness.

The beauty of the I Consciousness is that it does not depend upon the world. It draws everything from the invisible Kingdom of God even when the appearance is that you are in some way limited. There is no power to keep you in that state when you are in the I Consciousness. Nothing can limit the I for the I does not depend on the world. It draws from the Father. That's why the Master says, *"I am the bread of life. Whoever drinketh of My waters will never thirst."* The I of you is independent of the world.

Now, when I said you had to sort of be an actor or an actress, it was because you have to step back and to re-establish I, you have to see I in you teaching the disciples in you and that's how you get back to I. At least it's one of the ways.

"But these things have I told you, that when the time shall come, ye may remember that I told you [of them.] And these things I said not unto you at the beginning, because I was with you."

Now, let's suppose that a year or two ago, you had a Spiritual experience and somehow since that time, that particular experience never has recurred. Let's say one day, you looked at the grass and it was on fire in your consciousness. It was the greenest green you ever saw. Or one day, unbeknownst to you, out of nowhere, some force prevented you from being hurt by an automobile. Incidents that you never forgot. Now, there will come a time when the confidence engendered by those incidents will be needed by you. There'll be a time when you would need confidence and the remembrance of those incidents, in a flash, will give you the confidence you need at this very moment, even though they happened years ago. We're all sustained somehow by the flashback to another incident which in some way was miraculous to us and carries us through this particular moment of stress.

And so, Jesus says, *"These things I have told you, now so that when the time comes you will remember that I said them."*

There will come a time of doubt, when we grow faint but by living in the I Consciousness, you will build a backlog of experiences so that when the time comes for an even greater step, this backlog-of-experiences will serve as a source of inspiration and courage for you to take that greater step. Maybe you have already experienced a tragedy and yet for some strange reason, in that tragedy you developed a calm, a sort of awareness that this will pass and that you, not even knowing why except that that appeared to you in consciousness that somehow you could come through this. In the middle of all the turbulence there was this inner tranquility.

Someone recently told me that as he was transferred from jobs and didn't quite know what was happening to him and was going home to another city, suddenly he was aware of something independent of his personal self, saying, "That city isn't your home. No city is your home. Your home is everywhere." And while he was in this state of wondering what would happen to him, changing jobs or losing one, going home and not being sure what would be there, this inner Peace, this tranquility established itself without his conscious thinking telling him that home was everywhere and he lost all fear of the momentary sense of being misplaced or having no place or not knowing where he belonged. He knew he belonged everywhere.

Now, that experience will some day be very useful to him and I'm sure that experience only came to him because previously other experiences must have come building up to this one.

Now, as we live in the I Consciousness, these experiences come. They steal in. In a moment when ye think not, the bridegroom cometh and something from the Infinite is brought into your experience and you find yourself temporarily freed from the world mind in such a way that a Peace is established. It doesn't matter what's around you, a confidence is established. It may only seem like a second, a very fleeting one but you know there is a force at work. You're really finding your higher Self then.

Now the Christ in us is always doing this. "Before you ask, I shall answer. Before you ask, I go before you to prepare the way. The Father knoweth your needs."

And if we are sensitized enough to live in I, our antennas begin to pick up from the Infinite Invisible those things we need for the moment and everything we find that we need appears in Consciousness at the right time. The disciples had been sufficiently prepared in the outer.

"These things I have told you" but he said, *"because I was with you…. These things I said not unto you at the beginning, because I was with you."*

We have all been privileged without knowing it, of having I with us throughout all of our lifespans. Something has protected you and sustained you though you knew it not. The disciples were protected and sustained by the very presence of Jesus because it was the invisible I. It was always with them. Now, it says to them, "I was with you but now that I am not going to be with you visibly, I want you to know that I am still with you invisibly." You see how that is a teaching to us that always the invisible Christ is with us even though we don't see it? It became visible to them and then became invisible to show them that it was there. First, to show it was there and then to disappear and still be there. And they were to learn to depend on the invisible Christ as much as they depended on the visible Jesus.

You never see anything about the disciples being sick, do you or worried about money or how they're going to eat their next meal or where they were going to sleep? Because they always had visible Jesus with them. They weren't too worried about anything it seems. They could always turn to him and his very Presence was their immunity. And now, he says, "When I am not here, you're just as immune. Didn't you know that the power of immunity is in You? I showed it to you outwardly. Now, you're going to find it inwardly." And so, to the disciples in you, the Christ says, "Depend on your Spiritual immunity. It is always working. You are immune to evil but you don't know it. You are immune to death but you don't know it. You are immune to everything that this world calls error but you don't know it because you do not know the invisible Christ of your Being which is your immunity. And so, I, Christ visibly disappear for you to find the invisible Christ which is your immunity."

And so, we listen and we learn that where I am, the Reality of me is all that is here and it is immune to every evil in this world and the only way I can experience that immunity is to make the step from the personal mind to the Christ mind. In my Christ mind, I will see and feel and experience my immunity from the evils of the world.

"But now I go my way to him that sent me; and none of you asketh me, Whither goest thou? But because I have said these things unto you, sorrow hath filled your heart."

He could not share with them where he was going or how he would get there. They knew nothing of the events that were to follow. The idea of crucifixion entered nobody's mind. Where was he going? All they knew that was he was going. And they were worried about it. And they were sorrowful. When you lose your dependence on material power, on mental power, you are in the position they were in. We depend on our bank account. We depend on our automobile. We depend on various human, physical, material ways of doing things. We wouldn't know how to operate without them. We don't know any other way. And yet, along comes the Christ and says, "Well, I'm the other way."

— End of Side One —

"Can you travel through the atmosphere invisibly like I do? Can you make invisible loaves and fishes come into visibility? I can. Can you calm the tempest? I can. Can you open the eyes of the blind? I can. Then, what's the good of all your material powers if they can't do these things that I can do and I am your Self? I am your body. I am your mind and I am trying to teach you to rely on this I, Christ in you to do these things."

And so, it may seem difficult to give up your material ways of doing things as it is for the disciples to give up their dependence on their leader. He says, "I'm going away." And that's exactly why he's going away, so that they will not depend on their leader. That's why we give up our material desire for physical powers, mental powers, defenses because we learn to rest on, not the false sense of life, but the invisible power of the Spirit which can do all things.

"I live, yet not I…. Christ strengtheneth me….I can do all things through Christ."

And so, you're surrendering your accustomed mode of doing things for the way of doing the Christ way and you have to put your total trust in I, Christ by learning to live with I, Christ day by day. You're letting Jesus go away, knowing that Christ is not going away. You're letting material consciousness go away knowing that Spiritual Consciousness is present and will take its place. This is learning to live Spiritually instead of materially.

It was unthinkable for the disciples to live without Jesus near them but yet, it was the only way that they could come into Christ Consciousness. It's unthinkable for the world not to live materially and yet, it's the only way we could come into Christ Consciousness. Now, nobody said, "Get on a cliff and jump off." Nobody said, "Do it overnight." The teaching is to rest in the Christ mind day by day by day by day until you know what it means to rest in the Christ mind; until the Christ mind shows you the way. It's a gradual Spiritual evolution out of one way of life into another; out of the world into the invisible, finished kingdom of God.

Why would He disappear from them if he loved them? His loving them must have had something to do with disappearing from them. He did it because he loved them, to free them from dependence on outer aids, to make them self-reliant in Christ, to teach us to be self-reliant in Christ. That means whatever ails you, whatever material aid you wish to remove that which ails you, is hanging on to the coattails of Jesus. Same thing. You must learn to turn it over to I, Christ in you.

And, if you're practicing your seven steps, it's very simple. I, Christ am present. The power of I, Christ is here. The evil power cannot exist where I, Christ power is and therefore, there's no evil power here. It isn't here and therefore, there's no power here to cause the evil I'm suffering from. I know, I know how serious it appears but there is no power here to cause it.

The self-assumed power to cause the evil is the deception of the world mind in you. It's just the evidence that you're not in the I, Christ mind. That's all that evil is. It's the sign that we're not in the I, Christ mind. And the remedy? The I, Christ mind is all that's here. There is no other mind. There is only one mind. There is no other mind. The mind that perceives evil is no mind. It is the betrayer, the deceiver, the liar from the start. I'm looking at evil with a mind that isn't here and that's why I see evil. In the stillness of that mind that isn't here, the Christ mind says, "Behold, the Son of God, immaculate, perfect as the Father." In the stillness of the human mind, the deceiver can no longer betray us. In the stillness of the human mind, I, Christ reveal the Father's Son, - whole, complete, unseparated, living now, here under the government of God, perfect as the Father.

When you let the human mind go away, you're letting Jesus go away. You're becoming less form conscious, less mind conscious. You're not leaning on someone else. You're not letting the world mind fool you. Jesus is saying to his disciples, "You know me as a form, a man, come to bring you a kingdom on earth, an earthly kingdom but you're wrong. I am not a form. I am not a man. I am I, Christ, the Spirit of God and so this form must go. And yet, the very Power that you have experienced through me on this earth will remain here and continue to do the very same work when the form goes because the form never was here. Only the I, Christ was here which you looked at and called the form called Jesus. And when the form is not here and the work is still being done, you will know that I, Christ am still here doing the mighty works."

And then the great illumination, if the form of Jesus wasn't here but I, Christ was and still doing the works, what about my form? If I'm I, Christ, what about my form? Is it here? Is it really here and is I, Christ here too? If the form of Jesus goes away but I, Christ remain, isn't that all that was ever there? Isn't that what he's showing them, I, Christ is all that's ever here. You're seeing an image in mind called Jesus where I, Christ stands.

"But I've told you God is my Father and your Father and I Jesus can look at you and see only I, Christ standing where you see your own form." I, Jesus Christ can see I, Christ where you stand. I see no cripple. I see no blind man. I see no person. I see I, Christ, the Son of God and as you learn to live in I, Christ, I, Christ in you teaches you that that is the fullness of your Being. I, Christ teaches you that corporeality is an idea, a cosmic idea, that all person is, is cosmic idea where only I, Christ is. Without I, Christ mind, there is no way to know the Reality of Being.

Slowly, we're being led to rely less and less and less on human methods and on the human mind and to know that as we rely less on the human mind, however uncomfortable it seems at times, we are being led into the perfect Reality of our Being experienced. He's telling them these things so they will not be troubled, so they can endure difficulties, knowing it is for the good of their own Being that they must go through this change from sense consciousness to Christ Consciousness. He's told them it's not an easy way. He's told us it's not an easy way but he's told us where it leads to. It leads to the Life which is without end. It leads to the actual experience of the perfect, permanent Self and he has told us that the Kingdom of Heaven is here on earth to be experienced now, within you.

The great moment of Jesus announcing that he's leaving his disciples shows that all visible work on earth has been done. There's nothing for him to do in the visible anymore. His work is complete. And you reach the point where all human authority for you is no longer necessary. No human teacher is necessary. Christ within becomes your accepted Self. Here you are disciples, learn that we must go to Christ within ourselves in order to follow the Master's teaching and that Christ within ourselves train the disciples within us, until every Divine quality is brought forth.

Now, you may feel for a while that you really don't know where your feet are standing when you're going through this because your mind doesn't function the same way. It loses its capacity to run you in the same way it had in the past. It loses some of its authority. And it's a strange feeling but also with it comes the reassurance that because it's a strange feeling, something is happening. I am transferring power from the false sense of mind to the Christ mind and I feel something happening as I do that. It's an uncertain stage but a necessary one to go through.

"Nevertheless I tell you the truth; It is expedient for you that I go away: for if I go not away, the Comforter will not come unto you; and if I depart, I will send him unto you."

(Looks like we're going to skip the intermission, if it's all right with you.)

"I will send him unto you."

Now, the Comforter that he will send is the Holy Ghost. And who is sending the Holy Ghost? Christ is sending the Holy Ghost and therefore, we have this pattern. God, the Father is Christ in Jesus and Christ in Jesus is one with the Father, the Father is in Christ, Christ is in the Father. And then because Christ is in the Father, the activity of God comes through Christ, the will of God comes through Christ, the power of God comes through Christ and becomes the invisible activity of Christ which is the Holy Ghost. That is the Christ sending the Comforter. The activity of Christ comes through the disciple as the invisible Holy Ghost including within it the full Power and Will and Love and all the qualities of the Father. These are the new disciples.

This activity is the Holy Ghost which is called the Comforter which is sent by the Christ and when you depart from the outer world of material aids, material means and turn to the Christ in you, then, through the Father, through the Christ comes the invisible Holy Ghost to you to do what you were not able to do with human power or with a human mind. The miracle of the Holy Ghost transforms and brings the Word into flesh and you find the power of Christ in you is the activity of Christ called the Holy Ghost and it does the miracle work that you were laboriously struggling to accomplish in your own limited, human way. All this from I consciousness, living in I consciousness.

You let material means and powers go away, represented by Jesus and then Christ in you is where you live and Christ in you sends the Comforter, the Holy Ghost which performs the Divine will in you which is what Jesus in the visible had done to show the power of the invisible Christ. He's saying that "Everything you have seen Jesus Christ do, the Holy Ghost in you can do and greater works if you believe on I, Christ in you." We're seeing that these were not miracles of yesterday at all and that the finished invisible Kingdom of God is ever present here now.

(Maybe it would be better if we did take a break, so I think we'll do that right now and then come back in five minutes.)..

"And when he is come," meaning the Comforter, *"He will reprove the world of sin, of righteousness and of judgment. Of sin, because they believe not on me."*

Now then, there is still in the world false righteousness and false judgment and they exist because the world is still either denying the existence of God or depending on Jesus to do something about it. Here's Jesus trying his best to show them why he must leave and the world is insisting that Jesus is coming back. Jesus is saying, "The only way you'll ever learn the Truth is if I go away." And the world says, "Well, if you've got to go away, we'll wait till you get back here." He says, "If I go away, I will send the Comforter." Not Jesus Christ, the Comforter, the activity of Christ, the Ghost, that which is unexplainable to the human sense mind because it's like that individual who was displaced from his job and going back home and suddenly it occurred to him, independent of his own thought, over and above everything he was thinking, this invisible Presence saying, "Everywhere is your home." That was the Ghost. That said to him and did for him more than any human teaching can do and it was a comfort because it was the Truth. The only real Comforter is the Truth.

And sin, will be reproved, and righteousness will be reproved, and judgment will be reproved and the importance of the dissolving of sin and false righteousness and false judgment is that they are three barriers to what Christ Consciousness is leading us to.

First, sin is removed by a very simple process, the knowledge that it doesn't exist. Righteousness, if you remember, our human sense of righteousness, is a very limited thing. It's a self-satisfied feeling that I'm doing the right thing. It's a stagnancy in our own self- conceit. We feel we're being righteous and of course, that's a human righteousness and it may be fine on a human level but Divine righteousness is totally different. If you are being righteous in your own human way, that doesn't mean you're doing God's will. It means you're doing what you think is right and it may be nice, it may be moral. It may be helpful but he is revealing here another level of consciousness and a new kind of righteousness; a righteousness which is fulfilled only by Christ, that the human sense of righteousness is never sufficient, that Divine will can only be fulfilled in Christ and Christ fulfillment is righteousness. There is only Christ righteousness.

We see how easily two countries can each think they're righteous and end up on a battlefield and they're both so convinced that they're both righteous. In Divine righteousness, the will of the Father is functioning through Christ in you as the invisible Holy Ghost and his Divine plan in you is fulfilled, not your human sense idea of what it ought to be. We are lifted above all human error, human judgment, human miscalculation. We are lifted above the obvious paradox of a human, finite mind trying to fulfill the Infinite will. It cannot do it. And so, we need the Christ mind to fulfill the Infinite will and only that is righteousness.

And therefore, the Comforter must come unto you. If we're still waiting for Jesus to come back, what we're doing is we're throwing the whole teaching out the window because he already left two thousand years ago that we might receive the inner Christ. And when we receive the inner Christ, we are lifted above the belief in the presence of sin. All evil on this earth disappears in the presence of Christ. It is powerless and so, there's no flood to drown, no fire to burn. There's no disease to kill. Sin is reproved. The presence of Christ removes the power of sin by revealing that where Christ is present, sin does not exist. And it removes the false, human, limited, finite sense of righteousness that because I think it's right, it's right. And it brings in a new, higher level of government. It brings in the fourth dimension which is unlimited dimension and then Divine will is done in you. And that is Divine righteousness.

And then because you have the Christ mind, the activity of the Christ in you, you don't look out and make false judgments. You don't look out and judge this to be wrong and that to be wrong. You can look at everything wrong and say it's only wrong because I am looking at it through the separated human mind. It really can't be wrong because Christ in you reveals that all that is ever present is God. And only Christ in you reveals this.

Now, look carefully and see this. If Jesus must go away that we find the Christ and Jesus is saying, "Even Jesus can't be your intermediary any longer." You see the fatal error of going to a clergyman as your intermediary? Or going to a psychiatrist as your intermediary? Or going to any human being as your intermediary when Jesus himself says, "I can't even be your intermediary?" You see the fallacy of religion believing that it is our intermediary with God when Jesus says "Not even me?" Not even me. But Christ in You is all that can go to God for you.

And so, of course, that takes the complete foundation out of religion. And that's why religion has to teach that Jesus is coming back. Now you could call it ignorance or you could call it a lie. The result is the same. It's the total reversal of the teaching of Christ. There is no human intermediary between man and God because God is the Selfhood of the individual who thinks he needs an intermediary. Now, when he knows who he is, he understands why Jesus had to go away from the disciples.

Now, this is automatic. When the Comforter comes unto you, the activity of Christ in you removes the false judgments, false human righteousness and the false belief that sin exists, that evil and error are real. And this is necessary because this isn't the end. When this is removed, then you are ready for the mystical marriage. You are ready for your Soul to marry your Spirit. This is all the purification, the preparation for the great event when there is union.

Now, on earth, we have the human birth and it occurs through man and woman and all of this is an imitation of the actual union of the Soul and the Spirit for in the union of the Soul and the Spirit, you are witnessing the reality of union and in that union, Christ is born in your Soul. And the birth of Christ in your Soul is that which appears on earth to human sense as a birth of a child.

The union of man and woman and the birth of a child is the cosmic counterfeit of the union of Soul and Spirit and the birth of

Christ in you. This is the mystical marriage that is being led to by the withdrawal of the material aids, the outer, visible, external Jesus that man may turn to his inner Self to be led through the Spirit to the Reality of Being, to the marriage of Soul and Spirit, to the birth of Christ which lifts us into the next plane of Life. When you live in your I Consciousness, you are preparing the way for this ultimate attainment.

Now, I want to give you your assignment and it has to do with the next verse which is verse 12. *"I have yet many things to say unto you, but ye cannot bear them now."* This is what he said to his disciples after three years of being with them, things that he couldn't say to them even at that level. Why? Because they couldn't understand. There was no way for them to relate to what he had to say.

Now, you should know some of the things that he couldn't tell them and the reason is they had no way of anticipating the events that lay ahead. You have. You know what lay ahead and you know what happened. If he had told them certain things before crucifixion, resurrection and ascension, there would be no way for them to understand. For you know that crucifixion, resurrection and ascension is what the Bible says happened and therefore, on the basis of that, you should be able to know and through your understanding of the Infinite Way message what were some of the things he couldn't tell them at that time, which he would be able to tell them after the ascension, after the resurrection, when they had gone through that experience, seeing the return of the same form that disappeared. And this is your assignment then for your own benefit, not mine. Make a list to yourself. What were some of the things that Jesus couldn't tell His disciples at this particular point which is verse 12 of John 16?

"Ye cannot bear them," he said, meaning you have no capacity in you to understand them but later, he's going to tell them these things and why? Because they will then have had the capacity to receive them and what would that capacity be? It will be their new Christ faculty developed and therefore, why are we studying to develop this

Christ faculty? Because we're at the level where in order to receive a higher teaching, we must build the faculty to receive it. Just as they could not receive more at that point, we are at the point where we cannot receive more until we are living in the conscious awareness of the Christ mind as my mind. And that's how you receive more because the next verse explains that.

"Howbeit when he, the Spirit of truth, is come, he will guide you into all truth: for he shall not speak of himself; but whatsoever he shall hear, that shall he speak: and he will shew you things to come."

Your new faculty receives from the Infinite that which you cannot receive in a human mind. Your new faculty has the capacity for direct cognition of God. Your new faculty has the capacity to receive inner revelation regularly. Your new capacity in Christ mind has the ability to be fed, taught by God direct - without Jesus, without an intermediary, without a clergyman, without a human teacher. For *"I go unto my Father"* and this faculty must be developed consciously and daily. It's the reverse of dying daily. It's the being born daily. Each day you're being born into Christ awareness dying to the mortal sense of self as you are born into the immortal awareness of Truth.

Now, in your list, don't be afraid to state those things which Jesus couldn't teach his disciples at that time even though it would be a list you wouldn't want to show to many of your friends because let's presume that he wanted to tell them that they did not have any life in their human form. Would you want to show that to a friend who didn't know anything about the message? Don't be afraid of what you think he couldn't tell them because that is what we must learn in order to make every step into real freedom. Those things that he couldn't tell them are the things that we must learn.

You found many of them in the writings of Joel Goldsmith. In fact, they're all there. But you may not have seen them even though they're there or something in you, the mind that refuses to be the Christ mind also refuses to look at some of these things. You'd rather pretend or defer that until some other day. But know the time has come and we're going to discuss those things next time and we're not going to flinch from them. We cannot avoid the Truth. The things that were so difficult to explain to his own disciples, you and I must learn because we are those disciples. And the way we're going to learn them is to be consciously in I, Christ, more often than we have been.

Now, today, you may have found your Self in I, Christ more than at previous meetings because always when we come to this message, we find that we are having Invisible help. I can assure you that the Invisible help is very bountiful and very real because we are continuing in the Word of Christ and the Father says, *"Continue in my word.... and you shall know the truth, and the truth will make you free."*

And so, as we come to that which the Christ commands of us, if we make the effort to obey, you find your Invisible help is lifting you up.

And now, to sum it up, every difficulty that we have entertained in this world has been on the level of the human mind. It matters not how great the difficulty, if it was a flood in the ocean and you were on a ship and you thought you were in that ocean, on that ship, that entire scene is happening in your mind, even though you personally believe you're there and the mind in which it's happening is the only place in which it's happening and if you were in the Christ mind you would discover that is the Truth. You cannot accept such a ridiculous statement if you're in a human mind.

But if you're in the Christ mind, you discover the Christ mind says to the storm, "Be still. It is I." That's the way of saying that the Christ mind reveals that that which is real to the human mind is not real to God and that which is real to the Christ mind is not real to the human mind or as Paul put it, *"The things of God are foolishness to man,"* and vice versa.

All of the things that have been wrong have been in our human mind and as we are lifted into the new dimension of Consciousness called Christ mind, we discover these things are not where we thought they were. That is the miracle - not healing, not performing miracles - the miracle is that in the Christ mind, you actually witness the Kingdom of God on earth and the Christ mind in you is the only witness of that Kingdom. That's why it's invisible to the human mind. That's our transition period at this point. That's what we're stepping into consciously, aware of what we're doing. That's Jesus going that we may find Christ within. You might say Jesus is saying, "I'm going to leave you but I'm not going away. I, who am going away is Jesus but I who am remaining is Christ."

For further study, you can look into the Mystical I and see "The Two Ways of I" in Joel's, I think it's his seventh chapter, "The Two Ways of I". I Jesus am going, I, Christ am remaining. That's the reason. You've got to watch this carefully, this I.

"I tell you the truth; It is expedient for you that I go away: for if I go not away, the Comforter will not come unto you; but if I depart, I will send him unto you."

It's not the same I all through there, you see. One I is Jesus and one I is Christ and you've got to read it carefully to see which is Jesus and which is Christ. Then you find that sometimes it's I Jesus talking and another time he is saying, "I, Christ will do this but I Jesus will do that" and then you see that I Jesus is the outer, I, Christ is the inner. And every time he's talking of the I, Christ, the inner, he's talking about I, Christ in you. I, Christ in you sends the action of the Holy Ghost, not I, Christ in Jesus. I, Christ in you sends the Holy Ghost because I, Christ in Jesus and I, Christ in you are one and the same. He's awakening us to the power of I, Christ in us.

We'll start at that point next time. It'll be chapter 16 from 12 and 13 verses on, I don't know how far we'll get. If any of you are wondering just how long this is going on, I will tell you this, that there may be a week or two lull when we take a little time off around Christmas, before or after, and the whole thing will continue right on up to Easter and we may even finish the book and finish John but we'll continue with the thing called the Kingdom of Heaven and the highlights of Joel's work right on up to Easter just so that we know where we're going. Now what we want to do by Easter is to be in this I Consciousness so perfectly that the Comforter in you is sending the activity of the Holy Ghost.

There's so much more to say but we'll leave it unsaid and I'm sure the Comforter in you will fill in many of the gaps.

Thanks again.

Class 31

Your Second Coming to Christ

Herb: Let us assume now that we can safely say that, "I may not show it to the world and may sometimes not be capable of sustaining it but I definitely am a disciple of Christ." And in recognition that we are disciples of Christ, we know what we're really saying deep down inside that "This is my identity." When we say we are disciples of Christ, we are acknowledging that at this moment in our consciousness we have not reached that level of fullness but we know that within us is contained every Divine quality.

Now, I'd like you to see that these Divine qualities in you are the disciples and then to see that these disciples in you, these Divine qualities are branches, so that one branch is Love, one branch is Harmony, one branch is Peace, one branch is Truth, one branch is Intelligence, one branch is Integrity and so on. All of the Divine qualities in you are branches and the question I would like to ask you is, "How do you intend to feed those branches to bring up the fullness within you of these Divine qualities?" You know they're there. You know that they are complete and full and nothing is withheld. You also know that they are not appearing in the fullness in your human experience. The question then is, "How do you feed them? How do you nourish them? How do you give them food and drink to make these qualities expand within you so that you can bring them into your living consciousness?"

Now, first, the human mind, being unaware of them, overlooks them and so, in our human way, in our human thought, in all our human methods and even in our human solutions we do not nourish these Divine qualities. Rather, we walk away from them by ignorance of their presence.

And so, the mind we see does not feed these qualities. It misses the mark and that's the nature of what is called sin. The mind cannot feed the Divine qualities. The mind cannot make them grow. The mind cannot even express them. And so, in us, these Divine qualities lie present but dormant, un-expressing in our experience. And so, we age, we wither because we starve the Divine qualities until we are barren and our intellects, then becoming barren of the Divinity within us finally cut us off completely and that is why we are called mortal beings.

Now, the Father says, "There's only one way to nourish the Divine qualities in you and you cannot do it. Your mind has no capacity."

The consciousness of God alone can nourish the Divine qualities in you. The consciousness of God in you nourishing the Divine qualities brings them to higher levels of expression, finally opening your consciousness to the Divine consciousness so that the qualities of the Father in you are now becoming recognized, acknowledged by your Consciousness which has been quickened by the Divine. And the qualities do not grow. Your conscious awareness of them grows and as you become more aware of these full qualities in you, you bring forth out of your invisible substance those qualities into expression on what is called this human plane.

The branches are fed by the Divine consciousness alone. No human consciousness can feed food or drink to the Divine qualities within you. And so, there is a necessity to evolve from the human consciousness to the Spiritual. This Spiritual evolution is when the awakened Soul brings forth that which was only a branch into bud and into flower, into expression within you and the Divine qualities in you show forth. Your Light shines forth through material.

And so, we find that there is a method to awaken our human sense of consciousness to the awareness of the Divine consciousness in us which alone can awaken all our disciples. And that method is the bridge between heaven and earth and its name is Christ.

In the beginning was Christ, the Word and the Word, the Christ was in the Father and the Father in Christ. And the Christ then in you is that Consciousness in you which is the Divine consciousness in you expressing which feeds and nourishes and sustains and energizes your consciousness into a oneness with the Divine so that you become aware of the Divine disciples in you and as your consciousness of these disciples in you increases, it appears to you to be fruitage.

Now, all that God is within you is there. Nothing will ever be added. The finished Kingdom of God is attained when you become aware of the Divine consciousness which is I in the midst of you.

And so, "I go away," says the Christ, "but I shall return. And there are things that I cannot tell you now because you cannot bear them. The reason you cannot bear them," says the Christ, "is because you have no awareness yet to receive the Divine consciousness. You're still praying to an external God. You're still hoping God will favor you in some way. You're still looking to outside powers. You're still unaware that the fullness of God is within you already and there's no way for the Divine Infinite to convey to the finite. It must be a gradual development. There must be an awakening called the Spirit of Truth in you and you must prepare the way for that Spirit of Truth for as it awakens you to the Divine consciousness in you, the hidden splendor is released.

Always, we are being led to the self-containment in Christ that we need seek nothing outside. In fact, to seek outside is to deny that we are self-contained.

The things we cannot bear are the things we are not prepared to understand. If someone says to you, "You're God," you cannot bear to hear that because you know you are not God and yet, Christ in you is God. And so, we're not prepared, we cannot bear to hear what we're not prepared to understand and that understanding must be expanded day by day until the Soul is opened up, until we are ready to hear the Word not just from the mouth of a person but to hear the Living Word within ourselves.

"The Spirit of Truth will come and teach you all things." And so, the promise is that the finished Kingdom of God will be opened up to you, that all that it contains will be revealed unto you when you receive the Spirit of Truth. That is the descent of the Dove. We are being prepared to receive the descent of the Ghost, of the Spirit, of the Dove, the awakened awareness that here where I stand is the living life of God. And it is I.

This preparation is the intensified activity of Spirit in us because Spirit is speaking not to Pharisees. This message is given to the disciple. And the Christ says, "I will return, not to the Pharisee - to the disciple." When the Pharisee becomes a disciple, he will hear the message, "I will return." And then we have to see what does this mean that, "I will return."

Now, the mystery of "I will return" has to go back to your Life before form. We have to see that we are being led to the understanding that each of us is immortal Being, that we are living Spirit and that birth was the first entrance into form, out of the immortal Self, through birth into form, into a sense of mortality, out of Immortality into the belief that I am mortal being. But only into the belief. The immortal Self is always your Self. We walk out into mortal sense of form through birth.

And so, birth is the beginning of mortality. Birth is the beginning of that which must die. Birth is actually the beginning of death and what we call death is simply the ending of death. Immortality remains as the Life behind the appearance called mortal form. Your immortal Spirit, your immortal Life remains present even though you entertain a concept called birth into form and a concept called human life. And the Christ says, "Now you're looking at your concept of a human life called Jesus and you can no longer hold on to that because there's no way to teach you beyond this point." And so, Jesus must go from your consciousness. And then, I, who will return, I am your awareness of your own immortal Self.

You will return to Christ. Christ will not return to you. The second coming is your return to Christ. The second coming is never Jesus returning to man. It is man returning to his own immortal Self. The going and the coming of Christ is always a statement of where we stand. When Christ goes away, that means we are losing our awareness of Christ. When Christ returns, that means we are increasing our awareness of Christ. When Jesus goes away, that means we are able to reach that pinnacle of human level which is the awareness that I am not a form. Jesus goes away just as Judas has to go away. Judas was the losing of the sense of corporeality in Jesus and in us and then Jesus going away, is the losing of the sense of human mind. First, the lower self, the corporeal sense and now, the human mind.

We no longer rest on the capabilities of the human mind. We let Jesus go away. We no longer seek an outside power to help us. We let Jesus go away. We seek no help from external sources. We let Jesus go away. We seek no protection. We let Jesus go away. And we are assured that even though Jesus goes away, I will return and the I that will return will be your conscious realization that your immortal Self, which is Christ in you, has never gone away. The second coming is the return to your own conscious awareness that you are immortal Being, that you are immortal Life. I, Christ who will return, never have left you but you will now be raised in consciousness to recognize that I am your Life. It was I that you departed from when you went into the sense of form, into birth. But I did not go away and now, you are returning to I, Christ as your identity and that is the second coming.

And so, we learn that there is a Spiritual evolution going on now. We have passed the Pharisee stage. We are the disciples. We are aware that the tree of Life within us is the Divine consciousness. We are aware that it feeds the Divine qualities in us and that as we rest in the knowledge that I am the Christ, the life of God here and now, we are the actual second coming. We are coming to Christ consciousness aware that the Christ that I am is the bridge between heaven and earth, the connecting link with the one Self which is God which is its only Son, the Christ, and which I am. We learn to feel at home in the acceptance of Christhood, in the acceptance that all Divine qualities in me have ever been present, that the finished Kingdom of God within me is I, the Divine consciousness, that the tree of life where I stand is my own Being, that I am the Life, the Spirit of God.

This is the place where we should be even though at the time Jesus spoke the words to the disciples, they could not bear to hear the many Truths that he still had to tell them. Two thousand years in time is not too long to wait but shall we wait another two thousand years to hear these things or are we ready to open our ears to face what we really know but what we at times feel somewhat reluctant to face?

The disciples were unaware that before them standing in the form called Jesus was the individuality of God. They could not know this. Nothing could prove it to them, no words. Crucifixion and resurrection were a way of proving to them that he was the individuality of God expressing. Crucifixion and resurrection proved to us that the individuality of God expressing is always omnipotent and the Christ says to us that, "I in the midst of you am the individuality of God." And we learn that the Christ in the midst of our own Being which is our Self is God individualized and is omnipotent now. It's taken two thousand years in time for us to be able to know this so well that we can look at a suffering universe and know it isn't happening.

I, in the midst of you is God. I, in the midst of you am Christ. I, Christ in the midst of you and I, God are one and the same. I am the Divine consciousness that waters, that feeds, that sustains all the Divine branches in you and when you step aside from the human mentality to let I in the midst of you do this work without intervention, without interruption, without interference, without a second self, without a second power, without all human thought beliefs that there is something besides I, Divine consciousness then those Divine branches in you will bear fruit and they will appear as the health of your countenance. They will give you more than worldly riches. They will give you Spiritual riches. They will give you more than worldly health; they will give you Spiritual health. But above all, they will give you more than a worldly sense of life. They will reveal to you that you are the eternal life of God. The eternal life of God is the final fruitage of the Divine qualities in you as your Being.

And so, our Spiritual pilgrimage, our evolution ever pushes us beyond all forms of seeking personal improvements, human betterments. Instead, we are drawing from the Infinite to our own infinite expression through the realization that I, Christ is my present, immortal Self. We can bear to hear what the disciples then could not bear to hear because we have had the advantage of the crucifixion, the resurrection, the teachers, the two thousand years of learning. We are those who stood there then who could not bear to hear and we are here now and we are hearing.

And so, he says, "The Spirit of truth must be prepared for. It will quicken you. It will open you. It will teach you all things. And he will show you things to come."

Now, the things to come in the 13th verse of John, 16th chapter, are not a revelation of the future. The things to come are a revelation of the now which is contained within your Being. Things to come are impossible because All is already. The revelation of the finished Kingdom of God within your own Being is the revelation of things to come. All that you will ever be, you are and the revelation of things to come is the revelation of all that You are. When the Spirit of Truth moves through you, that which is the invisible, finished Kingdom of fullness now is revealed to you. And this is the revelation of things to come.

All that is, is brought to your remembrance. The infinite intelligence of Christ in you, already contains a full record of all earthly time. It is revealed unto you. It expresses. It becomes your living experience. You find your roots in a different level of yourself than just the visible. The omniscience of the Christ becomes the omniscience of You for You and the Christ are one.

And so, we can see there is nothing to fear. We can see there is nothing to be afraid of in any way. We can see there is no limitation. We can see there is no lack. We learn to look beyond the visible densities of things into that which is there. And this is the revelation of things to come.

The expansion of your consciousness removes the sense of evil, the sense of error, the sense of all suffering and tribulation, revealing the full joy of the presence of the Spiritual Kingdom on earth as it is in heaven. But this does not happen until we have opened a way for the Spirit of Truth, the descent of the Dove. It doesn't happen unless you're preparing the way, unless you are accepting identity, accepting the Word, accepting the Truth, hearing with the inner ear, loving God supremely, not sharing that love but loving God in all supremely, recognizing God everywhere. Recognizing God everywhere is going to become our main task now. We're going to see that unless we recognize God everywhere, we are denying the presence of God and we're going to see what that means and what it involves because the Master has given us a perfect example of what it means in just a few verses.

"He shall glorify me: for he shall receive of mine, and shall shew it unto you."

Now, we know Christ is speaking that the Holy Ghost, the activity of Christ, will glorify Christ, who glorifies the Father. All things that Christ is, through the activity of the Ghost, become the activity of You because You are the Christ. And so the Ghost, the descent of the Dove, the Spirit of Truth nourishes those Divine branches in You and they bud. They appear. They flow into your Divine awareness of consciousness as your Being and what is in your Divine consciousness then manifests in your experience as the flower, the fruitage, the expression, indivisible of your increased awareness of the Divine qualities in you.

You will notice that there is no human mind involved in this process. It is an instantaneous inner process of Divine revelation from the Invisible to the visible because the human mind is out of the way. We have transcended the mind in this area. We are in the Soul activity which expresses Divinity. This new awakened faculty then reveals Heaven on earth.

Now, it may seem that this is very remote still and so, the Master continues to tell the disciples to be patient. It can never be remote because the finished Kingdom of God is always where you stand. It can seem remote to a human mind and so, there is a step or two still awaiting in which the human mind loses its power to blind us to the presence of the full Kingdom of God.

"All things that the Father hath are mine: therefore said I, that he shall take of mine, and shall shew it unto you."

Now, that is the assurance that when the Spirit of Truth in You, flows into your prepared Consciousness, expressing of God, nothing is withheld. *"All things."* You can never feel that something is missing because the Christ tells you that *"All things,"* of the Father will flow into your experience. It isn't dependent upon your personal intelligence or your personal capacities. It depends only on your willingness to rest in the conscious awareness that God is present where you are and everywhere, no matter what you see. As you are willing to accept that God is present everywhere, no matter what you see, you are preparing for the descent of the Dove. The Dove cannot descend where there is a dual personality. The Dove cannot descend where there is one clinging to the belief that I am still a human selfhood.

The Dove descends where there is one who says, "The Father says I am his Son and that makes me the Christ now, not tomorrow. I will not become the Christ. I will not find Christhood in the future. It is my Being now, my substance now. I am the Light of the world."

Your fidelity to this in you, in your neighbor, in all that you see, is the willingness to see God everywhere, though invisible. To crucify that in you which would deny God everywhere, to crucify that mentality in you which insists that there is an evil person or an evil condition, that crucifixion in you prepares the way for the resurrection of your Spiritual, immortal Self through the descent of the Dove. Then you look out at the world and not only make the effort but insist that instead of identifying what you see, you identify the invisible God that is there. This is fidelity to Omnipresence. This is acknowledging Me in all thy ways. This is loving thy neighbor as thyself. This is the conscious effort to see God everywhere; in everyone.

And of course, there's no room in it for personal favoritism. There's no room in it for judgment. There's no room in it for condemnation. There's no room in it for the many, many human ways that we have of being snobbish, of looking down, of pretending, of segregating, of expressing quiet, silent hostilities while smiling in the face. All of that ends when we see God everywhere and we must in order to prepare for the descent of the Dove until everywhere is Holy Ground no matter what appears. There is no descent of the Spirit of Truth in you which opens you to direct cognition of God.

And so, "I go away," says Jesus, "Because my name is not Jesus. You have thought of me as Jesus, the man. You even thought of me as Jesus, the Son of God and it's not enough. My name is Christ invisible." And so, Jesus the form is going and this is mortality going that Immortality may be reborn in you. This is the disappearance of the human ego that you may discover the infinite, Divine Ego in your Self. This is the disappearance of matter that you may discover Spirit. I, who will return, am in you now as that which you are not recognizing and I who go away am the false sense of being that you are recognizing and I remove the false that you may find the True, the Real, the One in your Self.

"You could not bear it," he says, "If I'm to tell you now that I am the Spirit of God in you. You wouldn't understand it." And so, these are the things he cannot say to his disciples. They cannot understand that the man before them is not a man but is invisible Spirit which they see as man and that invisible Spirit is the Spirit of their own Being which performs all miracles on this earth when we have risen out of material consciousness.

And so, we drop the belief in corporeality. We let Judas go. We drop the belief in a human mind. We even let that human mind go and now, we're letting Jesus go. We drop the dependence on all outside powers to help us. We're making that journey which only the illumined can make; those who have felt the fire of Spirit within themselves.

And we know there's going to be an interval of time before the Spirit descends. It isn't going to be instantaneous. When we drop dependence on our sense consciousness, there will be a period of suffering, of tribulation and we must know that it is coming and be willing to undergo it. We must be willing to obey the inner commandment that God is everywhere and to drop all belief that God is not everywhere and to drop belief in the senses which testify that God is not everywhere until we are committed; not free but committed, living in that interval which is the dark night of the Soul, the interval of tribulation when we have left one shore but have not arrived on the other shore. We are in between, but, it is an interval of deep faith that the Living Word is my Being and though my human consciousness is not yet reconciled, though my flesh is not yet redeemed, the Word of the Father in me is so strong that I can rest in the assurance of his Presence here and there and in between as the only Presence.

And these are the conditions that Christ is setting to us as being requisite for the descent of the Dove, lifting us out of human consciousness into the Divine. He doesn't tell us how long that period will be and he knows that only those who have been touched by the Spirit will make the journey. Only those who have total faith in their own identity, total faith in the Word of God. They will make the journey.

"A little while, and ye shall not see me: and again, a little while, and ye shall see me, because I go to the Father."

Now, you remember the Two Ways of I. I, the human ego and I, the Divine Self. And here, he is speaking the two ways of I, the two ways of me. *"In a little while, ye shall not see me."* You shall not see Jesus. That means in a little while, you will lose your dependence on personal power, personal sense, material power, material sense, mental power, mental awareness. You will lose faith in the human qualities upon which you have depended.

"In a little while you will not see me any longer."

All of our human life has been a journey in which we depended solely on our own instincts, really on our own animal sense. We could see it and touch it. We could depend, too on our human thought. Now, the disciples have done all of that and they have transferred their total dependence on a man called Jesus. We have depended upon ourselves, our mentalities, our bodies, our strength, our intelligence to improve ourselves, to protect ourselves, to secure a better life just as they had depended on Jesus for that purpose. They had depended upon him to build a better physical kingdom, to liberate them. So, we have depended upon our physical and mental resources. He's pulling the rug out under them. He has asked them to follow him and now he's disappearing. He's pulling the rug out on us saying, "You have followed all of your physical and mental resources. Now, I want you to give them up. I want you to follow your Spiritual resources, the resources that I have taught you you have even though the Divine fullness of them has not yet become apparent to you. You must follow them."

"You will not see me for a while. It will be a setback. It will be difficult but you will see me. I will return if you will follow your Spiritual resources. Ultimately you will release the imprisoned hidden splendor of your own Soul. I will return. You'll become aware of Christ. Christ will be realized as identity but it cannot be done as long as you are pursuing a human sense of life. The human sense of life must be dropped. The disciple must walk in the Immortal acceptance. The disciple must walk in the Spirit, in the Light, in the Invisible with total faith that the Father is present in the invisible as the sustenance of all that they are with total faith that the life of God is the life of You, that it needs no protection, it needs no outer supply. It is Supply. It is the Life. It is the Protection. It is the Safety. It is the Fullness. This is the acceptance in the Invisible of your identity and the willingness to trust in that acceptance. And as you do, I will return."

The Jesus you saw will return to you and you will then recognize this never was Jesus. This was always Christ in you. The powers you depended on will now be revealed to you as just the dream powers, just as the man called Jesus was actually a dream. All that is present is I, Christ. I, Christ revealed in you will reveal to you that no longer do you need the powers of the world. The power of God, the fullness of the Father, all that the Father hath is revealed in I, Christ as your Being.

I will return. This is the assurance given to every disciple who steps off the shore of his mental and physical resources trusting his invisible, Spiritual resources.

I will return. This is a change in consciousness. It is a change in minds and the change must be done consciously. We cannot wait another two thousand years for I to return. Jesus is not coming back and Christ is not coming back. We make the journey in consciousness. In the interval of faith, in the acceptance that what is told to us by the Spirit is true and though we walk in temporary blindness, we are told we will be blind. That it will not be instantaneous. There will be a struggle and you must make the struggle. For I will return; Christ realized in you.

"Then said some of his disciples among themselves, What is this that he saith unto us, A little while, and ye shall not see me: and again, a little while, and ye shall see me: and, Because I go to the Father? They said therefore, What is this that he saith, A little while? we cannot tell what he saith."

And so, when you hear this within you, there is confusion, there is doubt. What is the Spirit saying to you? You wonder, you doubt, you flounder but in some ways it's because the human mind refuses to listen to what it does not want to hear. It is being told to crucify itself and it refuses. It has no way of knowing what to do about a thing like that.

"I've been depending on this human mind and this human body. How shall I crucify them?" You must go away from them or I cannot return. Jesus must leave. The human sense of life we entertain must leave. There must be a rising above the hypnosis of the flesh before we can become aware of the second coming of Christ. The Christ we were before the world was and the Christ we are, we are now becoming aware that we have always been. This renewal, this regeneration, this rediscovery of our immortal Christ Self, this second coming cannot happen while we remain under the hypnosis of the flesh in a human sense of life. We are being told to get out of the dying body and I who will return will show you your deathless body. Get out of the human mind and I who will return will show you your Infinite mind. Get out of all that is temporary. Get out of time and I who return will show you eternal Self. Get out of the human lifespan and I who return will show you Life without end.

The disciples say, "We don't quite understand."

We have said that for a long time. We might even have passed the point now where we are debating this issue. You see, what is really happening is the disciples are unable to accept his words without argument. When Christ says this, Christ means this and even if you don't understand what Christ says, you should follow. The disciples do not understand and therefore, they do not follow. But they should follow without understanding. Instead of rejecting the words and debating and asking questions, they should say, "Well you said it and that's it."

We are learning now to accept the words of Christ verbatim. The human mind ceases to question the Words. Often, we think we're questioning so that we can improve our understanding but very frequently, we're questioning in the hope that it won't mean what we're afraid it does mean. We're afraid to face the crucifixion of the mind and the body. And so, what we think is asking for light or understanding is really hoping in some sense that we won't have to go through with it.

But we may have passed the point now and come to the place where we want to go through with it. And so, I would say, we're passed the disciples who were saying, "We don't understand what he's saying. What's it all about?" We do understand what he was saying. He was telling us to step into our immortal Self, to crucify the mind and body, to crucify the senses, to crucify the belief in form, to crucify the belief in evil, to crucify the belief in false powers, to crucify the belief in disease and death and to look out and see that nothing could be here if God were not here and therefore, God being here, nothing else is here. We're seeing our concept everywhere of that which is only God.

And so, we look through our concept now and we see through the concept that all that is there is God and though we are not quite sure, though we cannot touch that God, feel that God, speak to that God or even hear that God, we're willing, because we have been to some degree enlightened, to say, "Only God is there and I'll go through this interval of faith when Jesus goes and Christ has not yet returned to my consciousness. I'll go through that moment, through that dark night but I will be true. I will accept that God is there and there and there and nothing else and I won't be a disciple who says, 'What's he talking about. What do you mean?' because I've passed the point of questioning the Word of God." This is where we should be.

He says, "Let Jesus go and I Christ will return." We say, "I'm letting Jesus go. I'm not going to ask Jesus to pray for me. I'm not going to pray to Jesus. I'm not going to ask Jesus to pray to God for me. I'm not going to call on Jesus Christ for help. I'm going to seek no intermediary with God. I'm going to depend on God within my own Being." That's what he's telling them.

"You thought I was going to bring you a better physical kingdom, great improvements in your human life. You thought I was going to speak to God and he would do these things for you. Forget it. I'm not going to speak to God for you. I'm not going to improve your physical life. I'm not going to free you from any human beings. I'm going to introduce you to your free, immortal Self which has ever been free, which has ever been God itself which has all that God is and I cannot explain it to you but I will remove Jesus so that you will find that which I cannot explain to you." That's our journey now.

And so, he hears the disciples speak this among themselves. Christ in us knows that we are still in a state of doubt and he says to them, *"Do ye enquire among yourselves of that I said, A little while, and ye shall not see me: and again, a little while, and ye shall see me? Verily, verily, I say unto you, [That] ye shall weep and lament, but the world shall rejoice: and ye shall be sorrowful, but your sorrow shall be turned into joy."*

Christ says, "If you make this inner journey, the world will rejoice about the disappearance of Jesus." Certainly, the world isn't interested in Truth. The world wants to revel in its own pleasures. The Pharisees didn't see Jesus as a Messiah. The disciples saw Jesus as a Messiah. They're both looking at God, one sees someone they ought to crucify and the other sees someone they think is going to help them in this physical world. Each one sees his concept and each one thinks of Jesus in a different light.

And so, the world rejoices when Truth goes away because it can now be in evil without being accused of it and the disciples who would follow this Truth as far as they knew how, they are sad and in deep sorrow. When we lose our dependence on outer powers, we feel like we're helpless. The world is striking and we're not allowed to strike back. There are evils and we're not allowed to try to remove them. And we weep and we lament. The reason we weep is because this is the inner weeping and the lamenting is the outer. It's a total sense of frustration.

Jesus is gone. They weep and they lament. We have no dependence on our human mind and our human resources. We weep and lament and yet, he says, "Don't worry. The world will rejoice. It will think it has won a great victory over you but your sorrow will turn to joy." This is the announcement that there will be a descent of the Dove. There will be an opening of the Soul. In this interval of faith, when we lay down all dependence on human resources, we are silent before the Father. We are meek. We are faithful. We are pure at heart. We are receptive. The way has been prepared and the Light of the Father dawns in consciousness and all that we thought was sorrow now disappears, dissolved by the sunshine of Truth. We are in the Joy. This is the promise of the Christ. The infallibility of the Word of God in you if you will be faithful to what it requires you to do.

And then comes this great analogy which helps us along the way. *"A woman, when she is in travail hath sorrow, because her hour is come."*

Now, that word "travail" if you look it up in the dictionary, it's spelled t-r-a-v-a-i-l but it's pronounced "travel." I used to call it "travayl" and then I call it "traveyl" but I find in the dictionary it says travel. I don't want you to mistake it. We're talking about the act of giving birth which is called here the labor pain or travail.

"A woman when she is in travail hath sorrow, because her hour is come: but as soon as she is delivered of the child, she remembereth no more the anguish, for joy that a man is born unto the world."

Now, you see how we are told we must go through the suffering as a woman must go through the suffering in order to bear the child. There's pain, there's anguish, there's concern but all this is gone when the child is delivered safely. Our dark night of the Soul is the same, like a woman in travail. The woman you see is your consciousness as it is making a change from dependence on human resources to your Spiritual resources and that change is difficult. There is pain. There is struggle. There is labor but you're laboring to bring forth a new birth and that man child is the realization that Christ I am. The new birth is your own true Self regained, the immortal Self you forgot about when you came into form, birthed as a human being. That is regained during this suffering, this period of anguish.

And it brings up the question, or rather, the revelation that pain is not evil. Just as pain is not evil during childbirth because it is necessary for the birth of the child. So, suffering in this world which seems evil to us, is necessary. Through it, we come into the birth of our own immortal Self which is the rebirth. All these things that you have thought were sorrow, in the Spiritual revelation of Self, the sorrows you thought you could never bear and would never forget, they're all washed away. In the rebirth of Christ awareness, all sense of sorrow is removed. You see that all so-called sorrow was no more than the anguish and suffering of a woman in childbirth and when the man child is born, when Christ is born in you, all else is forgotten. It disappears with a human memory. We stand revealed as the immortal child of God. This is Self-conception through the willingness to go through the dark night of the Soul, cutting the ties that bind us to humanhood, walking in the invisible.

Now, I think it's quite clear then what Christ is telling us and what Christ expects us to do and how we can do it. We are letting the separation of the human mind be released so that the Divine branches in me are no longer dependent on my human thoughts. I'm depending only on my Being to be what the Christ says it is. I'm accepting that I, here, am the invisible Divine consciousness. There is no second. And if I rest in the knowledge that there is no second, out of human thought, out of sense thought, out of concept, out of human beliefs, in the deep silence of my own Being, my own Divine consciousness will nourish my own Divine qualities and they will move through me preparing the way for the full realization of Christhood. In the deep silence of my peace, Christ will be born in my Consciousness as my own immortal Self. The labor pains will be over. The man child born is Christ realized. Mortality is no more. Humanhood has died that Christ may be born and then we do not look back.

This is the path we are moving into and we must be patient.

— End of Side One —

If you will walk through the streets of this world seeing God everywhere, no matter what appears, you will be doing what this is calling for. That is the struggle. It is a struggle to look at this world and see God. That's your labor pain. You consciously bring yourself to look at the world and see God behind it instead of what appears. That's your childbirth. That's the anxiety, that's the stress, that's the struggle. To consciously do this, no matter how to difficult it is for you to say, "I see that ugly so and so but there is only God." You must do this. This is part of giving birth to your own Selfhood.

No woman wants the pain of childbirth. She wants the child but the pain goes with it. Nobody wants the pain of giving birth to Christ but the pain goes with it. You must accept the pain as the companion to the event itself. You must be able to tear apart all of the pre- conceived notions of the human mind which says, "That one over there is better than that one over there." It isn't true and if it pains you to do it, it doesn't matter. You must know only God is behind both and God is there and only God. This is the struggle of the inner birth that we take into our conscious awareness day by day. We're sacrificing all of our delicate little human ways, all of the sacred cows of humanhood. We're sacrificing all our prejudices, all our so-called mental comforts, all of the grooves that we have worn so deep by human living. We're going into the deep travail of giving birth to Christ. And we must remain pure while doing it.

Silence, (pause) ...

And so, if you have to wrench yourself out of a conditioned response, who says you don't like the people in the deep south because of this or you don't like the people in the far north because of that, or you don't like people on one side of the ocean or one side of the tracks because of this, you must catch that tendency of the world mind in you. If you see a condition you disapprove of, you must catch that tendency in you.

Only God is there. Only God is there. Only God is there.

To the world, you will be insane. That's the world rejoicing and that's your sorrow but there will be a change and your joy will be forthcoming as the reward for your conscious fidelity to the All presence of God, no matter what appears to be there. Judge after no appearance. *"Henceforth, know ye no man after the flesh."* No condition after the flesh. Nothing after the flesh. God is not that flesh and God is there. This is a long period of gestation. In the world it's nine months. In the development of the Christ consciousness, it's ten years and plus ten lifespans. Now all of those lifespans are behind you leading up to this and in this lifespan, we can receive that Christ realization if we're willing to walk that space, that time between giving up the conditioned responses, correcting them, being faithful to the Allness of God. Let Jesus go even though you hate to let Jesus go, even though they hated to let Jesus go. Let Jesus go. Let all dependence on something out there to help you go. Place all your dependence on your own Being and walk that line quietly, confidently, silently until I am announces its Presence, not in your lips but in your Soul.

Remember the woman in childbirth every time you think your sorrows or your problems are too great for you because we're given that analogy which is one of the strongest that we have in the Bible. Without the struggle there is no birth.

So he says, *"And ye now therefore have sorrow: but I will see you again, and your heart shall rejoice, and your joy no man taketh from you."*

Through the struggle, we are led to that which is permanent, instead of transient. *"Your joy, no man taketh from you."* Not having made the struggle from material consciousness to Spiritual consciousness, we do not receive that which is permanent. We live in limited lifespans. That Joy which is permanent is the Life which is permanent. We're giving birth to that which is Life forever.

These are the words of the Father.

"And in that day ye shall ask me nothing. Verily, verily, I say unto you, Whatsoever ye shall ask the Father in my name, he will give it you."

Now, we're being told here that when the birth of Christ in you is realized, you will not depend on any outer being or power. Ye shall ask me nothing. Jesus, to his disciples, "When this happens in you, you will not ask me for anything." They thought Jesus was going to get them everything. He says, "No. When you are able to receive the Spirit of Truth, the Comforter within you, you will ask me for nothing." Meaning they will be so complete there will be nothing lacking. All that is will be revealed in their Being. Christ in you reveals you to be Self-complete. There's nothing you need seek outside. This is the promise of the Christ that you are Self-complete in your Christ realization.

Now, when we say Self-complete, we don't mean in a human sense. We don't mean you have all the money you need and you have the housing you need and the transportation you need. You may have all those things now. The disciples had all they needed really in a human sense. As long as they had Jesus, they had all that they needed humanly. But, we're not to be left at that level where we only have what we need in the human sense because the humanhood itself is taken away from us. We're told that we will have all we need in a permanent sense. In Christ, I have Life everlasting. In Christ, I have Wisdom everlasting. In Christ, I have the Intelligence of the Father, the Life of the Father, the Will, the Power, the Sustenance of the Father forever. In Christ, when this form goes, I do not go. In Christ, I outlive all that is transient. In Christ, I bow to no power on this earth. This is what is meant by, "You shall ask nothing of Jesus, of me, of any human being. You shall ask nothing of God."

"For all that you shall ask the Father in my name, he will give it to you."

In my name then, in Christ identity, you are Self-complete and there's nothing you need ask. This is taking us out of the human sense of life into Immortality now and this is obviously not in a future heaven for Jesus says, "I go away but I will return." He didn't say,

"You're going to come where I am." He said, "I will return." That means right where you are, you will discover Immortality now. You will discover that where the mortal seemed to be, the immortal Self that you are, always has been and in that immortal Self you will discover your full completeness in God with nothing to ask for. All that the Father has, already has been given.

We cannot humanly conceive of such a Life. And yet, here it is being told to us by the Christ of our Being for only the Christ knows of such a Life and only the Christ can reveal such a Life and only the Christ can experience such a Life. And we are told not to be satisfied with less than that Christ.

"Hitherto, you have asked nothing in my name."

Oh, what a statement. The world has asked nothing in the name of Christ. And yet, just think of the millions who are asking in the name of Jesus, thinking that they're complying when here the Jesus that goes away says, "You have asked nothing in my name because I'm not Jesus. I am Christ. I am the Christ of your Being and if you are not the Christ of your Being, you can't ask in my name because that is my name."

The dependency on the outer powers of the world is the false, deceiving human mind responding to the false, deceiving world mind limiting us to that which has no Truth, hoping to do something in our limited humanhood when here stands the invisible Christ Self, the immortal Being that we are.

Christ is breaking the bonds of mortality, awakening you to the one mind of God in you, lifting you out of all belief in limited human form, out of a transient world into the fullness of the everlasting Kingdom on earth, the Spirit of God. Nothing to ask for. Just be that Christ, that Spirit, that Self, that One.

"Hitherto have ye asked nothing in my name."

And that's the condition the world suffers from. It has asked nothing in the identity of Christ. That one verse sums up the problems of the world. The world has asked nothing. The world has not accepted Christ as their identity. That's the problem.

"Ask, and you shall receive, that your joy may be full."

To ask is to be that Christ. To go through the struggle of birth, to return to your immortal Self. That's asking; willing to put out whatever is required in your consciousness that is not the Truth so that the new child born is without blemish.

Now, Mary did this and so, Jesus was born. As you do this, Christ in you is born. Jesus himself, you see, was a symbol. He was a parable. He was not a man. He was the human husk which we see in our own mind where only Divinity is. He was a symbol that where we see humanhood, Divinity is hidden. Where we see humanhood in ourself, Divinity is hidden. The birth of Christ as you is merely the realization of the hidden Divinity of your Being where you had thought a human, mortal person was. The human mortal you is Jesus going away. The realization that you are the immortal Christ is, "I return." The symbol of Jesus and Christ is the symbol of all mankind, the immortal Invisible where the mortal visible seems to be.

This is what he is teaching. *"These things have I spoken unto you in proverbs."*

Now, your Bible, if its not the King James may say, *"in dark saying."* Some translators have made proverbs into "dark saying." "These things have I spoken to you in proverbs" or dark saying, meaning not clear to the human mind. Incidentally, that's why proverbs are not clear. They are parables. They are symbols.

"But the time cometh, when I shall no more speak unto you in proverbs, but I shall shew you plainly of the Father."

Now, if you thought you had difficulties understanding the Bible, it's because Christ here is telling you, "I have not spoken to you plainly. I have spoken to you in dark sayings, in proverbs. Why? Because there were things that you could not understand. But the time cometh when I shall speak to you plainly."

And naturally, the human in us says, "Well, I wish you'd do it right now. I'm ready to listen." And so the disciples do that. They say to him, "Speak to us plainly now." They are under the impression that plainly means that his mind will communicate with their mind. And that would be our intellectual assumption that plainly means that the mind of one will communicate more plainly to the mind of another - but it doesn't mean that. There's no way for the Infinite mind to communicate to a human mind. "Plainly" means that the Infinite mind in you, awakened in you, will hear the very same words but understand them. That's the plainliness of the Christ speech.

When Christ in you, when you are awakened to Christ, Christ in you will hear what your human mind has been unable to hear. And further, "plainly" means - and this is the announcement to the world - that it is possible to speak directly with God. To hear plainly is the announcement that you will have direct cognition of the voice of God within your Self. You can't get any plainer than that. Without an intermediary, without going through somebody to get to God. That is the meaning of "I will speak plainly to you."

Up to this point, all Truth has come to a human mind which reinterprets it as best it can. There will be no re-interpretation when God speaks to Christ in You. That is the speaking plainly and because Christ says, "I will speak plainly to you," that is your assurance that the day approaches when Christ in You, hearing God direct, becomes your permanent Consciousness.

That is the state of consciousness or Christ consciousness, the illumination, the enlightened moment, when I hear God direct, when the Father within speaks and the servant heareth and we are one and there is no human voice speaking and yet, the Infinite communicates with the Son in you. This will become permanent, a revelation which never ceases. A permanent source of guidance, a permanent source of intelligence, a permanent source of food and drink. This is how All that is of the Father comes into your expression. The Father in you speaks through the Christ which is God sustaining the Son, Infinity individualizing as your own Life. This is the promise of the Christ.

"At that day ye shall ask in my name: and I say not unto you, that I will pray the Father for you."

This is to the disciples, Jesus saying, "I won't pray for you." They can't understand why. He just told them why. Because the Father in you is present and you're not going to need someone to pray for you. The Father in you is there. You don't pray to the Father in you. Do you pray to yourself? Do you need someone to pray to your Self? Why do you pray to God? Because you believe God isn't here in you, as You. But when this day comes that Christ in You is born, You won't pray to God. You won't ask somebody else to pray to God. The God in you is You. There's no longer two.

And so, true prayer, real prayer, not praying amiss is the realization that the Father within me is my own Life. I cannot pray to my own Life. The acceptance of Divine life as my Life is perfect prayer. When I know that my Life and God's life are one Life, I am praying. The realization of one Life is perfect prayer.

And so, Christ says, "I'm not going to pray for you." It won't be necessary.

"The Father himself loveth you, because ye have loved me, and have believed that I came out from God." God loves you.

This is what Christ says to all of us. We don't believe it because we don't know what Love is. God's love never changes. God's love is always perfect. When God loves you, that means God has given you eternal Life. That's what God's love means. The mother gives the child a lifespan. God gives you an eternal Life. The mother's love brings forth that child. God's love gives you eternal Life. God loves you, not will love, not has loved or is about to someday but God loves you. *"The Father.... loveth you."* God has given you eternal Life and there is no other.

The knowledge that God has given me eternal Life is the acceptance of God's love. I don't need to pray to God because God has given me his eternal Life. When I pray to God, I deny he has given me his eternal Life. I'm still in that stubborn, finite, limited human sense of things which has not opened up to the fact that God loved us so much that God gave us his Life and that is our name, the life of God.

Now, what shall I pray for except to deny that God gave me God's life? I cannot improve God's life. It will not grow old. It will not grow sick. It's not going to have a problem tomorrow. In my limited sense of self, I may go through the belief in these things because I don't believe, I don't have the faculty to know that God's life is my Life now. But when I have that faculty, then I won't ask Jesus to pray. I won't ask the church to pray. I won't ask my human mind to pray. I will simply know that I and the Father are one mind. And if I can know it now, then I am asking in the name of Christ. I am accepting that I and the Father are one now. My asking is the accepting that the love of God is the life of God in me.

And because this is the Truth if I can live with that knowledge, I break the karma of the world. And if I can be willing to share that Truth, not to hold on to it for myself, then I malpractice no one who walks the earth, then I am true to the life of God which is the Life invisible of every individual who walks the earth whether he knows it or not; then I am recognizing God everywhere. I am faithful to Divine life everywhere and I am in a constant state of prayer. The recognition of God life everywhere is the constant state of prayer. We are no longer praying as humans pray. Our prayer is there and there and there is the one invisible life of God which the love of the Father in all of us ensures.

We are getting very close to being free of world beliefs as we continue to pursue that conscious awareness that the words of the Father in us spoken through Christ Jesus are living, accepted, lived in and that is living Spiritually, not talking, but living Spiritually, practicing the conscious awareness of the invisible life of God where the form seem to be.

"I come forth from the Father, and am come into the world: again, I leave the world, and go to the Father."

In this, Christ assures you that Christ which comes into the world and goes to the Father is never separated from God. And therefore, in Christ identity, you are never separated from God. And because, whether you know it or accept it or not, Christ identity is the only. You are never separated from God. You come from the Father, you go to the Father. You are never separated from God. You are always the individual selfhood of God expressing. So is your name and if you'll struggle through the birth of recognizing that in everyone, you will find that it leads to the birth of Christ in you.

"His disciples said unto him, Lo, now speakest thou plainly, and speakest no proverb."

They still thought he could tell them the things that you and I are talking about right here. Before crucifixion, before resurrection and he couldn't because without crucifixion and resurrection, there'd be no way to understand them. There'd be no way to understand there's no form in Jesus standing there. We can only see that now knowing resurrection took place.

And when we come to that, by that time I'm hopeful, that we will not only see it very clearly, we will be so prepared that we will know it is not taking place, that the illusion of crucifixion, resurrection and ascension is to teach us that only Christ is on the earth.

"Now are we sure," say the disciples, *"that thou knowest all things, [and] that thou needest not that any man should ask thee: [and] by this we believe that thou camest forth from God."*

In other words, no man need ask him. They could see he's fairly Self-sufficient. They know he comes forth from God. And he's somewhat amused. He says to them, *"Do ye now believe?"* He's repeating what they had just said that they believe. What do they believe? That's what he means. You believe what? You believe that I am the Son of God but you don't believe that you are the Son of God, so what do you believe? I'm teaching you that what I am, thou art. That I am the Son of God and you are the Son of God and you're not believing that, you're just believing that I am Jesus Christ, the Son of God, specially endowed, and the whole world is believing that and I am teaching you that the life of God is your Life and mine right now. But you're still going through the birth struggles so don't worry about it.

"Behold, the hour cometh, yea, is now come, that ye shall [all[be scattered, every man to his own, and shall leave me alone: and yet I am not alone, because the Father is with me."

Every man scattered. At the sign of stress, we scatter. We each run back into our own mortal consciousness again and now, we're not thinking of anyone else. We're thinking of ourselves. That's the scattering. He knows it will take place. Each will be saying within himself, "Oh my God, I've lost Jesus Christ. What am I going to do?" They will scatter each to their own house, to their own individual consciousness and when we have left all our human remedies and our human desires and our human ambitions, we feel that sense of having been scattered. We have nothing to hang on to. But Christ says, "Wait a minute now. That's how the senses tell you you are but I am not alone."

And while we're still in that state of being scattered, we're brought up sharply with the realization, "Well wait a minute? Where did God go? Did God leave me? Did the life of God go away? How can I be alone when I is God? Is God alone? No, God is All there is."

And so, in this sense of scattering, in the sense of great loss, we are saying "I am not the life of God." Only a human being has a sense of loss. I, who am the life of God can never lose anything except the false sense of life. There's a transference in consciousness from the self-pitying individual who thinks he has lost something or someone. There is no such loss. That's in the human sense of things which still denies the fullness of God as Being and thinks there is another being.

And then the great hope for the world. *"These things I have spoken unto you, that in me ye might have peace. In the world ye shall have tribulation: but be of good cheer; I have overcome the world."*

In the world, in the belief in humanhood, in the human mind, we have tribulation and that's the only place it occurs; but be of good cheer. Continue in the struggle to be reborn for I, the Christ in you, have already overcome all the tribulations of the world. When you find I, you will discover all of the tribulations of the world dissolve into the forgotten past. In the now of I, in the permanent state of Being, not in a future heaven, in Christ here now, I.

Every prayer of Jesus Christ was the recognition of his oneness with God. When we have prayed humanly, we have not prayed in the name of Christ. We have prayed in the name of a human being. We have prayed in my human name. I am asking God for. That's not praying in my name. That's not praying for the fulfillment of God's will.

But now, the great joy of knowing that Spirit, speaking on earth to men who were looking for Truth and preserved in this book and the scriptures of the world, assures us that there's no power on earth that can prevent us from realizing the Christ of our own Being.

Be of good cheer. No matter how the struggle or the tribulation, the lack or the limitation, no matter what the appearance, be of good cheer because I, who is your invisible Self in the midst of you, ever standing there, loving you supremely, I tell you and you can trust me, I have already overcome the world in which you are struggling. Rest in I and I will show you that the world in which you are struggling is only the hypnosis of the human mind. Your Father's kingdom is where you are looking at the world. Your Father's joy and happiness and perfection is where you are struggling. Out of this pain will come the joy of birth. If you are steadfast in the conscious awareness that your Father is now present everywhere including where you appear in form, where your friends appear in form. And as you practice the living knowledge that God is present, no matter what the eye can see nor the fingers can touch, and only God is present, you will be giving birth to your own Christ identity.

And so, that's the 16th chapter completed and still, he's not ready to be crucified. Somehow, in the Christ teaching, every eventuality is covered, every detail, every doubt is answered, not just by-passed.

And so, there's another chapter; the 17th. I'm not saying we're necessarily going to do it next week. We might do chapter 11 in Joel. I'd suggest you look at both, the 11th chapter of Joel which is "Lifting Up the I," and the 17th chapter of John which is the final preparation of his disciples as he walks out of form; teaching us how to walk out of form.

I had so many things I wanted to tell you today and the Voice said to me, "God doesn't need any human advice." And so, we'll be patient and accept what flows within ourselves knowing that I, who have overcome the world, am feeding you as quickly as you are prepared to accept what I am feeding you. I in you will give you as much as you're prepared to receive and you are preparing by emptying out that which is not true. That is your preparation. Emptying out all that is not Divine life and as you empty out, I, Christ in you, refill you with my pure Spiritual Self replacing your poverty of Spirit with the richness of the Infinite.

Let's be still now and wait upon the Lord. Silence, (long pause) …

Thanks a lot.

Class 32

You Are Eternal Life Now

Herb: Good afternoon everybody. We have a very rare privilege today, thanks to John.

A message has been preserved that is not available in any other part of the Old or New Testament. This is the message of the Soul receiving the Christ and the Christ speaking through the Soul of Jesus to God so that we are given an opportunity to know what our own Christhood is doing in relationship to the Infinite universe.

Now, I can tell you that if you understand the first five verses of the chapter 17, you have the whole Bible. There's nothing more important in the entire Bible, in the beginning of it and the middle of it or the end of it, in the Old or the New Testament. The first five verses of chapter 17 of the Gospel of John contain the complete Bible. They explain the riddle of the universe. They ultimately shock you and startle you and then when you think the shocks are over, the new ones begin.

And so, if we know these first five verses, we are on a different level than we were before and we're discovering a new universe, a new Selfhood in that universe. This leads us to the very essence of Being.

Now, try not to be too shocked. You've had, so far, only in the series on the Gospel of John, we've had fifty-two weeks. That's probably the longest class on the Gospel of John that's ever been had. Fifty-two solid weeks and we're still going strong and today, reaching a pinnacle.

This, the complete 17th chapter, is almost the only prayer in the audible of Christ Jesus to God. Until now, wherever there has been a prayer such as at the resurrection of Lazarus, it has been a very brief one, *"I thank thee Father that thou hast heard me."* And there have been three or four other instances where it could be said that Jesus was praying to God. At least it would appear that way to the human eye. But here is a lengthy prayer and it follows the end of the teaching to the disciples.

The direct discourses to the disciples are over and this is no longer a teaching from Jesus directly to the disciples. It is rather a communion between Christ Jesus and the Father. And this high communion is but an outer symbol of that which is ever taking place between the Christ of you and the Father. This is how you have access to that which no human being knows, through the vision and the understanding in John, to bring us this inner communion between Christ and the Father.

For now, the man called Jesus, who was to lead the disciples into the Kingdom of Heaven on earth, turns from the disciples and addresses himself to God. It's as if you were to cut away the exterior of a tire and look inside to see what it's made of, to get a cross-section of the inside of the tire.

Here, we're getting a cross-section of the inside of Christ, what goes on in Christ, and this isn't something happening two thousand years ago. This is what goes on in Christ in you now, the communion between Christ and the Father is the Oneness that is constant, unceasing. And what you are witnessing in the discourse between Christ and the Father is actually the constant prayer, the constant oneness of Christ in You with the Father. Every word that will be spoken by the Christ is a constant prayer in You, unknown to the human sense mind. Christ in You is always saying this to the Father. It is a revelation of the state of your own invisible Being as it is now.

Everything that we have learned, everything that we have in some way accepted, everything that we have rejected is brought now into high focus because this is an inner discourse of pure Love to God and pure Love of man. Everything comes into focus. Nothing can be denied after this inner communion.

"These words spake Jesus, and lifted up his eyes to heaven, and said, Father, the hour is come; glorify thy Son, that thy Son [also] may glorify thee: As thou hast given him power over all flesh, that he should give eternal Life to as many as thou hast given him. And this is Life eternal, that they might know thee the only true God, and Jesus Christ, whom thou hast sent. I have glorified thee on the earth: I have finished the work which thou gavest me to do. And now, O Father, glorify thou me with thine own Self with the glory which I had with thee before the world was."

These five verses are the Christ message.

"Jesus lifted up his eyes to heaven." The lifting of the eyes is the outer symbol of what is happening within. When you lift your eyes to Heaven, you are recognizing the indwelling Christ of your own Being. The lifting of the eyes is saying, just as he said previously, *"Lift up thine eyes... Say not there are four months to harvest.... The fields are already white to harvest."* When you lift up your eyes, you are seeing the Invisible fields. Lifting up the eyes is the recognition of the invisible Kingdom of God on earth. Lifting up the eyes is the recognition that there is an invisible Kingdom of God, that there is a Christ. Lifting up the eyes is the acceptance that I am that Christ and I stand in the invisible Kingdom of God. Lifting up your eyes to Heaven is the acceptance that Heaven is present where you are.

We are told to follow the Wayshower, and therefore we are told to lift up our eyes to Heaven, to recognize that invisibly, where the world appears to be, there is an invisible Kingdom of God, present. In our lifting up the eyes, we accept the presence of that Kingdom; all around us. We are walking in it. That Kingdom of God which indwells us, which surrounds this form, which is everywhere, is alive and present to those who stand in the realization of their own identity.

Jesus Christ, lifting up his eyes to Heaven, is saying that right where he stands is the invisible Kingdom of God, right where his disciples stand, right where the world appears and what was true at that moment - that the invisible presence of God was there, the invisible Kingdom was there - is true of this moment. As we learn to inwardly lift up our eyes to Heaven, we quietly acknowledge the presence of the Father, the Kingdom and the Father in me as the Divine Selfhood which I am. All this is embraced in lifting up the eyes to Heaven. He was not standing on a visible, mortal earth in a visible mortal body but neither are you.

The Wayshower says, "Follow me, accept what I teach you about my Self for it is the Truth about you." The Wayshower says, "I bring you knowledge from the inner realm for you to accept in what you call the outer realm but I bring you knowledge proven in the fire, knowledge that can be demonstrated, not opinions of men. I bring you Divine authority. I bring you Truth that you can depend upon and live by, in fact, Truth that you must learn to depend upon or perish for we're going to see that it is Christ or perish."

"He lifted up his eyes to heaven." We're looking now at Christ invisible and the outer symbols are the form called Jesus lifting up eyes to Heaven and the Christ you're looking at is the Christ of everyone who walks the earth, demonstrating at a specific time and place the presence of God as the invisible Christ appearing as Jesus.

These are Truths we learn to say, "Amen" to for it is the Truth of us and we will learn to walk with these Truths, to live by them and to dissolve beliefs in those attitudes and concepts which are the opposite of the Truths that we are learning to accept. Now, we're being moved into a higher realm of consciousness than the human three dimensions.

"The hour is come."

He has said that now, twice before, I believe. Once, when the Greeks appeared and once, when Judas, Judas was given the sop and departed. When Judas was given the sop and departed, the Master said, *"The hour has come for thy Son to be glorified and to glorify Thee."* Just as now. That was in the losing of the corporeal sense of life. Judas representing the corporeal sense.

Now, again, *"The hour is come."* What is this hour? And this hour, you see, is the key to the Kingdom. This hour is the revelation of more things than are known to a mortal mind. This hour is the revelation of things that we will be learning as long as we walk this earth. It is the hour to reveal the identity of the Christ as the identity of Jesus; the identity of the Christ as the identity of mankind. It is the hour to reveal the invisible Kingdom of God on earth. It is the hour to reveal the Allness of Spirit, the nothingness of form, the Allness of God. It is the hour to reveal that all who walk the earth are absent from the body though they know it not. It is an hour to reveal things unknown to the mind of man, things that cannot be known until the nearness of the consummation of the age and now is the time to know these things.

"The hour has come."

"The hour has come," for man to disappear and reappear. Think what that might mean if you were that man. To walk into the grave and out and step right back before your friends and say, "See, I told you all this time. It couldn't happen to me." Yes, that hour has come.

The question is, do we learn from that hour? Or do we go on believing in an external God that we pray to in the sky instead of seeing that the hour has come to reveal that the Self of man and God are one and the same, that God is within everyone. The hour has come to reveal that mortal form is not God created. The hour has come to reveal that Christ form is the form of everyone and that Christ form is indestructible. The hour has come to prove, to demonstrate that mortality is a myth, not just for Christ Jesus.

The hour has come to show that Immortality is the nature of every individual who appears in a form that appears mortal. The hour has come to show the nature of Divine life on earth as it is in Heaven.

This is a mighty hour. And because of it, we are given an advance key to the meaning of the resurrection. It is as if we are given instructions. This is what I am now going to do and watch it carefully because as I do it, I want you to understand it. And do not accept it as the world religions accept it; that a man who died was raised back into Life but rather see that no man died. Rather see that I am revealing to you at this moment the nature of the Christ is Life eternal, that the nature of the Christ which is Life eternal is the eternal Life of you, that eternal Life is the name of Christ, that eternal Life is the identity of Jesus Christ; that eternal Life does not die and is not resurrected, eternal Life simply does not die. It is indestructible and therefore, it needs no resurrection. I am the Life. The eternal Christ of you is the Life. It will never be resurrected because it will never die.

"The hour has come, glorify thy Son, that thy Son also may glorify thee."

Glorify. Reveal the name of your Son, the identity of your Son, the substance of your Son. Reveal that your Son cannot die. Reveal that God is the Son, that the Spirit of God is the substance of the Son, that the life of God is the substance of the Son and in revealing all this as the nature of the Son, the Son glorifies the Father.

But again, the Christ says, *"Follow Me."*

So now, we are given a very specific purpose, a very direct statement about the function of ourselves in this world, what we are to do. We are to reveal the glory of God individually. We are to show forth that life of God where we stand which is indestructible, beyond death. That is your function. And when your hour comes, it will be because you have prepared yourself through the acceptance of the

Truth taught by the Christ. Your function, too is to glorify the Father as the Father glorifies you and your function is to prepare the way.

The hour has come to show that reincarnation is over. The Christ will go forth proving, that is what glorification does, it proves that the Christ is the name of Jesus, that the Christ is the Son of God, that the Christ is the Self of man. We are to be given the proof. Not that God is going to raise Jesus from the dead, we are to be given the proof that the Christ does not die and we are to be let into that awareness that the Christ which does not die is my name.

And so, Christ in you now, is in this prayer, saying to the Father *"Glorify thy Son, that thy Son [also] may glorify thee."* And as the Father expresses through Christ in you and you manifest the qualities Divine in the outer, glorifying the Father, this will be the 'following in the footsteps of the Master.'

We are to be about our Father's business glorifying the Father through Christ in us, receiving of the Father, asking of the Father, seeking of the Father, learning how to dwell now in eternal Life, learning how to live now in eternity. And this is going to become very real to us, living in eternity. We're going to discover that unless we are living in eternity, we are denying omnipresence. We are denying the Christ. We are denying the Father. We have no choice but to live now in eternity as you will see.

"As thou hast given him power over all flesh, that he should give eternal life to as many as thou hast given him.

Now, we learn that Christ has power over all flesh. The nature of that Power should be clearly seen. Christ Jesus did not exert a physical power over those who would crucify him. That was not the kind of power. Christ Jesus did not defend himself against those who came to take him away. Christ Jesus did not, in any way, protect himself against the crucifixion and yet, Christ Jesus has Power over all flesh. What is that Power? Why is it Power over flesh if it doesn't use that power as human use power? It is power over flesh because of the one, incredible fact that there is no flesh. It is Power because it reveals the nothingness of form. There is no form. There is only Christ. Christ has Power over all flesh by revealing that flesh is not the creation of God.

"They have only the arm of flesh but we have the Lord Almighty."

The arm of flesh is nothingness. Christ has power over nothingness but Christ is you. The Self of you has Power over all flesh. The Self of you knows that flesh is not God's creation.

The Christ has Power to give Christhood to all those who seek it of Him. It says here, *"to all that thou has given to him."* That means to all who turn to seek the Kingdom of God. Did you hear the word *"eternal life"* in here? *"That he should give eternal life to as many as thou hast given him."* Now then, we're beginning to see that Christ and eternal Life are one and the same. If you are in Christ accepted, you are in eternal Life but if you are Christ now, you are eternal Life now.

And now, this new idea comes into focus. We are eternal Life now. If we are not, we are not Christ. If we are Christ, we are eternal Life now. If we are Spirit, we are eternal Life now. And once you know that you are eternal Life now, you can never really consider yourself to be a mortal being. Eternal Life is the name of Christ.

"Whatever you shall ask in my name…. shall be given you."

Now, in our re-identification, we found it difficult to accept Christ is my name. But we were assured that if you make the effort, you will receive invisible assistance and now, here is your assistance. You will find that eternal Life can be accepted without the same struggle you had in accepting the name Christ.

We know that God is Life, that God is the only Source, the only Creator, the only Life and therefore, the life of God which is eternal Life, being the only Life, it must be your Life. Now, do you come into eternal Life? How do you do that? How do you come into it? It is You. It's your name. It's your identity. We can see now why the Master had to stand before his mother and show us that he was not born of human parents. How could he be born of human parents if he was eternal Life? Does eternal Life struggle through the womb of a woman? Is eternal Life born if it's eternal? Can eternal Life be anything but eternal?

You see, your eternal Life is the only Self you could be and it's the only Life you can really live. The eternal Life that you are is the same Life you have always lived. Your Life was on this earth at the time Jesus walked this earth. You have always lived.

The Christ revelation that whoever learns their name to be Christ is given eternal Life is the revelation that eternal Life is the nature of Spirit, the nature of he who calls himself man or woman. And when we sit back and accept the words of the Father through Jesus that we are eternal Life, all of the boundaries of this frame of life are removed. We were never born into human parenthood. Eternal Life was never born through humanhood. Eternal Life reveals itself to be the permanent status of your Being. It matters not how far back you go in time, eternal Life was and is your name. It matters not how far you go into time in the future, eternal Life is your name. But eternal Life can never be destroyed. Eternal Life does not express as a human form. Eternal Life reveals that if I am one, I am not the other. I'm not part eternal Life and part transient life. I'm not part Divine and part mortal. I am totally Divine. I am totally eternal Life and that which is not eternal Life is not me.

Your sloughing off that which you are not as you learn who you are. You cannot be Christ, eternal Life and something else. The glorification of Christ Jesus is the revelation that he is not something else. He is eternal Life. *"I am the life,"* and the nature of your Being is ever declaring within you, *"I am the life."*

This eternal Life that you are is beyond disease, beyond destruction, beyond any problem known to man, beyond death itself. Why? Because it is eternal Life and nothing else. It embodies all that is of the Father because it is that eternal Life of the Father. This is the glorification in you of the Father, your realization that I am eternal Life - now, right here where I stand. This is the realization that the eternal Life of God is the eternal Life of me, for I and the Father are one eternal Life.

The whole book "Realization of Oneness" is to bring you to the realization that you are the eternal Life of God. And who said so? Listen again to the phrase, *"As thou hast given him power over all flesh, that he should give eternal life to as many as thou hast given him."* We can't pin eternal Life down to Jesus Christ alone can we? *"To as many as thou hath given him."* You can't pin eternal Life down to eleven disciples. Who is included? As many as turn to the identity of Christ within themselves and accept it. That's the purpose of the inner communion between Christ Jesus and the Father, to reveal your identity as the Christ which is Life eternal.

"And this is life eternal, that they might know thee the only true God, and Jesus Christ, whom thou hast sent."

The only true God is eternal Life. The only true God is the Father within you. Here, at a time when the world was totally unaware of the nature of God, Christ Jesus is revealing the only true God is the Kingdom of God within you which is your eternal Life. He is abolishing the concept of a God external to your Self. He is abolishing the belief that between you and God there is space. He is establishing that there is no one closer to you now than God, no one nearer to you than God. In all this world, no one is nearer to you than God because your eternal Life is God.

"And this is eternal life, that they might know thee, the only true God."

The glorification, the revelation that Jesus is not a man on earth or a specially endowed Son of God with an exclusive on the Spirit of God is to demonstrate that that Spirit in Jesus is his identity and it is eternal Life and is the nature of mankind.

And so, you should walk out of here today knowing that I, Christ am eternal Life. I have no transient life, no life that began at a certain time, no life that ends at any time, no life that in any way can be destroyed by any material force on this earth. You can't drop a germ in my Life. You can't cut my Life. You can't infect It. You can't influence It. You can't change it nor can you take it away. Your Life can never be taken away from you by any force on earth. There is no material or mental power on the earth. Not even God can take away your Life because God is your Life.

Now, this is to become our permanent Consciousness. I am eternal Life. And as you accept it, you'll find your meditations take a depth and also produce a new kind of fruitage. You find Peace is easier to find because it isn't the peace of the mind. It's the Peace of the Soul. You'll find your foundation becomes vast and deep so that you're really anchored in Truth that is unshakeable. You are eternal Life and whether you realize it or not, the fact will never change.

And as you learn to practice that you are eternal Life in your meditations, you'll find ways to practice it in your living of It. You'll find ways to demonstrate It, to glorify that eternal Life. You'll find that attitudes which are incompatible with eternal Life will be quickly revealed to you as attitudes that are untrue.

And so, in all ways, once you have accepted the new nucleus of Being, that I am Life eternal, you can begin to look at the things that would plague you, distress you, keep you up nights, those corroding acids of fear and you can dismiss things more quickly because everything that would in any way happen to you that is not Peace, Harmony, Beauty, Truth, the qualities of the Father are recognized quickly as world mind trying to convince me in some way, to tempt me out of the belief that I am Life eternal.

There are times when that understanding is so breathtakingly clear that you wonder how you ever thought you were something else. You are Life eternal and what the world has called life is revealed to you as the imitation, the sense mind separation which causes the belief in a changing, temporary life where only eternal Life can be. You don't have two kinds of lives anymore, the life of God and my life. There's only eternal Life and I and the Father being one, that is my Life.

The Christ having proven, demonstrated, glorified that Life as his Life saying, *"Follow Me"* is my assurance that I am that Life. *"Follow Me,"* in the acceptance, the living, the proving, the refusal to be a second kind of life for there is none. And then the wayward mind, the doubtful mind, the vacillating mind - all of those qualities in the mind that are ever changing, undecided - these begin to be the moneychangers that we put out of the temple.

We can really be at Peace. We can really rest in confidence, in silence and confidence, that God is the Presence of my Life, right here and another thousand years of time, it won't be any different. I will still be the same Life that I am now. I'm awakening now to the Life that I've ever lived and slowly I will become aware of more and more and more of what this Life really is. As my consciousness rises, as I am able to remove the veils of human belief, more and more of this eternal Life that I have accepted reveals itself to show me I am indestructible, to show me the nature of the illusion of matter, the illusion of form, the illusion of senses, the illusion of the world and to reveal that invisible Kingdom which is the imprisoned splendor ever present. But we must stand in that sureness that because the Father has revealed through Christ that I am eternal Life, I must be faithful unto this Truth.

It isn't enough to intellectually accept it. That's only a beginning. You work with it. You meditate with it. You practice the eternal life of God where you stand and you're not too shocked at the problems of the world because you recognize that what you've accepted for your Self is the Truth of everyone you know. Behind that mortal exterior is the invisible eternal life of God. It's not going through the rigors and tortures that appear to my human eyes. Release God from the belief that where eternal Life is, something else is also present.

Finally, you have come to a place where you could almost say and feel and know, "Why all there is everywhere, is eternal Life." And soon form becomes that which you are anxious and eager to see through because only when you have accepted eternal Life and have concentrated upon seeing through the form, not with human eyes but with understanding, only then do the invisibilities of the Kingdom begin to be visible. Only then do you find the vast, unidentified, ever present activities of Spirit that have been happening right under your unseeing eyes. Acceptance of eternal Life, the knowledge that form doesn't contain eternal Life. Slowly, the fog, the mist evaporates. The eternal Life reveals its newness unto you.

Now, so much more is being said that we have to be cautious that we don't glibly make statements until we can come to a place where each word is clear.

Now, suppose we were to say that we're watching a man on stage and he has this great big trunk and in it goes this little girl and then he takes that saw and he cuts that trunk in half and then he opens that trunk and to your relief, out steps the little girl whole. She wasn't cut in half at all. Now, would anybody say she was cut in half and then she was resurrected? You'd simply say that there was a compartment or there was a hole in the ground; in some way she disappeared into it. When he cut, he didn't cut into her and when he opened the trunk and there she was, nobody got the idea that she was resurrected. It was a trick.

Now, for some reason or other, when Jesus demonstrates that he's still alive, everybody figures he was resurrected, God brought him back. But he's teaching us that isn't what happened. He's teaching us that he is eternal Life. Not that he was brought back, not that he died and was resurrected. He's teaching us that eternal Life cannot die. There is no resurrection. There is the demonstration that eternal Life is deathless and it is interpreted by the human mind to be resurrection.

Now, the value of it when you see it as it was, is to teach you several things. First, the form that dies is never there. That's like the girl going into the box, getting cut in half and then stepping out whole. The form is never there. When you accept eternal Life, you're accepting that eternal Life is there and it is never in a physical form. Eternal life accepted is the rejection of the belief in the physical form.

The glorification is the revelation that where the form seems to be, the eternal Life is. Where the person seems to be, the Christ is. Where the earth seems to be, the Kingdom is. Where the world appears to be, the Kingdom is. The glorification is the revelation of what is and that carries with it the revelation of that which is not.

And that's why the 17th chapter here solves the riddles of the universe but only for those who have been prepared to listen within. Even those who say, "Yes, I accept that" are only beginning. Eternal Life is Divine, form is mortal. There is no Divine in the mortal. There was no Life in the form called Jesus: none whatsoever. That form never was there. It appeared just as other forms appeared. It never was there. It was never crucified. It was never resurrected. It simply wasn't there. What was there is what is there now; the eternal Life of God which was not crucified.

And so, this is the difficult part of the teaching. The revelation of eternal Life is the revelation that form is not on the earth. And because the human mind is bewildered by this, it must live with this idea for quite a while before it learns the power in that revelation.

Christ never is in a human form but there is a form and it is the form of the Soul and it and the Soul are one and that manifested form is invisible to human sense. It is never touched. You can cut it in half but you won't make contact with it. You can saw away but you cannot touch it. The Soul form, the Christ form, can never be touched by a material concept. You can drop a bomb in the middle of this room right now and it could not make contact with your eternal Life. You could drop a bomb all over this earth; eternal Life would not be affected in the slightest. All that would happen would be the changing concepts in the human mind.

We are to graduate beyond those changing concepts. We are to follow the Master who is teaching that when you live in eternal Life knowledgeably, through Spiritual consciousness practiced, through the Word accepted, received obediently, through a change in consciousness, you are so transformed that the Christ in you demonstrates its power over all flesh in the very same manner that it demonstrates that there is no resurrection, there is no crucifixion, there is Life eternal ever being itself untouched by any material power.

This is the kind of confidence that your acceptance of eternal Life will instill in you, the realization that I can walk now anywhere in the universe as eternal Life knowing that all there is around me is eternal Life and nothing else is there. There's no bomb here. There's no disease here. There's no potential death here. There's no problem here. All that is present where man sees earth is eternal Life. This consciousness is possible.

"This is eternal life that they should know thee, the only true God."

And forever, to those of us who have heard that word within ourselves, God ceases to be up in the sky. God ceases to be separate from us. God is the eternal Life that is seen through the eyes of man as this world. And the world ceases to be as the eternal Life of God replaces yesterday's concept in our newborn Consciousness.

This is a total new birth of Consciousness made possible by the supreme demonstration which follows this discourse between the indwelling Spirit and the Father. And it's given to us in advance so that we may understand the resurrection that will follow, as men will term it, so that we who have been opened by the Spirit will not make the mistake of the world in saying, "God raised him from the dead" but will know that he was never dead. He was eternal Life and he is demonstrating that that is the Truth of my Being right now. Never can eternal Life be dead. And this is eternal Life.

"I have glorified thee on the earth: I have finished the work which thou gavest me to do."

Again, your function and mine is to finish the work which the Father has given us to do. We can never leave this earth until we finish that work, until we are eternal Life demonstrated. Every reincarnating cycle in your life continues and continues until you finish that work that we are given to do.

Now, there must be work that you are given to do and it is to be the living Son of the living Father, to be the living Spirit, to be the living Life, to be all that the Father is. *"Son, all that I have is thine."* That is the work I have given you to do, to show it, to reveal it, to glorify the Father in you, to express God. That is our work.

Now, very few people on earth are interested in that work. Very few people on earth know about that work. To those who receive the knowledge that that is their work, there is a sacred trust and there is an unspoken command. "I have revealed my Self to you."

You can reject what you have heard or you can respond. You can deny that sense of self that you entertain. You can pick up the challenge, the command, the cross and instead of being like the world who says, "Well, if I die, I'll either go to heaven or to hell. I'll take my chances." You can say "No, no. There is no death. I can't go to Heaven. That's where I am. I can't go to hell. There isn't any. Hell is simply the unawareness that Heaven is where I am. And I will not say four months to harvest. I'm not talking about what I'm going to do tomorrow. I'm accepting eternal Life now. And then clearly, into your consciousness comes that understanding that when you are eternal Life now, before the experience of death, you will pass the point where death has any meaning. Death has no meaning to eternal Life.

To realize eternal Life before death is your function. This is the work we are given to do. This is the work that Jesus is finishing.

"I have finished your work. I have released Judas, the corporeal sense. I'm willing to lay down this mortal sense of life knowing it is not me. I am eternal Life and I'm ready to demonstrate it, to prove it and because I am eternal Life, there's nothing for me to protect and no one against whom I need to protect. No bug, no disease, no germ, no condition on this earth is a threat to my Self."

This is the work we have come to finish. And when you have reached that level and temptations are met, to believe that you are not the perfect, Divine, eternal Life, then you know that you are ready for the transition through the appearance of death. That is the work we have come to do and will do.

Just while we may have some doubts yet, and now *"Oh Father, glorify thou me with thine own Self."* Show who I am by showing that I am your own Self. Show that your Self is my Self, that my Self is your Self, that All of You is All of Me."

Put yourself in the Master's footsteps and see that Christ in You is saying to the Father, "Show that All of You is All of Me. Glorify thou Me with thine own Self. Show who I am."

— End of Side One —

Why? Because when you show who I am, the world will know who it is. For you are the Father of all. You are my Father and you are the Father of my disciples. You are the Father of all who walk the earth. Show who you are where I am and all who have ears will know who you are where they are. And then forever taking away the belief that your life is not eternal and that it began at a point in time.

"Glorify thou me with thine own self with the glory which I had with thee before the world was."

Before the world was there was a Christ. Before the world was, there was Life eternal. Where did it go when the world appeared? Nowhere. Before the world was, you were Life eternal and are now. The mortal sense of life slips away. It loses its power to persuade us that we are limited, finite selves in clay.

The Christ in us says to the Father, "Reveal that I am the Self that existed before the world. Reveal that I am pre-existent Being, that before there was a world, I was Life, that I didn't begin fifty years ago, that I won't end fifty years from now, that I am that Life which always was and let me live in that Life. Let me expand my consciousness to the place where I know my Self to be that life that never began and never ends. Take me out of this finite concept of a mind."

And so, your work is cut out for you. You are that Life which existed before the world. That Life is all that ever has existed and the life we have known to be life is the world concept or the re-created idea about Life which never was ourselves and which always persuaded us that we were mortal or dying creatures.

And that is the importance of these five verses, to clear the air, to open the eyes of those who are ready to see. They've been there so long that you know their meaning has been completely overlooked. The world has not seen them at all. The world has insisted this is all about Jesus Christ.

And Jesus Christ says, *"Glorify thou me that I may glorify thee. That I may give eternal Life to all those that thou hath given me."*

Now, then, the Life that you are now is the very same Life that was Jesus Christ on the earth. The Life that you are now is the Life of everyone who walks this earth. The Life that you are now is the Life of everyone who has walked this earth and that Life of everyone who has walked this earth is still their Life now. In other words, we are the Life and we must drop the concept of being the form. We become those who still walk in the appearance of form or we become righteous servants of the Life. We wait upon the Lord. We wait upon the Life. We rest in the Life consciousness, letting it move and activate the appearance called form.

No activity begins in the form. It begins in the Life. You rest in your Life consciousness and let the Life move the form. Ultimately, you'll find that the Life is moving its Soul form which will appear to you outwardly as your physical form although it is not.

The shift in identity now is eternal Life. These are the facts only. The application of the facts is what we might have some time to discuss today and what we undoubtedly will be applying. The remaining years that we walk this mortal earth, we will be applying the knowledge that I am eternal Life until earth is no more, until the place where I now standest is revealed as that Life itself, until Oneness is complete and there is no second, no two; no mortal life and immortal Life, only eternal Life.

Now, that you're accepting eternal Life, this will be your work: to learn what to do as eternal Life. How to live it, how to be it, how to accept it, how to be obedient to the Truth of it. This is how you build Christ Consciousness.

Silence, (pause) …

It is a challenge that demands the very highest capabilities within you. Silence, (pause) …

We'll have a short recess for about five or six minutes and then see how we can apply our knowledge.

(Class break)

I think it would be a wise idea to look at some passages. I think they clarify certain things.

Now then, we are being told in the 17th chapter of John that the invisible Christ stands where Jesus is and that invisible Christ is eternal Life and that eternal Life stands where everyone stands. That eternal Life is the reality of Being, that everyone is that eternal Life and that's the reason we're called the Son of God because we are the life of God and it is not a temporary life.

And so, the Life that we are must be an eternal Life to be the Son of God. And therefore, this visible, physical, changing mortal creature is not us. There is an invisible Self that is us and all we're seeing is our concept of that invisible Self through a human sense mind. But there is an invisible Self. There is a Christ and it is I and that Christ is the begotten child of God; the Son.

Now, for just those few who might still be in the lingering belief that Jesus was the only begotten child of God, we go to the 2nd Psalm. The 2nd Psalm, centuries before a Jesus appeared on the earth.

"Thou art my Son; this day have I begotten thee." In the 2nd Psalm, verse 7. Now, we know that Christ is the Son. And here it says, *"Thou art my Son; this day have I begotten thee."*

And so, the Christ which is the Son pre-existed the form called Jesus which appeared on earth later just as the Christ which is You pre-existed the appearance of your form here this moment. That pre-existent Christ never stopped existing and is your Self now.

Now, here's something you may have overlooked which was just called to my attention the last few days. It's in Matthew 12:32. The statement that's somewhat spellbinding to me. This is made by Jesus Christ.

"Whosoever speaketh a word against the Son of man"

Now, the Son of man is appearing here as the form called Jesus. The disciples are seeing this form and it is saying, "I am the Son of man." And it says to the disciples, *"Whosoever speaketh a word against the Son of man,"* which means this that you call Jesus, *"it shall be forgiven him."* You can say something, you can blaspheme the Son of man. You can blaspheme the form called Jesus. Jesus is saying it. You can do it. It will be forgiven.

"But whosoever speaketh against the Holy Ghost, it shall not be forgiven him, neither in this world, neither in the world to come." The invisible nature of your Being must be accepted. The visible form, whatever you say about it matters little. The visible form is not the You. It was not the Jesus. The visible form is the concept. "Anything you say about Jesus will be forgiven," says Jesus. But if you blaspheme and deny the presence of the Holy Ghost, the invisible activity of the Christ, then you are separating yourself from your Self.

There are some more passages to look at. They follow one upon the other. John 12:24, 25 and 26. Now, they sum up in advance of this last communion of Jesus Christ with the Father. They sum up the very things that he said but, in a way that we didn't see as clearly at the time.

"Verily, verily, I say unto you, Except a corn of wheat fall into the ground and die, it abideth alone" meaning separate not with God, *"but if it die, it bringeth forth much fruit."*

The form is that corn of wheat. You must die to the concept of it or else you live alone; separated from your Self. But, if you are able to overcome the concept of form by accepting I am eternal Life, that means then that the corn of wheat has fallen into the ground and is dead, then *"If it die, it bringeth forth much fruit."* If you overcome the belief in form, living in the knowledge of eternal Life, that Life manifesting is the fruit.

And even if you still doubt, again, *"He that loveth his life shall lose it."* He that thinketh, in other words that this mortal life is our Life. If you love this mortal life, if you believe that the mortal life is your Life, you shall lose it. That's obvious. We're all going to lose our mortal life.

"But he that hateth his life in this world shall keep it unto life eternal."

Now, to hate your life in this world is to overcome the belief that it is your Life and to see that right where your life in this world seems to be, your eternal Life is. That's hating your life in this world. Overcoming the belief that your transient sense of mortality is life is hating your life in this world. And then, you shall keep your life unto Life eternal. You're trading in your false concept for the Truth.

Again, if you doubt, *"If any man serve me, let him follow me; where I am."* He's showing you his name is the invisible self of God; un-crucifiable. That's where I am in the invisible because I am the invisible life of God. *"Follow me where I am"* means accept your Self to be that invisible eternal Life of God.

"If any man serve me, him will my Father honor."

You'll find those in your 24, 25 and 26 of John, 12.

Now, it becomes very increasingly clear, by repetition in every way, that the eternal Life of God is the only Life you could ever be, the only Life you ever have been and whatever else you may have thought, that was not your life.

When this comes upon you, you say, "Where do I go from here?" Because the idea in itself is so vast that the mind is sort of benumbed.

It just stands there gaping out and says, "Well, fine but what do I do about it?"

First, cherish that moment when the mind is benumbed. That's a glorious moment for once the mind is no longer on the throne, it has to be a bystander. It has reached the point where it is incapable of taking thought. Be grateful. Rest in that benumbed mind and let the mind of the Father supersede the mind of you which was only a sense of mind. Finally, it reaches an idea too big to handle and it stands there bewildered. It's taking no thought.

"I in the midst of you am the Life and I will do all the thinking. I in the midst of you have nothing wrong and I am your Life."

Now, we used the word Twin last time for the first time, or the time before. I want you to see that we're calling the Twin, your invisible Self. That invisible Self is your Twin. That invisible Self is the Christ and we're saying that you have an invisible Twin and every time you forget it, you're going to be back in the false sense of life.

Your invisible Twin is in the eternal Life now and the way to start into the knowledge that I am eternal Life is to remember that though I appear out here in the visible, I have an invisible Twin named Christ and that invisible Twin is ever present as I in the midst of me. And that same Twin of me is I in the midst of everyone else so I am in the omnipresence of my own invisible Twin.

And if I will wait and listen, my Twin, my invisible Self who is ever present, will guide me. Be still. Rest in the Twin and no matter what the circumstance, even if you're in a good situation, never act before you receive the conscious knowledge of the Presence of the invisible Twin. You will find you will be guided correctly. The Christ of you is the invisible Twin who will guide you correctly if you will wait upon the Lord.

The waiting then is first, to control the act of sense mind. Unless you control the act of sense mind, you are not preparing the way.

And as you control the act of sense mind to listen to your Twin, you find you're really doing that which was given in the Sermon on the Mount as "Ask, seek, knock." You're asking the Twin to speak. You're seeking the Twin. You're knocking in the invisible for the Twin. You know that every human action in the outer is a separated action. It doesn't spring from the eternal Life of you and so, you rest in the knowledge that present here now is my eternal Life; the Twin, the invisible Christ, ever present and within my eternal Life, within the Twin, every idea of God is embodied. It is omnipresent. I don't have to ask for the idea. It will pop to the surface if I am in the awareness of my Twin Self. Oh, it may seem like duality for a while but you'll get over that. My invisible Twin is ever present and I can guarantee to you that your invisible Twin is the Christ of God and your invisible Twin will always know every answer that is necessary for every situation. And before you ask, I shall answer and I have the answer here waiting for you but you must seek me. You must knock on my door in the invisible.

And when you do this, you become aware that your Twin is infinite and again, brought into clear focus is your function on the earth. You are here in a seeming human consciousness to be an outer expression of your invisible Twin. Your invisible Twin expressing through your outer consciousness is your function at this moment. If you are the outer expression of your infinite, invisible Twin which is one with you, everything you do will be Divinely ordained.

And so, if you know your Twin is present as the Christ eternal Life and that your outer consciousness merely must wait upon that Twin to be guided, then the infinite Twin will be guiding you locally and you'll find one continuous action from the infinite Christ to the outer, visible human type expression. Ultimately, the Twin will take over. The Christ will rise. But that Twin, seems like it's personalizing but I find it very effective. Effective because we can't hang on to nothing. It helps us to establish a specific, living invisible identity which we're calling the Twin, your spiritual Twin. You've lived without it, now, live with it and watch the difference.

Don't get ahead of yourself. You can't say, "But I am the Twin." Of course, you are. Just get into the habit of reaching to that invisible Twin and it will make all the declarations for you. Control the outer mind which is preparing the way. Listen for the invisible Twin and then, turn ye, be obedient. When you are in the outer obedient to that inner Twin, which isn't just where you're standing but is universal, you are fulfilling your function. You are expressing the Divine mind and whatever you do carries with it the benediction of the invisible Father within perfecting and performing all that concerneth Itself in you.

Make this Twin real to you and remember, it is the I that is in you that is greater than all who walk the earth. This Twin moves the mountain. This Twin parts the sea. This Twin has the answers. This Twin does the impossible but not your will. The will of the Father within you. Always, "What is your will?" is what you ask the invisible Twin until it is so real to you that you're in the Paul's way of life. "*I live yet not I.*" The invisible Twin, the "*Christ liveth my life,*" and that is why my Life is ever protected against the scorpion on the arm, against the Roman centurions, against every outer circumstance. Eternal life is its own protection. It is Real. It is Now. It is You. There is a Kingdom. There is a Christ. You are that Christ and you are in that Kingdom. Listen for the Twin.

Don't act from the outer self. Act from the inner Twin. Then look across the street at the neighbor coming down the street. Your Twin is there. Your invisible Twin is right where the neighbor is. Look up and down every street in the universe. Everywhere is your invisible Twin, don't care what the form is. Let that corn of wheat fall into the ground. Everywhere, identify your invisible Twin, the infinite Christ and wait. You will be guided. The words and the deeds will all be of the Christ. This is glorifying the Father.

What is happening to us? We are learning that we are eternal Life and that eternal Life is never in a form. When we are eternal Life understood, we are absent from the form but we are present with God. You must put "eternal Life" and "absent from the form" together to make them work. You are absent from the form when you know you are eternal Life. They go together. They take you out of the limited, finite boundaries. This is how you glorify the Father. You can't glorify the Father as a limited form. Man has tried and failed; he continues to die. You glorify the Father by living. The Father has no pleasure in your dying. You are his eternal Life.

Now what we have been given in these five verses then is a new kind of Lord's prayer. The Lord's prayer was given to the disciples along the way to lead them, to guide them, to bring them up to this point where the Lord's prayer, which is the Truth, is now explained as the revelation that the Kingdom of God is present.

At the beginning of the demonstration of Christ, man was given the Lord's prayer at the near end of the demonstration, he is given the communion with the Father which is the Lord's prayer again, expressed at a different level. It is the Christ prayer in you with the Father, the eternal, constant, unceasing prayer of Truth; the knowledge that I go to the Father, the Father with me is one. I am living that Lord's prayer when I live in eternal Life.

The Kingdom is come. The will is being done on earth as it is in Heaven. There is no temptation to digress into evil. All of the power is there, the glory is there because you are the living Kingdom of God. You are the living Lord's prayer.

The greatest word that comes to us now is obedience. Obedience to the Father within, the Christ; the infinite, invisible Twin - remembering that that Twin is always present.

Silence, (pause) ...

"I," says the Christ, "am never alone for I go unto the Father."

And now we can say, "I am never alone for I am always the invisible Christ."

And if I just remember, that relationship will be so completely cemented that it will become automatic. Everything will be referred to the Twin. The Twin will run your business and your home and your marriage, your relationship with the world and it will be in the image and likeness of God.

All this was predicted by Daniel; that there would be a Kingdom of God on earth which will be everlasting; that all dominion was given to the I of your Being. We shall even graduate out of these forms, out of this world of senses and that which is invisible will become the living, visible Kingdom of God for those who walk in the eternal Life.

Notice how easily you'll pick up people who now say to you they have a sickness that looks incurable or they have this problem or that. You'll see how completely they are out of tune with Truth. Quickly, something in you says they just haven't begun and then you'll wait upon the Twin who will say to you, "But don't you recognize that it is I standing here? not a person. Drop the concept. I, your invisible Twin, stand before you. Don't you recognize me? Everywhere I am. I am the invisible Self of the world, your Twin. Trust in me. Glorify me. Believe on me. The Father honors all who do this for I and the Father are one."

Now, we've got a good head of steam up on the 17th chapter. We're going to stay with it. Your meditations this week should be on your 'invisible Twin,' 'your name as eternal Life' and 'everything you ask in my name will be given you.' As you recognize your Self to be eternal Life, all that eternal Life is will express in your experience.

You see how the government is on the shoulders of eternal Life, not on a human mind? How you can begin to relax all the demands and pressures of the world knowing that your Twin knoweth your needs?

Silence, (pause) …

Study today's lesson very carefully. It's the complete explanation of all that is going to happen in the rest of the Gospel of John in the total mission of Jesus Christ. It contains everything and it is all about You.

Now go back with me two thousand years ago. You are living because your name is Life. You weren't in this form but Life was there. Life was here. Go back as far as your mind can think. You were living. Life never began at any one point. God never became your Father at a specific time. God always was your Father. And so, your Life always was. The forms it took into the appearance world are not what we are discussing. We're establishing that your Life always was and that Life is the same Life that is now and it will be the same Life forever. The original glory of your Life is forever.

Work with the knowledge that your Life is not riveted to this point, this place, this time, that your Life didn't begin in the twentieth century. Your Life doesn't end in the twentieth century. Your Life isn't confined within the shoulders and the hips and the ankles. Your Life is everywhere now and that is your invisible Twin which is expressing through you into the visible where you appear to be. Make this appearance of you obedient to your invisible Life everywhere and you will see the meaning of revelation, receptivity, meekness unto the Spirit, listening, waiting upon the Lord, direct cognition of the Infinite, tune to the Infinite.

All of this is saying, let the outer appearance of you be aware of the invisible Infinity of you and let the Infinity of you come through its way. Don't push it or press it or force it or demand of it. It knows what it is doing. The eternal Life of you is living with the total intelligence of God as its mind, with the perfect body of God as its body. Let all of this come through you. Be obedient to your invisible Self and you'll find that power which the world has missed.

Now there's much has happened today here - more than we can see at the moment. And many of you who do not practice will find that whatever has happened is of little value to you because the practice of these things is what brings them into play and tunes down the world mind. As you practice, you'll find the world mind loses its power and, in some way, you are raising the consciousness of the world. We have been given many blessings in this chapter 17.

Silence, (long pause) …

Thanks again very much.

CLASS 33

I AM NOT IN THE WORLD

Herb: Let us try in this lesson today that we're receiving from the 17th chapter of John, not to try to cram our minds with too many facts but rather to feel the essence of what John is communicating to us about this Soul communion of Jesus. He is turned from the disciples. He is communing within with the Father and we are privileged to watch through the eyes of John, through his Soul vision, that inner communion of Jesus with the Father so that actually we are witness to that which takes place within ourselves between Christ and the Father.

"I," says the Christ, *"have manifested thy name."* And that word manifest, we must understand. *"I have manifested thy name unto the men which thou gavest me out of the world: thine they were, and thou gavest them me; and they have kept thy word."*

Now, the importance of this verse is that there is no exoteric, orthodox religion on the earth that has understood it, in spite of the fact that it is uttered by Jesus Christ.

"I have manifested thy name."

The Christ is telling us that "I did not go around healing the world. I did not heal disease. I did not calm the storm. I did not walk upon water. I did none of the things that the world says I do. I did none of the things that religion will worship me for. I did one thing. I manifested Thy name. I, in the midst of you manifested the name of God on the earth."

You cannot manifest that which is not there. When you manifest Wholeness, it must be there. When you manifest Harmony, it must be there. You do not create it. You manifest what is there. When Christ appearing as Jesus walks the earth and manifests Wholeness and Harmony and Peace and Truth and Oneness, he is manifesting that which is invisible to human eyes but is present.

"I have manifested the Kingdom of God on earth. I have manifested Thy name. Thy name is God, the Kingdom of God, the presence of God, the virtues, the qualities of God. I have manifested on the earth. They were there always. They are here now and only I manifest them."

Now, then, no person manifested the name or the qualities or the character of God. I in you alone can manifest the invisible Kingdom of God. There is an invisible Kingdom and *"I, in the midst of you"* can manifest it and no one else. You have no power humanly to do it. No human authority has power to do it. The human mind has no power to do it. *"I, in the midst of thee."*

And so, the emphasis is that until and unless you find *"I, in the midst of you,"* you cannot walk here in the invisible Kingdom of God but when you have learned how to be lifted into I, then *"I, in the midst of you,"* walking here in the Kingdom of God will manifest that Kingdom where you stand.

I, Christ in the disciples, manifested to them the Kingdom of God. I, Christ in Jesus walked the earth revealing Wholeness where the world saw sickness, revealing Health where the world saw suffering, revealing Perfection where the world saw imperfection, revealing Abundance where the world saw lack and this Abundance, this Health, this Perfection, this Life without end, invisibly is ever present awaiting your recognition through Christ in you.

Now, when we awaken to this, we are no longer dead to Christ but awake to Christ. Awake to the miracle of I, Christ in the midst; awake to the fact that God lives here, not up there. We are being opened to I, Christ in the midst by the very Christ itself, saying that, "Where you walk is the full, perfect Kingdom of God."

"I have manifested the name of God on earth. I have revealed the Invisible for all who can follow that same invisible Perfection is available now."

"Unto the men which thou gavest me."

Very few were given to Christ then and the giving is that Love of the Father draws those who are seeking Truth to the Father. The drawing of Love which pulls you into the quest for Truth and ultimately to the discovery of Christ Self is the Father giving to Christ.

"Those thou gavest me."

And as you feel yourself drawn to a search for identity, this is the magnetism of Divine Love so that no matter how faint you grow along the way, this Love leads you, sustains you, strengthens you, enlightens you and ultimately reveals itself to you as your own Self.

"These thou gavest me."

And gavest also implies that these are those who have been taught by God. The teaching is given by God through Christ. *"They shall all be taught by God."* And these disciples, learning directly from Christ are learning from God for Christ is the individualization of God within themselves. We, too shall be taught by God and are being taught by God as we listen to the inner Christ who receives of the Father. This is God giving us enlightenment, sustaining us, leading us, opening our inner eyes, taking us behind a veil of the senses, behind the beginning of life and the end of life into that place where there is no beginning and no end.

And now, these few, these early pilgrims, are for signs and wonders to us, examples in other words. These have been trained.

These are opening their eyes. These God gave to the Christ to show man. More will follow.

"Thine they were"

Was Peter any more God's than you or I? Was John any more God's than anyone else on this earth? *"Thine they were"* because the substance of God is the substance of that which we call man. The substance of God being the substance of the disciples, *"Thine they were."* The substance of you and I, being the substance of God, we are of God. And that substance we're coming to know better and better as the I in the midst is lifted up, for this is part of the invisible revelation that you are the living substance of God.

"Thine they were."

The Father's you are. Whatever is true of anyone on this earth, whatever is true of them is true of everyone. There's no special Truth for any particular one. We are being taught the universality of God's substance called Christ.

"Thou gavest them me; and they have kept thy word."

They have kept the Word in the presence of Jesus. They have been sustained by that external presence. They don't all keep the Word when Jesus leaves them but they must learn to, as we must. The keeping of the Word is obedience to the inner Self. In many ways, more than just "I am the Christ." If we are merely saying, "I am the Christ," we're not keeping the Word. To keep the Word is to recognize Christ in All. There can be no place where you do not recognize Christ if you are keeping the Word. And the disciples, in the presence of Jesus, were learning to keep the Word and now he's going to teach them how to keep the Word in his absence.

We can all keep the Word pretty well when things are going good. That's easy. We can feel we are specially endowed. But to keep the Word through times of stress is even more important because that is a true test. And as the degrees of stress are heightened, this becomes even a greater test so that we who have accepted Christ identity for all must learn to look out upon a world which shows nothing of the Christ to the human eye and yet, we must reconcile that world without, to the Kingdom within, knowing always that there stands not a sinner, not a drug addict, not an alcoholic, not a murderer, not a good person, not a saint. There stands always the invisible Christ.

Today, we're going to strengthen that understanding because without it, we're not ready for the important journey into Life outside of form and this we must make. We must become conscious of the Christ everywhere. We must become aware, so aware that we never fall out of Oneness and that is not through reading. That is not through conversation or memory. Never to fall out of Oneness is a practice, a practice you inculcate, remain with, dwell with, abide with, under every form of tribulation. Oneness maintained is the requirement of keeping the Word.

Now, the disciples have to some extent kept the Word because it was easy for them to do so. They had a living Master walking beside them. None of us have a living Master walking beside us and so what are we going to do about it. We're going to do precisely what he's training them to do; to find the Master walking within us, who will teach us the way to never fall out of Oneness, to maintain a perpetual contact with the Infinite.

Now, he's establishing "I have revealed to these the invisible Kingdom of God on earth and the identity of every man as the Christ. At this moment they are living it as best they know how."

What are they being prepared for? Why couldn't they just go back to their occupations, do their jobs, live their domestic lives and raise their families? What is this preparation? Why are we even doing this? Why can't we just go out and get jobs and stay with them and build our houses, take our trips, enjoy our lives? What is the mystery behind this unrest that forces us to go deeper?

It is that somewhere deep within us, we cannot accept the transiency of life. We cannot accept the ending. We cannot accept putting forth our best efforts to attain, knowing that that attainment is going to be temporary; knowing that at the very height of any human nobility there must also be a depth. Something doesn't stack up right in our minds about that and this is what presses us on until we find that there is an eternal Self. And having found that there is an eternal Self, even though the proof to us is never definite, there are signs. There are assurances. And ultimately, there is conviction that there is an eternal Self and finally, the great discovery that the eternal Self is my true and only Self.

And this is the Self that I must manifest. There is no satisfaction that is enduring unless I manifest my eternal Self. As the Christ manifests the name of God which is eternal Self, I, too learn to manifest eternal Self. And then, I find I am out of the transient, out of the perishable, into the conscious awareness of a Self that is forever. Still without proof and yet, willing to move without that proof, convinced it is so; convinced by some inner knowing.

The Christ is leading us to the realization of our eternal Self. Not after death but before. While on the earth, while appearing in the flesh we shall know our eternal Self, taught by God. There's really no reason why you do not know your eternal Self this moment. It isn't a tomorrow Self. It is a here and a now Self and incidentally, if a single day goes by, even one day that you do not live in your eternal Self, consciously, at least for a moment, you have wasted a day. It should be our purpose each day to find and live in that eternal Self.

When Paul says, "*In him we live, and move, and have our being,*" who is that him but the eternal Father and is not the eternal Father your eternal Self? In your eternal Self each day you should live, move and have your being. Undoubtedly, we won't sustain it for twenty-four hours but to realize it some time during the day, the earlier the better, is to make your Eternal contact which will enable you that day to manifest the reality of Being, the name of God, the essence called Life itself.

We're trying to eliminate the tendency to seek a future realization and to convert that into the determination to realize a now Self, not a tomorrow Self. But here today, I stand as the eternal Self made visible only in flesh while I walk the universe invisibly. There should be a time of day in which you establish this. It won't matter if you fail a bit. It won't matter a bit because even in the failing, the effort put forth to establish it will ultimately produce the fruit. If you were to fail five hundred times, it wouldn't matter. It is the effort you put forth to attain the Truth that ultimately breaks the veil. And the Truth is, eternal Self should be a daily experience, not words in a book or a future attainment. *"I, in the midst of you,"* I will manifest the Name the moment you accept me as your identity.

"Now [that] they have known that all things whatsoever thou hast given me are of thee. [For] I have given unto them the words which thou gavest me; and they have received them, and have known surely that I came out from thee, and they have believed that thou didst send me."

If you think you're going to turn to religion or science or education or government or anything external, the Christ says, "No, that's not the way." The Christ says that, "I have come from God and only I have come from God and that if you wish the God experience, you can only receive it from I, who am come from God. It won't be in human prayer. It won't be in new technologies. It won't be in any peace treaties. The only way to experience the presence of God is through Christ within your own Being. The only way to experience Perfection, not its imitation, but perfection in Spirit is through I, Christ in you accepted, realized, lived in.

The importance of these verses here is to establish that only Christ is one with God. No man is one with God. No human mind is one with God. No person is one with God and deeper still, no one in a human form is one with God.

Now, you must remember we're at the pinnacle of the Bible revelation of Truth. We're at that place where if we do not understand Truth here, we're still down in the valley. If only Christ is one with God, then no human form is one with God. Christ is not a human form and Christ does not live in a human form. That is going to become a very important revelation to us; that Christ does not live in a human form. First, to instill in us the need, the desire, the vital urgency of accepting Christ identity and then to show us that Christ identity does not live in a human form. You cannot be a human form and Christ, too.

Christ is one with the Father. Spirit is one with Spirit. The human form is not one with Spirit. Matter and Spirit are not one, they are two. That is one too many. And so, the emphasis here must be on Christ identity, Spiritual identity and that means the concept of flesh is the deceiver.

There is no flesh in the invisible Kingdom of God. Only Spiritual flesh. Only Spiritual form. Only forms of the Soul, not of the mind.

"[But] I have manifested thy name."

What does that tell you about the so-called body of Jesus Christ? That body of Jesus Christ is manifesting the name of God. Is it physical flesh or is it a new species of man? Is it Divine Being? Are we seeing it?

"I have manifested thy name," which is spiritual Self. The Soul body of Jesus Christ stands there and no man can see it. That which is standing in the physical flesh is only our objective, subjective concept. There is no physical flesh standing there because *"I have manifested thy name."* I am showing forth the Spiritual body of the Soul which is deathless and though the world thinks they are looking at a physical form, they are wrong. That is why John put the 17th chapter here, to show us that the body of Jesus Christ was not a physical form.

But what was it? It is an image in the minds of men. How is it different than your form? It was different in two ways. He had reached the level of consciousness which could overcome the world mind and so that his body was not a world mind image. That's the first way in which his body was different than ours. It was not a world mind image. Our forms are world mind images.

And then his real body which was there, the body of Spirit, was not visible at all. And he was living in it so that he could move invisibly, walk on water, vanish in crowds, appear two hundred miles away to heal someone who thought he was just over here and didn't know he was over there too, so that absent healing was never really absent. He was always everywhere. He was in the Infinite Soul body. How could he be in it, if it wasn't present?

"I have manifested thy name."

I have shown forth that there is an Infinite Soul body and I am in it. But why did he show it forth? The same way he showed forth the invisible Kingdom of Harmony to all who came to him. He was now showing forth an Invisible Soul body that is infinite to all who came to him but no one could recognize it. It took at least a resurrection for them to realize there was an Infinite Soul body and only then, when blessed by the Spirit, did the disciples come to that understanding.

That Invisible Soul body which is infinite, which he revealed by walking through the experience of crucifixion untouched, is invisibly present here and now. It is also your Body and you are in it; unaware of it.

As you stand in a physical form which is the world mind image, you are in Reality in the Invisible Soul body which is infinite and as you turn to I, Christ in the midst of you which knoweth these things, it reveals that it is in the Infinite Soul body which is beyond death. This is how you come into your realization of deathlessness, Life without end.

Your Infinite Soul body is revealed to you through Christ in you, accepted, lived in, realized. All of this is presaged by the present inner communion of Christ and the Father. Not that we're going to come into this body some day but that it is and has been your Eternal body from since before the world began. You've always been in it unaware of it, without the capacity to perceive it through the senses. It is your Body now, it has no beginning, no end in time or space. It will be lived in on this earth while you walk in the appearance called flesh if you become Christ conscious. This is truly the ultimate purpose of all our work on earth.

"They have known that all things whatsoever thou hast given me are of thee. [For] I have given unto them the words which thou gavest me."

Now, these words which Christ gives to the disciples are actually the inner ordinations of God through Christ in you to the disciples in you, so that if you're living by revelation, Christ in you is giving you the words of the Father, teaching all of the disciples within you, lifting them up so that the qualities of God which are the disciples within you, through Christ in you, are being lifted to the fullness of Spiritual maturity. You're being taught by God but only if you're listening within through Christ. Not as a human being standing there listening but as the Christ listening. This is the difference between hearing the Father and going into some kind of mental psychism in which you imagine that what you're hearing is of the Father. If you're in humanhood, you're going into psychism. If you accept the inner Christ and dwell with it long enough to have the realization of it, then you hear directly from the Father and you become aware of your everywhere identity.

"They have received these words, and have known surely that I come from thee."

Now then, that word "surely" is to emphasize that Christ alone comes from God. No person does. Every one of us who has followed human authorities ultimately discovers the clay feet of that human authority.

I, Christ come from God and if you want the Word of God, you will only get it from I, Christ. Now, that's the complete theme through the 17th chapter to leave you with the un- shatterable conviction that Christ in you is the way. There's no second way. It doesn't matter how many religions you join. You must receive God through your own Christ identity.

"They," - these disciples - *"have believed that thou has sent me."*

Now, the importance then of these eleven is that they believe God has sent Jesus Christ. The importance of the teaching is to establish our conviction that without Christ identity, we must perish. Without Christ identity, we're simply waiting for an undertaker. It's that simple.

Unless we bury in our consciousness the concept of body, the body we fail to bury will be buried by somebody else. These are hard words to put out and to hear but they're important ones and we're not at the place now where we're going to turn away from harsh words. The world is waiting for an undertaker. We're not waiting. The world is waiting to be buried. The Christ says, "Why? I am Life eternal. Did I not show forth on earth, as a man called Jesus, who could not be buried? Did I not show you to do this while on the earth? Did I not say that those who follow me, my Father will honor?" We're not talking about going to Heaven after death. We're talking about living in Heaven before death.

And so, Christ becomes the way shown to us by the Wayshower. The miracle is that in spite of the fact that this way has been shown, you can't find a hundred people who will agree with you that they must live in this world not in form but in Christ's spiritual identity.

And after the assurance that this is the way we're going to travel, we won't mind the problems that arise. We'll regard them as the method of perfecting our capacity to walk in Heaven while the human eye sees the earth. No stone is left unturned by the Christ to carefully put before us a perfect plan.

"I pray for them," says the Christ, *"I pray not for the world."*

Now, the world, then, are all the human identities who walk this earth. How can Christ pray for us if we are not in Christ? I pray for them who have accepted that I, Christ am their identity and that prayer is not a human prayer. The Christ doesn't pray like a human being. The meaning of *"I pray for them"* is not that I, Christ ask God to do any good for anyone. Christ is a permanent state of Being which is a permanent state of prayer. The Christ prayer is the knowledge that I am Being. I and the Father are one. There's nothing more to pray for. I pray and when you're in Christ, I and the Father are one is the state of Being that is in effect functioning through you.

"But I pray not for them that are in the world." Because they are not in Christ. There is no way that Christ can be effective to anyone who's not in Christ. How can manna shine down? How can the Red Sea part if only the Christ can reveal the invisible Reality that there's no Red Sea to part? That all manna is already in your Being, that you already include All that God is. The prayer is the meaning of Grace. "I pray," says the Christ, "for them who are in Christ." Those who are in Christ are in Grace. That prayer is that Grace.

I don't think the Christ tells you, "Find the Christ. Live in the Christ" and then strands you there and says, "I'm not giving you any directions." Those directions are forthcoming the instant this is your undivided goal.

"I [only] pray for them….. which thou hast given me; for they are thine."

Now, remember years ago we talked about Divine sequence? Now you know that not everyone in the world is ready to accept Christ identity. No one can decide for you if you're ready.

But I, the Christ, I function only in them who are Thine.

Now, everyone is of God so everyone is Thine but here the meaning of "Thine" means those whom Love has attracted at this moment in Divine sequence to the Christ.

If your desire for Truth has lifted you to the place where you will not settle for less than Christ identity, then you will discover that your work is done. It's just a matter now of, in human time, going through the motions. Your work is done. There's nothing can sway you or distract you from the one, established purpose of living in Christ. The permanent prayer of Christ which is Grace on earth is already an established fact for you. That's to give you here such assurance if such final assurance you need. These words are infallible. Whoever is in Christ is in Grace.

"All mine are thine, all thine are mine; I am glorified in them."

When Christ says, *"All mine are thine and all thine are mine,"* this is a statement of Oneness; that Christ and the Father are One. If you want to be One with the Father, you must be in Christ to be One. Christ is not in form.

And now comes something you have never heard before in your life. In spite of all our studies, we have all walked past these words again and again and again. I'm quite sure there's not a religious individual on this earth who has seen these words even though they've been right in front of us.

First, we were told that "I have manifested Thy name. I have shown forth the invisible Kingdom of God." And now here's the reason that Christ could show forth the invisible Kingdom of God; *"And now I am no more in the world."*

You could read that ten times and not give it a second thought until one moment it suddenly hits you and all the bells start ringing.

"I am not in the world."

He hasn't yet been crucified but he says, *"I am not in the world."* Will you please ask yourself how could they get someone who's not in the world and crucify him? Ask yourself that again and again and you will see there the revelation that is contained in that verse.

"I am no more in the world."

It's true tomorrow they're going to crucify somebody but I am not in the world. And the world thinks they crucified I, who am not in the world. You see what is being told to you? There's a form there and its name is Jesus Christ but it is saying, *"I am not in the world."*

Now, is the form there or not? If the form is there, then *"I, who am not in the world,"* am not in that form because that form is in the world. Now get this because it's the key to the complete revelation of Jesus Christ on the earth.

The form was there. People could touch it. People could see it. People could crucify it but Christ could say, *"I am not in the world."*

Now because the Word of God says this, that means that Christ is not there in that form which is in the world. *"I am not in the world."* The form you see is in the world but I am not.

And then, the sublime Truth that this I, which is not in that form called Jesus which is not in the world is the I of you now and it is not in the world now; right now. And just as that I of you which is not in the world now, which is not in the world when the form of Jesus stood there, that I of you is not in your form. And yet, it is your name. It is your eternal Self and it is present but not in the world. It is right here but not in the world. It was right there but not in the world. How could it be there and yet not be in the world? How can it be here and yet not be in the world?

Is there a Kingdom of God and a world? Is the Allness of Spirit sharing itself with a world?

"I am the Lord thy God and beside me there is no other."

Spirit is All. Spirit is Christ. Spirit is saying, "I am not in the world. I am not in the form. I am eternal Life. I am your name. You are not in the world. You are not in the form. You are eternal Life. That is your name." And Spirit is saying, "Know this. Know this before the body is taken from you."

You've only got this human body on a lend-lease plan. I, Spirit am your eternal Self here and now and I am in the Invisible, imperceptible to the senses of that body which is temporary and I am asking you to transfer your consciousness from the body consciousness, from the temporary self consciousness, from the belief that you are flesh seeking God, seeking Spirit, to the knowledge that you are not flesh and you are not seeking Spirit. You are. I, here, now invisible, am your Self. This is the place where we must come. This is the realization that I, Christ is never in a physical form but is always present, is always living and never knows death.

Now when we come to crucifixion, we're not going to crucify the I that says, "I am no more in this world." We're going to crucify something else and the I which comes forth again in a form is not going to be resurrected because it was not in the form that is going to be crucified.

And you're going to learn that you're not going to be in the form that is going to be buried. That's why this is the pinnacle of the Christ message. You must learn you can never be in the form that dies and you will learn it only if you will take into your consciousness the understanding that I who could utter on the face of this earth, that *"I am not in the world."*

"While the world thought that they were going to crucify me, and while the world went ahead and did just that and then thought that God had raised me up again, all of that illusion you must learn to be illusion for that illusion is no greater than the illusion of you walking now in a form."

It's the same illusion and there is in you a level of Consciousness which can know this Truth without doubt; that you are this very I which spoke those words and said, "I am no more in this world." That isn't the I of Jesus Christ. It is the Infinite I. It is the I of Jesus Christ and the I of everyone who walks the earth teaching us, lifting us, opening our eyes that, *"I am not in this world."*

"But I am present here in the invisible Kingdom of God which I have manifested, first through the appearance called Jesus Christ then through the appearance called disciples, then through those who follow the disciples and now through whoever has the Vision, the Courage and the Love to be drawn to this invisible, infinite I that I am."

These words, the 11th verse, chapter 17 of John are your assurance that there was no crucifixion; that never is a crucifixion possible because the I of God is the only inhabitant on this earth. I, invisible am the sole inhabitant of the earth. I, Christ. And until you have come to that understanding, you are not living in the message of the Christ. You may worship a God. You may love Jesus Christ. You may have a religion. You may think you believe but until you know that you are the one inhabitant of this earth named Christ and are willing to live in that awareness, the message of Christ for you is meaningless as it is for the rest of the world.

Now this was the Word that religion did not see; that I who am not in this world obviously can not be crucified and that throws a completely different meaning on resurrection and on ascension because it reveals that the form which was crucified never was there. It reveals that all forms that walked the earth are not the creation of God.

At one time, we would have winced at this. At this level of the teaching, to some, it is a great joy because that which hitherto had been impossible ceases to be impossible. We can understand why we are told that "I in the midst of thee am greater than he that walks the earth." Your Spiritual identity is greater than every physical identity you could ever serve. You could come through five hundred more incarnations but they would all be for one purpose, to come to your realization of Spiritual identity.

"Now I am no more in the world, but these are in the world."

You see the disciples are in the world only because they don't know they're not in it. They still believe that they're in those forms. They're in the world. If we still believe we're in these forms, we're in the world. And presuming that we, most of us, do believe we're in these forms, we are at the place now of those disciples who are still in the world and so, they still are in school. They still have to go through a Spiritual seasoning; a series of trials. Just as we do. They still believe they're in the world and they're not. They have to learn through experience that they are not in the world.

Now, when he says, "I am not in the world but they are," he means, "I know I'm not but they don't know. They believe they are."

"Now I am no more in the world, but these are in the world, and I come to thee. Holy Father, keep through thine own name those whom thou hast given me, that they may be one, as we are."

Now, Christ and God are One. And you know that no corpse and God are one. No potential corpse and God are one. Christ and God are One and God keep these in Oneness with us. What does that mean? Teach them who they are.

But the words here that are important are *"Through thine own name keep these."*

"Through thine own name." Jesus is going. That's the signal for everyone of us to turn from the outer to the inner so that the Father within can keep us in our true identity. The Father within is thy name. The name of God in you is Father within or indwelling Christ.

Directly, in the Christ of your own Being you are enlightened to the fact that you never were in the world. Your form appeared in the world but you the Christ, never were in the world.

Again, the Christ does not leave us empty handed and so now we're going to be shown what must happen for us to come into the realization that I am Christ who is not in the world and not in a dying form.

I think perhaps it would be wise if we just had a moment of quiet and then took a little intermission.

— End of Side One —

Now some of these things right now are not new but the reiteration of them helps to reach a level of ourselves that we are somewhat reluctant to strive to attain. We are to know that we are Christ not in the world while we appear as form in the world. That's a pretty difficult way of life but after the intermission, we'll be opened up so that we see how we're going to further this goal.

For the moment, we're dwelling on the statement of Christ before crucifixion. *"I am not in this world."* And we will hear the echo of that Christ within ourselves saying, *"I am not in this world."*

And we will identify with that I which says this and that is the purpose of this silence.

I am that I which says, "I am not in this world but I am here now in the Kingdom of God."

We're at the twelfth verse, *"While I was with them in the world,"* emphasizing I'm no longer in the world. *"While I was with them in the world, I kept them in thy name: those that thou gavest me I have kept, and none of them is lost, but the son of perdition; that the scripture might be fulfilled."*

Now, at first blush it would appear that the son of perdition is Judas but we'll go beyond that.

In your 109th Psalm, you notice that there is a statement about the fact that there would be a betrayal and this is interpreted to be Judas. In fact, the whole 109th Psalm is about that betrayal but it's much more than the betrayal of Judas.

The son of perdition in us is Judas and it must be cast out.

We know now that the son of perdition is our material consciousness which must be cast out. The love of the world. The son of perdition in us is not the Son of God therefore, who is it the son of? We rediscover that the son of perdition in us is the world mind functioning as our corporeal sense. Our corporeal sense must be cast out. Always again, in many disguises we are told that all belief that I dwell in the form must be cast out. The son of perdition in you is your belief that you are living in a form. It must be cast out even as Judas was cast out.

"That scripture might be fulfilled" and it takes this even further than casting out the sense of corporeality. And this is something we have never discussed in this class until this moment. That Judas being cast out is a symbol of what you and I must do for that is a pronouncement of the end of the world. Corporeality is to be cast out. It isn't going to be prevented. Corporeality cast out or material consciousness cast out. Judas cast out is a preview of the end of the world.

Those who cast out the son of perdition, who lose the consciousness of form by rising to the Consciousness of spiritual Selfhood. Casting out Judas are those who are standing in the Light which is unaffected by the end of form. Just as in spiritual Consciousness, in the body of the Soul, you are not buried; so in spiritual Consciousness, in the body of the Soul, you are not buried at the end of the world.

These could be very unnecessary words for many but for some of us they're important. We are being prepared not just to step out of a body into a body of the Soul, into another realm; we are being prepared to survive the end of an old realm.

We are being prepared to be raised into three more worlds. We have the fifth world, the sixth and the seventh. We cannot stop at any one point for there are three to go. The fifth world will be our next realm and we have a preview of it while in the fourth and we attain it now by casting out the son of perdition.

I who am not in the form and therefore I am not in the world say to you, "Follow me." Cast out the belief that you are in the form which is Judas. Cast out corporeality for if you do not, Judas in you, corporeality in you, will destroy you just as it destroys Judas. The sense of corporeality must destroy itself because it is never real. It will always throw itself into the fire.

The sons of perdition translated literally mean total and utter destruction. Perdition means utter destruction.

Those who live in form, whether they like it or not, believe it or not, common sense tells them ultimately that form is destroyed and that's why we who live in form are called sons of perdition, sons of the devil mind, of the world mind, of the material consciousness. But we who live in the I, will discover that when Judas is cast out, that very same Judas who would betray us no matter how he tries, no matter how corporeality tries to betray you, no matter how it attacks, it is totally without power. It may seem to have power but it has no power.

"Now I come to thee....I come to thee.... and these things I speak in the world, that they might have my joy fulfilled in them."

And the joy of Christ is the activity of the Father in Christ.

And so, when the Christ says, "I speak these things in the world although I am not in it, that they might have the joy that I have," that joy is to know that you are not in a dying world. You are not in a dying form. And these words are spoken for you to know that. You are not in a dying form and you are not in a world that can be destroyed. You are not in it. You are in Heaven on earth and Christ in you can reveal that to you.

"I have given them thy word; now the world hath hated them, because they are not of the world, even as I am not of the world."

Now then, the disciples are not of the world; they are in the world. In it but not of it. They have at least learned that they are another substance. They think they're in the world but they know they're not of the world. They think that they are in the flesh and that in some way, they are of God. They're in an ambivalence. You cannot be in the flesh and of God. You really cannot be in the world at all. You cannot be of the world at all. You can think you are. The disciples are still under the belief that they're in it although they have learned they're not of it.

We could say that we are under the knowledge now that we're neither in it or of it. We're not between two worlds. We were between two worlds when we were in that level of consciousness but when you know that you are the Christ you cannot be between two worlds. You're between two worlds when you haven't yet learned your identity. When you learn it, you're not between two worlds. You're in the Kingdom of God because Christ is never out of the Kingdom of God. How can you be not in the Kingdom of God if your name is Christ?

Now there's a big question and even though unspoken, it's on every mind. But it's answered because "Before you shall ask, I shall answer." And the 15th verse answers that big question which you're not speaking. You're even fumbling to find the question when the answer already comes.

"I pray not that thou shouldest take them out of the world, but that thou shouldest keep them from the evil."

"I, Christ do not petition God to take my disciples out of the world but to keep them from evil."

Now what would that mean? This is the answer to the big question we're trying to frame in our minds. How do I become conscious that I am Christ? And here's the answer. Stay in the world. I, Christ do not ask the Father to take my disciples out of the world but to keep them from evil.

And so, this is the method. The Christ doesn't even say, "Father keep evil from them." It says, "Keep them from evil." There's a distinction.

In the world, we will meet evil in many, many forms but I, Christ in you, through the Father coming through I. Christ, keeps you from evil so that this is your training school. You must walk amidst the evil. You cannot go into seclusion and expect to find Christ. It isn't done that way. Christ comes by your walking in the midst of evil and seeing the Good. Christ comes by your walking in the midst of the suffering and seeing the Help. Christ comes by your walking in the midst of death and seeing the Light. In other words, you must walk through the evil of the earth. That is the training.

Anyone can be good if there's no bad around. Anyone can believe in Christ if there is no temptation. And then we don't go high enough; we don't go beyond just the intellectual belief. We must walk on the earth converting all that comes to us and the word is reconciling; reconciling all that we see to the invisible Christ in your Self.

This is the real way, the test, the trial, the initiation. You must pass through the school of seasoning. You must be inserted into the appearances of evil for that is how you develop the capacity to hold on to the contact of Oneness. And this is going to be our assignment.

A woman called and said she was trying very hard in her classroom to see that certain children were the Christ. She could accept it for some but these little wiggly ones over there she said,

"I'm trying so hard to see that they're the Christ, too." What was she trying for? It's a fact. You don't have to try. It is the fact.

You see, we're trying. Trying, trying instead of saying, "Well it is the fact. I don't have to try. It is the fact. I accept the fact."

The fact is then, that there isn't a person you can see that isn't the invisible Christ whether you like them or not and whether you hate them or not. And it doesn't matter who they are or where they are or how high or low they are on the scale of humanhood. They aren't there. And the form isn't there. We've learned that; but the Christ is there.

Now, your assignment is to live in such a way that you're in the Christ of you and in the Christ of them so that you turn from the Christ of you to the Christ of them, from the Christ of them to the Christ of the other so that you never come out of Christ. You're seeing Christ in All. This is how you maintain Oneness without falling out of Oneness. No matter where you turn, no matter who is there before you look at them, you are maintaining the constant awareness that only the one Christ is present.

And so, everywhere you go, you're in a state of Oneness with Christ no matter what the form presents. You see the assignment now. This is the test of living in this world.

"Don't take them out of this world Father. They haven't yet practiced Oneness through the Christ of everyone they see. They're seeing Johnny Smith over there as a cripple and they're seeing Mary Jones over there as an adulteress and they're seeing this one over there as a narcotic addict and they're seeing this one as something else." And we are not going to do this.

We turn to the Christ in each individual without even opening the eyes. We walk in the world through what the world calls evil knowing it isn't there and we must be tested in this fire of the world.

We must be tested again and again and again until we know that the evil that we are learning not to resist, cannot be there.

When we have come to the place where there is no evil in this world, for it is the invisible Kingdom of God, then the Christ will take us out of the world. But not before. That's why we're in the world. The only way you can get out of the world is to see Christ everywhere you go.

So that means there is not a moment, not a second, between your changing from Christ here to Christ there, because it's one Christ. Wherever you go, you're turning to talk with Christ. It doesn't matter what's before you. It doesn't matter what the weather is. It doesn't matter what the state of the nation is. Your test is to come to that place where you're in Christ in everyone. And that will be the duration of your stay in this world through as many incarnations as necessary. You cannot step out of incarnation unless you step into Christ.

That's the meaning of the 15th verse in the 17th chapter. We must be subject to trials and tribulations. Even the Christ doesn't say, "Father take them out of the world but keep them in it. Expose them to all of the so-called evils and keep them from the evil. Don't keep the evil from them. Dangle it in front of their nose everyday but keep them from accepting the evil as a present truth."

Where is the evil if God is the only Creator? Where is the evil except when you are not in Christ; in human consciousness? And because the human consciousness is what ultimately kills the body, we must be subject to the appearances of evil until we know evil is not there and then we are not in a human consciousness when we know that. And when we are not in a human consciousness, we discover there is no body to be killed.

The plan then - and there's no getting away from it - is that we will be moving in the midst of evil which is not there to the Enlightened one. And if you can see one person on this earth who is not the Christ invisible, you're going to stay in the appearances of evil.

Now, the technique of not falling out of Oneness is the acceptance of the universality of Christ. The so-called worst people in the world make no difference. The best people in the world make no difference. You live in the conscious awareness that all I can meet today is Christ. The rest is the test.

I'm going to meet forms and I'm going to erase them out of my Consciousness. I'm going to meet them from the within. I'm going to let the Father within introduce me to his Kingdom. I'm going to be taught by God. And once you let your personal sense of self rise up in some form of antagonism, hostility, resentment, even personal desire, you're out of Christ. You break the continuity of the one universal Christ. You're back in this world.

Now, that's the reason we have our coughs today. That's the reason we have these thunder showers. That's the reason we have the so-called problems, disturbances of the world. They're all part of that picture which is presented to us when we're not in Christ.

And they're necessary because as you establish Christ contact, lo and behold, these conditions are alleviated and then you know that the way, the way to Life eternal is the acceptance that I am that Life eternal, the Christ itself and never must I lose this contact, this awareness, even though everything in this world is working, it seems, in the opposite, to take me out of this awareness. That's how I am forced to maintain the contact.

That's why we're on this earth here now, in this level, in this fourth world. To develop the capacity, to look through the veil, through the mist, through the evils to the knowledge that they are only a test, to force me to the higher ground of Christ where the test becomes unnecessary.

In your incorporeal Christ Self now, you're not in this world. And like the woman who was trying to see that the little, wiggly children were Christ too but not succeeding, the answer is quit trying. There's no sense trying to make the sun shine, trying to make a fact become a fact. Accept, I am not in this form. It's as simple as that. There's got to be a place where you accept I am not in this form. You're not going to feel it. It's not going to suddenly become a great enlightening fact to you. It's a fact now. And only when you accept it and really go to the extreme length to accept it and dwell there for a while will you see that it is a fact.

The moment you accept you're not in the form, you're being forced to find where you are and then you'll see that you can live in your Self, experience your Self and even begin to see what was called an invisible Kingdom. I am not in the form and even if it's not a very comfortable fact, it's still a fact.

I'd like to finish this next week - rather than go through it all - and have a complete understanding of it. There is too many verses to crowd into the last ten or twenty minutes.

In our meditation now, there is a Self that knows no pain, no disease, no discord, no destruction, no hate, no animosity. It is the Self of Love. It is an eternal Self, an ever-present Self. You find it in your higher moments of Truth. You ultimately learn it is your Self.

And when you're not trying but rather accepting, then you are in the awareness that I am that eternal Love which is Life itself. I'm never going to become It. I am It. And I must learn to face the evils of the world aware that I am eternal Life and Love now; that all power is in my Self. All power is in my Life. All power is in my Invisibility and all that is visible on the earth is but a counterfeit of the invisible, present Self that I am.

I live then in my invisible Life walking through the evils of the world, not accepting them, not resisting them, not trying to change them knowing that they are not present because I, Christ am the only Presence.

When you honor the Father, you are honoring your Self. Now your way out, you're in a place where there's no way for the mind to hold on. To you, in this level, you're not concerned about form. In these moments, you dwell only in the Infinite, formless universe. You let go of everything. It is a total surrender of all human selfhood.

The seed of every tomorrow is sown in this moment. All Spiritual fruitage appears from moments of silence in which you attain a level of awareness that Christ invisible, infinite, eternal is the name I that you are. In that sowing there is a harvest and that harvest ultimately is the graduation day into the realization that all form is now without power. All matter is without power. Nothing to deprive me because I am that infinite Self which is I. I am that One and I am that One every moment that I walk this earth though I appear in form. The form is in the world but I am not. I am in the Kingdom of God while the form appears in the world. Thou seest the form, thou seest not me for I am not in the world. I am in the Father and the Father in me. I am everywhere now. Everywhere.

This deepening realization will ultimately take us out of incarnation, out of reincarnation, into the invisible Kingdom present with signs and wonders, with fruitage more than you can handle but always your supreme test and your supreme harvest is never to fall out of One. You must hold on to that One in everyone to stay in the One. It's wise to establish this very early in the day. I will let nothing take me out of the One no matter what forms appear, whether they're forms of plenty or forms of lack. Cleave to the One. That is sowing to the Spirit and you will reap of the Spirit. That One in everyone is your Being.

Now, as you practice this week, not falling out of One, you will be able to come to a full realization of the meaning of the 17th chapter of John.

Your second assignment for the week is to look back at verse 11 of the 17th chapter to realize that Christ Jesus is saying, *"I am not in the world,"* and to meditate a number of times to allow yourself to learn the meaning of that for you, what that revelation really means for you, that *"I am not in the world."* This will help you know if you're accepting that the Christ of you which is your name is not in the world. If you're not accepting it, you cannot go all the way. The 11th verse, *"I am not in the world."*

I don't believe we've had any more difficult assignments so don't be disappointed if you're not able to complete them to your satisfaction because you can know in advance that you cannot satisfactorily live in Oneness throughout the clock. You can make the effort but you have to creep up higher and higher.

The understanding that *"I am not in the world,"* is sort of the end of the line and when you dwell with that, it will help you to see the degree of Oneness that is required for you to totally be immersed in the one Self. You must know you are not in the world. And practice not being in the world in these meditations. You'll discover depths of your Self you hadn't realized.

"I am not in the world. I am not in form." Thanks for braving the rain. See you next week.

Class 34

Preparation For Gethsemane

Herb: Good afternoon again.

I was just given the title of today's meeting. It's called "Preparation for Gethsemane."

It's not a lesson that we anticipated when we began living the Spiritual life. One way or another, we anticipated many wonderful things. We saw an accumulation of Goodness, of blotting out of evil. We saw Harmony and Happiness ahead for us. But this lesson today is the preparation for Gethsemane.

If we were to limit the actual universe to the inventions or discoveries of man, we wouldn't have any heavenly bodies. We wouldn't have any planets. And if we were to limit the function of these bodies to what man can comprehend, the world would end in one minute. It would be all over.

In order for the universe to function, it must function at a level beyond the comprehension of the human brain. And similarly, if man were to decide what is the best way for him to live under the present society, he would go out and do things that he has done which are outside the rhythm of God. He has no capacity to live inside the Spiritual rhythm of the universe through his brain.

He would never, for example, decide to learn how to walk in the Kingdom of Heaven the way the Father has planned it. The Divine plan is so different than anything you or I would have conceived. We would not, for example, have included the preparation for Gethsemane in our work. That's the last thing we think of. It seems to be going in the wrong direction.

But the Father is always full of surprises and that is why the 15th verse of the 17th chapter is so surprising. We touched on it last week.

"I pray not that thou shouldest take them out of the world, but that thou shouldest keep them from the evil."

And in that we find the Divine plan which is the preparation for Gethsemane.

Now to understand it, we have to see certain factors about our lives and bring them into sharp focus. I'm going to read to you certain statements of Jesus Christ about you. They're all out of Mathew, Luke, maybe one in John, I don't know.

After the resurrection, when Mary Magdalene finds Jesus Christ in the garden, he says to her, *"Touch me not; for I am not yet ascended to my Father: but go to my brethren, and say unto them, I ascend unto my Father,"* and then he adds some words that are important to all of us, *"and your Father; and to my God, and to your God."*

Now there, Jesus Christ concludes your Father and his Father as the same Father. *"I ascend to my Father and to your Father."* These are the first instructions given to the disciples by Jesus Christ to Mary Magdalene to relay to the disciples. *"I ascend to my Father and to your Father; to my God and to your God."*

And a little later, *"Call no man your father upon the earth: for one is your Father, which is in heaven."* The emphasis again is *"your Father."* And so, the Wayshower is teaching us that his Father and your Father are the same Father.

Repeatedly, *"Be ye therefore perfect, even as your Father which is in heaven is perfect."*

"Let your light so shine before men, that they may see your good works, and glorify your Father which is in heaven."

"But I say unto you, Love your enemies, bless them that curse you, do good to them that hate you, pray for them which despitefully use you, and persecute you; That ye may be the children of your Father which is in heaven."

Again, *"Your Father knoweth what things ye have need of, before ye ask him."*

"And therefore, After this manner therefore pray ye: Our Father which art in heaven, Hallowed be thy name."

Always, you're being taught that God is your Father.

"But if ye forgive not men their trespasses, neither will your Father forgive your trespasses."

"Fear not, little flock; [for] it is your Father's good pleasure to give you the kingdom."

And again, *"Thy Father, which seeth in secret, shall reward thee openly."*

Now, every statement there is telling you that you are the son of God.

We have learned from the Scripture that the words spoken by Jesus are the words of God. "I say only that which I hear of the Father."

And so, God says to you, to me, to our enemies, to every person who walks the earth, "The son of God is your real name." Now, we have to take that into consciousness and we have to come to a place where we are living as the son of God.

And we say, "Well, I'm willing, I'm eager. And sometimes I'd like to remember that I'm supposed to do that but I always forget." And the reason we forget is because we do not yet know what it is to be the son of God. We don't really forget. We haven't yet learned.

And so, we say, "Well, what is the son of God if that is who I am?"

And now, I want you to come back to a statement that you have studied again and again in one of Joel's books and it's the major acceptance of what is a son of God. These quotations come from "Beyond Words and Thoughts" in the tenth chapter called "Incorporeality" and it tells you what is a son of God so you know what you are, so that you are willing to accept what you are, not only as a name but as a fact and to accept the nature of your true Being.

Now, if you haven't yet accepted incorporeality as the nature of the son of God, Joel firmly states as follows, you'll find it on page 138 of "Beyond Words and Thoughts."

"Those on the mystical path must remove from thought the image-man, the corporeal man, the man who has physicality because that man is not the man of God's creation."

The man of physicality is not the son of God. You are the son of God and therefore, you are either going to continue living in the belief that you are physical, structural being or you are going to accept that because you are the son of God you are not physical, structural being.

We're calling a spade a spade today because this is the preparation for Gethsemane. You are the son of God and therefore, not physical being and you have the word of Jesus Christ for it and you have the word of Joel Goldsmith for it and you have your own realization that it is true for it, too because by now there cannot be anyone who doubts this in our work.

Again, on page 140, 149 rather, of "Realization," *"There is,"* no, this is in "Beyond Words and Thoughts," remember, in "Incorporeality" chapter 10, *"There is no corporeal creation! It is we who entertain a corporeal sense about an incorporeal creation!"*

Again, on page 149, *"When you living out from incorporeality, you have attained the mystical consciousness out of which all form appears."*

And finally, I cannot be in that automobile on a crowded highway because I am nowhere between the head and the foot. I am not corporeal. I am incorporeal. I am Spiritual. I can stop worrying about the germs that cannot find me.

Now then, in answer to our question, "What is the son of God?" - the son of God is the non-physical, invisible, Spiritual Being who lives where God lives, who is one with God, who is the substance of God, who does not inhabit a human form, who does not inhabit a physical world. That is a son of God.

And the Christ, speaking in words that are clear, states that you are the son of God. And because you have not come to grips with that, there must be a Divine plan to make sure that you do and that is the 15th verse of the 17th chapter.

In the prayer of thanksgiving of Christ Jesus to the Father, in his high ecstasy of the Soul, he says to the Father, "Do not take them out of this world. Let them walk in this world which is not your Kingdom; but keep them from evil."

And so, you will find that by exposure to the illusions of evil, you will develop your capacity to be the son of God. You must be exposed to that which is not in order for you to learn what is. The plan is that to develop your Spiritual consciousness, you must walk in the material world, developing your sensitivity to inner Truth, building your capacity to trust your invisible Self, learning that you are an invisible Being, learning that the son of God is never in danger, that the son of God is always under Divine law, learning that you can depend upon the qualities of Divine Sonship to move you through the illusions of evil that surround you.

And so, this is the plan as announced by the Christ. We are to build a consciousness of Spirit. We are to learn to trust our own

Being to be whole, to be complete, to contain within itself the power of the Christ, the mind of the Christ, the presence of the Christ, the fullness of the Christ with nothing withheld. And therefore, to be a son of God involves the supreme test of proving that you are the son of God. You must prove that you are. You must prove the presence of God. You must prove the power of God. You must prove that you are the light of God.

It doesn't say go into seclusion. It doesn't say flee from the world. It doesn't say leave your home, leave your occupation. It says walk amidst the evil illusion learning that it is not there and the way you will learn that is by fidelity to your own Spiritual Sonship. Fidelity to Christ, fidelity to the Truth that I am truly the son of God now. And therefore, I am prepared to walk through the world overcoming every illusion of evil, non-reacting to every illusion of evil, non-resisting every illusion of evil, faithful to the fact that I, Christ is my name, that I am invisible Being, that I never drive an automobile. I never sit in the theater. I never walk in a form. I am the invisible son of God. This must be practiced in every way you know how.

We must ultimately come to a place where we can say, "I not only have been able to understand but I have been able to live out of the knowledge that I am Divine Being, Divine Life, not human flesh, not encased in a human form, that I am invisible to all who look at me, that I am maintained by the mystical bread and wine which is the living Word of the Father."

The word "ecstasy" in Greek means stepping outside of yourself and in some of the Far Eastern religions you will see the state of ecstasy often mentioned. It actually means stepping outside of your sense of physicality. The word "ecstasis," to step outside of self, to step outside of the concept and this cannot be done without continuous practice, conscious practice, conscious awareness that if I am not stepping outside of the concept called form, outside of the concept called matter, outside of the concept called world, I am not being the son of God.

And that is why the evil illusions must appear here. They force you to accept the challenge, to make the test, to wake up, to wake up to the invisible Power that is ever present, the invisible Life that is untouched, the invisible Self that can never be destroyed. They force you to prove that you are what the Christ says you are. They force you to be your Self and if you're not willing to be your Self, you're crushed in the process. It is the Father's will that you be the son of God.

Now then, you know the plan is to make you be the son of God consciously and so, you know why the illusions must appear as evil forms, evil persons, evil things, evil conditions because they can only be overcome by the knowledge that you are the living Christ, immune to all that appears to be evil and even when you're caught in it, having let down your guard in some way, the antidote is always, "I am the living son of God. I must rest in that Consciousness." And that Self is not the form that had the problem. That Self is never in a condition or a situation. That Self is never in a crack-up on a freeway. And that Self I am.

And when you do this, you're out of the usual sense comforts that you're accustomed to. You can't find a place to rest. The Son of man, the son of God has no place to lay his head. It's all rather strange until you feel the quickening and then the strangeness disappears and you find you're on a different level. It's slow before the Light really kindles and then that inner explosion and you know you have been lifted up. And you must be patient because it isn't a day, it isn't a week, it isn't a month. If you haven't been practicing "I am the invisible son of God," you've got months ahead of you. For some, years ahead of you. For those who've been trying, you may find that you have already experienced that Living sonship without any doubt in your thought to the point where you can really have the confidence that you are the living son of God.

All of this is to prepare you for that total trust, that total faith, that here, now is the full power of Divine Love. Wherever I go is the full power of Divine Love omnipresent and you must prepare again and again and again and continuously until that total conviction is yours.

They are not in the world. *"They are not of the world, even as I am not of the world."*

Now, when we are told that the disciples are *"not of the world,"* that we are *"not of the world,"* there's another way to say it and it isn't shattering if you have accepted your Self to be the son of God. You cannot be of the world because there is none. There is no world anymore than there was a human self. The human self is our corporeal sense about the incorporeal Divine Self that we are. The world is our corporeal sense about the invisible, incorporeal Divine Kingdom that is. And so, the sons of God are not of the world because they know there is no world and being the sons of God, they live where God lives in the Kingdom of God and that Kingdom is perfect. The sons of God therefore live in the invisible perfection of God's Kingdom, accepting it as the only present Reality and are non-resistant to the non-reality.

"Not of the world."

Now, you remember that at the beginning of the Christ mission, the disciples were promised, "If you follow me, Heaven will open up." In a larger sense, the whole New Testament is saying that it is possible and necessary for one individual, whoever he is, to bring together all his disciples into a Wholeness so that now, the disciples no longer are human beings. And Jesus Christ is the example or the symbol of your Self gathering together your inner disciples into a Oneness until you are a whole Being. And when you are a whole Being, you're prepared for the full test of Gethsemane.

Every character in the Bible is within you. You are the son of God and the characters in the Bible are the undeveloped Divine qualities within you, waiting for you to bring them into fullness to prove you are the son of God, to prove you are whole being.

And so, now we are told we will walk through the illusions of evil as part of our trial but we must know we are not of the world. We must be awake to our Invisible Self. And so, you're walking in the visible to the world but in the consciousness of your Invisible Self. Try it now and you'll see what I mean. In your Invisible Self you are like the Father who has no visible shape, no heart, no lungs, no brain, no physical structure and I and the Father are one and so I invisibly have no heart, no lungs, no brain, no physical structure and I must be willing to surrender all my concepts about physicality to be in the Consciousness of the Invisible Self that I am.

As you develop this capacity, you find you're building the awareness of Peace, of Tranquility, of Trust, of Assurance. All of these are the opening of the inner eyes that Christ Consciousness may enter in. The surrender of the human selfhood, the surrender of the human self is the sacrifice called upon to those who accept that I am the son of God. The son of God refuses to be a human self.

And so, very few walk this path, even those who have studied many years because now they're being prepared for something they didn't anticipate and at this level, all of the flaws show up. All of the fears, all of the doubts, all of the places where you found that you didn't have the time to practice your meditation, your communion, your study. This all shows up at this particular point. It also shows up for those who have done their work for they find that even though the ground beneath them isn't there, they're walking on the steadiness of their own Consciousness. They can feel the great adventure of walking in the Invisible.

They're saying, "Father, I trust your Omnipresence wherever I go. I trust your Power to be the only and I know it is Good power and I trust my own Selfhood to embrace every Divine power without any human effort on my part to make it so. I am not of the world."

We've been so far away from ourselves that coming back home seems strange and yet, continued practice of this invisible Selfhood does produce a feeling of well-being, of rightness and ultimately a complete at-homeness in your Invisible Self so that you can see the outer form is nothing but a vehicle which expresses your inner Consciousness.

In this Consciousness, your Invisible Self is the only Self in the universe. There is no other. All are the one, invisible Self. No matter what forms you see, they are your Invisible Self because the invisible Self of Christ is the only Infinite Son of the Father. Wherever you are going, the forms make no difference when you train yourself to let them make no difference because the Invisible Self where every form is, is your Invisible Self. Everywhere is your Invisible Self undivided, unseparated, always one with the Father, always being the perfect expression of God. Nothing changes it. Nothing in the visible changes your perfect, invisible Self.

And as we develop this Consciousness, we can accept the next verse, the next statement of the Christ. He says to the Father, *"Sanctify them through thy truth: thy word is truth."*

And the word "sanctify" now opens another doorway. To sanctify is to make you into a saint. I don't think you had any idea of becoming a saint. But the son of God is a saint.

On the pathway to Sonship realized, you must pass through sainthood. Do you see why we are to be without blemish? This is the call to sainthood. And even though none of us have reached the place where we thought of it that way, that we're being called to sainthood, this is why we must learn to walk in our Invisible Self as a living son of God.

The next step in your development out of humanhood is sainthood. These men Paul and John weren't named saints because they were good human beings; it's because they had passed through the portals of the visible, physical sense of life. Not by death but by surrender of the human sense of self into Spiritual sonship which is sainthood.

"Sanctify them." Reveal the Divine nature of their Being.

There's a place in Corinthians. 1 Corinthians, 1:2. A very strange statement which we all overlook even though it happened so frequently that we read it and never see it. There it has been all these years about sainthood. Right at the beginning of 1 Corinthians.

"Unto the church of God which is at Corinth, to them that are sanctified in Christ Jesus, called to be saints, with all that in every place call upon the name of Christ Jesus our Lord, both their's and our's: Grace be unto you."

"Called to be saints."

This is Paul saying that to the people that he is teaching in the city of Corinth. We have been *"Called to be saints."*

The funny thing is that it's in John, too, in the first chapter of John, right at the beginning. We have here in the first chapter, the twelfth and thirteenth verse, *"Which were born, not of blood, nor of the will of the flesh, nor of the will of man, but of God."*

And so, to sanctify, to call unto sainthood, is to reveal that you were not born of the flesh. You were not born of blood. You were not born of the will of the flesh nor the will of man. And so, the son of God is not born of flesh, is not born of the human processes but is born of God,

"And the Word was made flesh, and dwelt among us,"

Again, the sanctification then of you is to reveal what your human brain did not know that you were not born of the flesh. You were not born of the will of your parents. You were born before the form and you were born of God. That is why you are called the son of God.

And now these words, buried for most people in the Bible are coming up and demanding of us that we be what we are, born of God, not of the flesh.

Again, in 1 Peter, the 22nd verse of the very first chapter. All of this to support this moment in preparation for Gethsemane.

Now, there are several verses here that are important.

In 1 Peter 1, 22nd on to the 25th, *"Seeing ye have purified your souls in obeying the truth through the Spirit unto unfeigned love of the brethren, see that ye love one another with a pure heart fervently: Being born again, not of corruptible seed, but of incorruptible, by the word of God, which liveth and abideth for ever. For all flesh is [as] grass, and all the glory of man as the flower of grass. The grass withereth, [and] the flower thereof falleth away: But the word,"* and the that's the Word of which we are born, *"the word of the Lord endureth for ever. And this is the word which by the gospel is preached unto you."*

The corruptible seed then was the belief that we were born into form. The incorruptible is the correction that we were born of God, not of corruptible seed; that we are now the son of God, Spirit, which is not visible to human eyes and therefore, we are Invisible Self - now.

This is the meaning of "Sanctify them." Reveal to them, my disciples, that they are not visible flesh. They were immaculately conceived of God, of his Spirit. They are sons of God. They like I, are not of the world though they think they are.

You and I, who have thought we were of the world, born of the flesh, of the will of our parents, must learn that we are invisible Being, Divine, born of God, living under the government of God and this revelation, brought home to us to the point of realization, is the sanctification of the Self.

"As thou hast sent me into the world, even so have I also sent them into the world."

The Father sends the Christ into the world. The Christ, in the disciples, sends the disciples into the world but how was I sent into the world?

"As Thou has sent me into the world.... I have sent them."

Christ Jesus was revealed to be born of a Virgin. In other words, not born of the flesh, immaculately conceived. Christ Jesus was immaculately conceived and said, *"As you sent me into the world,,,, I have sent them."*

Whoever receives Christ within is Immaculately conceived. The moment you are in the realization that Christ is your name, you know that you were Immaculately conceived. This is the meaning.

When you accept sonship as a way of Life, you accept that you were Immaculately conceived and therefore, mortality becomes a myth. Death becomes an impossibility. All illness becomes an impossibility. All lack and limitation becomes an impossibility because there is no evil or error in the son of God and you look at all evil and error as an impossibility in your Being. This drives the wedge between our previous acceptance of evils and errors that we had to remove, preparing us to see that these are not to be removed. They have never made contact with my Being. They have only made contact with my fleshly sense of self. And when I rest in my Being, my fleshly sense of self benefits through the surge of all of the Divine qualities of my Being into the visible world.

Now you remember when Joel wrote about the fact that we all want things. We want health. We want peace. We want supply. We want possessions. But he said but you can't have the things without the fabric. Now in the human sense, we have the things. We're sure we have them but they are corruptible. They're transient.

In the Divine, when you are the son of God, you are the fabric itself and then from the fabric of your Being all things are added. And those things that are added from your fabric are different than those things that are built out of the world mind fabric. As the son of God, your fabric is the substance of God and the qualities of that Substance build into the visible as an expression of the Divine, those things which are ordained of the Father. Grace made visible becomes form built of the fabric of Reality and these things are not taken away. These things fulfill a Divine purpose. These things are ordained. *"The Father who seeth in secret rewards thee openly."*

And so, there's a different thing that happens between the things you have of the world mind and the things you have of the Spirit. Ostensibly they might appear to be the same but one can be taken away and one cannot. One can appear momentarily and yet not fulfill a function and the other always does fulfill a function.

And then the qualities of your Substance are your real protection, your real safety. Your real sword is no longer a pointed piece of steel; your real sword is your Spirit. Your real supply is no longer your dollars or your investments; your real supply is your living Consciousness. Your health isn't the chart of the doctor or today's thermometer telling you that your temperature is just right. Your health is Divine Sonship made visible as the health of your countenance.

There's no fluctuation in the Divine qualities. They do not depend upon the whims of the world. The Word made flesh is different than just the mind of the world made flesh.

"Sanctify them." Reveal their Divine essence. Reveal that Grace is functioning in their Divine Sonship. Reveal that they really are the son of God and as such, they really are Eternal Being. They really are forever. They really are beyond all of the evils of this world even though they would appear to be walking amidst them. They are on Holy Ground in the conscious knowledge of that Divine sonship practiced day in and day out. Prepare them for sainthood. Reveal to them the body of the Soul. Reveal to them the invisible body which we all share as the one Christ.

To be sanctified is the ultimate preparation for Gethsemane. For in Gethsemane you'll find the All-power as the only power and you rest upon it. Everyone walks to Gethsemane. No one is excluded. Each must present himself as a total human sacrifice willing to depend completely on Divine Sonship as the only protection. And as you pass that moment, successfully, that is the moment when you know your Eternal Self.

Now, we are all to be sanctified if we are willing to take the steps of living in our invisible Selfhood, trusting it, understanding it, building our awareness of what it means, letting the Spirit expand our awareness of who we are, what qualities we contain, letting the Spirit reveal the wholeness of our Being. If we take these steps, if we practice faithfully, we are to be sanctified which means the full, total realization of Oneness.

"Glorify Thou me Father with Thy name which was mine before the foundations of the world."

This glorification is the sanctification, the knowledge of who you are unshakable, revealed to you. The inner robe. The ring. That total confidence which needs no more words, no more signs, no more demonstrations.

You can say, "*I AM THAT I AM.*"

This sanctification awaits all of us and the prerequisite is to be You now the living son of God walking in the invisible universe in your invisible Body. Practiced daily.

"For their sakes I sanctify myself, that they also might be sanctified through the truth."

We have a Wayshower who did this first. Even saintliness is just a phase. It's the fifth world but in your saintliness, you'll find the total fidelity to the will of God in you. Only the saint lives totally in the will of God and that's why he's called a saint. We're learning to live totally in the will of God.

When you're out of the rhythm of God, out of the Spiritual rhythm, you're in a state of conflict. Many levels of your consciousness unknown to you are fighting against themselves, fighting against the Divine force. You feel these moments of unrest when you can't put your finger on what's wrong and yet, you're not quite where you want to be. Something's wrong and you don't know why and you don't even know what it is. Sometimes many things.

But suddenly there's a moment when everything seems right. It's when you find that Spiritual rhythm again. When you're running not through your own will but in the will of the Father.

And this walking in the illusions of evil invisibly as the Self that is the Self of All, this being the Divine son, this willingness to accept the words of the Christ that you are, all this is bringing you back, restoring you to your Spiritual rhythm so that you and the force of the universe are one; where there's no shadow between you and God; where there's no seam, there's no second. But I and the Father, one Invisible Self.

In Hebrews, we have something rather interesting along these lines. Into the 10th chapter and the fourth verse, then it goes to the ninth and tenth verse.

First, Paul tells his students, Hebrews 10:4 *"For it is not possible that the blood of bulls and of goats should take away sins."*

Then he goes on in the ninth and tenth verse. Then, he said, *"He,"* referring to Christ, *"Lo, I come to do the will of God. He taketh away the first, that he may establish the second."*

See what that means? As you enter the knowledge that you are the son of God, the first is being taken away. You thought you were the human being.

"He taketh away the first, that he may establish the second."

It's the surrender of the first, the human sense of self, the acceptance of the second, the Divine, Invisible Self. *"By the which will we are sanctified through the offering of the body of Jesus Christ once for all."* Each accepts the invisible Christ body. This is the sanctification.

In our meditation now, let us hold to this Truth of the invisible nature of your Being, that you can never be two and when you're not being the son of God, you're not being your Self.

The son of God is never visible. The son of God is never corporeal, never in a physical form, never in the world. Always in the Kingdom of God where earth appears to be; always in the body of Light where physical form appears to be. And because your five senses cannot cognize that fact, you must transcend the five senses, accepting the Word of the Christ which says it is so. And so, you're living beyond the capacity of your senses in your acceptance. You're not living in your universe to what your senses or your brain can tell you. You're accepting, with trust, the words of the Christ that you are that Invisible son now as the disciples were told; that they were not of the world; that they were to be sanctified; that they were Divine; that they were like Jesus Christ, the Son of God; that God was truly their Father just as God was his Father and that we now accept our perfection as the sons of God.

"Be ye perfect as your Father."

Your Father's perfection lies in the fact that there is no power other than the power of God. Your perfection lies in the fact that the power of God is the power of the Son and beside the power of your Sonship there is no other power. Beside the mind of your Sonship there is no other mind. And that mind being perfect and all-intelligent, all action of that mind is equally perfect and all-intelligent. And all action that is not perfect and all-intelligent is as much an illusion as the evils that you see around you. All that is not perfect as your Father is the illusion of the senses. There is nothing but perfection present in the invisible Kingdom of God and the visible world is but a distorted mental image of that invisible, ever present Perfection.

The Perfection never goes away. The Spiritual reality never disappears. The Sonship never changes. It's a matter of getting accustomed to living as that invisible Son in that invisible Perfection and looking out at the world with no fear or doubt or need to change what appears; knowing that your Substance realized makes all the necessary adjustments.

Your substance realized is the invisible, miracle worker of Grace. It's only when you realize your identity as Divine Son, Divine Life, Divine Substance, Divine Being that the adjustments are made. They cannot be made except through your conscious awareness of your identity.

But when you are in that conscious awareness, without sword, without might, without power, without manipulation, your very own Being removes the distorted sense appearances and reveals the harmony of your Being. It is effortless. The only effort is in being your Self.

— End of Side One —

Now continue the lesson we took with us for practice during the week which many of you may have forgotten, about resting in Oneness so that you live in an uninterrupted state of Oneness.

As one new person came into your life, you transferred your conscious awareness of Christ from your Self to that individual so that you still lived in the One Self. Now, that's what we're doing at this moment. We're trying to know that though there are forty or fifty forms present here, that only your Invisible Self is present here. And that's the realization of Oneness to maintain.

So that as you turn from one friend to another, you're never changing your conscious awareness of that one invisible Self of each individual. Wherever I go, only the one invisible Self is present. This is the one body of Christ.

The importance of this cannot be over-stressed. Whoever attains the ability to rest consciously in the one invisible Self regardless of what they're doing will find the law of Grace is the law of everything they're doing. You can't put in too much time on this. There's no sacrifice too great; to consciously know that though I speak to male or female, I am speaking to the one invisible Self.

Always to turn from that that you see before you to the next one who comes before you but never really to turn. It's always the Invisible Self of you and that Invisible Self of you is always the Invisible Self of the friend you greeted or the enemy who stood before you. There is only that Invisible Self. You must claim it and live in it consciously. This is all part of the pathway to the sanctification.

And so, we should be, even when we listen to a talk, even when we go to a theater, no matter what we do, always we never step out of the realization that one invisible Self is where all of the forms appear to be. And that Invisible Self, I always accept to be my only Self. All of this is your silent work. It's almost the same as world work, the knowledge of the one, infinite, invisible Self as your Self.

When you are sanctified, nothing happens to you for you are always the son of God. The sanctification mentioned here is the revelation that God individualizes as your Selfhood even before you come into form. The Selfhood of God is your individualization. The revelation of that is the sanctification. The acceptance of it is the preparation for the realization of it.

"Neither pray I for these alone," just these handful, just these eleven. Neither pray I just for the eleven qualities of God in the midst of me but for all qualities to be brought up to their fullness in my consciousness. *"Neither pray I for these alone, but for them also which shall believe on me through their word."*

The Word in you is Christ. Through your Word. Your belief in the Christ of you brings you into the same Oneness and sanctification as the disciples in the time of Jesus. This is the preparation so that your knowledge of Christ in you is automatically your knowledge of Christ in those you will meet that day.

And so, I Christ pray or prepare the way. The harmony of Christ in you becomes the Harmony of your relationships as you accept your one, invisible Self not as a limited invisible self where you stand but as the one Infinite Invisible Self.

Your Self, being everywhere, that acceptance brings into play Christ going before you, preparing the way. As the form moves in the visible, the Invisible everywhere Christ Self of you accepted, prepares the way in every other form that will be in association with you.

We do not drop our realization of Oneness for a second. We do not step out of Life, for that is Life. And the more you're conscious of it, the more you'll discover you have found that dimension which was lacking in all your previous years. The missing dimension was my conscious awareness that I am the one invisible Self of the universe. And it doesn't matter where I turn. It is still I, functioning, present and perfect and always the only Power. That is how you realize Oneness and that Oneness manifests as the Grace of the Father in your Presence.

"That they may all be one; as thou, Father, art in me, and I in thee, that they also may be one in us: that the world may believe that thou hast sent me."

The repetition of *"Thou has sent me"* again and again and again for you to know that only Christ is sent. Only Christ is of the Father. That which is sent of the Father is Christ and only Christ. Only the invisible Self of Spirit is sent and if you're not in contact with that invisible Self of Spirit, you're not in contact with that which is of the Father. You're separated.

We're learning to worship God within ourselves as our very own Selfhood and that God is invisible, incorporeal and I, that son of God am invisible, incorporeal, without boundaries, without visible form, without visible shape, without visible substance. You're taking yourself out of the body image and resting in your Infinity. And we can learn to do this to the degree that we're more at home in our invisible Infinity than in a body image.

That we may all be One.

"And the glory which thou gavest me I have given them; that they may be one, even as we are one."

Christ which is one with the Father says, "You are one with the Father for I have given you that glory" meaning I am Christ in you. You are assured that Christ is in you for you have that glory. It says, "I have given them that glory." Christ in you is an established Truth of your Being.

Now, we don't want to ignore these words which are beyond our own mind level but come to us from the Christ mind level because they are the eyes we need to take us beyond our own horizons.

We do not know that we are one invisible Body but we are told it by the Christ and so we follow the Christ which means we accept we are one invisible Body. But we're not another body. We're not a second body. We are one invisible body and when you drop the awareness of that, you're back in a second body which is not a body, which is not sustained. That's why the organs of our body can go wrong. They are separated from the one invisible Body. They're not controlled by

God. They're controlled by the world mind. But when you're in your one invisible Body in Consciousness, you find even the organs of your body are no longer controlled by the world mind. They *are* controlled by God. The power of your Spiritual Selfhood controls the organs of your body when you are not accepting yourself to be that very body in which those organs can be controlled by the Spirit. You must step out of the belief of it.

Realization of Oneness, now, is revealed to be a conscious attitude, a way of life lived in until it becomes an old shoe, a way that you're accustomed to. Not something new or shocking or something you heard about and you're going to try someday but something you're doing all the time and always holding the thread of Oneness - that I and that Invisible Self, while you're shaking hands with a prospect, while you're saying to the butcher, "I'll have two pounds of that"; while you're saying to the delivery man, "Thank you for this." Always, the words that are coming out of your mouth are not what your consciousness is saying within you. You're saying "I am the Invisible Self of every individual I shake hands with, or talk to, or address in any way. I am that One. That One I am that is everywhere. I will not let go of that Oneness. And that one is invisible Spirit. That one is the Christ. That One is the child of God, one with the Father and that One I am everywhere no matter what forms come in to my consciousness visibly."

Never dropping that thread of the One builds your awareness, sensitivity, consciousness until finally, the Essence itself is realized and that's the substance or the fabric of all things. That Essence realized can give you all the forms that you will ever need out of the infinite reservoir of Spirit and they will pour forth in profusion. They will move mountains. They can do anything required if you are in invisible Oneness with the Selfhood of God everywhere. No longer divided.

"I in them, [and] thou in me, that they may be made perfect in one; and that the world may know that thou hast sent me, and hast loved them, as thou hast loved me."

Always, he who was called Jesus Christ emphasizes that he is not the exception; that the power he demonstrated is the universal Power in everyone.

"[That thou] hast loved them as thou has loved me."

The universal nature of Sonship is stressed so that you can never make the mistake of religion in worshipping Jesus Christ as the one and only Son of God. That is a tragic error and it is equally a tragic error to assume that a mortal being is going to become an Immortal one or that a material being is going to become a Spiritual being.

We are being told that the Father loves us and the Father has said, *"Cease ye from man."* The Father has said, "I am no respecter of persons." The Father doesn't love a mortal being. The Father loves you because you are his son and his son is an immortal Being now. When you're told the Father loves you, you are being told you are the son of God again in another way.

And you'll find that hidden in all of the words is the constant reiteration that you are my Son. When you take that to heart, all human heredity is thrown out the window. That's why Jesus had to overcome the sense of human heredity.

I am the son of God and for lifetime after lifetime, man has been saying, "I am not the son of God." And he's been suffering for it. And this handful who can come to the realization, "But I am what they say I am" will not suffer for it but will accept Divine heredity as the fact of life now and with it, all that Divine heredity embraces. The Father's life passed on to you as your Life doesn't include susceptibility to any problems on this earth and your problems therefore are based on the false assumption that you are not the child of God.

Correction in consciousness practiced, shows that all evil in the world is impossible. Evil is not here. The son of God is here. That is the glory of the Father in you, in your Oneness.

"Father, I will that they also, whom thou hast given me, be with me where I am; that they may behold my glory, which thou hast given me: for thou lovedst me before the foundation of the world."

Now, when the Christ says, *"Father I [wouldst] that they be with me where I am,"* this is the will of God expressing. The will of God expressing as Christ says, "I want you to be where Christ Jesus is." That's the will of God expressing and you either fulfill that will and you're in the rhythm of Spirit or you refuse to, through ignorance or otherwise. And if you are to be where Jesus Christ is, it doesn't mean tomorrow. The son of God is where Jesus Christ is now. There's only one way you can be where I am. I am in the Kingdom of God.

"Father, I will that they also, whom thou hast given me, be with me where I am."

I, Christ am in the Kingdom of God and I will that you be with me, in the Kingdom of God. Now, you try to enter the Kingdom of God in that form that you call your body. You cannot be with Christ in that form.

"I will that they…. be with me where I am."

You can only enter the Kingdom of God by relinquishing the belief in the form. And the will of the Father is that you do just that for there's no other way for you to be where Christ is, out of the form concept.

Now, if you're not in the form and are in the Kingdom of God where Christ is, it's because that is who you are. That is who the son of God is. You see how you're getting ready for Gethsemane? If you're in the Kingdom of God, out of the form, can you be in Gethsemane, too? Gethsemane is a place. You can find it on the map. It's a physical place.

But *"Father I will that they.... be with me where I am."* He had previously said, *"I am not in the world."* Pretty soon, there's no one where you are to be in Gethsemane. That's your preparation for it. You withdraw from the physical sense of life as you build the Spiritual awareness of identity.

"That they may behold my glory."

To behold the glory of Christ is to behold the glory of your own Being as incorporeal, invisible, eternal Self and it's all about now; behind the atom; behind the world; behind the images of the mind. He's taking us into the realization that you can and must learn how to step out of the mind universe. The universe of the mind is this world. The universe of the Kingdom of God is all that is here where the mind sees this world and only the son of God in you is no longer dominated by this world. This is a now possibility and soon becomes a now must.

"Righteous Father, the world hath not known thee: but I have known thee, and these have known that thou hast sent me."

There's a world meaning behind that. *"Righteous Father, the world has not known thee."* *"[God,] the world has not known thee."* God is Life. The world has not known Life. He is saying, "The world is dead," and the world says. "God is dead."

The world has not known God. The world has not known Life. Religion has not known God. Mankind has not known God. You see the meaning of raise the dead? Those who do not know God do not know Life and they are dead and to raise the dead is to lift us into the knowledge of Life, into the knowledge of God. And that knowledge is that I am the son of God. Then, I know Life. I know the Father. To know the God aright is to know the son which is God in you. God in you is the son of God. And you can only know God aright through knowing God in you which is the son of God or Christ. That's why it is said that only through Christ can you know God.

"The world has not known thee: but I have known thee." I, Christ have known Thee.

And when you know Christ in yourself, you are coming alive. You are stepping out of death into Life. You are stepping out of mortality. To walk in your invisible Self is coming alive.

"I have known thee, [and] these have known [thee,]that thou hast sent me."

Again, Christ is sent. You must know Christ to know God. You must know Christ in you to know God. You must know the son of God is your name and then you know God in you which is Christ.

"And I have declared unto them thy name, and will declare it: that the love wherewith thou hast loved me may be in them, and I in them."

The Christ will continue to declare it through you. "I will continue to declare Thy name."

The name of God is Christ in You. The name of God is your identity. The individualization of God in You, Christ, is the name that Christ declares all the time and will continue to declare it so that as you come into your acceptance and you're living in the invisible Self, you will show forth the fruits which are the declaration that is the continuation of declaring it. You will declare it. I, Christ in you, through the fruitage of your living in your invisible Selfhood continue to declare to the world my Presence.

And so, the 17th chapter is over. It is the preparation that everyone goes through to come to the realization of Self. That Self which now, when you realize it, enables you to walk out into your Gethsemane where you're ready to surrender your total humanhood. The supreme trial of saying, "I am ready to give up humanhood, mortality, the dying self, the dying form and live in the living form, the living Self, the living Kingdom." That's Gethsemane.

All of this is preparation for the moment of total surrender where you become a human sacrifice to accept your Divine Being. That's why we don't give away bulls and goats or pigeons or tithes or make promises or little sacrifices. The only sacrifice is the sacrifice of the human selfhood. Few that be who enter that straight gate.

And so, the Wayshower is about to do just that and the disciples are going to make many mistakes in that process and that's where we're going to learn how we, too faced with similar circumstances this day would react pretty much the same and through their errors, we can correct our own potential errors and eventually come into the full acceptance, the full Spiritual maturity of being Immaculately conceived and never otherwise.

We are drawing all our inner disciples now together to come to a place of Wholeness where I can say, "I am the son of God and there are no human remnants. This is my name." And then for you, Gethsemane is your next step.

Now, your Gethsemane won't be next Sunday. It might not happen in this lifetime for some. It might be five years ahead for others. It really is an everyday event. Every day is Gethsemane if you're living as the son of God. Every day, you're proving that you need no defense in this universe except your own identity. And so, Gethsemane actually is the daily experience of trusting your identity to be Self-sustaining.

You've started and now we will reach a climax in this understanding of the Self-sustaining son of God that I am who needs no outer assistance. All flows forth from the very web of your Being.

Again, this week, deepen your conscious awareness that I will maintain the thread of one, invisible Self in every personal relationship throughout the day. The telephone won't surprise me into finding

Mary on the line. It's the One Self I'll be talking to even if it wants to call itself Mary and the doorbell won't surprise me. The only one who's going to be there is the Invisible, one Self and everything you do, everywhere you go, hold on to your Invisible, one Self as the only identity there. Don't lose the thread of Oneness. You'll find it very valuable in the final realization that I am the living Son.

He promised them Heaven if they would follow him. They had followed him and now he's taking them into his own apparent death in Gethsemane but you know he promised them Heaven. The turn of events is most amazing. It is the way to Heaven, the complete annihilation of the human concept of life.

Now, we are all the One this minute. No matter where you go, how much distance seems to separate us, we will still be that One and that will always be the fact of your Life. No matter where you go, no matter whom you seem to be separated from or whom you seem to be with, only the invisible One will be your name forever. That is your eternal and only Self. That is the reason through Christ Jesus we are told "*Call no man your Father....but be [ye] perfect as your Father*," the One Invisible Self. This is where the consciousness must rest.

And so, as we were told at the beginning, we were today discussing the preparation for Gethsemane. One Self.

You might again look at chapter 11. We're not going to do it next week. We're going right into Gethsemane. There are some things in it that might help you in the "Realization of Oneness" in chapter 11. We'll go into chapter 18 in John this coming Sunday.

Thank you.

Class 35

Your Triumph In Gethsemane

Herb: We're going to begin right in your consciousness, not outside yourself and we're walking out of Jerusalem which is the traditional state of orthodoxy, a belief in a God external to ourselves and we're walking away from Jerusalem.

Now, we're walking over a brook, that's called a brook of Cedron. And as we walk over the brook, we notice that the waters are rather murky. The waters of this brook represent the clutter and the confusion of the world mind that we're walking over.

Then we come to the Mount of Olives. The Mount of Olives stands for the love of God that we entertain within ourselves. We mount the western slope of the Mount of Olives and we come to a really shaded part, the Garden called Gethsemane. We have made a journey in consciousness, from orthodoxy, over mortal mind, guided and led by love of God to this inner sanctuary in the Mount of Olives called Gethsemane which is the place, the arena where we are ready for the supreme test.

Here the forces of the world which have dominated humanity are going to meet in us the awareness of identity and here identity stands, letting the forces of the world explode as they will and identity says, "I need no defense against nothing."

This supreme test in Gethsemane is that arena of consciousness in which we reach the peak of all of our activity building the Spiritual consciousness to the point where we are ready now to let the old man die. We're ready to accept the Allness of God, the one Power of God, the incorporeality of Reality. We're ready to accept that Spirit is and matter is not.

And in this place, this secret place, we are prepared to meet any adversary, regardless of its name or nature or whatever disguise it may wear because we have learned now that there are no adversaries at all. They are all the disguises of the world mind. They are never real. They have no substance. They are not God created or sustained.

Here in Gethsemane, we are prepared to face what the world fears knowing the illusory nature of it. Here we stand knowing the Truth, being the Truth. Here we say, "I am the Life itself." Here we need no sword. Here we need no offense. Here we need nothing to protect ourselves, nothing to run away from, nothing to fear, nothing to change.

Gethsemane is where Christ in you is born. This is where the real crucifixion takes place. You crucify the world mind in Gethsemane. You suffer the agonies that the world thinks you're suffering but to you, they are the ecstasy of knowing the truth of Being.

Everyone is moving toward Gethsemane. Everyday you have been experiencing the dying of the unreal, that within you, you may become conscious of the Real. And every true disciple finally comes to the place where unarmed, and undefended, he takes dominion over the world, alone, without any human aid; merely by being He.

Now you know that many changes are taking place in your life at this time. Many have reported to me that quite a number of changes are taking place in their lives and I've never seen such an increased amount of change in our students, in the outer world of effects. New jobs, new homes, new relationships, promotions, going to new cities, new understanding. All of this is the outer revealing the new activity within and if there is no change going on in your outer, it is because your inner is stagnant. Always, the outer will reflect the inner change. And because we, at the moment, have been in a great inner change in this work, everywhere it seems, I receive phone calls and letters about people who say this is happening and that is happening; there's quite a great deal of happy excitement about it. It's a sort of a yardstick to measure how we have progressed within.

And now, another progression. The Master has made his talk. From the Last Supper until this moment, the disciples have been exposed to the highest Truth on the earth. How much they have absorbed remains to be seen. How much we have absorbed remains to be seen because when we read about the disciples, the Master, Gethsemane, this isn't because we're interested in history. We're here to extract the message of today out of the words that appeared yesterday knowing they are Now words, a Now message. They are to guide us this moment. We are to make them ours.

And so, we join this little group of early disciples but we're really watching our Self in a figure called Christ Jesus and our Self in other figures called disciples who are the full, Divine qualities of God invisible coming into visibility through the careful cultivation of the Christ within. All of this is us. All of this happening within each individual here, all the time and we are given this externalized picture so that we may find that which only Spiritual Consciousness can reveal even before we have developed that Spiritual Consciousness.

And so, we see Gethsemane as the Christ mind. We see the brook as the world thoughts that we pass through to come to the Christ mind. We see the Mount of Olives where Love is the law. We know that Gethsemane means - it's formed of two words, the "Geth" is actually "gath" and that is an oil press; a press. They took the olives from the trees and pressed them to get the oil in the press and the "shemen" which became "semane" is the oil. You press out the oil from the olive and oil is the symbol of the wisdom, the Divine understanding. And there's Gethsemane, the place where the olives are pressed for the oil to be distilled. Gethsemane, the place where the world is pressed out of you and in the pain and the so-called suffering, we find that out of our pain is pressed the wisdom of the Father.

You remember the first series of temptations? Just coming out of the wilderness? Those were the temptations of power and of pleasure.

Now, in Gethsemane, the second series of temptations are the temptations of pain and of sorrow, of bodily harm, of life being torn away. Another series of temptations. There will still be another series later. And so, these are the temptations we are alerted to be prepared for.

And now, let's follow this little band remembering this is all happening in your consciousness whether you're conscious of it or not. And is being externalized to show you that you, too, who must travel over the brook, up the Mount of Olives, the Mount of Love, to the Garden which would seem to be a garden of sorrows but it unbars the gates to Glory.

This garden now, this Gethsemane is the sacred place of the Most High. Within you it is the oasis of Truth where you're prepared to meet all that is untrue knowing it has no place. Here, you meet the serpent but unlike Adam, you will not be fooled. Here you will be given an opportunity to accept the Tree of Life or the tree of knowledge of good and evil. And because you are not the first Adam but the second, coming into Christ, we learn here to look at the serpent, Judas, to look at good and evil, the attackers, the world of effects around us, the threat of powers and instead of succumbing as Adam did, we overcome the temptation.

We do not overcome our enemies. We overcome the temptation to accept that there are enemies in the Garden of Truth within your Consciousness. Our Gethsemane is meeting the temptation to believe that humanhood is there.

Watch how subtly the Spirit leads us.

"When Jesus had spoken these words, he went forth with his disciples over the brook Cedron, where was a garden, into the which he entered, and his disciples."

Cedron, you'll find in the Old Testament, too, it's spelled there K-i-d-r-o-n and here it's C-e-d-r-o-n. In both places, it means mortal mind. David fled over the brook of Kidron when he was fleeing from Absalom and in 1st Kings, there's something about Kidron in reference to Solomon.

But now it's coming into clearer focus because we know exactly what the disciples are doing. They're stepping out of mortal mind. They're walking out with the Master out of mortal mind, out of world mind, out of hypnosis, out of material consciousness.

An historical truth about this brook is interesting. It actually empties out into the Dead Sea, a sort of a forerunner of where the Truth would ultimately be found as it was in the parchments found in the Dead Sea.

And now, we learn to let Gethsemane, it was a headquarters for Jesus and his group; even after he long departed, it remained the headquarters for Mary and John and other disciples. They all came to this high mount for the meditative periods when they were opened to the Infinite.

Whenever Jesus and his group came to Jerusalem or Bethany, rather than go directly into the temples, they pitched tents here. They rested. It was their favorite spot for regeneration and yet, even though it's an outer spot, a physical spot on a map, it's the inner spot that we all find that place where we rest for regeneration. And this signifies now that we're coming into that place where we are to meet the Divine Word within ourselves instead of the world thought of the brook of Kidron. We cross over that brook. Love draws us, that very Mount of Olives where the Sermon on the Mount was delivered, another sermon of Love.

And here we rest now inside ourselves. We have passed out of a false consciousness, a consciousness which sees evil where only the Kingdom of Perfection is.

In Gethsemane, we are not in the false consciousness and yet, still, there are two Gethsemanes. There is the Spiritual Gethsemane and the physical and if we only go into the physical Gethsemane, we're still going to see evil. We, dwelling in the Secret Place, go to the Spiritual Gethsemane where there is only one Life, one invisible, everywhere, infinite Being; Life itself that I am. Our Spiritual Gethsemane is a realization of Oneness.

And now, if you're prepared to rest there, it won't matter if Judas comes. Judas is on the way we know. What is not reported in the Bible is that coming to Gethsemane for Jesus was a second stop along the way. The first was in Mark's mother's house. That's where Judas thought they were. That's where he left them. That's where he received the sop. He got his little band of soldiers. He wanted to make quick work of this. He made the arrangements with the Romans. He was going to lead them. He made the arrangement with the Sanhedrin. He was going to lead them. And so, he got his little band together. He went to Mark's mother's house. It was going to be very quick because nobody was armed except Simon Peter and Simon the Zealot, just two men. The rest would have no way of counteracting this quick maneuver and in the quiet of the evening when the city was asleep, Jesus would be taken without any great tumult.

Who was this Judas doing this? He was our corporeal sense. He had been dismissed but like the serpent, he was still ready to come back. To his surprise, the little band wasn't there. He thought to himself, "Now what am I going to do? They've probably gone to their favorite headquarters, Gethsemane."

And so now, he had to do something different because whereas in the first time he was going to just take a little band, he knew that in Gethsemane many people came to visit Jesus. This was where he often entertained Nicodemus and even other members of the Sanhedrin who privately came for instruction. This was where sufferers came for deliverance. This was where the world came to Jesus, just as you and I must come to Gethsemane frequently within ourselves. It is there that you find your Twin.

If you've been trying to find your Twin, you'll find your Twin in Gethsemane. That is where the invisible Christ resides. Only in that Consciousness where there is nothing to defend against or to fear, where there is only One, where there is no second, that's where you find Christ.

Judas now had to get a little larger group together. So now, it is even rumored that he awakened Pilate in the night and said, "We need some Roman soldiers." And now they had a larger garrison because they knew there was a larger group waiting in Gethsemane for them. They didn't know what to expect, how many people were armed. The Greeks had by now joined Jesus in his group in Gethsemane, too. It was a large park, you see.

Now, it isn't known but Jesus was waiting for them and not with his group. He was all alone. He actually went and sat on an olive press and he waited. His reason was, he knew they were coming. He wanted as little activity there and he wanted no opportunity for his group to in any way resist. He was all alone waiting.

Meanwhile, here's Judas, with a pre-arranged idea that "I will kiss the man you are to take" because of course the Roman soldiers knew very little about who Jesus might be. The Sanhedrin soldiers did. The guardians of the temple did. But to be sure that he was identified properly, the pre-arranged signal was a kiss and even then, Judas was very cunning. He walked well in advance of his crew. He hoped within himself that he could be so far in advance of them that his former colleagues would think that he was coming to warn them, that he wasn't connected with this group but was running ahead of them to warn them. But it didn't work out that way at all.

And now, we come to some interesting things here, little subtleties that are important. We find Judas leading the pack.

"Judas also, which betrayed him, knew the place: for Jesus ofttimes resorted thither with his disciples."

Having gone to Gethsemane with Jesus and the disciples before many times, it was natural for Judas to know that because he wasn't at Mark's mother's house, he was here. And now, he was on his way.

"Judas then, having received a band of men and officers from the chief priests and Pharisees, cometh thither with lanterns and torches and weapons."

Do you notice that he received his weapons from the chief priests? In Matthew, we're told those weapons were swords and staves. He received them from the chief priests, those great lovers of God - gave him weapons to take the Christ. And this is telling us that corporeality in us, which Judas symbolizes, will always attack the Christ of you and even think it is doing a holy thing.

This is a great statement about the betrayal of the church, that not knowing the invisible Christ, it attacks the Christ; that world mind, not knowing incorporeal Truth, attacks the Truth and these human methods, the lanterns, the torches would indicate they are coming at night which is a state of darkness, a lack of Spiritual discernment. In their state of darkness, they are coming to attack the Christ. The lantern would refer to the intellect, the torches to the reason. Human aids, human weapons and all under the guise of authority, so does mortal mind come to us disguised as religious, political and forceful authority by might and by power, in some way, ever attempting to stifle the Spirit. All this is within us. It's not outer. The reason, the intellect, the human sense of righteousness, the human sense of what is the correct way to do things comes with lanterns and with torches, with the letter of Truth, with human weapons, saying, "We are doing the right thing," weapons given by the priesthood.

And what is the great crime that they are attacking?

In the visible world, the only crime they are attacking is that the man has done good. That's the crime. The man has done good. What harm has the man done? Nothing but help. Nothing but love.

And so, "We can't have any of that," says corporeality. That's in our way. Corporeality wants to manipulate and convert everything to its own selfish interest. Don't make the mistake of thinking these are Pharisees and soldiers with lamps and lanterns and torches and weapons. These are the corporeal disciples within ourselves. These are the disciples of world mind within us attacking Christ and they are led by Judas, the serpent in the garden. And who is Judas? Our own physical form. Your own physical form leads the attack and bands all the rest of its own disciples together to make the attack sure to succeed.

You're being told here that the greatest betrayer of your true Selfhood is your sense of body and your sense of mind for it cannot see the invisible Christ and therefore ignores or attacks that which it cannot see. This is the false consciousness of humanity that is being described as Judas coming with a band armed with weapons and with lanterns and torches. This is the false consciousness of each individual human being. The consciousness we're going to meet in Gethsemane and overcome.

"Jesus therefore, knowing all things that should come upon him, went forth, and said unto them, Whom seek ye?

This great act of compassion has been unnoticed before. The purpose of it was to prevent Judas from making the betrayal, for Judas' sake. He hadn't yet kissed Jesus Christ, the kiss of death. So, to save him the trouble of making himself into a visible betrayer, the Master said to those who came, *"Whom seek ye?"* He was going to give himself up rather than let Judas be a betrayer.

But of course, there's deeper meaning there. Way back at the beginning of his discipleship, when he picked those who would follow him, he said, *"What seek ye?"* When Andrew came and John came. *"What seek ye?"* "Well," they said "we seek where thou livest."

And of course, the meaning, though they weren't quite aware of their meaning, the words were placed within them; the meaning was we seek where Christ is, where Christ lives and that should be always the quest, to seek where Christ lives because Christ lives within you and if that's your quest then you find Christ within you, you've found the living Kingdom of God.

But to these men, he now says, *"Whom seek ye?"* It's the other side of the same question. To the disciples, the answer would become, "We seek the Christ" but to those who are not disciples, they don't answer, "We seek where thou livest." They're not seeking Christ. He's pointing out the difference between a disciple and a non-disciple. These seek Jesus of Nazareth. They're not looking for Christ. They're looking for a man, a form, a corporeal creature. That's what they came to find. That's what the lanterns were for and the torches, so that they could see and get the right man. But they were looking at Christ and seeing a man. They were looking at the Spirit of God and seeing a man. They were looking at their own Self and seeing another form. They were blind as mankind is to its own Self. They were attacking their own Self. The absurdity of the attack is that we are doing it every day. Each day, with lanterns and torches, led by Judas, we corporeally attack our own Self.

"Whom seek ye?" "We seek," they said, *"Jesus of Nazareth."*

Each day, when we identify ourselves as person, we are committing the same folly. We say that we are person, mortal being, a human self, a Jesus of Nazareth or a Mary of Alameda or a John of Palo Alto. We identify ourselves as the person, as they did in seeking the one they would crucify. They were seeking a form. Actually, they were seeking a deadness because there was no self there other than the living Christ. So do we act out of deadness in mortality.

Now, you'd expect the disciples of course to know better. He doesn't correct those who've come to take him away. "Fine, you're looking for Jesus of Nazareth. That's fine. I am he." And of course, there's that double statement again just like "Render unto Caesar that which is Caesar's unto God that which is God's."

"I am he."

To you who come to take me in the night, you only see Jesus of Nazareth but *"I am he."* I am the life of God. I am the Invisible Self, visible to your limited consciousness as Jesus of Nazareth. *"I am he,"* the eternal Self, the Infinite Being, the one who was never born, who will never die, the One who with a snap of the fingers could dismiss every soldier who stood there.

And while he was saying, *"I am he,"* not running from the soldiers, not defending because Christ needs no defense, there was a bond of Love established that they were unaware of. He who said, *"I am he"* was Love itself and he who said *"I am he"* was the I Am of those very soldiers who came to take him away. Love was recognizing Self. Love was being Self. There was only one Self there to him who said *"I am he."*

That's your Gethsemane, standing in the midst of many even under visible attack of form, *"I am he."* And those who apparently are attacking me, can they be there if *"I am he,"* who is the Infinite Self? Is there another here than I? *"I am he"* does not fall into the trap of form, matter, movement, humanhood, mortality. *"I am he"* knows only *"I am he"* and knows no other is present. Divine Love expresses as Self-realization.

And before the scene goes any further, we see the power of Divine Love. We see the power of Truth in Consciousness. We see the power of only identity as defense.

What happens? The soldiers fall back. They're unable to do what they came to do. They have absolutely no power to move and take him. They cannot touch him. Why? Because there is only one, Divine Consciousness present. There is no second consciousness. There is only the consciousness of *"I am he."* The divided is gone. The second consciousness is gone. It cannot externalize as force, as power, as hate, as destruction.

In the one, Divine Consciousness present, *"I am he,"* we see what Gethsemane means. It means resting in our Oneness, knowing only our Oneness is present. There is no second. Where I stand or where he stands or where she stands, one with God is All that is there and therefore, it is the majority.

"I am he" is your answer to every problem you consider to be present in your complete and total environment, in all ways. The problems that you experience are the externalization of that consciousness in you which is not *"I am he."* That false consciousness shows forth as your problems, as those things which threaten the harmony of your Being.

And so, this is how we stand in Gethsemane and we learn from this that the soldiers always fall back.

Judas, which betrayed him, stood with them. The importance of that statement is that Judas wasn't standing with Jesus. Jesus Christ stood in *"I am he"* and Judas stood with the soldiers. There was no Jesus and Judas standing together. There was no *"I am he"* and corporeality. *"I am he"* is the total absence of the belief in corporeality; the total awareness that there is no Judas. There is no force. There is no flesh. There is no matter. There is no other power. There is no activity. There is only the Spirit present. Spirit alone is present, is *"I am he."*

When you can stand on only Spirit is present, you have found where to stand. You are ready for your real Gethsemane. Judas is over there standing in the false consciousness, not in your Consciousness of *"I am he,"* here.

Now, this is the clear picture that we are to walk away with. If we do not, it is because we are still in the Peter consciousness. Peter should have known all this by now but as he watched, there was a growing anger within him. He loved this man Jesus.

He said, "I will give my life for you."

And the Master said, "Will you Peter? Will you really? The cock will crow three times before you deny me."

He loved the man. Just as they came to attack the man, Peter loved the man and there was no man. There was only *"I am he,"* the Spirit of God.

And so, in your Gethsemane, while you are standing resolutely against one side of your consciousness which says, "The problem is here," there is another side in your consciousness which wants to attack the problem, release you from the problem. That would be the good side against the bad side. But that's the tree of good and evil. There are no good sides and no bad sides.

In your true Consciousness, there's no love of matter that you need to preserve and no fear of matter that you have to defend against. You are spiritual Being and matter does not exist in the Consciousness of *"I am he."*

Now, if it were not necessary to teach us, there would never have been a Garden of Gethsemane. The scene could have even stopped at this point. But we had to learn that even though Jesus Christ could stand there, free, protected, without any defense, that Divine Love was the only force he needed. We who are incapable at this point of living at that level, who still have an active Peter consciousness within us, something in us is then going to want to remove the attacker. And so, Peter reaches for the sword, cuts off the ear of Malchus and breaks in you the protection of the Light. The moment you attack another creature, you break the law of Love.

That's the teaching at this point; the breaking of the law of Love and then you are open to attack and then the problems come in like a landslide. But if you do not break the law of Love, you are under the protection of the Invisible Light of Love for there is nothing there to be protected against except the illusion that something else is there.

Peter breaks both commandments, the first and the second. That impulse in us which would defend breaks the first commandment because it acknowledges something beside the Spirit of God.

"Acknowledge Me in all thy ways. Heart, mind and soul; acknowledge Me, the Spirit of God." Don't acknowledge these attackers with lanterns. Don't acknowledge these false thoughts within you. Don't acknowledge the things of the world that seem to be attacking. The first commandment says acknowledge that Spirit is present. *"I am he,"* and *"And beside me there is no [other.]"*

So, Peter broke that and because he broke that he automatically broke the second. *"I am he"* was loving the neighbor but Peter wasn't. Peter couldn't love the neighbor because the neighbor was attacking the One he loved. And Peter was a very practical man, a natural man, a materialist. Here he was and an innocent man was being led off to death. What was he supposed to do? Stand there and watch him? But he was in the false consciousness which saw an innocent man being led off to death. The so-called innocent man had already declared, "I am the Life. I have power over all flesh. I can come and I can go. Destroy this temple and in three days I will raise it up again. Whom did thou say I am, Peter?" And even Peter had said, *"The Christ"* and now he had forgotten. He didn't know what he had said or what it meant.

Defend the Christ? That would be like standing there to defend God, wouldn't it? But we are the Christ. Why do we defend ourselves against anything? Because we think we're not the Christ, we're not for the Spirit. Because we think the things that are threatening us are actually happening.

So, day by day, through Truth in Consciousness, through the awakening of the Spirit, we are lifted higher and higher until the moment when we can enter, across the brook, up the Mountain of Love to the sacred place and know that whatever comes now will be an illusion of the senses. All that exists is the Spirit of God. You're in your daily Gethsemane, daily solidifying the Truth of Being and watching the soldiers fall back, watching the non-power of what had seemed to be a power.

Now, this is what we should be proving to ourselves every day.

"As soon [then] as he had said unto them, I am he, they went backward, and [they] fell to the ground. [Then again he turned,] Whom seek ye? And they said, Jesus of Nazareth."

Now, between those two questions, Jesus had been kissed by Judas. Judas not taking advantage of the Love that was giving him an opportunity not to make the betrayal, presented the kiss, identifying Jesus as the one they would take. And again, though, he emphasizes, *"Whom do ye seek?"* To emphasize that they are seeking a man, a person.

Now, in our human lives, we are seeking things. Just as they were seeking a form, we are seeking forms and our mistake is that we are reaching out for that which is not there although we can feel it and touch it and put it in our pocket and put it in our bank and put it in our homes. This is what we are seeking - forms, and we are fooling ourselves. The forms aren't there. You can get all of them you want, pile them up high. You can store them in barns. They are not there. They're not even perishable. They simply aren't there. For all that is there is the Spirit of God. This is to alert us to the non-reality of matter. No matter what form it may take.

In Gethsemane, you live in the Cause and you let the effect of forms bombard against the Cause in Consciousness and you stand there unperturbed, watching those soldiers fall to the ground. They are only the arm of flesh but we know only the invisible, living Spirit.

You see how Adam is dying and Christ is being born? The serpent is losing its sting. The Tree of Life is being selected instead of the tree of knowledge of good and evil. The same writer who wrote Genesis, the same writer who wrote the complete Bible wrote it from Genesis to Gethsemane: the Spirit of God. One writer. And only one actor under many disguises called Biblical characters.

And all this, an outer expression of the inner conflict within every man. The conflict he doesn't even know is going on to make it visible so that he becomes aware of this conflict and knows what to do and what is expected until we come to the purpose of our lives. It is to serve your own Spirit and when you're ready to serve only your Spirit, to love your Spirit supremely, you have found the complete purpose of everything that has happened up to this point. You have found the cup and the meaning of the cup.

Peter's about to find the meaning of the cup. He strikes off the ear. John doesn't tell us that the Master put the ear back on. Maybe it wasn't necessary for us to know that or maybe he felt it would be mentioned in the other Gospels but basically, he gives us what you don't find exactly the same way in the other Gospels.

This Malchus, whose ear is struck off by Peter, is the bodyguard of the chief priest. The ear of this bodyguard is struck off. The ear of the servant of the priest is struck off. You see the symbolism? The ear struck off is a symbol of deafness. The priest is a symbol of the church. The deafness of religion which is attacking the Christ. It has no ear. It cannot hear the inner Word. It is deaf to Christ. It is deaf to God. It is deaf to Spirit. It has an outer ear only to hear the letter so the ear is struck off and there's only one way for that ear to get back on to religion so that it can hear. And that's why Jesus puts the ear back on. Only the Christ can restore the ear of the church. Until the church finds Christ it has no ear. See that? There is no listening capacity, no Spiritual discernment, no receptivity until the church turns every member of every congregation to Christ within. Then it has an ear and only when it has an ear can it obey the Divine will. So, the removal of the ear from Malchus is the statement that religion has no ear for the Divine Word and is not obeying the Divine Will. And this is a current statement.

These are the disciples here, now. The ear of religion is not listening to Christ. It is coming with lanterns and torches. It is looking to make a better, corporeal world. *"Whom seek ye?"* We seek to make better human beings, not spiritual Reality.

The church has not yet been to Gethsemane and isn't ready. And while we are not in Gethsemane, we are not listening to the Word but rather, we are walking over the brook of Cedron, over the corruptible, turbid waters of human thought. And sometimes, we fall right in. They're not the living waters of the inner *"I am he."*

"Peter, put up thy sword unto thy sheath."

I thought you were a disciple? Who are you going to attack with that sword, Peter? Aren't you aware that this man over here, this soldier is a mental image in your mind? And you think there's a soldier there? Haven't you been learning about incorporeality? About the Spirit which is All? You still think there's a soldier, Peter?

Now, we are all to be reprimanded for we are all reaching for that sword every day. It may be the sword of words, the sword of plans, the sword of ambition, the sword of anticipation. We have so many swords in our scabbard and we need none; for *"I am he."*

"Put up thy sword unto thy sheath."

We are learning there is an effortless way to live in the Kingdom of God, *"Not by might or by power but by my Spirit."* But if the damage is done, if you still believe in corporeality, if you still take out the sword, lo and behold, the soldiers who had fallen back, who had no power to attack, now they have the power. You're in division again. You're in duality again. It externalizes as a pro and a con, adversaries for you and someone else. Matter and the Spirit. This world.

Now, if that's clear to us then we are being alerted to the real test of living in the Spirit.

"Must I not drink the cup that my Father gave me?" says the Master.

What is this cup? You're going to have to drink it, you might as well know what's in it. We must all drink the cup that the Father gives us. Usually, the cup refers to its contents. The cup, he could have said, "Well, this certainly can't be the will of God that I let them take me away to die."

And so, he said in another place in the Bible, *"Take this cup from me."* But then came the realization, "But this cup is my Will. This is what you are to do." *"Nevertheless,"* he said then, *"Thy will, not mine."*

And so, now he says, "I must drink the cup my Father gave me." He didn't say, "It isn't the Father's will that I should die." He could have. No one would have, in any way, said anything bad about it. In fact, most people would have agreed. Certainly, he shouldn't die. It's not the Father's will.

But the cup you must drink is not to die. That wasn't the cup he was drinking. The cup he had to drink was to be exposed to the threat of death, to the temptation that death is reality. That was the content of the cup, temptation. In the cup that you must drink is the temptation to believe and to accept that you are a human being. The cup he had to drink was to drink it to the very bottom, to not accept the temptation that he was a human being.

And because he is the Wayshower, ultimately, you must drink that same cup. He said as much. He said to his disciples, "You must walk with me in my temptations. To him who walks with me in my temptations, I give the Kingdom."

You must walk through the temptation that you are human, even to the point of a threat on your life. That is the cup we must drink. Each must be brought to that total understanding that I am not this human form.

In Gethsemane, you meet that temptation. In Gethsemane, that is the end of the conflict between the matter and the Spirit and when you have ended that conflict by the total steadfastness to the Truth of your Being, you have passed the test of Gethsemane. That means if somebody comes in with a revolver to shoot you and you don't want to defend your life, you're doing a good job of knowing the Truth in Gethsemane. That means if the doctor says, "You're going to die," you stand there knowing, "I am he," and you're meeting the Truth in Gethsemane. That means regardless of the severity of the crisis confronting you, you have no desire or need to defend or preserve yourself because your Self is the Self of God. That is Gethsemane and we who have not stood there, maybe more than once, are not ready for that mystical interval between resurrection and ascension where even higher things are revealed.

And so, let us see then that this is the clarification of what is expected of us. We cannot make the mistake of Peter. We cannot make the mistake of Judas. We cannot make the mistake of mortal mind, religious mind, human mind, natural mind. We know that the Divine Self being the only, that no other self is possible anywhere in the world. Everywhere you're looking at Divine Self. You're loving that Divine Self everywhere and one day, you're forced to prove your Love, to stand on your Love, not human love but Divine Love. So that, unlike Peter who would defend the Master himself, who has the power to summon legions, who has power over all flesh, willingly submits.

"*I am he,*" he says "And if I am the one you seek, therefore let these others go."

When he says "*I am he,*" and "I submit, let these others go if I'm the one you seek," he is telling you another secret. That only in the death of your corporeal sense do the disciples in you come alive into freedom. The Divine qualities in you cannot be liberated while you are still unwilling to submit your corporeal sense to the acid test of non-existence. You cannot uphold your corporeal sense here and expect the Divine qualities to burst through.

"Let them go," he says, "If you want me. You want a man? Well, here's a man. Take the man." And this is the freedom of the Divine qualities. The old is dying that the new may be born. The old man dies. The old concept of self dies that the new may walk the earth as the Invisible Christ. When Jesus asks the band of soldiers to let the disciples go and take him, he's making way for the new understanding, the new age of Spirit. He is sacrificing the nothingness of corporeality that the Allness of Spirit may be understood.

— End of Side One —

Don't think he's being punished by God or accepting the sins of the world for anybody's sake. He is demonstrating that only Spirit is present.

There are no sins. There's no suffering. There's no punishment. There is the Allness of Spirit being demonstrated and all that is not Spirit must die in our consciousness.

In our consciousness then comes the death of the corporeal sense and that is the birth of the Christ awareness. It's a see saw. As one diminishes, the other expands. As one goes down, the other comes up.

This is all by way only of explanation. The implementation of it follows.

So, finally the servants of the soldiers bind him up, the band and the captain and the officers of the Jews took Jesus and bound him.

And so, the Self of man is bound while the non-self takes over. As we live in the human sense of self, we bind our Christ Self.

Meanwhile, the teaching has been given and the world has bound the Christ Self so that the opposites of Truth can continue to dominate the mind of man. This is taking place within all of us. We know what Gethsemane is. We know what's expected of us. We know our purpose is to live in Divine Love.

And so now, our entire quest is how to stand in that consciousness called Gethsemane, in the Garden of Truth, in the Christ mind, watching all that would declare itself to be real when it is unreal; ridding ourselves of the false consciousness which sees what isn't there.

We'll pause a little now.

We'll go to our Gethsemane and in our Gethsemane, we have no flesh. There simply is no flesh there. No matter. No person. And in this realm of Consciousness, whatever enters to defile, to lie, distort, deceive, persuade us that something beside pure Spirit exists, we meet with the knowledge that only Spirit is here. There is no flesh. There is no person. There is no human. There is no matter. There is no corporeal world. There is a Spiritual universe, peopled by Spiritual Being. This becomes our daily Consciousness in which we rest. This is how we face every outer circumstance.

We're following the Wayshower who faced his outer circumstances in the same way. My identity is my sword and your identity is my identity everywhere. There is no flesh in the Kingdom of Heaven on earth.

Silence, (pause) …

This must go beyond a mental lesson into consciousness and so we have a few thoughts that will help that after we have a brief period of rest.

Silence, (pause) ...

Let's take that rest now and start over again in a few minutes. (Class break)

In the 9th verse of the 41st Psalm, "*Yea, mine own familiar friend, in whom I trusted, which did eat of my bread, hath lifted up his heel against me.*"

"*My friend....I trusted....ate of my bread, has lifted up his heel against me.*"

And then strangely, in the 13th verse of John, 13th chapter of John, the 18th verse of the 13th chapter, "*I speak not of you all: I know whom I have chosen: but that the scripture may be fulfilled, He that eateth [my] bread with me hath lifted up his heel against me.*"

Now, that's the serpent in Genesis. That's Judas in the New Testament but who is it in your human life? Who eateth your bread? Who turns up his heel against you who is your friend? Your physical self eateth your bread and your physical self is your friend and it turneth against you. It leadeth you to death. And this the secret of that 41st Psalm verse repeated in John, that your physical body which you consider your friend, even yourself, is not your friend. It eateth your bread and you trust it but it will be the chiefest attacker when you enter the Garden of Gethsemane. It will lead a band against you and don't take this lightly because corporeality is the enemy, the adversary we are to learn to agree with by understanding it.

Now, we're at a place in this teaching where if you're new, you're puzzled. If you're relatively new, you're confused. And if you're a veteran, you're still saying "I heard it but I don't believe it."

But number one, is that there is no flesh because flesh is a friend who eateth your bread, whom ye trust, who will lift up its heel against you. Flesh will keep you imprisoned unto death.

And so, we come to the grip of the Truth which says, "The only flesh there is, is pure, invisible Spirit."

One, then, I am not this flesh.

Two, all flesh is a mortal dream. And yet, this mortal dream of flesh is made up of little building blocks.

And those are the third point, these building blocks called atoms, invisible to the eye, come disguised as forms, persons, places, things, objects, conditions and we reach for the sword against these forms not knowing they are invisible atoms of the world mind appearing as flesh.

And when we have been enlightened sufficiently to know the secret of this false flesh, we come to the fourth point; that all that is false exists only within your false consciousness. The flesh you see is not external. The objects are the not external. The conditions are not external. The people are not external. *"I am he,"* is the Infinite Self that is present without opposite and the mortal dream exists only within your false consciousness of it.

And therefore, you never go out there to heal those out there. You learn to dominate your false consciousness. You will find that every evil in the world, every wrong in the world, every discord in the world falls back. War falls back. Famine falls back. Poverty falls back when you are able to see that its only location is within your false consciousness. No flesh. No matter. No healthy flesh. No diseased flesh. All, a mortal dream. Two.

The dream is made of the invisible building blocks called atoms which we react to and call form. That's three.

Four, they exist only and the world exists only within the false consciousness that perceives it. There is no external world.

And then the secret is to learn to overcome your false consciousness. You don't have to overcome the evils of the world. They only exist in your false consciousness and it is a false consciousness and therefore, the overcoming of it is simply to step out of it. It doesn't matter what the evils are that beset you or the groups you know. They are in your false consciousness and you can step out of that consciousness and you will discover that when you step out of that consciousness, you come to the fifth point.

You are in the new Consciousness. You have changed Consciousness. You are in the Divine and the evils of the world are not there even though you haven't moved an inch.

Those are your five points to practice this week. They're a little more detailed than the simplified structure we gave you several weeks back.

Now, if you're not consciously aware that there is no flesh, you're going to fall into the trap Peter fell into. You're going to see things attacking the ones you love and you're going to run to the medicine chest. You're going to run for the x-ray. You're going to run for the human aids with lanterns and torches. You're going to follow Judas, the material sense of man.

We make a mockery of the Bible when we read it and then turn away and proceed to do precisely what it's teaching us not to do. You may even have to take the teachers of religion and put them in the pews and become their teachers by the example of the Light you shed because we must come out of the false consciousness which perceives evil.

Your Gethsemane then, is standing where the evil is, where the oppression is, where the tyranny is, where the liars are, where you are considered to be a victim of something and knowing that exists only in your false consciousness. It isn't happening in your Being and then, because you must come to the total, ultimate trust of Spirit to need no defense, you withdraw your belief in the consciousness that is presenting the evil to you. No sword. No words of Truth. No remedies. No quotations. Just the moral courage to trust that you truly are your Spirit. And then nothing else exists.

There is no flesh.

And in the quietness of your Consciousness, the invisible transfiguration will show you the power of resting into One Self in the new Consciousness, the *"I am he"* Consciousness, which refuses help. Can God be imperfect, can my Life be imperfect if it is the Life of God? Can Spirit be imperfect? Does omnipotent Spirit need to defend itself against anyone or anything? No. These are all the illusions of the Judas consciousness.

Again, and again and again, you walk over that brook into the Garden. You make it your home, your headquarters, your home base and you take a day, and specifically test out the principle that there is no flesh. You look at it and say to your Self within, "It isn't there." And watch how Love springs up where flesh had seemed to be. That's how you awaken from the deep sleep of a fleshly universe that God did not create.

You may find that you're really taken to the real Gethsemane in the Invisible. You may find Christ lives there always, that Christ never left. Nobody took Christ out of Gethsemane, I can assure you that. And what you meet in Gethsemane may surprise you, what you see there and what you hear.

Gethsemane is where the real crucifixion takes place. This is where regeneration reaches its peak test and all that is not You dies in Consciousness. All that is You is born in Consciousness. Every test up to this has been for that purpose, to where you can know the Invisible Self that is not flesh as the only Self that exists.

Silence, (pause) ...

Your false consciousness is the money bag that Judas carried. In this bag he threw all the objects that had some value to him.

This money bag is a bag of memories, it's the accumulated false consciousness we carry around with us, with all of our yesterdays. It's the accumulation of concepts in the conditioned mind.

Get rid of your money bag. Get rid of your false consciousness which includes all of the defects and problems of human flesh by getting rid of the belief that the flesh itself is there. Look through it to the invisible, building blocks of atoms and then through them to the Invisible Spirit and you will see how human mind through world mind has distorted Purity into that which perishes without changing the genuine, original that is always invisibly present.

The importance of today is for you to know without doubt that your Father is perfect and your Father is everywhere without opposite and that whatever you see as imperfect exists only in your false consciousness and that when you fight and attack and defend, all of that is done only in your false consciousness. Step out of it. Enter the arena of Truth and let your Truth in Consciousness dispel the false human consciousness you entertain. When you drop your human consciousness and are in the Divine, you will know that Life is present and perfect without flaw.

I want you to learn to meet "There is no flesh." This is where you make your true demonstration.

Silence, (pause) ...

To clarify that, whatever is wrong, see that it exists in your false consciousness and nowhere else and then step out of that false consciousness, just like you step out of a garment that doesn't fit. When you step out of it, you're really seeing that the false consciousness has no real existence and all that it contains is equally untrue, unreal, un-present; only seeming to be. False appetites are in the false consciousness. Weaknesses, vulnerabilities, lacks, limitations, fear, false ambitions: all in the false consciousness. Death is in the false consciousness. Sickness is in the false consciousness.

Every imperfection is in the false consciousness. All that is present is Divine Consciousness in which all is maintained Divinely and the false consciousness is the cosmic veil, the veil that separates us from the perfection of our own Being.

As you stand here, you'll find you're finding a link between time and eternity. You're finding a pass-over from the false, mortal sense to Immortality, from the visible imperfection to the invisible, ever present Perfection. You're being born into your own Reality.

The false consciousness and the human mind are almost identical. The human mind is that false consciousness if you include all that has made the human mind possible, if you include all of the past human minds you have had which have poured concepts into your bag, if you include all levels of that human mind, if you include the human levels of yesterday before you came into this form in a previous form. This accumulated concept of the human mind is the false consciousness giving you a past you did not have and veiling a present that you do have a Now, that is eternal.

The great difference is Life never becomes human form, never becomes human flesh, never becomes a mortal anything. In Gethsemane, I am Life.

We're moving now out of Gethsemane. We don't stand there forever. Once we prove that *"I am he,"* the soldiers can come and take us away. That's happening in the mortal dream. They're not taking I away and this is how you continue to live in the I, watching the human picture, unbowed and unwavering with unfalterable faith that you are I, for the final curtain has still to be lifted.

That which you are accepting that I am not human flesh, that there is no human flesh must be proved. And the way it is going to be proved is not your way or my way but the Father within has a way, a very joyous way. And that way is what we're preparing to witness, the way in which the Father takes us beyond Gethsemane to say, "Son, you have lived the true Life, the knowledge that there is no flesh that dies. For I, the Creator create nothing that dies. And now, I will show you the reward of your faith. I will show you your real Body. I will show you a Temple that was not formed in the womb, not formed and not made by human hands. I will show you your Spiritual body and I will teach you to walk in it. But first, go to Gethsemane and then when you have stood fast, the Father who seeth in secret will reward thee openly."

Let the soldiers take you. Don't defend. Don't defend against the problem. Don't defend against nothing. Rest in identity and watch identity through Grace, through Love dissolve what never was there. Treat every problem that way.

The missing ingredient which we have all missed is Divine Love. First, to love the Divine is to give Love and then the Love you give you find you receive in abundance and you receive the quality of Divine Love expressing in you. Divine Love will lift you above every human adversary, every material adversary. The power of Divine Love will show you that every adversary is dissolved. But first, you must love the Divine which is the giving of the Love and then the Divine will return that Love to you multiplied. That missing ingredient. And every time you remember that is the missing ingredient, you will look right through the false consciousness which is presenting a conflict and know it is not aware of Divine Love. That is it's real problem. It is separated from Divine Love and so it's in fear. It's in doubt. It's in jeopardy. But once Divine Love is recognized as being invisibly present, the sunshine comes right through the blinds and all of the little dark crevices are lit up. The miracle worker is Divine Love recognized as omnipresent.

Why don't you take that thought and see if you can pursue it, on your own, in certain circumstances that you either dwell with it inwardly or meet in the outer but place that Divine Love there in your conscious knowledge because it is there invisibly waiting for yourself to recognize it as present.

In its presence, evil dissolves. Divine Love prevented the soldiers from laying hands on the man they came to take. Divine Love released every healing that appears in the Bible and a victim walked or talked or saw. Divine Love in you recognized, felt, accepted, is where Gethsemane leads you.

There's more to say but see if you can say it this week inside yourself and we'll all come prepared to experiment in areas unknown to us of Divine Love as we go through the tribulations of the trials before the high priest, loving them supremely as our neighbors.

My work is cut out again and it's more difficult every week but I feel a softening of the shock. I feel that we've come to a place where we can place the areas of problem right where they belong, in that bag that Judas carried, in the false consciousness. And I feel we can learn to just rest outside of that false consciousness and watch that it's becoming more effortless now to live in Truth. You may find that the hardest work has been done. You may be coming now on the other side of the mountain.

At any rate, we're at a period now where more of the pieces are coming and less of the climbing effort. I think you're winning your stripes.

Divine Love, to dwell with the understanding that it is always present no matter what you see, those five points which are strong ones, and to dwell in the Gethsemane which stands firm on the truth that *"I am he."*

It's quite a week's work. You'll find it's probably ten year's work. But it's clarifying and all the activity reported to me indicates that something's happening inside our group consciousness that is Light itself. Maybe it's a sign that we're moving out of time into eternity a little better. We just had to change our clocks in time.

Much love and thank you.

Class 36

Where God Is · Flesh Is Not

Herb: Good afternoon everybody. We are in a very beautiful and a very strange place. The lesson of Gethsemane was to stand fast in the realization that there is no flesh created by God. Having been introduced to this experience, although vicariously, we at least are aware that we must come to that understanding which can look at the world of matter which is not the Kingdom of God and not be content to live in that world which is not the Kingdom of God but rather to seek the Kingdom which is invisible.

And always, along the way, every trial is followed by another trial. And always, we are building karma if we are not meeting that trial with the knowledge of the Allness of Spirit, the Allness of God and that includes your Being which must therefore be Spirit. You're being honed to that fine point of Consciousness which can say, "First I learned that there is a Christ. Then I learned that I am that Christ. And now, I am learning how to live as that Christ that I am." And even though the footsteps are small, every new stride is building another invisible, Spiritual muscle.

Now, we've come to a place in the Bible - we really have passed that place but we're going to point it up today - the place that is again different from the way the Bible is being understood by billions of worshippers all over the world. And the difference is so momentous that it changes the entire meaning of Christianity. It makes us understand why we were told, "Awake from the sleep of mortality." It makes us understand why even a Master of Love could speak as he did to the Pharisees who still control the religions of the world.

Now, John is going to weave for us a very subtle tapestry, almost like a symphony. He'll be matching up instruments, harmonizing them and contrasting them and every word is going to have three different meanings so that we have to look at all sides of everything he says.

We must remember that John, who writes this Gospel, knows what he has written. When he says something in chapter 18, he knows what he has said in chapter 17 and if we pass by as the world has, we are unaware of John's purpose and we fall into the trap.

The first thing we want to point out is the 12th verse on which we concluded last week in chapter 18.

"Then the band and the captain and officers of the Jews took Jesus, and bound him."

And he's going to go through a number of trials, a number of humiliations, a number of painful activities. And if we accept this as a happening, we're falling into the trap.

Now, remember, John wrote this 12th verse, let's see what else John said earlier.

Let's look at John 16:33 in which John reports Jesus as saying *"I have overcome the world."*

And so, we have I, who have overcome the world, in the next chapter or two, being set upon by a band of soldiers and bound. Does this sound very probable to you, that I who have overcome the world am at the mercy of a band of soldiers?

Now, go a step further. Let's go to John 17:2, speaking again of the Christ. *"As thou hast given him power over all flesh, that he should give eternal life to as many as thou hast given him."*

The Christ has power over all flesh, even power to give each of us eternal Life. And again, do you think this Christ is being bound by a little band of officers?

And finally, all over are many more. In 17:11, *"Now, I am no more in the world."* The very same one who says *"I am no more in the world"* in verse 12, we are told that he is being bound by a captain and a band of officers.

Now, if the first is true, the second is not true. And we made that same mistake in Genesis. When the first chapter of Genesis told us about the perfect, Spiritual creation, the perfect Divine man in the spiritual creation, we went right on to chapter two and we accepted now an imperfect Adam and an imperfect Eve, just as if chapter one had never been written; not realizing that they were placed next to each other to show us the Reality and the mental distortion we entertain of the Reality.

Here is the identical maneuver in which John places one before the other to show you the Truth and the mental distortion of the Truth. First the Truth. "I am not in the world. I have power over all flesh. I can give eternal Life to all those who accept me. Am I now being bound by officers?" Is that what's happening? Did God create officers to harass, humiliate, destroy the Christ? Did God create flesh? Can the All power of Christ be bound? Can Divinity be bound? Can Spirit be bound?

What is being revealed to us? The dream of the mind. The dream of the flesh. That which is not in the world is untouchable by those who think they live in the world. Can we, in the world, reach into the Kingdom to bind Christ? Could these soldiers reach into the Kingdom of God to find the Christ who is not in the world and bind him? What were they doing? They were binding their own mental concept.

And this is where you learn to stand because this is the revelation of the non-reality of mortal flesh. They were doing what cannot be done which is hypnotism. The mesmerism of the world places before you a collage made of a thing called matter which is not God's creation and it appears as soldiers binding Jesus Christ. And religion has accepted it and the worshippers of religion have accepted it. They have thought the begotten Son, living in the Kingdom of God, who has declared, "I am not in the world" could be bound in the world. And if God is no liar, then these men were merely wrestling with shadows. They thought they saw flesh. And they thought they were flesh. But look at it as it was seen through the eyes of the Christ and what was happening there was totally different.

The Christ who walked through Gethsemane now walks through the same scene, only with different appearances. Suppose you were seeing the scene through the single eye instead of the naked, human eye? Suppose you were not standing in the belief of the three- dimensional world but were living in your fourth-dimensional Consciousness? Suppose you could see that God has created no flesh? Then what is there before me? The illusion called flesh. The illusion called soldier. The illusion called captain. The illusion called a band of soldiers and you would see that because you would know that here where I stand is not flesh. Here where I stand is the living Spirit of God and when I am able to see through the nothingness of my flesh, what can be external to nothing? The moment I abandon the nothingness of myself, there's nothing external to that nothing called the band of soldiers. The material world dissolves when you have eliminated that nothingness which is called your own personal self.

The Christ walks not in the form. The Christ walks not in the world. The Christ walks in the Kingdom of God and there is no mortal being who can reach into that Kingdom of God to bind, to slap, to bruise, to kill, to crucify, to cause suffering. There is no contact. The Christ is untouchable and the untouchable Christ looks forth and sees only the Kingdom of God.

And so, in your higher Consciousness, the consciousness you are developing, the consciousness which you are achieving as You walk through the trials of the flesh, You stand in the midst of the band of soldiers, who to You are not there. And they are not there to You because You are not there. The form that stands there is not

You. The form that stands there exists only in the false consciousness of the world, not in You. Christ Jesus does not stand there at all. A new man stands there. Divine man stands there and the secret is that Christ invisible is never in a place, never in a place although the appearance of form seen in the three-dimensional world sees that so-called Infinite Christ in a place.

Now, the secret for you is that You are never in a place. You never meditate from a place. You never close your eyes and sit in a chair and say. "Here am I and I'm going to meditate." You never walk in the Kingdom of God by knowing that you're in a physical place. You dismiss the world hypnotism which puts you in a place. As the Spirit, as the Christ, You meditate upon your Infinite nature.

I am not in this place. I am Infinite Being. I am not in this place. The Christ could not stand in a place, then nor now. And only when you learn to dwell frequently in your Infinite Self are you accepting Sonship.

I am not in a place. I am Infinite Being. I am Christ, the Infinite Son. I am Christ, the Infinite mind. Christ, the Infinite Body. I cannot be in this place if I am Infinite. I am in every place. And when you have not accepted this, you cannot understand why it was impossible for a band of soldiers to pin Christ down in a place. The supreme illusion of the mortal mind is that it is in a place and it is never there. Neither the soldiers were there to the Christ nor the Christ. The Infinite Christ was All that was there and is All that is here. You can relax in that, resting in it with confidence until you begin to know the power of the Infinite functions in your acknowledgment of it.

Now, once you have established this, you can see the difference between the way Christ knew Christ to be, through the single eye, through the eye of the Soul, through the Christ mind and the way the soldiers saw the scene and the way the world has seen the scene same as the soldiers saw it and they never had a Christ there to bind.

They never had a form of Jesus there to bind. They were binding empty air. They were not there and the form of Jesus was not there. We are seeing a sequence in the dream of this world made up of two different levels. The third-dimensional consciousness seeing what it can in the fourth and interpreting it down to the three-dimensional level called form or Jesus but there was no one there to bind.

The Christ says, "I am not human flesh. I am the new man. I am the Divine Self. I am not physical man and I stand among you. I am revealing the presence of non-physical man on earth, who even when he appears to be bound is not bound. When he appears to be crucified, is not crucified."

Non-physical man walks through Gethsemane untouched, although the world thinks they've touched him and bound him and struck him and captured him and this is the sign for you that as the non-physical Self, you are to walk through the world.

Now, there are many subtle things here. You will notice that in the resurrection of Lazarus, there was a technique used to show you what was going on in the consciousness of Lazarus for him to be resurrected by showing you what was happening in the consciousness of Mary and Martha. Through their consciousness, you could see what was happening in Lazarus and now, through the consciousness of John and Peter, we're given a glimpse into what is happening in the Consciousness of the Christ. And through the glimpse of what is happening to Annas, Caiaphas and Pilate, we're given an insight into the consciousness of the world.

The world thinks in terms of the fleshly creature. The Christ is teaching us that the non-physical Self of you is present waiting to be lived in, waiting to walk through matter, to walk through all appearances out through death itself and the Christ lets an image be bound. The miracle is not that the Christ isn't there in a form, the miracle is that there is a Consciousness transcendental to all human consciousness which can place an appearance called a physical

377

form within the world consciousness and move that physical form untouched through the world. That is the miracle, that there is such an Intelligence which can do that and place it right before our eyes and even fool the world until the eyes are opened to see that this is the teaching that is happening. This is not an historical event. It was historical only to those creatures of flesh who do not exist.

This is the teaching leading us out of Egypt, out of flesh, out of matter, out of form, into my Kingdom which is invisible to the human eye. And to do this, there walks One who was not in that form and the form is the decoy to the world, to the world of the human mind who thinks it has this form, has bound it and discovers after all of this that it has bound empty air. The form ultimately walks free as if it had never been touched because it never was there. All that was there was another image among the images to show us the foolishness of the perishables called matter.

The soldiers see the flesh and the Christ sees the Christ. The Christ walks in the Invisible and the soldiers see their concept of that Invisible and they capture their own concept.

The non-physical man is all that is there.

Now we are going to learn that so well that we, too, living in the non-physical Self can walk through the illusion of a physical world.

"[They] led him away to Annas first; for he was father in law to Caiaphas, which was the high priest that same year."

Annas. You won't find this again in the other gospels, this Annas. At this particular point, in the other gospels, Jesus is led to Caiaphas. John has a different idea in mind. He is setting a pattern and the pattern is very interesting.

On the Mount of Transfiguration, the Master shows the non-fleshly Self, the eternal, permanent identity as pure Light, Spirit. Present with him are John, James and Peter. And now, we want to see these three in a new light, something we hadn't noticed before. These were the three qualities necessary for you and I to attain that same transfiguration. John, Love. Peter, Faith. James, Action. Through Love, we engender Faith which leads to Action. And these three were present as the symbol of that which is necessary for you to come into the awareness of your Invisible Self. Through Love, through Faith and then through deeds or Action.

Now, in order to set the opposite of this up, John takes us first to Annas, not just to Caiaphas. Annas, Caiaphas and then Pilate, the three opposites of John, Peter and James. Annas represents the human will and this is the core to the inability of man to find his own Invisible Self; the human will. Annas right now is not the high priest. He was. He was appointed roughly three or four years after the birth of Jesus Christ so that when Jesus was three or four years old, Annas was then high priest. And it was he who was responsible for the den of robbers in the temple. Most of his revenue, a good deal of it, came from this sacrificial ceremony in the temple where they sold pigeons and animals as sacrifices to God. He was an aristocrat, member of the Sadducees. Actually, he represented something even higher than our Justice of the Supreme Court because all of Judaism was religion and the high priest was the very incarnate symbol of Divine Law. He was the supreme authority.

And in this case, this supreme authority was misusing his sacred office. He represents the world mind in us which is our human will and that human will is born of a personal me in the flesh so that that human will in us must preserve this flesh, must direct it, must establish it in the community as a figure of importance.

The will in us is Annas and because Annas is a human being, although occupying what seemed to be a sacred seat in the highest tribunal, he already had pre-judged Jesus. He had reached the state of knowing that this man had to go. Why? It wasn't any difference to him that Jesus was an innocent man. This man had to go for several reasons. He was jeopardizing the power of the priesthood.

He was revealing the Spiritual barrenness of the priesthood. He was healing people and the priesthood could not duplicate these healings. They were being disclosed as incompetent, impotent, barren, without Spiritual power. He was upsetting the authority of the Hebrew church. He was upsetting the power and he was cutting in on their revenues by showing the people through his teaching that you can't sacrifice animals to God. There's no external God. The Kingdom of God within doesn't need animals. Everything that the man-made doctrine stood for, Jesus did not stand for. He had to go.

And so, Annas, looked from the standpoint of human will. What's good for me and what's good for me is that I get rid of him. What's good for this Hebrew nation is that we get rid of him. And so, the will is formed out of personal motives. The will couldn't say, "This man is bringing Heaven to earth. This man is healing where human beings can't do it. This man is exposing us to a new, Spiritual power." He couldn't do that. He can only see his revenue, his authority, his position jeopardized. And so, he had to be included by John to show us first that the human will, the very crux of our mistake is number one on the cause of the evils we encounter.

And then he passes him on to his son-in law, Caiaphas who now is the high priest. He was the Chairman Emeritus of the board but Caiaphas is the actual high priest now during the trials and out of deference to the older man, he first let Annas stand before Jesus and now, he's sent to Caiaphas. And that's very interesting, too because Caiaphas had already predicted that Jesus had to die, not just stated that Jesus had to die. He had predicted it and the word is used by John with intent. We're going to look at that in a moment.

"[They] led him away to Annas first; for he was father in law to Caiaphas, [which was the] high priest that same year. Now Caiaphas was he, which gave counsel to the Jews, that it was expedient that one man should die for the people."

It was Caiaphas who actually had engineered the whole thing. His logic was very simple. It was easy to inflame the members of the Sanhedrin. All he had to do was tell them that if Jesus continued doing these miracles, why, the people would become riotous and if they became riotous, Rome would have to send in some troops and Rome, in doing that might even harass the Sanhedrin itself and upset everything. The whole nation was in jeopardy. This was the story Caiaphas pointed and he said, "All there is to do about it to save our nation was to get rid of this one man. It's very simple."

There was some dissent. Nicodemus for one. Joseph of Arimathea another but there were seventy members in the Sanhedrin. And even though, most of them were against Jesus and he had a few supporters, there are many ways in which the Sanhedrin had been hurt by the activities of Jesus. And one of the most unnoticed but most important is that Jesus once sent out seventy disciples on a healing mission, two by two. Seventy. Do you know why he sent out seventy in the Bible? Do you know how many members there are in the Sanhedrin? Seventy. The seventy who couldn't heal were in the Sanhedrin. The seventy he sent out who had nothing to do with the Sanhedrin, their names were writ in heaven. That was a sort of a needling of the Sanhedrin and there were other ways in which their impotence was underscored by the activities of the Christ.

Annas now says precisely what you would expect of the will of a man who already has reached a conclusion before the trial is even submitted to him. After all, he's the father-in-law of the one who has predicted that Jesus must go.

And so, he says, "What is your doctrine and your disciples?" He hasn't the slightest interest in Jesus' doctrine or disciples. He does have a purpose in asking. He wants Jesus to incriminate himself. He wants him to say something which in some way will convict himself. And what are the charges? The charges, we know, are one, the real charges are the hidden charges. The ostensible charges are, one, that he declared he would destroy this temple but in three days he would raise it up again. They accepted that as a charge that he had said that the temple would be destroyed, the temple of Jerusalem. He had said, "*Destroy this temple,[of my body] and in three days I will raise it up [again].*"

The second charge was that they said to him, "Are you the Christ?" And he said, "*I am.*" But the Christ means Messiah. He had declared he was the Messiah. That was the second charge. And then you take Messiah and you convert it and you make a very simple charge that he said he was a king, king of the Jews. And now, even though you cannot tell the Roman Empire why you want him killed, you have something you can go to Rome and say, "Look what he said. He's competing with your emperor. He said he's a king." And you know only the emperor of Rome governs. There's no other king. And so, this was the subterfuge whereby they could present it to Rome.

Now, there was a new law passed. There was a time when the Jews were able to kill but they weren't after this law and that law came in even after Jesus had declared, "*Destroy this temple, and in three days I will raise it up [again].*" The new law was, and it was a Roman law, that the Jews could not impose the death sentence upon anyone. They could not kill.

And so, even though the Sanhedrin met at midnight and decided that Jesus must die, even though they had him in custody, they had no legal power to kill him. There was no way. They needed the power of Rome to enforce their will. Their will was to kill him and they needed the power of Rome to carry out that will.

Do you see the symbolism that brought this to a head? The will of the mind, the will of the intellect and that's always the symbol used of the Jew, the intellect. The will of the intellect must turn to the force of the Roman and they must come together so that the will invokes the force. The will invokes the power and carrying the symbolism further, the mind asks the body to do the killing.

And so, the mind and body of man are the symbols of the Jew and Rome. The mind provides the will; the body provides the power and this kills the Invisible Christ. We turn from the Invisible Christ as the intellect and the body of force conspire in their ignorance of the presence of the Divine Self. We live this way constantly in a state of ignorance of the invisible Self, constantly killing the Christ by unawareness of the presence of the Christ.

The Christ isn't killed but we are dead to the Christ. So, Judaism was dead to the Christ. Rome was dead to the Christ and together they combined forces to externalize that deadness to the Christ by the sentence to kill the Christ. And the Christ could not be killed. You cannot kill Divinity. You merely blind yourself to it. And always, the Christ that is being killed is personalized as a visible form of flesh called Jesus who isn't there. And all this takes place within yourself as you walk in the body of flesh. All that was done in Rome, in Jerusalem, we do every day. The Sanhedrin, the ruling body of the mind and the body, the Roman empire, join forces and we walk in a body of flesh where there is no body of flesh, where only the Invisible Christ is. And so, we walk in the wrong identity, in the wrong world, in the wrong lifespan, in the wrong activities and ultimately to the wrong death.

Annas, the high will of an individual, must turn Jesus over to the understanding which is Caiaphas. First, the will and because the will restricts everything within its own limited motivations, that which cannot satisfy the human will is never accepted and so the understanding is equally restricted. Caiaphas now looks at Jesus with a limited understanding because the will in him is the same as the will in Annas. His will is that Jesus be killed. He's not interested in anything Jesus has to say. I think we ought to look at this place where Caiaphas predicts what will happen to Jesus or should happen. It's in John 11:47. He's being brought now to Caiaphas who way back then made the following prediction. 11:47

"Then gathered the chief priests and the Pharisees a council, and said, What do we [do]? for this man doeth many miracles. If we let them alone, all men will believe on him: the Romans will come and take away both our place and our nation. And one of them, named Caiaphas, being high priest that same year, said unto them, Ye know nothing [at all], Nor consider that it is expedient for us, that one man should die for the people, and that the whole nation perish not. And this spake he not of himself: but being high priest that year, he prophesied that Jesus should die for the nation."

Now, the word "prophesied" is used to show that he was misusing his sacred office. In other words, it was if he had said, "I heard the Voice say to me, this man must die." He didn't say, "I believe he should die." He said, "This is the word of God." He prophesied so that the people would think this was the will of God.

And now, what good is bringing Jesus before this man? That's a kangaroo court. Nothing can happen except that they'll try to humiliate him some more, draw him out some more and try to make him say things that aren't true.

All the while this is happening, between him being brought to Annas and to Caiaphas, Peter is going through his own trials; three trials. Now, let's look at Peter. We know then that Annas is the will of man. Caiaphas is the understanding which must follow within the limited range of the will and finally, they're going to send him to Pilate and that's going to be the end of the line because the will and the understanding being limited, the activity or Pilate, the action, the civil power is going to be equally limited.

You see how those are the three opposites of Love, Divine faith and Divine action? John, Peter and James went to the Mount of Transfiguration, the very opposite of Annas, Caiaphas and Pilate who are the mortal counterparts, who because they have no Divine love, no Divine faith, no Divine understanding are restricted to human, limited function in this world.

Peter's three trials are between the first two trials of Jesus with Annas and Caiaphas.

"Simon Peter followed Jesus, so did another disciple: and that disciple was known unto the high priest." John is telling us that he was known to the high priest. *"He went in with Jesus into the palace of the high priest. But Peter stood at the door without. Then went out that other disciple, which was known unto the high priest, and spake unto her that kept the door, and brought in Peter."*

Now, John is Love. Peter is Faith. When you take an orange and cut off the peeling you can see what the orange is made of. Now, we're taking the outer appearance called Jesus and we're cutting off the peel to see what it's made of. It's made of the Love, the Faith and the Action.

John is the Love. Even though Jesus is led into the presence of Annas - and this is where you come in and I come in - Jesus is loving Annas. That is why John goes in with him, to show that the activity of Love does not stop in Jesus though he is subjected to these trials. There is this illusory form called Jesus and it is actually Love itself, in spite of the appearance of an ex-high priest who has determined that this form must die. You do not stop loving if you are living in the Christ. You love your enemy. You pray for your enemy. Why? Your enemy isn't there. Annas sees Jesus but Christ does not see Annas. Christ does not even see Jesus. Only Christ is there and we must learn this. The presence of John is a sign to you that once you let go of Divine Love, you're living back in the illusion of flesh. There's no love in Annas. There's no love in the human will. The Love is in the Christ of your Being and it accompanies you wherever you go. If you're not in that Love consciously, you're back in flesh.

Peter stays outside the door. Peter is outside Christ. Why? John goes out to get Peter in. Why does John do it? Because Love is first. All your faith without Love will perish. With Love, Love will take and lift your faith up and bring it in because if you do not have love of God as the only living Being, ever running a perfect universe, how can you have faith? Faith is born of that Love. John has to come out for Peter and bring Peter in. Human faith is not enough then. There must first be the love of Reality, of Truth, of the Spirit and it in turn, spawns Faith.

From that is born the activity of Grace or Divine action. And we come into the transfiguration, the knowledge that I am not the flesh. You see the ascending scale and the descending scales, the subtlety of John's presentation?

"Agree with thine adversary."

And here the Christ is showing us how to agree with our adversary. How do you agree with Annas, with Caiaphas, with Pilate? They're not there. They are not there. That's how you agree with them. That's why Love is there. Love is seeing the Invisible, Divine Self everywhere and that Divine Self everywhere that you're seeing and knowing is not possible when you think you're in that place. That's why you get out of this place, out of this chair, out of this room, out of this form.

I am Infinite Christ and all of this that is here is the cosmic charade. You're looking at the thought forms of the cosmic mind, cosmic thought patterns and you walk through them in your love of God, in the faith engendered by that Love and you discover the non-power of the cosmic thought forms that we call persons, conditions, things.

Only when you are not in the flesh but are absent from the flesh, knowledgably in the infinite Self of you, the Invisible Christ of you which is everywhere, can you walk through the thought forms called the world. The ability to do this grows when the will of you is centered on doing it. Then the understanding is not limited to the limited human will. The understanding expands with the Divine will in you and finally, the action follows. Our scale will not be

Annas, Caiaphas and Pilate. It will be John, Peter and James to the Transfiguration.

Whenever you find that you're having difficulty getting the message, getting through, making the contact, finding your center, one good thing to remember is that you have limited yourself to a place. There was a me here struggling to get it and there is no such me.

The Infinite Way means you are Infinite Being and only when you take that literally and are out of place in your consciousness, do you begin to find that Infinite feeding itself back into your consciousness. Every time you forget that, you begin to restrict yourself into a little ball and that's the problem.

Christ was not standing in front of Caiaphas, in front of Annas, in front of Pilate. Christ was not in that form and that form was not there and this is the supreme message that we are to have. He was knowing no man after the flesh, not even himself.

"I am not in that flesh. I, Divine Being, am the new species on the earth. I, in the midst of you, am Divine Being and I am your name. I am your substance. I, in the midst of you am the son of God and I cannot die and I cannot be hurt. I cannot be touched by mortal being."

When you accept the Allness of God and also think that there is flesh, you are denying the Allness of God at the very same moment.

And so, here is the one that makes it very difficult but which will remove the stone. When you accept yourself as flesh, you are denying the presence of God. God cannot occupy the same space as flesh. When you say, "I am here and I am flesh," you are saying, "God is not here," and you are separated. The only way you can accept the presence of God is to remove the belief that flesh is where you stand. God is not flesh and therefore, it cannot be there and if you believe it is there, you do not believe God is there. I cannot be both Spirit and flesh.

Just like God and evil cannot occupy the same place. How can God and evil be in the same place? So, if evil is there in your belief, you've said, "God is not there." When religion says, "These people have this problem and these people have this and the other has famine and poverty and these have cancer and these have TB," religion is saying, "In all these places that we have found these evils, we have said God is not there." And so, strangely enough, you see Jesus was teaching that religion does not believe in God.

Annas, the high priest did not believe in God. He believed in killing Jesus. That's not believing in God. But Annas is the human will and the human will does not believe in God. Caiaphas is the human understanding and the human understanding does not believe in God and therefore, Pilate, the human action can say, "Take him away. Crucify him."

You see then, you must come to that root which is the human will. If your human will is not determined to move, live, have your Being outside the flesh, all that follows will be within the limitations of your double-minded consciousness which wants to worship God but also wants to live in the flesh. And this conflict makes it impossible to find God. Where your flesh appears to be, God is and God is not that flesh. And we must dwell with this deeply in our meditation to know that God and flesh cannot occupy the same space.

They couldn't crucify the Christ because God and flesh do not occupy the same space. God was standing everywhere and those who had the concept of flesh saw flesh and one called Christ Jesus had the concept of God everywhere and saw, only God everywhere. And if, for one moment, there had been a single withdrawal from that knowledge, that only God is everywhere and God is running a perfect universe, even in the midst of all these apparent trials, if there had been a moment of wavering, that measure of wavering was the very judgment that would have returned and we would not have had the Christ message.

The judgment that we send out is the judgement that returns. The judgment of the Christ is that God is running a perfect universe and that is what was eventually made manifest. God is running a perfect universe. I am ascended. Throughout these trials, the Christ maintains the one knowledge that God is here running a perfect universe and there is no other. And then, no judgment can return to you other than that judgment whether it's lack or limitation or health; that is a mis-judgment. But God is running a perfect universe - there is no flesh. There is nothing that can deteriorate and this is the judgment that returns as the health of your countenance.

Poor Peter had to learn these things. The girl at the door said, "Don't I know you? Aren't you one of his disciples?" "Oh no, not me." You see the division in consciousness that is pointed out to us?

Christ says, "I am He. Who are you looking for? I am He." The wavering consciousness says, "I am not."

If the Consciousness within the Christ had said, "I am not," there would be no form walking through the illusion of death and coming out alive. There would be no teaching to show us that we can walk through the illusion of flesh and come out alive. And all these problems of the flesh, we can walk through them and come out alive because I am He and beside He there is no other.

I want to meditate on the knowledge that wherever there is flesh in our belief, we are conversely saying that God is not present. Once you understand that this is the ultimate denial of God and the daily denial that we are making, you will learn that something must be done about it.

Where there is a germ, where there is a malignancy, where there is a thorn, where there is a problem, wherever there is the acceptance of something that is not God then we are saying, "God is not there," and we have stepped right out of Gethsemane, right out of the Kingdom into the world of duality. Right there where I see the butcher and the baker, in my fourth dimension of Consciousness, I know there is the Invisible Spirit alone and there is no butcher, there is no baker. This is a cosmic thought form which I do not accept.

Right here where I stand is a cosmic thought form called flesh. It is not God and so I cannot accept it because I must accept God as being present, not the opposite.

The world mind, my adversary, says "My flesh is here," and the world mind in me, my human mind, says "My flesh is here." But my human mind saw soldiers. My human mind thought Jesus Christ was bound. My human mind thought Jesus Christ went through all those tribulations even though God had said through Jesus Christ that Christ was not in the world. My human mind calls God a liar every day. The liar is not God. The liar is the world mind and my human mind conspiring to call God a liar. God is not a liar.

And God says, "If you believe on Christ as your identity, you will see God face to face."

He that calls God a liar must be overcome. That's why we go back to Annas, the will in you, must be dedicated only to the will of God in you, not to the will of the flesh. As long as you have flesh, the flesh will have a will wanting to express. The mind will want to express its will in the flesh. When the flesh is crucified in Consciousness and we live in the will of the Father, not the will of what the body wants to do or the mind wants to do, then we have the cornerstone from which the Kingdom is discovered.

Don't mind if it takes you ten meditations before anything happens. It isn't what happens while you're meditating on this. It's just uncluttering, getting material beliefs out of the way. The time comes when, without thought, Spirit begins to flow back to you and you find powers that you never knew you had, very subtly showing forth in your daily experience, effortlessly. The moment you're willing to crucify the flesh, you have released the binding of the Christ through ignorance of the presence of God where you stand.

Don't mistake it. It doesn't mean you stop eating tomorrow. It doesn't mean you fast for the rest of your life. It doesn't mean give up the joy of living. It means be conscious that God's presence means that everything that is not God is not present. And then the will of the Father will gently enact itself in you.

— End of Side One —

We want to look now at some Biblical passages with this thought in mind. We're establishing today that where God is, flesh is not and the human mind will find it very difficult to first accept; second, to stand with that; and third, to face a world of matter with the knowledge that the matter isn't there. And yet, that is the Christ message.

Now, we want to see that this has also been disregarded by us and by religion and by the world at large even though more than fifty percent of the world believes in God. Always, in the Old and the New Testaments, the knowledge that there is an invisible Kingdom which is not flesh, which is here and which we must learn to live in, to be an inhabitant of it as a non-fleshly creature, as a none physical being. This has been the hidden secret of the Bible and it comes into focus more and more as you become aware that the final trials of Jesus Christ are establishing that there is no one there in the flesh, in spite of the fact that the world is lamenting all the suffering that allegedly is taking place.

He who has passed through the illusion of flesh is not in the flesh and walks in the Kingdom of pure Spirit and the reality of that Kingdom must be impressed upon us again and again.

In Daniel, we find it. In the second chapter, the 44th and 45th verse. *"In the days of these kings shall the God of heaven set up a kingdom, which shall never be destroyed: and the kingdom shall not be left to other people, but it shall break in pieces and consume all these kingdoms, and it shall stand for ever."*

And that kingdom which shall stand forever is the invisible Kingdom of the Christ which is the message of the New Testament.

"Forasmuch as thou sawest that the stone was cut out of the mountain without hands."

The stone which breaks all the physical temporal kingdoms is *"the stone cut out of the mountain without hands;"* not born of woman, not born, never dying.

"The stone carved out of the mountain."

Your consciousness that where God is, flesh is not and God is everywhere; your conscious realization of this until it is your actual Consciousness. This is *"the stone carved out of the mountain."*

Daniel 7:14. *"There was given him dominion, and glory, and a kingdom, that all people, nations, and languages, should serve him: his dominion is an everlasting dominion, which shall not pass away, and his kingdom that which shall not be destroyed."*

Christ walks forth as Jesus revealing the presence of that Kingdom. Christ says to you, "I am the Light. Ye are the Light." That is our Kingdom and that is the Kingdom of God within us which is not of this world. It has dominion over the material world. It breaks the material world to pieces. It melts all matter. It speaks and the earth melts. Your Consciousness that where God is, there is no flesh. And where flesh is accepted, we are standing away from the presence of God. We are declaring there is no God.

Now, this is referred to later as the Cornerstone or the Headstone which the builders rejected.

Isaiah 28:10, 28:16. We today do not want to reject this cornerstone. We are to understand it. Bring it out into the open in our consciousness, understand precisely what Isaiah is telling us and what each prophet is bringing to our attention. 28:10.

"Therefore thus saith the Lord God, [Behold], I lay in Zion for a foundation."

Zion is not a place. Zion is the high Consciousness. You can't go and build a nation in a place and call that Zion. That isn't the Zion of the Bible. There is no place. There is no matter. There is no flesh. Zion or Israel is the high Consciousness of the Allness of God's presence. You're in Israel when you know that only God is present, not flesh. That is Zion.

"I lay in Zion for a foundation a stone, a tried stone, a precious corner stone, a sure foundation."

And so, your sure foundation is the knowledge that God being All, flesh has no existence. For you, the material world is but a world of effect. You do not go out seeking effect. You do not reach for effect. What's the point? You can't hold what isn't there. You must give it back.

We sow to the Spirit, the origin, the original cause of things, the Source. We keep our consciousness to the Allness of the Source. We live in the Kingdom. We do not reach for the effects. We live in the invisible Consciousness which is called Zion, Israel, Christ Consciousness, fourth dimension, transcendental, the illuminated, the enlightened, the Buddhic consciousness, the Christ mind. All saying the same, where God is, flesh is not. That was Isaiah 28:10, no, 28:16 is correct.

We come to the Psalms, the second Psalm, 6th verse. We could go on a little further in this Psalm. *"The kings of the earth set themselves, and the rulers take counsel together, against the Lord, and against his anointed."* There you have Annas and Caiaphas taking arms against the Lord.

"Let us break their bands asunder, and cast away their cords from us. He that sitteth in the heavens shall laugh: the Lord shall have them in derision. Then shall he speak unto them in his wrath, and vex them in his sore displeasure. Yet have I set my king upon my holy hill of Zion."

It doesn't matter what's going on in the world of matter. *"Yet have I set my king upon the holy hill of Zion."* The conscious knowledge that only God is present is your Christ Consciousness, the Temple not made with hands. This is sitting on the throne of the holy hill of Zion.

The whole 118th Psalm, I almost missed the very next phrase, even though it wasn't meant or it wasn't listed in my...

After he says *"I have set my king upon my holy hill of Zion. I will declare the decree: the Lord hath said unto me, Thou art my Son; this day have I begotten thee.... this day have I begotten thee."*

You see, when you have accepted that only God is present, that there is no flesh, this is the meaning of *"This day have I begotten thee,"* this is the actual birth realized. Begotten of the Spirit of God and in the moment of realization, you're in the world where there is no flesh.

Flesh is not begotten of God. *"This day have I begotten thee."* Dig deeper, deeper than the human will. Rest that will and you will find the Self which is begotten of God which is your Self and live out of the will of that Self and the whole sequence that follows will be of the Divine, not the mortal.

All mortality is being revealed as a myth without substance or law or father. Mortality has no Divine Father. The acceptance of mortality is the statement that I have no Divine Father.

I'll ask you to read the 118th Psalm in its fulness, just for your own joy. But I'll only give you at the moment the 22nd verse of it. The whole 118th Psalm is a pane of joy, telling of the glorious Kingdom of God on earth. The 22nd verse says, *"The stone which the builders refused is become the head stone of the corner."*

Those who built religions built it with the knowledge of good and evil and they've always been trying to get rid of the evil. And when you accept that only God is present and where God is there can be no flesh, you've got rid of the evil. Where is it? The moment you accept there is no flesh, you have eliminated all of the cancers and all of the TBs and all of the multiple sclerosis and all of the mental and emotional and physical disorders in the universe. There is no flesh.

Where are the disorders? In the flesh that isn't there. Where is the flesh? If it isn't there, where is it? It's only in the false consciousness of the mortal being.

But you are the begotten Son. This wasn't speaking about Jesus Christ. This was five hundred years before Jesus Christ. *"I have begotten thee."* There is no mortal there. What is a mortal consciousness? It is a nothingness. A mortal consciousness is the denial of the Allness of God. A mortal is the denial of the Allness of God. The duality becomes shorter and shorter. The shadows diminish. The one consciousness of God as your Consciousness is going to displace the divided consciousness. The human will, will diminish and dissolve. *"Thy will be done,"* in me becomes the only creed you have and you reach far back beyond that human will. You refuse to acknowledge it or to obey it.

These are the disciples of Christ then who are moved only by the Christ will who are conscious that flesh is a cosmic illusion; who can walk through the illusions of matter knowing them to be cosmic thoughts, cosmic thought forms, false sense of powers, non- existent, only in the cosmic thought forms. All of the world of thought breaks past you without touching you.

Take a look at the 118ᵗʰ Psalm when you have some time.

Now look at Genesis, 49ᵗʰ chapter, 24ᵗʰ verse, speaking about Joseph and it says, *"The archers have sorely grieved him, and shot at him, and hated him: But his bow abode in strength, and the arms of his hands were made strong by the hands of the mighty God of Jacob; (from thence is the shepherd, the stone of Israel.)"*

The secret of Joseph then was that he knew there was no flesh. He had found the stone carved out of the mountain without hands; Spiritual consciousness. His reincarnation, as Jesus Christ was but a continuation of the same Invisible Christ which was Joshua, and which finally becomes the invisible Consciousness of us all. *"The stone of Israel."*

Now, you might say, why are you even stressing this? Because the Master stressed it.

In Mathew 21, the importance of what we had been stressing is emphasized by Jesus Christ. 42ⁿᵈ verse, *"Jesus saith unto them, Did ye never read in the scripture, The stone which the builders rejected, the same is become the head of the corner: this is the Lord's doing, and it is marvellous in our eyes?"*

He was teaching the world to accept Spiritual consciousness, the stone of Israel, the secret of the Masters, the secret of Joseph, the secret of Moses, the secret of Buddha, the secret of all who have walked with God, not in the flesh, though they appeared to human sense to be in the flesh.

And now, we see a magic transformation. In the Acts, our friend Peter was going through his three trials. He's going to do something very beautiful afterward. Starting with the 8th verse of Acts, we find that the disciples have been captured and look who captured them.

(Acts 4:5 - 7) "It came to pass on the morning, that their rulers, and elders, and scribes, And Annas the high priest, and Caiaphas, John, and Alexander, and as many as were of the kindred of the high priest, were gathered together in Jerusalem. When they had set them in the midst," - meaning the few disciples who were preaching about Jesus - *"they said, By what power, by what name, have ye done this?"*

They had had the effrontery to heal a cripple. And they said they did it by the power of Jesus Christ and once more, the rulers of the Sanhedrin assembled, took Peter and John and the disciples in their midst and now they were going to put them through the grilling.

But *"Then Peter, filled with the Holy Ghost, said unto them,"* - this is the very same Peter who just back a few weeks denies Christ three times - Peter says, *"Ye rulers of the people, and elders of Israel, If we this day be examined of the good deed done to the impotent man, by what means he is made whole; Be it known unto you all, and all the people of Israel, that by the name of Jesus Christ of Nazareth, whom ye crucified, whom God raised from the dead, even by him doth this man stand here before you whole."*

Now Peter may not have had the right words but he certainly now had the faith.

We've learned much since Peter uttered these words. But now, the third crowing of the cock, you see, was the end of that era for Peter. Deep repentance had followed. He, who had denied the Christ now could stand before the very same tribunal and affirm *"I am he."* The Spirit of God cannot be denied. Even though you crucified Jesus Christ, you think, I'm ready now to go through the crucifixion that I wasn't ready then.

"This is the stone which was set at nought of you builders, which is become the head of the corner [stone]. Neither is there salvation in any

397

other: for there is none other name under heaven given among men, whereby we must be saved."

Now, that stone is still Christ Consciousness, not healing in the name of Jesus Christ but healing in the name of I, Christ where I stand. I, Christ in the midst of me, in the midst of you, in the midst of Annas, Caiaphas, Pilate, in the midst of the executioner. I, Christ.

There is no flesh. There is no executioner. There is no evil. It has no flesh in which it can function for God is there. That Consciousness is the pure in heart Consciousness we are developing.

In the 16th verse of Acts, the high tribunal says in their privacy, *"What [are we going to do with] these men? for that indeed a notable miracle hath been done by them [is] manifest to all [all who] dwell in Jerusalem [know it]; we cannot deny it. But that it spread no further among the people, let us straitway threaten them, that they speak henceforth to no man in this name,"* meaning Jesus Christ.

And so, they call the disciples now and commanded they not speak at all nor teach in the name of Jesus but Peter and John answered and said unto them, *"Whether it be right in the sight of God to hearken unto you more than unto God, judge ye. For we cannot but speak the things which we have seen and heard"*

Today, maybe, our faith waivers. We cannot walk in a world without flesh. Neither could Peter. Once, twice, three times, "I do not know him. I am not his disciple. I have nothing to do with him. I am not the Invisible Spirit of God. I am flesh."

But now, look at this new Peter. The very Master he worshipped was crucified and to the very same people who crucified him, he can say, "You can't make me change my story because I have seen the Invisible Spirit of God within my Self. I know there is no world of flesh. I know I'm not talking to flesh. I know that you who are trying me are not flesh." That's what he's saying. "All there is, is the Spirit of God and I'll teach that." That was his transformation through the renewing of the mind. It is ours.

Romans 10:11 *"For the scripture saith, Whosoever believeth on him shall not be ashamed"*

And so, however difficult it may be to accept the all presence of God means the absence of flesh, the Christ is not flesh, the Christ is All. The Christ is the begotten, infinite Son which I am, whoever believeth that I am the Infinite Christ within himself shall not be ashamed, meaning you can stand before the highest tribunal in the world and declare "All that is here is the Spirit of God." You declare it within your Self. You don't make an open show. Peter didn't say that to them, "You are not flesh. You don't exist.' He said, "What I know I know."

And so, we stand before the world who appears to be flesh and within our Self, we declare the Truth, "Flesh is not present. The Spirit of God is here." And that is All that is here.

Peter, just to show you the total transformation, in his First Epistle, the 2nd chapter and this should be a conclusion that we finally reach within ourselves. 2nd chapter, first Epistle of Peter, 6th verse, *"Wherefore also it is contained in the scripture, Behold, I lay in Sion a chief corner stone, elect, precious: and he that believeth on him shall not be confounded."*

I think it's clear then that the Allness of God and the non-presence of flesh is the way.

We're going to John now. John 12, for the way to the realization of this is given us by the words of Christ. This is what I call the blessed promise. In the 12th verse, the 12th chapter, the 32nd verse, *"And I, if I be lifted up from the earth, will draw all men unto me."* This is the way you come to the realization that all is Spirit and there is no flesh. *"I, if I be lifted up…. will draw all men unto me."*

In Gethsemane, *"If I be lifted be up,"* before any trial in the world, *"If I be lifted up,"* before every problem that confronts you, before every mountain that rises before you, before every stormy sea. *"If I be lifted up,"* I will lift all men into the Stone not made of hands but carved out of the Infinite Consciousness. And so, we walk through the Red Sea. We push the mountains into the sea. We calm the sea. Why? It is flesh and flesh is not there and there's nothing to do about it. It isn't there. *"If I be lifted up,"* you will know it isn't there.

That is the blessed promise.

In a moment he will say, as he stands before the high tribunal, in response to their question, "Are you king of the Jews?" He will say nothing. He will not answer. He will not say, "I am," he will not say, "I am not." Why? Who is asking the question? The world mind expressing through Pilate. He has been teaching he is not king of the Jews. He is the universal Christ. Shall he honor the world mind and reply to it? Shall he say to the world mind that you are the king of the Jews, you are the king of the world that isn't here. In silence, he makes no reply and then, he utters the classic words, *"My kingdom is not of this world."*

Is your kingdom of this world if his was not? If the Christ says, *"My kingdom is not of this world,"* and Christ is your name, is your kingdom of this world? And when Christ says, *"But my kingdom is not from hence,"* the double negative, *"not from hence."* My Kingdom is here. Where is your kingdom but here, *"not from hence."* It is a kingdom of no flesh, the Kingdom of Spirit. Your Kingdom is here, invisible.

Your assignment during the week is to read in the "Parenthesis in Eternity, My Kingdom is Not of this World." If you happen to have a tape on it, you can listen to that too. "My Kingdom is not of this World." You'll find it in the third section of "Parenthesis," in the mystical section and for those of you who don't have the book, take the words into consciousness. Commune with the Father. Go into your Kingdom within which is not of this world and rest there letting the Father within explain the nature of My Kingdom, the Infinite, eternal, ever present Kingdom of true Being where all is perfection, where imperfection is revealed as non-existent.

We'll stop at that place. *"My kingdom is not of this world."*

And one day, without you taking conscious thought, you will know, you will say within your Self, at everything you see, "My Kingdom is not of this world of flesh, of matter, of transiency. My Kingdom is the present Christ kingdom and there is no power on this earth that can destroy it or my Being or take from me that which I am, for nothing is here but that Kingdom." The concept called world disappears over the false horizon when you come into the conscious awareness that your Kingdom is All that is here, the Kingdom of God and you walk through world thought untouched.

That's a fitting ending to our class. Thank you again.

CLASS 37

WHAT IS NOT SPIRIT IS NOT REAL

Herb: We're going to explore the meaning of truth and the meaning of "My Kingdom is not of this world" and this is not for the faint-hearted. It is for those who have accepted the Christ message wherever it leads them.

Though we have introduction, I want to take you back to Isaiah, 44th chapter in which he makes the following statements, full of very unusual, oriental imagery.

He's speaking about those who have stepped away from the knowledge of their Source and he does it this way. *"The smith with the tongues both work at the coals and fashion it with hammers, work with it with the strength of his arms, yea, he's hungry and his strength faileth. He drinketh no water and is faint. And the carpenter stretches out his ruler. He marketh it out with lines, presses it with planes and he marketh it out with a compass and maketh it after the figure of a man, according to the beauty of a man, that it may remain in the house. He heweth him down cedars and taketh the cypress and the oak which he strengtheneth it for himself among the trees of the forest and he planted an ash and the rain doth nourish it. Then shall it be for man to burn for he will taketh thereof and warm himself, yea, he kindleth it and baketh bread, yea, he maketh a god and worshippeth it, he maketh it a graven image, and falleth down thereof. He burneth part thereof in the fire, which part thereof he eateth flesh, he roasteth roast, and is satisfied, yea, he warmeth himself and saith, Aha, I am warm, I have seen the fire."*

He shall far remove the man comes. Now he's got that fire which is keeping him warm, forgotten is the tree which was planted, forgotten all the work into that, forgotten all the preceded the tree, forgotten is his seed. He comes further and further away into the material world so that in oriental imagery, burning wood, burning coals is a symbol of being separate from source.

We're back in Isaiah, forgetting there is one Being, one, spiritual Self, man walks out into the material world and in the oriental mind, this comes in one form as burning wood or coals.

You're going to see this in the 18th chapter of John again.

Now, we go to Peter and we see in the 13th chapter of John, Peter makes the following statement to Jesus, *"Wither I go, says Jesus, thou canst not follow me now but thou shall follow me later and Peter says, why cannot I follow thee now? I will lay down my life for thy sake."* I will lay down my life for thy sake.

Now in the 18th chapter of John, the damsel that kept the door said unto Peter,

"Aren't thou not also one of the man's disciples?" and he said, *"I am not."*

And then, the next phrase, *"The servants and the officers stood there, who have made a fire of coals for it was cold and they warmed themselves and Peter stood with them and warmed himself."*

Peter was separate from his Source. He was burning coals, warming himself, not with the inner light but with the outer light. Not with the inner love but with the outer sense of matter. Now the demonstration there is that even though Peter, had great faith and great love, he was mentalizing faith, not realizing faith. We want to see the difference between mentalizing and realizing. We all can mentalize and very few can realize.

Peter's faith was the mental kind. He asserted he would lay down his life and he really meant and when it came time to do so, he was willing to pull out the sword but there was a moment when suddenly, he was completely lost in the world of flesh and he feared for his own safety. The life that he'd said he would lay down, he feared for. Why? Because his faith was insufficient? No, it's because he never had the right kind of faith. He had the faith of the mind, the faith that rests in what the mind thinks it knows. He had reached the state of mentalizing without realizing. He hadn't passed over the memory patterns of the mind.

Now, this week, someone said to me, "I have read in the Contemplative Life on page 132," I think he said, "Joel says that the secret is to know the non-power of all appearances and I'm trying to do but they always get me down anyway. What am I doing that's wrong?"

Now, that's like burning coals to keep warm. That's the obvious thing to do so you do it and it's also obvious to know truth with your mind so you do it and then it fails and the reason it fails is because the mind has no capacity to know truth. What it thinks is truth is never truth. It's only its own concept of truth and you have to go deeper than the mind knowing truth because it always knows the illusion of truth.

And so, you finally come to a place where you see that your mind cannot take you into the Kingdom of God and it doesn't matter how hard you try or how dedicated or how intelligent. Even though you know all the words, even though you stay up all hours to read and cram it in.

And then the secret is that you have to know Christ in you for Christ in you realizes but your mind mentalizes. Your mind will always mentalize and until it surrenders to Christ in you, there's no one, no self in you to realize. Only Christ can realize and Peter's faith at that level is our own mental faith which has to be transcended. You of your own self cannot have faith in God. You must reach the Christ of you which is faith itself.

And so, if you're trying to remove a lack or a limitation and all your mentalizing won't do it, it's for the same reason. The mentalizing can only grapple with the problem in its material aspects and the mentalizing itself is part of the illusion. So, we have to go further and further in all ways. Instead of walking into that particular problem, we walk into Christ and turn the problem over to the Christ of our own Being which then realizes what our mind couldn't realize. It realizes the non-reality of the problem.

Now, we're going to deepen in that aspect as we go along.

"The servants and the officers stood there."

Now, servants and officers referred to the principals of the mind which are inadequate. The thoughts of the human mind are the servants and the principals and they are inadequate. So, it's the servants and the officers who stand in there warming themselves. Our thoughts that are mentalizing is insufficient.

"They warmed themselves. Peter stood there and warmed himself."

Once more, there will be another denial by Peter and these three denials represent the final, complete denial of the mind of God. The mind has no capacity to know God.

"The cock crows."

And this is the dawn of a new era. When the cock crows, this is the moment when Peter becomes totally repentant, meaning at that moment he learns the futility of the mind. His repentance begins with the crowing of the cock because it is a signal given to him about three denials.

In each of us then, there is a continued denial of Christ as we continue to utilize the mind to understand God and you keep trying and deepening into the illusion as you want to understand but you do not know you cannot know God aright with the mind so you keep trying in every fashion you know. And one day it dawns on you and that dawning upon you, that you cannot with the mind, realize the Kingdom of God, that is the cock crowing in your consciousness.

The moment you reach the realization that I can no longer go in this direction of the mind, you have heard the cock crow and now, you're going to turn and live. You're going to say, "This that faces me is not something I have to overcome with the mind at all." That would be a double illusion. First, the illusion of the thing to overcome and then, the illusion that you can overcome it with the mind.

You don't heal a condition. You never heal a condition and you never heal a condition out there.

This week, we had a call from a little girl in Wyoming, a student of our class who got married and went to Wyoming, who knew some degree of this work, enough so that there's a degree of fidelity to the truth within the girl and we heard that she had a broken bone, wasn't healing and it was growing in the wrong direction. And so, the doctor decided that unless they operated, that poor girl wouldn't be able to use that arm at all.

And so, an operation was scheduled and we were called and just before the operation, this girl did something that very few people do and which we've never asked anyone to do. She said to the surgeon, "I'd like you to take another x-ray just before you operate." He said, "It won't do any good." But she said, "Just do it just to please me then."

And so, he did and when she called yesterday in the morning, she said, she was crying and she said, "You just called me and told me I would be doing you a disservice if I operate on that arm because healing is taking place."

Now, this is Wyoming and nobody healed her arm. Nobody went into Wyoming to heal her arm and nobody knew she had a broken arm. That which is called a healing is now her consciousness becoming aware of her invisible perfection. Her arm isn't healing. She's becoming aware of the perfection which is her Divine birthright. If somebody had tried to heal her arm, she would have been under the knife of the surgeon that morning. If somebody had thought she had a broken arm in Wyoming, she would have been under that surgeon's knife that morning.

And the message is that you don't meet the so-called condition which you think is in Wyoming. You meet it where it comes to your attention. It comes to your attention where you are. It is brought to your conscious awareness and that's where the healing takes place. It doesn't take place in Wyoming.

Now then, somebody tells you they have a broken arm and they're in Wyoming and you're called upon now to forget them in Wyoming. They have passed to you the world mind belief that there's a broken arm in Wyoming and that belief is now right in your consciousness where you are and that's where it must be healed. So, you don't have her to heal. You have you to heal. You must heal your consciousness of the belief that there is a broken arm in a place called Wyoming.

Now, I cite this because the realization of healing within your own consciousness and not in the external world where the problem seems to be is going to be very useful to you. It might be your foot or your hand or your head and you want to heal those but that's not really what you must do to get rid of that nagging appearance. You must heal your consciousness of the illusion that this is the condition that you are suffering from. You're never suffering from a condition.

The condition is not what you're suffering from. You're suffering from the belief that you have the condition. Get the distinction because if you work on the condition, it lingers. You see, you're chasing after the illusion with the illusion that you can remove the illusion or that you're trying to remove something that your mind tells you is supposed to be an illusion but is bothering you.

It's the same thing as Peter. The faith of the mind is not enough. He's mentalizing and when you're trying to get rid of the problem, the condition, you're mentalizing. You're not in a state of realizing and realizing then is different in that you dismiss the condition. And you say, instead of what caused the condition, you asked yourself what caused the belief in this condition. The cause of the belief is the world mind which has now placed a sense or a condition in your consciousness. Forget the body. Get into your consciousness and there, erase the belief in the possibility that such a condition can exist where God is. And you find that this does the interesting thing of removing what appeared to be a condition.

Several others in this last few days are important and I must repeat them for your benefit. I told you about the individual whose blood pressure was up and then after calling for help, the blood pressure instantly went down thirty-six points and the patient still felt terrible. And so, he went to his doctor and the doctor said, "What's happened to your blood pressure? I don't believe it. It's gone down thirty-six points overnight." And the minute the doctor showed him the chart that his blood pressure had gone down, he felt fine again.

It's like Joel's story about the rain that had stopped. After a hundred and eighty days, this country called him and the rain was stopped but the condition of rain still remained and they couldn't understand why the rain wasn't falling when all of the sky was so angry and the same thing happened here. The man was still in a state of discomfort and pain and that sort of thing, but his blood pressure had dropped and he didn't know it and when he discovered it through the doctor, then he felt good again. Always, it's the belief which is the father to the condition and the world mind is the father to the belief. And so, you've got to get inside yourself and remove the belief.

Now, a third case this week and I don't know if we've often talked of this without a purpose. It was a brain tumor and this brain tumor was called to our attention seven days before the operation was scheduled and in the seven days that we worked with someone who actually was not at all in this work but was advised about us by the fellow whose blood pressure went down and the tumor didn't disappear in the seven days so the operation went forth as scheduled. Now, if this had been one of our students, who like the girl in Wyoming could say that the doctor wanted to take an x-ray just before you operate, we might have found a different case. We don't know. But in the course of the meditations for this girl, who was having a brain tumor surgery, we were given this information which is always a sign of everything is finished, in right. The information was this woman would be sheathed in light during the operation and although you might say, "Well that's not very much to go by." It really is all you need if it's real, if it's a realization, not a mentalizing. If it's just a psychic thing, well, it's nothing. But if it's a realization of the actual Spirit itself, then that's it, you see because what happens in Spirit today happens in the physical world tomorrow, the next day or a hundred years later but Spirit always precedes what comes out in time, in matter.

And so, the morning after the operation, there was a call from the husband of the woman to the friend whose blood pressure had gone down, who in turn related to me that they had a perfect operation and that everything is benign and so on. They had no problem whatsoever. She actually was sheathed in light, the presence of Spirit realized.

Now again, that's not a condition out there. It's a condition of a spiritual realization within yourself. All of this is what Peter was still unaware of at this particular point. He was still in the awareness of flesh, not of Spirit and we all must come to the place now where when the Master speaks and says, "My Kingdom is not of this world," we've got to look that straight in the face. What is he saying to us? His Kingdom, the Christ Kingdom is not of this world.

Now, I want to give you a principle which is very stark and startling because it leaves no alternatives but it is a true principle.

"My Kingdom is Spirit. My Kingdom is truth and only Spirit is truth. Only Spirit is real. Spirit is the Kingdom of God. The Kingdom of God is reality. Spirit is all that is and that which is not Spirit is not real".

Now that's stark in that whatever is not Spirit is not real and that's an absolute principle that you can depend on even though before you come to the place where you learn how to depend on it, you may struggle quite a bit.

"Spirit is all that is real. My Kingdom is not of this world" is the statement that My Kingdom is Spirit and the world of matter is not my kingdom. It isn't a statement that you will graduate from the world of matter and eventually enter into the Kingdom. It isn't a statement that mortality can become immortal or that matter can become Spirit. It is saying Spirit is and matter is not.

When the Master says before the world, "My Kingdom is not of this world," he is stating that this world does not exist. That My Kingdom of Spirit is all that exists and I know from my experience that you can learn to live in this awareness even to a minor degree and see wonderful things happen. Only Spirit exists.

And so, let's go back to all our personal conditions. You look at any one of them or any ten of them and they are not Spirit and that is simple, right there, they do not exist. If your faith is mental, you'll discover you can hold this today and then you lose it tomorrow. But if you practice this and learn to look at this world and all it contains as non-existent, you'll find yourself coming to a place where you can realize that behind the non-existence of the world, there is an existence which is real and permanent, of Spirit, and you will realize the presence of that Spirit. Something in you responds, makes contact, something in you radiates the actual awareness of the spiritual universe. And then you know you have found My Kingdom which is not of this world and although you're just a babe in the Kingdom, your higher than all those who walk the world of matter.

And we learn to live as babes in this Kingdom. We learn to struggle as little tiny infants holding to one truth, only Spirit is present. Whatever is not Spirit, has no existence. I don't have to overcome it. I don't have to see through it. I don't have to avoid it, defend against it, resist it, maneuver, manipulate it. It isn't there.

Now, this is an absolute principle and a total one and it would leave you, it seems, with nothing. All your material possessions exist in the world. The world is not reality. If your material possessions are in that which is not reality, are your material possessions real?

We even include our bodies. When you know that only Spirit is, then your body becomes like your automobile. You have an automobile. You use it to transport you. Now, you learn you have a body and your spiritual Self is the invisible activity which to your visible sense appears as body. You learn that your visible body is a very small concept you entertain about your invisible body. Your invisible body is infinite and we're at the level in consciousness now where the concept we entertain about that infinite, invisible body appears as a physical, visible body. It is only our concept about our invisible body but our visible body is in the world, therefore, it has no reality because My Kingdom is Spirit.

Now, I know this is a very difficult place to be. I also know what it does when you make the effort to be there. That's why I mentioned these cases to you. I want you to know that when you rest in the activity Spirit as the only present reality, you feel a subtle change in your consciousness. It loses beliefs in matter. You are lifted above your human consciousness, right out of it and you are given information, inside intuitive awareness of another realm, the realm of Spirit and it then expresses as the harmony of your body or your purse. You find that when you are willing to follow the Master in the knowledge that only Spirit is present, and take the time to dwell in that consciousness, the whole world of matter is redeemed. You are reconciled to Christ. Whatever is necessary is transformed even in the visible world and you will discover miracles happen which seem to be miracles to others which you begin to realize are the normal procedure of Grace functioning as the living Spirit of your Being. Things that you cannot conceive of as being possible happen because the Spirit of your Being is always in a state of Grace.

Now, when we accept My Kingdom is not of this world, we are accepting that the state of Grace which is the state of Spirit, is always here functioning. Whenever you are under the illusion that you're not in a state of Grace, you are not accepting yourself to be Spiritual being. Your Kingdom is Spirit. Spirit is under Divine Grace. Spirit is here. Your Kingdom is here. Grace is where your Spirit is and as you rest in the knowledge that I am Spiritual Being and transcend the mind which stops at a certain point, coming to the point of realizing, you will find that Grace functions in your Spirit right where you are as a permanent dispensation. This never stops.

As long as you are true to the truth that only Spirit is, and go through the trials and labors of coming to that conviction so that it matters not who or where you are or when things occur to you, you know only Spirit is and therefore, only Grace is functioning no matter what surface impressions of the world may appear through your five senses.

Now, we've discovered something interesting in the Bible and everyone who is a lover of the Bible and its truth will understand why it's so interesting. When we come to this statement of Christ Jesus to Pilate, Pilate has said, *"What have you done? If you're not king of the Jews, what did you do? Why did they deliver you to me as a criminal?"*

Now this Pilate, this civil power of the law sets itself up to judge the Christ. And finally, he wants to know why Jesus isn't defending himself and the statement made by Jesus may not be correctly translated as far as the world goes and that has posed a very major problem.

Now here it is in the King James version. I want you to listen to it very carefully because I think part of the inability of Christianity to understand Christ is right in this statement. *"My Kingdom is not of this world. If my kingdom were of this world then would my servants fight that I should not be delivered to the Jews."* And here's the part I want to call to your attention. *"But now is my Kingdom not from hence."*

Now, I know what that means and I find that as I go through certain other Bibles that the translator hasn't the vaguest idea what it means and also, I don't think that from the King James version, "not from hence," Christianity has caught the point of what it means either.

Now, here's another translation in the Stonefield Bible. He says *"My kingdom does not come from that source"* instead of "not from hence." *"My kingdom does not come from that source."*

Now why would he use a different phraseology? It's because they're both translating from the Greek, which in turn has been translated from the Aramaic. *"My kingdom is not from hence"* says the King James version. The Stonefield says *"My kingdom does not come from that source."*

Now, here is the Goodspeed version, and that's 18:37. *"My kingdom has no such origin."*

You see the difficulty the translators are having with whatever the Greeks says. One says, "My kingdom has no such origin." One says, "My kingdom is not from that source." And the King James says, "My kingdom is not from hence."

And then, in the Moffat, still the same passage, *"My realm lies elsewhere."*

Now isn't that strange? Four accredited Bibles and here it says, "No, my realm lies elsewhere." Another says, "My kingdom is not from that source." Another says, "My kingdom is not from that origin." And the King James alone says, "Now is my kingdom not from hence."

Each one, Moffat, Goodspeed, and Stonefield have omitted the word "now" and they have also tried to figure out what "not from hence" means and so they have said "not of this origin."

What they have all neglected to say was what Jesus Christ was saying here. "Hence" means here like in Medieval times, in Shakespearean characters say, "Get ye hence." Get out of here.

Well, "not from hence" means not from here and you see the great discovery then that comes to you when you see that Jesus Christ is saying, "My kingdom is here." "Now," he says, "my kingdom is here." And they've all missed it.

And so, Christianity says, if you want to go the kingdom of God, you have to die and go to heaven and Jesus tries to say, "No, my kingdom of God is right here, now. Now is my kingdom, not from hence." He's revealing the spiritual Kingdom of God on earth is the only reality here. He's revealing the world isn't here but the Kingdom is.

My Kingdom is not of this world but now my Kingdom is here. My Kingdom is here, the world is not here. My Kingdom is Spirit and that is why I can walk through the experience of the torments of the world. There is no suffering. There is no pain. This is the illusion of the world. There is no disease. This is the illusion of the world which does not know that reality is My Kingdom of Spirit, here, now.

Now, you and I are at the place where we are going to learn that when we live in the knowledge that My Kingdom of Spirit is here, now, that this becomes the living experience of the all-power of Spirit. And all worldly powers, underline that word "all," all worldly powers are revealed as powerless.

When you are aware consciously through all the efforts it takes you to reach that awareness that Spirit is all that is here, you will discover that the whole battle is taken out of your hands. It all becomes a new consciousness in you which no longer has to warm its hands over the fire made by coals, which stands in the midst of the condition and isn't lured into overcoming the condition. The condition is not Spirit. There is no spiritual tumor and only Spirit is here. Therefore, where is the tumor? The tumor is in the belief that such a condition exists and if you know that only Spirit exists and rest in that spiritual knowledge, the Grace of Spirit removes the illusion of tumor.

The Grace of Spirit is present and the words, "My kingdom, although it is not of this world, is present here, now, not from hence." Right here and now. That word "now" and not from hence, meaning here. Now and here is Spirit and only Spirit. You are now in the Kingdom of God and instead of trying to make God change your human illusions, instead of trying to use spiritual power to get rid of the bad conditions and bring in good conditions, you overcome even that. You don't say, "Get rid of this condition and bring me some of those nice conditions." Instead, you live in your spiritual awareness and let Spirit manifest in its own way. It may give you four other tires instead of the money to buy tires.

One of our students told us about a load of cement tossed right outside his house. He hadn't even asked for anything and it wasn't his cement. For some reason, they just tossed a load of cement out there. Well, he used it to build something he needed. Nobody wanted it and he needed it. He needed cement for six months before somebody just dumped a load of it there. He could have used the money to buy it but he got the cement. Nobody missed it or wanted it. They were getting rid of it.

You'd be surprised how many things are brought to your door that you've needed but if you thought about it, you would have needed the money to get them and they come there anyway without the money.

Always, the way of Spirit cannot be anticipated and if you outline to Spirit, you waste your time and you also break the continuity. And so, whatever the limitation may be, when you know that you must overcome that false sense of self which says "I need this." That was all right in the earlier stages of spiritual living or the attempts to live spiritually. But there is no "I need anything." You don't even need a pair of shoes. You don't need good health. You don't need anything. You see, when you talk from a need, you're denying "My kingdom is not of this world." You're saying there is a "me" here who needs and you're denying your spiritual Self which is your only Self.

So, this is the class in which we establish for ourselves that Spirit is all there is. Beside Spirit there is nothing. The moment you need something, you think there's something beside Spirit. Now, when you get that new pair of shoes, it's going to be an illusion just as much as a lack of the shoes was an illusion before that.

"My kingdom is Spirit and henceforth, know ye nothing in this world after matter, after flesh."

If you want to live in the Christ truth, you have to live in the knowledge that only Spirit is present and it isn't something you mentalize. You must face the world with that knowledge. Only Spirit is present. I'm not trying to change the bad illusions of matter into good illusions. I'm not trying to make the spiritual universe make my world a happier place. We are walking in the Spirit itself as the Spirit, living in and by and through the Spirit. And whatever manifests in the outer world as a material this or that is but the evidence of the spiritual consciousness you are living in. The evidence of things unseen. We're not trying to make our lives better. We are spiritual beings who are now perfect.

And so, when the Christ says, *"My kingdom is not of this world but now my kingdom is not from hence"* we are being told that we are spiritual Being; that the Kingdom of Spirit is here; that we are living in it and that the law of Grace is functioning and because of it, the Christ needs no protection against the powers of man because the powers of man do not exist. They are part of the world illusion. You and I as Spirit can walk through the powers of this world knowing they have no existence. Only the Kingdom of Spirit is here. Matter is the mental imitation entertained about and all the suffering that we can ever undergo is only in the imitation. Reality never suffers. You only suffer in the imitation. Every sickness is in the imitation form, never in your reality. Don't treat the imitation.

And so, back to healing, when you see that Spirit is all, Spirit then is the only truth and therefore, when there is something that is ailing or imperfect, it is an untruth because Spirit is perfect and Spirit is all. Now why would you want to treat an untruth? The way to overcome an untruth is not to treat it but to know the truth. When you know the truth that Spirit is all, all that is not Spirit whether it's ailing or not, loses its power over you.

Now if this stays in the mental state or the memory state, it will be meaningless and powerless and it takes time and initiative and a willingness to stand before this crystallizes into living consciousness that Spirit is all there is. What is not Spirit does not exist.

And this world is not Spirit and all this world contains is not Spirit. Spirit is invisible and Spirit is all there is. If you're wondering then, "How do I know what is good or what is bad or what is real or unreal?" The answer is Spirit is all and Spirit is invisible. Nothing visible is real. Nothing visible. There is nothing excluded. Anything you can see with human eyes is not real. If you see the Christ, you have to see the Christ within your Soul. If you see the spiritual universe, you'll have to see it within your Soul. You cannot see it with your eyes. You cannot see reality with your eyes or touch reality with your eyes and you are reality. You are invisible Spirit.

And as you notice, you will see why Christ walks through the evils of the world, untouched. That which we see and call the Christ is not what is there. Christ is invisible. Even though we see a form called Jesus, we are not seeing Christ. Even though the world sees a form called you, they are not seeing the Christ that you are and you must know that is who you are. Your Kingdom is here. It is your invisible Self, your invisible universe and that is the consciousness, the Christ consciousness which realizes what the human mind only mentalizes.

Now this is another dimension to live in, not to pay lip service to as Peter did. You have to practice this very carefully and I can assure you it's a very frustrating experience for a while. But you find the more frustrated you get, the closer you're becoming to the place where suddenly, it's so easy you can't believe it. I mean, it's just as if, why there's no effort involved. All of a sudden it just, there it is. Why of course, there's only Spirit. How could God turn us loose in the corruption that we see? The forms, shapes, figures, the objects, the things, all of nature, everything that can deteriorate or die or be diseased is a world illusion.

We have sown to this illusion, to this flesh, to this matter and we have reaped the death of the body, the diseases of the body, the malfunctions of the body, the difficult human conditions and they are all part of the illusion of the senses, of sowing to flesh when there isn't any. Sowing to the bark of a tree, to the blade of grass, to the weather. There isn't any. There's no weather in the Kingdom. There's no bark of a tree in the Kingdom. There's no liver and lungs in the Kingdom and all that is present now is the Spirit of God. That is your name, your identity. That is your habitation. It is right here but it is not this world. You learn to live in it. You learn that you are the Life which lives in the Kingdom of Spirit. You're not the form that lives in the world. The form that lives in the world is the degree of your limited consciousness made visible. Your consciousness translates into this form and its experience.

Now, while we're on this subject of healing spiritually, living in the Spirit, Spirit being all, it must be seen that no material condition changes anything in Spirit. There is only Spirit and so, a tumor isn't changing Spirit. Spirit or reality doesn't change because a tumor appears. Reality doesn't change because anything appears. Nothing in the visible changes the reality. The reality is always itself and therefore, you never have to improve the reality. You have to find the reality.

And so, the solution to living in the Spirit, to living independent of the conditions of form is not to try to bring Spirit into the world. That's part of the mental illusion. You cannot bring Spirit into an illusion. You must step out of the world and live in the Kingdom. When you step out of the world; that's where the condition is, in the world, the condition isn't in the Kingdom, so instead of trying to improve the condition in the world, improving the illusion, step out of the world where the condition is into the Spirit and you find it isn't there. Then, that which appeared in the world will disappear.

Now, then, stepping out of the world into My Kingdom is the healing consciousness. It isn't improving the condition of the world; it's stepping out of the world into your Kingdom. In other words, stepping out of the belief in matter, into the acceptance that only Spirit is here which then becomes your spiritual consciousness.

Is that clear? You step out of the belief in matter to get rid of it. A head cold or a sprained ankle. The belief that you have a head cold or a sprained ankle is a belief that matter is there. But Spirit is only the presence, only the reality. You come back to the acceptance that only Spirit is present. You seem to be walking away from the problem rather than meeting it and that's fine. You're coming to the reality. You don't have to meet that problem. You come to the reality only Spirit is here. I am Spirit. I am the life of Spirit and the power of Spirit; the power of God is functioning in the Spirit of my Being now.

You find the conditioning of the mind which had been, for a moment, drawn into the belief of the ankle or the cold or the tumor begins to be drawn into another area of consciousness. It is almost if you feel yourself walking over a line, something in you straightens up, something in you disappears. One belief goes and you find yourself strong in something saying to you within, "I am the Spirit. I am come. Where you are, I am now and I am the Spirit of your Being."

You begin to feel this. Now, you're away from problems. You're just aware of the presence of the Spirit. You see what you had tried to mentalize is now over you. You're past the mentalizing. This is the beginning of the realizing. The realizing is of the Spirit and as the Spirit begins to work with you, finally you're out of mind. You're just resting in pure consciousness and pure consciousness is that which said, "My kingdom is not of this world. I am ruling my Kingdom right here."

Everything then in the invisible becomes a living force in your Being and the visible world is no longer governing you. You're no longer under the law of matter. You're under the law of spiritual Grace, in the invisible Kingdom of your own Being. Your Kingdom is invisible Grace of Spirit, not this world and I don't care who you are or where you are, whenever you discover that you are Spirit and that Spirit is all there is and you are faithful to this and do not commit adultery by thinking there is Spirit and matter, do not step out of spiritual reality and adulterate truth with the belief that there is both Spirit and matter, then you won't be in spiritual adultery. You'll be in the single truth of being, the great truth announced by the Christ that My Kingdom is here now and it is pure Spirit and where it is, the world is not. Then you're a babe in the Kingdom and you can leave all the successful adults in this material world, pay their own miseries.

You really will find the great glorious power of living Spirit. You'll find that your rent is paid for your entire lifetime. You'll find that your health is assured for your entire lifetime. You'll find that you are truly an eternal Being. You'll find that every word spoken by the Christ about Spirit is the truth about you and about everyone you know.

You won't forget the two commandments that Peter forgot. You'll know that in accepting only Spirit is, you'll fulfilling the first two commandments and there's nothing more to fulfill. When you're loving Spirit supremely and accepting no other, that's *"Acknowledging Me in all thy ways."*

When you're knowing that Spirit is the identity of your neighbor, that's *"Loving your neighbor as yourself."* There's nothing more to do when you know that only Spirit is. You're fulfilling the Bible. And if every day, on this earth that you now spend is spent in living in the knowledge that only Spirit is, you'll discover the power of transition is forming in your consciousness.

"If you continue in my word," and my word is *"My Kingdom is not of this word but it is not from hence."* Now, it is here. *"Continue in my Word and you will know the truth and the truth will make you free"* and that freedom is freedom in eternity. Not just freedom from momentary discomforts. That is permanent freedom in eternity and that is the truth.

— End of Side One —

I think it's a good place to meditate now.

Where Spirit is, there is no opposite. Spirit is everywhere. Everywhere there is no opposite. Only Spirit is. That is the name and identity behind every visible person, creature, object, animal, flower, tree, river, mountain, star or sun. Behind every visible is the reality of it which is invisible Spirit and that invisible Spirit is all that is there.

As the world mind brings forth these surface impressions which we call matter, we have been lulled into accepting them as reality but they are but a shadow. The mental picture of the cosmic mind projected from its concept about the everywhere-ness of Spirit, which is all that is present. That shadow mind, that cosmic shadow mind puts forth a shadow called the world.

You are the Spirit and this is your Kingdom and you are the King in this Kingdom and you have dominion in this Kingdom if you will live in it and not let your mind be drawn into the world except for amusement, to watch the TV images, to know while you watch them, the spiritual nature of the universe without opposite.

You'll feel from this why Joel repeatedly brings us that great truth that you need no power. If you think you need power to overcome anything, you don't realize yet, that Spirit is all that is here and because Spirit is all, there's no power that we need except that knowledge. You actually rest in the knowledge that Spirit being all, I need no power to overcome the condition. The condition cannot be here. I need no power to overcome it, just the knowledge that only Spirit is here and then wait for the realization which takes you over what you thought you knew into a place where it knows through you. That great realization is the actual Spirit of your Being, Christ realized and you see how gently it shows you why you needed no power ever. All that's here is my Spirit.

There never was a material anything and in that knowledge, you know why there is no power needed. That is why Spirit is omnipotent. It needs no power. It is all there is. And when that comes into your realization, that's when you say, "I didn't know it was that easy, that simple and that beautiful."

You need no power, just be aware that you are spiritual Being in a spiritual universe in spite of every appearance that besets you and it won't be long before these appearances lose all their sense of power that they had entertained over you. There are no exceptions.

With death imminent, the Christ could stand there and say, "I don't take back any of my words, Pilate. I have nothing to defend against." He was calm. He was poised. He had nothing to apologize for. Simply to tell us the glorious truth that all that is present here is Spirit, My Kingdom. There's no Pilate. There's no soldier. There's no crucifixion coming up. Don't let them fool you. All that is here is my Spirit and I am the Spirit of each one who stands before me.

That is the truth of you then. Your Spirit is all that is on this earth and there is no earth. There is only your Spirit where man sees the earth. That is why the earth is the Lord's, because it is all invisible Spirit and the fulness is Spirit and there are no exceptions. It is all Spirit. Nothing can enter Spirit to defile it because there is nothing. We are babes in this Kingdom of Spirit and what the Father has prepared for us still remains to be seen. It remains first for us to be willing to be children in the Spirit. You'll find the power of the child is greater than any mature adult in the physical world.

To trust the non-power of Spirit to be all that is here will enable to you to react to nothing that challenges you as every challenge is a lie. It isn't there. No matter where it comes from, there's only one Source that you recognize as being present and that Source is the everywhere-ness of Spirit, which is here. And gently, we rest in that knowledge without defense. There is no power needed for only my Spirit is present. You'll feel the turning within yourself.

Let's have a brief recess.

When Pilate hears, "My kingdom is not of this world and so forth," he's quite bewildered by it. While he says, "Aren't thou a king then?" the reply of Jesus is *"Thou sayest that I am a king. To this end was I born. For this cause came I into the world"*

Now, this is Christ telling us the purpose of Christ. This is your own self telling your Soul your function, your Identity, your purpose, your way of life. This is the inner disclosure of the Christ to the Soul of all who listen, who they are, where they are and what they are doing.

"To this end, this cause came I into the world that I should bear witness unto to truth."

He has just stated the truth. *"My Kingdom is not of this world but it is not from hence."*

It is here now. My kingdom is Spirit. It is not matter and I have come to bear witness of the truth that my kingdom is Spirit and it is not matter and I, being yourself, have come to bear witness in you so that if you wish to live in the Kingdom of Spirit, you must surrender to yourself. You cannot do it with your human mind. You must accept the identity of Spirit before you can live in the Kingdom of Spirit and if you're not receiving the Grace of the Kingdom of Spirit, it is for that reason. There are no mortal beings in the Kingdom of Spirit. There are no human beings in the Kingdom of Spirit. Grace only functions in the spiritual Identity and therefore, when you accept yourself to be Spirit, you also accept yourself not to be its material opposite. Whoever seeks then, the fruits of the Spirit must be Spirit and not matter.

"I have come to bear witness of the truth."

The truth is that I am the Self of every individual on the earth. I am that Spirit which Rome cannot crucify and I have come to tell you that you are the Spirit that Rome cannot crucify. I have come to tell you that you are the Spirit that no germ can crucify, that no disease can crucify, that no material condition can crucify. That Spirit I have come to attest to as the presence of your own being.

This is the revelation of Identity and the omnipotence, the dominion of Identity, the Grace of Identity, the allness of Spirit and the nothingness of all that is not Spirit. You quickly identify anything in this world, is it Spirit? If it isn't, it isn't there.

Look again and you'll see something is there you hadn't noticed, the Spirit of being. You hadn't noticed it because you were looking through human eyes. In your spiritual awareness of Self, you'll begin to feel the presence of the spiritual nature of all that is around you. You will see why you've had an affinity to some and a lack of affinity to others. There were different levels of spiritual awareness there. You'll begin to feel that great invisible force which makes all unlike itself impossible.

"Everyone who is of the truth heareth my Voice."

Whoever is living in spiritual Identity, hears the Voice of the Christ, receives impartation, is directed by the Christ. Whoever is in spiritual Identity is under Grace. Hearing my Voice is being under Grace. That is why the complete demonstration had to first be made, of immunity to the laws of matter, to the world's powers and then the Christ could say, "You've seen my immunity. It is your immunity. I have come to attest to this truth that my immunity is because I am spiritual Being and I recognize no material world, no material power, no material person, no material condition and therefore I walk through the world and it cannot touch me. I walk through the world of lack and limitation, never concerned about tomorrow because I am always the living now of Spirit and that which I am doing as the living Spirit, I am prepared to do in you as you accept my Identity as yours."

"So, Pilate says, what is truth?"

He has told Pilate the truth and the ears which could not hear then say, "What is truth?" If he had stopped to answer the question, he could have said, "Pilate, I'll tell you the truth you won't believe. Six years from now, Pilate, you won't be walking this earth. You'll be what is called a corpse. You're one now but you don't know it. Six years from now, Pilate, they're going to call you back to Rome and you know how you're going to die? You're going to kill yourself. You're going to commit suicide. And here you are standing here, judging me today."

Pilate said what is truth of the flesh that he saw before him. It wasn't there. He couldn't care less about what that truth is because he then turns to the crowd and says, "I find no cause of evil in this man, no offense in this man." But you see the point the human mind admits it doesn't know truth which Pilate did when he said, "What is truth? I don't know what truth is the same thing as saying "What is truth?" Even though he doesn't know what truth is, he proceeds to act anyway. Now, he's not following truth if he doesn't know what it is and so what is he following? He's following untruth. His question is admission that he doesn't know truth and that's the admission that the human mind does not make but that is the truth about the human mind. It does not know truth and not knowing truth, it proceeds to act anyway.

And so, its action is not based upon truth, just as Pilate's. Truth would have been, "This man, if he's innocent which I believe he is," as Pilate said, "well then he should be dismissed and released." But the human mind says, "Well, he's not innocent but what of it? We have to do the wise thing here. We have to please the high priest. We can't get him against us."

In fact, all the while that Pilate is making his decision, he's got his eye I on his job. Rome had been very, very angry at Pilate. He's been sort of a boob on the job. He stumbles and bumbles and he's made mistakes. The way he finally commits suicide is, the word gets out that there's a prophet in Sumaria. This is six years after the crucifixion, and that this prophet says that on the top of the mountain in Sumaria, Mount Gerizim, buried at the top of the tablets of Moses, not only that, he's going to dig him up. They set a date and the crowds come, they're all chanting him, some songs.

What does Pilate do? He thinks this is terrible so, he had his soldiers planted around there and when they tell the people to disperse, there's a sort of a bloody massacre instead. Gets back to Rome, next thing you know, they call Pilate back. They tell him he's an irresponsible governor. He's got into so many different predicaments that could have been avoided if he had just used tact or some kind of common sense and he's deposed. He's just taken out of his job and in fact, he's banished by this Caligula and in that banishment, in_____, he commits suicide. Six years after the crucifixion.

When he said, "What is truth?" Christ Jesus could have told him all that. He could have told him many things but none of them would Pilate have heard because the human mind is closed. Jesus turns away. You cannot speak truth. There's no way. Spirit is truth and that's all there is.

The poet said, "Beauty is truth and truth, is beauty and that is all you need to know."

But that isn't true. Beauty isn't truth. Material beauty is not truth. Material beauty fades. Material beauty can be scarred. Spirit is truth, not beauty. Spiritual beauty is truth, yes. Spirit is truth and truth, is Spirit and Pilate and the hundred thousand Pilates around the world have no knowledge of that truth and so, the human mind continues to act without truth. We see it as war and hate and violence and lack and limitation functioning without truth. This is the condition of the world. It is not saying it but in itself, it is saying "What is truth?" It doesn't know what truth is and so, it functions without it. Spirit is truth and there's no other truth.

Pilate now turns to the mob. "*When he had said this, he wnt out again to the Jews and said unto them, I find in him no fault at all but you have a custom that I should release unto you one at the Pass-over. Would you therefore that I release unto you the king of the Jews?*"

The king of the Jews was the term he used because it had been placed in his mouth by the high priest, who wanted him to feel that Jesus was committing treason against the by calling himself a king. When Jesus was asked by Pilate, "*Are you the king of the Jews?*"

He says, "*Thou sayest it, not I.*" He had no earthly kingdom, no material kingdom.

"They cried out again saying, not this man but Barabbas. Now Barabbas was a robber."

Again, here, we have to fault the translators. The beautiful symbology here is lost in the English translations of the Bible. Way back, before there was an English translation, this will startle you, the name "Barabbas" was "Jesus" and Pilate said, "Which Jesus will you release? This one or that one?" They were both named Jesus. The church fathers got squeamish about it. They changed the name "Jesus" to "Barabbas" in one of them. You won't notice unless you can get hold of some early Greek editions of the Bible.

And so, when they named Barabbas, "Barabbas" they were true to the meaning of the word "Jesus". It means "son of the father." That's what "Barabbas" means and when you pursue that a little further, here's what comes out, it isn't one world like it's printed in the King James version and in many other versions. It's two, Bar-; bar means son and arabas means of the father. Son of the father. There are other, Bar-Jonah, son of Jonah, Bar-Joseph, son of Joseph and so forth.

And so, it was brought together or e-lighted and it became Barabbas. But it meant son of the father and the symbology is, "Which one shall I release? Which son of the father? This one or that one?"

And so, when the crowd made a choice, release Barabbas, they were saying, "The son of the father who was named Jesus, don't release him. The son of the father who is named Barabbas, release him."

You see there is only one father, the divine Father and that which is not the divine Father is the devil. In the releasing of Barabbas, they're releasing the son of the devil. When you will not release Christ in you, you automatically are releasing the son of the devil.

We are each given a choice of Heaven or hell. If you accept spiritual Identity, you are releasing Christ. If you do not, you are releasing Barabbas. Son of the devil is the human identity which is controlled totally by the world mind. That is Barabbas and its correct pronunciation is Bar-abbas, son of the devil father, not son of the Divine Father.

When we do not release Christ in ourselves, we are that Barabbas. That's why it said Barabbas was a robber. The false sense of identity robs us of our Divine heritage. Every quality of the Father then is present in you now, awaiting only your acceptance of Christ in you as the only Self you can be. You go over with that to your neighbor and Christ of you is the Christ of your neighbor.

One, you've got your spiritual universe and that's what you live in.

The denials of Peter were possible because he had not yet reached the will to live in the Spirit. Anas, Caiaphas and Pilate represent those actions in Peter which were the result of his will being still material, personal, living out of personal motives.

Now then, if your will then is to live as Spirit, you'll find everything will fall into place. Your Identity being established as the one anchor of your life, your understanding will flow from it. The pathway to Grace is the pathway to spiritual everywhere-ness accepted.

For some of you, it may be easy to know that you are not the form but you are the Life that is invisible. Always, Christ was the Life, not the form that men saw. The Life that is invisible is you and if you hold on to that, you find that you are living in your spiritual Identity. The form that appears is just the automobile used to get around in. the Life is never touched by the mob. The Life is never touched by world thought. The Life never has a tumor. The Life is never sick. All illness is in your mortal sense of self, never in your Life, only in your form. Just as you are Spirit and not matter, you are Life and not form and this form comes under the dominion of Life when you live as Life.

Now, if you've read Joel's chapter, I think I have the book here.

"The spiritual life is not the overcoming of evil but the recognition of the nature of evil. Evil is not ordained of God. Evil has no law of God to ordain it or sustain it. Evil has no God existence, no God purpose, no God life, no God substance or God law. It is the arm of flesh or nothingness. As long as we are praying for God power to overcome evil, we are resisting. We re not anchored in the truth."

And so, there is no evil. That's important to establish. There are other passages in there. We won't have time to discuss but I think next time, we should discuss the passages in here and so, I'm going to ask you to study this very closely in preparation for next time. Those of you who have studied it, look at it this next reading and realize that what you have heard today is the story behind what Joel was saying in the chapter, the story he couldn't put into print. I assure you, that that which you heard today were in this book, not in a parable form, but directly stated, the message of the Infinite Way would be dead. The world wasn't able to accept that. But the message of the Infinite Way cannot be dead within those who know the Christ for they hear the Voice.

And when you read Joel's book, that chapter and if you're ambitious, go on to "By and through the Spirit" as well and when you read the Bible, remember, it is telling you that only Spirit is present and that if you limit yourself to the mind that does not understand this, you will always release Barabbas, Bar-abbas, instead of Christ.

I spoke to a woman this week and she asked a question and in response to the question, I told her the truth and her reaction was, "You're asking me to go too fast."

Now, I'm not asking anyone to go too fast. I'm finding out who's ready to go that fast. Whoever isn't ready to go that fast is not accepting the message at its present level. We must go fast and we cannot say, "My mind has to sit here and linger on these things and decide what I want to accept and not accept." That's putting the mind there as a block. The mind has no rights. Only the Spirit is present and that's very fast.

Now this week, when you read "Living in, through and by the Spirit" and review the "Kingdom of God, My Kingdom is not of this World," remember, the Kingdom which is not of this world is within you and the Kingdom within you is your spiritual Self and your spiritual Self is here, is not tomorrow.

Now then, if you're living in your spiritual Self, isn't it like planting a seed today? If you plant a seed today, what comes tomorrow? You get the flower or the tree begins, something takes root. How are you going to get the tree tomorrow if you don't plant the seed today? When you're living in your spiritual Self today, isn't that going to take care of tomorrow? Isn't that the meaning of sowing to Spirit, living in your spiritual Self today? And then the fruit from the tree becomes what happens in the material world tomorrow. It's the evidence that today you lived in the Spirit.

Now, two hours after you have found some kind of spiritual release, you'll find you're back in the Peter consciousness. You're not even aware of yourself as Spirit. You've fallen into another trap and there's some feeling within you that, there's something you need or desire or want.

Now every desire is another division. Every desire is another sign of duality; every want, every wish, every hope. Every time you seek something materially, you are stepping out of your spiritual Identity. Every time you accept a material appearance, you are stepping out of your spiritual Identity.

There's a place in spiritual Identity where the humanness of you all disappears. Even the mind of you disappears. You actually cease to be and when you reach that point, you'll know you have found yourself, where you totally cease to be and yet, there's a consciousness.

It's not conscious of form. It's not conscious of condition. It's not conscious of the day or the time. It's not conscious of the place. You cease to be as a person. It may be an instant or ten seconds but you cease to be and you know you cease to be. There's no person there anymore and the Infinite flows and it is you. You are that Infinite Spirit flowing.

Now that is the state of consciousness in which the entire universe and your Kingdom are one and the same. That is your Kingdom. When the only barrier that is here, which is you, is lost and the infinite nature of being is found. You don't conquer the world like we've been trying to do humanly. Instead of conquering the world, you conquer yourself. When you conquer your human self, you find you have conquered the world. You don't conquer a disease. You conquer your belief in it. You don't conquer a bad business. You conquer your belief that there is such a thing. Always, the perfection of Spirit without an opposite present is your living consciousness and this is conquering the human self.

What is truth? The truth is that you are truth. Your spiritual Self is the only truth.

In our final meditation, for those of you who won't be able to get up at 6 a.m., let's just dwell in the nowness of our spiritual Selfhood everywhere, knowing that our spiritual Selfhood is in Holland at this moment. Holland is in us at this moment. We won't have to wait till next Sunday to be spiritually alive where the world calls Holland. Right now, Spirit of our Being is the only Spirit in the universe.

We are the living Spirit of all those who will appear in Holland at a meeting. There's nothing there but our Spirit now. It is the one infinite, invisible Spirit that is my Kingdom, my Being. It is not of this world. It is all that is present.

And when there ceases to be an ocean between us or forms between us and you feel the nowness of your Being, to you Holland is here. One, invisible Spirit, present everywhere and the law of that Spirit is the harmony of Being.

Without the actual experience of it within you though, you don't have the realization and there's no power so you must wait until there is a realization within you. When you have it, you will know that you have attained the contact, the dropping out of humanhood into the spiritual Self and then the power of Self must manifest.

I am the only Life in the universe. Beside my Life there is no other and my Life is the Life of God. You're one with the entire spiritual universe as the Spirit descends upon you.

It is done.

Thank you so much.

CLASS 38

52 SECONDS OFF THE GROUND

Herb: As you are no doubt aware, the world has felt that there was a great suffering inflicted upon Jesus Christ and because of this, the teaching has been lost in that area.

Every time Jesus Christ was slapped or tortured or pierced with a sword, the world says, "Look what he's doing for us."

I hope we can now come past the point where we feel that the Christ is a physical being so that we can clear that away sufficiently to see what is being taught to us by the sufferings of Jesus Christ.

The message here, at this point, enables us to remove those levels of karma of which we are unconscious. You will see that every slap, every lashing, every humiliation is intended to show you that in the unconscious mind of you, in the world mind that functions through you, this is what is being done to the Christ. This is the universal lashing of the Christ and even though we are not conscious of it, we are all permitting this violation of Divine law within ourselves until and unless we consciously do something about it.

And so, the great method of bringing this to our attention is first: you remember, there's John the Baptist and he says, "*The one who follows me is preferred before me. His shoe latchet, I am not worthy to unloose.*"

And we all thought he meant Jesus Christ and he does at one level of the teaching but what he actually means is that the one who follows him is his own Spiritual Self. First, his physical self and then the one who follows him is his Spiritual Self. He's talking about the second Self of John the Baptist. We have all thought he meant Jesus

434

Christ but he's saying, "No, first comes physical man and then comes Spiritual man." The first self and the second Self.

Now, I want you to look at this. This is a magnifying glass and I want you to see that all the light comes down through the top and this would be the Light of the world; the Light of the world streaming through the top, rays of Light and because this is a certain kind of a glass, turning a certain way, all of these rays of light then are pointed to each other when they come out of the other side of the glass. And so that above, they're individual rays of light and down below, they're all combined and all of the light coming through is pointed to one specific point.

And now, if you change that, you see that all the light comes down through the top and then the concavity of the glass points all the light in one direction and conceivably, if the light were in patterns, the magnifying glass would point all the light and form a figure.

And I want you to see then, that above the glass is the unformed light and below the glass is the formed light. Above the glass is the light which is invisible and below the glass is the visible light.

Spirit, coming through mind, is formed into the appearance called matter. Above is the pure Light. Below is the formed Light but the pure Light never ceases to be pure so that all the Light above the glass is always pure Light and the figures, the forms, the objects made by that Light as it passes through the mind, which here is the glass, becomes forms. But the forms are only in the mind as the Light comes through them.

So, these would be the two firmaments, the above and below. Now, bear that in mind. We have the glass, the magnifying glass or we have the world mind which is the magnifying glass and above it, is the Reality of Spirit. Below it, is the concepts of the world mind. The above firmament could be called the Christ Consciousness or the fourth dimension of consciousness and the below could be called this world consciousness or material consciousness.

Always, the pure Light is pure. What the mind does in its concepts about it does not change the Light and so, the mind receiving the Light throws forth projected images. Above is My Kingdom. Below is this world.

John the Baptist, appearing in this world, says *"The one who follows me is preferred before me"* meaning, "I appearing to you now in physical form in this world am not that Self which is complete. There is a real Self here which is an invisible Self which is in my Kingdom, of pure Light and I, John the Baptist, am going to make way for a second Self." And that Second self will be John the Baptist reborn to his original Self of pure Light. The first self, below must make way for what appears to be the second Self but is really the Self that is above. The Self of you above is buried in this mortal consciousness as you come into form and now the form must make way for the Self of you above and so, you must return to your original Self. The returning to your original Self appears to be a rebirth to a second Self. It is a return to your original.

John the Baptist is making way for his second Self but this is a message for everyone that the first self in form must make way for the second Self in form and the second Self will be the Divine image made visible.

Now, along comes Jesus Christ and his birth is totally different than your birth and my birth. It's different in the sense that he is born not to the first self. He's already past that stage in previous reincarnations. In this one, he is born through the pure Consciousness so that he is not only a form but he is actually Life itself. Life comes into appearance and this Life is the second Self and it is also the first self at the same time because it is born of a pure Consciousness which is not a consciousness of form but a Consciousness of Life. It is born of a consciousness of Mary, which is pure at heart or virginal, knowing the Father aright.

And so, in this appearance comes a second Self which is also the first Self which is also the original Self and it is able to show the power of that original Self. It has complete mastery over all flesh, over all nature, over all matter. It has mastery over human life. It has mastery over all world powers and it demonstrates that it has this mastery and we watch it and we see the Christ within a cripple, relieving that cripple of a concept of being crippled. We see the Christ within a blind man, removing the concept of blindness. We see that the Christ within, represented by the outer Christ of Jesus, is always able to dominate matter - completely.

And now, after establishing this mastery over matter, we come to a phase of the Christ demonstration which is totally different. Now the Christ, having established that I have total dominion over matter will now show you about the reason for your suffering in the world. I will make visible to you the causes of your own suffering. I, who have mastery over matter, can submit to matter, letting it appear to master me knowing that it cannot and therefore, I will draw out of matter that which is hidden to human sense.

And so, Christ walks the earth drawing out of matter what we call lashings and beatings and torture and crucifixion only to reveal the invisible nature of our adversary. There is no physical Christ to undergo this torture.

And so, let's not be squeamish about it now as we come into scourgings. Let us see that the human below is unaware of the nature of his problem and the Christ which has shown mastery over the world now wishes to reveal the nature of the human problem in another way. He's going to reveal the activity of world mind in man of which man is unaware.

You are not aware, for example, that you are lashing the Christ. You are not aware that you are smiting the Christ. You are not aware that you are crucifying the Christ. You are not aware that you are committing suicide and the Christ is going to show us that we are all, as mortal beings, daily committing suicide and the ingenious method is almost incredible.

A form is placed in the world and there's no person in that form. There's no person there to suffer. There's no person there in any way to shed one drop of blood and that non- person which appears as form, draws out of the world all of its hate, all of its animosity, all of its hypocrisy to show the world just what is happening inside every individual on the earth even though the individuals on the earth have no knowledge of this unconscious, involuntary, inner activity of the world mind which makes them individually do within themselves to the Christ of their own Being precisely what the Christ is making us do outside in the visible lashing and crucifixion of Jesus Christ. The outer is being a mirror to the inner so that you will know how the inner workings of the mortal mind are.

And every time a hand reaches out and slaps the Christ, you're being told that mortal mind in you is doing that now in ways you know not of. And every time you slap the Christ within you, even though you are unaware of it, you're committing suicide. You're inflicting wounds upon yourself.

And so, let us remember the mirror is the outer Jesus Christ to reveal the invisible activity going on in the world mind which functions in each of us as a human mind to alert us that we must step out of that area below and be reborn of the area above; that unless we stop slapping the Christ, crucifying the Christ, piercing the Christ knowingly, consciously, specifically, we will continue to fall into the trap and we will not benefit by what he is revealing.

Now, Pilate, undecided, is trying to shift responsibility. The mind and the body each take turns denying the Christ. The intellect and its body, which it uses, each turn away from the Christ because they're both controlled by the world mind. The world mind in you controlling your mind unless you're Christ conscious, therefore controls your body. And so, Pilate, the material power, is torn between many forces.

"Pilate, therefore, took Jesus, and scourged him."

That's a lashing. But there is no physical Christ. Now, who is scourged?

Christ is Spirit. The whole teaching is that I am the Light. How do you scourge the Light? The deception then is that mortal mind in us makes us by our unawareness of Christ within, scourge that Christ. When you are unaware of Christ within, you are lashing the Christ.

You see, you don't have to take a whip and strike somebody. It's the unawareness of Christ within you which is the lashing. Just when Christ said, *"Give me to drink,"* unless you are aware of the living waters of Christ, you're not giving Christ to drink. Unless you are aware of the Christ, you're lashing the Christ.

Pilate is unaware of the Christ of his own Being and because of it, that appears outwardly as him lashing the outer visible Jesus Christ. He thinks there's a Jesus Christ there and the world has thought so. And he lashes out. He has the Christ scourged. But that represents what he's doing to Christ within himself. Because he doesn't know he is doing it, he is doing it.

It represents what all physical might in the world is doing to Christ within. When we send a collective army somewhere, we are all lashing the Christ within ourselves and you must take yourself out of that because that is a collective karma and we suffer from it.

All of our sufferings have to deal with the denial of the Christ within every individual. For instance, if somebody hurts somebody else, you may think you're not suffering but you are because the hurt that they have perpetrated on another isn't from them to that person.

It's from the world mind in them and that same world mind that you do not see in them is also doing it in you to the Christ.

Every time another individual on earth denies the Christ, the world mind in you is doing the same and so, you must consciously be aware that Christ is your identity. That's the only way world karma does not hit the individual. Otherwise, the individual is part of world karma and all of the suffering we go through is largely the world karma which we suffer from plus that individual karma which we have earned by our own individual ignorance of Christ.

Everything is geared on: are you in the Christ or not? Are you in Spirit or not? And if you're not, even though you're good, you're sharing, you're humanly a fine person, the same world mind functions in you denying the Christ anyway and you're in violation of Divine law without even knowing about it.

Now, Jesus Christ, through being able to draw out upon this image called Christ, all of the hate and venom of the world, is revealing what is in the world mind and those who had no awareness of what he is doing think that he is suffering from the cruelty of mankind. He's not suffering from their cruelty and they're not being cruel. He is pointing out to you the real hidden adversary. It is not Pilate. It is not the Jews.

The Jews aren't cruel to Jesus Christ. Pilate isn't cruel to Jesus Christ. The world mind is the Jew and the world mind is Pilate. The Jew doesn't say, "Crucify him." Pilate doesn't say, "Crucify him." The rabble doesn't say, "Crucify him." World mind in Pilate says it. World mind in the Jew, world mind in the rabble says it. He's telling you who your adversary is and if it wasn't the Jew, it would be another. If it wasn't Pilate it would be another. If it wasn't the rabble it would be another. The world mind wears every face and every form.

To agree with your adversary, you must see that Christ is making your adversary commit visible acts so that you will understand that these people who allegedly are crucifying Christ, they're as much a victim as the one they consider their victim. They are victims of the world mind.

And now, watch. Every time someone attacks the Christ in some way, it's as if Christ were holding up a sign and saying, "Now, watch carefully. This is what's happening in you. See 'em hit me?" Now watch this sign. It says, "Just as he's hitting me now, in you, you by the ignorance of my Presence, you are hitting me." He's alerting us. "You put this crown of thorns on my head and this purple robe on my shoulders and you mock me? No, that isn't you mocking me. That's the world mind which mocks the Christ." How much longer will you let that world mind run your affairs? That's what he's saying.

And so now, this is the reverse. First, he showed his power over all mankind to raise people back to life, to tame storms, to remove diseases. Now he shows why we don't do it. We don't do it because we have not come to our Christhood. And when we're not in our Christhood it's because the world mind in us is separating us from our Christhood. And we can never come to our Christhood as long as we do not recognize the world mind in us. That's what's going on now in this chapter.

Universal world mind is where the problems of the world are. This magnifying glass with the light above it and then the forms beneath it formed out of the light, this magnifying glass is the world mind. It re-interprets the Light of God into the forms that we call matter so we see through that glass darkly. That which is below, that which is human, is not there. There is nothing below. There is nothing in the world mind that is. All that is, is the pure Light. There is no Pilate. There is no Jew. There is no Gentile. There is no material selfhood. There is only the pure Light of God.

And so, he wants us not to fight the wrong enemies. And so, you find Jesus Christ completely unmoved by all these forms. Pilate can't understand why a man can be so calm in the face of a vicious attack. So strong, so unafraid and it's because the Christ, is actually God. What else is Christ but God individualized? You think that God was being beaten up? It's a teaching on the vast screen of time and space for you and I to understand what is happening within our consciousness. The only way you can purify your consciousness is to understand what is happening in the invisible nature of the world mind, to understand its methods of deception, to see that the world mind makes all that appears to you as form.

Above the glass is the pure Light but below the glass comes the experience we call birth. The Light is never born. Is God ever born? Can the Spirit of God be born if it already is? Are you the Spirit? The birth that takes place below never happens. It seems to happen. The pure Light is always there and that is why after the birth of the form, a John the Baptist must say, "He who follows me is greater that I, preferred above me. He who cometh after me is preferred before me."

You must learn to say that. The form that I came into, is not the Light of my Being but the Light of my Being which was first is preferred. I am not the form. I am that Light, that Life and so, I must rise out of the belief in birth and form and I cannot do that while this world mind in me makes me continue to believe that I am form, that I was born into form, that I will die in form.

And the Christ is saying, "Now, watch carefully how world mind is going to act. It's even going to crucify me who loves God supremely and it's going to say to you, it's going to do the same to you that it did to me. If it's going to crucify the One who is the great teacher of the world, what do you think it's going to do to you?"

World mind in you is going to bury you. That's what it's going to do unless you are aware of how it works. He's teaching you that world mind in everyone births us and then commits suicide, killing us and we let it happen because we're not aware that that is what is happening. We call it death. It isn't. It's world mind dropping its concept which it conceived as birth. World mind exerting powers that do not exist and the answer is always to find that capacity in you which is the Light of the world which is the second Self and that salvation is not by faith in God but by faith in Spiritual identity. Your Spiritual identity. Once you have faith in your Spiritual identity, then you have the secret of salvation which is to be reborn from the lower to the upper, to be born from above.

"I," says the Christ "am from above. You are from below. You are the formed light. I am the unformed Light, the undifferentiated Light. I am the infinite Light and to be born from above, you must accept your Infinite identity. You must overcome the falsifications of the invisible world mind in you."

Now, everything the world mind here is going to do to Jesus Christ in the visible, the world mind is now doing to everyone in the invisible mind of their own Being. Daily, the Christ is being crucified by our actions and unless we stop it, the world mind will bury us. It buried our parents. It buried everybody who has ever walked this earth. Whoever has been born into this world has been buried by the world mind and whoever wants to step out like Enoch or John or Moses or Jesus Christ has to step out of the world mind which is that functioning body of thought in them and they step out of it, the lashings stop, the tortures stop, the suffering stops. They were all unnecessary. They existed only in the world below. Never in My Kingdom. Never in Christ.

All suffering on earth, he is pointing out, is illusory and unnecessary. Every minute of suffering you have ever undergone has been unnecessary. It has happened only because of the unawareness of the nature of error which is universal world mind and the nature of God which is Christ, the substance of your true Being.

Now, you don't come from below and go up. You rise in Christ Consciousness and as your Christ Consciousness rises, you find the magnifying glass disappears. The world mind is obliterated. It has no power in you and you break all the seven veils.

Christ in you breaks the veil of time, the veil of space, the veil of form, the veil of matter, the veil of motion, the veil of human will and the veil of human ego. The complete human personality which is only world mind in the disguise is broken and death becomes an impossibility.

Now, we're going to deepen with this understanding of Christ here once we have eliminated the personalized human belief that Jesus Christ is going through a great torture chamber. This is the inner activity of your consciousness that is being described.

"The soldiers platted a crown of thorns, and put it on his head, and they put on him a purple robe."

So, we have the thorns on his head and a purple robe. We know they're mocking, of course, but world mind is always mocking the Christ. The crown of thorns; we know that in order to come to the crown, you must first come to the cross. We know the thorns are necessary. We know we must go through the thorns in order to receive the crown.

You see, here, these people are the actors even though they themselves are unaware of it. Many people come into your life and have very little apparent function Spiritually and yet they are used in some way by Spirit. Someone who dropped a book you need. Someone who'll do something else. They have no intention of doing these things other than that Spirit has brought them to your doorstep in one way or another. And here, the rabble, the soldiers, Pilate and the Jews are the actors. What they do, they cannot help.

I have here a little passage. This is from the Gospel of Nicodemus. It's the apocryphal Gospel. It's also called, "The Acts of Pilate." Pilate is speaking privately in this Gospel to Jesus and he says, "What shall I do with thee?" And Jesus says, "Do as it hath been given thee." And Pilate says, "How hath it been given?" And Jesus says, "Well, the prophets foretold concerning my death and resurrection."

The point is, the Jews had to crucify Jesus. Pilate had to crucify Jesus. Jesus had to be crucified to reveal the non-power of the world, the non-reality of the world, the illusory nature of the human form and of the material objects of the world. It was a teaching and the beautiful and magnificent part of the teaching is that we do not understand that for that teaching to come into our experience visibly, there had to be an intelligence bringing it to us, a great Infinite force, putting on the screen of time and space a teaching to tell us not to stop at the level of form. Man wants to stay at that level. Man loves that level. He wants to be successful. He wants to survive as fleshly creature. He wants to perpetuate his own incompleteness even though he doesn't realize that's what he's trying to do.

And the Infinite Spirit is saying to us, "Don't stop at that level. You must go beyond form. You must be born from above, from the Light. The second Self must replace the first self. That which came before you must now come after the form. You must return to the original Self."

And the mind of man struggles against this and so it scourges the Christ. It says, "I want to remain a physical creature." And the soldiers, the servants of material power, they mock the Christ. The soldiers within us mock the Christ, put a crown on its head, raising human intelligence above God. Human wisdom is rated higher than Divine wisdom and the purple robe, another sign of mockery, human wisdom is rated above Divine. Human righteousness is rated above Divine righteousness.

You see how Pilate represents all the physical force of the world and the Jews represent all of the pseudo-spiritual force of the world. Who is higher in Spiritual awareness than the Jews? Nobody. Who is higher in physical might than Rome? Nobody. You take the two great forces of the world, the so-called religious power, the so-called physical power and Christ is showing that neither of them know God. Neither of them know identity. Something greater has to come and only John the Baptist gives us the clue at the beginning, "[*He who follows me is greater than I.*] *His shoe latchet I am not worthy to unloose.*"

Only Christ can reconcile the conflicts of the world and then, the great physical power of Pilate, Rome, the great religious power of Judaism - both are totally rejected by Jesus Christ. Jesus Christ rejects Judaism. Jesus Christ rejects Rome. As great as both are supposed to be, only the invisible child of God is present. The visible power of Rome and the religious power of Judaism are both non-existent. They are world mind disguised. They are both anti-Christ.

All of the powers in the world that ever will be in the human world, on a physical level are represented by Pilate and all of the religions in the world that ever will be are represented by Judaism. The highest represents them all and the highest represents them all. Both cases represent the allness of all the religions, of all of the physical might.

Now we're being told that we are independent of these forces. They will always lash out at the Christ. They will think their righteousness is correct, their power is insurmountable and they are not what they appear to be. They are the world mind which in us is doing that very same thing.

The adversary has beautifully disguised himself as Judaism and as religion, as armies, as nations going off to war, defending democracy. That's still world mind. You can't go off to defend democracy. You can't go off to kill anything. Only world mind does that.

Now then, we have our adversaries identified, whether it's Jew or non-Jew, whether it's religion or whether it's science or whether it's any form of government. Anything that believes in matter is world mind posing as that which believes in matter. We cannot have a material world formed of good anything or bad anything. There are no good religions. There are no bad religions. There is no material world. There's no good power and there's no bad power. There is no power. There is only the pure Spirit, the pure Light of God, present and that's all that is in this world. The invisible Light of God is all that is present. All the rest is the screen on which the concepts of world mind appear and only a Jesus Christ who is actually God itself and who is God itself in you, shows you how to walk through these screen- of-concepts knowing that there's no substance or power there, not being fooled by the material concepts that appear as form, not reaching out to get that which perishes. Showing here the non-power of Judaism over the Christ, the non-power of Rome over the Christ and therefore, the non-power of the world over the Christ in you. Christ in you becomes salvation.

"Hail, King of the Jews!" say the rabble. *"And they smote him with their hands."*

All human thoughts, whether they're good thoughts or bad thoughts are turning away from the Christ. They are not the thoughts of God, are they? And so, all human thoughts are smiting the Christ. When they smite him with their hands, this is not them smiting the Christ; this is human thought automatically mocking the Christ. All human thought which is an automatic turning away from Divine thought is mocking the Christ.

"Take no thought" because when you take thought you are mocking the Christ and when you take thought, when you do not do something consciously, to step out of human thought, you are building your karma.

And so, while we continue blissfully to ignore Christ Consciousness, thinking, "Well we can put it off for another hour or day or month or that life will go on, things will happen well anyway whether I do something or not." While we're doing that, the karma within is building. You see how our inertia permits karma to build up even while we think we're worshipping God? That's how important these few phrases here are.

"They smite the Christ with their hands."

When you do nothing about knowing God, you are harming yourself even though you're not aware of it.

"Pilate therefore went forth again, and saith unto them, Behold, I bring him forth to you, that ye may know that I find no fault in him."

You can even say, "What am I doing that's wrong? I've not done anything that is faulty. I haven't stolen. I haven't lied. I haven't cheated. I've been friendly to people. What have I done that's wrong?" And even while you're doing these nice things, you're building negative karma and don't know it.

When you're not one with Christ, you're building negative karma. And so, you may have led a beautiful life for sixty years in which you did all the right things that people think are right and built negative karma while you were doing it and can't figure out why at a certain time you go through certain sufferings. And so, we're jolted again and again and again out of our complacency that just being good isn't enough and that religion cannot just satisfy the Spirit of God by teaching people how to be good human beings. It isn't enough.

They must be the Christ and when we're not being the Christ, we're crucifying the Christ by not being the Christ. These are the self-inflicted wounds that you have permitted yourself to undergo even though you were unaware, even though you thought you were such a good person. And this would go on again and again through more reincarnations unless the meaning of the Christ message is clearly pointed out that this is what the Christ is doing at this juncture, not suffering, not being self-tortured but bringing to Light that which is happening in the invisible world mind.

Now you take a psychologist who probes the mind. He's not aware that Christ is the greatest psychologist of all time for Christ shows you that the mind which you're probing is the cause of everything that is of a material nature. The cause of both birth and death and the false lifespan in between. Christ just takes that line and turns it upside down. He says, "Look at it. Don't probe this corner or that corner. Look at it. This is the murderer in our midst smiling at you in one way while killing you in another."

And so, this teaching has been lost to the masses. It's too difficult a teaching. You can't tell it to normal people. They won't understand. They won't know what to do when they do find out about it. It'll only perplex them and frustrate them.

But mortal mind is the person you're looking at. There's not a person you see who isn't mortal mind made visible. That's what persons are and where person appears and mortal mind is making that person appear, when you step out of mortal mind in you, you become conscious of the Invisible Christ where the person had seemed to be. And you still see that person but you _feel_ with the inner soul sense the Presence of something besides a person. You no longer hold them in the tomb of a body and while the rabble, the Jews, Pilate and the soldiers are hating this which they call Jesus Christ, Christ is loving them. Christ is not holding them in bondage to physical form. Christ is not seeing them as an enemy. Christ has no human enemies. Christ knows only the one adversary, the world mind and isn't fooled by the physical disguises.

Similarly, if there were lack or limitation, Christ wouldn't be fooled by those disguises. They, too are the world mind. Every evil on this earth, whatever its name or nature, is the same one world mind. And when you lick it, you've licked all the evil there is and you only lick it by accepting Spiritual identity. And until you do, world mind will completely devastate your life in one way or another because it is the nature of world mind to continue to lead us into committing all forms of violation of Divine law until we accept the Spirit of God as our own Being. It's only when we do, that the world mind loses its power to manipulate us, to torment us, to deceive us and to present things to us that are not true and have us accept them as if they were true.

And so, the plan that Jesus Christ is revealing world mind as the only oppressor, the only place where problems exist and that world karma continues and that this karma continues whether you're aware of it or not, whether you voluntarily contribute to it or not and it only stops when you consciously seek, ask, knock at the door of your own Christ within yourself. When you accept that here stands no mortal being - that is how you defeat the world mind.

Here stands what you have called a mortal being only because you've been looking out from the eyes of mortality but invisibly, the child of God stands where you are and that child of God is the Light which you know when you're in the upper firmament of Consciousness. Then there are no lashings. There are no beatings. There are no tortures. There are no diseases. There are no misgivings. There are no oppressions, there are no lacks, no limitations. Once you have accepted the Light as your name, you may go through the period of thorns and thistles but the Light will take you through them safely, effortlessly.

Now, then, as he was able to look at the Jews and Pilate and soldiers without hate, later saying *"Forgive them; they know not what they do,"* he was acknowledging only the Presence of God. He was demonstrating that this that you see is not the true picture. He was demonstrating that only God is present. The Allness of God. He was demonstrating that one who knows that only God is present is the majority. One with God is a majority. He was demonstrating that I, the living Spirit of God, am the only Self that is present. There are no Jews, no Pilate, no Roman Empire. There's no pain. There's no suffering. This is the illusion of the world mind, the knowledge of good and of evil. It isn't present.

And just as it wasn't present at that moment, in that day, it isn't present in this moment, in this day. There is no lack. There is no limitation. There is no famine. There is no overpopulation or underpopulation. There's no war. There's no Pilate today. There's no dictator today. There's no Jew today. There's no non-Jew today.

There are not twenty-five or eighty-five religions on the earth today. They're all mortal mind wearing its many disguises.

All that is here today is what was demonstrated there in that day and that is the invisible God. That's all that is present in this room and on this earth. Only God is present and all of this that happens therefore is finally shown to have had no effect whatsoever. It only seems to happen and the corpse is not a corpse. It never happened. That's why.

The illusory nature of the mortal world, the illusory nature of the mortal body, the illusory nature of mortal conditions is the revelation that only God is present and where God is, is Holy Ground and the place whereon thou standest is therefore Holy Ground because God is present there and the invisible name of God, is Christ in you. Until this is accepted, invisible world mind continues, birthing us and then killing us.

"*Christ in you,*" is the very same Christ that is making this demonstration of Christ on the cross.

Jesus Christ is healed of mortality. Jesus Christ is healed of the belief in the power of the world, healed of the belief in the existence of anything unlike the Spirit of God. But the world mind, acting as the various forms, that continue to beleaguer him show forth that which is in the world mind - the hate, the distortion and this continues in each of us even though we don't share in the outward physical being of the Christ. To be forewarned enables you to do something about it.

"*Then came Jesus forth, wearing the crown of thorns, and the purple robe. And Pilate saith unto them, Behold the man!*"

He was really playing to their sense of pity. He didn't want to crucify Christ and yet he did. He didn't know what to do. This was a hot potato. We learn in Matthew that the wife of Pilate was a sort of student of Jesus Christ - Claudia. We learned in Matthew that she said to Pilate, "Don't have anything to do with this man's death. I had a terrible dream and I suffered a great deal in my dream because of him." In some way or another, she had become aware of him as a force and Pilate didn't really know what to believe anymore. Maybe this man was a very special, privileged man. He didn't know. He just wanted to get rid of the whole thing and now, he's hoping that when they look at this sorry figure, they will have some compassion and say, "Well, let him go. He's had enough punishment."

But mortal mind, you must remember is writing the whole script here. It's being forced to show forth its contents. They won't have any of that.

"When the chief priests therefore and officers saw him, they cried out, saying, Crucify him, crucify him."

The chief priests were saying, *"Crucify him."* This was then the greatest religion on the earth saying, *"Crucify him."* This was the religion that had in the Ten Commandments, *"Thou shall not kill,"* saying, *"Crucify him."*

You see how mortal mind poses as religion, makes its own laws, turns upon itself? And this is the ugly nature of mortal mind in us.

"Pilate [says], Take [ye] him, and crucify him: I find no fault in him. The Jews answered [him], We have a law, by our law he ought to die, because he made himself the Son of God."

Well, let's look at their law. You'll find in the Leviticus. You'll find it in Deuteronomy.

In Leviticus 24:16, here is the Judaic law about attitudes toward God. *"He that blasphemeth the name of the Lord, he shall surely be put to death, and all the congregation shall certainly stone him: as well [as] the stranger, as he that is born in the land, when he blasphemeth the name of the Lord, shall be put to death."*

Put to death and yet it said stoning, not crucifixion.

452

Now, in Deuteronomy, we have a little further discussion on that. The thirteenth chapter of Deuteronomy, the first verse says, *"If there arise among you a prophet, or a dreamer of dreams, and giveth thee a sign or a wonder"* then we'll skip over to the fifth, *"And that prophet, or that dreamer of dreams, shall be put to death; because he hath spoken to turn you away from the Lord your God, which brought you out of the land of Egypt, and redeemed you out of the house of bondage, to thrust thee out of the way which the Lord thy God commanded thee to walk in. So shalt thou put the evil away from the midst of thee."*

If this prophet then has all these signs and wonders that have something to do with blaspheming God, he shall be put to death. And so, its in their law and according to their law, Jesus blasphemed.

Now, specifically, here were the blasphemies he made. In John 5, the 18th verse, we have one of the blasphemies, *"Jesus answered them, [and said] My Father worketh hitherto, and I work. Therefore the Jews sought the more to kill him, because he not only had broken the sabbath, but said also that God was his Father, [thus] making himself equal with God"*

Now, when he said that God was his Father, they interpreted that from their Leviticus and Deuteronomy laws as being a blasphemy against God.

— End of Side One —

That was the crime they called blasphemy. And later, in 10:33 of John, *"The Jews answered him, saying, For a good work we stone thee not; but for blasphemy; because thou, being a man, makest thyself God."*

And so, we can see why they would be feeling self-righteous about what they were doing. Their law said so, this man said he was a Son of God, God was his Father. And then suddenly it hits you, didn't they think God was their Father? And the answer is; they certainly did. That's the name of God, the Father of all mankind. They didn't really think he had blasphemed at all, did they? Because they too thought God was their Father. They were using blasphemy as a very convenient way of getting rid of he who had renounced Judaism. He who would not bring them a kingdom on earth. He who had said, *"My kingdom is not of this world."*

And so, we find that religion is being exposed here as having no interest in the Truth, no interest in God when it suits religion's purpose to have no interest in God.

But why? Because religion isn't religion. Religion is the same world mind that crucifies. Religion is the same world mind that sends boys out to be shot in war, the same world mind that says to this group of boys, "You need heroin today." You're either in it or not in it. You're either serving it consciously or not or serving the Christ mind. If you're not in the Christ mind, you're in the world mind and just by not being in the Christ mind, you commit every act of infamy that is in the Bible. It all goes on in your sub consciousness and eventually, it surfaces in one way or another, some greater and some lesser. We're all feeding out of the reservoir of the world mind unless we're in the Christ mind. That's why we have these funny tendencies that we can't understand.

Why does a man steal? Some people even steal when they don't have to. They just, it's a habit. It's a way of life or it's a weakness they can't control. And they don't want to but something puts the hand out there and takes what it shouldn't take. Why? The world mind. The person never does it. The world mind is the hand. The world mind is the body. The world mind is the flesh. The world mind is even the object that it steals. The world mind is the world and we who are not in the Christ mind are in that world mind of good and evil. We who are not in the Christ mind are in the world mind which kills the human race. Each successive generation is killed by the world mind because it is a murderer from the start. It is the false creator of a false world and there's no hope to make this a better world. The only hope is to come into the Christ mind and to walk in the Kingdom of God on earth. That is the meaning of salvation. Otherwise, it's an empty word. Just making good boy scouts out of us isn't salvation.

This was the nature then of the charge of the hypocrisy, to say that God had blasphemed against God. The religious mind does not know the nature of Christ. You find examples who do know and they are the rare exceptions. You find books for example, by a Catholic and you say, "Well this is the Truth." Yeah, the book is and then you find examples of the Truth by a Protestant and you say, "Well this is Truth." Yes, the book is. And you find some by a Muslim, by a Hindu, by a Jew. The book is but you're talking about millions of people who know nothing about what is being said in that book. There are over twenty billion Bibles that have been sold in the world and most people still think that Jesus did all this to in some way make it unnecessary for us to come through the Christ experience ourselves, that all we have to do now is be good and die and we'll go there and we'll find him.

This empty teaching has existed in spite of all the Bibles. You can find a great, big Bible in the middle somebody's living room. I have some friends who collect Bibles. They have Greek Bibles. They have early Bibles. They haven't read one of them. Haven't even read them, not even interested. It's just something to collect and there it is. People see it. And they're collectors of Bibles. They don't know what's inside the Bible, either good or bad.

And when the church reads the words of the Bible, everybody says, "Oh, that poor man. Look what he went through." We're going through it ourselves right now. Every day. This woman who had the brain tumor, she was a believer, a faithful believer. She couldn't understand why she had that brain tumor. How could you explain to her this was the collective karma of the world appearing in her through the world mind; that she had nothing to do with it? She was just the recipient of something that was caused by a world mind and then the psychologist might probe her mind to find out if she was mean to her mother and that caused it or something like that and that wouldn't help because the world mind is going to keep pushing itself through what she calls her mind anyway. She never can identify her adversary because religion doesn't teach her that. It doesn't teach her that there's a world mind. And it doesn't make any difference what religion you go to. The adversary is never identified. Some come very close to it and then for some reason or other, duality enters in and there is always God and me or there's a power of evil.

Did you read what the Pope said the other day? I couldn't believe it. In fact, I've written the Catholic monitor to give me the full statement. It was so incredible to see this statement in the papers. This isn't the full statement. That'll come later. The Pope said whole societies have fallen under the nomination of the devil. He said sex and narcotics provide openings for Satan's infiltration of mankind. He said the devil exists and people should be on their guard against him. He said the defense against the evil which we call the devil is necessary, that our greatest need is the defense against the devil. He said the devil does exist and is a dark enemy agent. Evil is not just a deficiency but an efficiency. It is alive, spiritual, perverted and perverted being. It is a terrible, really mysterious, fearsome thing and then he said Satan was responsible for man's falling from Grace. He is the enemy number one, the tempter par excellence, the hidden enemy who sows errors and misfortunes in human history. The headline is the Pope says the devil's role is spreading, that the devil really exists.

Now, people read that and have been brainwashed on that for so long that we can say safely that at least, fifty million people in that over-all congregation believe there is a living devil somewhere. And you try to take that devil away from them, they're going to get mad at you. They really do because this is what they fight. They fight the devil.

And you know something? I wouldn't want to ask all the religions of the world if they believe that because I'm sure they'll tell me they do. You'd find that that's not just part of any one religion. The world believes there's a living devil and that the devil causes these things and of course, that means that the devil must be operating under God's permission, under God's will because God is the power of the universe. It must be God's will that the devil do this then and if it's God will, then you can say that all of the evil on earth is God's will.

Now, how in the world can you pray to God then? If it's God's will that there be evil, what are you going to pray about? And if it's not God's will, how can it happen in the first place? How does the devil get away with it if it's not God's will? And these are the questions that are unanswered.

And so, we live in this kind of hazy, in-between unawareness and this becomes, this is what world mind is. I could tell you world mind speaks and makes these statements. This is a statement by the world mind. And whatever is not Truth, is a statement by the world mind and that is fed back into the collective consciousness of every individual. You may not even see it in the paper but one way or another, it comes into you and you begin to feel that there's some powerful sinister force working and you may not call it Satan or devil. You may have another name for it but you think it's there, it's existent and there is no such force. There is no such power. All that is present is the Spirit of God. There's no devil and there's no power of a devil. There is only that which is below and that which is above.

And these are the two levels of consciousness. One is pure Consciousness and the other is human consciousness and human consciousness itself does not exist and all that it knows is equally, non-existent. And when you step back out of it, you find you're in the pure Consciousness. There's no devil. There's no deviltry. There's no evil. You see through the illusion of the form, through the images. Time and space, is lifted out of your consciousness and you stand in the One, in the pure, in the real. And then you know, all that is here is the Light. It is all pure Light. The illusion only exists in the illusory mind, the mind that perceives the evils of the world itself is the illusion. That illusion mind perceives its own illusions and when it's the world mind which is the illusion, then all within the world mind perceive the same illusions.

Christ doesn't. Christ stands in the midst of the attackers, seeing no enemy. That's why Pilate's puzzled. "What kind of a man is this? Maybe my wife was right. She said I better watch out for him. I better not monkey with this man. He must be a very important man for all these Jews to want him killed."

He thinks Christ is a half-God of some kind and while he's thinking that, he's got another problem. They're going to threaten to send a report back to Rome if he lets this man go. He's torn between what his wife told him and his fear of Caesar and his fear of the fury of the mob and he's a very typical human being; torn between all of these different forces. Why? Because he has no anchor in Christ. He doesn't know the Truth. He even said so.

You see how necessary it is to come to grips with this world mind? That Christ in you, just as Christ in Jesus could walk through the world mind which was threatening to kill him, unafraid, knowing it doesn't exist, that Christ in you can do this with every problem you have? Do you see the great symbolism there? That just as Christ in him could walk though an intended crucifixion knowing its impossibility, knowing the non-existence of form and matter and material power, Christ in you this minute could walk through every lack and limitation you think you know as a fact in your life. It doesn't matter what it is. Christ in you sees it as a non-reality which it is.

And then finally, why this Christ in you? Is there a you that contains Christ or you this invisible Christ your Self? Doesn't Christ in you finally become Christ I am?

There's a very interesting consciousness that does something unusual to you. It actually takes you out of your human self. It's like that fifty-two seconds of the Wright Brothers off the ground. It gets you out of yourself and once you feel your Self out of yourself even for those fifty-two seconds, the great fiction of human selfhood is revealed to you: that there isn't any.

Once you become aware for those fifty-two seconds of your true identity, you feel your Self as something totally different than the one you had lived with all of your human lifespan. It's as if you really are a Spiritual form, a vast form; so vast that all of the physical events around you are walking through that form and not touching it. These little pygmies of human events seem to walk through the vast, physical Spiritual structure of you; you feel your everywhere Being, off the ground, out of matter.

In a flash, you might even know that everything that exists is right where you are. It doesn't matter where it was in time or in space, it is right where you are because where you are is the Infinity of God and everything that's happening in any part of the universe is just part of the mortal mind picture that isn't there. What is there is the Infinity of God. The Infinity of God is right where you are at all times and nothing else.

It doesn't matter where things seem to be happening. The Infinity of God there is the Infinity of God here. One, Infinite God. One, Infinite identity and when you feel it, you know that Christ is revealing the nothingness of the entire material world and the Allness of the Infinity of your own Spiritual Self.

There are times when this can be so strong in you that you don't want to do anything but revel in it. Just resting in the Word that the Infinity of God, I am, and it doesn't matter if something seems to have happened two thousand years ago. Whatever happened two thousand years ago could only be a Spiritual activity because there's nothing else there and that Spiritual activity is happening now. Whatever will happen two thousand years from now can only be a Spiritual activity and all Spirit is now therefore, two thousand years from now is happening now. That is the Infinity of your Being so that the world of time is in the now of your Infinite Self as an experience, as a living knowledge. And the world of time did not exist because the Infinity of Christ is all that can ever happen. Nothing else can happen. You rest in it. You feel that there's no space outside of you. There's no time outside of you. There's nothing outside of you.

Infinite Spirit is your name. Infinite Spiritual power must be functioning. Infinite, Spiritual action is all that can happen. Nothing can enter to defile or make a lie.

There can be no human punishments. There can be no human pain. There can be no human lack or limitation. You are Infinite Spirit and there's a moment in your fifty-two seconds off the ground when you don't have to be told that again. The experience replaces all the words you've heard. In fact, there are no words that can really awaken you to that experience, no words that you can truly believe in. You can only believe that experience and when you have it, then you know why the words were unnecessary. The only reason you hear the words is to enable you to know that the experience is waiting to be lived in and when the experience happens, you know that you truly are not this physical form.

Christ was not the physical form there. All of these events were happening in time, in visible form but they're all happening inside the world mind, not in the Christ identity. You walk free of this world mind. Those fifty-two seconds off the ground are going to be a very important experience.

Infinite Christ, not finite Christ, not Christ in this room or this body, not Christ in any century, not Christ in any place but Infinite in time and space and in fifty-two seconds off the ground, you don't get to feel that full Infinity but you get out of this limited self enough to know that that was a promise of things to come into your fullness of Consciousness.

We seem to have gone quite a bit over the half so I think we'll continue.

"The Jews answered him, We have a law...When Pilate therefore heard that saying, he was the more afraid; He went again into the judgment hall, and said unto Jesus, Whence art thou? But Jesus gave him no answer."

He wanted to know where Jesus came from. The human mind cannot understand Christ. Christ cannot speak to the human mind so he gave him no answer.

"Pilate [said], Speakest thou not unto me? knowest thou not that I have power to crucify thee, I have power to release thee?"

The human mind thinks it's a power. The world mind, expressing as the human mind is a power over all those who do not know their own Christ mind and the Christ says that very strange statement, *"Thou couldest have no power [over] me, except it were given thee from above."*

You see that above part? The Light and then the forms. Here's the forms. These forms don't exist. All that's here is the Light. These do not exist. Where you appear in form, it does not exist. All that's there is the above Light. As it comes through mind, it becomes form.

"Thou couldest have no power [over] me, except it were given thee from above" and then this great revelation, *"Therefore, he that delivered me unto thee hath the greater sin."*

Now, that line means, *"He that delivered me unto thee hath the greater sin."* Who delivered Jesus Christ to Pilate? The world thinks Judas did. World mind delivered Jesus Christ to Pilate. He's trying to show us again and again and again that world mind is the culprit. Who deprives you of the things you need? World mind. Who fools you into thinking that you suddenly got them? World mind. Who takes them away again? World mind. Who makes you sick tomorrow? World mind. And who makes you well? World mind. You go up and down like a yoyo in world mind, never knowing what's causing it and what's causing it is he who delivered thee unto the sickness, the sin, the lack, the limitation is the world mind. And then the world mind recovers you and you say, "Thank you."

And when the religions of the world go to pray, they are praying to this world mind. That's who you pray to. Dear world mind, which I am calling God by mistake, make me well and God never made you sick so how could God make you well? God is your name. Your invisible identity is Christ, Son of God. You don't have to pray to God to make you well. God is always well. You have to step out of the world mind and you're well. You don't have to pray to anyone. Your prayer is the acceptance that I am the living Spirit of God, the Life of God now, called Christ. That acceptance is your prayer. That's the Lord's prayer.

This then is revealing the universal nature of evil coming through the world mind. *"He that delivered me unto thee hath the greater sin."* Not Pilate, not Judas - the world mind. If your business is bad, it's the world mind. If your business is good, it's the world mind. But if you have Spiritual business, you'll find it doesn't waver and it will appear outwardly as a permanently good business, a permanently good health, a permanently good income, a permanently good relationship, a permanently good life.

When John the Baptist said, *"He that cometh after me is preferred before me,"* he was giving us the clue that we are to find not this temporary sense of life. We are to find our permanent Life. *"He that cometh after me.... preferred before me"* is our permanent Life, our permanent identity.

When you find your permanent identity, world mind collapses. It hasn't a leg to stand on after that. The illusion of the world mind is gone. It'll catch you once in a while. It'll tempt you. It'll fool you but by and large, its teeth are gone.

And so that's the whole purpose so far of the 19th chapter, to show us that the adversary, the cause of every evil in the world is not man's inhumanity to man. It's not man's greed. It's not his selfishness. It's the world mind posing as these things and Jesus never met a claim in that person for that reason. That's why Jesus didn't defend against the so-called enemy. He wouldn't go for the decoys.

We're being taught to avoid the decoys of form, person, place, condition and thing and get to the root of all evil which is the mind that is not the Christ mind. For only the Christ mind can see, experience, live in the Reality of God on earth.

Well, there's a lot of deception that follows. We'll get into it some other time.

I'm interested in your having the experience of knowing yourself to be a Spiritual Being and the way you might go about it at this particular point in our study is to know that God is the Allness demonstrated here by Christ Jesus and the acceptance then of his demonstration that God is ever present and is all there is, is always the beginning point of your day. God is here and the Spirit of God must be my name.

There is no evil in the Spirit of God. It is not the will of the Father that there be evil. The will of the Father is goodness and because there's no power to push aside the will of God, it is functioning and goodness is functioning. The will of God is that I have all that God has. The will of God is that I be perfect and that will must be functioning. Nothing can stop it.

And so, we accept the Word. We rest in the Word rather than in our own personal, human experience. My human experience tells me there's many other things here beside God and beside the will of God. But because world mind in me wants me to do just that, I've finally come out of that deception and rest in the Word of God rather than in my own human experience which says there are other things here. In other words, your faith is in the Word which says, "Only God is here." That's what Jesus Christ was demonstrating. "There's no power in you, Pilate, over me. I'm getting out from underneath the magnifying glass. I'm not living in the below, in the form. I am the Life. I am from above and there's no evil in God's universe and this is it. I'm not going to be in a universe that isn't God's universe because there isn't any and there is no lack in God's universe and there's no limitation in God's universe and there's nothing finite in God's universe. I'm not going to try to become what God tells me I already am. I am the child. I don't have to become the child. That means I am the Spirit. What can Spirit become? The mere trying to become is the denial of Being the Spirit. The effort to get is a denial of having the Allness of Spirit."

And so, there's nothing more to desire or to seek or to find. Nothing to become. That Spirit of God is where I am. I am in the Kingdom of God now. There is no other. I am in the universe of God now and there's nothing in it that's finite so I'm not a finite anything in the universe of God.

And now, slow down a minute. I cannot be finite and be Spirit. There is no finite Spirit. I can't begin at one place and end at another place. I can't begin in time with a birth and end in time with a death. That's finite. Where do I begin? I have no beginning. Where do I end? I have no ending. Does God have a beginning? No. Does God have an ending? No. I have no beginning. I have no ending. Was God born? No. Then I was not born because God is All. Does God die? No. Then I cannot die because God is All.

Where do these ideas come of a beginning and an ending? They're false ideas of the world mind. I have no beginning and no ending. I am Spirit and if I have a beginning and an ending, I am denying myself to be the Spirit. The nature of Spirit is without beginning or end. It has no beginning in space or in time and no end in space or time. The moment I have a beginning or an end in space or time, I'm saying, "I'm not the Spirit," and I'm divided again.

World mind has divided me from my Self. These characters in the Bible who were crucifying Christ are not doing that at all. They're crucifying themselves. They are turning away from Christ in them which is all that this is made visible to show us and we don't want to be like that. While they crucify the outer Christ, they were crucifying the inner Christ by turning away from him. And by we turning away from the inner Christ, we're crucifying the Christ the same way.

But now, we're not. We stop crucifying Christ when we know that's my name, that's my being and Christ said, *"Before Abraham was, I am."* Therefore, before Abraham was, I am. Christ said, *"I am the Light"* and therefore, I am the Light. Christ said, *"You have no power over me world power of Pilate"* and therefore, I can say to the world mind, "You have no power over me." The minute I know the world mind and recognize it, it ceases to be a power. Its power lies in the fact that no one recognizes it. When it's recognized, it has no power. That's the only power it has. It's invisible to human sense. It works through the unconscious. But when you recognize it, it loses its power.

And so, every report that comes to your consciousness which says something is wrong is the world mind. It can put ten ambulances out there and clang ten fire engine bells, they're all put there by the world mind. It can have a flood. It can have a storm. It can have an epidemic. It can have every kind of calamity. Don't believe it. And that's all the same world mind. It's all part of the initiation, the testing for you who have been in the wilderness, unknowing that you are the Christ and when you know it, you can say to the world mind which is Pilate here, "Thou has no power over me. It wasn't given thee from above. The only power is my ignorance and if I have ignorance, you have power. If I have awareness of the Spirit, the power is gone." That's your freedom.

Salvation is faith that you are the Christ, not faith in God. That faith has not been salvation. That's been the prolonging of all the superstitions the world has known. The faith that Christ in you is God, is salvation.

And then world mind is powerless. It can never tell you again what you lack, what you need or what you should have because you can always know, I Spirit am Self-complete. Everything I need is right here. This is Holy Ground and the hereness that I speak of is my Self. All of me is here. All of me is here because the universe is here and the universe is All of me. Nothing can be added or taken away from the Spiritual reality and nothing else exists.

We have then the will of God being good, only goodness can be. The substance of God being Spirit, only Spirit can be. The action of God being perfect, only perfection can be. And if the human mind keeps trying to catch that and accept that, it fails. Again and again it fails because it's the human mind which must be crucified, not Christ. When you crucify the human mind, Christ in you rises and the Christ mind reveals to you that mortal mind is dead. Instead of being dead to Christ, you're dead to the deadness of a world that never was.

Instead of crucifying the Christ, we have learned to crucify the mind which is the outlet and the inlet for an illusory world mind and then the murderer of the world has no one to murder.

Now, if you keep using that mind, you're saying to the murderer, "Work through me." If you crucify that mind, you'll find the mind which was in Christ Jesus is your mind and things will instantly clarify themselves. You'll find you're out of this form. You're aware of a vast Spiritual form which is yours and you can feel that all of the winds that blow, all of the forms that walk, all of the powers that make noises are not making contact with you anymore. Just as they couldn't make contact with Christ. The one was unreal and One was real.

Then you're taken outside of this human selfhood. You're lifted right out of it. You're off the ground and you find that all of the laws of Spirit are working, maintaining a perfect Kingdom through your entire Being.

Now, this experience of not being in this limited capsule does for you what no words can do and it doesn't come because you're thinking about it. It comes because you're true to the fact that God is truly All there is.

If you can be true to that Truth that God is All there is, every time you meditate, you'll find this new power takes you your 50 seconds off the ground.

Well I think that's our story today.

I wish you all a very pleasant Thanksgiving.

CLASS 39

INVISIBLE MANSIONS

Herb: Presumably, in this meditation, those of you who are not familiar with Joel's teaching about the rose may have lingered on the material values or material appearances of the rose and those of you who were able to see the rose as a doorway, went through that doorway and found you were touching something invisible, ultimately touching the Infinite.

Now, the way we see a rose, whether with the naked eye or with a Spiritual Consciousness, it's the way we read a Bible. And so, today, we want to see if we are reading the Bible correctly. Many of us still read it as if we're talking about characters named Pilate and Jews and Nicodemus and Jesus Christ and John. That isn't the Bible at all. Those are just names. You could take the name Pilate and throw it away and call him Gregory Peck; it wouldn't make any difference. Who was he? What does he represent? What do the members of the Jewish council represent?

And then, we come to this place now where we can say that the Bible is not about people at all. Oh, they walked the earth. They had forms. They said and did things but they're not in the Bible for that reason. They are not external people. There's not a character in the Bible that is there for that purpose. Their purpose in the Bible is to show you the multitude of ideas, thoughts and conditions that exist in your mind.

Now, take the name of Pilate away. Who was this individual? Pilate was an administrator. Not just an ordinary administrator but an administrator for Rome, an administrator for all of the material power called Caesar. And where was he an administrator? In the land of the Hebrews. In the land of the intellect. Pilate administrated in the land of the intellect. In you, in your intellect, there is a Pilate. Pilate represents that outer action, that administration in us which is a tool, which is used.

And now, as we begin to read our Bible correctly, we see that Pilate in us is a tool used by both Caesar, world power and the Jew - the intellect - so that mind and material power conspire to force something in us to act a certain way so that Pilate in us must make a compromise.

And every other character in the Bible is to be seen not as a name but rather as a mortal power within us, forcing us to do things that turn us away from the Divine nature of our Being. Oh, there are good characters too, who turn us to the Divine nature of our Being.

But every character in the Bible then, is no longer to be read as an external person. Some of us have already discarded that old habit anyway. We see Pilate here now, in the 19th chapter as a tool or an instrument of two forces and he cannot make up his mind. He is forced one way and then the other because he is not anchored in the knowledge of his own identity. All he knows is he gets a paycheck from Rome and so, he has to do what Rome wants. He also knows that the Jews can in some way unhinge him from that job. All they've got to do is to tell Caesar that he's unfaithful to them and to him and the next thing you know, poor Pilate who does not know who he is, has to turn around and do things for the Jews that he doesn't want to do.

And so, you find your inner administrator. That which makes you decide to walk right or left, or forward or up or down. The administrator in you which lives today for you and will live tomorrow for you, who does he answer to? Does he answer to Christ? Does he answer to Caesar? Does he answer to the intellect? Does he answer to the Jew? Does he answer to Rome? Who does he answer to? And if he does not answer to Christ, he's going to compromise.

And we can still further clarify whom this administrator should answer to because the Jew and Pilate, the administrator in jury for Rome and Rome itself, all represent a material world - totally barren of the awareness of the presence of God within. And if our inner administrator is unaware of the God within, we're going to make a decision like Pilate and six months later or six years later, we're going to be forced into suicide as he was or we're going to make a decision like Judas who acted from somewhat similar motives on a different scale and he was forced into suicide. But worse than that, these were visible, ostensible suicides. There is that suicide in a man which is not visible.

And now, in the 19th chapter, some of the highest teachings take place before the crucifixion to show us that man is daily committing suicide. Pilate, in every man, unable to make the right decision because he knows not himself, goes forth and worships at the throne of matter. And not only that, but the intellect goes right along with him. The Jew turns on the Jew. The Jew turns on himself. The intellect turns upon itself and tears itself to pieces. Don't make the mistake that you're looking at characters in a book. You're looking at the thoughts that are in the mind of the world today, in the religions of the world, in the sciences of the world, in the psychology movements of the world, even in metaphysical movements in the world. You're looking at ideas and thoughts and actions and conditions that exist in the world mind and they're given names like Pilate and Herod and Annas and Caiaphas. You don't see Herod in the Gospel of John at this point. You see Herod only in the other Gospels.

Here Pilate makes a decision. In the other Gospels, Pilate turns Jesus Christ back to Herod. He gets rid of this difficult decision when he learns that Jesus is a Galilean and he has no control in Galilee. Herod does. He also has had a lot of difficulty with Herod and he thinks by turning Jesus over to Herod, he can patch up his personal difficulties and also be free of making a decision that he thinks he might regret.

Why does John not tell us about Herod? The reason he doesn't is very important and it indicates why John is so trustworthy as a witness. John was absent when Pilate turned Jesus over to Herod. John was sent to get the mother of Jesus. You won't find it in here. You see, he was taken so quickly that his own family knew nothing about it and only one disciple went with him; John. Only one disciple was inseparable from him; John.

And just as Pilate means nothing as a name, neither does John. But the meaning of that inseparability from Jesus will be clear to you as you dwell with that inner Self which clarifies all things. It was John to whom the Master said, "Now fetch my mother. Bring her here that she may watch me die." And it was John who then went and it was then that Pilate turned Jesus over to Herod. And John, because he wasn't there to witness that did not report that but he knew about it. John reported only what he witnessed and you will discover that the very Spirit of Jesus Christ directs us to John for the Truth. But again, not to an external John but to John in you and that should clue you in to who John in you might be.

We'll begin approximately at 12th or 13th verse of the 19th chapter.

The 12th tells us that, "*Thenceforth, Pilate sought to release Jesus: but the Jews cried out, saying, If thou let this man go, thou art not Caesar's friend: whosoever maketh himself a king speaketh against Caesar.*"

And so, mind is using its pressure against the administrator. Pilate has tried every way he can not to have to have Jesus crucified. Not because he believes in the Christ but because he's a coward. He doesn't want blood on his hands. He also hates the Jews. He despises them. He hates to do them a favor. And yet, he's forced to do what they tell him. He doesn't want to. This is a thorn in the side that Paul speaks about. "*That which I would not do, I do.*" Why? Because there is a force working through us, making us administrate in a way we do not wish to administrate and we cannot identify that force and so, we do what we would not do.

We sort of file down the edges a little bit here and file the edges down a little bit there making little concessions until they become great big concessions and always, the concession is we believe in the existence of matter.

As we're pushed closer to the crucifixion, we're pushed closer to the decision we must make. Do we drop the belief in matter? Or do we let matter crucify us? We're going to have to make that decision and then we're going to have to keep that decision once we've made it.

Pilate is squirming because he has not faced such a decision. He's unaware that such a decision must be made. He does not know what forces are compelling him to act. Everywhere he turns, matter gets him this way and mind gets him the other way. He's in between.

Now, the Jews won't let him release Jesus Christ. He wants to. He'd like to leave this town and go back home. They say, "If you do this, let a man go, who is no friend of Caesar, what about you? Are you a friend of Caesar?" So, this hits him on his weak side again. If he were Christ, he wouldn't have a weak side. If he knew Spiritual identity, there would be no weak side. He couldn't be persuaded or influenced. He would be willing to say, "Because this man is innocent as far as I'm concerned, he is free."

When we stand in our Spiritual identity, we can face the torments of the mind or the body. We can accept them as conditions which must pass but which have no power. When we do not stand in Spiritual identity, then the conditions of the world around us swarm in and they have a sense of power compelling us to do that which we do not want to do.

"When Pilate therefore heard that saying, he brought Jesus forth, and sat down in the judgment seat in a place that is called the Pavement, but in the Hebrew, Gabbatha."

The administrator brings in Jesus Christ in the place called Gabbatha, the pavement. And this means a pavement of stones; a pavement of stones and these stones are literal truth. The truth of the sense mind. Jesus Christ will be judged by the truth of the sense mind. That is the pavement called Gabbatha.

There will be no Spiritual judgment present. The administrator in us judges by the sense mind. And so, today's decisions are based upon what our sense mind tells us and this leads to a false decision. It invariably leads to a decision not based upon Truth and however right it may appear to be, in time it is shown to be wrong. If a decision in your life is made not based upon Spiritual Truth, even if you have a temporary advantage, you will discover that this is reversed by later incidents. This is the delusion of making decisions with the mind which is sense bound.

The cardiogram says you have a bad heart. That's a sense bound mental decision. The Spirit of God says *"Be ye perfect as your Father."*

And so, the administrator in us, Pilate, says, the cardiogram says, "I have a severe heart action," and now, the rest of us accepts this and fear begins to sway us. Decisions are now made and these decisions are all based not upon Spiritual identity but upon material identity. And so, the operation finally comes off and it's a success and we're very happy. We think we've done the right thing but we're still just as far away from our permanent Self.

The purpose now of these characters is to show us what mistakes we should not make. How to avoid these mistakes, how to come to that sense of Self which is the permanent Self which is perfect now as the Father. There are big decisions to make at this point of the path because if you haven't decided that you have a permanent Self and that you are at all costs going to live in that permanent Self, you're going to withdraw and be battered and buffeted on both sides by the material world and the world mind. It's only when you have riveted your goal to living in and as your permanent Self, not the changing day by day material self, but the unchanging, eternal Self, the Life Self. When that is your goal you find the administrator in you becomes not a Pilate who ultimately is forced to commit suicide but the Father who doeth the works. Then you have the Divine administrator, the Father within and Grace flows, making perfect decisions, perfect expressions of the Divine where you stand.

"It was the preparation of the passover, and about the sixth hour: and he saith unto the Jews, Behold your King!"

There is a secret in the Bible here which we may have spoken of many times in which people who have no idea that they represent God, in some way are used to utter words of Truth. You'll find Pilate, though he's unaware of it, in some cases, he is a spokesman for the Divine word. The words are put in his mouth. He has nothing to say about them.

"Behold your King!"

What he's saying is really a taunt, a mockery and yet, he's saying the Truth though he knows it not. His hostility to the Jews is now being revenged. He's taunting them with this appearance. They know this man is not their king and he knows this man is not their king but they have seen fit to accuse him of saying he was their king in order to get him crucified. And so, he turns his taunt back to them and he says, *"Behold your king!"*

Matter doesn't want to do what mind is telling us and it tries to fight mind. He's now in his own way attacking the very mind which is controlling him.

"Behold your king! But they cried out, Away with him, away with him, crucify him. Pilate saith unto them, Shall I crucify your King? The chief priests answered, We have no king but Caesar."

Now, we are given an insight into the human mind. If there was one person on earth that the Jews hated worse than Pilate it was Caesar. If there was one person they feared, it was Caesar. They hated him and they feared him. Now, they say, *"We have no king but Caesar."*

Caesar is their oppressor. Listen closely within yourself to those words, *"We have no king but Caesar."* The intellect of man says, "Caesar is our king." The intellect of man says, "Matter is my king." The oppressor of the Jews was Caesar and the Jews declare Caesar is their king. The oppressor of man is matter and man still worships matter. Man worships that which oppresses him and destroys him.

Caesar represents the epitome of material power in the world and there's hardly a man on the earth who doesn't worship material power. What destroys man? Material power. The material power of sin, of disease, of sickness and of death destroys every man but that's what he worships. He worships the other side of that coin, the good material power, the health. He worships all of the so-called positive side of material power and while doing it, it's like asking Caesar for favors. The Jews never got a favor out of Caesar.

We think we get favors out of matter. Now, this is how at this point John is teaching us that we commit suicide worshipping matter, seeking matter, striving to attain matter, striving to live comfortably in a material world. This is saying, *"We have no king but Caesar."*

Where is Caesar today, the man the world feared? A corpse. They were fearing that which would be dead but they were really fearing that which was dead. The message of Spirit is that matter is dead. Matter is a corpse and when you seek matter, you're seeking a corpse. Even when you acquire it, you've acquired a corpse. This is how we commit suicide daily and that is the reason this occurs before the crucifixion.

The Talmud of the Jews declares we have no god, we worship no man but God. No man can be our God and now, *"We have no king but Caesar"* is turning away from its own Judaic God, showing how the human mind can be perverted and distorted under stress. It has no anchor in itself and as this mind here says, is forced to declare, *"We have no king but Caesar"* which it doesn't mean at all, so do we every day worship at the throne of the material world.

Now, if you dwell with this awhile, you will see that Caesar represents that which mankind worships and fears. Material power, material possessions, material health, material bodies, material conditions, all that has the capacity to turn and oppress us, we worship.

In the tenth deca, only thirty odd years after the crucifixion of Jesus Christ, there were more Jews hanging on trees from the sacking of Jerusalem than you could count. The entire city was destroyed. The same suicide which took place in the statement, *"We have no king but Caesar"* ultimately led to that oppression.

Now, throughout the world, we know that the Jews are noted for their being oppressed. This is true. Do you see the vaster symbolism, though? That the mind, the intellect is always oppressed by Caesar, material power. That's the decoy the mind follows. The oppression throughout the world of the Jews is a vaster symbol of the oppression of material power over the intellect of man.

Just as in the days of Jesus, the Jew and Pilate and Caesar symbolized humanhood in its various levels. So, it is today. The world ruling power is still comprised of those facets of intellect and matter which are the suicide of the human race. These are facts that never change. They always stare us in the face until we come to Spiritual identity, until we stand in the midst of these powers of the Jew, of Pilate, of Caesar unmoved as Jesus Christ was. And this is the symbol of standing in the midst of all worldly power in Spiritual identity knowing that Spiritual identity is untouchable for Spiritual identity is the permanent Self. Then the intellect, the false sense of world power will try to manipulate the administrator in you but the administrator in you will be God, the Father within unmoved, uninfluenced and just as Jesus Christ walks through a crucifixion, we walk through the sin, the disease, the death, the bad health, the sickness, the conditions of the worldly mind.

The symbolism is very clear because we're reading the Bible now as John wanted us to read it, not with the human mind. It was written from Soul to Soul. This is the vast panorama which is on every page of the Bible, always with new names. Before the full picture emerges, you are given the strength and the foundation stones so that when you come to the real trial, you know that you have learned how to stand on one fact, that there is no person where you stand.

It's easy to say God is All, but what stands on the cross is the false sense of self and everyone has to come to that place where the false sense of self is put on the cross. There is no person where you stand. The Allness of Spirit, the Allness of God, the Allness of Divine Selfhood is the only You and these trials and tribulations of all for the purpose of transmuting all that is unlike God out of our system until you are willing to stand on your own Divine Selfhood as the only Self you are. That is your permanent Self as you overcome the feeling of a personal me, as you release the belief in a material me.

And before this crucifixion takes place, all of the suffering and torment we go through is because we still worship Caesar. We still worship the material power of the world. We still fear it and we still try to seek favor from it in some way.

I had expected more than a year ago that most of our members in this class would have dropped out. Continuously, we emphasize that Christ offers you nothing in this world. Christ isn't trying to offer you a better human world. Christ is saying that "When you look at that rose, learn to look through it." Christ is saying "When you look at that person, learn to look through that person. See that every object on this earth is a doorway to the invisible, spiritual Kingdom."

Now, this minute, everything you see is a doorway to Infinity. You must cross out that which you see and walk through it to that which you do not see and you must develop the habit, the capacity to walk through the material world around you, to walk through Caesar, to walk directly into the invisible Spirit always.

And yet, in spite of the fact that we have repeatedly told you that Christ offers nothing in this world, many haven't turned away. And it may be because it took eight or nine years before we could come to face this Truth within ourselves. It wasn't done overnight. We had a foundation.

And today, when we say "There is no person," it's still a difficult thing to say. It's still a difficult thing to accept but it's still as necessary as it was the day that Jesus stood upon a cross. He was demonstrating there is no person here.

Pilate couldn't crucify the Son of God. Caesar couldn't crucify the Son of God. No Jew could have the Son of God crucified. Neither mind nor matter nor material power can crucify the Son of God and this is the teaching that you are that Son. That means no germ, no sickness, no disease, no lack or limitation can crucify the Son of God and you are that Son.

And ever you think you're being crucified, you're saying, "I am not that Son, I am material being." No one can do to you anything except it be the will of the Father and it is the will of the Father that you be perfect as your Father.

These are the issues behind the forms and the conditions that we now see at this particular point of the Bible. Identity being revealed and false identity being revealed. Everything coming into sharp focus for those who have made total illumination their only goal. The doorway which is called a rose, the doorway which is called a river, the doorway which is called a mountain, the doorway which is called a fruit or a pear or an apple or a tree or an animal or a person; that doorway is only the doorway to the Invisible that is there. And standing at that doorway always is the Invisible Christ saying, "I stand at the door."

As you look into the doorway of matter and accept the invisible Christ there, you're crucifying matter instead of Christ. And if you look at matter and see matter and accept matter and know only the matter that you see, you're crucifying Christ. If you see a person, you're crucifying Christ and this must be seen. When we are not accepting Christ, we are crucifying Christ.

When the churches of the world believe in the reality of evil which is material, material evil, the religions of the world are practicing atheism. They are saying, "There is matter, it's bad matter. We've got to do something about that." John tells us if God didn't create it, it doesn't exist. God didn't create bad matter. And if we've got to do something about what God didn't create, we're accepting it as being there, created there. That's not worshipping God. That's worshipping Caesar.

All belief in evil is turning away from the Allness of God and is pure atheism and it doesn't matter who is the atheist, what religion he runs or doesn't run. If he believes in the existence of evil, he is an atheist and it's best to face it. And we can truthfully say that we have most of our lives been atheists while thinking we believed in God. But we believe in a God in some form. We didn't believe in God as the only Reality of the universe and that wasn't believing in God. It was believing in our false concept of God. In our skull, we had an idea called God and that's what we worshipped.

And so, the handful of us who straggled through this have come to the place where we can worship God, and finally get the message that God that we worship is 'individual identity'. You worship God everywhere you look for that is the only One who is present. Everywhere you look is God and you either worship God or crucify God in your mind.

Jesus Christ had the fantastic capability of drawing forth two things in this world. First, to reveal Divine action; the great, invincible power of the Spirit. And then, having revealed this power is on earth, to reveal the nature of the world mind so that this world mind, acting through men with names would turn and crucify its own Savior.

"We have no king but Caesar."

This is the mind of the world expressing through the Jew, through the intellect in which man would rather crucify its Savior and worship its tormentor than crucify its tormentor and worship its Savior. This is the choice between matter and Spirit. If you choose matter, you crucify the Christ of your own Being. If you choose the Christ of your own Being, you must then crucify matter. One will be crucified and you make your choice by who you are. If you are material being, you have crucified Christ. If you are Spiritual Being, you must crucify matter. That is the choice we all face.

Many of us are ready. Some of us, it would be premature to expect you to make such a choice. You have had to go through many things before such a choice can be made. You can't make it mentally because your mental choice would have no power behind it. You'd find you'd have to stumble. The only way you can make it is if you know who you are, if you know certain principles, of how to live in that choice and then you've got a struggle. And if you do not have those principles and if you do not know who you are, to say, "I make that choice," would be as futile as five thousand people stepping up to the podium and saying, "I pledge for Jesus Christ."

The words won't mean anything. It won't keep a germ away. It's that conscious awareness of the presence of Christ where the flower appears, where the animal appears, where the person appears, where the tree appears. It's that conscious awareness that you walk, move and breathe in a Spiritual universe. It's the conscious knowledge that all around you is the One, living Life of God and nothing else.

And however difficult that may seem, out of the mouth of babes sometimes, we learn that these things that seemed so remote from our consciousness at one time or another are not as remote from the consciousness of the young.

In this classroom last Wednesday, we had about twenty people. They were students of a high school and half of them were Chinese, one Japanese. Others were American boys and girls. I suppose the age group might have been fifteen or sixteen. They were here with their teacher. They wanted to learn what this was about and so they said, "Give us a little talk." And then, there was a question and answer period and the Japanese boy raised his hand and he asked the strangest question I had ever heard. I don't think he'd ever heard this message before. I don't think any of them had but he said, "Well, is there only one Life then?" And I just couldn't believe what I was listening to. We worked nine years to get across that message and I don't know what it is that was said before but he just looked at me and that was his question. "Is there only one Life then?"

Now, how would a seventeen-year old boy who had never heard this message or any message like this, how would he come to the place of asking, "Is there one Life?" And being willing to accept such a thing.

Now, if you're Jesus Christ, you're not seeing Pilate and Jews and Caesar. You're living in One Life and One Life doesn't turn upon itself. It doesn't crucify itself. It doesn't make itself sick or diseased or destroy itself. If you're living in the One Life, you're living in that which is immune to any form of destruction. And therefore, anything that appears to you that is unlike the perfect, One Life reaches you as a temporary condition existing only in the false consciousness. It's just a sign that for the moment, you're not in the consciousness of One Life.

And so, you go back into the Consciousness of One Life and wait for the illusion of such a condition to be dissolved by the Father within. The moment you're in the consciousness of One Life, your own identity passes judgment not Pilate. All judgment is made righteously by the Spirit of your own Being through Grace. And once more, the conditions that beset you are shown to be without power, without substance, without law, without Divine ordination.

"I and the Father are one." One Life.

No person stands where you are. The Spirit of God is there. The Christ is there. The Light of God is there. The Life of God is there. The Perfection of God is there. What is this physical person? It's a cosmic collage of many different ideas and thoughts in the world mind which we now crystallize into the appearance called form.

"This," says the mother, "is my baby. And this is my baby grown up now to young manhood." There's no mother there and there's no man grown up to young manhood. There is the invisible Spirit of God. Who says so? God says so. God is not the Father of a growing, human child. You find many of those under tombstones. God has no human children. God is not the father of persons. God is no respecter of persons. It's time to take God's Word and not the word of the intellect or of Caesar or of Pilate.

Now, you're fighting for possession of your mind. Either it's possessed or you possess it. Either it's dominated or you dominate. Possession of your mind means you must stand at these opposing forces of Reality and unreality. The Tree of Life, the Spirit. The tree of the knowledge of good and evil, false belief in good matter and bad matter. Where you stand and how you stand determines which dominates you and which you dominate. And if your mind is not your own possession, it is possessed and you will go out worshipping Caesar, even unaware that that is what you are doing.

Now, at this point, that issue has been clarified sufficiently so that what follows will only confirm what we have discussed. And it is necessary for you to find that confirmation in the Bible to see that

Spirit is leading you to, not the crucifixion of Jesus Christ but the crucifixion of your false sense of human selfhood.

John walking with Jesus through the trials, through the crucifixion is a sign that he has attained in this world the crucifixion of the false sense of self. Jesus demonstrates it. John records it. They're working as one team. John is the only Son of God on earth when Jesus walks off the earth.

And John represents your Soul. Jesus represents your Spirit. As Spirit steps out of the belief in form, Spirit can only communicate through your Soul. Jesus communicates to the world through John. Christ communicates through your Soul. You'll find the age of John is the next age we're going to live through.

We've had the age of Jesus Christ and it will continue but now there will be a magnification of the work of John. John represents the Soul of mankind, the universal Soul of man. And unless you find John in you, you continue to live in Pilate in you.

John is now designated by Jesus as the Son of God. Jesus calls his mother and says, "There is your Son." To John, "And there is your mother." And we are told that everyone who comes to Christ is the Son of Mary. Whoever comes to Christ is the Son of Mary. She has no human sons. "There is your Son," pointing to John but John isn't her physical son. She didn't bear him in the womb. He is her son because he has accepted the Christ. He has crucified the personal sense of John. He is unselfed.

To Peter, who had quibbled something about John, the Master said, "What is it to you if I would have him tarry awhile here?" This tarrying is John remaining on this earth when Jesus goes off the earth. For John is the only one who can receive the Voice. John is the symbol of your Soul which receives the Voice. So, the Gospel of John is the Gospel of your Soul.

Salvation is not through faith in a person made into a God. Salvation is not through faith at all. Salvation is through Spiritual identity accepted and the instrument through which you accept Spiritual identity is John, your Soul. Your Soul takes you above the Jew. John takes you to the place where your Soul receiving the Light of the world, removes you from the darkness of matter. Otherwise, the Light is in the world and the darkness receiveth it not.

The whole Gospel of John is the Gospel of your Soul. Just as Revelation is the Gospel of your Soul and Living revelation is the inner Self speaking to you through your Soul. Then you transcend the mind. Then you come into the unconditioned mind of Reality. Then you live in your permanent Self and you're led into the body that is imperishable.

Now, these are some of the highlights of this chapter. We'll look at a few more of them. I think we can stay with this awhile yet.

Important to note is that the chief priests answered, *"We have no king but Caesar."*

Now this is still true today. We are told that religion still believes in matter and material power. We are told that religions today are worshipping Baal, that religions today are not going to lead us to individual, spiritual Selfhood. They are preaching faith is the way to salvation and it isn't. Only your spiritual Self is salvation. There's no permanent Self achieved after death. The permanent Self must be achieved before death in consciousness and lived in.

"Then delivered he him therefore unto them to be crucified. And they took Jesus, and led him away."

And so, Pilate succumbs. The administrator in us yields to the world mind, material powers of the world and the individual mind of us is forced to make this action, *"Then delivered he him"* so we're delivering now, Jesus. We're delivering Christ, *"unto them to be crucified. And they took Jesus and led him away."*

They, the Jews, led him away. The Jew, being intellect; intellect leads the Christ. It's turned around for we know the Truth; Christ leads us. we do not lead the Christ.

But you see, this is the report of the condition of the world. Intellect is leading the Christ. It is turned around. That's the meaning of repent. We're turned around and so we must turn around again. Turn around. Don't lead the Christ like the Jews led the Christ here but turn around and let the Christ lead you.

You see, that means there's no personal self where you are. If there's a personal you, you're always leading the Christ. You've got to take care of that personal self instead of letting Christ live itself as you.

"I live yet not I. Christ liveth [my life,]" says Paul. He's not leading the Christ. Christ is leading Paul because there is no Paul. There is only Christ. There is no personal self. Now, how do you face such a situation? No personal self. Go back to the rose. It's a doorway. The rose you see today is gone tomorrow. It's dead. The person you see today is gone tomorrow. He's dead. What are you going to do? Wait for that to happen? Go through the doorway. Sure, it's a beautiful rose. It won't be less beautiful because you say, "Spirit is standing there, not a rose," and sure that's a nice person to have around. But that person will still be standing around. Go through the person. Find the permanent Self that is there. Sow to the Spirit. Recognize, live by, acknowledge in all thy ways the Invisible Spirit until there's something in you that is rising the capacity to acknowledge the Invisible Spirit.

John in you was rising. The Soul is rising until the Soul of the world is risen, until we recognize the Invisible, spiritual universe around us, now. We must walk through that rose. We must walk through that person. We must walk through every Pilate, through every power, through every condition. And as you develop and train yourself through this discipline of walking through the material appearance and condition and the material person. By not doing so, your keep crucifying You who are the Christ. With Pilate it's six years between his crucifixion of himself and his final suicide. With us it might be twenty or thirty but it's inevitable. If you crucify you, that finally appears in the visible as your death and if you don't crucify You, you find you are deathless. And what appears as your death is no more a death of You than it was a death of Jesus Christ. The death of You is simply an appearance if you learn to crucify the you that isn't and live in the You that is; the Self that is perfect now as the Father.

Now, this is where the difficult discipline is a daily thing. It isn't something you hear in a class. You practice it with every bug you see, with every insect, with every flea, with every newspaper headline, with loved ones and hated ones. You practice it with the fellow who takes your money behind the teller's cage at the bank. You practice it with the butcher and the baker. You practice it with that which stands on your plate for you to eat today. You look through it to the Invisible and then you stand in front of the mirror and you look through that image and declare yourself to be the Invisible Self.

— End of Side One —

That Invisible Self in you starts to talk to you. "Yes, I am You. I am come. I am here. I am your Spiritual Self. I am real. I exist. I am the Self of you and I can walk through the fire."

There must be that continuous, daily reconciliation to Self, that daily redeeming of the appearance, that wrestling with the material condition until you're blessed by Self-identity realized, until you know that the One that is the Spirit of God, I really am. Then Christ in you is no longer crucified.

And all of the hardship of doing this is rewarded. The easy path is not to do it and think you're getting all of the beautiful rewards the other way and to suddenly find they're taken away. It is harder to do this than not to do it and only the belief in the ultimate Truth of it will make a person do it.

"He, bearing his cross went forth into a place called the place of a skull, [which is] called in the Hebrew Golgotha."

There's the skull. To bear your own cross is the sign of your guilt. That was the custom. You had to bear your cross. Actually, it was a cross beam but you didn't bear the whole cross. They already had the stakes planted in Golgotha. This is the tranverse, cross beam and you bear it because the Jews wanted the world to know that Jesus was guilty. That's why they wanted him to bear the cross which was a Roman custom. Even crucifixion was a Roman custom. They could have had him stoned but that wouldn't have been severe enough.

But you see this is a boomerang because now, what you see called Jesus suffering, this is the method whereby we are given insight into the consciousness of the world. The mind wanted Jesus to appear to be guilty. He had to bear his cross. The boomerang is that this is precisely the Christ method of revealing to us the nature of the world consciousness and this is the world consciousness which is guilty. This is telling us that what is guilty here, what is really bearing the cross is the world consciousness and then, to underline that, they go to a place which is known as a skull.

If you think Jesus was crucified on a tree, you're mistaken. All that was crucified happened in that skull. The skull of man is where Jesus was crucified. That skull is the empty- world consciousness, empty of Spiritual awareness. That skull represents the nature of the consciousness that crucifies Christ in us every day. That skull is barren. That skull is hollow and even though we think we have five senses and we trust these five senses, one day we find it's only a skull. It only seemed to have intelligence. It never had. The only intelligence in a skull is false intelligence. Golgotha is where we crucify ourselves. That is where the skull or the world consciousness which is hollow, barren, empty of Truth buries us every day.

That's the meaning of the skull. That's where the religions of the worlds are worshipping today, in the skull, in the outer ceremonies, in the words, in the concepts, in the beliefs but the church of God is Christ in you, identity, not a skull. The intellect buries Truth in its skull. It worships that Truth in its skull and ultimately, it is too late. All that's left is that skull.

You see the vast hypnotism of the human mind that is intended by having the Christ appear to be crucified in a place called Golgotha, the skull? That's why it is Golgotha, the skull.

And this crucifixion today is the same, the skull of science, the skull of religion, the skull of psychology, the skull of government, the skull of personal sense is where we crucify the Christ. We have our twentieth century Golgotha on the top of every person's shoulders.

"Come out of her," says the Voice. "You are Infinite Being. You can't live in a skull. You can't be guided. You can't have your administrator in a skull. You are the Light of the world; Shine!"

So, person - which is nothing more than the creation of that which happens in a skull - person is the effect or product of the activity in the skull. Just as the skull rules us and creates the illusion of person, so do we impersonalize and step out of the skull. We transcend the skull, the mind, the barren, hollow vehicle which is not a vehicle for the Spirit of God. And we stand outside of that body, outside of that form, outside of that sense of life which says, "That's me walking down the street. That's me going to the office. That's me getting married. That's me having children. That's me having my fiftieth wedding anniversary." That isn't me at all. The skull wants me to think that. Golgotha wants me to think that and it's going to crucify me with that belief. No, that's not me.

Son of God is never going to have a fiftieth wedding anniversary. Son of God had his fiftieth wedding anniversary five trillion years ago. Son of God is forever. Son of God has ever been alive, ever will be. Don't settle for fifty years when the Father says, "You are eternal." Don't settle for life that began yesterday when the Father says, "You are as old as I am. You have ever been. You are my Life without beginning or end."

And so, we're getting out of the skull. We came through a fish. We came through a lizard. We came through apes. We're coming through a skull. We're coming out of the belief that we are mortal. We're accepting the Father's statement that mortality is never the child of God and we are crucifying mortality with Spiritual awareness.

Let's be still for a moment before our intermission.

I'd like you to take it as a personal task for yourself to wrestle with the Truth that where you are, there is no person. I don't expect you to like me for it and I expect you to have many problems with that task. I expect you to stumble and hurt your knees many times but I hope you will remember that that is your problem that is your real task. And if from within you receive the assurance that this is so, and as you course through the Bible and your books, you find more assurance this is so, you will find that again and again, as you stray from that task, finding new problems or a repetition of old ones, new fears, new lacks, new doubts, it will always be because you have not come to that agreement with yourself that there is no person where you stand. You're being fooled be the drama in time and space, the world broadcast called person, the image which is nothing but a replay in time of all that you already are.

And every time you forget this, or succeed momentarily and think now you can forget it, you will make another mistake. There has to come a time when Christ in you is no longer crucified. Then you're perfect as your Father. Then you're the One, realized. The Father won't accept any less. You may as well face it.

That's the cross we all must bear individually. The cross of personal sense must be crossed out. If you're having trouble, let the

Soul of you, the John consciousness receive of the Father for you. Rest in your Soul above your mind. Wait upon the Word. The Infinite Power of Love itself will always translate to the momentary need of one who says, "There is no person here but the Life of the Father" and rest in the Soul awaiting the expression of that Life where you stand.

Each daily task that you look through as a doorway to Christ enables you to reach the pinnacle.

It's hard work but it's Divine work. Silence, (pause) ...

And ultimately, it's much easier than laboring for the meat that perishes.

We can take our little interlude now. See you in about five or six minutes. (Class break)

I think somene gave me some good advice a moment ago. They said, "Just give us a little something now, not too much because what we've got is just fine," and I thought about that and I agree.

And so, this is that little something.

We're going to skip in order to do that, only momentarily because whatever I skip, I'll come back to at another time.

In the 27th verse, Jesus says to John, *"Behold thy mother!"* In the 26th verse, he says to Mary, *"Woman, behold thy son!"*

Now, actually, it's very probable that this Gospel was written about 65 years after it happened. John had written some things earlier. It was called a Jerusalem Gospel but the way this final Gospel ended up is written by the mature John who already had transcended all humanhood. There are some omissions here which are intentional.

Now, John knew who came with Mary. He knew that Mary had been summoned by him at the will of Christ Jesus to come to the crucifixion. He knew that Mary came with one of her daughters and one of her sons. She brought Ruth and I think she brought Jude. But he doesn't say that they were here with her because that wouldn't fit the text of spiritual identity. You notice who he does say are here with her in the 25th verse. *"Now there stood by the cross of Jesus his mother, and his mother's sister, Mary the wife of Cleophas, and Mary Magdalene."* Three Mary's and all following the Spiritual path. He was witnessing Spiritual identity only.

"And when Jesus therefore saw his mother, and the disciple standing by, whom he loved."

It doesn't say he saw his younger brother and his younger sister there. *"He saw his mother and the disciple standing by, whom he loved."* *"He saith unto his mother, Woman, behold thy son!."* And the funny thing is that years before that, he had said to the same mother, *"Woman, what have I to do with thee?"* He then said, "I am not your son" and now he points to John and he says, "John is your son." Isn't this strange?

Mary had eight children but he says, "This one is your son. Even I, Jesus am not your son." He had said that to her three years earlier when he had been at the wedding where water was changed to wine. *"Woman, what have I to do with thee?"* meaning there is no relationship between the I, Spirit of God and a material woman and now he is showing her the other side of this, who her real son is. Her real son in identity realized is always he who has received the Christ.

"And John, this is your mother."

But they were not mother and son in a human-flesh relationship. And so, this again is similar to his teaching us to leave mother, brother, father, sister for my sake. He is renouncing all human relationships and announcing the era of spiritual relationships and he is telling the world that John is the Son of God. John is the real Son of God. Oh yes, Jesus Christ was the Son of God but Jesus Christ now is leaving as an appearance in the minds of men. Who's left on earth who is the

Son of God? To whom shall we look? Shall we look to Jesus Christ? "No," he says, "look to John."

"If I go not away, the Comforter will not come unto you."

How will you receive the Comforter? You will receive the Comforter through John. Now, Let's see what he meant by that.

Let's retrace several steps and pin this one real tight so we understand it. Now, you remember in John 13:23, *"Now there was leaning on Jesus' bosom one of his disciples, whom Jesus loved…. Leaning on his bosom."* You may have remembered, you may remember that when we discussed that we pointed out this was not a physically, a physical fact that he was reporting. This is a spiritual Truth being revealed.

And now, we have its sequel. *"Leaning on his bosom."* We go right back to John 1:8, way at the beginning of the Gospel. That's 1:18. For a moment I thought I missed it but we have it. 1:18, *"No man hath seen God at any time, the only begotten Son, which is in the bosom of the Father, he hath declared him."*

To understand God, you must be in Christ. Christ is said to be *"in the bosom of the Father."* John is said to be on the bosom of Christ and so, there's your sequence. God, the Father to Christ, which is God the Son, to John, which is God the Soul. From the Infinite Father to the Infinite Son through the Soul to you. John leaning on the bosom of Jesus who is in the bosom of the Father. This is the direct chain of command. Oneness is attained then through the realization of God, knowing God aright, through Christ in you which you receive through your Soul faculty. And this is why Jesus says, "Son, there is your mother and mother, there is your son."

The world is to receive its Christ initiation through its Soul faculty. The new age of the Soul is the entrance to the fifth world.

Now, there's one more detail and I've got to go to it. It just seems important right now. On the cross where they divide his garments in four, *"Then the soldiers, when they had crucified Jesus, took his garments, and made four parts, to every soldier a part; and also his coat: now the coat was without seam, woven from the top throughout."*

Now, you won't find that coat in two of the other Gospels. But John has it there for a purpose. Now, his garments are divided into four and this is the revelation that we are in the fourth world. This is the fourth day of Genesis. This is the fourth level of consciousness.

The total Truth, the garments of Christ are the fulness of the Word and when they are divided into four parts, you are being told that you are, as a human being, in the fourth level of consciousness. The fulness of the Word is broken down and we have had four worlds. This is the fourth.

John, just a moment later is designated as the Son because John is the entrance. The Soul is the entrance to the fifth world and that is why John included the coat.

Now, the garments that are divided are the outer garments. Presumably, the sandals, he wore a turban - although people don't usually see a picture of Jesus wearing a turban - the girdle and the cloak. The four outer garments. The four outer garments are divided. There's an inner garment. That's the tunic and this, the soldiers say, "We will not divide this garment. We'll draw lots to see who will have it, who will own it." This is predicted in the Psalms, the 22nd Psalm.

But you see, no garments of Jesus can remain because no matter can remain. Just as the physical form must go, so must all that is material go to show us this is a Spiritual Being. This is Spiritual identity and as these four garments are divided, indicating we are in the fourth level of consciousness, so, it is that throughout the four corners of this earth, in the four elements that comprise this earth, the Truth is divided everywhere and there is no Truth in division. There is only Truth in wholeness.

And so, we must look to Soul to lead us into the next body which is the body of the Soul and that will only lead you to another body which is the body of the Spirit, in the sixth world. And that will lead you to still another, to the Divine Light which is the body of the seventh in which you are a complete, full Self.

But always, the body of Light, the body of Spirit, the body of Soul are always present in the Now, awaiting your entrance if you will walk through the doorway of matter.

So, John now becomes very significant in all our work. We're told there is an Aquarian age to come. It is the age of John. It is the age of the Soul and of the Soul universe. It is the dawn of the Soul universe in our consciousness when the garments which were divided are no longer divided, and we are lifted high into the fifth realm. So maybe that's just the little extra something that will not take away our conscious awareness of the work we ought to do.

Other things omitted by John, you'll notice as you compare the other Gospels and they are because of that period when he was away fetching the mother of Jesus. And whatever he did not witness, he did not report. That doesn't mean these other things didn't happen. It means that he would not report on what he did not witness.

And your assignment for next time - I know I'm jumping you around a bit it seems - but I'd like you to look again at "Transcending Mind" and "Unconditioned Mind" in the "Thunder of Silence." When you read "Transcending Mind" and "Unconditioned Mind," you will see why it is necessary for you to live with the knowledge that only through Soul can you become Self-aware. Then you won't divide his garments.

Now, the outer garments were divided. But Scripture said they would cast lots to own the inner garments and that's how it happened and the reason is that you can only divide the literal meanings of Truth, the outer garments. The inner garment is the imperishable Truth which is not affected by the intellect of man. Man's intellect can divide the outer garments but they cannot divide the inner. That's why John alone could include the inner garment which was indivisible.

The inner garment which is indivisible is You. The indivisible One Self. It is never separated in spite of what man's mind may do. In spite of what may appear, your invisible Self is indivisible because it is the infinite Self. When you have found the inner garment of your Self, which is indivisible, which is the One, Infinite Spirit, then Pilate has no power. Then Caesar, through Pilate has no power. Then the intellect through Pilate has no power. The administrator of the world of powers no longer rules. The indivisible garment is individual identity as the living Spirit of God. God, your individual Selfhood realized. That is the inner garment which is indivisible which is pre-shadowed in the 22nd Psalm.

The world around you may be awry. Everything may seem to be shattered. You can't pull things together. Those are the outer garments of the mind. The inner Self is always One, Infinite, Invisible Being. That inner Self can never be divided. It is always You. It is imperishable and your realization of that One is your realization of Oneness. Then, you're listening through the Soul.

Now, you're having troubles in your human life like everybody else, no matter who you are. They're big ones or small ones. Jesus Christ had a lot of troubles, too. But you stand in this Invisible Self because those troubles are there to make you stand in your Invisible Self. That's what they're for. They're there so that your Invisible Self may erase the illusion of them and only when you're standing in that Invisible Self are you erasing all of the appearances that beset you.

We've only got two or three more chapters now in the Gospel of John and just two chapters in "Realization of Oneness." And so, we're at the place now where you've got to reach a firm awareness that the Invisible Self which could not be divided by the soldiers, by the thoughts of the world, by the thoughts of material power; that Invisible Self is always inviolate. It is always your Infinite identity and you must learn to live in it, to be it, not to just come to it when you're in trouble. Where you are there is no person. There is only your inviolate, infinite, indivisible, incredibly wonderful, glorious, Divine Self.

Live in it, consciously. Look at "Transcending Mind," "Unconditioned Mind," chapters 5 and 6 again in "Thunder." And we'll have a few surprises next Sunday. We'll end with a meditation.

Silence, (pause) ...

But if you are not there as a person, you cannot meditate as a person. And so, just do it that way.

You see, it's effortless when there's no person there to do the meditating. Then you're closer to that realm called John the Soul. You're letting Spirit do all the meditating for you.

Silence, (pause) ...

Much love and thank you again.

Class 40

Hidden Power of Scripture

Herb: I think we'll start today at the 19th verse of the 19th chapter. It reads as follows:

"Pilate wrote a title, and put it on the cross. And the writing was JESUS OF NAZARETH THE KING OF THE JEWS."

Now, I've checked that out against the other Gospels and they read as follows: In Matthew, *"THIS IS JESUS THE KING OF THE JEWS."*

In Mark, *"THE KING OF THE JEWS."*

In Luke, *"THIS IS THE KING OF THE JEWS."*

And only in John do we see *"JESUS OF NAZARETH THE KING OF THE JEWS."* So, we have to say that Nazareth was inserted there by John with a purpose. We also have to see that they can't all be right and that may give you an insight into these differences that occur in the various Gospels at crucial points.

Now, it is agreed that only John was present at the crucifixion of Jesus Christ. It is known that the other disciples scattered to the wind. And you can be sure that they didn't come out of hiding to go up there and look at the cross to see what the inscription read. So, everything they have to say has to do with what they have heard from someone else and John, being an eyewitness, could give us that which he saw with his own eyes. *"JESUS OF NAZARETH THE KING OF THE JEWS."*

And then, the significance of that must be searched for and very quickly, you discover that Nazareth is where Joseph and Mary went after the death of Herod. If you recall, they had gone down to Egypt to get out of the clutches of this madman who wanted to kill every child of two years and under. And then, when Herod had died, and they learned about it, they returned and they went to live in Nazareth and that was where the boyhood of Jesus took place.

Herod is the symbol, you know, of the world mind and Nazareth is the symbol of those who sup with the Christ, those who sip from within. There was a sect in Nazareth, the Nazarites and I suspect that with a little research, we could connect them up to the Essenes because their teaching was almost identical.

The Nazarites, very strangely enough, had no belief in matter, no belief in evil, no belief in destruction and no belief in death. They lived at Nazareth and if you recall at the early part of the Gospel when Jesus was still picking his disciples, either Nathaniel or Philip said, "What good can come out of Nazareth?" And this is what good could come out of Nazareth, one who could lift the world into Divine Sonship.

Nazareth, in the Greek, translated from the Aramaic, means a branch growing out of, and so, Jesus of Nazareth means a branch growing out of and you know what the Christ grows out of; God, a Divine branch.

And so, you see, even those who are not on the path of Spirit are used by the Spirit so that Pilate was obliged through no desire on his part to be a Spiritual teacher, to write a Truth, that this was a man who was a Divine branch.

But further the word "Nazareth" here beside that connotation, is emphasizing that this was a human being. He came from a place on this earth. He could have said this is Jesus of Alameda, Jesus of Palo Alto, Jesus of any city where he had been to emphasize there was a form there and the city that it came from. But the city being Nazareth, is the city which is on the path to Divine Consciousness.

And just as Jesus of Nazareth, upon the death of Herod, was able to live his boyhood in the city which makes one a Divine branch - that city within - so the pathway was opened to all who realize that every person on the earth must go to Nazareth. There's no one here who must not go through Nazareth in order to reach the inner Self. In other words, we must now come to the place where world mind in us has no power, where the only authority is the Spirit within, where we are fed, where we drink deeply from the Truth of our own Being. That is Nazareth.

And that's why *"KING OF THE JEWS"* becomes an important title because it's a symbol. The Jews being at that time the only religion on earth that treasured the idea of one God, they were then a symbol of all religion and the *"KING OF THE JEWS"* though not so accepted by the Jews was not the man named Jesus but the inner Christ, the inner Self of every man. And this was the revelation of a new dimension on the earth, a higher Self, an Invisible Self, an inner Spiritual Being which was King of all religions, of all mankind. And for that reason, it was written in three languages. Pilate wrote it in Hebrew - actually, it says Hebrew - I presume it was Aramaic - in Latin and in Greek. And just as language here means all civilization, you know, like the arm of the Father means the power of God; here, the three languages mean all over the earth. In the language of culture of the Greeks; in the language of religion of the Jews; in the language of power and law, the Latin, all of the three major languages on the earth at the time symbolize civilization. And of all civilization, Jesus of Nazareth who raised himself beyond the concept of mortality into the knowledge of the inner Christ, the Self; that Self was the king of all languages and this was a foreshadowing of the new language that would come. The inner language of the Spirit which all mankind would learn to live in, dwell in, abide in and ascend in, out of the mortality, the matter, the flesh, the form, the limited lifespan of humanity.

And so, Pilate was an instrument without design on his part. And we're going to see how many people are instruments though they know it not. The soldiers here, piercing the side, fighting over the garments; they are instruments. And a very strange thing shows up. We find that it was possible to crucify Jesus Christ but it was impossible to break his legs. They could make him suffer every form of humiliation. They could strike him physically. They can make him bear the cross through the streets. They could spit upon him but, it was impossible, even though they could crucify him, it was impossible for them to break his legs. And for you and me, this is a very vital point.

The reason they could not break his legs is because Scripture said so. The soldiers would have broken his legs. They had been asked to do so. They broke the legs of the two thieves but when they came to Jesus Christ, they couldn't break his legs. We want to look in Scripture. We want to reinforce our understanding there and see how that applies to us.

Here's how it reads in John. First, we want to establish the coat without seam woven from the top throughout, the casting of lots, the parting of raiment. *"These things therefore the soldiers did."*

Now let's look in Scripture and we find that all of this was presaged in the Old Testament.

We find for example, in the 22nd Psalm the following statement - this is 22:18: *"They part my garments among them, and cast lots upon my vesture."*

Now, this is happening more than five hundred years in the Bible before it becomes a visible event in the life of Jesus Christ on the cross. In other words, that which is spoken in the Psalm, through the Spirit, must eventuate as a visible event in the life of Jesus Christ. There's nothing can stop it. Everyone around that event had to act the way they did. They had no choice. They may have thought that they decided to divide the garments or not to divide the inner garment but they absolutely had no power to do otherwise. They were a visible expression of these words which were uttered more than five hundred years before the visible expression. The words and the expression in the visible were one and the same, separated only by what we call time.

And again and again and again, the pattern of this happens *"that Scripture may be fulfilled,"* is repeated until to you and to me, there comes an understanding that whatever is revealed as the Word of the Spirit must ultimately appear in the visible. And there's nothing any human being can do about it. A Pilate can be used. A soldier can be used. A Herod can be used. All those who function in the material flesh are subject to the Word of Scripture even though it may have occurred two thousand years before they appear in the visible world. And no one knows who and where and when those Words of Scripture will come forth in an individual. But one thing you can be sure of, the words of the Father will not return void. The Spirit says, *"Heaven and earth will pass away but my words [will never die]."*

And more and more, you become aware that every commandment given to us by the Spirit must be visibly fulfilled by you. You absolutely have no choice. The Spirit teaches you to love your neighbor whether you know how or whether you want to. You must. And although you seem to delay it, there is no power on earth that can prevent you from ultimately doing just that.

Finally, you will see that your Divine destiny is to become that same individual for whom it was written, *"[THIS IS]JESUS OF NAZARETH KING OF THE JEWS."* It is your Divine destiny to become the living Spirit of God realized because the words have been spoken in Spirit already. *"Be perfect as your Father."*

And the more you become aware that there's no turning back, there's only a false delaying in the dream world of time, the more you are assured, the more you receive signs within for confirmation, the more you will finally set your sights on one goal. Precisely as he worded it, "Pick up your cross and follow Me."

Now, we see Christ going through the streets with a cross on his shoulders. But what is really happening is we are being told that everyone of us is carrying a cross. Your cross is the belief in a material world. You're carrying it with you every day. And now, the time comes to take no halfway measure. The time comes when we must stop digging our grave. And this is done in a different way than we had anticipated. We thought we could learn some Truth. We could memorize some Truth. We could meditate. We could be moral. We could study. We could do everything required of us and also live the lives we'd like to live. This is the place in the Bible where we discover we have no human rights. We discover that the only thing expected of us is to pick up the cross of matter and stop crucifying ourselves.

Carrying your cross through the street, believing in matter is the problem in the world today. The religions of the world worship God in their fashion and while they are worshipping God, the Bible tells us that they are also crucifying their own Being. The belief in a material selfhood is the crucifixion of your Spiritual Self. The Bible has to show us visibly what we have no way of knowing with the mind. It has to bring into the visible those things which we cannot understand unless we see them with the five senses.

And so, we pierce the side of the Christ. What does that mean when water and blood spurt out? It's telling each of us that we have a job to do. We must reach the place where the meaning of that is the attainment of our Consciousness. When the water and blood flows from the Christ it is because that place where the side was split by the piercing is really a sacred lance used by soldiers who had no idea of Scripture whatsoever but again fulfilling Scripture.

They pierced the side by the heart, the symbol of Love. When Divine Love in you is released, the water is transformed to the wine of Spirit. The first birth is changed to the second birth. The first covenant is exchanged for the second covenant and we are reborn not by water but by water and Truth, by water and the Spirit. The water and the blood, is the sign that there is no human being in that body. The water and the blood flowing, is that Love is released this individual from the belief in form. This individual is now ready to move invisibly into foreign countries and to earn a master's wage in the body of the Soul.

And we, who are told to follow the Christ, we too, travel in foreign countries, in invisible mansions, in the Soul body to earn a master's wage, we must now release Divine Love that it may transform the first birth, the water of Truth into the wine of Spirit and there can be no holding back. There cannot be a divided consciousness.

You find that in the vinegar that is given to the Master's lips. In Mark and in Matthew, he's not given vinegar. He's given vinegar with myrrh in one and vinegar with wine with gall in another. And in both cases, it is said, he refuses them. He will not take a mixture. He will not accept wine with gall. He will not accept wine with myrrh. There cannot be mortality and Immortality. There cannot be matter and Spirit. This is the way Spirit shows us that the way to the Kingdom of Heaven is through the realization that I am Spirit; I am not material being. You cannot mingle the wine with the gall, the vinegar with the myrrh but when in John - and John takes us out of the other two Gospels that have a mixture given to him on the cross - he is offered vinegar. It is pressed to his lips. A sponge is placed inside the vessel full of vinegar and the sponge is placed on a reed and that reed in Mark or Matthew is clarified here by John alone. That reed is hyssop and the sponge and the hyssop make the vinegar palatable to the Christ.

Now, this hyssop is another symbolism for purification. It's actually a plant of the mint family and it was used in the Mosaic rites for purification. Now, see the symbolism then. We have a full vessel of vinegar. That's the world mind. But why does the Christ accept the vinegar? It's not pure, living water. It still isn't pure living water. It simply isn't mixed with the myrrh or the gall and the answer is that even though it's not pure, it's coming through the sponge and through the hyssop. And you're being told there that the world mind, the vessel full of vinegar, must be understood. The sponge is part of the purification. The hyssop is part of the purification so that Truth, if your motives are pure, will be transmuted and finally will be acceptable to lead you to the Christ. The difference here then, is the motivation. If you have a pure motive in seeking the Christ, you will gain entrance into the Kingdom. If your motives are for a personal, human reason, you will not.

And so, the vinegar is accepted. You can put it on a sponge with hyssop. You can continue even though you are ignorant of Truth, if your motive is to know Truth, to know God aright, you will find your way into Christhood. But if you're lingering in a sense of division, that you can combine the wine and the gall, the wine and the myrrh, the mortality and the Immortality, the matter and the Spirit, then there is no way to enter into the Kingdom of God.

Always, the Kingdom of God is that Life which is perfect and eternal.

And so, all of this symbolism takes place in John now to show us that the rising of the Christ in you depends upon stepping completely out of the belief that you are now a mortal, material being. You may not have the full understanding of it. You may not have reached that place where you can live totally in that belief, but if you are willing to set that as your goal, to reject the belief in matter, the belief in form, the belief in evil, the belief in every form of error, the belief in destruction and the belief in birth and death, then you too are in Nazareth. You, too, even though you're still not in the purest essence of Being in your consciousness, are fulfilling the law, fulfilling the Scripture. The Scripture that must be fulfilled is your identity, is the living Spirit of God. And whoever, with pure motive, tries to live from that focus will discover that this is acceptable as the vinegar was to Christ on the cross.

That is how Christ in you wants you to approach Christ. Not as a physical being, not as a mortal being, not as a creature in time and space but as one who accepts himself to be without any hereditary past, without any human birth because now, we're at the place where every division in consciousness is a barrier that keeps you out of the final acceptance of Christ in you.

The miracle of Christ must be fulfilled and when you believe in matter, even though you believe you are worshipping God, you are crucifying the Spirit of God within yourself and within your neighbor by your unconscious awareness - your unconscious lack of awareness is more accurate - by your unconscious lack of awareness of the presence of the Spirit of God. That's how we crucify the Spirit of God everywhere. The belief in matter is an automatic crucifixion of the Spirit.

At other levels of our work, it wasn't necessary to be that definite. We had to learn this but now we see that the entire world says, "We worship God," but it also believes that God is guilty of creating evil. It believes that God is guilty of creating matter that deteriorates and at this point, we must know clearly that if you believe in the existence of matter, you are crucifying Christ. You are crucifying the Spirit of God within you which says, "I am the Only." Just to believe that a material form is real is crucifying Christ because there is no Christ and a material form.

And so, the Nazarite, the Essene, those who dwell in the Truth, have this sacred inner duty to perform. They crucify matter instead of crucifying the Spirit of God. This crucifixion is done in the Consciousness. We cannot worship at the throne of matter and worship at the throne of God. And when we reach the sublime height where one individual is able to be crucified in the appearance called flesh without dying, he is demonstrating that this crucifixion without dying is possible to every man. Only he has done it the hard way. Our way is to be crucified in the Consciousness that matter has no existence. This is the inner crucifixion of all those who walk the path of Spirit without opposite.

Again, we cannot worship the written Word unless we are willing to go through with the outer action to conform to that written Word. We cannot, for example, be very anxious to obey certain material laws or even certain religious laws while killing an innocent man and we're given that degree of hypocrisy here. We find it's the Sabbath and it's also Passover and you cannot, in the Judaic religion, leave a man hanging on a tree if he's dead overnight.

In Deuteronomy we're given the law, "no man shall hang on a tree if he's dead overnight." And certainly, no man shall hang on a tree if he's dead on a Sabbath and this is the high Sabbath, a Passover. And so, they want these men down but they're not dead yet. And so, the order is given, "Break their legs." It will hurry it along. That will hasten the death. We don't want them up there desecrating the Sabbath.

You see the hypocrisy of not wanting to desecrate the Sabbath but killing? And the Father has said, *"Thou shalt not kill."* And this is again the way our intellect deceives us. Our intellect says, "Break the legs." And then they go to break the legs and they take one thief and break his legs because they found him still alive and they want to hurry up the death. They go to the next one and they break the legs. They want to hurry up the death so they could get them down before darkness sets in. They come to Jesus to break the legs but he is dead. There's no need to break the legs. But that's what Scripture said five hundred years ago. "No bones will be broken....No bones will be broken." It says in Exodus, in the Psalms and here, the crucifixion of Jesus Christ, in a strange way, it so happens that no bones are broken and the man is taken down. And where is he put? He's put in a tomb. When? On the Sabbath.

Again, the soldiers are being used. They don't know the Scripture. They're centurions. They're Roman soldiers. They had no knowledge of the Old Testament. And they put the man in a tomb on the Sabbath, the eternal rest of One who has found the Spirit.

We are to find that eternal rest. Our eternal rest is when we come to the place of Spiritual Sonship and then not only are the legs not broken but we have found that One Self which is woven from above without a seam, that Indivisible, One Life. That One Life which cannot be crucified, whose bones cannot be broken, who cannot be diseased or sick or deteriorate. This new dimension is being revealed when those bones cannot be broken. Mind you, the man is dead on the cross but his bones cannot be broken. What Spiritual Power is preventing that? The same Spiritual Power that uttered the words way back in Exodus, "No bones shall be broken."

Who uttered those words? The Christ uttered the words then and now the Christ stands in the appearance called death on a cross and the Words cannot be taken away. Their power is still there. *"Heaven and earth shall pass away but my Word shall [never die.]"* The power is forever even on the appearance of a dead man, the power of the Spirit maintains the power of those Words.

Have you heard the Word within you? The power of the Word you hear within you is forever and nobody can take it away. Nobody can oppose it in any way.

Some years back, I heard some Words that were important and I feel I can share them. I was told that "Whenever you ask, I will sup with you" and I have discovered that whenever I ask, whenever I ask the Spirit within by acknowledging its Presence as the only Presence - that's the asking, no division - then that Spirit sups with me. It feeds me. It leads me. It opens my eyes. It removes the blindness of a mortal man. I can depend on this and the reason I can depend upon it is because the Words were spoken to me within. "Whenever you ask, I shall sup with you."

And no matter what the situation may be, I find I can go within and speak to the Christ which is my own Being and rest in the conscious assurance that the supping of the Christ is the Divine Word which is all Power, all Presence, all Intelligence, all Love, all Truth without opposite. That Word needs no human implement, no human instrument. It functions by Itself, though invisible.

And for all of you who have heard any Divine Word within you, you have discovered, I'm sure, that that was a force which could not in any way be obstructed by any human being on this earth. There is no human being nor human condition that can stand in the way of that force of the spoken Divine Word in you. It could prevent the legs of a dead man from being broken because there was something even greater being revealed.

Now then, every word in Scripture, though it was not spoken to you within, to your inner ear, was spoken to you and when you realize that these words, though you did not hear them are being spoken to you now, they are saying, "Scripture in you must be fulfilled."

The Divine Word which says, *"Acknowledge me in all thy ways....* *Love thy neighbor as thyself,"* must be fulfilled. And the promises of those words, "When you acknowledge Me in all thy ways, I will direct thy paths," that is an automatic phrase which functions and there's no power on earth to prevent it because it is Divine law. Scripture must be fulfilled. When you fulfill that in Scripture which is demanded of you, every corollary goes right along with it moving the Red Sea out of the way.

There is a man now crucified and there is no power on earth that can kill him because one with God is a majority. There is a you that is expected to do the same, to reach that level of Consciousness in which you know death is an impossibility because I and the Spirit are one and the same.

The importance here, at this juncture of the Bible, is the complete revelation of the new man, the necessity for Spiritual evolution. There's no way you can forestall it or stop it or prevent it. You can only draw out your own miseries, put yourself in a position where you are divided into good and evil, whereas if the Spirit has touched you sufficiently, to make you brush aside every objection of the human mind, you will see that the only possible way for you is to make every day a conscious fulfilling of the words of Scripture so that you become a living Bible. You are no longer to read the Bible but to live the Bible, to be the living Scripture fulfilled. Christ in you must be fulfilled.

And if you were to spend every day putting it first in the order of business, you would discover that even those things that were so important would still be done well so that you go through the Scripture, you pick out the words of the Christ and you know that these words are commands. These words are like the early days of Exodus or Genesis or Deuteronomy in which certain words were pronounced and then five hundred or a thousand or two thousand years later, they become visible events.

So, these words in Scripture uttered by the Christ are to become visible events in your life that Scripture be fulfilled. That's why John, again and again and again, reverts to that theme. They did so and so, that Scripture might be fulfilled. Now, the they who did it didn't do it for Scripture to be fulfilled. They did it because they had no choice and they had no choice so that Scripture would be fulfilled.

Now, the Spirit has made many pronouncements about you and the only thing that has prevented their actually happening in your life is that you didn't realize that these are Divine law. They must happen and you must come into the rhythm of that to see that you do not try consciously or unconsciously to prevent their happening. And then, you're moving in the Infinite rhythm of the Spirit of God.

"Deny thyself." Thyself is physical being, mortal being, human being with a home and a business and a family and this is the denial. That isn't You. And as it continues to be you, you are standing in the way of Scripture which says, "Deny thyself."

And so, at this point of our work, we very carefully watch every word, every thought, every idea, every action that is taking place on the cross because every word, every eyelash is telling us precisely what we are to do. If they drive five nails into his hands, that means the five senses bind us to this world. If they pierce his side and water and blood flow out, that means, we must in Consciousness do the same. We must come to the heart. We must learn to overlook all that is not Love and come over to the side where all that is Love flows through us to let the subtle transmutation of Divine Love transform us into the image and likeness of the Father.

Now, this is no longer a work for beginners or just veterans. This is a work for those who turn their entire love to God. Loving God supremely means only. You love God in your wife. You love God in your husband. You love God in your child. You love God in your enemy so that all are to you the visible expression of the Invisible Spirit of God and you are sowing only to the Spirit of this universe. We cannot sow to the flesh. We cannot sow to the form. We cannot sow to matter. We cannot sow to evil and by sowing, we cannot accept the belief that that which is not Spirit can exist.

The fulness of the demonstration here on the cross is the fulness of the demonstration that we are to make. We must stand aside from our mortal self and let God make the demonstration of God where we stand.

"And now, the work is finished," he says. That means the work that is finished is the fulness of Divine law revealed on the earth. There's nothing more to say or to teach. It has been said. It has been taught. It has been demonstrated and that demonstration is that there is no mortal being on the earth.

Every healing that you witness should now mean to you something totally different than you thought it meant. People say, "Thank you for healing this one. Thank you for healing that one." And sometimes they say, "What's wrong that you didn't heal this one or that one?" But a healing now means something quite different. If, for example, you were ill yesterday and through Spiritual work, you are not ill today, healing was only the periphery of what happened. What really happened is your Spiritual identity was revealed to you. That's why you are what is called healed. The awareness in one's Spiritual Self that that Spiritual Self is the Only and is the Self of you becomes the Spiritual activity within you breaking through the crust of human consciousness and that healing is the sign to you that you are the living Spirit of God. No matter who is healed Spiritually, that is the proof that they are Spiritual Being and that's the importance of the healing. It reveals your identity. And every healing of Jesus Christ was revealing the Spiritual identity of the victim. This one thought he was 38 years in such a condition. But when he was healed, the revelation was that he was Spiritual Being, not mortal being. Whoever is healed is being revealed as Spiritual Being and that is the meaning of "The work is finished."

He has revealed that all there is on the earth is the Spirit of God. All he's done is take a cross sampling. One here, one there. Two here, two there. But each one is a symbol of all the rest. Every Spiritual healing is the revelation of Spiritual identity and this is the Allness, the Oneness of Spirit everywhere. That there is one Spiritual Being is being revealed by the Christ. The work is done.

And although the work is done, it remains for those who become aware of the nature of that work to now follow in the Consciousness that everyone, everywhere is Spiritual Being, to follow through on that which was revealed by the Master.

His work he says, "*is finished.*"

And that means that the very plan for us to attain the awareness of our Spiritual identity is also completely finished. That in the words of the Christ, in the Bible, is the complete plan of your Spiritual Sonship with God. Some may interpret it for you. Others may explain it another way but the words are there, the demonstration is there, complete, and whoever is turning full love toward God above all is led to the meaning of those words and the way to implement them in our daily living.

If today, we were to accept that I cannot be both Spirit and matter, we would find that a great void would come upon us after a while because of our transition in consciousness. And that void, however uncomfortable it might be, is a very important void because it's a cosmic

vacuum. That void enables you to empty out the old. And that transitional period of emptying out the old is what is called here, *"I thirst."*

"I thirst," says the Christ. This is the transitional period in all of the Spiritual evolution of every individual. As they turn to the Christ within, recognizing the Christ within, they are quenching that thirst. Christ is never quenched within you by your mortality, only by your Immortality accepted.

"I thirst."

Within you, Christ says, *"I thirst."* Turn away from your mortality. Acknowledge your immortal Christ Self and that will quench the thirst of the Christ.

And then, he *"gave up the ghost."*

We have used that expression, "giving up the ghost" but not in the sense that it is meant here in the Bible. They could break the legs of the thieves but they couldn't break the legs of the Christ and yet both appear to be forms. One was a mental image and one was a Divine image. One was a physical concept about an atom body, the other was a physical concept about a Spiritual body.

The flow of blood and water is an ancient sign, much older than Jesus Christ. It signifies the new Soul body is complete. It signifies the individual is living in the Soul body. And the giving up of the ghost then is the yielding of the image called physical form. You and I are to give up the ghost. We cannot walk in the ghost if we were to follow the Christ.

Now, think for a moment of the Essenes, the Nazarites, other sects who had learned the non-existence of the form and realized that however strange this seems to you, there have been men on this earth who have known it and who have lived by it. And there were those who followed the Master who taught it. And this body that could not be broken while on the cross is revealed there not to be like other bodies on the earth.

We are to build the Consciousness of a Divine body which is indestructible, which is immune to all forms of error, all forms of disaster, immune to death and we are told that such a body is a body we already possess and we cannot attain the awareness of that body until we learn in Consciousness to give up the ghost; this form that we think we're carrying around.

In your deeper meditations, you will discover that there was no person in that form on the cross. The water and the blood that spurted out says that there was no person there. In your deeper meditations, you will find a way to know that this is the Truth of you now. All that is lacking is the realization.

When you are able to give up the belief in matter, you will find this ultimates in the externalized awareness that you are not in a material form now. You will be aided in your effort to give up the ghost.

As long as you consider yourself to be in a material form, at this level of the Bible, you are rejecting the Christ. This is what the world is doing. This is what religion is doing. This is what every individual on the earth is doing who is not aware of his own Spiritual Selfhood. And so, we are really a very small, small minority. Perhaps, larger than we realize, once we begin to find many of those who are in sacred and silent teachings.

Once you are in this awareness that you are not in the body, not in the form, you'll find you have a new awareness of the Invisible, something that no words can describe. You will understand why this is a secret teaching up to a point and why for you, it can no longer be just a way of worshipping words but must become a living, daily activity, not in the form.

So, the Wayshower demands of us to give up the ghost.

— End of Side One —

Now, let's meditate for a moment.

We've seen a lot of characters in the Bible with names. We've seen a lot of healings. We've seen a few raised from the dead. We've seen an individual who, though he could be crucified, could not die. Although he had no defense, his legs could not be broken because the power of Scripture had determined that in advance.

And we have heard the Spirit say, through the lips of that One, "*Call no man on earth your father: for one is your Father, which art in heaven.... Ye are the light of the world.*" Not "Ye are the flesh" but rather, "Flesh is grass." "*Ye are the light of the world.*"

And while we're doing this, let's think for a moment of science, in its great projected plans, how it has the world's hoping it would make atomic energy available in the next decade; new plants, new thermonuclear energy to be released and always, the world is hanging on the promises of science or on the promises of religion that we're going to find some great promised land someday.

And here, in our Bible, the Spirit is saying, "Now are you the living child of God." Can you follow science? Can you follow religion

514

if you are now the living child of God? You can follow the Spirit which makes such utterance and it says, "Where you are, I am. I will never leave you. I am the very substance of your Being. I am you."

And now, this wayward mind which is the mind that follows either religion or science or some kind of –ology; this wayward mind is what we separate ourselves from. We see that on the cross, there are two thieves, one on each side and there is the symbolism of the world problem. That's not a man on the cross and that's not two thieves, one on each side. That is the world consciousness hanging on a tree. The world consciousness is brought into visibility as two thieves, one on each side of a man in the center. And we look at it and if I continue in mortality, I'm going to be that one in the center. If I continue in materiality, those two thieves are going to bury me. One is mind and one is matter. The belief in mind and the belief in matter buries the Christ within. This is the nature of the world situation.

Everywhere you go, invisibly, no matter who you're looking at, there are two thieves on the cross and in between them, they are burying and crucifying the Christ. It doesn't matter what their names are, how important they are in this world, they are crucifying the Christ within themselves by the belief in mind and matter. These twin-beliefs are the thieves on the cross, always crucifying the invisible Spirit, turning that individual away from his Self. This is what you're looking at all over the world. Every individual is crucifying himself, unaware of it and yet, this is the symbolism of the two thieves on the cross.

Now, we are to be taken out of that. We turn to one of those thieves. We recognize no human mind. We recognize the Divine Self. We take that thief into Paradise. We recognize the Divine mind there and automatically, in the recognition of Divine mind, there can be no human body. There is only Divine body.

And the Christ within is no longer thirsty. The Christ within is quenched. We recognize the Divine nature of all Being. It doesn't matter what each individual does to himself, we un-crucify him in our Consciousness. We un-crucify ourselves. We un-crucify our children. We un-crucify the world. We do not accept the opposite of that invisible Christ. We do not let the two thieves surround us, one on each side. We're putting on the robe of Immortality. We are accepting Sonship and this is a daily practice, a conscious practice every day until world mind hits this conscious awareness in you and makes no headway.

If you put yourself first as a human being, you're putting Christ second and you'll find that you cannot violate Scripture. You must acknowledge Christ first.

The understanding of this is only a prelude to the living of it, the daily living of it. And even if you put it off one day, that day you will crucify Christ and you'll pay the price for it. This becomes to us the most important work we have. It's more important than the success of anything we think is in our human lives because without this, you're removing the Reality of your Being and you're going to have a paper castle.

With this, you'll find there substance in everything else that you do. You must, each day, un-crucify Christ. Put the vinegar up to the lips of the inner Christ. Recognition, that the inner Christ is your permanent Self and _live_ in this permanent Self every day. Then all the symbolism is taking place, the water and the blood is spurting from the heart, the transmutation is taking place, Christ is being born in your consciousness.

We'll have some very specific suggestions after a few moments recess. (Class break)

See if you recognize this passage.

"And the angel of the LORD appeared unto the woman, and said unto her, Behold now, thou art barren, and bearest not: but thou shalt conceive, and bear a son. Now therefore beware, I pray thee, and drink

not wine nor strong drink, and eat not any unclean thing: For, lo, thou shalt conceive, and bear a son; and no razor shall come on his head: for the child shall be a Nazarite unto God from the womb: and he shall begin to deliver Israel out of the hand of the Philistines. Then the woman came and told her husband, saying.."

And the whole story is pretty much the way it was with Mary. Now, Samson, the Nazarite was born here and you see how this was a foreshadowing of Jesus the Nazarene. There are many foreshadowings and one of the most important at this moment, you'll find' in Isaiah. That incidentally was Judges, Judges 12. (Edit note: Judges 13)

In Isaiah, in the 53rd chapter, we find this. Now, the interesting thing about Isaiah's long-suffering servant is that this again happens five hundred years before the cross. *"He is despised and rejected of men; a man of sorrows, acquainted with grief: and we hid as it were our faces from him; he was despised, and we esteemed him not."* It goes on describing the feelings and the activities that later took place on the cross. *"He was oppressed, and he was afflicted, yet he opened not his mouth: he is brought as a lamb to the slaughter,"* and so forth.

Now, because you begin to know that the Spirit of Christ which speaks through Isaiah is the Spirit of Christ which appears on the cross, that the Spirit of Christ which utters these words in the Bible, in the Old Testament and in the New Testament; this is the Spirit of Christ in you that is going to do these things. And then you begin to see that you have a job, a function. The Divine plan is for you to let the Christ do these things in you without your human interference.

Everything the Christ says in the Bible is to happen in and through you where you are and the Divine plan released to all mankind through the activity of Jesus Christ is that you are to let the demonstration of God take place by renouncing any selfhood, any life, any sense of being that is not Divine.

"Say not, There are four months, to harvest. For now are the fields white to harvest."

And everywhere the Christ walked, the earth people were saying, "Tomorrow there will be a harvest when the Messiah comes" and the Christ was saying, "I am the Messiah. Now is the harvest. Now open your eyes. Now stretch forth your arm. Now is the Red Sea parted. Now does the troubled sea subside. Now is the woman healed of hemophilia. Now is the leper cleansed. Now, now, now are the fields white to harvest." And these are the words of the Christ in you saying, "Now."

The sowing and the harvest are now. Now are you the Sons of God, not tomorrow. Now are you perfect as your Father. Now is there joy and harmony and fulfillment where you are. It is all present, invisible in your Spiritual Selfhood now. The long-suffering Servant in you, the invisible Christ, whom you have starved, who is thirsty, who takes all of the abuse without a word because, we in our ignorance, stand away from our Self; that long-suffering Servant in us is teaching us that now, everything you seek, you are. There is not a promise in the Bible, not one. Every statement of Truth is now in your invisible Spirit, functioning.

And so, the suggestion I'd like to make is that we now come to grips with being living Scripture. We've had enough reading of Scripture. You are that Scripture and your whole life, your whole activity must be the demonstration of living Scripture, the release of the imprisoned splendor.

You say you have a supply problem? God says you haven't. God says, "Now are the fields white to harvest. Where you are there are loaves and fishes invisible." You say you've got a business to run. God says you haven't. God is running the only business there is and that manifests as a perfect business when you know yourself not to be a mortal human being trying to run that business. You say the marriage isn't working or the children haven't caught the idea of their function? You're wrong. They're perfect children. You have to invisibly accept the field is white to harvest now. Not tomorrow. In everything you do. If you're waiting for better health, you're wrong.

If you're waiting for better supply, you're wrong. If you're waiting for new developments, you're wrong. Now are the fields white to harvest.

And if you will re-translate your life at this present moment so that every level of it in which you seem to be lacking in some way or limited is changed in your consciousness, not out in the outer world, removing the belief of every lack and every limitation whether it's health or business or supply or what not. Remove the belief because humanly, you cannot see the invisible harvest that is there and build yourself the faith that the Christ which speaks and says, "Now are you perfect as your Father," is telling you a Truth. That means perfect in every way.

Please make a list to yourself in order of lack and limitation and take a great big cross in your consciousness and cross out that list. Sit with it if you have to spend hours until you can agree this limitation, this lack, this problem, this error, this that I'm trying to accomplish is already accomplished. When you can agree that this is the Spiritual truth of your Being, you will find that the Scripture must be fulfilled when it is accepted in your consciousness. And if you accept it, you will find new beliefs, new seeds, new thoughts and these new beliefs, these new seeds will come forth. They will show you what you thought was lack was only your lack of awareness of the Spiritual nature of your Being, your lack of awareness that the Scripture was telling you the Truth of who you are.

Now, let's take any specific case. Let's take health. Everybody's interested in health. None of us want to be sick. None of us want to be sluggish. None of us want to be drained of energy. Do you know the biggest problem in our health is that we still haven't learned that there is no bad health? We still think it can be. Just think of yourself, how many times you say, "Look what I've got" as if you've got it. You accept it as a condition. The least you can do at this stage is to know that it's an illusory condition. That's the very least you can do. You can't set yourself as knowing more than God. When God pronounces you perfect, when God says, "All I have made is good and you are my

Son," you can't talk about your bad back. You see, that's still a belief in you. You've got a bad back. You can't do that. You can't have a bad back. Otherwise, you're saying "God doesn't know what God is talking about. I still have a bad back." And that belief that lingers is the dream. That's the hypnosis.

You say, "My business isn't good." Or "My children aren't doing what I'd like them to do." You're wrong. You have no right to like them to do anything. They are perfect as your Father, as their Father. Your function as a Spiritual Being is to live in a Spiritual awareness, not to pass human judgments about yourself or others. And unless you precede everything you do with the knowledge that the field is already white to harvest, that right where that problem or that problem or that other problem seems to be, there is invisible, Spiritual perfection and nothing else is there. Right where that bone seems to hurt, there is invisible perfection and nothing else is there and you must hold to that Truth that the fields which are white to harvest are your own Spiritual Being and the Spiritual Being across the way. Everywhere you must hold to that and you will discover the fields are white to harvest. Then, you will be crucifying the problem, the belief and not the Christ of your Being. This is the suicide we come out of when we start to accept the words of Scripture above our own concepts. Scripture must be fulfilled in you. Christ in you must be fulfilled.

Now, that's a pretty simple and definite Divine law. Christ in you must be fulfilled.

Another weakness we have, a very big weakness: is there's always a me there trying to get something done. There's always a me trying to even understand the Truth and when you may not be aware of it, you completely feed this me. You want this me to have certain harmonies. You want certain things around you to change so that the me over here can be more comfortably situated. That's all the wrong focus. You want this me to have a better job. You want this me to have a happy marriage. That's the wrong focus. You're working out of a false sense of self. You must learn that there is no me here. There is only the Christ of God here and that means, at this level, we have no personal desires, no earthly desires.

Before Jesus gives up the ghost, he bows his head. The bowing of the head is the complete surrender of the human ego. Everything is significant. He bows his head to tell us that you must learn to bow your head. The complete surrender of the human selfhood and as long as there's a human selfhood there, there's going to be a bad back or a bad child or a bad relationship. There's going to be good and there's going to be evil in human relationships. When there's no human self, you have bowed your head and then, you can give up the ghost. There must be no human self in your consciousness.

I was up at 4 am this morning and it took me two and half hours to even make a dent before I could feel that something was happening and I remember when we first started in this work and Joel used to say, "Well, we've got to have two or three meditations a day."

Now, you discover that if he had told you what you had to do, you might never have continued in your work. You don't have two or three meditations a day. You live in the Truth all day. You don't step out of the Truth. Your whole life is a meditation. Everything you do is a meditation with your eyes opened or closed. And then, he had ten second meditations for those who didn't have the time so they could just blink an eyelid and say, "I am the Christ" and go on their way.

I want to recommend to you that you take a day, and get up before the world does and don't mind if the first two hours are a problem to you. Don't mind a bit. Don't mind how much you feel you're getting nowhere. Just keep knowing the Truth in various ways about who you are until all of a sudden, out of nowhere and you can't explain why or when, there You are. Suddenly, it's taken right out of your hands. Suddenly, someone else is driving the wheel, it's not you. You don't know how it happened. Something lifted you right out of your thought, right out of your contemplation and now, you're in My Peace. We've been trying to get peace in our lives and the Spirit says, "Oh no, that's not the right way to do it. You want the peace of the world, human peace. It won't work. My Peace is not as the world giveth."

There's a new dimension of Peace when you are able to get to the place where it's taken out of your hands and then the soft, gentle Spirit calls you because it now is You and there's no human being there. In that moment when there's no human being there, you are meditating and not before. All of your statements, that's not meditation. Even the psychic trance is not meditation. It's when suddenly, there's no you; only the Spirit is there. Then you're in meditation. You're in the Father. And then you see why the fields are white to harvest because in that Spiritual you, everything is happening the way it should be. Scripture is being fulfilled. Everything in Scripture is happening. The promises are Being, not becoming, Being.

Now is the time for work then. Time to know that because I am accepting that I must step out of the sense of mortality, I've got to work at it and I won't be able to close my eyes for three minutes and come to that conclusion and go on my way. I've got to really put in the time.

And so, if you haven't yet come to that conclusion and are ready to, you've got to take one day a week to see what I really mean. One day in which this is what you're about to do. There's nothing else on your mind that day. You get up before the world does and you go to work. There's nothing else you have got to do that day. If after two, three, four, five hours you find you've got it, great. It'll take care of the rest of the day. You can go about all the things you wanted to do. You'll find this new dimension makes you sail through those things. But put in this two, three hours stretch. If you're lucky, if it's so meant for you, you might find in twenty minutes you've got it. But if you don't, that's par for the course. Don't worry about it. Sometimes we go two or three days before this thing gels. There's no miracle meditation. It's work. Hard work. And it only becomes easy work when you're finding yourself doing it every day.

Now, then those of you who haven't yet had the great pleasure of meditating before the world is awake, contemplating, resting and struggling too; get with it and don't mind the struggle. And make your object one thing. I'm putting my mortality on the cross because that's what we're about to do. Putting my mortality on the cross and I'm going to have to wrestle with this thing in the wee hours of the morning, two, three, maybe four hours. With a little rest, I might have to go out and get some coffee. I might have to keep the pot percolating. I might have to do all kinds of things just to break it up a little bit so I just don't fall into a trance but I'm going to stay with it until I can come to a conclusion. Mortality was never my Self.

You are joining, uniting with your pre-existent Self which is simply the removal of the sense of mortality. When he gave up the ghost, he was telling you he was re-joined with his pre-existent Self. All he was, was what he always was. Nothing else.

Your pre-existent Self is your present existent Self and only when you go through this inner scourging of this sense of mortality will you suddenly find lifted out of your hands and you'll be on that flying carpet of Spirit.

Now, I know meditation is supposed to be an effortless thing but it only gets to be effortless after you've gone through a great deal of effort. And you've got to put forth that effort. You've got to be a striver with God. You've got to wrestle with the intruder. You've got to find a way of being just as persistent as the world mind is in you and quench the thirst of the inner Christ.

Now, start with Scripture and remember, it applies to your Being. It's not about ten other fellows. It's about your Being and take it into your early morning contemplation, wrestle with it, till you can agree; this that I have read in the Scripture, I am doing. I am a living Bible.

And then each day, add to your armament of Truth that way. You'll find these depth bombs will really unseat the world mind in you like nothing else.

You are lifting up the I. Don't complain about world conditions. There aren't any. Don't complain about the noise of the neighbors. Don't complain about anything. These are human judgments and there's no human there where you are. Judge not lest ye be judged. You judge yourself every time.

Now, then, make the effort to overcome the sense of mortality, to bow the head for the plan is complete. The Divine plan is clear. You must accept that you are immortal Being and all that goes with it is true, now. This that I am suffering from cannot be a fact. This must be a supposition, a concept. This that is wrong in my business cannot be a fact. There is no such thing as a bad business. This is for mortals.

Everywhere you go, everything you do comes out purified. Put the hyssop on the sponge. Feed it to the lips. Purify everything you do with the knowledge that invisibly, this is perfection and it is here now. And you'll find there is a rainbow that is going to come into your Consciousness. In other words, you're Spiritualizing everything you know because it is already invisible Spirit. You can take this as far as you're willing to take it, as far into time as you care to go because the complete harvesting of the field is already complete where you are now. There's nothing for you to do but to go through the effort, the action in the visible of harvesting what is there now in the Invisible by the silent acceptance of Christ within, everywhere, everyone. There is no mortal. There is no matter on the face of the earth.

And that's what the Father says to us. That's what we learn to say, "Yes, Father." I have no pain in the back. I have no financial problem. I don't care if I haven't got a dime. That's not what I go by. I go by the Father's Word. "All that I have is thine, Son. Be still. Thou art ever with me."

Thank you, Father. I have all that there is in the Father's house now. And never will I waver and let another thought enter where another thought would not be the thought of the Father. It would be mortal thought and where there is no mortal, there can be no mortal thought. Even while the tears are running down your cheek, you must learn to do this.

Then suddenly, the agony of Job is changed. The living Spirit heaps upon him all of the glories of the invisible Kingdom. Everything is recovered double. Why? Because Spirit multiplies. Matter is always division. No good matter. No evil matter. Only pure Spirit.

Put matter on the cross and the Christ will announce Itself where you stand.

Next week, please come prepared to, within yourself, listen to the Spirit's understanding of the chapter called, "Lifting the I" the eleventh chapter in Joel's book, "Realization." You've read it three or four times by now. At this point, we want to see that "Lifting the I" means the crucifixion of mortal sense. Crucifixion is the only way to resurrection. The path of the cross is the path to resurrection.

Well, a happy December and a happy holiday season to those who we won't see this month again, and to all of you who will be here next week, we must pursue this path of resurrection now to the point of realization.

We'll see you soon and thanks again.

CLASS 41

TURN OFF THE WORLD

Herb: First, an announcement about our class schedule. This series is going to end on the second Sunday in January. That's the 14th of January. We'll go right through, that means this year, we continue every Sunday. This is the 10th. We'll be here on the 17th, the 24th, the 31st and the 7th and the 14th of January. Then there'll be a month recess and we start again on the 11th of February which is the second Sunday in February. We stop the second Sunday. That's the last class in January. We begin the second Sunday in February.

Now, when we begin there are only going to be seven classes. In other words, we go straight through the end of March. And those seven would be a special seven and that's going to be the termination of our work in San Francisco at the end of March.

And so, what we want to do now is to spend these five sessions and then those seven, if we can, together and I think today's lesson, "Lifting up the I" is probably the nature of all the work we will do until the end of March. "Lifting up the I."

Now that is the title of the 11th chapter in Joel's book, "Realization of Oneness."

"Lifting up the I" was given to the world by the Master's statement, "I will give you the keys to the kingdom." And when we realize that this *I* he spoke of was not his person, not his human selfhood but *I*, the Christ of you, will give you the keys to the Kingdom, then we see that lifting up the *I* is learning to recognize Divinity in yourself, in everyone you know throughout the world.

Now, let's go back to a time when as a girl, you hadn't yet worn high heels or as a man, as a boy, you hadn't yet put on long pants. I know how girls are. They just can't wait for that first time that they can step into those high heels. And then, one day it happens. Now, when you are wearing those high heels, you're not wearing the low ones and usually, as you become more mature, that becomes the accepted way for the woman to dress except when she's walking somewhere or shopping and that sort of thing. You don't turn back. When the man changes into his long trousers for the first time and then grows up, that's his way of life. He doesn't turn back.

And similarly, in the Spiritual work, when you turn to *I*, when you learn who *I* is, you learn that you cannot turn back and this is hard. We want to turn back because there are so many pleasant memories in the world but you cannot wear high heels and short heels at the same time. You cannot lift up the *I* and then turn around and honor the me.

And so, this is a commitment. As you learn to lift the *I*, you're pushed further and further. There comes a moment when you realize that mortality has got to be abandoned and this may be that moment for all of us. There is a world consciousness now which is being shattered. Possibly, typical of it is the way a magazine like "Life" can fold up.

Certain things are happening and they should be recognized. "Life" gave us its reasons for folding up – three. One, that that it had too much specialized competition; higher postal rates - I even forget the third one - but it didn't give the real reason. It didn't fold because of these reasons. It folded because the consciousness of the world is changing and it hasn't kept pace. You can't just show a photograph of women's lib and think that is covering their needs or a photograph of the new activity at colleges and think that is covering their needs. The world consciousness keeps changing and when a woman's liber looks at "Life" magazine, there's nothing in it for her anymore. When a person learning what life is really all about looks at "Life" magazine, it's just something for ten minutes and then you throw it aside. The truth that sticks to your ribs isn't there. And so, the magazine folds, oh yes, advertising, it didn't have advertising. But the reason it didn't have enough advertising, the reason it likes to say postal rates put it out of business and the new era of specialization, is simply that it has not caught a way of fulfilling the need of mankind.

We find that everywhere, we're being forced to take a new inventory of our own consciousness. Things that at one moment seemed so right, a moment later appear to be not quite as right. We're growing up Spiritually and we don't seem to know it. In this growth, we're learning that there is a Divine Self and although this has not surfaced into the consciousness of everyone, this is the cause of much of the unrest that goes on in our world. The invisible nature of the Divine Self asserting itself on and through the human consciousness causes unrest and it's wise for us to see that we have been given an invisible pathway out of this world.

We were in a home the other night and the woman wanted to show us the hunting trophies of her husband. They have been very successful. She had been very successful, too. They were both career people but they're not together today. He passed on five years ago and her statement was "They've got to do something about that disease." And the question is, what can anyone do about it? She who vehemently sought some way to find something to do about that disease would not even understand or recognize what has been taught to the world to do about it. As much as she desires to eliminate that disease, she's not prepared to do so when given the information on what she should do because she does not know how to lift up the *I*.

The only way that disease and countless others are eliminated from this world are through an enlightened world Consciousness, through Spiritual understanding that here where we stand, there is an invisible realm and that Spiritual law cannot be ignored.

Now, I don't know if this woman thought of where this particular disease came from that took her husband away but I know one thing and that is God did not create that disease. And I do know who created it. The universal consciousness created it and we have allowed the universal consciousness to imprison us in these bodies that deteriorate and are subject to all forms of error. By one word alone – infidelity. Our infidelity is to the Divine Self that we are. By not abiding in your Divine Self, you become a separated self and in the not abiding, in the becoming separated, we lose all contact with the Grace of God so that without realizing it, we're really hanging on by a thread which we call a lifespan. And because Scripture tells us what to do, which is Divine law, and we do not do it, we create the very diseases we try to avoid. Karma is the effect which comes about through mankind not abiding in Divinity and whoever in a measure abides in Divinity which is the I of your Being, the I of everyone's Being, you find you nullify the karma, the ignorance, the superstition, the false powers of the world.

Now, right in this room right now, there is an invisible thief - that's the carnal mind. It wasn't invited but it's always present and if you are not abiding in the Divine Self of you, it will steal you away into that realm which is not Reality and you will find yourself asleep, walking in a dream called mortality. And in that mortality, you will suffer all those things that are not God created which we call the destructive elements of this world.

And only by abiding in your Divine Self do you step out of these destructive elements. When that becomes clear, we finally choose Immortality as the nature of Being. You cannot be Divine Self and mortal self and to lift the *I*, you begin peeling away all of the false, the conditioned, the inherited concepts of the world consciousness.

Scripture comes to your aid. Your righteousness must exceed the righteousness of the scribes and the pharisees or else you cannot enter into the Kingdom of Heaven which is a very oriental way of saying, "Unless you abide in your Divine Self, you cannot experience the perfection of Reality." The place whereon thou standest is the invisible realm, unseen to human eyes and while you are not abiding in Divinity, the thief functions through your senses and your senses become a channel for the mirage and that mirage is where every error and problem of this world is contained.

And so, we're beginning to face one important fact. To lift the *I* out of mortal sense, out of human sense, out of the belief that there is good and that there is evil, to go beyond the voicing of Truth for the Father has told us that you must be reborn of the water and the Spirit, of the Truth and the Spirit.

And so, we must go beyond truth as we know it humanly. We must leave the lulling pleasures of the senses, the lulling pleasures of matter, the lulling pleasures of the world. We must go beyond into the realm of Spirit, out of the high heels, out of the long pants, out of the humanhood and we must pass into the next realm of Being.

I will give you the keys to Reality. You come face to face with *I* in the midst of you and you are told, "Abide in *I* and you will bear fruit richly." And the word "abide" says that doesn't mean part time or halfway. You cannot abide in *I* while you're abiding in a mortal sense of life.

To abide in *I* means to yield, to surrender, to make of yourself a living sacrifice. The Master set the tempo for us. "I give my complete humanity as a living sacrifice." There is no mortal selfhood left as you learn to accept the *I*.

Now, it would be foolhardy to look at the testimony of Jesus Christ and pretend to ourselves that he said less. We clearly see a total crucifixion made visible to human eyes so that even human eyes cannot deny it. There is no Spiritual Self and a material self. There is no Immortal Self and a mortal self. There is no permanent Self and a temporary self. And you don't have to be a detective to know that the forms we inhabit are temporary selves.

Right here, where the temporary self is, there is *I*, the permanent Self. *I*, the Self that existed before there was time and space, before there was a world, before there was a human being on the world - *I*, the Self that will always exist - and we must lift the consciousness to know that this *I*, I am. This second that *I*, I am. When you live in your Infinite *I*, consciously, you are nullifying every discord in the world. You are abiding. You are sowing to the *I*, the Spirit. Sowing and abiding are one and the same.

If you sow to matter, if you believe in the existence of matter, though you be humanly righteous, though you be a philanthropist, though you be kind and merciful, though you be compassionate and cooperative, you must reach the place where you see that one hundred percent human perfection is not acceptable to God. Your righteousness must exceed one hundred percent human perfection. Otherwise, somebody will be looking at your trophies and wondering why you're not there to share them and enjoy them with them.

There is no such thing as human perfection. It's as much a mirage as the good and the evil of the world. There is no good matter. There is no evil matter. "There is only my Spirit," says the Father. And the *I* of you is the Spirit of God. The Spirit of God which is your permanent Self is named *I* and *I*, that Spirit, that permanent Self which you are, is the key to the realm of this perfection which is invisible everywhere on this earth.

And so, we're sowing, abiding in *I*. *"Abide in me....* and you will bear fruit richly.... Acknowledge Me in all thy ways and I will direct thy paths." The Father taught that the first commandment is to acknowledge *I*. To acknowledge God in all your ways means to acknowledge the *I* of your Being as the Self of you and to recognize that you are that Divine I, that Divine Life and to abide means that because I am that Divine I, that Divine Life, I accept no opposite and no substitute. I am the *I* which the world knows as God. That is my permanent Self and I have no temporary self. *I* have no self that is subject to material powers. *I*, the Spiritual Self which is the Self of God, which is otherwise known as the Father within, I am not subject to material powers. I am not subject to disease. *I* am not subject to death itself.

I cannot be crucified. *I* cannot die or be sick. *I* cannot be hurt. *I* cannot be limited or lacking. *I*, is your name and to abide means that you cannot accept conditions which deny who you are. How can you hurt if your name is *I* and therefore, what is this hurt? It is the mirage of the world mind and it is using your senses as a channel for you to declare that you are not *I*.

In every area of your human lifespan, by the sheer belief that you are material being in a material world, you deny who you are and this is the human separation from Reality.

Now, the habits that must be started to abide in *I*, to lift up the *I*, to sow to *I*, to acknowledge *I*, to realize that *"I and the Father are one,"* and the same *I*, are very difficult habits to start because that invisible thief in our midst is always working and you can't find him. You can't draw a blueprint and put it on a piece of paper. You can't put a searchlight on this invisible thief. You can't padlock him. He's always present as a spur and yet, unless you are aware that he is present, he will always outwit you.

And so, you accept the invisible presence of the world mind. You can give it any name you like. You can call it carnal mind, world mind, the glass darkly, universal belief, the thief, the deceiver, Satan, the devil, but you must know that this invisible, universal mind of man is ever functioning and all of the evils in the world and all of the good in the world are contained within it.

God never made a volcano. The world mind makes volcanoes and they are mirage. God never made poverty or famine. They're made in the world mind and they are mirage. God never made a disease. They're made in the world mind and they are mirage. God never made physicality. It's made in the world mind and it is mirage. *I*, which existed forever and will exist forever, I am not in the world mind and if you stand in *I*, you are out of the mirage. You are awakened out of the cosmic dream in the world mind.

Only *I* can give you the keys to the Kingdom. We learn to accept, my name is *I* and all that *I* is, I am. The Father tells us, "*Be still and know that I am God.*" Therefore, *I* is God because the Father says so and *I* is my name because the Father says so. And "*I and the Father are one,*" because the Father says so and that is who I am. I am *I*, the very Self same *I* that is the I of God. And when I am not abiding in this knowledge, I become a branch cut off, a separated branch and I find myself vulnerable because I am living in a false state of myself. In that separation, the powers of the world to me are power even though they are no power to *I*. I'm out of center. I'm in a false body, a false series of relationships and a false world. I cannot control my own destiny. I am controlled by the world mind, the invisible thief.

The moment I am separated from *I*, the invisible thief controls me and may even make me appear to be very successful and healthy and then wipe it all away. And so, I make a living sacrifice of this mortal me which was created in the world mind. That mortal me created by the world mind through birth is not *I*. My past is not a true past. All of the destructive elements in that past, all of the sin, all of the errors are untrue. They were world mind appearing as a me that wasn't me. They were world mind appearing as a mortal self and there is none, for *I* is my name. *I*, is your name and there can be found no mortal being in *I*. *I*, is the name of every individual you know. Divinity is the only Self that is present and only when you stand in that Divinity do you render null and void the false powers of the world that use the senses and the mind as a channel through which they project those disturbances which ultimately lead to final death.

The fact that it was done by the Master and taught to his disciples and practiced by those who secretly have studied the Word of Truth for centuries, the fact that a Joel Goldsmith appeared to preserve this Truth in a record or twenty-nine books and nine hundred tapes and to demonstrate in his life that we can demonstrate it in our lives, is ample evidence that this is the way through which we move through the false world consciousness of death.

We're learning to abolish disease and destruction and death in our lives and we're being trained for a higher purpose. And I do believe that when we have finally completed our work here together, that many of us will be prepared to do successful world work. We'll be independent of the false consciousness of the world. We will be able to move in Divine Rhythm, in an awareness of our Divine Body, our Divine Mind, our Divine Life, free of the tribulations of the world.

Just to give you an idea of how we're being forced to it, there was a man phoned this morning about his cattle. Four fell dead. Some weeks back, two fell dead. And by this time, he was becoming quite frantic. However, he couldn't tell what was wrong. It wasn't the frigidity of the air. There was some kind of an epidemic of some kind and he couldn't put his finger on it. In fact, he called me before he called a vet. I think he called from Nevada. I'm not sure. I don't know the man.

But the point is that I learned, that this man was studying our tapes. He's not a student of our class in the physical sense but one of our students has been lending him some tapes and so he was impressed with the possibilities that lay ahead for him. He simply hadn't yet reached that Consciousness where his consciousness was the Divine Consciousness so that his head of cattle could benefit by this awareness. Next problem is, suppose the other hundred and fifty head were contaminated? He'd be wiped out.

Now, that man is being forced by this invisible thief to come to a higher level of himself. If he didn't know about the Infinite Way work, he'd probably wonder what in the world can he do about it. He knows there is a way and I'm quite sure that he's going to find that way because he's forced to. It's a matter of complete failure in business or success and so, he's forced to do it on a human level. But one advantage is his that isn't available to many others, he at least knows that there is a way and now he'll be forced to find and cultivate the higher levels of that way. This is the karma of an individual who has been part of the world consciousness. And had he been one hundred percent perfect humanly, it wouldn't have made any difference. The world consciousness plays no favorites.

And if you've been pushed, your back against the wall, too, you'll find its because knowing the way and not taking advantage of the way, but rather trying to live sort of midstream, riding two horses, you're being forced to accept that the only way is *I*, the Divine Self of you. There is no second way. Lot's wife couldn't turn back - when she did, she was through.

"Two will be on the field and one will be taken away." The mortal is taken away. The Immortal remains.

Finally, it's crystal clear, Immortality is the nature of Being. There is no mortal on the face of the earth. There is only Divine Self and whoever is able to abide in that consciously, day in and day out, discovers that *I*, my own Divine Self, makes me Self- complete, Self- fulfilling, independent of the conditions of the world.

Now, what you are also tells you what you are not. Every quality of *I* is every quality of God. *"Son, all that I have is thine."* I have all that God has because I am that *I*.

Now, because *I* have all that God has, the opposite condition cannot be true. Although the opposite condition is what appears, it cannot be true. *I* have all that God has. That is the Divine law and your name is *I*. The *I* that you are has all that God has right now. Therefore, whatever denies it is a lie. If you live in the conscious acceptance that you are *I*, the Son, and that the Son, *I*, has all that the Father has because the Father has said so, then you accept that here where *I* stand, all that God has, *I* have. And whatever God does not have, *I* cannot have. God does not have disease. *I* cannot have disease. God does not have poverty or famine. God does not have old age. God has nothing except perfection therefore, *I* have nothing except perfection.

But the thief says, "Look at this, you cut your finger." The thief says, "Look, your tires are wearing thin." The thief says, "Look, you've got an old car. You need a new one and you don't have the money to buy one." The thief says, "Your parents are suffering." The thief says, "Your children are on drugs." The thief says everything except what God says and the human mind trained to believe at face value what it hears and sees, accepts the thief which steals away your Divinity.

The enlightened One, however, can recognize the thief for every expression of imperfection is a denial of your own Being. Every expression of imperfection is a temptation to you to make you not abide in *I* which is the key to the Kingdom.

So, there's this little something in us now. We'll call it our consciousness. It's like a lawn mower. You've got these lawns of grass, let's say the grass is three or four inches high and you push the mower through the grass and you cut a swathe. That swathe depends upon the width of the mower, the sharpness of the blade and so on. That is like your consciousness. Your consciousness cuts a swathe through the invisible and what it comes up with is what appears. The quality of that consciousness determines what expresses, what appears. If that consciousness is living in *I*, when it cuts its swathe through the invisible, it expresses the qualities of *I* and then in the visible, you find I am the Peace. I am the Wine. I am the Water. I am the bread of Life. I am the Harmony. All that I am, thou art because we are one and the same and all that appears not to be what I am, is mirage. The broken bone is mirage and the bone that isn't broken is mirage. There is no good matter. There is no evil matter. There is only *I*, the invisible Spirit.

Absent from the mortal sense of life, we are living in the *I* and daily, you pick that *I* up, up, up, never letting it fall down.

Five seconds from now, after you hear something, you will do what you've always done in spite of hearing it. When you were told to look at your neighbor and know that only Divinity is there, you will do it and five seconds later, you'll be seeing Mrs. Smith and Mrs. Jones again instead of Divinity. But that's the thief in you who sees Mrs. Smith and Mrs. Jones. We must learn to look at Divinity, not at the appearance called form. You see the form of the I with your physical senses but you see the invisible Divinity with the *I* of your Immortal Self and that is the *I* to cultivate. You can only greet a Divine Being. You must see Divinity everywhere. You must abide in *I*. You cannot see humanhood anywhere and be abiding in *I*. It's an absolute point that the Divine law says, "Abide in *I*."

And so, it's departing from the old habits. You must change and the change is not partial. The change is total. This is the change which says, "Take off the garment of mortality. Put on the robe of Immortality." Do not try to patch up the old consciousness. Do not pour new wine into the old mind. It's a completely fresh start from a new focus and it's a conscious, continuous awareness that I am *I*, Divine Self, not living in a mortal form. I am that *I* which never knew physical birth. I am that *I* which can never know physical death. I am that *I* which is the Christ which could be physically crucified on a tree without dying. That *I*, I am. I am the deathless *I*, the *I* that is never sick, the *I* that can never be hurt by man or beast. This is identity, lived in, not for a minute or an hour or a day; a total change of consciousness. And as we live with it daily, abiding, rejecting all that denies it, we find we are never denying the presence of God anywhere. There is no place in Heaven, on earth, in the sky or in the wild where God is absent, for *I* is the Infinite *I* and that Infinite *I* is everywhere. In that Infinite I that is everywhere, there is no evil. There is no disease. There is no matter. There is no mortality. There's no place to go except into *I*.

If you do what comes naturally, you identify with people. You have four cattle that were killed. Your pipes break because of the frost. Your car breaks down. This is identifying not *I*, not abiding. This is accepting the opposite.

As you continue, that which at first seems like a denial of obvious facts, turns out to be a revelation of the nothingness of all error. It makes no difference what the error is. All material existence is the error. And there's nothing you can do about it. It will continue to be the error. Any belief in the existence of matter is not abiding for abiding means abide in Spirit.

If you believe in the existence of matter, you are breaking Divine law and if, in your life appears a series of problems, that is the karma which you have accepted, which you have invited by your belief in the existence of material world.

This is where we must now stand. You must know that if you choose to believe that matter exists, you are denying the Allness of God which is the Spirit of the universe. There cannot be the Allness of God and matter, too. There is Spirit or matter and your life, your experience, depends on which you accept as Truth. Allness of Spirit or Spirit and matter or just matter. If you're divided, your divided consciousness brings back both good and evil. If you're Oned with Spirit, out of the divided consciousness, you find that all that comes back to you is that Oneness with the Father which expresses his qualities in you.

Finally, the decision is always yours - if you know the facts and I think you should know the facts by now. You are making the decision about tomorrow. You're saying my tomorrow will be with good and with evil or my tomorrow will be perfect. And you're making that decision by whether or not this instant and the next instant and the next instant, you are accepting that only Spirit exists or you're accepting that there is Spirit and matter.

When you're single pointed to the knowledge that only Spirit exists, you're following the Master's teaching. And that's half the battle. The acceptance that only Spirit exists makes possible the development of ways and means and techniques to be true, faithful to the fact that only Spirit exists. That fidelity to Spiritual identity enables you to look past the errors of human beings and to recognize that they are nothing but the invisible, universal thief appearing.

And so, the whole world is taken out of condemnation in your eyes. You don't have good and bad people anymore. You don't have good and bad children. You don't have good and bad anything. You can even know that four cattle were killed and yet, you can see this is the universal lie. Somehow out of that, good will show forth Spiritually. You can't anticipate how. It may be that you're lifted higher and that will be the good.

In one way or another, nothing has happened because that which God does is all that can happen. The self-crucifixion is the birthing of *I* in you. When you are birthed in *I*, rebirthed, you are returning to *I* that you ever were. This mortal self is now seen to be a shadow of thought.

It's not a question of, "Don't I have a heart or pair of lungs or ears?" It's a question of who I am. I am Divine Spirit and therefore I am not living in lungs and heartbeats. The change is total. I am being lived by the Spirit of God independent of the world of matter and if the world of matter were to crucify this body *I* would still be standing here. This must be the conscious knowledge that *I* can never die. I am the living Spirit of God and in this knowledge, in your fidelity to it, in little things and big things, you begin to sense that there is a new law functioning in your whole Being - a Divine law, with Divine action, with Divine rhythm, with Divine intelligence. The change of consciousness becomes the change of life.

Now, the habits you start then are very specific. If I am to obey that Scriptural command which says, *"Abide in me,"* I must know who me is. God says, *"Abide in me."* For God is Spirit and I must abide in Spirit and the name of Spirit is *I*. I must know that I am *I* and that's how I abide and if I abide in *I*, that's who I am twenty-four hours a day.

The old-world ways will keep giving me a human name and a human description but I am to be faithful to the Father and so, *I* do not answer to that human name and that human description and *I* cannot be moved by human desires and human ambitions. *I* already have all there is.

Now, as I meet those who walk in form, the *I* that I am is the same *I* that they are. What they know or do not know makes no difference in my injunction to abide in *I*. I must transfer my abiding in *I* where I am to also abiding in *I* where they are. Whoever I meet, I still must continue to abide in the *I* of them. And so, I'm abiding in *I* in me and *I* in him and *I* in her and *I* in the tree and *I* in the river, *I* in the world. *I* in everything there is. You abide in *I*. There's no breaking of that abiding consciousness. No matter where your *I* lifts you, there's still only *I* there. No matter what you touch, there's only *I* there. You continue the unbroken *I*. You're only greeting Divine Self no matter if it's a person or a bird or a fowl or a fish. All that's there is invisible Divinity named *I*. You're meeting *I* everywhere. You must move in this direction.

And what else is there? Nothing, only *I*. What qualities are there? Only the qualities of *I*. Whatever qualities of God are there and there are no others no matter what appears and that is your test. Can you walk abiding in *I*? Can you abide in the qualities of *I* without opposite? Can you look at imperfection and know because I am there, imperfection cannot co- exist with *I*, the Spirit of God.

Therefore, imperfection is a world mirage. Death is a world mirage. Sickness is a world mirage because I am abiding in *I*, the Spirit of God which is there. I'm abiding in *I*, the Spirit of God which is here and then you watch the quiet way in which healings occur. Because all is *I* in your Consciousness, that is what your Consciousness begins to out-picture in the visible world around you. The transition in Consciousness becomes a transition in experience. You are abiding in *I* and the Scriptural law is fulfilled. You do bear fruit richly. You are sowing to the Spirit and you do reap Life everlasting. You are not sowing to the material world of flesh and you do not reap corruption. Spiritual law is firm, true and invariable. And when you abide in it, fulfill it with fidelity, you find every activity that is promised in those Scriptural decrees becomes your experience.

All evil is wiped off the face of the earth in your Consciousness. There is no evil power. There is no evil condition. There is no evil person or thing because all is the invisible Spirit named *I*.

Here is an exercise you may find very good. I call it, "Turning off the world." In your consciousness, you want to reach a point where there is no invisible thief, where the world mind, the carnal mind has no outlet in you. And so, you go into an awareness of who You are. You are the Self of God. There is no mortal being where You are. You are pure, Immortal Spirit. And therefore, there is no world where You are; there is only the Kingdom of Heaven. You are really accepting the robe of Divinity without ands, ifs and buts and learning inside that Divinity means perfection in all things. Divinity means this that was born is not You. Divinity means that You are not a human ego, that You are not a human body; that there is no human here.

You see, in this acceptance, in this "Turning off the world," this is your crucifixion in consciousness, accepted in meditation. Here, there is no mortal being. There is only *I*, the Immortal Self. Your permanent Self is here, your Divine Self and your Divine Self here extends without interruption throughout Infinity. It is never separated from that Divine Self which is God. Your Source is ever present. You are one with your Infinite Source, here and now. Nothing else is present except your One, Source, Self, the Self that is You forever.

You learn to accept this inside until something in you reaches a point where the world is turned off. You don't feel a world. You are not aware of a world. You're only aware of Infinity, totally Divine and nothing else.

This becomes stabilized as a vast, inner Peace. Even the Truth of it begins to register as an unconscious feeling within. If I am Divine and my neighbor is Divine and everyone is Divine, then all must be the same Divine One and that Divine One is the Self of each one. That Divine Self, I am and *I* cannot be disconnected from Infinity because it is the Divine Self. I am that Infinite, Divine Self; until the Truth of this to you is not a quotation but an acceptance within. And when it is, the powers of the world cease to be for you. When it is, you are inviting all of the qualities of God to flow in their natural sequence and express where you are. They reveal the absence of the desolation, destruction, discord, despair, disaster and death that works through the false thief of the world mind.

You find you need no power against anything. The world can say, "This can't be done or that can't be done or this is an obstacle or we're facing this kind of a condition over here" but when you register inside with this feeling of the Infinite, Invisible Self of You, all of the statements of the world about what can't be done for You have no weight whatsoever. You can break down any door without trying. Every obstacle is demolished. The Spirit of You reveals that there are no obstacles. There never was an obstacle. They're all part of the mirage. Spirit of You reveals that you truly are in the perfect Kingdom now. The *I* is lifted and the *I* reveals the Infinity of God's Kingdom as a present Reality.

I and the Father. *I* abide in the Father and the Father abides in me. We are One and, in that Oneness realized within, I am free. Free of a temporary lifespan, free of mortality, free of all the confining ideas of the world mind, free of error, free of false beliefs. For all that *I* has, is mine. The world is gone.

— End of Side One —

On page 176, "*The Infinite Way begins with an infinite, ever present, omnipotent God.*"

Now, the name of that God is *I*. I am God. "*Be still and know that I am God.*" The Infinite Way then begins with an ever present, Infinite, Omnipotent *I* in the midst of you. Therefore, in our acceptance of this Truth, I can say that where I appear to be, there is *I*, an Infinite, Omnipotent, ever present God and it is appearing to your sense as a person here and a person there and a person where you stand and your consciousness must switch from the person where you stand to that Omnipotent, ever present, invisible *I*. And when you switch to that *I*, you have changed from the age-old false idea that you are mortal being. The mortal self that we have been taught we are, we are not. We are *I*. This is the teaching of Jesus Christ. It is the teaching of the Infinite Way.

And as you make that switch in consciousness to the real identity, you are also changing from the world to the Kingdom without having to do anything else about it and you are moving into eternity, into timelessness without doing anything more about it. You are moving into Divine law. The minute you move from mortal me to Immortal *I* in your consciousness, you are under the law of God.

And all of yesterday's errors, all of yesterday's mistakes are karmic debts that are wiped away. The moment we are *I*, instead of me, we are white as snow and we fear not any mortal condition for we are no mortal being again. We are *I*.

And when we experience this, we know that we can learn how to maintain this.

The mirages of the world cannot function in that *I* consciousness. They cannot out- picture for you all the threats and limitations of mortality.

Actually, this teaching right at this point, in this one sentence that Joel gives us here, when we know that God and *I* are one, that teaching is the passport to Heaven on earth. All it needs is a worker, someone who will accept it and work with it and live with it and wrestle with it until it becomes living Consciousness. You don't need a whole lot of new Truth beyond that.

Once you make that transition in consciousness right where you are, all of the Truth you need flows right out of your own Being. You might use a few helpful hints on how to stay there but ultimately, you see you're going to come to the place where no one on earth can help you because you don't need any help. You know that I am *I*. You know the Truth that makes you free and because God functions in *I*, which is the Son of God, the Father says, "*Son.... all that I have is thine.*" In doing this, you've automatically agreed with your adversary. That step is already taken care of without you making a conscious effort to do it. Where's your adversary? There is none. The only adversary you had was when you were not in *I*. When you're in *I*, the adversary is gone.

Now, when you're in *I*, will you be guilty of judging? No. Will you be unrighteous? No. Will you condemn anyone? No. Will you love your neighbor automatically because *I*, will love your neighbor? In other words, all of Scripture is fulfilled when you stand in *I*, instead of in me, and then all of the words of Scripture that we're trying to get you to come to *I* are no longer needed because *I* wrote those words.

Realization of Oneness. I am that *I* which is God.

So, "*Infinite Way begins with an infinite, ever present, omnipotent God.*" Its premise is that there is no imperfection in any part of God or of God's creation. None whatsoever. God is being perfect and so, therefore is God's creation.

"*No one has ever been born, no one will ever die; no one ever had a beginning, and no one will ever have an ending.*" All of this you see is mortal belief. The birth, the death, the beginning, the ending is all a denial and ignorance of the fact that I am that *I*. And suddenly, the birth, the beginning, the death, the ending are moved away from *I*. There seemed to be cosmic shadows of thought, impacted into an appearance called form: but I am not mortal. I am that *I* which is the permanent, Immortal *I* and that Immortal *I* did not go through birth and will not go through death and that is my name and identity. You learn how to stand in that until you're at home in *I*. This is returning to the Father's house.

"Thou seest me, thou seest the Father whose name is *I*." Thou seest the Son whose name is *I*. The Son and the Father are *I*, one and the same. Without beginning in time or space, with no division in time or space and no ending in time or space. That *I*, I am. That is the Immortal *I*. I am not the mortal me. In my capacity to remain, consciously that *I*, while the form walks this earth doing its human chores, will determine the experiences that that form undergoes. If I have this open end with *I*, consciously there all the time, the appearance called form will be under the law of *I* and that law is Perfection in all things. That law is Grace, a sufficiency for every moment.

Do I or do I not stand in that *I* is going to determine every tomorrow. It will even determine whether or not I reincarnate or make a transition to a realm in which physical form does not appear. It will determine if loaves and fishes rain out of the sky or if my table can in some way be barren. It will determine if I live in the miracle of the presence of God or the absence. I have that power to stand or not to stand in *I* and I make my own bed. I make my own karma. I make my own freedom. If I stand fast, I find that all that the Father has is never withheld. This *I*, is your secret place, the Immortal Self.

Let's repeat that line, "*No one was ever born, no one will ever die; no one ever had a beginning, no one will ever have an ending.*" That's mortal talk; beginning and ending, birth and death. I am Immortal.

Wherever you do not accept Truth, you're accepting karma. Wherever you're told, for example, "Judge not, lest you be judged," the moment you judge, you're in karma. And the reason is because nothing can enter to defile or make a lie of Truth. Truth is forever and it has no opposite and when you're not in it, you're in untruth. When you're not in Truth, you're in karma because truth is all there is. Karma is living in unreality. There's no karma in Reality. The only reason we experience karma, cause and effect, is because we're not living in *I*, which is Reality.

I, does not live in this world. *I* lives in the Kingdom of *I*, the Kingdom of God and therefore, *I*, the *I* that I am, am not in this world now. *I*, living in I, which is in the Kingdom of God receive of the Kingdom. If I haven't hitherto, it's because I was not living in the Kingdom to receive the gifts of the Kingdom. All that the Father hath is in the Kingdom of Spiritual Reality and is experienced in the appearing mortal world only when we live in that Kingdom consciously which is known as *I*.

This is the *I* which is your identity and has existed for billions of years and will continue to exist without interruption for many more billions of years. Just think, when we entombed ourselves in the belief that this is my life, this span, we were denying the *I* that I am, which is billions of years in each direction. You were denying the Infinity of your own Being and losing the Power of it, the Grace and Truth and Beauty of it, but the minute you're out of this mortal shell, in the *I*, all of those billions of years are living now. They're not dead years. They're not yesterday. The *I* that existed for billions of years means: exists unto Infinity in every direction and that is all living now. You become Infinitely alive in *I*. Who can even estimate what that means with the human mind, to be Infinitely alive, now? But I am. The *I* in you is Infinitely alive, now and when you are that *I* and there is no second, you can truthfully say, "I am Infinitely alive."

In that Infinite Life, is all the Power of the universe. All of the health, all of the success, all of the human baubles that we have valued so much are all included but so much more. In your Oneness with *I*, you are one with the Spiritual universe. There's nothing to heal, is there? Everything is perfect in *I*. To be Infinitely alive is to live in *I* and who knowing this, would wander off into a little, mortal me?

"[This is] the I which I am and the I which is God and [they] are one and the same I." This is Joel's statement, *"[They] are one and the same I. Therefore, I is immortal…. God can no more begin than He can end and if God and I are one, the I of me, in that oneness has never begun and will never end."*

And so, there is an *I* that I am, which *"never began and will never end."* When I lose sight of it, I'm in the karma of the world. When I don't lose sight of it, you cannot destroy me for it is the only Power. But it must be lived in. You cannot live outside of *I* and experience that Power. So, we are lifting up our conscious awareness that *I*, without beginning or end in space or time, is my present identity and I'm living in all of it, even though all that appears here is a little tip of the iceberg called a human self.

And the beauty is that if you know the Truth, the Truth will make you free. You don't have to go beyond knowing it but you can't stop knowing it either. The minute you stop knowing it, the minute it's out of your conscious knowledge, you're not knowing it and then, you're not free.

It does another beautiful thing, when you're resting in this *I*. We know your mind isn't dwelling on your ailments or your lacks or limitations. You can't dwell in both. You're either in them or you're in *I*. Which are you? If you're in your limitations, you're not living in *I*. If you're living in *I*, you're not dwelling on your limitations and pretty soon you find that the *I* you live in has no limitations. You become conscious of the nature of that *I*. You're taken right out of the limitations of the mortal sense of self.

Of course, we say to ourselves, "Well, how often can I do this? I've got a human life to live out here. No one's going to put my shoes on in the morning for me. I've got to do it. I've got to brush my teeth. I've got to get ready. I've got to go out, down to the office. I've got to go out to the school. I've got to go out and do this and that. I can't be thinking of *I* all the time."

The Father says, "Oh yes, you can and you will... *Abide in me.*"

Somebody gives you a passport to heaven, do you tear it up and throw it away because you've got to go down to Safeway today? *"Abide in me,"* while you do whatever you have to do. Abide in *I* and you'll find it's very normal to abide in *I*. It becomes your permanent consciousness just as this consciousness we had in a mortal sense was our consciousness, we have this new Consciousness which abides in *I*. The old is gone. The new supersedes and everything derives a new appearance to us because of it. Everything has a new animation because of it. There's a different glow in the things around us because of it. The inner Light begins to suffuse right through. We feel the new texture of Spirit invisible seeping into our daily lives. *"I am the way."* This is your lifeline to Infinity. Why should you let go? Only the thief is trying to make us believe we can't do it. We can do it so well that there's no power on the earth that can stop us. And you can do it for others as well as yourself.

As you become strong in the *I* consciousness, you find you can reach out and embrace those who need a little help. You find that you weren't doing this work just for a you for there never was such a you. You find that others reach out and the *I* consciousness of you lifts them up to the *I* consciousness of themselves and then you know that you have caught the Spirit of the Master, the real inner Teaching. You're walking with God. You have substance. You're out of quotations. You know that the *I* of you is the answer to every problem on the earth and to everybody's problem. You just can't reach them all fast enough and so you stand in that *I* and let it draw unto you your own household.

Like the Master, you don't go out and heal the world for those who come to you are lifted to the *I* of their Being. *"I, if I be lifted up.... will lift all men unto me."* *I* truly am the key to the Kingdom and all those who seek that Kingdom in your household are drawn to that *I* in you which is the *I* of them and you walk arm in arm.

We're living in One, not two.

Says Joel, *"....when the parenthesis is removed we live in the full circle of immortality. It is true that while we may be aware of ourselves as living only in this particular parenthesis, slowly or rapidly moving from birth to death, actually it is possible for this parenthesis to be removed and for you to become aware of our true identity as one with the entire circle of life and its immortality and eternality. Once we realize ourselves as I, separate and apart from personality, separate and apart from a physical body, as I, the incorporeal, spiritual I, we will have the secret of the eternality and immortality of life: without beginning, without birth; without ending, without death."*

He's interpreted for us the Truth in words we can understand, that Jesus was demonstrating the Immortality of Life as the Reality of all who walk the earth in form. We appear in form but this is not the Truth. It is the Infinite I of our Being interpreted by world mind into the appearance called form and where the form stands, only I am. And because that is true of you and your neighbor and all who walk the earth, only *I* stand everywhere.

And so, when you are one with *I* where you are, you are one with *I* who stand everywhere, you are One with the Infinite I and that's the power. Never divided from the Infinite I by accepting the *I* of your own Being, is your realization of Oneness. One *I* here, one *I* there, indivisible *I*. I and the Father, One. *I*, the key to the Kingdom. It's really clear and the disciple lives in that *I* awareness and the fruits of the Spirit follow as the night the day.

Every quality of *I* is present in your consciousness even though you're not conscious of these qualities. When you are accepting *I*, the omnipotence, the omniscience, the omnipresence of *I* is functioning in the *I* itself and you do not have to go into detail about it. The *I* of you is present everywhere. It is omnipotent everywhere. It is all knowing everywhere.

Simply by being aware that I am that *I*, now, forever, releases all of the Intelligence that is necessary at any given moment and all of the Power that is necessary at any given moment. This is the unconditioned universe and because *I* know all that must be known and can perform all that must be performed and am doing it now, that Perfection appears outwardly as the added things. The necessities of life as we know it, appearing visibly because *I* who know all things and can do all things, am always a sufficiency unto my Self wherever *I* am realized and accepted.

I, is the best artist in the universe. *I*, is the best scientist. *I*, is the best composer. *I*, is the best author. Wherever you stand in *I*, the world will stand in awe of what they think are your mortal achievements. They may say Da Vinci did that but it was *I*. Michelangelo did that but it was *I*. This composer did that but it was *I*. Always the *I* released is what the world calls a genius.

And yet, that wasn't enough for many geniuses because they didn't know that only in that level of their work had they attained the *I*. We may not appear to the world in that level of genius - we may; but if we attain the *I*, whatever is necessary in the Divine fulfillment of our Being must flow. Not just as an isolated event but as a continuous dispensation so that always, you're walking in Divine fulfillment, needing not the plaudits of man anymore because Spirit doesn't need the applause of mankind.

Isn't this what Scripture is telling us? And so now we are united in one *I*, Immortal Self and the thief cannot enter to defile. Nothing can enter to defile or make a lie in the *I* accepted. The thief is unemployed. The thief is removed. The thief can no longer say, "You lack and you're limited." You're on the high ground of *I*.

Tomorrow, you're going to have to do this all by yourself and just as well as we're doing it here today as a group because *I* will teach you. If you *"Come unto me... who are heavy laden, I will give thee rest... I* will open all the invisible doorways. *I* answer before you ask but come unto me without ceasing and this is how *I* abolish the belief in death, in disease, in sickness, in lack and limitation."

Everyone has this key to the Kingdom. Don't lose your key.

"All that is of God," says Joel, *"is of you and of me because the I of you and of me and the I of God are one and the same I."* And that means no question about the fact that *I* of you and *I* of God are one and the same.

"And all the qualities of God are the qualities of spiritual, eternal, immortal man: of you and of me.... all that constitutes the I of God constitutes the I of you and of me for we are forever one with the Father. All that is of God is ours."

Nobody's chasing us out to the lions yet. We're being built up to the place where we can stand on anything. Gently, we're being eased up and up in *I*. Many of our tribulations have been monumental to us but we're still here, aren't we? Each of them has been a preparation for the moment when I am come, whose right it is to sit on the throne of your consciousness. For when I am come, this world becomes your playground.

Now, Joel is giving us pure Truth here. If we are receiving it, we have no barriers to the acceptance of it. If that something in us says, "And I will live this Truth," you will discover that every word of it becomes living experience.

One of the by-products of it is that you realize that all personal ambition is a denial of your own identity. You want to be this and you want to be that. Can you be more than *I*? Is there anything more than God? And if *I* is your name, to simply be *I* is a fulfillment beyond every mortal dream and then *I* appears as that which you must appear to be in this human world. That *I*, expresses the Divine plan where you stand. It may change you from all of the things you thought you ought to be but what It appears as where you are is what you must be. Many of us changed quite a bit that way. Some of us want to be tycoons and we find, we lose that. We find we always were a greater tycoon than we could ever become in this world.

When Infinity expresses as your Being, you step aside as a mortal and say, "*Thy will be done.*" The perfection of Infinity is all I could hope for beyond every mortal idea or aspiration.

"*Thy kingdom come.... on earth as it is in Heaven.*"

And there *I*, expresses in ways beyond every human capacity.

Beautifully, *I*, laughs at the sins and diseases and germs of the world, laughs at the grave, laughs at all these mortal barricades that we have accepted as realities. We're taken right out of the tomb of a limited lifespan while we walk in the appearance called mortal flesh. There isn't a miracle in the Bible that isn't part of the *I* of your Being.

"*Every moment of every day,*" says Joel, "*determines what our tomorrows will be. As we sow, in this moment, so will we reap tomorrow; next week, next year or ten years from now.... But if we accept the world's belief in two powers, its belief in Spirit and matter, in good and evil, then we're going to experience both good and evil.*"

The emphasis here is that when you accept *I*, don't let that face in the mirror fool you again. And don't let that person coming up the street fool you. There will continue to appear all forms of disturbances in the world but don't let them fool you. They're not there - I am. *I*, is the invisible identity everywhere which you have accepted where you appear to be. One, invisible, indivisible *I*.

Now, there are levels of this *I* awareness. There are degrees of coming to the higher awareness of it and there are places where you learn this will never be taken away from me now. I have reached this level, it cannot be taken away.

Now, we want to come to those levels where it's not a mental exercise, where it's substance; your actual Being realized and that takes practice. And I know you won't be able to succeed in what I'm going to ask you to do but I want to ask it anyway. I want you to see how difficult it is and then you will learn how to succeed in it.

I'm going to ask you to spend just one hour of any day you choose identifying nothing except the Divine Self in that one hour, wherever you may happen to be. If there are fifty people present, coming and going, if you're crossing on a street corner where there are five hundred present, spend one hour doing whatever you have to do but identifying nothing but Divine Self for one hour.

Don't make it easy for yourself by closing your door and sitting in a chair for an hour but do it when you're out among people and things and conditions as if you were walking in the park or at a theater where there are people but be conscious for one hour of Divine Self - everywhere.

For you it will be a very instructive teaching - far greater than anything that anyone can say to you. If you've done it, you'll know. If not, you'll say, "Oh my gosh, just to know that this fellow was Divine and that one is Divine." And why while this person was dancing on the stage, to know that they're Divine, you'll even improve their performance for them. You'll find you're lifting all those around you. You may never have direct, tangible evidence of it but in some way, you'll know something different is happening in your life and so, that's a very important exercise.

I was going to ask you to do it for a day but I know how difficult it is to do it for an hour. An hour is at least within reason. Now in that hour, just think, we're going to really be living in Heaven because you can't have any judgments if you're judging Divine. It doesn't matter who gets on that telephone. That's the Invisible I. It doesn't matter who's angry at you or what you happen to see in the newspapers or what comes off the TV tube. In that one hour, you identify all that is Divine.

Then what do we do after the hour? Do we go back to "It's not Divine, now? The hour is up." You see what it leads to? It's forming a habit, a way of life and if you are true to Spiritual identity, that's what returns to you. That's exactly what returns to you because your fidelity is the mirror and your infidelity is the mirror. When the Master speaks about adultery, he's talking about just this. Are you faithful to the Invisible I or not? If you're not, you're married to mortality, to this world and this is the Spiritual adultery which is the karma of the world.

All right. We'll do it for an hour. Nobody's keeping score on you but yourself. And I would like to suggest that when you fail, that you begin and start the hour at that point of failure until you complete one hour of identifying everyone and everything, even a flea, as the Invisible, Divine I and if you don't get through one hour, during the entire week, well you just are saying to the Father, "You said abide but not this week."

Correct yourself. Start again when you fail. If you fail at the 59th minute, begin your hour over again. <u>You must go through an hour</u>.

The Bible says, "Go twain if someone asks you to go a mile." So, some of you who want to can go two hours. But that's not the lesson.

"While we are part of this human race into which we were born, we're sowing to the flesh, we're going to reap corruption even if we obey the Ten Commandments to the letter... what we accept into our consciousness is going to determine our experience."

And so, we're learning to accept in our consciousness the Invisible, Divine Self everywhere. When we accept that into our consciousness, our righteousness exceeds the righteousness of the scribes and pharisees. We're not judging after the appearances. We're not judging after the flesh but we're judging righteous judgment that only the Divine Self is here. God is One. God is All. That is the nature of Being that is present wherever I am. And in this, you'll find you have turned off the world. You have turned on the Kingdom. Your key is fitting the lock, opening the door.

I think we'll stay with "Lifting up the *I,*" because if we can come to a place where we are properly aware that *I* is not only in this room but in every other room, in every office, in every city, on every street, the miracle of *I* will yield fruit beyond imagination.

So, that will be today's lesson. We have five more until our recess and remember the last, we're going to go right through New Year's and Christmas, every Sunday, so we'll be leaving the day before Christmas and the day before New Year, the 7th and the 14th of January. And the 14th of January will be the last of this series and by then, we're going to finish this book, "Realization of Oneness" and the Gospel of John. They'll all be finished and that last lesson is when we'll finish both the Gospel and the book.

Thanks very much.

Class 42

Perfect Faith In A Perfect God

Herb: Can't help but comment today on the many smiles we've noticed. It's supposed to be a dreary day but it's hard to prove it just looking around at the happy faces. In fact, this is one of those classes that in some way is almost finished before it begins. There's a real feeling that we have all brought with us a very special consciousness which permeates all around us.

We want to look at the chapter which we began last week, "Lifting up the I." The first thing we want to look at is a very unusual statement made by Joel. It's almost a statement which is so complete in itself yet, when it is understood, you have the complete and total secret of the nature of error.

I think it could begin right here on page 189. Joel says, "*Through conscious realization, we must establish the truth of our oneness with God, our oneness with spiritual perfection.*"

We're going to assume now that we have established this to a degree so that at least we know that this is the nature of our Being. We may not be able to demonstrate it a hundred percent of the time or even perhaps twenty percent of the time but we know we are Spirit, one with the Father, one with each other as one Self.

And so, this has to be established before we can go further with his next statement. "*Then from there on, we are not dealing with persons or conditions: we are dealing only with the world of appearances or illusion.*"

Now, here is the important phrase, "*The illusion in one place may be a lake, the illusion in another may be a city, but it is all illusion, and the substance of an illusion is nothingness, whether it appears as a lake or a city. The substance of illusion is the same, whether it appears as a cold, a headache, a cancer, tuberculosis, a broken bone, poverty, or unemployment. It is always nothingness, the 'arm of flesh,' appearance. And behind it is the activity of a universal malpractice or hypnotism, produced by the universal belief in two powers.*"

Now then, the big statement is that this illusion on the left and that illusion on the right and the third illusion up there and the fourth illusion down here are all one and the same illusion so that if in the office, everybody is saying "There's going to be an earthquake at 9 pm or 9 am on January 4th," that's one illusion but it's no different than the illusion on the other side which says, "I have a head cold." They're both the same illusion. And if you come across someone beating a dog and your heart bleeds for the dog, you're trapped into an acceptance of the third illusion which is still the same illusion. The cold in the head, the beaten dog, the earthquake are one illusion.

And so, Joel's statement is that when you learn the nature of one illusion, you've learned the nature of all illusion and then the alertness to the universal illusion is a path to freedom.

So, let's look at the three human type illusions which we see as three separate illusions when they're really one. The earthquake, the beaten dog and the head cold.

We know that God has not created earthquakes. We know that God is not standing by watching people beat dogs and we know that God didn't give anybody a head cold. And if we have perfect faith in a perfect God, something happens in us. It's like putting starch in the collar of a shirt. Something starches up your awareness so that you can stand without being moved out of position. You think with a sense of conviction. There is a lucidity in your thought as if it were coming from another level and you find suddenly, you can understand the nature of illusion as something which normally persuades you to accept it as a reality. The talk is hot and heavy and the fear jumps and the next thing you know, all of your teaching is out the window. All you can think of is where can I put this body if that earthquake comes or the head cold is there and you're angry at yourself because you're supposed to have known better. But here it is and then you can't help but wince when you see somebody lash that dog. You want to tear it out of his hands. You want to cradle the dog. You want to stroke it. In all cases, this is material sense presenting different pictures to the one who is not alert to Reality.

Now, let's go back to our perfect Reality. Let's see that the real problem begins long before the physical birth. Infinity is so vast. There's no way that it can present Itself to the finite mind. And so, Infinity presents itself to the finite mind through many veils, through many segments; so vast that in one lifetime, you can only get a little bite out of a big apple. And so, you see Infinity but don't know you're looking at it. You see a little portion in one lifespan and another portion and another portion and then another. And every time you look out, you think you're seeing what's there because the human mind has no capacity to see Infinity.

And so, right at the start, we're pressured into an illusion. We cannot see any further than our human eyes can see and they cannot see the wholeness that is present. And so, with our other senses, we're limited again and again and again and we learn finally, that these limitations are not limitations at all unless they're accepted as senses which convey to us reality. When you know they have no capacity to convey reality, then you are lifting yourself above the sense of sight and sound and touch, knowing that always, Infinity is present. And finally, you know that you're in what may be called the fourth level or the fourth world. And because you're in the fourth world, looking at Infinity, you find that you are to be lifted up to three more levels.

Into this fourth world comes a Light, always present but there is one to receive it and so, Jesus becomes Christ. And now, you have a higher level made manifest in the fourth level and it comes to show us that there is a way to a higher level, a fifth level, a sixth and a seventh. The seventh being the eternal Sabbath or rest in which you live in Reality, without seeing fractions of Infinity but live in Infinity itself.

And this Light, made manifest as the Christ Jesus, now gives us a perfect preview of what happens when you are willing to place your perfect faith in the Father knowing that Reality is perfect and present. It does not create bodies of flesh that die. It does not envelop these bodies of flesh in earthquakes. It does not give them head colds. It does not beat them or beat animals and it is always present.

You begin to see that there is a universal illusion and that its presence is there for a purpose, to help us develop perfect faith. Our perfect faith accepts the perfection that is present and looks through every form of that universal illusion, even to the point of looking through all that is material until we see that the nature of the universal illusion is to create a fourth world and our Soul, hungry for union with its Source, is taking us forever, leading us, guiding us, driving us to find that union with Source, which lifts us beyond the false sense of power that exists in the fourth world.

And so, we follow that Light which was made manifest. We saw One who could walk through the fourth world untouched and we try to cognize the secrets that enabled him to do so. And one is, we discover, he learned that he was not present in a material body. He learned that there were no material conditions; that there were no material objects; that all that was present was the invisible Light.

And he discovered a carnal mind, a universal sense of the fourth world which re- interpreted the Light into the appearance of form called matter and that all belief in matter emanates from this carnal mind and that all belief in the evil of matter emanates from this carnal mind; all belief in the goodness of matter emanates from this carnal mind; and that this carnal mind which recreates the Light into an appearance called the fourth world, is a universal illusion itself and that only through stepping out of the effects of that world illusion could we receive that Light which guides us through the fourth world, lifting us into the fifth.

And so, that is what our work consists of. It is learning how to express the Light by stepping aside from that which the carnal mind places before us as a world of material form. To express the Light is to express the invisibility of God into this fourth level. When we look at Jesus healing, we see that he never was dealing with physical forms. He learned that the secret was to stand in the Light of his own Being as an Infinite Self and to let the Light reveal itself where the world saw material being.

This might be a good time to see that there are seven levels of body. In each world there is another level of body and in the fourth world, that level of body is a human body, for us. But it isn't a human body in the fifth level or the sixth or the seventh. The human body is the world appearance, we assume, only at this level of consciousness.

And so, as the Master did, in perfect faith, we accept the body of Light as the only Body and we can look at the body of flesh into which we have journeyed in the fourth level as a temporary condition imposed upon us only by the universal belief in material bodies. And we begin to lift ourselves simply by stepping aside from material sense. We do not deal with physical bodies or physical conditions. We step aside and by stepping aside, is meant we step out of the belief of the mind that physical form is present in any way. We cannot bleed for the beaten dog. We cannot fear for the earthquake. We cannot be angry at ourselves for having the head cold. We learn that we must step aside from this human sense of things; that we must take a Sabbath from mortality.

And as we step aside, as we find the capacity to find a Soul center, instead of a five- sense chilling fear, there is a quickening and that's when the system begins to see the miracle of that which we had feared dissolving right before us. This quickening is the oil of the Soul, the

Soul substance forming Itself in your consciousness and it releases us from the illusion of the world.

And most of us, when we have attempted to heal ourselves or another, have been trapped in quite a number of ways and the one way to finally get out of all of the traps is to not try to heal that condition or that person but to recognize that you're dealing with a universal belief.

Now, you may want to get rid of your head cold but the best way not to get rid of it is to try to treat it as a head cold. You may want to remove the fear of the earthquake but the best way not to remove the fear is to keep thinking you're going to, in some way, eliminate that earthquake. What we're getting at is that there's no earthquake to eliminate and there is no head cold to get rid of. If you've gone that far that you think you've got to get rid of the head cold, or protect against the earthquake, then you have not caught the idea that a universal illusion is not something you try to get rid of and you don't try to get rid of it where you stand. Once you localize that illusion and think you're trying to get rid of it where you stand, you find your efforts are thwarted.

What we want to learn today is that we meet the illusion on its universal level, not on its local level. When you meet it on the local level, you're not ready for the greater works. You've got to meet it on its universal level.

And so, if we were to meet the earthquake, we would not meet it as an earthquake in this area of California. We would meet it as, "*The earth is the Lord's and the fulness thereof*" and we would have to know that the earthquake is an impossibility in God's Spiritual Kingdom. We don't have to determine where it might strike or when it might strike. We have to determine the Truth not the nature of the illusion or the nature of the lie. And if we know the Truth, this knowing will be that God, being Spirit, being All, is not material and that matter has no existence in God.

There is no matter to quake. That earthquake is going to be a mental idea before it ever seems to be a physical tremor and when there is a receptivity to the carnal mind which says "It's possible that there is a material world and that it can quake," then that individual is part of the group illusion, the group unawareness of the Allness of Spirit. God is not in the whirlwind. God is not in the earthquake, meaning Spirit is not in matter.

Now, the importance of knowing that Spirit is not in matter about an earthquake or about a head cold ultimately takes you to a more important knowing; that when you know Spirit is not in matter, you know that Spirit does not die. When you've solved the illusion of earthquake, you've also solved the illusion of death. In fact, when you solve any one form of the illusion, you've solved all illusion. It only appears to human sense that some are bigger than others. The earthquake is no bigger than the head cold because they're the same illusion.

Now, we're going to be prepared before our series is over - before this, before the next four classes - we're going to be prepared to be able to participate in world work effectively. And our participation will be on the basis of knowing that where the world appears to be, my Spirit is and we're going to know that well enough so that whatever occurs in our communities or in any part of the world, that is brought to our attention, can be met not as a local event but as a universal lie, a universal nothingness so that you don't meet a head cold in your head. You meet it as a universal lie and then, not only will your head cold disappear, but many others and you will not even know who has benefitted by your work. But that is the reason for the lie coming to you, for you to stand in the Light, not just to release yourself but to see always the universal nature of the lie and then you become a permanent Light working in world work all the time. It doesn't matter what illusion touches you, you remove the belief in the universal nature of that lie, not the local nature of it alone. And you'll find suddenly, you have discovered deep wellsprings of power.

Now, there has been much talk and some fear has been expressed to me about this earthquake because it seems to be prognostication time again. And so, the experts have set us down for 9 am on January 4th. And I think this would be a good time for us to begin our world work. It's getting ahead of the next chapter but we'll call this a tune-up.

We have here then a condition in which world belief is that God, in some way, is either absent or permissive or impotent. And so, all we have to do is to ask ourselves one question: do we believe in the omnipotence of God or do we not?

Now, if you don't believe in the omnipotence of God, then more than an earthquake can terrorize you but if you begin to accept omnipotence as a fact, then all that remains is, how can you and that fact become one? In other words, how can you in this fourth level of the world extend your awareness into a higher level so that you are not a separate human being in a separate human body but are One with the very power of God. For when you are One with the power of God, then all that appears to be the power of an earthquake is rendered null and void.

So, this is an excellent opportunity for us to take a second look at what may be called a Divine blueprint. What are we here for? Humanhood has been thought to be the nature of our Being and we were always seeking human ways to make a better humanhood. But now, let's look at humanhood as a seed that we have to plant something while we're here, something that takes root in God and lifts us beyond the appearance of humanhood so that as the seed of our Being takes root in a higher level, let's say just the fifth level, the activity of Christ begins to function more noticeably in our experience lifting us, dissolving mortal sense, material sense, limited sense, finite sense, belief in good and evil, belief in the powers of evil. Finally, this Light within from the fifth level establishes Itself as the very Light of our Being.

Now, we can see that where the man Jesus became aware of the Light called Christ, that was evidence that this everywhere Light is the Light of us waiting for our acceptance and as we accept it, as we learn it is present where we are, that it is alive, that Christ is always living, that wherever God is, Christ is, then we accept God is where I am and wherever God is, Christ is, Christ must be where I am.

We're beginning to take root in the Light of Being. The human seed is dissolving, personal sense is stepping away. We're taking root in Christ here, where I am and we find that as we become more aware that God is here as the living Christ that I am, we begin to get a knowledge that I cannot be in a mortal body because Christ is not in a mortal body. Christ here is in an immortal body. Christ here is in a Spiritual body and Christ here I am, the root in the fifth level, dissolves the false beliefs in the fourth level. The human mind, which is controlled by the universal, carnal mind ceases to accept the beliefs of its false father.

I learned that one of my great secrets is never to deny that I am the Light of God, never to deny that I am the Spirit, never to deny that I am the Christ, never to deny that you are the Christ, the Light, the Spirit, never to deny that anyone on earth is.

In other words, fidelity to identity deepens the root and it begins to sprout. The fifth level begins to feed you the oil, the substance and soon the living will of God begins to move you and there's a great secret there. When carnal mind moves you through your human mind, you're in the carnal will and it moves your physical form. When Divine will moves you, it moves your Spiritual form and so, the Divine will functioning in you moves your Spiritual form in God ordained acts and then they appear in the fourth level as the movements of your physical form. Without that step, without the Divine ordination coming from the higher level of Divine will, all that moves your physical form is carnal mind without any connection whatsoever to true Being. You walk through an entire mortal lifespan completely outside of Reality but when the deeper root of Divine will moves through you, that which moves your physical form, the carnal mind, is without power completely. Your acts are ordained.

And now, you can discover that where you are walking under Divine will, under the awareness of Spiritual Self, there can be no earthquake. It is impossible. There can be no head cold. There can be no pain. There can be no limitation. There can be no lack. The oil of the substance is forming itself from the higher level and the miracle of a Jesus Christ is happening in your own Being. The very Light shown through Jesus is shining through you. You're dissolving mortal sense and the fifth world is beginning to open its doors.

The *I* is being lifted and the *I* is doing the lifting Itself. The Light that came through Jesus was the death of mortality and the birth of Christ. The Light that comes through you is the death of mortality and the birth of Christ. A new mind, the Christ mind, replaces the human mind just as Jesus was replaced by Christ. As the false self falls away, Christ takes over as your Being. You discover that everything you've been doing has been a preparation for Christ in you to take over. You are opening your consciousness to the One, that Christ may take over and lead you into the fifth, the sixth, the seventh levels of consciousness, out of this world, out of good humanhood and bad humanhood, out of the carnal mind illusion called humanhood, out of carnal mind itself into the purity of Being. This is a Spiritual transfusion that takes place and sometimes very quickly. The quickening shows you that you're in a new level of thought.

And now, there is no illusion on the face of the earth regardless of its form or its nature that can hypnotize the Christ of your Being. To deny Selfhood is to accept an earthquake. To deny Selfhood is to accept the head cold. Even when it's there, it isn't there. Even when the earth trembles, it doesn't tremble. These are cosmic suggestions. You can have the head cold visibly and physically feel it but it isn't there. And when you know it isn't there, you're being faithful to identity, through the sniffles, through the wet Kleenex. It isn't there because God didn't create it because there is no material universe, because there is only the body of Light. And in your fidelity to this identity, which is *I*, the Light, which expressed through Jesus, which is expressing through you, you find you're lifted to a place where you're ready for the greater work. And those greater works cannot be anticipated but they come whenever you have been able to discard the belief that God could be present where evil appears to be or that God could countenance evil or that God could create evil or that God could be impotent in the face of evil.

All of those beliefs are the belief that God is not where you stand, that you are something separate and apart from God Self and as long as you rest in that false belief, then the whole world of illusion appears to you as separate, different conditions of human form and material form and you're a complete, vulnerable subject for all of the so-called evil on earth. A change of thought, a change of identity, an acceptance through perfect faith that the words of the Father are true, that God is your Father, that you are the Child, you are the Spirit, you are the Light, you are the Life and that quickening process begins.

Of course, you can see the earthquake then in its true Light. A large group of people aware only of the material universe, separated from their own individual identity, unaware of the Light of Christ, walking the earth in bodies of clay, in material senses: they are victimized by the carnal mind of the world. They have no defense. The carnal mind functions the human mind. It controls it. It enslaves it and through that human mind, it projects its concepts.

Once we're caught up in it, it's difficult to see our way through but when we are in identity, when we know who we are, when we practice living in and as that which we're told by the Father we are, the Child of God, the Son of God, what right have we to say, "I, the Son of God, can be hurt by an earthquake." The contradiction is so obvious then. The acceptance of the earthquake was the denial that you are the Child of God. Not living with the knowledge that I am the Son of God, we succumb to all the suggestions around us.

Now, Joel has taught us that there is one illusion and so, we don't have to try to figure out, "What about this? Is this of the carnal mind and what about that?" This world is of the carnal mind and in our work, we must come to that conclusion which states that nothing in this world is created by God; nothing in this world. There is nothing in this world that is not created by the carnal mind. It is a complete carnal mind creation; all of it, because it is the fourth world, the fourth level and only when you let your human sense of self be a seed and rooted in God which is identity everywhere will you find relief from the fifth level taking you up above the cosmic illusion called world.

If you start making exceptions thinking this is not of the carnal mind but that is because this is good and that isn't, you're wrong. This world is the carnal mind made visible and all evil that exists in this world exists only in the carnal mind that projects the evil. It has no rise in God, no law to sustain it and when we live in this world, we're not living under Divine law.

Now, that doesn't mean when the dog is beaten, you don't want to help the dog. It doesn't mean you don't try to get rid of the head cold. It means that you add your new dimension always. That dimension from which you live, the dimension which is invisible, which is Light. That Light made visible through Jesus Christ as a force. That Light is the Light of your Being. And when you accept it, then *I*, the Light and the Infinite Father are One and there is no power needed anymore. The knowing of that Truth consciously is the Power. It does all the work. If you know that I am the Light which is one with the Infinite, you cannot now turn around and expect an earthquake in the Infinite life and so, you're standing on the knowledge of what you are with a need for no power whatsoever: for what you are, is the only Power. And when you experience that it really is, you'll see why to know the Truth is sufficient.

Sometimes you'll think you know the Truth and you'll be dismayed to find that something happens which you thought might not happen because you thought you knew the Truth. And that's because your knowing of the Truth is simply mental. It isn't the Consciousness of Truth, the Spirit of Truth. It hasn't been lived in long enough to take root so that you have perfect Faith.

Now, most of us by now can heal things but fear will always crop in and the reason it does is because it is alerting us to the fact that our consciousness is still in a semi sense of separation. You couldn't feel that where I am, God walks and have fear. And so, there is still that unawareness of the presence of God where you are. Not practicing the Presence, is practicing the absence and carnal mind is very quick to find all of the gaps in your consciousness and then you're forced into a false sense of separation and before you know it, here comes the tidal wave.

Now, in our world work, we're going to look out upon the world not to improve it or to heal it because that's part of the trap of the carnal mind. The minute it gets you to want to heal something, you've been trapped into accepting something that exists which is not the Spirit of God. When we do our world work then - and we've had now many years of preparation for it - it will not be to improve the world because that would be the trap. That's what carnal mind always wants to force you to do. But rather, you're to know the Spiritual nature of what is present where the world appears to be. You're really to discover your Self everywhere in your world work. We won't be praying that God remove a condition from the world like war or that God takes away the flood from the Gulf of Mexico or that God prevents certain conditions or that God empties out a hospital ward.

Rather, we will be knowing first, that where I stand, is the Light of God. Without that as a beginning, you have no fulcrum. You have nothing to tie onto. You can't just have a God out there. You must begin in the hereness of your own Being. Where I stand is the Light of God and no other.

If you're going to do successful world work, it's going to be by beginning at that level. Where you stand is the Light of God. This is a 24-hour Truth and if you practice that truth no matter what you do, you'll find it takes root until your conviction is fully established and then you aren't forced to use words to drive home the point. You find that you have that total conviction. It needs no verbal reinforcement.

Where you are is the Light of God. Why? Because the Child of God is the Light of God. Where God is, the Light of God is and the Light of God is where you are because God is there. That Light, you are. As this deepens, you are one with the Light everywhere in your Consciousness. Now you, in the Light, as the Light, one with the Light everywhere can find nothing in the Infinite Light of your Being except the Light and that's your Consciousness: living Light where you stand, connected to everywhere Light so that all is the one Light.

"I and the Father are one.... I am the Light of the world." Where the world appears, there is no world. There is only *I*, the Light. I am the Light where the world appears. This becomes your awareness.

Now, you stand in that and whatever comes into carnal mind, into human mind to present to you a suggestion that you are not the Light where you are, which is one with the Light everywhere, you look at this suggestion and you find there's no place for it to take root. It comes into the Consciousness which cannot accept it. This is the Consciousness of Light which is too pure to be defiled, too pure to behold iniquity. Nothing can enter to defile it or make a lie. You don't need any power. You don't need any statements. You have this daily building of the Consciousness of the Light here is the Light everywhere and nothing else exists. And through this Light, the power of the Light dispels the false presumed power of the darkness.

The earthquake's lines are unwrinkled. The floods are dried up. The diseases are dissolved. You stand in that Truth. You don't go out to dissolve those diseases or to repair fences or to raise the dead. You stand in the Light of your own Being knowing that Light is everywhere. One Light and let the Light do its own revealing. That's the kind of way in which we will do our world work.

And then, one day, when we're in different parts of the world and not grouped together here in a room, you'll find we're still doing our world work so that you are doing it in one city and someone else in another. And whatever comes to your attention in your particular area, you meet the same way and you're doing world work because you're never meeting it as a local situation. You're meeting it by knowing the Light I am is the Light everywhere and it needs no further power other than to know the Truth. The Light I am here, is the Light everywhere and this becomes a law unto you. All karmic law is broken. Your Soul is finding conscious Oneness with its Source and all of the patient years of mortality are finally bearing fruit as the Soul is now lifting you to the next level of Consciousness, the fifth level in which the Light that you are dispels the total darkness of the fourth world.

Lifting the *I*, the rising Christ of your own Being, lifts you out of this world and when Jesus was lifted out of this world that way, his form still appeared in the world. They now saw a fifth level form in the fourth level. Your form will continue to appear in this world. Don't expect to disappear, but you will find that your form in the visible is now working as an outward appearance in conjunction with a new, invisible form. That one is the outer expression of the Inner and your form isn't taking orders from the carnal mind of the universe. It doesn't get a cold just because everybody else does. You find your mind is replaced. It doesn't fear. You find that the false goals of humanhood do not tempt you anymore. Your goals are totally different. They are simply to be faithful to let the outer serve the Inner. Your perfect Faith says to you, "I have no personal goals." The Light is complete. The Light is whole. The Light is not lacking. The Light isn't trying to become. The Light accepts that it already is.

And so, if you find yourself striving to become, you're caught in the trap of the carnal mind, trying to be a better or more successful human, and the temptation of the world mind is functioning in you only because you are still rebelling against identity. If you find you've still got that yen for success or for greater comforts in the world or for some kind of personal improvement, you're still under the hypnosis that you are not the Light.

"Seek ye first the Light which is the Kingdom."

Now, this is a going away from the world, not a better human way. This is the meekness which is the strength: the great disguise for strength is the meekness unto the Spirit. All of this world is an illusion, for right where this world appears to be, is the Light of Being. And as you walk in that Light consciously, you will find you are being lifted to new levels of consciousness which will culminate in the seventh level, the level of full awareness of a permanent Self, a permanent Life as the pure Spirit of God.

If we're not in our daily Divinity, we're in daily karma. Whenever you step out of Divinity, you're stepping into karma. Whenever you step into Divinity, you are crossing out karma. And that is the reason this carnal mind of the world is here.

We've never questioned that we grow up from children. We don't say, "Why wasn't I born an adult?" We do question and say, "Why wasn't I born as a perfect Spirit of God then if that's what I am. What's the sense of all this illusion? Why don't we just start right out with all of it." Well, then you'd have to say, "Why do we ever get born as children at all? Why don't we just start out as perfect adults?"

Infinity is too vast. You must let your Soul continue its journey through Infinity and at the present level of our journey, we're in that mortal sense of the world carnal mind. And we're being lifted out of it by fidelity to the Light of my own Being where I stand. Whoever holds on to the Light of their Being will find that the Light is the way. It will illuminate you.

Now then, you'll still have head colds. You'll still have fears. You'll still find things go wrong. You'll find you're still disturbed, you're still resentful but these diminish and diminish and then the head cold that you have doesn't last the whole week. You manage to shake it a little quicker than someone else. The fears diminish. The disturbances diminish. We begin to see the utter nothingness of our human resentments.

More and more and more, we're lifted into the perfect Love of the perfect Father. Don't ever be ashamed of your difficulties in this work. They only happen because they're necessary. They're necessary for you to know that that difficulty is there because you are not standing as the Light. You are rejecting fatherhood of God, identity as the Light of the Father. Make the adjustment. Accept yourself and know that this Light that you are is one with the eternal Light, the Infinite Light and all of that Light, the Infinite, eternal Light is right where you are, always.

Nothing is impossible unto it. It is functioning and carnal mind finds that you are now no stranger to the Light, it cannot manipulate you. Mankind is stopped at this human level but we go beyond it. We do not stop at it and it is our function not only to lift ourselves out of it but to lift the world with us. We are to lift the world out of its humanhood. We may not hide our Light under a bushel.

The same Light that Christ says to you, "You are the Light" you inwardly are saying to your neighbor, "And ye are the Light." There's no victim there. The victim is the illusion of the carnal mind. Right where the victim appears to be, you recognize the invisible Light of your own Being. Place your own invisible Light wherever the world presents an illusion, until you have one, Infinite, homogenized, perfect Light everywhere. And you will be led. This is the bread of the Father instead of the bread of this world. This is the Spirit of the Father instead of the might and power of this world. This is the meekness.

Suddenly, you know this power of the Father has always been present. It was never absent. You know the world suffers only from its illusions and you are standing above the illusions of the world. You are ready to be a Spiritual worker in the Father's Kingdom.

— End of Side One —

You have substance, the bread of Life, the very Light itself flowing as your own identity everywhere.

It takes a great deal of courage to stand in the face of something that you fear and to stand on it knowing I am the Light and this that I fear has no power over the Light. But when you've done it, you know the Truth of it. It takes great courage to stand on the Light of someone else's being and know, "No, this cannot take place over there where that person is for there is the Light." And every appearance is met that way. Perfect Faith casteth out all fear. Not faith that God is going to do something but faith that God has already done it. God's perfection is already the fact in all things. That's your perfect Faith and the reason the world suffers is because it has not been taught perfect Faith in God's presence everywhere.

And so, you've got to stand for the world, for your friends, for your loved ones. You've got to present that perfect Faith to the Father for them. When you pray, pray not for that person. Pray by recognizing the universal nature of perfection in which that condition which is presenting itself has no Reality and you will free more than meets the eye.

Just to review it quickly, let's take the head cold. It's not that *you* don't have the head cold, it's that there is none, anywhere. Don't meet it on its little, finite level. There isn't any, anywhere. There's carnal mind presenting the illusion of head colds in five million different places. That's all they are. They're five hundred million places saying that "God isn't there," and you know better. That's what your function is, to know better and that even though the appearance may have localized itself where you are, you're knowing it on a universal level will remove it on your local level and other local levels. Don't know it just locally. That's the point of this recognizing carnal mind as the tempter, the assassin, the evil doer, the devil. Don't bring it down to local levels.

As Joel's work increased in tempo and as he was coming into the homestretch of his mission on earth, more and more he brought to our attention not to meet the problem at the level of a local situation but to recognize it as a universal, carnal mind temptation and even though humanly, we may not quite understand why, when you do meet it that way, you do understand why because you banish the whole power of carnal mind by meeting it that way.

And the power falls away, the presumed power and you find you're in the clarity of Truth. I don't think in one lesson we're going to resolve that technique but I'd like to get it across today because by the 14th of January, we're going to have completed our lessons in world work and I'd like to spend that month between the 14th of January and the 11th of February, when we're not together, I'd like to spend it doing world work with each other so that we're prepared to meet these things.

I think we could probably pause now and resume in a short time. I'm sure there's much more in the chapter here now that will reinforce our study on this aspect of the work. Let's be back in about five minutes.

(Class break)

Now, some of these things that we're discussing should be very normal and basic with us. Some of these things should be very basic. I mean, we ought to have them behind us in a sense I almost feel that it shouldn't have been necessary to even discuss them today but the questions that have been put to me through the week indicate that there are weaknesses still at this level and maybe that's why we're still in the 11ᵗʰ chapter of this book which strangely enough is totally dedicated to the false appearances of the world.

Now, this statement from Joel, "*In 'this world,' where an ignorance of truth predominates, we are constantly being faced with sin, disease, death, lack, and limitation, with evil of every kind.….If.…we have been spiritually taught, we will instantly recognize that these suggestions [that come to us] are appearances like the mirage on the desert.….Do not accept appearances of good and evil at face value. Accept them only as mirage, illusion, a form of malpractice, or hypnotism, and above all things, do not accept them as something that has to be healed.*"

Now, the reason for that statement is once you've accepted the mirage of evil, you don't go around healing a mirage. So, if you want to heal it, for you it's r-e-a-l, a reality, not a mirage and you miss the first step which is: the mirage is caused by our material sense coordinating with the world mind.

And so, there's that pause now, that inner Sabbath, that resting in the Word that the material sense produces the mirage of matter and the evil condition in the mirage of matter must be as much mirage as the matter itself.

And so, your conclusion finally is there is no matter in God's universe and there are no material conditions in God's universe. And as the child of God, you're committed to living in God's universe, not in the world of the carnal mind.

And so, this is a new lifestyle, isn't it? There is no matter and there are no material conditions. And even though you're going to go around in a world of matter and material conditions, in your lifestyle as the Child of the Father, the Light of the world, this must be your constant knowledge.

Jesus didn't say, "I won't make the cripple walk because there is no cripple" and then turn away and forget about it. He accepted it on the terms that came to him from the world as we learn to do but we re-interpret it on our own Divine term. We do not walk away from it and pretend it isn't there but rather, we reveal that something better is there by the knowledge that where the mirage appears, I do not have to remove that mirage but rather, that which is where the mirage is, is the Light of Being. The recognition of the one, invisible Light always centering in the Light where you are so that you're connected and that Consciousness becomes the health of every detail of your life. That's the miracle of Spiritual recognition. That's the new dimension of Life that we learn to live while we walk in the world.

We're not pretending that things aren't there. We're recognizing that something else *is* there. We're not telling the world that man isn't sick. We're knowing that all that is there where that man appears to be sick is the Light of God and our knowing is within ourselves not on the tip of our tongue. It's a permanent knowing.

And so, don't try to improve the mirage. Just rest in being Spirit, being Light and you'll find that when you are resting in being Light, the Light reveals Itself. Our weakness is that once we have established that we're the Light, we want to still do something which is a denial of that which we have just established. We are the Light which is perfect. We are the Light there which is perfect as well as here. There's nothing to be done but rest in the Word.

It's amazing how many things that you thought were real and then uncovered as mirage as you do this. You find the enchantment of walking in the Spiritual universe is yours.

"Nothing has to be healed, reformed, changed or corrected.... We really do not have to get rid of any of the sins, diseases, lacks, or limitations of the persons who come to us. We merely have to refuse to accept the appearances and realize that whatever is presented to us is a state of hypnotism producing an illusion, a mirage."

Silence, (pause) …

There are two kinds of persons who study this work. One kind says, "What is there in this that is good for me?" And you'll find that person cannot really put this message into practice because the very nature of that type of consciousness repels Truth. The other individual says, "What is the Truth? Wherever that is, that's where I go." Now, that individual can put this into practice because they haven't narrowed it down to what of this that I have heard is good for me. They are not conflicting their personal sense with Truth and interpreting that which is Truth only in the nature or degree to which it helps their personal sense.

If you still have yourself, lingering in this, "What is good for me attitude," you will miss a great percentage of what is coming across. It must be an unconditioned quest for Truth alone and then you'll find the personal me is out of the way. There was no personal me where Christ expressed as the visible Jesus. There was an unconditioned Self. There was a One which was One with All. If it was what's good for me, the message never would have reached this level that we have it at now.

I mentioned this because those who are still in the "What's good in it for me?" may not realize that they're blocking the Light of their own Being. This is above personal improvement. You don't try to improve the mirage you call your human body or your human self. That's an obstacle. You accept your perfect Self where the human body appears and that perfect Self is never going to be tarnished, never going to in any way be less that its perfect Self. This is different than a better human you. Your perfect Self is there and unless you're living in your perfect Self, you're living in a second or false self which cannot benefit by Divine law.

Every problem you have is in that imperfect self you have accepted to be you which isn't there. Your perfect Self does not contain problems. Your perfect Self is walking in Reality. Your perfect Self is permanent and the mirage of physical form, human life cannot be accepted if you wish to accept the fatherhood of God.

These are issues that must be met or else you spend the rest of your years improving, or trying to improve, that which is invisibly perfect.

If you work with the present perfection of your Being, you won't need as many words to convince you. It has a way of identifying Itself.

"In God's kingdom, there is not a sin, disease, death, lack, or limitation."

Now, if there's no sin, disease, death, lack or limitation in God's Kingdom, that's another way of saying that there is no sin, death, disease, lack or limitation anywhere. The Allness of God's Kingdom means that there is no sin. There is no lack. There is no limitation. There is no disease. There is no death. And when the Master says, "Raise them from the dead" it means from the belief that there is death. You raise someone from sin, you raise them from the belief that there is sin.

Always, all that is evil is the belief, never the fact. The belief is all that is there and it is made visible as what we have accepted as the fact. Where the fact appears to be, we are looking at our own belief made visible. And the eradication of the belief eradicates the mirage which we thought was the fact.

Then you can say, "Ah, carnal mind, I recognize your method. You place a belief in me which I subconsciously accept then it becomes a conscious belief then it becomes a fact and now, I think I've got it. But this that appears to me as a fact which I'd like to get rid of, isn't a fact at all. I can't get rid of it. It is a belief made into a visible mirage."

Get behind the mirage to the belief and replace the belief with Truth. The belief is you have this thing. The fact is God didn't create this thing. What is sustaining it? God isn't. Your belief is sustaining it and carnal mind is making you believe that. Carnal mind is making you accept that. You're a victim of carnal mind.

The Truth will make you free. What God did not create is not here. That's the Truth. This thing that disturbs me is not here. I don't have to get rid of it. I must get rid of my belief that it is here and I do that by knowing the Truth that God did not place it here and therefore, it is not here. It can be a world war holocaust. It can be an earthquake. It can be a germ. It can be anything that God didn't make and it cannot be here. It's the world belief hanging in space, waiting for me to say, "Yes, yes, yes" and I refuse to. You don't remove it. You recognize its non-reality.

Now, we should be clear then of a lot of things and able to shuffle off most of the things that superimpose themselves in our consciousness one way or another. We should be almost free enough that we're ready to say, "Thou seest me, thou seest the Father." Even if there's a momentary flaw brought into visible experience, it has nothing to do with you; it's just world thought traveling by. Why detain it. Let it go. Let it go right on its merry way. Don't stop it and claim it for your own. Let it go. It has nothing to do with you.

Then we have an open consciousness. We're not a repository for the world's false beliefs. The instant you're faced with a false belief in your consciousness, recognize it. It's just world thought traveling through. Let it go. You'll find it continues right past you and the false belief that this was going to be bad or that was going to be bad or this was not going to be improved, all of that goes right with the world thought. Perfection has ever been there and when the cloud of world thought passes by, it shines through again.

We come unconditioned. You don't have to sit and anticipate problems or worry about what might be or come to face every day with that funny feeling that, "I wonder what today is going to bring to me that I have to combat." We start the day in a fresh consciousness of the perfect presence of God everywhere.

You don't carry anything from yesterday into today to worry about. Wouldn't it be marvelous to begin every day that free and clear that all of the yesterdays with all of the problems they presented are behind you? And yet, that's the Truth, isn't it? Spirit is never carrying over memories of this material world into this minute of today. Who's doing it? Our unawareness of the world mind that functions in us, as us. When we are wise to it, we can begin a day completely free of all worry, free of all concern, knowing that I am the living Light of the Father now and forever, I'll open a new book.

When you start your day with that awareness, you don't have the seeds of yesterday's problems to grow into great big oaks today and you don't have as much to combat or get rid of. It's a fresh, new, beautiful, Spiritual day and if it isn't, you're still in duality, still accepting the mirage as something you've got to live with.

Speaking of the fact that many of the healing works do not come off as we'd like them to, Joel offers two reasons. The first is a very simple reason; the practitioner hasn't got what it takes. He says, "Let's face it. Our practitioners aren't living in the truth all the time and because of it, they don't have the truth to be witnesses all the time." But there's a second reason, he said and this is the second reason. "The other reason is that the patients will not yield. They usually have it in mind the changing of an evil condition into a good one and this acts as a barrier." Spiritual healing is not changing an evil condition into a good one. Healing is really the changing of consciousness and very often there's a reluctance or unwillingness to yield up whatever it is that is acting as a block.

Now, I have met that, I have known that there were certain blocks in certain individuals but it's a delicate subject. You just can't say to a person, "This is your block." First of all because you never really can be sure what the block is. You can only think you know and secondly, as Joel points out here, people resent being told that they have this point of view. They may hate someone very desperately and don't know it. They may fear a condition very desperately and don't know it. They may be hanging on to an untruth.

I know one person who had a sense of guilt about something and really there weren't any words you could give to that person that would make them lose that sense of guilt and as long as that sense of guilt remained, the work that had to be done couldn't get through because the point here is to change the individual's consciousness and if the sense of guilt is there, that's the consciousness.

Now, what are they guilty about? It was a personal sense there. Guilt is of a personal nature. Guilt was the feeling that they hadn't done something they should have done. Well a change of consciousness would mean that there's no me here to do or not to do. Thou seest me, thou seest the Father. Here is the Light of God. This person having the guilt complex refused to accept their Identity as the Light. I may be the Light but look what I did. Well, the Light has nothing to do that could be wrong and so by insisting on a guilt complex, taking the blame for something, this individual was rejecting the Light of God as their own individual selfhood and that was a block.

Oh, there are many other blocks. We hold many people in a state of malpractice because we see them as they appear to be and we insist that's the way they are and then we may want them to be healed of something but we're still holding them in that light, that false sense of humanhood. We've got mortal beings on our hands, physical bodies on our hands and then when it comes to us, we haven't really come to that total acceptance of ourselves as the Light. When we do, then we're not a barrier.

There are some people who can call you for help and all you've got to do is hear their voice and before that happens, you're all aflame with Light. It's as if there's just nothing between you. It's the one Life. There's some people who invariably call you up and say, "Every time I call you it's always almost instantaneous." And you're thinking to yourself, "It's not me. I can tell you that. It's you."

There's something that some individual has as a block and something that others have is not a block and as Joel points out, that's only the second reason. The first one was the practitioner in the first place. Sometimes, the human element enters. Certain people will affect you and shouldn't. You shouldn't be affected by them, so you get desperate and you say, "Oh, I can't have that happen to poor Mrs. so and so." And right then you've hurt her and so on.

Now, continuing his thought, *"In Infinite Way healing work, we are not turning to God to heal anybody. We do not have the kind of God who would let anyone be sick if it were within His knowledge."*

And since all in Reality is in the knowledge of God, God isn't letting anyone get sick. Now, who's sick? The personal sense of self and the personal sense of self when we are lifted high enough being out of the way, there's no one there to be sick. Finally, there's no one there to be sick forever, cause there's no personal sense of self.

So, you see why healing is just a part of the work, an incidental part. It's a part of the way on the path to being lifted above the personal sense of self. The ultimate is that Christ takes over where you are and lives your Life. And when Christ takes over and lives your Life, you have fulfilled your mission. You fulfill the Divine blueprint at this level, yielding to Christ. When Christ lives your Life, you have your own personal physician.

"If we recognize God to be Omniscience and Omnipotence then surely we could not find anyone outside of God's knowledge."

So, who can we heal? It would be just as much of a mirage just to think you're healing someone as for them to think they're being healed because then practitioner and patient would be both in a false sense of self.

But suppose patient and practitioner are both in the knowledge that I am the Light? Then whatever temporarily seems to need healing yields very quickly. Two or more in the Light.

Now, in your world work, people will be reaching for the Light of their own Being and you will bring to it the knowledge that you are the Light of their Being and that will be two or more. For the Soul of everyone is yearning for the Light, driving us to that conscious union.

Now, our healing work takes a new turn. No sin, no disease are supported by a law of God. You see just hanging out there without God's support, what is it? Is it there if God isn't supporting it? It may seem a vast thing in the cosmic fourth world because we're just a little entity as a human being looking at this fourth world. And so, to us it's big, it's hovering, it's there - but it's not there. If we could remove personal sense of me and I be the Light, this vast thing would just vanish. It only hangs there because there's personal sense looking at it. That's what makes it hang there. That's what makes cancer stay on the earth. That's what makes earthquake stay in the earth. That's what makes all disease stay on the earth. You're looking at them out of our personal sense perpetuating that which isn't there.

As you withdraw from personal sense, you withdraw from the diseases of the world. You don't heal them. You recognize they aren't there. They do not exist in the Light of God which is all that is present.

Sin, disease: never supported by the law of God because if they were, they would be eternal. We never hope to change anything supported by God.

The fact that we do break through our sins, diseases, lacks is sufficient proof that there never was a law of God supporting them. It was only a law of matter, a law of mind. But these are not laws of God. And for this reason, any form of evil can be dispelled. Therefore, we need never be afraid to try to heal regardless of the name or nature of the claim because to begin with, we have the awareness that there is no law of God supporting it, no law of God maintaining it because it is an erroneous condition and we know that no law of God created it.

This is all part of the purifying of our consciousness.

We're finally exonerating God from creating evils and from supporting evils and from countenancing evil.

Now, in my own work, it's easy to get caught up in all these words even while you're learning, it's difficult to assimilate it into a practical way of life. And I find the best way to assimilate it is that no matter what you face, whatever its nature, don't waste your time trying to figure it out. The fact is that only God is present. Whatever comes at you and labels itself this or that or the other thing, go to your knowledge that God is present. That's accepting Omnipresence.

The minute you've accepted that God is present, you get a whole new perspective about it because if God is present, what are you going to do about it that God hasn't already done? The minute you know God is present, there's a new stability. God is present.

Now, where's the earthquake going to be in God's presence? You see how the belief in the earthquake is atheism? The belief in the reality of a head cold is atheism? The belief in the reality of any form of evil is atheism? God is present and the earth is the Lord's and the fulness of the earth. Is that earth going to quake? What's going to quake? The world mind's going to quake. That's all. That's where the earthquake's going to take place: in the world mind. That's where the head cold takes place: in the world mind. That's where every evil takes place: in the world mind and all you've got to do is stay in the world mind if you want to share in those evils. That's where the mirage takes place, in the world mind and when you have accepted God's presence where you are, where the world is, strangely, those evils do not come nigh thy dwelling. It's all in accepting God's presence everywhere and where you are.

And as you stand in that, you know God has the power to maintain a Perfect universe so where can evil be? That world mind is knocking on your Christ mind. It can't enter.

Whatever God has, you have. Wherever God is, you are. In that Consciousness, you are not open to that which defiles. And so, instead of reaching for that little jar in the medicine cabinet, suppose you reach for that little conscious awareness that God is where you are and see if that doesn't do the job.

There was no earthquake in the Christ and if you're in the Christ Consciousness, there's no earthquake in you. It goes right around and makes a detour leaving even one little rose to bloom, if necessary.

Silence, (pause) ...

We are not dividing his garment as the soldiers did when the Master was on the cross. One seamless garment, the invisible Light everywhere and there's no place in it for division. God is never divided. God never divides himself. There's no place in it for material activity. There's no place in it for evil activity. That Consciousness is the realization of Oneness.

"And so anyone," says Joel, *"can [practice] healing.... at any time if he will realize the basic principle that he is not trying to heal a disease, a condition, a sin, or a false appetite. The moment anyone tries to do that, he's trapped, and there will be no healing.... We are not dealing with condition, [we are dealing with] universal belief in a selfhood apart from God."* A universal ignorance, a universal hypnotism but only an appearance. There is no self apart from God and therefore, there can be no evil anywhere.

Now, you have the capacity within your Self to heal alcoholics and drug addicts. Now, I'll tell you exactly how. It'll shock you because it's so simple. When you can reach the realization that there is no liquor, you'll find you have the way to heal any alcoholic who comes to you. Liquor does not exist. When you find that you know that drugs do not exist, you'll find you have the answer to healing a drug addict. There is no drug. Did God create them? If you believe they exist, you're going to try to heal the drug addict or heal the alcoholic. You can't heal them. You have to know the unreality of the person, the unreality of the condition, the very unreality of that which seemingly is causing them to be alcoholics and drug addicts. God didn't make liquor. God made nothing material. There is no liquor. That's how you'll heal an alcoholic when you have the realization of it: that there is no liquor, period. Stop right there.

You want to heal smoking? There are no cigarettes. They don't exist. Oh, you reach for the illusion and you puff an illusion and you think you're smoking but when you know there are no cigarettes, you'll find you will not smoke if you don't want to. That's how you'll break it.

There is no material world. There is no cigarettes. See, we can't go on thinking there's a material cigarette, there's a material bottle of booze. There isn't any. You want to enjoy it? Go ahead but it isn't there. And if you want to break the habit, it isn't there is the answer.

This'll come to you someday (sound of click of the fingers) as a quick realization, a conviction, an awareness of the non-reality of matter and you'll see why Joel says, *"Anyone can heal."* All you've got to do is know the Truth. But you've got to know it all the time. Stay with it.

Finally, *"In the Infinite Way, we never give a treatment to a person. We give the treatment to ourselves. We are the one under treatment because we are the one to whom the appearance has been brought and it must be made in our own consciousness going immediately to the I of our Being."*

When I said, "We go to God," this is another way of saying, "We go to *I.*" God where you are is the Light, going to the *I* of your Being, meaning accepting that *I*, the Self of me is the Spirit of God. That's going to be *I* of your own Being. That's the beginning of treating you instead of the patient.

"And it must be met in our own consciousness.... go immediately to the I of our being, abiding there until we come to the conclusion that [I, here, the Light of God] and my Father [the infinite] are one." [I, here and the infinite are one] this then is a universal truth. We wrestle with this truth within ourselves until we now come to the point of conviction that all there is, is Spirit."

Now, we haven't told that person stop smoking, stop drinking, stop taking drugs but that person has come to you for You to help them stop and you recognize this Truth here in your Self. All that's here is Spirit and there is Spirit.

Finally, comes "Ah." You know that is true. In a few moments comes a deep sense of peace, a click, a deep breath, something or other and I know that God is on the scene. *"That's all there is to it,"* says Joel, *"as you can see I've had nothing to do with the patient.... That's all there is to it."*

Over 16 years, he was able to establish that *"That's all there is to it."* But he established it. And as we put in our time, we'll discover that we can say, *"That's all there is to it."* As long as there's a me here trying to heal a you there, we're getting nowhere.

And so, self-crucifixion which is what the practitioner learns is also the secret of your living free of the horrors of the world. When you remove the personal sense and have only the Light of God where you are, which is One with the Light of God everywhere, you won't have to remove those evils. You will watch the Invisible Light bear witness to Itself in the visible world.

I think that's pretty clear. He made one more statement that seemed important to me. I think I'd rather look at it in the book. It's the last statement in that chapter.

"It is possible to bring the very presence of God to earth if you will meditate, make contact with your Center, and let that Presence be released into the world."

587

The words to me that are important there is, *"It is possible"* meaning, I, Joel have done it. Others before me have done it. Others with me have done it. Others will do it. It is possible to bring the very presence of God into your experience.

And that should be our single-centered goal: to bring the very presence of God into our experience as a permanent dispensation. Don't wait to suffer. This is a always job, a constant job. You should always be the living presence of God where you are. The Light of God must be your constant companion as your Self and it is the Light of everyone else that makes you One with the universe. You're moving in the Grace of his Presence.

Next week, we're going to look into the resurrection of Jesus Christ, the 20th chapter of John. We've come to the place where lifting up the *I*, seeing the nothingness of self as person, is the accomplished fact of his demonstration on the earth, and now we want to understand entirely that with our own Spiritual progression, we want to find what the religions of the world have missed; that the Light of the world which came forth as the permanent Life of Jesus Christ was demonstrating that the permanent Life of us is right where we stand.

We are overlooking our permanent Life as long as we stand in the sense of a second or material self. When that is cast aside, like Lazarus, we walk in the invisible body of the Soul.

Resurrection should take us into the conscious awareness of the invisible body of the Soul. That's a Christmas present we owe ourselves. That will be our work next Sunday, chapter 20 of the Gospel of John.

And then we'll increase our capacity to do world work in the remaining three sessions.

Thanks for bringing the sunshine where the world thought there was rain.

Class 43

Going All The Way

Herb: I want to extend a very cordial welcome to all our friends.

We have a very unusual lesson today. It is the lesson of the Resurrection and I believe you will discover that as you dwell within your Self with the meaning of Resurrection, you will find that you have the key to every so-called problem on the face of the earth here in one lesson.

In the Resurrection of Jesus Christ, is the meaning of the entire mission of Christ on earth, the meaning of your Life, the meaning of all those who have walked before you and all those who will follow you. And in the realization of that meaning into an actual living experience, you'll find that for you, the problems of earth, even those that are not your individual problems but the collective problems of man, for you begin to lose any sense of validity at all, whether they be war or famine or overpopulation, death itself. You can look at them and see that when you know what Resurrection truly means, that all evil on the earth for you no longer has any meaning at all.

Now there was a first Easter and I presume you might call the first Easter when Mary Magdalene came to the tomb, looked in and to her amazement, there was no body. And that was Easter. He has risen. "Someone has taken my Lord." And the misinterpretation of the first Easter has caused us to live not only misinterpreting every other Easter but those 364 days in between Easters have suffered accordingly.

"I give you the keys to the Kingdom," said the Master, who had answered to the name Christ. "Yes, Peter, thou art right. I am the Christ and I, the Christ, give you the keys to the Kingdom." And then this I which says, "I am in the midst of you and I, give you the keys to the Kingdom" also said "I am in the midst of you and I am the Resurrection. I, in the midst of you am the Resurrection."

And if you go with the world who has misinterpreted the first Easter then every day thereafter is spent in turning away from the message of the Christ.

First, we know that God is All. And then the question is, how do you crucify God? And then the question is, can God be resurrected? Is Christ in a human form, resurrected from what?

And we see that a false label has been put on this meaning and it is because of an unawareness of a fundamental fact that rarely is pointed out. In fact, you won't find it except in what may be called the Mystery schools which are not known to the world, in the inner teachings and that inner teaching makes understandable the Resurrection.

I think you can get to see it in another way if we look at two passages in the Bible. One is in Peter and one is in Revelation.

Peter says, "The Gospel has been taught to the dead," and in Revelation, it says, "You have the reputation of being alive but you are dead." You'll find that in 3:1 Revelation. "You have the reputation of being alive but you are dead." It's disguised as a letter to the third church or to one of the churches, the Church of Sardis. "You have the reputation of being alive but you are dead."

Now, this is that which the human mind has failed to accept. When we come into incarnation through birth, this in Scripture means the first death. Incarnation is not birth in Scripture. Incarnation is death. Reincarnation is return to that death. The real birth in Scripture is Resurrection, when you are resurrected out of the first death.

Peter understood that mortal life is called death by Spirit. John understood that mortal life is called death by Spirit. And rather than tell us that we were dead in words that we understood, many allusions and hints were made. Always to let us know that death is actually what we have called birth and it is death because the Soul is imprisoned in matter. Never is the Soul actually imprisoned in matter but matter becomes the place where we are separated from the awareness of our own Soul.

And so, the incarnation into flesh, into matter, the first death is that state called humanhood. That state which is what we have called birth and it was necessary for a teaching to come upon the earth to show us that incarnation into flesh is only halfway home and the other half is Resurrection out of flesh. And so, you have the birth into flesh and then the birth out of flesh. The first birth, incarnation and the second birth, is Resurrection. One into body and one out of body.

You might compare it to a group of people who decide to motor from California to New York. They're going to spend, let's say, five days on route. When they get to Chicago, one of them says, "I can't wait till I get there" and the rest of them say, "No, this is as far as we want to go. We'll stay in Chicago." And that one insists, "But you haven't arrived at your destination. You've only come halfway." And they say, "Well, it's nice here. We want to stay here. We don't want to go any further."

Humanhood is that state of starting out to New York but stopping in Chicago, not knowing that our distance has not been fully travelled. We think this is where we belong and we want to stay. And the Spirit says, "No. We started out to go to the Seventh Heaven. That's where we're going."

We're making a complete tour of Infinity. We start from God. We go out into incarnation and then we return to our starting point. You cannot stop midway. Resurrection is to push us out of Chicago into New York all the way to make us complete our journey from

God the Father into the state called mortality and back to God, the Father. We cannot imprison the Soul by stopping in this fourth world.

And so, for those who receive that deeper insight which permits them to know that there is a way to go beyond mortality - which is not the way of human death but is the way of transition, the way of second birth - we find that Resurrection takes on the meaning then of being born into Life before human death. And this for us then becomes the greatest accomplishment for which we can spend our time, our effort, our concentrated and total human lifespan, to reach that great pinnacle of achievement in which we can be born again. First, having been born into mortality and now to be born out of mortality, to become the Word of God made flesh instead of the physical appearance of a world mind made flesh.

Now, either Jesus was resurrected or he was not. It's either a fact or it is not. If we worship at the shrine of Christ within ourselves, we understand then that Resurrection is the raising up of Christ Power within each individual. When Christ in you is accepted, realized, understood as the very nature of your own Being, there stands the Son of God and you are resurrected and you are still in the flesh on this earth, not having yet come close to the point of a grave.

Resurrection must precede the grave. We must step out of the first birth into the second, out of the first death and whoever does, finds that they have become Masters for the way of Resurrection is the way of Self-mastery.

Resurrection is the mastery of land, the mastery of sea, the mastery of air and it follows that it also gives you mastery over sickness, over age, over untoward conditions that are called evil and over the illusion of death. You discover that all death is, is a word and that the only one who experiences death are those who remain. The one who goes on knows nothing about it. There's not a person who has gone on to death who knows what death is. We who remain think they have died. All that happens is the illusion of death continues to baffle us.

But now, we see One who not only goes through the death: having helped others to come into their second birth, having raised a child into her second birth, having raised one out of the coffin into his second birth, having raised Lazarus into his second birth and now the greatest achievement of all - that which is the achievement of every man on earth, to raise ourselves out of a dying body.

And here, it is made visible. Now, if it's true, we must pause. We must study. We must listen for the Word from within to teach us what is the meaning of this that could not die. The world has benefited little from the Resurrection of Jesus Christ but we are to benefit from that Resurrection. It was a great teaching, the greatest teaching on this earth.

Now, there was a Soul body there. There was one who had passed the point of a mortal body, but this who passed the point of a mortal body was the Christ made manifest to men. And the Christ which is the nature of your own Being, is saying, "I must take you now past the concept of a mortal body. I must resurrect you from the myth of mortality. I must show you another realm, a Kingdom of God on earth as it is in Heaven. I must lift you to the point where your consciousness can leave behind the grave clothes in which mortal body is buried and the napkin over the face so that a new mind and a new body walk where the old man was."

Resurrection from the body of flesh, from the mind of matter is possible on this earth and when we finished our last chapter, Joel's statement was just that. It is possible to bring the experience of God on earth and the Power of God and the Presence of God and the Love of God because they are on earth and when Jesus steps aside, miracles are performed by the Christ.

When mortal you, steps aside, the Immaculate Conception takes place. Then the Self of you is all that remains. The sense of duality is gone. We are resurrected from duality, resurrected from material sense, resurrected from the concepts of a human mind, resurrected from the belief that we live between birth and death alone, resurrected from the belief that we live in bodies that must die. All of these are inherent in the Resurrection.

There are many startling conclusions that we must face. We know that God is All. God is not human flesh. And the Resurrection teaches us one of the most strangest things that can ever be said. The illusion of the human race.

Only One stands and that is the invisible Christ revealed as the deathless Being, the invisible Self of all who walk in bodies of flesh. To see it as Jesus, the Christ, to be worshipped by men has done us no good whatsoever. To see it as the revelation of your own invisible Self, made manifest, is the turning point for I in the midst of you, I am the Savior. I am Salvation. I am the Resurrection. I am the Life which is imperishable. And your function on this earth is to be resurrected out of a dying body into I, the Life, the Self, the Reality of your Being. Not in a future Heaven, but now, here, on this earth to walk in the knowledge that you are the living essence of the Father.

Without this meaning, Resurrection is pointless. It is nothing but a personalized deity. Whereas the Christ is teaching that all Life is impersonal. All Life. You are the Life and your function, is to be that Life, not the person so that the outer person becomes nothing more than the echo of the Life which you are.

Self-mastery is when the outer person is the echo of the Life that is your Being. When you're living in your Life, the outer person conforms to the law of the Divine and the outer person is nothing more than the innerness of Being expressed into visibility.

And so, if we're going to accept the Resurrection of Jesus Christ, it must be on the terms of the Christ which revealed that there is a Self in every man which is forever and that this Self which is forever is not to be resurrected. It already is. Resurrection is not future. Resurrection is an established fact. Resurrection is dropping away all that denies identity, the Now of Resurrection, the Is of Resurrection. It wasn't something we are to become. It is a revelation of what we already are.

"*I am the resurrection,*" says Jesus, long before the body is placed in a tomb, long before Mary Magdalene comes to the garden, long before the Master walks into a room, through a wall. While appearing on this earth, the invisible Christ through Jesus says, "*I am the resurrection.*"

Then how could the Resurrection occur later if it already occurred. The Resurrection was not the body returning. The Resurrection was stepping out of the false belief in mortal sense. All of the miracles were possible because Resurrection had already been completed. The miracles were the revelation of the invisible Christ Presence everywhere, resurrecting those who seemed to be living in bodies of flesh. Each of these was Resurrection performing an active revelation of its own Presence that the Christ in each individual is resurrected when the consciousness opens up and as you open your consciousness, Christ in you is resurrected.

In other words, you become conscious of Christ in you. As your consciousness of the Christ in you is raised, you are being lifted to that pinnacle when, I am the Christ, speaks through you as you and Resurrection is an established fact.

Until we have been resurrected, until we are conscious of the Christ of Being, our work on earth must continue and we must incarnate again and again, always coming back to the tomb of flesh until one day, we enter the tomb of flesh like Mary Magdalene and we can see that there is no Divinity in the tomb. There is no

Divinity in a human body. When you know there is no Divinity in your human body, the startling conclusion is reached that there is no Life in form. There is no Divine Life in a human form and only Divine Life is.

And so now, Mary Magdalene is going through this great opening of her consciousness. She comes to the tomb and the body isn't there. Actually, she is a pawn. She's being used by the Spirit to demonstrate what everyone must go through. We must all enter the tomb of our bodies. We must finally come to the conclusion that the Lord is not in the tomb. You will not find Christ in your human body. *"He is risen."*

There is no Divine Life, there is no Divine Spirit in your human body. And then Resurrection is, if I have no Divine Life in my human body, am I in one? Am I Divine or am I mortal? If I am Divine, can I be in a human body? What is this human body? Well, that's what we're being resurrected from. That's the purpose of Resurrection, to lift us out of a sense of human body, out of the material sense of a mortal world, to leave our nets, to fish on the other side of the ship.

And so, Resurrection says to you directly, "How far are you going? Are you stopping at the midway point? Then, you don't want to study about Resurrection. Going all the way? Good. Then you're interested."

And therefore, for those who are going all the way, we can't stop even at having a religion because in the Spirit of God, there is only one religion and that's the only religion on this earth. Christ is the religion. You either are or you are not the Light of God. And the Light of God doesn't have any kinds of creeds or colors or shapes or sizes. You can't say the Light of God is a Christian or the Light of God is a Jew or the Light of God is a Hindu. The Light of God has no labels put upon it and we, who are going all the way, can only accept that I am the Light of God and we can accept only that the Light of God walks this earth invisibly everywhere and it is our function by correct awareness to participate in the Resurrection of mankind. The Resurrection of everyone who walks this earth in a human body is our function by recognizing only the Light of God.

Now, into the sepulchre goes Mary Magdalene on the third day. The third day is when he had promised to raise the body. And here on the third day, there were these women coming to the tomb with spices. They were going to anoint the corpse.

The world was unprepared for the meaning of "On the third day, I will raise this temple." The world was unaware that he who had said, *"If I go not away, the Comforter will not come to you"* was now putting them through the experience for even while she said, "My Lord is not here" the very Christ was there. There is not a moment in the life of any individual on the earth when Christ is departed.

No matter what state we find ourselves in, Christ is always identity. Mary Magdalene was the invisible Christ but unaware at that moment and Peter to whom she ran and said, *"They have taken our LORD away"* and John, started to run to the tomb. It says that John out ran him, and he got there first but he didn't go in. And then, when Peter came, John let Peter go in first.

Now, you've seen in the Resurrection of Lazarus a similar symbology. Noteworthy is that first, Mary the mother of Jesus, is a symbol of the highest level of unselfing that is possible to womanhood. Mary Magdalene is not of that level but she, being a fallen woman, represents what is called the fallen female principle. Whenever you find that feminine principle, you're really talking about matter. We all come to earth through woman as matter and matter is what we must be raised up from.

Mary Magdalene - she would have been the lowest and yet, not condemned by the Spirit of God - is now the first woman on the earth to come to the tomb of Jesus Christ. She's actually the first person on earth and that's the symbol then that the material sense of life, which is the feminine principle of life, must be lifted up in man. And as she comes to the tomb, the feminine principle of life is being lifted up symbol[icly] and this activates Love and Faith. The moment you are moving aside the belief in a material sense, raising up the mortal material sense of life, Divine Love and Faith begin to flow into your consciousness and that's John and Peter running to the tomb. Love gets there first.

Intuitively, the heart outraces the mind. The Soul, the awareness of God Presence, the Love of God is released when you are willing to step outside of sense conviction and this intuitive sense, this new formed Love within you awakens your Faith. Love doesn't need to be shown. Faith does. So, Love doesn't enter the tomb. Love steps aside and lets Faith go in to examine. Love already knows. Faith represented by Peter goes into the tomb and looks and examines and over there, just as Mary Magdalene had said, there were the linen clothes, very neatly folded. Nobody in them. And over there, on the other side, there was the napkin worn around the face, neatly folded. Nobody there.

And then, John goes in and he sees and he believes. But what do they believe? They believe exactly what Mary Magdalene has told them. "They have taken the Lord, our Master away." That's what they believe. They cannot understand and the world cannot understand that there was nobody there to take away.

"*I am the Resurrection*," the Master had said. The body that they think was put in the tomb was never put there. It didn't have to come out of a tomb. It didn't have to have its rate of vibration so increased that it could now disappear. "*I am the Resurrection*," long before you tried to put me in a tomb.

And so, the startling conclusion is that there was no physical Jesus there to put in a tomb. Why? Because the Christ was all that was there and the Christ is not a physical body. Then what did they put in a tomb? And that's where we have to really stop and take a long, hard look because that's where you're being shown that not only was there no Jesus to be put in a tomb, there was nobody there to put him in a tomb. There was no one to be buried and no one to bury him. There was no physical body on the earth. If there was one physical body on the earth, then God is not All. Spirit is not All.

To go all the way means to see that Jesus was not entombed. Jesus had died on the banks of the Jordan. He had died when he could say, "Thou seest me, thou seest the Father." He had died when the dove descended. The very physical body of Jesus had been stepped out of and the body of the Spirit had been stepped into, all in one great, redeeming realization and it continued to walk the earth appearing to men's minds as the form of Jesus, until the men's minds buried the form in their own minds, in a tomb that existed in their own minds. You were looking at the complete, mortal dream and only one had stepped out of that dream.

To further understand that, on your five-day trip to New York, the reason you're going there is because you know it's there. You know that space is there, it's called New York and you're driving to it. Even if you had not gone there before, you know it's there and it's going to take you five days to get there but you're not worried about it not being there when you arrive, even though it's five days away.

And there's a very strange assumption you make in that trip. You assume that you will have five days to do it, that that time which you have not yet experienced will come to you. You don't question the fact that you will have the days, the time. But where is that time? It hasn't arrived yet. How do you know there'll be five days? Where is that time? It's in your future and yet, you blithely accept it as a fact. You accept future time as normal, something you will be able to live in and then you go through that future time and lo and behold, it does appear and in those five days that appear, you finally arrive at this space that was always there.

Now Resurrection is telling us something like that. It's saying that just as if there was space that you knew existed and you went to go over it and there's time that you know will appear to give you the time to go to it, there is also an invisible Kingdom right here and it isn't in the future. That space that exists before you go exists now and five days later, you would have covered space that existed before you started on your journey. The time that you think is in the future is already existent just as that space is already existent and the invisible Kingdom, the Infinity of it, the Allness of it, exists right now and Resurrection doesn't mean that I'm going to become an immortal Being in the future for the immortal Self is a now fact that I must learn to live in and out of, not in the future of it but in the present of it. I'm not going to be resurrected. I am the Resurrection. I am that immortal Self now.

And, when Jesus accomplished this by stepping out of self into Self, out of mortal form illusion into Soul body, into Spiritual Selfhood, he also stepped out of the illusion that you could go across the country in five days. For him, there was no country anymore. He stepped out of the illusion of time and when you are living in your immortal Self, you're in the nowness which has nothing to do with the illusion of space or the illusion of time.

In the illusion of space and in the illusion of time, there will be bodies to be buried and people to bury them because we're all moving with that time. None of us have tomorrow yet. No one on this earth has tomorrow but everyone believes tomorrow will come. That's because we're all moving in the illusion of the one time.

Jesus stepped out of that illusion, into Christhood. When you step into Christhood, you're not moving with the other illusions that take place and one of the greatest of those illusions is the illusion of matter. Just as we all move with the assumption that tomorrow's time will come today, that future time will come into the present, so we move with the illusion that matter is a reality. And as long as you're in the illusion that future time will come into the present, you're going to move in the other illusions that are part of time; matter, motion, all physicality, all conditions, all good and all evil. All that is not God created moves with each of us in the one world mind, in the illusion of time, space and all it contains. And only when you are the living, Spiritual Self are you out of this moving illusion of time and space in which the images of the world are contained.

When Jesus was able to not die, he was revealing the presence of a realm which makes the realm in which men live, a different world than we had ever imagined. That's why it is said, "We must preach the Gospel to the dead." That's why Paul says "To be carnally minded is to be dead." That's why Paul says, "When will we be taken out of this body of death?" That's why Jesus teaches, *"Raise the dead."*

Always, deadness and human life are one and the same. The moment we came into birth, incarnate in human flesh, we had entered the death. We have called it life by mistake. Knowing it as life, Resurrection means nothing to us, except maybe some future Heaven and it doesn't work that way. We have to see mortality as not the creation of God. The word "death" is merely to describe it is not the creation of God; it is a world image. And all that it contains, the illusion of space and time, the illusion of growing up, the illusion of then giving away your life, all of that disappears when you know yourself to be the living Christ who needs no Resurrection for, I am the Resurrection. You stand on the nowness of Being and watch the clouds drift by.

Let's take a look at this passage here (John 20:1) and see how beautifully the Spirit is trying to open us up to the meaning of living as the Christ or the resurrected Self.

"The first day of the week cometh Mary Magdalene early, when it was yet dark, unto the sepulchre, and seeth the stone taken away from the sepulchre."

Now, that sepulchre or tomb means life on earth. That's the symbol of it. It means the earthly life. It also means the human body. The stone taken away from it is this great big stone door that runs on grooves and they roll it through the grooves like a millstone and then they put these vast ropes across it and they fasten them to the tomb and they seal the ropes with wax. They want to be sure that nobody's going in or out. They don't want that body stolen because they're afraid - at least the Sanhedrin's afraid - that if the body is stolen, the world will think that Jesus is the Son of God or some kind of a great person. That's the last thing they want. That was why they wanted him crucified. They didn't want him to be a miracle man. And now they've got to be sure he's not a miracle man and fasten that tomb so securely that nobody can get in. They want him dead. And the Romans have been asked to put extra soldiers around and they do that. Every precaution is taken. It's impossible. You couldn't bribe a Centurion to get in there. It would take quite a number of people to even open the door.

And of course, they're all pawns of the Spirit to show us that there's no way for a human being to go in or out.

But here comes this fallen creature, the adulteress, who by now, we know is well on the way to her total illumination. It was she who poured oil upon the Master. It's a sign of the recognition of the Soul body. Next to Mary, she is the highest illumined on the earth.

But she is now alarmed. The body isn't there. She runneth. She cometh to Simon Peter. *"They have taken away the LORD ... We know not where they have put him."* She thinks they have been, in some way, instrumental in removing that body and putting it somewhere. But you and I know that's not what he's teaching. That body which is the same body that was shown in Transfiguration, that body of Light, is not buried in that tomb. It never was. You couldn't squeeze the Infinite Christ into a physical tomb. You can't squeeze the Infinite Christ of your own Being into a sepulchre, into a physical body.

From this we are to find our Life elsewhere than in our physical bodies. We are to become conscious of the Life that is not in the physical body. We are to become conscious that this Life which is not in the physical body, which never was, is perfect and every situation that the physical body must meet, we have to first meet in the invisible Life which is revealed to us. As we meet these situations in the invisible Life first, then the outer body becomes an echo or reflection of that perfect, invisible Life and moves in the Grace and Harmony of the Father.

"Stand ye fast."

This situation is also described in Zachariah. The early part of the day when it was not yet dark, when it was still dark rather. This is a fulfillment of a prophecy of Zachariah.

14th chapter verses 6, 7 and 9.

"It shall come to pass in that day, and the light shall not be clear, nor dark: But it shall be one day which shall be known to the LORD, not day, not night: but it shall come to pass, that at evening time it shall be light."

This is a transitional state when just as you and I are discussing that we have no Divine Life in this physical body, that is the state of mind of Mary Magdalene. *"They have taken away my LORD."* You don't know where to go. You would blithely assume Christ is in your body. You assume that you were the Light of God in some way in this body. But this body is revealed here esoterically as the sepulchre. This physical body is the sepulchre that she's looking into and the Lord isn't there. There is no Divine Life in the human body. And there's no other life than Divine Life.

Now, you're coming face to face with the almost epical revelation of the Resurrection, that there's no one living on earth in a human body. No one. But it isn't yet day. We're not in the full consciousness of the meaning of that. It's still dark.

Zachariah was well aware of that. *"And it shall be in that day, that living waters shall go out from Jerusalem…. And the LORD shall be king over all the earth: in that day shall there be one LORD, and his name one."*

This transitional stage when you say, "They have taken my God away," when you don't know where to go; when you realize that there really is no Divine Life in a human form. Then you can go further and understand the linen grave clothes and the napkin.

So, Peter and John run and he, Peter, following John, they come to the tomb *"And he stooping down, and looking in, saw the linen clothes lying; yet went he not in. And then cometh Simon Peter following [him, and] went into the sepulchre, and seeth the linen clothes lie."*

Now, these linen clothes were the symbol that Christ Jesus no longer wears physical clothes. This is a definite, inner experience you will undergo when the Soul is unwrapped; when you lay aside the garments of physical flesh in your consciousness. This is the linen clothes folded neatly on the side.

When you reach the conclusion, the understanding, the deeper revelation that only the mind wears a garment of flesh and the mind is not the mind of God, then you will transcend that mind and in your transcendental awareness you will know that you are setting aside the linen clothes.

You see, we are buried in and by bodies of flesh and the linen clothes that you set aside are the bodies of flesh which you realize do not contain Divine Life and therefore, you are not in those bodies of flesh.

And over here there's a napkin, the same way. They put these originally on the corpses. Now, this corpse somehow folded the linen clothes and folded the napkin, put them in separate places and isn't there. Again, the Spirit is revealing that the napkin, which covered the face, no longer covers the face. That is the sign that now, we see him face to face.

Lazarus had come forth from the tomb. He, too was in grave clothes and a napkin over his face and the Master said, "*Loose him [and] let him go.*" And only then, was the napkin removed. Christ in you removes the napkin from your face. Christ in you enables you to see him face to face. Christ in you, with the napkin removed, is the Christ mind; with the linen clothes removed is the Christ body.

When in your consciousness, you come out of the sepulchre, out of the sense that I have a mortal body, then the linen clothes, the grave clothes are removed. You are in the Christ body realized. The napkin is removed from the face. You are in the Christ mind realized and you are the Resurrection. This is an experience that must take place in our earthly experience before the grave.

I lay aside the linen clothes. I lay aside the napkin. I accept that I am the living Christ body and the living Christ mind now and no other. And though I have no full capacity to live in it knowledgeably, to release the totality of it, the fulness of it, as Zachariah said, "That day will come when the Lord is one." But where do you begin? You must begin. You must start on this trip and then, not stop midway.

All the way means to step out of the body of flesh as a fact. It isn't there. Out of the human mind that sees it as a fact because the human mind which sees the illusion must equally be an illusion. Take off the napkin.

This is a turning in consciousness. This is pausing to accept or reject. And when you accept, even the brief time lived in the awareness that this body of flesh here and that body of flesh there are but pathways on the road to the fulness of Being. We're not to stop in them. We're not to be content to make them better. Our function is to outgrow them, to come out of the tomb.

If you have tried to face individual problems of some kind, even physical ones, with the knowledge that you're not in a body of flesh and therefore, the physical condition had nothing to do with You: if you've done this, you know that it is quite startling to see how you are separated from these pains. It's very startling.

This developed Consciousness that I am not in the flesh and nothing in the flesh is mine and then to look over the earth which in the fulness is the invisible Spirit is to remove the concept of flesh everywhere: to look over the fields, to look at the rivers and the mountains and the forests and the grass and to know this is man's concept of the invisible Spirit of God which is there and only the invisible Spirit of God is there is to bring you into the Oneness with Spirit everywhere. This is all part of coming into the Resurrection before the grave.

And then you find that it's almost when problems break around you, sometimes it's very hard for them to register on your awareness. You just don't catch it as a problem. You catch it as some kind of false concept in the air. It registers with you quite differently than in your normal mortal consciousness. There it hits right into you and it sticks there and it wriggles around and demands attention.

But when you're in the atmosphere of the resurrected Self, the ground is higher and these problems seem sometimes so far below you can hardly see them. They don't make contact. They don't have the urgency and strangely enough, they dissolve because they cannot penetrate the Self which is not in the flesh. There's nothing left to feed these problems. And then, you know you have found a different level to live in.

Now, just to read about the Resurrection is nothing. The Resurrection is an experience that takes place within yourself and it's a daily experience and it's a continuing experience. And you know it's happening when it's happening. And through the continuous

Resurrection within, you know you're being reborn to that Self which can say, "Before Abraham was, before Adam and Eve was, I am."

Somebody discovered just the other day that the world was at least 70 billion years old. That means Christ must be older than the 70 billion years because "Before the world was, I am." You lose these tight, confining, finite idea of life which is actually death. There is no tight, confining idea called life. It is death. It's the shadow that we live in as we look out of the mind that perceives what God did not create.

Then it says all the disciples or the three anyway, John and Peter, after they had looked and believed that Jesus had been taken from the tomb, they went home. And that means they went back to this consciousness, this mortal sense of life. The old consciousness was their home. They returned home.

He had told them, "[If you believe on me,] the works that I do, you shall do.... If a man believes on me, though he were dead, yet, shall he live."

— End of Side One —

"If man believes on me, though he were mortal, yet shall he live."

Always, when you find the dead burying the dead and you find that word "dead" in here, we're being told that that is the nature of the human race. And it's a false state of being.

Now, if you'd been present and seen the Master in the garden as Mary and if you had been sufficiently versed in his message to know the Truth, you would have known that before the crucifixion and before the Resurrection and after the crucifixion and after the Resurrection, Christ had not changed. Christ was the same before and after. All that had changed was in the world mind. And to this minute, Christ has not changed. Christ never changes. Christ is always the same. All that can change is the world mind in you or the consciousness of Truth in you.

When you know the unchanging Christ in you, the Resurrection becomes experience instead of words in a book and that Resurrection experience is what most of us are going through and have been going through for some time until we emerge into the pure Light and mortality is no longer a myth to baffle us, to frighten us, to deceive us.

I'm hopeful that today the Spirit of the Resurrection will dwell in every heart, that we can learn to accept within us the Truth that the I of our own Being is already the resurrected Self, free of the material world, independent of form and that we can learn to live in and accept that I resurrected Self, not as a future event but as the present Truth of Being that we are all joint heirs in I, the resurrected Self.

This is about our midway point and so we'll meditate on this.

As we close our eyes, our function is to know that the Resurrection of Jesus Christ was the teaching that I, Spirit is my name. I am that Christ which was teaching Resurrection. Resurrection isn't an event that happened in the past nor is it an event that will happen in the future. Resurrection is the revelation of the identity of mankind, that all I can ever be is the living Spirit of God.

It is the consciousness that must be resurrected so that my consciousness must be lifted out of its false beliefs. This is where I dwell.

Silence, (pause) …

Go into the tomb of body now. Enter your body. Look around. You will not find the Lord there. You will not find Christ in that body. Christ is the Life of God. Resurrection says, "I cannot continue to live in this body. Christ is not here."

Resurrection says, "I am the Christ." This body has no existence except in mortal mind. I'm living in a dream body and as long as I continue to, I will have only relationships with other dream forms.

I am an invisible body made of Infinite Spirit. I am going through this level of the world mind. I'm not going to stop here. I'm not going to be imprisoned, entombed in a body not created by God which does not contain his Life. I am stepping out of world concept. I am Divine Life itself and if I have any body, it must be a Divine body. It cannot be this mortal body. I am living in my invisible, Divine body now and this concept that the world sees is but a level of human consciousness, a mental image. I am proceeding beyond it.

I and the Father are one Life. One Life is revealed as the only Life there is and that Life can never be put into a tomb, can never be put into a grave, can never be put into a sepulchre. That Life has no beginning, that Life has no end and that Life, I truly am. To become conscious of that Life is my Resurrection. That is my life work, to become conscious of the Life that can never be entombed and that is your second birth. When you become conscious of that Life, you are reborn of the Spirit and the Word, not world mind, but the Word of God is made flesh.

Silence, (pause) …

Let us pause a moment now.

In the 9th verse of the 20th chapter, there's a very important statement. John says,

"For as yet they knew not the scripture, that he must rise again from the dead."

Those who believe they're living in mortal forms are the dead and they knew not the Scripture that he, Christ, must rise from the dead; that Christ must be realized in the consciousness of those who think they're walking in mortal forms. This is the next step in all evolution of man on earth. And the importance of it is this: Scripture must be fulfilled.

You've noticed that the Scripture may be fulfilled is spoken always and always there's an appearance that our response to a prophecy, that goes way, way back to either Isaiah or Ezekiel or Daniel or someone of that Spiritual Consciousness and then out here in the physical world it appears because Scripture must be fulfilled and the Scripture says, *"If I go not away, the Comforter will not come unto you."* But this I who goes away is your physical sense of self. If the personal I, goes not away, the Christ in you will not raise you from the tomb of mortality and Scripture must be fulfilled so you're in conflict with the Spirit and the will of God unless you are cooperating. Unless you can say, *"The Father worketh hitherto and I work,"* whatever the Father's will, is in me, I am doing and not putting roadblocks in the way or not ignoring, you're in conflict with the very Spirit of your own Being.

And so again, Scripture says, *"Sell all thou hast."* All. That means every concept that is in conflict with Scripture must be sold or put aside. Every belief that we have is part of all that we have until you're willing to accept that only what the Father gives me, do I have and what the Father does not give me, I do not have. Then, you have sold *"all that thou hast."*

The Scripture in you that must be fulfilled is that you *"Be [ye therefore] perfect [even]as your Father,"* and therefore the one Divine Life is revealed as your Life now. That one, Divine Life is not going to be resurrected. Christ has always been alive.

"I am the Resurrection," says Christ and by believing that the Resurrection could be resurrected, religion has lost its way. By not knowing the identity of he who says *"I am the Resurrection"* as the indwelling Spirit of every man, religion has missed the point. I in you must be accepted and you must pass beyond the mental acceptance. Christ in you must be raised from the dead sense of a material being.

And now, then, we're interested then in the Christ experience which is the Resurrection experience and you'll notice that nobody goes into the tomb as a group. Each goes in individually. You are faced with the necessity for meeting this in your own individual consciousness and there's no one who's going to do it with you in that consciousness. You either are going to accept that I, in the midst of you am the risen Christ or you are going to continue to believe that in some way, God created mortal, material beings and then you're going to be watching the heartbeat and the pulse beat and the temperature and the blood pressure thinking these are an indication of whether you're healthy or not.

In the midst of you at this moment is the meaning that Christ where you stand is all that is there, that there is no mortal being there, that there is no physical body there and this was true of your mother. And this was true of your father. And we discover that Resurrection tells us that parents aren't parents as we have known them to be and children aren't children as we have known them to be and people aren't people as we have known them to be. And we're alone when we come to this realization. There's nobody to hold us up. This is the single narrow pathway that you walk through. And until you are ready to banish the material concept of the world and walk this path, you are rejecting Christhood. That's fine if you just want to get to Chicago. But this class is whittled down to those who want to go all the way and all the way means out of humanhood.

Then Christ will walk through the wall of your consciousness and enter the room which is the room where you are waiting on the Lord, where you are in the Sabbath of the mind and you will be lifted to that Sabbath which is called the eternal Sabbath and you will learn how to go through the mystic death. The mystic death takes you to that place where you have reached the level of Consciousness which no longer is earthbound, finite, material, mortal, living in space, living in time, living in any form of lack or limitation. You are pure, Spiritual Consciousness realized. And that has nothing to do with a mortal person. That Spiritual Consciousness never needs

Resurrection. It is the Resurrection. That Spiritual Consciousness is the only Self we can ever be.

And so, the Master says, "My peace passeth understanding" because Resurrection revealed, takes us beyond all of the known methods of living, beyond the emotional, beyond the mental, beyond the physical, beyond the rational. It takes us into a realm of Spirit. Where all of our normal reactions are absent. Where nothing that we can quite comprehend is taking place. We're in a different atmosphere.

Mary was in that atmosphere for a while. It was then that she was able to bring forth that image which would be the leader of mankind. She was out of the way. She was not in the sense of matter or materiality or mortality or humanhood. She was dwelling in the Spirit of her own Being as a pure Soul. Unless you have the experience of being a pure Soul, there is still a dual you, another self that isn't and you will experience that other self, you'll be lingering in the midway mark, unwilling to walk into the tomb and make the great discovery that the tomb only exists in the mind of the world.

"Father, forgive them; [for] they know not what they do."

The word "forgive" also means erase. You are being told to erase from your consciousness the belief that they are out there external to your Self. You are truly the one, Divine Self. There are no divisions in your Being between you and someone else. You can never come to that place while you still inhabit a mortal form in your consciousness.

Now, suppose you were to take this as your assignment for this week. Not to dwell in the consciousness that I am not a mortal being for 24 consecutive hours, but to establish 2 meditations a day, every day in which this becomes the purpose of your meditation. I am not a mortal being. I am that Life which exists before Adam and Eve, that Life which was always living and ever will live. I am the Resurrection. I am the One that is the Only. I am not a passing self in a passing form.

Now if you make this the subject of your contemplation to be followed by the Sabbath of the mind, the Silence, you will be lifted by the very Spirit itself. And then if you make that your second meditation of the day, and repeat this spontaneously, without any formula so that twice a day for six or, seven days or whatever it's going to be until we meet again, you are prepared for five to ten minutes, twice a day, resting in the awareness of who you are and then signing off the mind so that the inner Spirit can establish its identity in your consciousness. You will at least be trying to accept the meaning of Resurrection not as words in a book or as an event in history but as the living experience that every Self must come through until it knows its self to be the only Self, the One, Infinite Self.

This is our real Resurrection, the experience that I am the One Self and beside me there is no other. My Self is walking this earth everywhere, appearing as the forms that I see. I am that invisible Self. I am the Life of everything that moves and the Life of everything that is still. I am the Life of inanimate objects. I am the Life of every form. I am the Self behind every visible condition. I am the Resurrection. I am the living Kingdom of God on earth.

This is the nature of your meditation twice a day and I know it will lift you. It will teach you. It will open you and you will be fulfilling Scripture to that extent.

The great work we have ahead of us is the announcement within by the Spirit itself that "I am come." And it will say this to you many times, at many intervals but it is always saying this to you and the times that you hear it will be when you rise to these higher levels of self-awareness to bring into consciousness That which is always present saying, "I am come."

Forgive the world. Erase from your consciousness all that you thought was happening. *"Sell all [that] thou hast,"* and listen for *"I, in the midst of you,"* for *"I am the Resurrection and the Life,"* and *"I am the Way,"* and "I am the seventh Heaven," and "I will feed you Spiritual bread."

Then we will find that Christmas day for us will be that moment when the new substance of Spirit which was ever present is born in us again, reuniting us with our eternal Self. That will be the moment of Bethany, the House of Substance when the living bread of the Spirit in you becomes your awareness that I am the living Christ, the Infinite Christ. This will be our Resurrection and it will continue and continue and continue until that moment called Christmas, Christ born in you, becomes a Reality.

That Resurrection means all incarnation is over for the second birth is the end of reincarnation. When the true Self is realized, your mission on earth is nearing its close. You can stay. You can continue to fulfill the mission of the Light. You can even return, if you wish, as you know, but learning the lesson that I am the Light of God on earth is what you're here for. And when you live in it knowingly, you will find that you are a pillar in the temple of the Father and you go no more out. That's what we've all been preparing for and it's worth many, many seeming problems on the way. It's even worth a few tragedies because in the moment of illumination, you will see that every tragedy was an illusion. All that is present is the Presence. All that is present is the eternal perfection of Being. There is nothing else present.

In your Resurrection experience you can say, "Thou seest me, thou seest the Father. We are One."

And so, this is the way we face our real Christmas. Christ in you born through the Willingness, the Love, the Faith to release mortal sense. Not half way. That's *"Selling all [that] thou hast."*

I assure you it is lonely and yet, Infinity has a way of bringing to you many glorious surprises once that tinge of loneliness is overcome for in the fulness the loneliness disappears.

And again, and again and again you're raised back to that fulness until it is sealed. You have no way of knowing how short the time may be - nor have I - for the new age is very closely upon us. We're learning about what we had thought was our individual Resurrection but we're really not. It's the Resurrection of the world.

And that Resurrection of the world is just as close as the Resurrection in your consciousness is. You are playing that role in the Resurrection of this world out of the false sense of corporeality into My Kingdom, realized.

Our theme will continue to be the 20th chapter, Jesus walking through the wall, Thomas being converted, but all of this will be a further heightening of our own Resurrection experience and from there, in the mystical interval between Resurrection and Ascension to see the difference between the two.

And finally, from that strength to stand in world work, so that perhaps when we meditate here about the earthquake we know can't occur, we can include Nicaragua and not limit our consciousness to that place where we stand physically. Always, we'll be learning that we must dwell in the conscious awareness that the carnal mind of the world is the only adversary. And never localize down to a head cold or a pain in the arm. And if you remember in our meditation on the earthquake, that's where we were. I would call that my error. But we learn by these errors.

And so, before we disband which will be - let's see we have three more classes in this series - we must learn to be more omnipresent in our consciousness when we do our world work.

Now while you're accepting, "*I am the Resurrection*," that Omnipresent Consciousness that you must be in must accept that I am the Infinite Resurrection. You can't localize down to Resurrection on the place where your feet are. I am the Infinite Resurrection. My Self is the only Self in this entire Spiritual universe. I am the One,

Infinite Spirit. That's quite a jump out of being mortal matter for all these years.

So, make that your meditation and be prepared through your reading of the 20th chapter of John to go into some interesting details about the Spiritual nature of that chapter. It would help if you have read it because then you will find you have a deeper capacity to hear what Spirit wishes to reveal.

Maybe this is a good time to say, "Thank you," to so many of you or maybe that can come next week. But I do want you to know how grateful we are here that we can share these beautiful Truths together and that in some way, your response to the inner Spirit of your own Being has made this possible. It has been a very moving year for me, more so because we have seen great changes in the students who have worked with us. We have been invited to share with them their living experiences and we know that the Spirit has definitely made a great entrance into the consciousness of our group. From that point of view, we are deeply grateful.

To all of you, a very joyous Christmas. Thank you.

Class 44

Invisible Man Revealed

Herb: A very happy New Year for tomorrow and the eternity to follow. We know that in our Spiritual Self there is no New Year for we're told that eternity already is. The I is not experiencing a New Year. The I is our identity and so, we know that in time, we're merely living out our concept of the I and if it's a limited concept, it's a limited life. As the concept is lessened from the mortal sense and the Spiritual enters, we find that we're not living in a year or in a physical form but we are Life itself.

Now, in this 20th chapter of John, it's safe to say that there is very little in it that the world has known about. It can trace the footsteps. It can say, "He is risen." But I'm quite sure you'll agree that even we who have studied this long and hard could not understand this particular chapter unless we have had a full preparation for it. And we have had that preparation and for that reason today, we can look at the experience of Mary Magdalene, of the disciples and especially of Thomas and we can see things that have never really been revealed to the minds of the millions who walk this earth, who have studied this Bible.

As a matter of fact, as we enter certain levels of this chapter, you're going to find that you don't have a place where you can hold on. There's no sure footprint to follow. You'll have to walk in your own Spiritual footpath. You have to find your own invisible way and, in this sense, Mary Magdalene is leading us now because she is going to do something very strange.

Peter ran into the tomb. Peter saw there was no body. Peter saw grave clothes and a napkin and then Peter believed that Jesus

Christ had risen and then he went home; went back to his material consciousness.

Now, Mary had announced that Jesus wasn't in the tomb. She was the first woman disciple to know this before the men. But now, she doesn't go home. Something rivets her right to the spot she won't leave. So, as we pick Mary up here in the 11th verse, Mary stood without at the sepulchre, weeping.

".... and as she wept, she stooped down, and looked into the sepulchre, And seeth two angels in white sitting, the one at the head, the other at the feet, where the body of Jesus had lain."

Now, there's going to come a time in the life of every person here when we go through this experience if we have not already done so. Something is going to say to us, "You're ready for a new level. You're ready to let go of what you thought you were. You're ready to ascend to the Self that you are. You're ready to be restored to your own Reality."

And that happens when, like Mary, we're willing to weep. She could have gone home. She could have said, "He isn't there." But you know, that his not being in the tomb was not the cause of her weeping. This would rather be a cause for rejoicing. It would seem that weeping means quite a bit more than human sorrow.

Humanly, she would have said, "Why he's not here. How wonderful. He's risen." But instead, she's weeping. And that is because Mary has seen something that Peter could not see. Mary is weeping means the Christ in Mary is weeping for her recognition. The Christ in Mary is weeping to lead her into conscious union with the Infinite. And Mary is standing fast. Something in her tells her that Christ is near. She doesn't assume that he is risen in a physical form. She's really now in an inner experience and all that is within her is saying, "Christ is right near. You're almost breaking through into Christ Consciousness." She's weeping for union with Christ.

Now, Mary at this point represents the entire will of an individual. When the will of you is weeping for Christ, weeping for Truth alone, you'll find you're standing not in the tomb, but outside. In the tomb, you will be bound by your sense perception. Outside the tomb means that Mary is outside sense perception. She is transcending her senses. She is not imprisoned within the senses.

You will recall that John did a strange thing. When he outran Peter to the tomb, John did not go in. Peter did. Mary is now doing the same thing. Before she goes into the tomb to look, to investigate, she stands outside and this is the procedure which is called living outside the body image. This is the high esoteric teaching at this point that before you enter any place in this world, you must learn to remember that you cannot enter as a physical form. The moment you enter anywhere, even this room, as a physical form, you have come in a state of duality. You are a divided consciousness.

Mary could not enter that tomb until she had first found her inner Self and so she was weeping to find the inner Christ. She was Soul searching. She was reaching out beyond the mind, refusing to accept what the mind saw and because of it, as she rests within herself, knowing that I am not in this form, I am not living in this physical body, I am the Spirit of the Father. She's outside the tomb, the sepulchre called body. She's outside the concept of mortal life and only when she establishes that, is she ready now to look inside. And she does that. She does it and the procedure is called stooping and looking. She stoops and she looks.

When she stoops, she's expressing that humility of there is no person here called Mary. When she looks because she has already stooped, because she has obliterated personal sense, when she looks, she is looking with the inner eye not with the outer eye.

Peter ran in with the outer eye. He saw the grave clothes. Mary comes in with the inner eye and sees not the grave clothes at all but two angels. And John is showing us the difference between the personal sense of loss experienced by Peter who lives in material consciousness and the high, transcendental awareness of Mary Magdalene who lives by Divine Will and Love.

Divine Will in her is expressing its wholeness and it shows forth to her as two angels. One at the head and one at the feet where the body of Jesus had lain.

Now, these two angels are not visible to human eyes. They are Divine communications. They appear only to the inner Self. Mary is introducing the world at this point to the great Truth that beside the five senses of the physical nature, we have the senses of the Soul which can perceive that which is invisible to and untouchable by the human senses.

Mary had achieved the inner senses and with the inner senses she is now able to discern those qualities of the Spirit which are unknown to the mind of man but not to John who had already been in that tomb long before he arrived at the tomb. John who had already transcended his personal self, who made way for Peter to show us the distinction between one who knows the Spirit and one who knows the flesh.

The angels represent many things. The two, one at the head, one at the foot, is expressive of the total regeneration, the whole man regenerated, from head to foot. And the last is returned to the first, so that first and last are now One. I am the beginning and the end, the Alpha and the Omega. This is the sign that one has returned to one's pre-existent Self and these two angels further tell us a secret that will only develop in the twentieth chapter as we go along through it very carefully. We will see it as a sign of two different kinds of bodies that are going to be presented to us. One might be called a Spiritual body and another a still higher body called a Celestial body.

The two angels are a promise of new developments to come. They are the sign that Mary, within herself now is being Christed.

It hasn't fully happened but she has opened the way by her weeping which is yearning for Christ Consciousness, putting Christ first, last and always so that there is no personal Mary there, there is only the desire to live in Christ.

"Blessed are they that mourn."

This weeping and this mourning are one and the same. Those who are ready to be dead to that self which is not, are mourning and ready to be alive to that Self which is, are weeping for reunion with Christ and they shall be comforted. They shall receive the Holy Ghost, the Comforter and Mary will receive the Comforter.

Now, she turns outside. The angels have said to her, *"Why weepest thou?"* And she says, *"They have taken my LORD away."*

She cannot find the full expression of Christ within herself but she lingers. Something holds her there. This inner communion with the angels of the Father within is an experience in which you know you are on the path of Truth. Within you is the complete, total awareness that I am now being guided and, in a moment, an eternal moment, something will open up, a new horizon, a new consciousness, a new age. I will be lifted up into the seventh Heaven.

When she goes outside the tomb now, she sees one but she can't quite tell who it is. This is that in between state now when we're coming close to the Christ Consciousness but have not yet been fully lifted up to perceive the Christ of our own Being. We may feel the presence of the Spirit without any specific identification and again, comes the question *"Why weepest thou?"* But this time it comes from this vision that she sees in the garden. *"They have taken my Lord away."*

And then comes the word, *"Mary."* That's all he says, *"Mary."* And as that word is spoken, this is the Christing of Mary. This is Christ within her recognizing her entire Being.

When Christ within you speaks your name, Christ knows you and in the moment that Christ knows you, you have the capacity to know Christ. As we are known by the Christ, we can know the Christ.

In that breathless moment, when she hears the word, *"Mary,"* her entire Being is being Christed and her recognition of this is her response, *"Rabboni....Master."* She recognizes the Christ of her Being. It would appear as you read this that she sees Jesus in the garden and recognized him to be the Christ. But this is the inner experience of Mary in which she recognizes Christ within her Self.

She may not know she has found Christ within her Self. She still thinks this is a person out there but she has seen the incorporeal Christ, the incorporeal man. She's swept with ecstasy. She wishes to throw herself at his feet and embrace him, to clasp his knees to her but he says, *"Touch me not;[for] I have not yet ascended."*

And again, this would seem to mean that Jesus, the Christ had not yet ascended. But it doesn't mean that at all. It means that I, in the midst of you, have not yet ascended. I have not been fully lifted up within your consciousness if you still want to touch me, if you still think I am a person out here to be touched.

And Christ is telling us all at this moment, "I am incorporeal Being in the midst of you. Do not be deceived by the senses again. Do not reach out to touch that which is within your Self. Do not fall back into the deception of the physical senses. You have found Christ in you, not outside you."

And so, know the incorporeal Christ of your own Being and that will be the Ascension. "Do not reach out and touch. I cannot be touched. That would be an illusion. I am not yet fully ascended in your consciousness and I will not be until you overcome the illusion that you must touch that which you seem to think is out there."

Mary was finding her own Christ Self but not yet fully aware of that until the Master says, *"Touch me not."* There is still inner communion until total Oneness is attained.

Now then, Christ will appear within you one day but only after you have prepared yourself and then Christ will re-appear, perhaps many times. And finally, there will come the moment when the Christ who appears within you will be accepted by you as the Self of the universe, as the Self of your Being and not as a separate individual from your own Self. When you know that, when you have been so favored to receive that Inner Bestowal, that the Christ within you that you see with the inner eye, is known to be but an image in your consciousness of your own Infinite Being, then you will have passed the point of *"Touch me not for I have not yet ascended."* And we must pass that point.

This inner illumination is the end of the quest.

Now, think back, those of you who have witnessed the Christ within, those of you who have had the Voice within, and see that here, Mary is giving you a lesson. She's being used to teach you that the Voice of the Christ that she hears in the garden is an inner Voice and Mary is taking us way back to the Garden of Eden where Adam and Eve, the un-Christed, living in the garden, were unaware of the invisible Christ. Mary in the garden finds the invisible Christ.

And this is the revelation that all mankind is incorporeal, that Christ is the invisible, incorporeal Self of mankind and that the world, living now, is in the Garden of Eden unaware of it. It is miserable in the Garden of Eden, still listening to the serpent, still listening to mortal mind when invisibly, to those who have made the preparation, Christ is present and can be experienced as Divine Selfhood. We are walking in that garden now. We have always been walking in it. But we have not stopped. We have not wept. We have not stooped. We have not looked. We have not listened. We have not discerned. Because we have not yet developed the will to love

God and only God within. This will, this living, active will is Mary Magdalene in you.

As you accept this will in you to know only God aright, first, last and foremost, you will find you are aided to rest, to be meek unto the inner Spirit, to have the inner eye opened, to be lifted out of and above the five senses of the mind, to witness the incorporeal nature of all Life and finally, to know it is you. And where did it all begin with Mary? When she was cast at the Master's feet as a sinner, told to be stoned but the Master had seen her Incorporeality and now, she is seeing her own Incorporeality. The cycle is complete. She never was what the world thought and no one is.

And so, as we accept the will to know only God in ourselves, in everyone we meet, we are staying outside the senses, outside the sepulchre, outside the tomb of matter, outside the tomb of mortal life, resting in the word that the invisible Christ is here in the garden, ever present, always present and we are weeping for conscious union with that Christ until the Christ says *"Why weepest thou?"* until that Voice opens the heart.

The angels had searched the heart of Mary for her motives. They were found to be pure. Her inner goodness enabled her to receive the awareness of the Inner Self. Mary wasn't seeking anything of the world. Nothing. Mary wasn't seeking anything for Mary. Mary was seeking Christ salvation. Mary was seeking Divine Truth and Mary attains that which she is seeking because her motives are 100% pure.

Now she is told to go. *"Go to my brethren."* Tell them what you've seen. Tell them that I go *"to your Father and My Father; to your God and my God."* He emphasizes *"Father."* He emphasizes *"God"* because Mary had called him *"Rabboni,"* which means *"My Master."* He's telling her, "I'm not your Master. I am your Self and tell my brethren that I go *"To your Father and to my Father."* We're one and the same. We have the same Father. *"To my God and your God."* We have the same God. My Father and my God are one and the same.

Your Father and your God are the same. We are the Self, we are not two, Mary. Neither are my brethren separate from us. They are the One Self, as we."

And now because the Will has been established to live in God, that Will, runs to the disciples. Without the Will to live in God, the disciples cannot be alerted or awakened. Mary had to come first and this is now Mary, in the midst of the disciples who must be awakened. Mary in the midst of us must be awakened to awaken the disciples within us. Unless the will of you is established to live in God, the disciples in you will remain asleep.

This, too, is a promise of the Christ which was fulfilled from the 22nd Psalm. We'll just look at it a moment because it's necessary to know that always, every Divine promise must be fulfilled.

The 22nd Psalm and the 22nd verse. *"I will declare thy name unto my brethren: in the midst of the congregation will I praise thee."*

And here, in chapter 20, just as in the 22nd Psalm, "Go to my *brethren, and say unto them, I ascend unto my Father, and our Father; [and to] my God, and your God."*

So, the very Christ who spoke the words through David in the Psalm now speaks the words to Mary within her own Being. And if you have heard words of a similar nature, you have heard the eternal Word, words that unite you with all who have walked in the Spirit throughout all eternity. If you have heard these words within you or similar words, at that moment, you were One with every prophet who ever walked the earth and that Oneness has never stopped remaining in Oneness. It can never be broken.

We are being opened beyond this tomb of a physical form to know that we are not walking in it. The incorporeal Christ was not confined in that tomb and neither is the incorporeal you and only through the recognition of the Invisible Christ in the garden around you are you accepting Life not confined to the body image.

That is how we are lifted out, far and above and beyond our mortal concepts, out of the limitations of form and time and space because I, the Christ of you, I go unto my Father and your Father. This is the Divine surgery whereby in the attainment of Christ awareness, you are One with the Father which is Infinity and that little tomb of a body ceases to be your habitation.

This is the new Consciousness. It is also the first day of Resurrection and is still only the morning. We learn through Christ, accepted as invisibly present, as my incorporeal Self, I am in the first day of Resurrection.

The complete teaching of Jesus Christ comes to a pinnacle at this point; for Mary, for those who understand what is happening to Mary, for those who can walk the same path.

So, Mary goes. She is now entrusted to alert the disciples.

"Mary Magdalene came and told the disciples that she had seen the LORD, and that he had spoken these things unto her."

Now, to whom could you give this inner experience had it been yours? The only ones she could give it to were the disciples of Christ. It seemed natural for her to do this rather than go out and broadcast to the world.

And similarly, when you have been lifted to the point of inner Light, there are very few people to whom you can divulge what has happened, only to disciples of Christ and even then, only if the inner Self has directed you in some way to do this as it often does.

Now, it is evening. We can imagine what happened when she arrived and told them what had happened to her. She found them in the upper room of Mark's mother's house. Even Peter was there who had run home. But now they learn that something has happened, something beyond their wildest dreams. First, they had learned - probably from Peter - that the Master wasn't there and they had assumed he had risen. Now, they learn that he has spoken to one among them, he has spoken to a woman. Just as for the first time when he divulged his identity on this earth, it was to a woman at the well of Samaria. She said, "I know when Christ cometh he will do these things." And he said to the woman at Samaria, "*I am he.*"

And now, to Mary Magdalene, who has passed the point of the five senses just as the woman of Samaria had passed the point of the five husbands or the five senses and was in that in-between stage, transcending the five senses, so Mary Magdalene in us, reports to the disciples within us that "I have spoken with him. I have seen him. I have been entrusted to bring you this Truth." And the disciples assume that he has risen from the dead. Mary Magdalene has learned that he has not risen from the dead. He has risen from the deadness within her.

Now, you'll find that Christ never changes. When Jesus appears in the garden or when he appears to the disciples, he's never really appearing. Christ is always present but as others become more conscious of that Presence, he is said to appear to them and each receives Christ within at a different level of their own awareness. Mary, in her way, and now the disciples find as they are at, in a prayer with the doors shut, that this form appears. It was just as present before it appeared through the door or through the wall. It was present in the garden when Peter was at the tomb but he couldn't see it. The angels, he couldn't see. The Christ is present in this room but you cannot see the Christ unless you are in communion within.

If suddenly, the Christ walked through the walls, it would not actually be an event of the Christ walking through the walls. It would be you and I or someone here lifted high enough to perceive that Christ which is ever present.

And so, the symbol of the walls being so thick that no human could walk through but only the Christ is the statement that these disciples now having known that Jesus is actually alive are in deep inner communion. And when Christ appears, his words are, *"Peace be unto you."*

Their assumption is that Christ is risen from the dead. They still had not caught the inner Christ of their own Being is being experienced within themselves. They still see an external Christ coming through a wall. Christ is never external to you. It is impossible for Christ to be external to Christ.

But there is sufficient inner awareness now to perceive this incorporeal form. They need no further evidence. They don't say, "Let us touch the wounds." Their visual evidence is enough for them. They are satisfied this is Jesus Christ.

Not Thomas. He's not satisfied. Thomas has to touch. So, we see three levels. Mary, who doesn't see him in any way imperfect. The disciples, who still see him as an imperfect form return to them still as he was, with wounds. They are not yet in the fulness of Christhood. They see an imperfect Jesus Christ. There is none. And then a Thomas, who is the lowest level of this inner knowing, who sees but isn't even convinced by seeing. And so, he says, "I must feel. I must thrust my hand in his side."

These are the various levels that are given to us at this point. What does he say to Thomas? "Blessed are those who can believe without seeing, who don't have to touch the wounds."

Now, why, if Christ is Christ, does Thomas see the wounds and have to touch them and the disciples see the wounds and believe that he is resurrected and Mary sees the incorporeal man without wounds? There's no mention of wounds when Mary sees him; different levels of awareness to show us that we all see Christ in different ways but always, Christ never changes. Christ never has wounds. But if we see wounds, if Thomas sees wounds, what is he seeing? He's seeing his own consciousness. If the other disciples see wounds, they are seeing their own consciousness. They're not seeing wounds in Christ. They're seeing wounds in their own sense awareness.

If you're seeing an earthquake, you're seeing it in your own sense awareness. If you're seeing a disease, you're seeing it in your own sense awareness. The deception of the senses see imperfection where Christ is and no imperfection can be there. It's never external imperfection. It's always within the visible senses of the beholder. All the diseases on the earth are within the senses of the beholder. The whole world is within our senses. The Christ is never in the world. The Christ is never in our senses. The Christ is never imperfect and "blessed are they who believe without seeing" is telling us that when you can accept that the Christ is present and perfect, then you can look through all visible imperfection which Thomas couldn't do, which the disciples couldn't do but which Mary could do.

You can look through every visible imperfection in your so-called human experience to know that that is but the denial that Christ is present here in the garden. It isn't happening outside your senses. It doesn't matter what imperfection you know. The only place it's happening is within your five physical senses.

And when your Soul is opened, you will perceive that these five, physical senses had deceived you into thinking something was present beside the perfect Christ. Christ is revealed as the only Presence. There is no other.

When Mary finds the Christ, Mary ceases to be. But there's still a Thomas. There are still male disciples to be lifted up.

The importance here is that Thomas represents the level of the world today. The highest religious world today believes as Thomas did, that he rose from the dead. Why? Because the senses of Thomas said so. Thomas was deluded twice. First, by the crucifixion and then by the Resurrection. Neither had occurred. The world of religion today still thinks Jesus was resurrected. Why? Because judging from the Bible, Thomas and the others, some five hundred, saw Jesus resurrected. But what was happening is they were being lifted to perceive that which had never died and each was seeing it in his own level of consciousness. If they could have all seen him as Mary saw him, they would have known This was never wounded: that was the world illusion. And then we, in knowing that would know, there was never a disease on this earth: that was the world illusion. There was never an evil on this earth: that was the world illusion. There was never a Managua-Nicaragua earthquake. There was no plane came down in the Andes. There were no human corpses eaten by their colleagues. All this is part of seeing the wounds in the side, seeing the print of the nails. This is seeing the evils of the world with our senses and believing they are there.

So that Thomas in us, the reasoning, the understanding of the human mind says, "Well, I finally saw it. It must be true." Then Thomas gets on his knees and says, *"My LORD and my God,"* to the Master. But on a false assumption that the mutilated Christ has now come back in a mutilated form. That's the limit of Thomas and it's the limit of the religious mind of the world. It's also the limit of the congregations of the religions of the world.

"But go, tell my brethren….. that I go to my Father and your Father," not with a mutilated body - as the perfect Child of God. And when you have found me in you, you go to your Father, not with a mutilated body but as the perfect Child of God. That going is the acceptance of the now Self.

We overcome Thomas. We overcome the disciples. We walk with Mary. We are joined into Oneness with the Invisible Self. For us, the Garden of Eden is the Reality, for Christ is the only inhabitant. And this earth is Christed in our Consciousness. Christ is the only inhabitant. We can look out. No matter what we see and we judge not. We don't have to feel the wounds of the world. We don't have to see the prints of the nails and the hands of the world.

Instead, we learn that when the Master comes to the disciples, his hands stand for his Power. His side stands for his Love. They were glad when they saw him because he showed them his hands and his side, not physically, he showed them his Power and his Love. They were feeling the Power and Love of Christ within themselves. When you feel the Power and Love of Christ within your Self, you have found the hands and the side of Christ.

So, this is our 20th chapter. Let's see if we can rest with it a moment. What have we learned out of this?

If you have reached an important conclusion with yourself, never to deny the God Presence where you are, then you're in that Will which lingers and will not go back to the old consciousness. The five senses are not revealing the Kingdom of God. They're revealing the wounds, the nail prints, the errors, the imperfections that aren't there. They are making Thomas within you reach conclusions that are untrue.

On the other hand, if you are true to the presence of God everywhere, then we must be cautious so that in no way are we fooled by the senses in denying that Presence; Truth of God as the only Self.

Now, watch how easily you fall out of upholding the presence of God as the Only. You judge. And whatever your judgment, big or small, even if it's a good judgment, that judgment breaks the continuity of the One mind. When you judge, you are saying that "God is not present." Whatever you judge is unrighteous. The only judgment is righteous judgment and that judgment is that God is present.

Now, if God is present, and I judge something to be wrong somewhere, then I am saying that "God is not omnipotent," that "God is not omniscient," that "God is not omnipresent." If I have accepted the newspaper headlines of the day, or the tragedies of the past, or anticipate tragedies of the future, I am judging that God is not present because in the presence of God, there can be no tragedy. I am looking at tragedies and, in my consciousness, I am accepting the wounds as real; falling into a trap.

There can be no tragedies in the presence of God and therefore, there can be no tragedies in your Life no matter what appears. The illusion is the tragedy. The Reality is the invisible presence of God and although you'd like some sign or something to aid you to make God reveal God before you make the acceptance that God is present; it's the other way around. You must make the acceptance before God can reveal God. Unless you're living in the conscious awareness of that Presence, there's no way for the Presence to reveal itself through you.

You can see that Thomas is being shown to us as the opposite of Mary with the disciples in between. Thomas could not stoop down. He could not permit himself to accept what he, personally could not verify. Mary could stoop down. Thomas couldn't have seen two angels. Thomas couldn't see the Christ in the garden. That's why Mary came first and then the disciples and then finally, Thomas.

To uphold the One presence of God as perfect is to know that we are living in Perfection now. There is no power to change it. We will see the invisible form of Jesus from one point of view or another and this body we now see within ourselves, if you see the Christ within your Self, will be from a higher realm than the realm we've walked in as human beings. And then later, still another realm and always the form you see will be but a symbol for Christ is Infinite and you cannot see an infinite form. You're going to see an image of the infinite form within your Self.

You're going to live in the Soul senses or human sensations depending on whether you uphold that only God is present. And if you are fooled by your senses, you will accept that beside God something else is present. And then, the meaning of Mary seeing the angels in the tomb and then outside the tomb, finally seeing the invisible Christ will be of no value if you still persist in believing what your senses see. Her senses did not see the Christ. It was the absence of those senses which enabled her to see the Christ. It is only when you overcome the belief that you have material senses that you will see the Christ. You cannot have material senses. They are unreal and all they can report to you is the unreality which they are forced to witness.

Our conclusion at this stage should be there is an incorporeal universe and an incorporeal man ever present, ever perfect, ever infinite. *"Peace be unto you."* When that is repeated for the third time by Jesus Christ in this chapter, it is the sign that he is coming to the place where he will reveal the fulness of his mission. The third time he says, *"Peace unto you"* means I am now reaching and preparing you for a new age. Three is the beginning of completion and that new age is the incorporeal age of Spirit in which there is only One and you know your Self to be that One. You never deny it. You never deny its Perfection. You do not let the five-sense world fool you into believing that any but the perfect One is present.

This may be the first day of Resurrection in the Bible and for those of us who have faithfully found that inner rest out of the world of appearance, out of the world of sense judgment, so that we ourselves are past the point of being judged for we judge not and therefore, we are not judged. We are not separated from the One who is the Only.

During our intermission, you might give a moment's thought to what conclusions this experience of the 20th chapter should lead you. What Truth can you depend upon if you accept this chapter and the interpretation of it? What Truth can you depend upon to live by so that a New Year is actually a new Consciousness?

That's what we're going to do in the second part of this meeting and so let's have a little rest now before that. Thank you.

— End of Side One —

In the earlier chapters, when the disciples learned that their leader was going to leave them, he said to them, in John 16:22, *"Ye now therefore have sorrow: but I will see you again, and your heart shall rejoice, and your joy no man taketh from you."*

"No man will take your joy from you when I see you again."

Now, this is a promise then that when you are able to transcend the senses, and receive the Christ, no man can take your joy from you.

And now, in the 20th chapter, *"Then said Jesus to them [again], Peace be unto you: as my Father hath sent me, even so send I you."*

Now, something happens then when you receive the Christ. As Christ is sent by the Father, you are sent by the Christ. Now we know that "Christ sent by the Father" means that the Infinite individualizes as Itself and it is called Christ. The ocean individualizing as its waves.

When Christ is sent, everything that Christ expresses is Divine. It is the Source expressing Itself at a given point called Christ. When you are sent by Christ, everything you do is the Infinite Source through Christ expressing Itself as you so that you are sent. You are ordained. That which you do is the result of your Source doing it. Christ has no obstacle because Christ is the expression of the Source It is sent. You have no obstacle because you are the expression of the Christ when you have received the Christ.

So, the Master says to the disciples, *"As my Father has sent me, even so send I, you."*

And then, we are given this great insight to that which happens when you are sent and how it happens. *"When he had said this, he breathed on them, and said unto them, Receive ye the Holy Ghost."*

This is the fulfillment of the promise that they would rejoice when they saw him again. This is the fulfillment of the promise that, *"If I go not away, the Comforter will not come unto you."*

When you drop the personal sense of a you, of a material self, of a human lifespan, of all that your five natural, physical senses report and have divested yourself completely of the belief in corporeality, that's when the physical goes away and then the Spirit of the Father within you breathes upon you and this is the Bestowal of the Holy Ghost or the Comforter.

The Comforter comes unto you when you have dropped all physicality and belief in physicality because what is physicality but a five-sense belief? I see it, I touch it, I feel it, I hear it but I have no physical senses to do this with. They are mortal. They die. They are not of the Father. What can they tell me about God? What can they tell me about Christ? What can they tell me about my permanent Being? Nothing. They can only tell me about the world; recreation. So, when you drop belief in the physical senses, you are enabled to be lifted into creation instead of re-creation.

So, the Holy Ghost is bestowed which is that You are now sent by the Christ. You actually are that Holy Ghost. The Holy Ghost sends Itself as You. God sends the Christ. The Christ sends the Holy Ghost. That is the Holy Trinity of One and that One is your Being. The activity of Christ is the Comforter, the Holy Ghost.

And how can you have the activity of Christ, the Comforter, the Holy Ghost unless you have the Christ? And you cannot have the Christ while you're still in a five-sense world, in a five-sense concept. That's the sepulchre. That's the tomb, the five senses.

So you're outside the five senses when you disbelieve in their evidence but rather you believe in the evidence of things unseen, untouched, unheard. Then, Christ in you, sends the Holy Ghost. That is the activity of Christ in you expressing Itself as the Divine qualities of the Father where you stand.

And you discover there is nothing corruptible. Nothing that can decay. Nothing that can die in your Being. Nothing that can be limited. Nothing that can lack. Your Being does not see the wall. Your Being does not see the door. Your Being does not see the physical obstruction. Only your senses do. Your Being does not know what it means to need anything; only your senses do, and this sense perception is the denial of Christ identity and it is a barricade we build which prevents our being sent or ordained by the Christ so that Christ expressing the fulness of the Father is the invisible Holy Ghost finally appearing in the visible as the health of your countenance.

The line of communication is clearly established that unless you transcend the belief in the senses, there is no Bestowal of the Comforter or the Holy Ghost: the invisible activity of Christ cannot manifest in your experience.

But here it is, being bestowed upon the disciples of Jesus Christ. In spite of all their fears that he had left them, in spite of their doubts, even in spite of their belief that he had now returned, they hadn't yet come to the realization that they were being lifted up to witness the Reality of their own Being.

Every time we think that the Holy Ghost is just a word in a book or that Christ is something we're going to attain tomorrow, we are really saying that "God's on a vacation. God's taken two weeks off. God's gone fishing." But God is the invisible activity of the Christ every moment. And whatever is un-Divine is non-existent. There is no such thing as un- Divinity. It is but a sense illusion. Whatever is un-Divinity, is actually deadness for the Divine is All.

Now, because we are sent, ordained, we have a mission and that mission is to let Christ in you heal the sick, feed the hungry, feed the dead. You find - and this is a great lesson in the practitioner work - that there is no healing takes place within your senses. In order for healing to take place, it must occur outside your senses and then it will appear within your five-sense appearing world. The actual healing is always outside the senses. There could be no healing inside the senses.

And that's where we prove out for ourselves that all of the work of God must be outside your senses. You must learn how to live outside them, not inside them. The Within of You is living outside your senses. The Above of You, the Transcendental of You, the Reality of You and then suddenly, the senses are revealed as the world mind in disguise. That's where we've been imprisoned, in the world mind that surrounds us as our own five physical senses which then report unreality as unreal as the senses themselves. They report a physical form where there is none. They report physical experiences where there are none. They report a physical life where there is none.

Once these five walls are walked through, when you walk through the wall of the five senses, there's a new world waiting, a complete, new realm and now, the Soul senses become accustomed to it and open you up. The things you hear, the things you see, the things you do, the things you experience are totally different than the world knows.

When the Master says, *"Peace be unto you,"* that is what he was saying. He isn't saying, "I hope Peace comes unto you." Christ in you is the Peace unto you. Now, is Peace unto the disciples when the Master says, *"Peace be unto you."* As they receive the Christ, Peace is unto them and Peace means the end of all conflict. The end of all confusion. *"Peace .... unto you"* is the end of the warfare between the Spirit and the flesh. *"Peace .... unto you"* is the end of duality, the end of separation from your own Self and your own Source.

Whenever the inner Voice says, *"Peace .... unto you"* that is the actual experience of Oneness with God. That is the revelation of your own Immortality. You may hear this within your Self, *"Peace be unto you."* This is the revelation to us, that now the disciples have lifted up the I of their Being. They have been drawn by the Christ into the new realm.

"Many other signs truly did Jesus in the presence of his disciples, which are not written in this book: But these are written, that ye might believe that Jesus is the Christ, the Son of God; and that believing ye might have life through his name."

As Christ becomes more real, not just an idea, and then not just an experience but the Reality of your Being, then you are believing in his name, for his name is his identity in you and then as the sent Holy Ghost of the Christ, you will walk forward, letting the Light shine. It is now our function to lift the world, to let the Light shine through the religions of the world, through the races of mankind, to demonstrate the Christ and your capacity to reject all sense evidence, finally to know the One Divine Life where you stand, where your neighbor stands.

You have the capacity now to malpractice the world or to bless it. You have the capacity to release in the world the sense of evil. And that was given to you when the Master said to his disciples that he had given them the Power to remit sins. *"Whose soever sins ye remit, they are remitted unto them; and whose soever sins ye retain, they are retained."* Only this group had that Power because this group had been given the Comforter.

Now, if you were a priest in one of the holy orders of the world and you thought you had the power to remit sins, this would actually be a sin on your part. If you thought you could lay hands on some and remit their sins, this would be a sin on your part. No holy order can give any man the power. There is no such thing as human forgiveness of sins and this here is teaching us just that. The only way that sins are remitted is through the Power of Christ, not through a human hand. And it is not a person who can remit the sins of another person. It is the Christ within the individual who remits the sins. The moment Christ in you is risen, your sins are remitted.

The remission of sins then is really the end of separation from God by the final realization of Christ identity. That's the only way sins are remitted and all sins of course, are the belief that I am a personal, human being. That sums up all of the sins of the world.

This passage where Christ remits sins has been so misconstrued that you've got thousands of men in cloaks going around the country putting hands on people's heads and shoulders and saying "Your sins are remitted," and then the poor fellow goes out and trips down a manhole ten minutes later. He's immune to nothing. He hasn't received the Christ and the one so-called remitting his sins hasn't received the Christ and Christ is the only Redeemer.

But you, as you are willing to weep until the Christ announces Itself in the garden of your consciousness, the Power of remission of sins comes unto you. Your capacity to stand aside and recognize the incorporeal Self of every individual is the way you remit sins. There's no sin in the incorporeal Self of the world, only in the five-sense corporeal self we see.

So, we're going to now intensify our capacity to remit the sins of the world, not through personal effort, but through the impersonal Christ.

Your next chapter is the last chapter in John - other days of the Resurrection. And we're going to begin with that, our world work. That world work will teach us how we are to face this world of earthquakes and typhoons and diseases and limitations and dying people and restore the lost years of the locusts in our consciousness.

Now, I think we owe Nicaragua a recognition that we haven't given her. They say typhoid is supposed to break out there or already has. And so, let us now discern the Reality. Let's get out of the tomb, out of the sepulchre. Let's see that there is no material self that can have typhoid anywhere in God's universe.

There are no diseases in the Kingdom of Heaven on earth. My sense mind knows nothing about that but fortunately, we don't have a sense mind. Fortunately, we know that Christ is the only mind. And so, we have nothing with which we can perceive disease. We have nothing to behold disease with. If it appears to us, we still cannot behold it or accept it for the Christ mind knows nothing of this. The Christ mind only knows Reality.

And so, we're accepting no earthquake in Nicaragua or in any part of the globe. We're accepting no typhoid in Nicaragua or in any part of the globe. We're accepting no disease. We're accepting no suffering. We're accepting no human being. We're accepting the incorporeal Christ everywhere. That means your Self is there and your Self is Christ and your Self is free; the perfect image and likeness of the Father. And your Self is here.

Silence, (pause) …

We're accepting the Resurrection of Christ in the consciousness of those who live in the country called Nicaragua. The I of you, the I of me is the I in every individual and as it ascends in our consciousness, it ascends in them. I am ascended, in the consciousness of the world as you accept Me in your consciousness, as Infinite Being.

Silence, (pause) …

"Fear not.…. it is I." It is always I. All fear is a sense mechanism denying the omnipresence of God.

We're out of the tomb.

And in our consciousness of the Presence, we are playing an important role in the development of the universal Resurrection of Christ in the consciousness of mankind. This is the part you are playing. It's the part you have been playing since you undertook this work.

We are walking with the disciples of yesterday in the presence of Now, sharing with them the same knowledge that was transmitted to them that "I in the midst of thee am the invisible Christ." And then, the bestowal of the Ghost comes unto all those who remain faithful to the universal Truth that only Christ is expressing on earth. There is no second.

There is only Christ where the world sees Nicaragua. There is only Christ everywhere and there we rest until the Father within establishes the deep-rooted Consciousness of this Truth as an experience, not a statement.

Silence, (pause) …

Resurrection is never an outer experience of a physical body returning to a physical form. The two angels within were the announcement of an inner Resurrection. That is the inner Resurrection that takes place in our own consciousness and lifts us to higher levels until we find that Sabbath which is eternal, the eternal Sabbath of the senses when the veil of the senses is completely pierced and never returns.

Silence, (pause) …

Only Spiritual flesh is present everywhere and the senses have deceived us from the first. All is the Light. That Light is the One Being that you are. That Light is expressing where all forms appear.

Mary transcended all appearances when she said, "Show me where my Lord is and I will take him away." There was no physical appearance of the Spirit of God, the Christ Jesus, and yet, she said, "Show me where my Lord is." She transcended all appearance. We are being asked to do likewise, to transcend every appearance on this earth, ever saying, "Show me where my Lord is that I may take him away, that I may be one with the Christ of my own Self."

Thanks to Mary, we can say, "Thou seest him when thou seest me." Mary was the Christ she sought and later, that which appeared to her as the Christ would be revealed to her as her own Being. That we can accept now. The Christ you seek infinitely is your Being. There is no personal self. There is only your Infinite Christ and to accept this and to live with it, faithfully, is finding Christ in the garden, though unseen but accepted in your consciousness; in every garden for there is only One. In every country, in every race, in every religion, find Christ in the garden. Know that you are the invisible Self of every church in the world.

Silence, (pause) …

Then the signs that follow will show you, you are truly sent. You will receive the Bestowal. The Comforter will announce, "Henceforth, there is no flesh in your Consciousness for all is the One, Divine Self."

This is the preparation of the Christ for the new era when all who walk in the flesh will walk out of the flesh as Moses and Enoch, Bhagriath, Buddha, Jesus, laying down their coats of skin and walk into the new Universe which has ever been present awaiting our existence in the next realm of Life. Those who have walked before us are all awaiting our entry into this new Realm and the help you're receiving is beyond calculation.

We have two more meetings, the 7th of January and the 14th then a month off till we meet again on the 11th of February for the Special Seven classes which end on, I think it's March 24th, the last Sunday in March.

If you know some people who might be planning to come here between the 14th of January and 11th of February, try get word to them if it's convenient for you because there won't be any notices mailed out about it nor will there be any notices about the Special Seven classes because we don't want to encourage people who haven't been attending to attend these Seven. We won't reject them but we don't want to influence them in any way.

These Seven classes will be the capstone of the work. Now, please read the 12th chapter of "Realization of Oneness" and last chapter of the Gospel of John. Those two chapters will constitute the work for next two sessions.

A very joyous Christ New Year. Thank you.

CLASS 45

THE INNER FLAME

Herb: We're going to take a look today at a passage which began the Bible of Mark and which culminates the Bible of John. So that we see one being descriptive of the faith of man at the beginning of starting on the path and the other being descriptive of the faith of man after he has awakened to the inner Light. Now the first passage is in Mark in the first chapter, the 10th and the 16th verse.

"Now as he walked by the sea of Galilee, he saw Simon and Andrew his brother casting a net into the sea: for they were fishers. And Jesus said unto them, Come ye after me, I will make you to become fishers of men."

At the first awareness of something higher than your own human selfhood, Christ says to you, *"Come ye after me, and I will make you to become fishers of men."* You may not be conscious of Christ saying this within your Self but there is some subtle inner Guidance and now you find yourself on a path in which you are leaving your old nets behind you. You are grafted away from your old ways, your old beliefs, finally to a higher level where you're even grafted away from the very mind itself upon which you depended. And you are made into a fisher of men.

Now that was a prophecy and as that prophecy was made to the disciples, it was also made to each of us. The Christ has spoken this to mankind, *"Follow me.... and I will make you fishers of men."*

Now we look at it in Luke because in Luke we have it a little more detailed and then we can have a good comparison to the way it comes in the last chapter of John. In the 5th chapter of Luke it begins as follows:

"It came to pass, that, as the people passed [pressed] upon him to hear the word of God, he stood by the lake of Gennesaret, And saw two ships standing by the lake: but the fishermen were gone out of them, and [they] were washing their nets. And he entered into one of the ships, which was Simon's, and prayed him that he would thrust out a little from the land. And he sat down, and taught the people out of the ship. Now when he had left speaking, he said unto Simon, Launch out into the deep, and let down your nets for a draught. And Simon answering said unto him, Master, we have toiled all the night, and have taken nothing: nevertheless at thy word I will let down the net. And when they had this done, they enclosed a great multitude of fishes: and their net brake."

Launching out into the deep, we have learned through our progress in the Scripture, was departing beyond the five senses and all the sense mind was the shallows. And there they caught no fish. We in the shallows of the sense mind catch no fish; and at this point fish is a symbol of Divine Truth. Through the sense mind we are not receptive to Divine Truth. And now we go out beyond the sense mind, into the deep. But being novices even though our catch is great our net breaks; we find that the mind of man is unable to receive Spiritual Truth. And this is our introduction to the transformation that must take place in a man. And as this procedure continues we find that;

"When they had this done, they enclosed a great multitude of fishes: and their net brake. And they beckoned unto their partners, which were in the other ship, that they should come and help them. And they came, and filled both the ships, so that they began to sink. And when Simon [Peter] saw it, he fell down at Jesus' knees, saying, Depart from me; for I am a sinful man, O Lord. For he was astonished, and all that were with him, at the draught of the fishes [with] which they had taken: And so was also James, and John, the sons of Zebedee, which were partners with Simon. And Jesus said unto Simon, Fear not; from henceforth thou shalt catch men. And when they had brought their ships to land, they forsook all, and followed him."

Now these men then were motivated by some inner Impulse now to follow Christ although to their minds they were following a man named Jesus. And this is our faith at the beginning of the path. If you just cast your mind back a little, you find that there was a time when suddenly you knew there was another way and then you went out and for some reason or other, even though the quick results of the new way were magnificent, somehow you couldn't hold all that you received; your net broke, you needed help, you had to call another ship to you and even then the great weight of a new Truth coming upon was so heavy it seemed that the mind was sinking like a ship.

At the beginning of the path we have what is called the faith that is not anchored in that which it needs. We have a new kind of faith. A faith in a God, a faith in a way, a faith in something but we don't know how to define it and we don't have the net to catch the fullness of the Truth.

But now after three years with Jesus Christ something has happened. They have learned much Truth. They seemingly have caught much fish. Even to the point that twice after the crucifixion they have been visited by the Master. Once the Master has appeared to them in a closed room and again later when Thomas was present the Master appeared. You would think now their nets would hold and yet a funny thing happens and only John puts it here of all the Gospels. And so he begins his 21st verse with what appears to be a repetition of these incidents that began in the beginning of his ministry with the disciples. So that you might say they have fallen back. And you might compare this to your own experience as you go forward, as you're lifted, sometimes even into Spiritual ecstasy. And then there are moments of shattered faith, there are the ups and downs, the upheavals and the uplifting. The earthquakes within, the volcanoes and then the great doubts. And here is a very strange thing full of surprises. Twice visited by the Master, the disciples who had left their nets, who no longer relied on even a profession for their livelihood were going back to fishing. They had returned to their old consciousness. They had gone home as you remember, the old consciousness, they were starting again. And the strange thing is they'd already twice seen the Master.

And so Peter says, *"I go a fishing."* So with us you can see that we may rise to sublime heights but somewhere, somehow that faith with which we start is insufficient. Peter had it, if you remember when he tried to walk upon the water and he fell through. And the teaching there was, as the Master said, *"O ye of little faith,"* that Peter had little faith. And yet the heart was willing and eager. There was zeal, there was desire to follow but the faith could not support him. So with us, we may have a great human faith but it cannot support us and we fall through and we wonder why is my faith insufficient? And this 21st chapter is going to tell us why. And so it is that now for the 3rd time the Master comes upon the disciples.

"After these things Jesus shewed himself again to the disciples at the sea of Tiberius; and on this wise shewed he himself. There were together Simon Peter, and Thomas called Didymus, and Nathanael of Cana in Galilee, and the sons of Zebedee, and two other of his disciples."

In other words seven disciples were present. These seven were the advanced disciples. They were ready for this third visit. They were ready now to become fishers of men. And they were together, it says. They were joined in one purpose.

And now the symbolism begins. It's not just an ordinary fishing trip. *"I go a fishing,"* said Peter. Let us remember that even though it would appear on the outer, that they're simply going fishing as they did when they were fishermen, there had been two appearances of the Christ after crucifixion. And now you may know that this fishing trip was on the inner plane. A new kind of faith has come upon them. And to teach us about it we have to see it on the outer and the inner. We'll see it on the outer as a fishing trip. We'll see it on the inner as a Spiritual experience in which the disciples have come aware of the Invisible. Their new senses have developed. They can now see the invisible Christ and even make out Invisible objects. And they themselves may not even be aware that they are doing this. As you pass from sense vision to Soul vision you are not always aware that you have stepped over the veil. It all looks the same to you except a little brighter, a little clearer, a little more beautiful, maybe a little breathtakingly beautiful at times but you can't be sure what you're seeing. Is it with your inner senses or your outer? And that is a state of awe which is described in here.

"I go a fishing," said Peter. And that Peter saith. Peter says, *"I go a fishing"* is a very important phrase. Now when the seven are listed Peter and Thomas are listed first. Peter the will, the human sense will, Thomas the understanding. And when Peter says, *"I go a fishing"* that means the will of you is going fishing. Now everything of you then must follow that will. When that will of Peter says, *"I go a fishing"* the other six must go along and in turn you see that they do. They say, "We'll go with you." Everything follows the will of yourself. And if your will is human then everything follows your human will. If your will is Divine everything follows Divine Will. And the distinction is now being brought here that Peter is the spokesman of yourself. The will of you is the spokesman of the rest of you. Peter says, *"I go a fishing."* You say, "I take a drive," you say, "I go to the mountains," the rest of you must follow. The will of you is decided. And let's see what happens to this will of Peter.

And *"They say unto him, We also go with you. And so they went forth, they entered a ship immediately; and that night they caught nothing."*

Wherever your will goes the rest of you immediately goes and in this case they catch nothing, they're right back to the 1st chapter of Mark, the 5th chapter of Luke - what have they learned? It would seem they have learned nothing. And there will be times like that in your life and have been, when you think, "Oh my gosh, I've studied this for so many years and right now I feel bankrupt. It's as if I've never studied the Word or never had an experience or never knew a Truth, I just feel barren." So it was with them; they caught nothing.

"But when the morning was now come, Jesus stood on the shore: but the disciples knew not that it was Jesus."

Now the symbolism begins in earnest. This morning that was come could not have come without those three years. Even though at the moment they had caught nothing and seemed barren that was only the outer picture. That maybe your outer picture. But there will come a morning, and this is a strange and beautiful morning because it is really a mystic dawn. A mystic sunrise. This is the morning within. The morning when without their being aware of what is moving them, they are in some way conscious of the Radiance of Christ. They don't recognize Jesus, you see. He's standing on the shore and that shore if you can draw back and see this vastness of the shore and the sea and the land, you see the symbolism then that they are on the sea. The sea of world thought. But out here where the sea meets the land which is the shore, on the brink of their consciousness rising just like the early sun may just hit the mountain tops and yet itself may not be visible; so rising within them was an awareness of an Impulse. Really outskirts of their consciousness, on the shore was this Impulse called Jesus or the invisible Christ. They could see maybe a form but not recognize the Essence at the moment. And so we are moved by this invisible Power. All our years are coming into fruition in the mystic dawn within ourselves. The beginning of a real golden harvest, when without being able to define that which is happening, we know it is happening. We can feel the rising Christ, and it matters not what we have caught, what we have understood, what we have comprehended, what we have been able to grasp, we are now being lifted in a strange way. We are the fish and the fish must be caught in the ocean and lifted out of the ocean. And just as the fish are caught and lifted out of the ocean by the fishermen, we are caught by the Christ and lifted out of the sea of world thought.

To be caught up by the Christ is to be saved from mortality.

And this is the experience now which the disciples are going through. They are the fish. They were the fishermen, but now they are the fish and they are being raised up by the Christ. They are being caught. They are being saved. They are being redeemed. Each is becoming aware of the inner Light and though they're still in the sea, that Light which is within them is seen to them to be on the shore and they are approaching it. So it may seem to you that the Goodness that you have been seeking is out there to be touched and felt, but if it is a Spiritual experience it is happening within you and projecting what you call Goodness into the external but it's really an inner event made visible. We are approaching the shore but we still cannot discern the nature of the Christ.

"*Then Jesus saith unto them, Children, have ye any meat? And they answered him, No.*"

That which is on the shore which is deep within their consciousness not quite clearly defined yet is saying within, "*Have you any meat?*" And first addressing them as "*Children,*" meaning Spiritually immature, meat meaning substance and of course the substance is Spirit. The question then comes to you, "Have you accepted Spiritual identity? Have you any meat? Or are you still a child?" And it's a great moment when you can say, "No, I have no meat." When you can confess that you have been Spiritually poor, you open the gateway to the Christ. Only when we are aware of our Spiritual poverty are we replenished. If we think we are rich, if we think we are worldly wealthy, if we are not aware that without Spirit we are nothing then we are that which the Old Testament calls vanity, "*All is vanity.*" We are intellectually alive and yet dead.

The disciples know, and that's a great stride, that they are Spiritually barren, "No, we have no meat. We have no food of the Soul. We have no Divine substance. That's why we're out here with no catch. That's why our lives have been fruitless. That's why there have been discords and upheavals. That's why we lack. That's why we're limited. We have no Spiritual substance. No Spiritual vision. No Spiritual awareness."

They were men in physical bodies of flesh. They were living in this world. On the sea of human thought but they were headed to the land. We are headed to a land, another realm which coexists right where the sea is, adjacent to it. And we have to cross out of the sea into the land.

Out of world thought, out of the sense mind, which says, "You caught nothing. Your life has been meaningless." or "Your life has been a fragment." or "Your life has not been fulfilled. You have not fulfilled your purpose on this earth." This is the sense mind talking, and the answer comes, "Because I have no meat, because I am Spiritually barren, because I am poor in Spirit." And always the Christ within is forcing you to reach these inner conclusions if you are being moved by the Christ.

Now this should be the path then, the confession of duality. "Oh yes I've had some Spiritual moments but I've also been of this world. I've also been motivated by improving my human welfare. I've thought about how I could get along better as a human being." That's not meat, that's division. That's why the disciples were out there with no fish. They had not gone all the way.

"He said unto them, Cast the net on the right side of the ship, and ye shall find."

In the original, at the beginning of their journey into Spirit, he had told them to *"Launch out into the deep."* Now he tells them to *"Cast the net at the right side of the ship."*

Now the ship is the mind. We sail along in our mind and we sail in the sea of this world. There's another sea there that we don't see. There are two seas - the sea of the world and the sea of Spirit. And in our mind we travel in the sea of the world. When he's told to cast his net on the *"Right side of the ship,"* Peter is being told that the *"Right side of the ship,"* is not his mind but his Soul. When you dwell in your Soul instead of your mind you are casting the net on the *"Right side."* And that *"Right side"* enables you to move in the sea of Spirit instead of the sea of world mind. That's the only way you make it to the shore. In other words, unless we step out of the five sense mind consciously, transcending it, disbelieving all evidence of the senses - you're not going to take a pair of scissors and cut off your sense of touch, or put something over your eyes so that you don't see - you're going to look through those eyes and hear through those ears but you're not going to accept what those senses bring to you, for one good reason: God is All and the senses have no capacity to see God. The senses have never heard God or seen God or touched God.

And if the senses cannot find God for us what do they find but the lie? To find God then we cannot rely on senses, we must step out and above the senses. And that means we stand in the senses rejecting the evidence of the senses until that inner stirring opens us to the Christ Radiance which leads us to the shore of the new senses. The senses that can, not only see the form, but see the Essence. The senses that begin to look and find objects that exist.

Now when the Soul senses take over two things will happen; mostly they will replace the senses of the mind. so that you'll be seeing what eyes do not see. There is also a time and only for instruction when you have what is called double vision - you can see both the one that appears to the naked human eye and you can see the inner that appears only to the Soul eye. It doesn't happen very often. Now when it happens, having heard about it or having had this double vision perhaps, you may find that you now understand it and I'd like to explain to you what it means.

To a geologist we're in a world now where the rocks have formed through the ages. And if you've gone into the caves, some places out in the West here where you can see various strata of rock that have over the years become hardened and atrophied. You would agree with the geologist that this has taken place over thousands and thousands of years. That's untrue; that's true only to the human sense mind. Actually this instant everything that is in this world is being manufactured. Every rock that allegedly was there even millions of years ago is being manufactured this instant by the world mind. And if you ever have a glimpse of that you will understand that this is a *Now* world in a counterfeit sense. There isn't a single thing in it that happened yesterday. The complete counterfeit is happening at this present moment. And also at this present moment that which it is counterfeiting is present. Both the original genuine in Spirit and the counterfeit of the world mind are both this instant. And you live in one or the other,. And there is a moment in your double vision when you see both, and you can see how it's possible to stand in the midst of all of the ravages of the world untouched, because they're only happening in the one sense mind and they're not happening in the Soul sense. Whatever you happen to be experiencing is the one you're in and for you the highest is the majority with God.

Now I'd like to explain that more fully but the best thing for it is to wait until the experience touches you and you'll see that there are times when you're actually looking out through a Soul sense and don't know you are. That's how subtly and effortlessly you move from one to the other even though you may not be aware of it. And then ultimately of course you become more aware of it.

Now the disciples are not aware of it. They are looking out through Soul senses. That's why they're beginning to discern the presence of a man called Jesus. He's not in a physical body you know. He's already demonstrated there is no physical body and yet they're seeing Him for the third time. They're looking through their Soul senses and now they're seeing things they never saw before. In one moment no fish. Why do fish suddenly appear? Because they're stepping out of the physical universe into the Spiritual universe through their Soul senses. They're being lifted by the inner Christ.

It's like the loaves and fishes for the multitude. One moment just a few fish, a few loaves; in another moment five thousand people are lifted into a vision of something they couldn't see a moment ago which was always there even though they couldn't see it. In a moment they all were in their Soul senses but didn't have the vaguest idea that they were, and they saw supply interpreted to them as loaves and fishes. So it is, you'll find the miracles that occur in your life are not because God suddenly decided you were a good person, but because through some instinctive awareness of the inner Christ you were open to your Soul senses and that which was ever present is now presented to you, through your Soul senses in a way you can comprehend and utilize.

Now there is a transition or a transformation in the nature of faith that is taking place in Peter and the disciples. Your repeated experiences change the nature of your faith. At the beginning it was blind faith and that's why the net broke. It was faith that could only see and be amazed and say, "Isn't that marvellous," and yet go out and do likewise? No, it couldn't do that because the mind couldn't hold the meaning behind what had happened.

Now we're going to learn how to hold the meaning of what is happening. Your faith is going to be joined together with some other quality, to make it a Faith that will no longer be called by the Master, "A little faith." And this Faith will be such that the nets will not break regardless of the load. This is the Faith that is being built in us now.

"Cast the net on the right side of the ship, and ye shall find. And they cast therefore, and now they were not able to draw it for the multitude of fishes."

They were not looking through the mind anymore they were looking through the Soul and the Soul experiences that which is necessary at every moment. The Soul is ever in complete rapport with the infinite Spiritual universe. If you need fish there are fish. If you need clothing there is clothing. Grace flows through the Soul. Suddenly there are fish. Now these fish are not to be interpreted only as physical, tangible fish. Fish also means new Truth. The inner Truth, the Fish, represent the new levels of wisdom that are welling up within. Great Fish, great Truths. Truths that the human mind would never even know about. You know how people ask questions in this work, question after question and yet not one of the questions of the human mind even begins to anticipate the new Truths that come up when the Soul is open. There are no questions from the human mind about these Truths because the human mind knows nothing about them. Now the Truth that passes all mental understanding is brought into play.

Now what's happening here? There's more than just Peter there, there's more than disciples there: there is Christ. Christ on the shore is the Invisible activity in the consciousness of the disciples. Christ on the shore of your consciousness changes you. Your vision changes, your hearing changes, your understanding changes. You are lifted into the awareness of a realm not known to mankind. You are lifted behind the veil, behind the veil of all religions on the earth, behind the veil of science, behind the veil of the human mind, behind the veil of the atom, behind the veil of Darwin's theory, behind the veil of human evolution, behind the veil of human death, behind the veil of everything that the human mind knows, as Christ rising in you, awakens you to a new Self of your own Being.

We begin to vaguely know that we are finding another level of our Self, a higher level where Heaven is a realm within our own Consciousness and that transformation from the self who lives in the human senses and in the human body is taking place. Even though in a small measure sometimes, this awareness is destined to grow. It depends on your capacity to listen to the inner Christ and then to obey the Divine Impulse that comes to you.

I'd like to underline two words: Divine Impulse.

Sometimes you find it difficult to realize that God is everywhere or that the Allness of God is everywhere. Perhaps it's too big, too much of a project to know that I here am the Spirit of God and my Spirit is everywhere and nothing else is there. This should become normal consciousness, but you certainly can remember and even test out that the Divine Impulse is everywhere. So that if you're confronted with a situation that would seem to be frightening or despairing or in some way causing you grave concern, this would call for an immediate readjustment to the fact that wherever this situation is emanating from, there is the Divine Impulse invisible. Right there my net is catching no fish. I'm just catching world mind as a problem and yet right there is the Divine Impulse and if I can rest in the conscious awareness that the Divine Impulse is there, and accept that it is there without any great affirmations about "God is everywhere" and "God is wonderful" and "God is perfect" and "God is all power," without any words in me the acceptance that the Divine Impulse is there lights the spark of that Divine Impulse in me here.

And there's an inner Radiance begins. You can almost feel the beginning of the rainbow. The omnipresent Divine Impulse never fails. You're casting your net on the *"Right side of the ship."* That's how you begin to enter the Soul realm: to accept the omnipresent Divine Impulse. Knowing it's invisible to human senses but it is present awaiting acceptance; recognition, and the recognition cannot be with your eyes or your ears; it must be with a quality in you. And you find that quality in you which recognizes the Divine Impulse becomes your Soul. As you accept it this is your recognition and then your Soul is kindled. Christ rises and sometimes quickly, startlingly quick, you find a healing takes place because the Divine Impulse you've accepted was right where someone else was accepting a problem. That Divine Impulse out there is really a Divine Impulse within you.

It's always present. You simply do not see it or notice it or acknowledge it and so you cast your net, your mind on the wrong side of the ship. But the moment you are aware that even though you're not in conjunction with the Divine Impulse, it is there; then you re-adjust and you accept that which you cannot see. The fish you cannot see you accept and you cast your mind into the acknowledgement that the Divine Impulse must be here because God is. Everywhere is God, everywhere is the Divine Impulse and that Impulse listened to, accepted, acknowledged, begins to beat its own drum and you are listening to the unlistenable and you find that it's there all the time. You have now another level of faith, Faith in the unseen, not just faith in what you could see with your eyes like Peter but Faith in what you cannot see with your eyes.

Everywhere the Divine Impulse: you're walking through it, and then as you listen - which means you step out of the mind that does not see the Divine Impulse - you give your Being over to this Divine Impulse you cannot see. You're coming into the early dawn of Love. Love is when you give your Being to God, sight unseen. And this Love united with Faith becomes the new dispensation. This is the missing ingredient, faith without Love is empty. Faith with Love walks on the water. When Faith and Love are united in you, you have the key to all scripture, the key to the meaning of Christ. When we love God enough to accept Gods presence, where our senses do not know Gods presence, we're going beyond human faith. We are opening Love.

The disciples are learning that now. Their human senses tell them that they have caught no fish. The inner Christ is saying, "Get out of that mind…. *Cast your net on the right side of the ship.*" Don't believe what your sense mind is reporting - ever. No matter what your sense mind says it's the wrong side of the ship. You must go beyond it to the *"Right side,"* you must launch into the deep beyond the sense mind. You do this on the knowledge that God is present as the living Divine Impulse and the moment that Impulse touches you and you touch it, it fans out and becomes the complete spectrum of everything God is; the Power, the Presence, the Love, the Truth, the Beauty. That Impulse is an Infinite One. And all you do is rest in it. You don't have to catch the fish. It catches all the fish for you because the fish were already there and caught. The fullness of your Being is already present but you must get beyond the sense mind. Then your net is filled with all that God is. Something in you tells you when it's time to go beyond the senses and that something is now happening in Peter.

"Therefore that disciple whom Jesus loved saith unto Peter, It is the Lord."

The human understanding didn't know this was the Christ telling them to cast their net on the *"Right side."* Peter didn't know this was the Christ; John did. The awareness of the Christ comes not from the human mind it comes from Love. Love spontaneously responds to the Christ and alerts the human mind. And if you try to skip that step and try with the human mind to climb the gates of Heaven it doesn't work. Peter knows nothing about what is happening but John does. In other words, Love in you is aware of the Christ and your mind must be aware of this Love. That's the connecting link, the bridge between the understanding, the human will and the Christ.

If you got a Love centre that is low then the mind continues in its material intellectual ways. But you cannot manufacture this Love. You find then that the reason Love is mentioned here, as John alerting Peter, is that when you find that the Love is in you, this is a sign that you are in that progression of consciousness which is Illumination. When the Love in you awakens the mind, you are in the illuminated state. Illumination and Love are one and the same. You will recognize that state then of Illumination by the Love you feel. The Love not only of yourself but of all that exists throughout the universe.

You will look at all created things and say, "Well this is much different than it appears to be." It would appear to be that there are no fish here, no fish there but just as there are fish everywhere so there is perfect Essence everywhere. And when this overwhelming awareness of the invisible Essence everywhere is yours then the human understanding which was faith without knowledge is now reinforced by Faith confirmed by Love. This is the Faith that never wavers. This is the Faith that takes you into Heaven on earth.

This Love now alerts Peter, *"This is the Lord."* Up to this point Peter could only believe what he saw with his own senses. He saw more fish and he was excited. Now he sees Jesus. He sees Jesus because something in him has awakened him to the fact that there is someone there called the Christ. He's very excited. It is said though that *"He was naked"* and now he girds himself with the garment he had discarded. We have to see that very carefully.

"When Simon Peter heard that it was the Lord, he girt his fisher's coat unto him, (for he was naked,) and did cast himself into the sea."

Now we are naked just as Peter was, and that nakedness is human faith. When you're naked you're without Spiritual Faith, you have all the human faith and then the water does not support you. Now Peter is adding Love to the faith that couldn't support him and something beautiful happens. And that Love means that Peter is getting out of Peter. You see he's not loving Peter anymore. The arrogant, over zealous, over bearing qualities within him have been refined. John is alerting us to the fact that Peter becoming aware of his Christ Self is now able to generate that Faith which he didn't have at the early part of his ministry.

There's a deeper meaning though. Simon Peter was naked and now *"He girt his fisher's coat unto him."* The true meaning of naked is more than just lacking in Faith, it's part of the meaning but when you're in a mortal body you are naked. All who walk in material bodies are naked biblically. His fisher's coat means that he suddenly became aware through Christ of his other body, his Soul body. And you see now he can cast himself into the sea.

You remember last week that Mary Magdalene paused before she entered the tomb and that pause was to teach us this great pause never to enter a room until we are consciously aware that not a physical body is going to enter; we're not in such a physical body.

And here it comes in another way; Peter girding himself with his fisher's coat. Your fisher's coat is your body of the Soul. Now if you're conscious of yourself as a physical body you're in the state called naked. If you're conscious of yourself in a Spiritual body you are wearing your fisher's coat. One drowns in the sea, one can walk in the sea.

Now this has to be a conscious activity; you cannot decide that it will take care of itself, because it doesn't. Through Love your faith must rise beyond what your senses know to the acceptance consciously that you are in a Soul body that is Invisible and can never be destroyed. And you must consciously live in the awareness of it, so that you're never caught in the belief that you inhabit a physical form. Now that can only be taken on a different level of Faith than the blind faith of a human mind. It must be taken through the experience which confirms that Faith. You can't have the experience unless you are making the effort to understand it, to witness it, first in the words of the Bible and then as a living experience in your Self. It isn't enough to read that Peter is doing that. It wasn't enough for Peter to read it somewhere; it had to become experience, living experience over a period of time.

And so we should be bending ourselves toward the experience of the Invisible body by casting our net on the *"Right side of the ship,"* taking our mind out of its creation called this physical form, rising above that mind into Soul which is conscious of the Soul body. And in the interim while there is a gap in the passage from mind to Soul, being willing to accept that the dispensation of the Christ was to lift you into the Christ body which was ever present where the world saw Jesus just as it is ever present where the world sees you. This changeover in consciousness from the belief that I am mortal man to the knowledge that I am Immortal Self is casting your net on the other side.

If you are not ready to make that decision then you must go back and study a little harder. Read the Sermon on the Mount several more times. Practice what it says. Read more of the books. Hear more of the tapes. There are many things you must do until you can consciously say, "I've reached the place where I'm willing to consider that I am not in a physical form, that I am not in a physical world but I am Spiritual Being in a Spiritual Body right here and right now. And then hold the Consciousness frequently on that level until that inner Christ which is on the shore of your consciousness develops into a more living experience and the Essence becomes part of what you know to be present. Then you'll find your ship comes out of the sea onto the shore. You'll find the Inner quality of John in you alerts you that Christ is leading you into the invisible Kingdom on earth.

This new Faith is to replace the faith of the seven disciples in you. You have the faith of the will in Peter, the faith of reason in Thomas but you have the twins in there, the Zebedee twins and they are the symbol of Faith and Love united as One. This is to take place in us. There was a faith of Nathaniel in Wisdom. There was the faith of the other two disciples in external life. And now your faith is changing. All types of faith in you are becoming the Faith that God is present as individual Christ Selfhood. There are no seven disciples. The knowledge of Oneness is coming into focus. Christ on the shore of your Consciousness is leading you into the realization of the One Divine Self everywhere.

Silence, (pause) ...

"The other disciples came in a little ship; (for they were not far from the land, but as it were two hundred cubits,) dragging the net with fishes."

It was Peter, the will, jumps into the sea and then the other disciples follow in a little ship. The will is always the leader. You can see that if your will is God centered everything will follow in a little ship, if your will is not God centered that little ship will follow humanly. Always Peter represents the fullness of your Being, the little ship with other disciples represents all other qualities in you following the will of your Being.

When Peter is not just human will, but is human will lifted by Love, then the ship comes to the shore because the shore is always close by; only two hundred cubits away. In other words the veil of the senses is all that separates us from the shore, from Reality. And now this new quality in Peter the illumination of Love should be functioning within us. A Love that is selfless. A Love that is not seeking personal welfare. A Love that has learned that all seeking on the material level that is not preceded by an awareness of the inner Christ, is a detour. An act that will never yield fish. What at first seemed to be turning away from the things we wanted is revealed to us as the only way to live. To turn away from the world, to harken to the Inner Christ, to let the Inner Christ guide our consciousness. Listening not with the sense mind but another quality called Soul, deeper within, higher within. And then we come to the land.

Now the land here means out of the sense mind, out of world thought, out of all material beliefs which was shown to be transitory. The land is the Kingdom of Heaven on earth. The land is Reality. When Love and Faith are combined we are lifted by the Christ from the sea to the land. And there stands a fire with coals.

— End of Side One —

Now then the surprise comes at this point when you would expect that he would say, "Now come and have these, have this Heavenly feast."

But when they land on the shore, *"Jesus saith unto them, Bring of the fish which **ye** have now caught."*

And this is the crux of the message at this point. Before you can sup of the Heavenly bread and fish on the fires of Divine Love you must bring something of your Self. Now this is the wedding of instruction in the letter with inspiration in the living Divine Word. So Peter and the disciples are asked to bring the fish that they have caught. "What Truth do you know? What are your beliefs? What is your understanding? Bring that; yes. But don't stop there. We've all had instruction in Truth and now with that instruction must be wedded inspiration; without it you'll always be off shore.

Inspiration now is when having through Love of God supremely, being willing to yield your complete effort, not to better your humanhood but to seek only the Kingdom of God within yourself. In trust that the Kingdom of God within you will yield its fruit and that it being All-Power will completely cover every so-called human need.

As you're willing to do that - launching out into the deep beyond the senses of human faith - then Love and Faith lead you to the shore and there you find the Christ has drawn you to the Heavenly feast which is the new Self. The fish on the coals of the fire is Divine Love revealing your new Self and the bread is the substance of that Self and there are many meanings in the fish and the bread because you see he doesn't have fishes and loaves he has one fish, one cake. One is sufficient to mankind. One Self. And like a fish that One Self increases into many appearing. That bread is the new bread, the new substance you live by. You live by Grace. In the new Self you are the fish who has been plucked out of the sea of world thought and you are now the incorporeal Self. And you live by the bread which is cooked on the fire of Divine Love by the Master within you. And that substance increases and increases and increases your living experience, and now as you draw the Truth you know to this fire, living inner inspiration opens you to Truth you couldn't know any other way. It isn't enough to continue as a memory student or as an intellect. You must have living revelation and you can only get it from Divine Love – Christ, in you. This is a total inner turning to Christ in you. With total confidence, total trust that there is a Self of you. This is the land where the Self of you is where you live. This is the transformed Self. The transformed Consciousness.

They're not seeing physical bread anymore or physical fish; they're seeing the One Divine Self within themselves as themselves. They are the fish and they are the bread. "I in the midst of you am the Fish. I in the midst of you am the Bread, and I am the sacred

Fire of your own Divinity." This invisible journey through the sea to the shore to the land is the transformed Consciousness accepting Divinity as Self. Divinity which multiplies as fishes do. One Self fulfils all needs.

The acceptance of that One Self now is the level of Consciousness which Peter is being led to and the other six disciples with him. They are being awakened to who they are. They are going through a temporary experience of the real Self. But it is being presented to you and to me because it is our Way-shower. All that is happening out there visibly in the written word is a living experience within you when you are willing to cast out beyond the five sense world.

That means if you continue believing certain things about yourself that are not so, you're not launching out into the deep, you're not ready for the Peter experience, for that renewal of Faith with Love, so that Faith and Love are united in one. And this is a necessary experience. *"Sell all thou hast... Cast thy net on the right side of the ship,"* and now bring the fish you have caught to the Christ. Lay everything you think you know at the feet of the Christ and say, "Now you show me. I know nothing. All the fish I have caught are of no account. I come to you completely open."

This is the Divinity acceptance within yourself. You cannot accept Divinity and still have human concepts. You cannot trust Divinity and still have human concepts. And even at this late date, at this point in the transitional consciousness of Peter he has not reached the pinnacle. It's only a glimpse that mankind will have of itself before it further solidifies by learning the true nature of Love, and so the Master must now say to Peter, "Do you love me?" And again "Peter, do you love me?" And again, "Peter, do you Love me?" And there's a meaning there - just as Peter three times had denied the Christ so now three times does the Christ lift Peter above those previous denials.

Now one thing you won't notice in our text is that the three questions of "Do you love me?" are not identical. They seem to be but they are not in the original. And only by knowing this can you find a fuller meaning in these questions. Now in the Greek, "Do you love me?" the first time is said by a word that means, do you love me not as a mechanical robot, or as a human emotion but "Do you love me, the Christ?" Not Jesus. In other words the question is, do you love Jesus the man or do you love Christ the Spirit of God? And Peter always says, "Oh yes, I love you," but Peter isn't aware of the meaning and so again the Christ says, "Do you love me," meaning do you love Jesus the man or do you love Christ the Spirit of God? And again Peter asserts his love, and the third time the Christ now says the word which is not "Do you love the Christ," but do you love as a mechanical man another human being. And Peter doesn't even know the difference and the change that is taking place. He still says, "Of course I love you."

And the Christ is revealing that all Peter really loves at this moment is not the Christ; he was lifted to it but he can't grasp it still. He still has a sense of loving Peter. But we are being taught beyond that. "Do you love me?" means do you love Christ within yourself more than you love your human self. "Peter, do you love Christ within you more than you love Peter the man?" And Peter not understanding says, "But I do love you." The question is phrased to you then and to me and to every individual in this world, "Do you love Christ in you more than you love your human selfhood?" On that you make or break your demonstration and the fulfilment of your very purpose in this world. If we still love our human selfhood more than we love Christ within ourselves, it's quite clear that we're in a state of duality.

And still the message is incomplete for now Peter must turn and say, "What about him over there?" pointing to John. Even having been blessed by the new experience of finding Self, which he couldn't hold onto, having found some degree of Christhood, Peter turns and says to the man called Jesus, "What about him over there? What about John? What's he going to do? If I am to follow you what about him, what's he going to do?" And this is a teaching to us.

The Master says, "What is it to thee if I wish him to tarry until I come?" Just as the Master on the cross could point to John and say to his mother, "There is your son," and point to John and say, "There is your mother." He reminds us now that Love must remain a living factor in your heart. Peter, the will, must now follow the Master but Love must tarry on the earth. And then translated again you see that Peter the mind must go, Love must remain: the Soul is all that can redeem you. Peter is ready to now go deeper and deeper but the Soul remains on earth as the way through which the Word will enter every human heart. John must tarry on earth meaning Love within you will open your Soul. Mind won't do it.

You can't get to Heaven through Peter you must get to Heaven through John.

The mind stays in the sea the Soul comes up and lands on the shore. The great teaching of the Bible finally culminates with the knowledge that only through your willingness to resist the world mind expressing as a sense mind in you, living beyond it in your Soul, accepting yourself as Invisible Being, the invisible living Christ - the Spirit not in a body - will your Soul be open to receive the inner confirmation of that which you accept through Faith and through Love. This union of Love and Faith will not waver and will enable you to walk upon the water of Truth. The fire of Love which contains the bread and the fish has been prepared for all of us. It is in the land of Reality behind the veil of the senses now. We are being asked to partake of that Heavenly feast.

"If you hear my voice and you open the door when I knock, I will come and sup with thee." And this is what I bring; the bread and the fish.

The new Self, the new Body, the new Life which is Christ eternal and your receptivity to all this is made possible only through the awareness that within you is John; the Soul. The Soul receives the Christ. You cannot do it through instruction. You do it through inspiration. Instruction leads you to inspiration. Inspiration takes you across the sea of world thought. Inspiration brings you Truth that can be received in no other way. The whole Gospel now takes you to the point where you must know who you are and live in that knowledge.

If we had tried to do world work before we came to a knowledge of identity, before we came to a place where we were able to receive living inspirational revelation from the very Christ of our own Being, we would be going through some kind of form without substance. You may have noticed in the last three or four weeks that we have been doing a little world work. Enough to maybe give you some evidence of the fact that when you know yourself to be who you truly are then you are given only Truth that works. Not Truth that is opinion. And then you are in world work. What is the answer that the Master says every time Peter professes his deep love?

"If you love me feed my lambs. If you love me feed my sheep. Do you love Christ? But Christ is You. Do you accept Christ as loving Christ? But if you accept Christ feed my sheep, feed my lambs."

And so we must know what we're to do. We must give the evidence that we accept Christ identity by feeding the lambs. Who are they? There are two meanings. The lambs are just....well first of all lambs are innocent, they're distinguished from the sheep who are a little more mature and they're more advanced you might say. Innocent, in a sense that they do not yet know but they are on the way with blind faith. And so those who are coming through blind faith are the innocent lambs and in our world work we must feed them, we must help them. And then there are those who are more advanced; their faith is not blind they are now sheep. They're not innocent lambs their faith has been confirmed and they're more advanced along the path and we must help them. But that isn't all that was told in "Feed my lambs, and feed my sheep."

The real lambs and the real sheep are the Divine thoughts in your Self. Those thoughts within you which are just budding - still undiscerned but there are the lambs - those which have taken firmer root in you are the sheep and by feeding them means you must let them grow. You must accept them, you must listen to them and be obedient for they are the methods through which the Divine feeds us. The Divine does the feeding. Our accepting of the Divine thought within us is feeding the lambs and the sheep. And if you're not listening to living revelation within your Self you're not feeding the lambs and the sheep. You're doing it by rote. You're only bringing your fish but you're not finding the coals with the living Fire of the living bread and the living fish of Spirit.

"Eat of my flesh and drink of my blood" again is the same as the fish and the bread. Another symbolism for the same thing.

Now then, if you have caught more than words in a book, if the spark is ignited in you, if that fire is a Fire within you, a Fire of living coal; the bread and fish are now within you on that Fire and you are receiving Invisible lambs, Invisible sheep, Invisible guidance, Invisible impulses. You are receiving the constant Divine Impulse and you are turned within to It, listening to It and obeying It. Then you're tending those sheep. Then you're about your Father's business. And then you can find the capacity to do effective world work, not just an outer charade.

Now your next chapter is world work. We have to, in that chapter which is the last of "Realization of Oneness," tie it all up together. Today is a New Year, the first meeting of a New Year. It's a new Consciousness. It's the new Consciousness that has come onto the shore. And in this new Consciousness we find that within us is the Divine fire which we must listen to and it will show us its way. But we must be there listening out of self in the human sense. If you're listening it's because your Faith is deeper than human faith. And if you're not listening it's because you're still in that blind human faith which cannot hold still; it has no Love. Now if you're listening you'll find that there's nothing goes on in this world that can persuade you that you are not now in the living Kingdom of God. And that you yourself are the living Kingdom of God. And that the perfection of this Kingdom is all around you, invisible as the Invisible fishes but ever present. That which we cannot see is here. That which we cannot touch is here. That which is called God is here. That which is the Power of God is here. That which is the Wisdom of God is here. All of it is here and all of it is available in Christ Self.

Now then, whatever is happening in the world is a sense activity whether it's good or bad. Whatever's happening in you is Divine activity and it is always Good. It can only be released to replace the outer world experience if you are living in that center of Soul called John - listening. Peter had to follow commands. Not John. John lay on the bosom, on the breast of the Master meaning they were connected; they were One. And so he instinctively and automatically followed the Christ; there was no thought taking. And then Peter would follow after John would automatically follow the Christ. We must be in the John Consciousness that automatically follows the Master instead of the Peter which has to wait for a visible command. We must live in that Self which automatically is lying on the breast of the Master.

Now when you do world work whether you're living in Self or not, we show up in what the results are. That's why this message is so important. It doesn't leave you hanging. If there are no results you are not in the Consciousness. It has a way of showing you where you are. And so that's why we want results because they show us that we're in Christ or not. This is a message with Power.

Now let's meditate then on the Bible meaning because we should all be now at a point where we're even higher than the Bible. It is the in-struction but its instruction should lift you to a place beyond itself, to the point of inspiration. Within you is the sacred Fire of Christ. You have passed the dawn, you're into the sunrise which actually becomes a visible event within you rising out of material sunset, out of materialism, out of the belief in all that is unlike God. In our Consciousness only God exists. This is the rising Christ. This is the mystical Easter. This is the Resurrection of Christ in you. All that is not God does not exist. We're true to that sacred Fire of identity and unless you can stand there when all around you attests to something other than God, you're still in naked human faith. Get out of the form, get out of the belief in form, get out of the worldliness, out of the material sense of life. Seek ye first, last and always, nothing at all in the world, for your Father is not in the world. And have the confidence to rest in your Father, the invisible Christ, as your own identity. Trusting It. Being willing to let anything happen that might while you maintain your trust. This is loving God supremely. Lo and behold, all these great catastrophes that seem to be striking lose their sting. *"Death is swallowed up in victory."* Either the message is true or it's untrue and we owe it to ourselves to come to the place where we can say, "I follow it," or "I do not."

I've seen so many catastrophes that turned out to be false alarms when someone catches the rising Christ within themselves.

Finally when the word "Amen" is spoken it means "I accept that Eternal Life is my name." In my Eternal Life is Christ here and Christ there. The moment you touch the sacred Fire of Christ within your Self, you have found the multiplication of every loaf and every fish in this world. The fish increase; they multiply. Grace becomes the law instead of material law.

"Do you love me?" or "Do you love you?" That is the question Christ is always asking within you. Three times the question is asked and this is the indication that the message is finished. The book is closed. Those who can see beneath the surface of the words are ready to walk out in the deep. Ready to bless their fellow man.

So we're going to do our world work next week together and that will be the last class of this series. That'll give you a whole month to move back and forth over what you have come into in Consciousness, refining that Consciousness unto a workable state so that when we hit the Special Seven in the second Sunday of February we should be able to work on the level of the Inner senses instead of the outer. We should be able to experience the walking on water. We should be able to understand how the Invisible universe works around us.

Next time we'll prescribe some things that should be done during the intervening month. Your work now is to *"Cast your net on the right side of the ship."* Stop trying to figure it out with that mind. Rest in Faith. Reject the sense testimony until the sacred Fire bursts and the living Radiance of Christ is your living experience with its living wisdom. Believe it, it happened; only two hundred cubic feet away.

They caught a hundred and fifty three fishes when they did this - add them up - one, five, three - nine. In other words they had progressed beyond mortality which is six six six. We had to come beyond six six six, the symbol of mortality to nine which is the symbol of the transformed man. And because John is remaining on the earth as the Soul, as the symbol of Love, there must be a reason for John remaining to tarry until the Master comes. What is the reason? There must be a remnant on the earth who can receive through that Self.

John's tarrying on the earth is a statement that there are still seven thousand who have not bowed to Baal. Those who consider themselves to be among the disciples of Christ are the remnant who will find through the experience of Soul that Christ comes to earth in them if we will tarry in John until Christ realization comes.

Let us be grateful that such a teaching exists. Let us not make the mistake of the world in seeing it only from the human eyes.

And so with that, you can join me, we can say, "Amen." (Audience says, "Amen")

This is our teaching.

And to all of you, the best of our Spiritual mansions in this coming New Year. Thanks again.

Class 46

No World Out There

Herb: Welcome again.

It would be a perfect meeting today if we were all at a certain place in the Bible which is signified here by the 12th verse in the 21st chapter of John:

> *"Jesus saith unto them, Come and dine....and [then he] taketh bread, and giveth them, and fish likewise."*

Now there are other translations of *"Come and dine,"* which are more accurate. The world today, as then, has been in a form of fasting from Truth. Just as we are to fast from untruth, we have been fasting from Reality. And when the Master says, *"Come and dine,"* he is really saying to his disciples, "Break your fast." He isn't saying, *"Come and dine,"* he is saying, "Let us have break-fast. Let us break our fast now from the unreality. Let us sup now on that which is Real." And so he takes fish and bread to them. This breaking of the fast is where we should be. In our consciousness we should be breaking the fast from mortality, from materiality, from that which is not of the Father. We should be ready to dine. And this is now exemplified further in the 18th and 19th verses.

> *"Verily, verily, I say unto you, When thou wast young, thou girdest thyself, and walkedst whither thou wouldest: but when thou shalt be old, thou shalt stretch forth thy hands, and another shall gird thee, and carry thee whither thou wouldest not. This spake he, signifying by what death he should glorify God."*

You'll find that later in Peter, the 2nd epistle, the 1st chapter in the 14th verse.

"Knowing that shortly I must put off this my tabernacle, even as our Lord Jesus Christ hath shewed me."

Peter acknowledges that he must put off this tabernacle as Christ showed him. Now old and young here refer to Spirit. When you are Spiritually young and Spiritually mature. When we were young we girded ourselves and walked where we wished; we were in human will. But as we become Spiritually mature we are girded by another. In short, the Christ takes over and we walk in Divine Will. And this is where the disciples are as the gospel ends, walking in Divine Will, the New Man released, the old self Impersonalized. And today when we take up World Work we'll find a few secrets about it.

We have been in the process of learning Truth. And as Joel points out as he begins the chapter 12 in "Realization of Oneness," there is now a point where many are able to avoid the disasters of the world. And he says, *"That's not enough."* There's no problem avoiding the disasters of the world if you're in Truth. *"It shall not come nigh thee."* But now he says, "You haven't been learning just so you can avoid the disasters of this world, now you must become a centre of Light unto the world. A place where Truth is demonstrated not as an individual alone but as a Universal Truth."

And so when he bids us to take up World Work the first thought we have is, "Oh, we're going to now help the world." And we must learn that we're not going to help the world at all. World Work is quite different than helping the world. The secret behind World Work is two fold.

One is that you are learning that the world is the veil where your Self is. Your World Work is to unveil your own Self. We have been thinking in terms of our human selfhood and even when we accept Spirituality we still think in terms of a limited personal Spiritual selfhood and there is none.

World Work is the expression of your Infinity as Being.

When you rest in the Word and know the Truth of the world, you are merely finding your Self as an Infinite Being. And therefore in every book when Joel speaks of World Work the real secret is, is revelation there to those of us who have eyes that we are not to live within the boundaries of a mortal concept. When you are able to, through the knowledge of the One Self, reveal the non-existence of material powers on the earth you are really finding the One God, you are believing in God.

To believe in God takes a new turn now. You cannot believe in God only where you are or around the corner, you must believe in Only God. There can be no second belief. Our World Work is the expression of our belief in God as the universal Self. And there is a further development as we deepen and make a greater penetration into Reality.

Now then, we have been ordained, we have been chosen. We have been chosen through Scripture although we have not realized that we were chosen. We have been chosen to walk a separate path than the world. We have been chosen to bear witness to the activity of God in human consciousness. And if you do not accept the fact that God has chosen you to function as a Light upon the earth, then this is not believing in God, because the words of Scripture are very clear that you may not hide your Light under a bushel. That you are here to be a faithful witness. That you are here to be a transparency. That you are here to Christ the world. Not to love it or hate it or fear it but to Christ it. You are here to bless the world.

And as you survey the activity of Christ on earth appearing as Jesus, you will see that by words and by deeds everything that was done was to make you aware that this is the Christ of your own Being appearing in what we call mortal flesh. The words of the Christ were the words of your Self, the deeds of the Christ were the deeds of your Self, and they were words and deeds to show you the nature of your own Being. We must now look at Jesus Christ in another way, as the outer expression of your own Self. And the ordainment comes from that Christ of your own Self saying, "Now believe on Me. Follow Me. Deny your own mortality. Pick up your cross of mortality. Do not hide your Light. But walk in the footsteps of the Invisible Christ." This is the ordainment and it must take us out of the desire to improve our personal conditions. That is the very purpose of World Work. It is not to improve the world. It is to lift you out of the belief that you are a finite being and that where the world seems to be, You are.

Now when you practice World Work it may seem to you that you're doing a favor to someone somewhere, that you're helping them behind the Iron Curtain or you're helping them in the White House or you're helping someone somewhere - but you're not. Until you are willing to step outside of the mortal boundaries of the mind and without desire for personal reward, do World Work you are not accepting the Infinity of your own Being. It is a subtle way in which Joel has lifted us up to look face to face at our own Infinity and either reject it or accept it.

Now while you are doing World Work you may not seem to be meeting your own personal problems and yet that is the way to meet them. The World Work you do will take you out of the false sense of self which has the sense of personal problems. And so Joel is stressing again and again in more ways that meets the eye, that you must be taken out of your own sense of self. You must learn to give of your Self to something bigger than a person. To something bigger than helping persons anywhere. Giving the universe back to God.

Now in our World Work then, we're going to find that we're not thinking of ourselves. We're not thinking of my lot in life. We're not thinking of my physical condition. We're not thinking of our finances. We're not thinking of anything that will make us enjoy life more. And if you've been touched by the vision of Truth you know that is the way in which all of the doors of the inner mansions open. As long as there's a remnant of personal self left in us which is still saying, "What about me?" we have lost the way and we are separated. Among the last words of the Master within were, *"Feed my sheep."* But who are my sheep when all is One Christ? Do you see how that has been hidden from the world? We could open kitchens for the poor, that wouldn't feed the sheep, you would still leave them in dying bodies. Always the desire to help and to over-help and to be a crusader has hidden the fact that feeding my sheep means: to recognize the Universal Christ.

Now as you sit back and think of the many teeming ideas that come to you all day about how you should improve yourself, remember you are living in a limited sense of self when you do that. The great vision of un-selfing is brought to mankind by the Crucifixion. When Joel says *"Impersonalize"* and Christ Jesus walks forth and shows Crucifixion you are hearing the same word. To Impersonalize and to Crucify are identical. Every time you Impersonalize you are crucifying a false concept. One word is more harsh but it is also more total. It is the word we have to face. In order to be free you must live in Truth. And you cannot live in Truth as long as you believe that God created human flesh.

Now then, if we're going to do World Work we're not going to improve human flesh. As Joel puts it, "We're not going to go behind the Iron Curtain surreptitiously because Christ is already there."

Now are you ready to make a turn that will be very significant? If you are accepting Truth, if you are willing to agree that because God did not create human flesh that flesh is not here, that whatever God did not create is not here, but something else must be here; and it is a Universal Spirit.

Your World Work is to rest in the conscious knowledge that Universal Spirit everywhere is the only Presence and is unopposed.

There is nothing for you to do beyond the recognition, the acknowledgement of the Universal Christ. That will encompass loving God supremely. It will encompass loving your neighbor. It will include everything that is taught as a principle. The recognition that only Universal Spirit is Present.

And now in Universal Spirit there can be no sickness or war, no death or disease, no lack, no limitation and therefore we're not trying to remove these things; we're recognizing their non-existence. We are maintaining a transparent Divine Consciousness which is unconditioned, which knows no mortal powers, no material powers, no human powers. It does not acknowledge evil. And therefore it does seek to remove evil. It does not resist evil. It does not try to dissolve evil. We recognize only Invisible Spirit in which evil has no existence. And knowing this Truth you rest in this Truth. And that Spirit which you recognize to be Universal is the Spirit of your Being.

Now if these facts are clear then we must find: where is this human flesh? Where are these world conditions? Where are the evils? Where are the problems? Where are the limitations? Where are the errors?

The martyrdom of Peter was that he was going to die to the flesh to be born of the Spirit. The Father has no pleasure in our dying. Our death is the glorification of our Spirit. Our death is the death of all material concept. In the death of material concept we are obeying the Scripture which says, "The Father takes no pleasure in your dying, wherefore turn ye and live."

Now the turn is - and this comes fittingly at the end of our long journey opening a new door - the turn for us must be that the world out there is not there. And there is a practice for you which must be begun in earnest. If you have glimpsed it from time to time or practiced it from time to time now is the time to accelerate. *"Turn ye."* There is no event in this world that is out there. And there are no exceptions. Whatever you see out there is within your mortal mind.

Now we want to learn how to place it correctly within our mortal mind and then dismiss it.

It may be an army but it isn't out there. It may be an epidemic but it isn't out there. It may be an ocean but it isn't out there. There is nothing out there but God. And all that you believe to be out there with the mortal mind exists only within the mortal mind. And you can tuck it safely into that mortal mind and forget it.

Now at our pinnacle of this work, we must take the events of the world and locate them within ourselves; never outside. And so I mean that wherever you look, whoever you see, is within you. There is no outside. There was no outside to Christ. There is no outside to you for the Spirit of God has no outside. Now the in-Self of you is the everywhere. The Self of you then which is here is also there and everywhere and there is no outside to everywhere. The moment you have something happening outside your Self you are not believing in God. You are not believing in your Self. You are not believing your Self to be Spirit. Spirit has no outside.

Now perhaps you own some property; it is within your mortal mind. Perhaps you own an automobile, or a home or some land, or a business: they are all within your mortal mind. Perhaps you have children or parents: they are within your mortal mind. Perhaps you have a physical body: it is within your mortal mind. Everything in the world is within your mortal mind. And there must be a conscious knowing of this from time to time to time. Daily, there must be periods of knowing, that which I see out there, whatever its name or nature, is within my mortal mind.

The entire world is within my mortal mind. And to consciously take events, incidents, things, people, forms, conditions, objects and to quietly know, that which I see out there is within me. It has no power other than the power I have given it.

When I know it is within me and rest with that knowledge within me, until a realization of that Truth comes that there is no outside, everything is within me, then that which is outside visibly loses its power.

That was the secret of Hezekiah: "They have only the arm of flesh," meaning they are nothing but my own mortal thought: all form, all person, all event, all condition. And as you dwell with this, contemplating it, swiftly acknowledging it to be not an external something but an inner idea or thought and resting with it for a moment to wash it with silence, you will discover that there is really no world outside. And you are turning, you are opening the way for a new Life, you are learning what Peter learned that day from the Master. "Here is bread and here is fish – come and dine, break your mortal fast, dine on the Truth of Being."

To live Mystically is to recognize the world has no existence except in human thought. The acknowledgement of this must be followed with the abiding in it; consciously, daily. There must periods of abiding in this Truth before you have the true Inner experience that the world in the outer has always been a concept maintained only by world mind in every individual Being.

That is why there are no powers. That is why there is no disease. That is why there is no death. But this means nothing unless you learn to live with this awareness. And when you do you'll find that you don't have employees or employers. You don't have students or teachers. This is all external and there is no external. Bring it back into the within of your mind, recognize it to be your conscious awareness of an outer which only exists in your conscious awareness and then you have located the trap of mortal mind. And rest in the Word.

God is not flesh and God is All; where is the flesh? God is not a blade of grass and God is All; where is the blade of grass? God is not an ocean; where is the ocean? God is none of this world; where is this world? It simply never was there. Your Self is there. And until you are willing and ready and able to tuck the world within your mortal mind and rest there until you know that's where it always has been; it could never could get out of there. When you have done this many times it will dawn upon you that Christ Jesus lived in heaven where men saw earth, and that all of the miracles were the revelation that what we thought was outside never was there. Our concept was changed by the Christ and we saw a different outside and called it an improvement. We were still looking at the good instead of the bad. And Joel has taken us to see that neither the good is there nor the bad. And so now living Mystically, you have this way of Life.

First you must know the unreality of all evil: it isn't out there. If it were then God wouldn't be there. Step number one; *the unreality of evil* which must be followed by *the unreality of good*. When you have neither evil out there nor good out there, you are believing in the omnipresence of God's Spirit. And then you rest in the Word. And the Truth you know that neither good is out there nor evil is out there, quickly or eventually sets you free. Or if you know the Truth that there is no world of good matter or of evil matter, no good conditions and no bad conditions, no good people and no bad people, you are living in the Inner Spirit which is the Allness. You are accepting that only God is.

Now we're closing the gap between God and man. We believe in God but do we believe in God's Self as our Self? Are we willing to close the gap into One? Are we willing finally to take the book and accept what it tells us that God is One and beside God there is no other and therefore to exist at all I must be that One. "You believe in God now believe in me," says the Christ, "You believe in God now believe in your Self." And finally the last form that you Impersonalize may be your own. It never was there either. It too is a mortal concept. All that you could ever be is the Mystical body of Christ.

We have tucked the world in where it belongs, in the world mind. We have tucked the world mind into our own little mind knowing that our mind and the world mind are one and the same. And the world now is safely tucked within us. It really has no power when you know that. "Pilate, you do not exist out there, you seem to be, but I know you're not out there you're simply an idea in the world mind, you're an idea in my mind and that's why thou couldest have no power. If I thought you were a person out there you'd have lots of power." All disease is seen the same way; it only has power because we think it's out there. Tuck it into your mind, that's the only place it is, and you can say, "What did hinder thee?" There was nothing out there to hinder you except the Spirit of God. Tuck your business into your mind, tuck your students into your mind, tuck your employees into your mind; they're not out there. The only place they exist is within your mind and rest in the knowledge that all that is out there is your Self. And this is the way you release Grace into your life.

Once the world is no longer there, there's no more duality, there's no more separation. You don't believe in separate lives. You don't believe in people who are growing up and dying some day. You're not mal-practicing the world, watching it and believing in mortal bodies, you're accepting the dispensation of the true Life.

Now whoever reaches the level then where they can accept and realize the non- existence of an external world is one who can answer the call that says, "*I have chosen thee.*" That one is prepared by those who have attained and have become Invisible already, and is lifted up to the point where they enter the realm of Soul and can behold the activity of Christ in the consciousness of the world. They become a witness of Christ and they find that in their new dispensation their sole function is to leaven the consciousness of the world by living and abiding and dwelling in the Truth of Spirit as an omnipresent Reality without opposite. Nothing comes nigh their dwelling. Nothing attacks them. They're not limited because they have discovered that all that exists is the One Self. They have reached the realization that the One Self that exists is their name. And they see this as a Universal Truth. Wherever you look you are looking at your Self. And wherever you are not aware that you are looking at your Self you are in duality because there is no other Self than your own. In this One undivided Consciousness you find that Christ is truly living Itself as the only Power.

First, the unreality of evil - tuck it within you in your mortal mind and see that that's the only place it is. Oh, you can give it a hundred reasons why it can't be there because you know God is there. And now tuck the good and see the unreality of that in your mortal mind and then rest in the knowledge that only Spirit is present - there is no outside world. This practice, as many times a day as you find you can, will deepen you unto the knowledge that you have found the river of Truth. You'll finally remove the shadow of mortality. And then you will be prepared to fulfill your function on this earth. Our function is manifold: we are here to bear witness of the One Light, we are here to be faithful witness to the Truth that only God exists, we are here to demonstrate the Universal nature of Christ. All of this takes us out of the personal self, the personal ambition, the personal desire, the personal need, the personal want. That was yesterday's mortal mind consciousness for those who have graduated, who have turned and are living Mystically. They're moving toward the next world which is the True universe behind this world in which we all live not for personal selfhood but simply to express Divinity.

If a person were deeply ambitious it would now be wise to take a good second look at the complete gospel of John – privately, by yourself. You will notice how every deed is a revelation of the Invisible nature of Christ where the world had seen form in the outer. How every word is a statement by the Invisible Christ which the world interpreted to be the words of Jesus. And you will find that every word spoken by Christ is the Truth of your Being. There is not a single Word spoken by Christ that is not true of you because that Christ speaking those words is You. "*I am the life.*" Where is the other life? What other life is there if I, Christ am the Life? We lose all belief in separated human lives. We find there is no life on this earth that can die. We find death is the belief in separated lives. There is no life to die, "*I am the life.*" All human death was a mortal mind concept; a sense illusion - but so is human life. We must see that there is no reality to the evil and no reality to the good. Always present is the Invisible Spirit of your own Being.

Now we share then One Invisible Spiritual Being: this is who we are. What's bad for you is bad for me. What's good for you is good for me. Whatever you know is going to have some effect on everyone else. We never seek personal good anymore. There's nothing to seek. I already am that Self. You're not concerned about time two thousand years ago. It never existed. The Self that I am now is the Self that always was and always will be. You see this is the Consciousness you need to do the World Work and this is the consciousness that is developed as you do the World Work.

The Christ controls what we have thought of as weather, what we have thought of as conditions, as epidemics, as plagues, as floods and fires and in the knowledge that these are in the external only in the mortal mind and nowhere else, we are now in a position to join those who have walked before us and who Spiritually, Invisibly now are doing World Work. We can actually be One with our own Invisible Self which are termed the Invisible Spirits of the world. Many of the higher dimension Consciousness have come down behind us to help us and fortunately some in this dimension can rise up to a higher. And we are all joining that one household now, to live not in the world of effects.

Now Grace is not going to come by prayer to God in the sky. That outmoded method of life is over for us. And as we develop now accepting my Spirit is omnipresent, my Spirit is omnipresent and omniscient, my Spirit is the only Power; we countenance no opposite. We know that every opposite to my perfect Power, my perfect Presence, my perfect Knowing is a false concept in a human mind. Never getting outside that mind even though it appears out there.

You might see it this way. On a screen of a movie you're looking at How The West Was Won and a half hour later there's another movie there, all about The Godfather. But they're both appearing on the same screen. Where are they actually happening? In that little millimeter film, which contains everything that goes on the screen and no matter how the scene shifts on the screen - you may see fifty different scenes on a screen - it's all in that little millimeter of the film. So it is that no matter what you see out there in this world, it's all within the mortal mind. That's the only place it is. The rest is consciousness objectified.

Always bring it back into the little film; that's the only place it is. It has no power there when you recognize that's where it's located. And as Joel said "If it's an atom bomb what difference if you get it back into the film." If you get it back into the world mind, into the individual human mind and see that's the only place it is. It never is out there; there is no out there. Only God is out there. And now close the gap and see God out there and God where I am are One and the same. All that's out there is my Spirit. Don't make God a separate self. There is no second to God. There's only God Life.

Now you're qualified as you develop this capacity to do World Work. You're ready to be a Light. You can be a transparency for the Truth. And it makes no difference what world conditions come into view. One with Spirit is a majority.

And so we have been trained to bless the world by knowing its non-existence, by releasing man from the belief that he is a creature who walks under two powers; under material law, under world karma. We're saying, *"Get thee behind me, Satan"* You only exist; the only devil there is, is material sense. And because material sense paints a picture of an objectified world out there, when I lose material sense that world is dissolved. It may continue to appear but it will slowly undergo a transformation as my consciousness rises. Yes, you can escape the disasters of the world individually but now you're putting that knowledge into practice to lift the world above the disasters.

Now the way we can practice World Work is to consider that the world is our patient. Up to now individually we have been treating one person here and one person there to learn that your real patient is the world. And just as you may have witnessed some success with one here and one there, now we must witness success by accepting the world as not the creation of God and therefore only an inner idea. We can rest. That is all inclusive, we don't have to pinpoint.

We might take an outer situation which seems to have occurred right out there, right outside right now and see the nothingness of all that appears externally. The presence of God is all we acknowledge. Here, there, is the One Spirit.

Silence, (long pause) ...

Now try to know that there is no out there and then be still. Silence, (long pause) ...

Now over the next few months we're going to set up a program so that instantly we can recognize conditions that appear in the world and come into a realization of their non- reality as external events. Oh, you can think of many kinds of such conditions and wherever you are it will be your function to live in the Truth of your own Being knowing that your Self is where the forest fire seems to be, your Self is where the hurricane seems to be, your Self is where poverty seems to be. There won't be starving children in India to you; they'll be your Invisible Self; One Invisible Self where many starving children seem to be. And don't look for the children to stop starving because you did that.

This is your way of acknowledging One Self. This is your way of acknowledging God supremely. We won't turn back and say, "Now, is it better?" We won't get out a yardstick and measure the wound. But you'll discover as you proceed in this method that Grace begins to envelope your own life in a new way because the bread you cast out through your recognition of One Invisible Self without an eternal world comes back and expresses as the One Self and its Divine qualities in that which appears as the world, in the world, as your Self.

You'll find many people are healed that you don't know about, but someone somewhere through your work reaching out for Truth is touched and lifted. And that is why this is a self-less work. You're not trying to help a specific person ever; you're trying to live in Truth. It's a broader vision which Joel brought us, that as we live in Truth, it makes us free.

Let's take a brief intermission and then let's explore the chapter very carefully.

— End of Side One —

Today everyone embarked on a Spiritual way of life should have a concern far greater than the demonstration of his own daily harmony and that concern should be for the survival of the entire world. The question now is, is there a principle of Life, a Spiritual Principle that will govern the world? Is there a Principle which can now be realized and relied upon to prevent the destruction of civilization and the extermination of mankind?

That raises many important questions.

At this particular level of the message, in that particular year, we were using words like, "the extermination of civilization" and "the extermination of mankind." Even the Christ in the Bible speaks of *"the end of the world."* But when you have located the world in your mind it is the end of the world. When you have located civilization in your mind that is the extermination of civilization for you.

We want to see that Joel is speaking not at the Absolute level at this point in this book; that came later. But through the preparation at this level it was possible to then come to the mind of man at the Absolute level with the teaching of Incorporeality which followed the year later. We who have had the advantage of seeing the later book can accept that this would not be the language for you at this particular moment. You should be past the point of believing that civilization can be exterminated or that the world can be obliterated.

Just as God has no pleasure in your dying and only the death of mortality in your consciousness is the acceptable death of the God, so only the death of the world in your consciousness is acceptable.

"If I go not away, the Comforter will not come unto you."

Now the Comforter is finally revealed to us as the realization of your Christ Self. When you have accepted your Christ Self as the only Self in the universe the Comforter has come unto you. What else made you accept the Christ Self but the Comforter? But *"If I go not away,"* you cannot reach that realization. And now I is revealed not to be Jesus but the world mind. The world sense of self must go away. You must rise above the world sense of self, just as I is Christ, and then the little I is Jesus, this little I that must go away is the mortal selfhood of the world.

When Jesus appeared saying, *"If I go not away,"* this is the statement that mortal selfhood universally must be obliterated in consciousness; that is I going away. When you obliterate mortal selfhood as a universal fact in your consciousness, I have gone away. And then the Comforter which is Universal Christhood can come unto you.

There's no extermination of civilization is there? There's no civilization to exterminate. But these were words that were necessary in 1963. They're words that are also necessary in 1973 for most of the world. They're not necessary for you anymore. You don't need words anymore that give a sense of reality to this world because you have travelled a higher path than the path of those in the first and the second degree. You're at the point where, to you, the world never did exist because *"I have overcome the world."* But this is not the I that must go away for the Comforter to come unto you: those are the two natures of I.

There is I - the world I, the mortal I - which must go away for the Comforter which is the I Christ which has overcome the world.

Now if you have not overcome the world think for a moment - where are you? Can you truthfully say that *"I have overcome the world?"* If you cannot, then you're not in the I are you? Because *"I have overcome the world."* And if you cannot say, *"I have overcome the world,"* then you're not in the I - then where are you? You're divided, you're separated from I. You're separated from the Christ. You're not accepting yourself to be the Christ and that is why you cannot say, *"I have overcome the world."* But you must come to the place where I in you says, *"I have overcome the world"* and that is why you must do this World Work to come to the place where the world has no fear for you. Where there's no life in the world to die.

When you have realized I which has overcome the world, then you will realize that you have no life that could ever die in the world, or be sick in the world, or be limited in the world. You recognize that when Jesus walks through walls or walks on water, this is the revelation of the nature of your Being. That the I of you, the Spirit of you, the Self of you is ever walking through the walls and windows of the world; even now. But how can you know this if you are still believing in the presence of a world? And so the World Work which ostensibly begins to help the world is actually a deeper thing. It's to make us be lifted into the realization of the I of our Being which has overcome the world.

For us now, we must live in the absolute realization that the world has already been overcome, it has no existence in I, Christ. And because I, Christ is your name, the world can have no existence in you. You are sowing completely to One Infinite Spirit without opposite.

And so for others it's called World Work and they may think they're improving the world but at your level you should know the difference. We're living differently than anyone on this earth, except those Invisible Selves who know the Truth of One Self and those visible ones who from time to time retreat into the silence, sometimes for long periods when they're never seen anywhere. They too are knowing the One Invisible Self which is the All, the I which has overcome the false concept called world. That's why we're not looking at our own daily harmonies.

Joel says, *"Is there a principle of life, a spiritual principle, that will govern the world?"* And then he says, *"There can be no question but that an individual can rise so high above the immediate circumstances on earth as to make himself immune to the disasters of this world."*

And so there are those on earth who today can walk immune. We in some measure find that we're not subject to many of the things that other people are. Now he says, "[*That's not enough. Is that all that is concerning him? If it is we*] *may find that the world is a lonesome place to be in. This is the age in which everyone who is seriously on this Path should forget his own problems.*" And mind you, he's saying that to his students, "Forget your problems." And something in us says, "Well, who's going to take care of me, doesn't charity begin at home? Who's going to take care of me while I'm taking care of the world?" And I want to make that very clear: you're not taking care of the world. You're accepting your Infinite Self. And that's who is taking care of me, You are. You're taking care of your Infinite Self not your visible body, and all things are added unto you. You see the difference in the focus?

"[*Not only,*]" says Joel, "[*should we be ready to*] *forget our own problems but even be willing to lose our life, if need be, in the search for, and the demonstration of, that principle which will mean life for this globe. All of a sudden we are face to face with this.*"

Again when he says, *"Lose our life,"* he's talking about a life which has no existence isn't he? That's why we can lose it. You cannot lose your Divine Life. You can lose your mortal sense of life and that's what he means.

Somewhere in here it becomes clear that most of us in the world have rejected the Supreme Gift that we have been given. God has given us the Supreme Gift, which is Himself and unless you accept Divinity you reject the Supreme Gift of All and want to protect mortality, which only exists in the mind and so you protect the illusion and reject the Reality.

Perhaps fifty lessons ago this might have been a difficult thing to accept. But we've been through sixty six weeks of the Gospel of John and that followed on many other things. We are learning to Impersonalize the world.

"There is no such thing as personalized evil," says Joel. *"If you have worked with the principles of The Infinite Way, you have already proved that the impersonalization of evil is three quarters of all that is necessary for healing."* Three quarters. In other words, when there's no outer world in your consciousness, you're very close to that inner Peace which is beyond human understanding but which is the dissolution of the illusion.

Now so far we've added something to this chapter that you haven't seen in the chapter: that is that there is no outer world. I do suspect that toward the end we have a quotation here that brings that into focus, but it's much too important to just come to us at the end of a two hour meeting. It's something that we've got to learn to live with and so I've been stressing it for that reason.

Instead of Impersonalizing evil and saying, "There's no person there," we're going that extra step and we're taking that person there and bringing them inside and saying, "They exist only in my mind." That is how you Impersonalize them.

You can't say, "They're not there," with words: you've got to take them inside and see where they do exist. They exist only in your mind. You Impersonalize them by knowing that they exist only within your mind. And I mean literally: that no matter who you look at they exist only within your mind. That is your Self and you are not seeing your Self; you're seeing a person. That is God Self and you're not seeing God; you're seeing a person. You cannot have a person and God too because God is One and there is no other, there is no God 'and.'

Every chapter in this book has brought us to the place where we can say, "There is no person there. There is no form there. There is no tree there. There is no valley there. That is all within my mind and it's within the mind of everyone else who sees it."

There is no evil on the earth because there's no person in whom evil can be and that's the Impersonalization of evil: there's no person there in whom the evil can be. And so we see there is no evil in a person because there's no person and therefore there is no evil person there and there is no cause for evil because the only cause is God. You're taking the whole world and not bothering with the left side and the right side and the high and the low and the in between, the whole world and putting it in your mind were it belongs and seeing that's the only place it is and automatically you are Impersonalizing and Nothingizing when you do that without having to go through steps.

Joel had a meditation in this chapter which I think we can do now. His meditation says...and we'll do it with our eyes closed but I'll have to read it to you because I like his words, the words of the Christ.

"Thou alone art power. Thou alone art presence. In Thy presence is [fullness of joy] fullness of life - here, there, everywhere. In Thy presence there is only the Spirit of God, the Spirit of Love, the Spirit of Truth, the Spirit of Life, and besides this there is no other, so I am not going into meditation now to use God or direct God, but to realize God.

Here where I am, God is: there where thou art, God is; and God is Spirit, and [God is] Love, and besides Him there is none other."

Now as you dwell with the idea that here where you are is God and there where someone else is, is God, you have Impersonalized and you're down to that which is present here and there which is

God: which is I, the Invisible Christ, appearing to human sense as person here and person there where only the Invisible Self is. And as you rest in that you're in Oneness; you've realized the Invisible One. And in the presence of the Invisible One realized, you are free. You are free of every human need. The Law is that Spirit flows where Spirit is recognized. You're in Divine Will. You are recognizing the Invisible Presence of Divine Will functioning Itself. And it makes no difference what had appeared in the visible; it is known to be unreal, totally imaginary.

The world has moved aside and then Divinity expressing through your transparent Consciousness becomes a new visible world in which the added things are present. The Goodness, the Harmony, the Love of the Invisible makes Itself manifest. You are One with the One. And yet you've asked for nothing, you have simply witnessed the inner Truth and that is how you bless the world. That is how your Light is not hid. That is how you accept the supreme gift of God Life as the only Life of you and your neighbor.

How different than all of this running around we do as human beings trying to fill all the gaps. It's really believing in God.

Mortal sense goes away and we are Christed. We learn to accept Christ identity, obey Christ identity, serve Christ identity, live in Christ identity. We walk in Christ and then every disturbance that arises is met the same way, "Who are you? Who convinceth me of a disturbance? Where is it? It's in the mind. Be still in the mind. Know the Truth. All that exists in the mind is not of the Father. The only Truth is God presence here and now." And rest.

Now these are the weapons we have been given to accept Divinity.

"We do not have to penetrate the Iron Curtain." says Joel, *"God has already penetrated it. But without our conscious realization of this truth, the presence of God will not function there [now] any more than the presence of God has functioned there in the past. The presence of*

God functions only where and when there is conscious recognition and realization."

That leaves it squarely up to us. We must furnish that consciousness recognition. We must abide daily in the Invisible Self. We must tuck the world in where it no longer exists as an external fact.

Now if we could accept the following statement all of the world's troubles, as far as we are concerned, would be over. Page 202. *"There is no power.... in armies."* You wonder what kind of an intelligence could make that statement. *"There is no power.... in armies."* Could you tell that to Hungary or Czechoslovakia or Poland? *"There is no power.... in armies."* And yet here it is, a statement of the Christ. Only the Christ could make the statement because only the Christ is power, and only the realization of the Christ reveals the non-power of the army. He might just as well have said, "No power in disease or sin or famine or poverty or death," because they're all the same Truth. The power of them exists only in the mind. That is not the Christ mind. The Christ mind in you realized, reveals the non-power. "Pilate, that hast no power over me. There's no power in death you can't entomb me. There's no power in arthritis, pick up thy bed and walk. What did hinder thee?" What hindered you was the belief that there's power in the mind. That there's power in things and conditions and persons and material objects - but there aren't. There's only power in the Christ mind. In the absence of the Christ mind all these false powers are rampant.

"There is no power in... armies.... I say unto you that this is a law and a principle. It operates in your personal life, if and as you make a daily practice of realizing: Where I am, God is. God in the midst of me is mighty, and all those who are opposed to the purpose of God have but the "arm of flesh," and nothingness. The Lord God in the midst of me is mighty, and there is no might external to me.... no might external to me - not in the mind of man or [in] the matter of man."

Which is another way of saying, "There's no world out there."

That army which has power out there isn't out there. What human being can say that? None. There has to be a Christ standing there. And Christ isn't just going to stand there if you're not practicing Christhood. Why else would a statement like this, so contrary to all human understanding, appear if it were not possible to attain that Consciousness which could know that there is no power in armies? No power in anything of the material world. No power in matter. No power in mind.

World Work will open you to that realization - and only World Work. When you work on individuals, persons, yourself you don't open to this because you're always limiting and finitizing. That's how valuable World Work is. It opens you to the place where you finally can see when they invaded that country, someone stands in World Work and someone in that country reaching out for God finds help unexpected.

Our function is to be that Consciousness which is available for someone to reach out and touch.

"Where I am, God is." That is the Truth of all of us now. But *"Keep this truth as a "pearl of great price," …. within you, then, abiding in this truth, praying the prayer of realization of God's grace, God's omnipotence, God's omniscience, God's omnipresence, and understanding the nonpower of what is not ordained of God, you will be fulfilling your function in this world, and you will watch the breaking up of error all over the globe and the gradual restoration of harmony."*

I cannot accept that these words are spoken in vain. I can only accept that these words are spoken and that they will eventuate into exactly what they say. The break up and the restoration of Harmony, meaning the Kingdom of Heaven revealed. Not patching up the world; revealing the Invisible Kingdom of Heaven, the change of consciousness. The change from mortal sense of life to the revelation of a Spiritual universe as a living fact. But only by those who can sit and say, "Where I am appearing God is," and being willing to live with that conscious awareness as a universal fact. Where my neighbor is appearing God is, wherever anyone is appearing God is, and that God everywhere is my Self, for I and the Father are that One Self. That's what we've been trained for. That's what we've been chosen for; to let our Light shine. For we must have some Light to let shine - Divine Light.

Statements of Truth will not save you. "*You must abide in [this] truth, dwell in it, live in it, hour by hour, day by day, night by night.*" That means even while sleeping we must know, before we enter the sleep, that Consciousness is God and ever alive. That's the only way we can comply with the statement, even "*night by night.*" We must know that Divine Self, Divine Life is never asleep, all that goes to sleep is the sense form and we must consciously know this.

"*Until it is a very part of your being, and then all of a sudden a spiritual light dawns within you …. 'Whereas I was blind, now I see.' Now I know that Spirit is really the substance of all form, the law of all form, the cause of all form. My error had been that I have been believing in a power outside, a power in form, a power in thought, whereas all power is spiritual power.*"

Once you get rid of that outside, then the inner and the outer are one and the same. "*No power in…. armies.*"

Finally he goes a step further. "*As you abide in this Word, remember always there is still one more step, that is, that after contemplating the truth about God,*" and also about your Self for they're One and the same, "*Be still, listen:*" as if to say, "Speak, Lord; for thy servant heareth. Thou uttereth Thy voice, and the earth melteth.*"

In other words always your contemplation of Truth must be followed by the Silence. Quite a number of people have failed to follow their contemplation with Silence. And an equal number have failed to contemplate before entering the Silence. So that they try to go directly to the Silence sometime and they find it's a very shallow silence. They haven't plumbed the depths through recognizing Truth consciously first. And if you will recognize Truth consciously, accepting One Self without a world and then dwell in the Silence the so called powers of the world will subside.

You see we've been doing World Work without really recognizing it. Whenever you enter Truth you're doing World Work, you're leavening the consciousness of the world: but now we're doing it consciously. There's no reason to wait any longer. If there's a mudslide around anywhere in the world and you have allotted one meditation a day for the quiet realization of the non-world and therefore the non-power of the world, take it into consciousness, rest in it. You don't have to wait for the world to join you. There's always ten righteous Invisible Selves working. Join the Ten. Make it your practice once a day. And this is Joel speaking, not me, although I'm not reading it. "Make it your practice once a day to meditate on the nothingness of the world. Whenever you are faced with any form of condition in the world that you recognize as being not of God. And then you're blessing your fellow man, you're recognizing his Divinity and you're blessing your Self."

Joel suggests that we have one meditation daily on World Work: every day. And when you know that this is not just to protect the world or save the world but rather to recognize your Infinite Self, I feel you're more apt to respond to that suggestion.

I personally would feel that if a day went by that you were not doing this that would be a day in which for some reason or other, you were rejecting your Self. Too busy to find your Self.

Now it comes. *"Error is not in the external; power is not in the external; all power is in the "still small voice." There is no power in sin, there is no power in disease, no power in tyrants, no power in external conditions: power is in the still small voice."*

He has told us there is no outside world. If it were there, it would have plenty of power.

Inasmuch as this is going to be the end of this book, here's Joel's final statement to us.

"In the midst of threatening world conditions, I say to you: Think in higher terms than your own health, your own supply, or your own happiness. For some part of every day give yourself to the realization and the practice of these principles through which you have witnessed healings of minor or major problems, principles that have helped you or your neighbor, begin now to think in terms of a principle revealing itself on earth as the presence of God, universally."

That would be of course the Realization of One, Divine Self as the only Self in the universe.

Now you have a month in which nothing new will be coming from this pulpit and so you can either take it upon yourself to review the past, put into practice daily some of the things that have been suggested and if you want to keep very current, to take today's lesson as your monthly work, every day for thirty days: one period of the day to do World Work as follows:

Face the situation that you have heard is impending or coming or present, somewhere in the world. Face it with the knowledge that there is no world there, that there are no conditions, for there's no world to contain conditions. There are no evils, there are no fires, no floods, no epidemics: there is no problem out there. It's a world mirage. It's not ordained by God. It's not sustained by God, it has no law of God for its continuity. It wasn't caused by God.

Take any phrases that you like until you can come to an instant agreement within yourself: "That's true. What is out there? The Spirit of God. What is here? The Spirit of God. Is there space between? No, it's all one indivisible Spirit. My Self is all that is out there."

They're trying to tell me My Self, my Spiritual Self is not out there - and it is. And I'm not going to have to remove that condition, or improve it, or change it, or correct it. All that is there is my Divine Self, God's Divine Self, the Divine Self of the Universe is all that is there. And when you can find some inner Peace from this you'll know that your own consciousness of mortality has melted away. And even though the human mind doesn't understand a word of it, it makes no difference.

When you find your inner Peace this way, just be still. That is when the Still Small Voice comes upon you, that is when Realization comes upon you, that is when Inner visions come upon you, that is when my Peace comes upon you and what happens in that Inner Realization becomes the Law. And then something gives you the release and says. "It is done," or the sigh, or the rainbow, or something within that says, "My Presence is now the only Presence here." And then you rest in that Presence.

And your World Work is being done. You've overcome the world by finding the Invisible Presence.

Russia won't declare peace and release the satellite nations but you are helping Invisible Beings everywhere. You are leavening your own consciousness, you are letting your Light shine. If the whole world could've been lifted up into paradise instantly Christ would have done it in the form of Jesus. It's a slow leavening process but it's our job and it's a silent job and it's the way to Self-realization. Every day that you do this, you are accepting the Infinity of your own Being as the only Reality. And as Joel says, "Until there is a dawning." Something happens to awaken you to the actual experience Itself. Oneness realized manifests as the Grace of God on earth.

Now as you do this during the month, when we meet again you'll find that we're all at different levels than we are at this particular moment. That month of leavening will take us to a new precipice. We are opening ourselves to what may be called The Special Seven.

They only function at the level of our own consciousness and as we are sowing to our One Infinite Self we are preparing the way for us to receive higher guidance than hitherto.

So this month I think is a perfect time for this World Work to be upon us. We should know each other better when we return. There is no other assignment for you during this month.

You must learn to recognize that the Invisible Will of the Father is ever working no matter what appearances seem to be there. And when you accept that Invisible Will as working now in the One Self which is here without opposite and there without opposite, it will manifest and you will have the God experience.

This culminates 66 weeks of the Gospel of John and our next series begins on the 2nd Sunday in February, I think it's February 11th, it's called the Special Seven, and that culminates the work of Immortality House in San Francisco. In those Seven we will have much that is new and this month will make it possible.

Thanks very much.

I hope to see you in February.

The End

of

Volume 2

Lightning Source UK Ltd.
Milton Keynes UK
UKHW011315130123
415295UK00005B/498